AN EYEWITNESS HISTORY

WORLD WAR II

Carl J. Schneider
and
Dorothy Schneider

Facts On File, Inc.

For Thetis and Larry Reeves
Always the best of friends

NOTE ON PHOTOS

Many of the illustrations and photographs used in this book are old, historical images. The quality of the prints is not always up to modern standards, as in many cases the originals are from glass negatives or the originals are damaged. The content of the illustrations, however, made their inclusion important despite problems in reproduction.

World War II

Copyright © 2003 by Carl J. Schneider and Dorothy Schneider
Maps and drawing p. 392 © 2003 by Facts On File

All rights reserved. No part of this book may be reproduced or utilized in any form or by any means, electronic or mechanical, including photocopying, recording, or by any information storage or retrieval systems, without permission in writing from the publisher. For information contact:

Facts On File, Inc.
132 West 31st Street
New York NY 10001

Library of Congress Cataloging-in-Publication Data
Schneider, Dorothy.
    World war II / Dorothy and Carl J. Schneider.
        p. cm. — (An eyewitness history)
    Includes bibliographical references.
    ISBN 0-8160-4484-8 (hc : acid-free paper)
    1. World War, 1939–1945—United States. 2. United States—History—1933–1945. 3. World War, 1939–1945—Personal narratives, American. 4. United States—Armed Forces—History—World War, 1939–1945. 5. World War, 1939–1945—Causes. I. Schneider, Carl J. II. Title. III. Series.
    D769.S36 2003
    940.53'73—dc21   2002015268

Facts On File books are available at special discounts when purchased in bulk quantities for businesses, associations, institutions, or sales promotions. Please call our Special Sales Department in New York at (212) 967-8800 or (800) 322-8755.

You can find Facts On File on the World Wide Web at
http://www.factsonfile.com

Text design by Joan M. Toro
Cover design by Cathy Rincon
Maps by Jeremy Eagle and Patricia Meschino

Printed in the United States of America

VB JT 10 9 8 7 6 5 4 3 2

This book is printed on acid-free paper.

CONTENTS

PREFACE

Certainly the generation of Americans who fought World War II did not at first talk much about it to their children. But they have talked and are talking—and writing—about it to their grandchildren and great-grandchildren. The Internet throbs with their reports and those that their descendants extract from them. Scholarly and anecdotal accounts of "the good war" map its campaigns, and former GIs and Rosie the Riveters portray its heroes.

This book provides its readers with the materials to understand what it felt like to be an American during World War II and the years that immediately preceded and followed it. Eyewitness accounts of history are like flashes of lightning on a landscape—what one sees is brilliantly illuminated but lacks context. To provide a sense of the whole, the authors give the readers overviews in the chronologies and chapter sections devoted to historical backgrounds. The excerpts from documents in appendix A flesh out the eyewitness accounts and offer insight into the attitudes of the time. They show especially what people took for granted and their need to justify or denounce war and its cruelties. The biographies in appendix B more fully describe the more prominent participants. Appendix C gathers maps to help the reader get bearings in this wide-ranging war. Appendix D sets forth a glossary of World War II terms, and appendix E relates the wretched history of U.S. attempts and failures to help refugees.

These days, revisionist historians and peace-loving citizens find much to criticize in the decisions made in the course of World War II—especially the treatment of refugees; the treatment of Japanese Americans, Italian Americans, and German Americans; the greed and selfishness exhibited by some Americans; the inefficiencies that bottlenecked government and industry; and most of all the decision to drop the atomic bombs. Some conscientious objectors feel that they were unfairly dealt with or are still underappreciated.

Beyond a doubt Americans individually and the United States as a country blundered in the course of this catastrophic war, committing both cruelties and errors of judgment. Nevertheless, to the minds of most Americans who lived through it, World War II remains an unwanted war that had to be fought, a war that forced them to new and often disagreeable undertakings, and a war in which they did the best they could.

ACKNOWLEDGMENTS

To the interested researcher, information about World War II presents itself on every side. The scholarship on it is extensive, both in published form and on the Internet; anecdotes abound from anyone born before 1930. We are grateful to the many fine scholars and the many participants who have illumined it for us.

We particularly thank the librarians at the Kennett Square, Pennsylvania, public library, who have procured so many interlibrary loan books for us, and the reference librarians at the public library in Wilmington, Delaware, as well as the librarians and curators at the Library of Congress, the National Archives, the Truman and Roosevelt Libraries, and the various U.S. military historical centers. We owe much to the many individuals who have allowed us to interview them and to talk to them informally and to borrow from their unpublished manuscripts and photograph collections, particularly Barbara Ambler, Charlotte Bartlett, Ed Brubaker, Penny Caccavo, Mildred Corey, Kate Hobbie, Eve Karr, Jane Lyons, Ruth Malone, Walter Naegle, John Noyes, William T. Paull, Anne and Caleb Penniman, Larry Reeves, Robert Wells, Dan and Rosalie Wilson, and Denise Wood. We appreciate also the endeavors of our agents, Elizabeth and Ed Knappman, and the folks at Facts On File, particularly our editor Nicole Bowen, her assistants Seth Pauley and Laura Shauger, and skilled copy editor Doug Burke, all of whom have done their best to hold to a minimum whatever errors we have committed.

1

The Debate: Isolationism v. Interventionism
January 30, 1933– December 11, 1941

HISTORICAL CONTEXT

Less than 20 years after the end of World I in 1918, the American people again confronted wars and threats of wars in distant countries. The rise to power of Benito Mussolini's Fascist Party in Italy in 1922 and of Adolf Hitler's Nazi Party in Germany 11 years later destabilized and eventually destroyed the European order created by the treaties that ended World War I. In Asia, Japan began its bid for empire with its occupation of Manchuria in September 1931 and its invasion of China in 1937. Meanwhile the European powers, both separately and as members of the League of Nations, hesitated to challenge the aggressors, even with serious economic sanctions. While Europe lunged toward war, the United States was embroiled in a debate between the *interventionists,* who fervently believed that the United States had a vital interest in preventing Hitler's domination of Europe, and the *isolationists,* or *noninterventionists,* who insisted with equal fervor that America's interests were best served by holding aloof. This debate, perhaps up until then the most bitter in American history except for the debate over slavery and the Civil War, divided families and friends unpredictably, some liberals and some conservatives ranging themselves on either side.

Isolationist Arguments

Until the Japanese attacked the U.S. naval base at Pearl Harbor, Hawaii, on December 7, 1941, poll after poll showed that Americans overwhelmingly opposed entering a foreign war. The Neutrality Acts passed between 1935 and

1937 reflected the isolationist mood of the country by outlawing arms sales or loans to nations at war.

In September 1939, Germany invaded Poland, and Great Britain and France declared war. The United States immediately declared its neutrality. On June 20, 1941, thousands swarmed into the Hollywood Bowl to attend a rally sponsored by the isolationist America First Committee. As late as August 1941 an audience estimated at 15,000 at a rally in Oklahoma City cheered Charles Lindbergh, the aviator whose solo nonstop flight from New York to Paris had made him a hero acclaimed worldwide for his courage and modesty. In the late 1930s he had put his fame in the service of the isolationist cause, becoming the foremost noninterventionist in the country and the principal spokesperson for the America First Committee. Just four months before Pearl Harbor the House of Representatives came close to abolishing the draft, finally passing it by a vote of 203 to 201. The controversy, wrote historian Wayne Cole, "extended from America's greatest cities to every small town and main street in the land, from every bar and barbershop to the halls of Congress in the nation's capital and to top-level Cabinet meetings presided over by President Franklin D. Roosevelt in the White House."[1]

Opposition to U.S. intervention against Hitler came from many sides. Some Americans harbored a lingering sympathy for a Germany whose aggressions they attributed to Hitler's effort to reverse the wrongs inflicted upon Germany by the vindictive policies of France and England after World War I. They perceived Germany's and Italy's war aims as limited, just more moves in continental balance-of-power politics. If Germany sought only to dominate Central Europe, they did not care. If it ventured closer toward the Soviet Union, the war would end in a draw, or one of these dictatorships would rid the world of the other.[2] Until England's declaration of war, they believed that war could be averted by a policy of appeasement.

Just such thinking had led the European democracies to accept Hitler's annexation of Austria in March 1938 and the dismemberment of Czechoslovakia in the Munich Pact of September 30, 1938. Believing Hitler's denial of any further territorial demands, British prime minister Neville Chamberlain announced that he had achieved "peace in our time." It was not worth going to war, he said, over "a quarrel in a far-away country between people of whom we know nothing." Many Americans agreed, including the American ambassador in London, Joseph Kennedy. Appeasement lost credibility when less than six months later, on March 14, 1939, Nazi troops invaded what was left of Czechoslovakia.

Nonetheless, isolationists continued to argue that the United States must in its own interests stay neutral. This nation could not solve the problems created by Europe's power struggles, they asserted, pointing to the American experience in World War I. In 1934 a congressional committee chaired by isolationist Senator Gerald Nye had announced that munitions makers and international bankers—"merchants of death"—had somehow manipulated the United States into that war for their own profit. The committee's sensational revelations persuaded many Americans that if the country had only remained neutral in World War I, it would have been spared unpaid war debts, the wasteful sacrifice of blood and treasure, and the cynical betrayal by Britain and France of the idealism that sent the American Expeditionary Force overseas. Indeed, Senator Nye and his supporters had little use for the European democracies, seeing them as selfish, outmoded colonial powers.

Throughout the 1930s and up until Pearl Harbor, isolationists were determined that the United States should not again be maneuvered into a European war by the British and French, who they believed had gulled the Americans into pulling their chestnuts out of the fire. They harked back to George Washington's farewell address of September 19, 1796, in which he warned against "permanent alliances with any portion of the world" and advised the new nation to have as few political connections with foreign nations as possible: "The great rule of conduct for us in regard to foreign nations is, in extending our commercial relations to have with them as little *political* connection as possible. . . . It is our true policy to steer clear of permanent alliances with any portion of the world." Lindbergh, in a radio address shortly after the outbreak of war in Europe on September 1, 1939, described it as a continuation of "an age-old struggle between the nations of Europe" and warned that the safety of America "does not lie in fighting European wars."[3] Isolationist resentment against the British was fueled by Britain's failure to repay the money it had borrowed from the United States during World War I; Senator Nye, from his seat on the Senate Foreign Relations Committee, denounced Great Britain as the "greatest aggressor in modern times."[4] And Frank Waldrop, editor of the *Washington Times-Herald,* wrote on September 28, 1941: "Those of us who are isolationists believe Churchill is bossing Roosevelt and leading us down the road to a profitless war as a mere British Empire goonsquad."[5]

A similar note was struck by Senator Arthur Vandenberg in a speech to a Republican rally in Grand Rapids, Michigan, on September 17, 1939. "The last war cost us 40,000 American boys killed in action, 192,000 wounded, 76,000 who died of disease, 350,000 who now deserve and receive disability allowances. It cost us $40,000,000,000. Our erstwhile allies still owe us $18,000,000,000 twenty-five years later, and all but Finland have given up any pretense of payment. We did not 'make the world safe for democracy.' . . . Our supreme obligation to democracy and to civilization is here in our own United States of America and in the Western World."[6]

In any case, isolationists argued, neutrality was the only way to keep the United States safe and prosperous. Intervention would be foolhardy because Germany was too well prepared. Charles Lindbergh, who had personally inspected Germany's military forces, believed them superior to those of any coalition that might dare to oppose it, whereas the United States was ill-prepared to wage war successfully. In the early 1930s the U.S. Army, with fewer than 150,000 officers and men, was smaller than the army of Czechoslovakia, or of Poland, or of Turkey.[7] Even in 1939 the U.S. Army had only 188,565 soldiers on active duty and 199,491 in the National Guard.[8] American participation in the war would only add to the bloodshed and carnage in Europe and obliterate democracy and liberty at home. Col. Truman Smith, U.S. military attaché in Berlin, warned that war with Germany would "only result in a blood bath and . . . the dissolution of society as we know it."[9]

Moreover, the isolationists asserted, the security and welfare of the United States did not depend upon the defeat of Hitler or the survival of Great Britain. America's distance from Europe and the Atlantic Ocean would protect the country. If after conducting a war in Europe Hitler turned on the United States, the American navy could fend off invading forces, and the United States by then would have had time to strengthen its defenses. Accordingly, Lindbergh and the

America First Committee lobbied for a strong military defense in response to Nazism and criticized President Franklin Delano Roosevelt (FDR) for weakening the defense capabilities of the United States by his efforts to aid Britain. "Our survival," said Senator Vandenberg in his September Grand Rapids speech, "is far less contingent upon the outcome of European battles than it is upon our success in stopping the Administration with its profligate deficit-spending here at home, which has more than doubled our national debt in seven years; which has pushed our annual Federal peacetime spending to $13,000,000,000 this year, as compared with $4,000,000,000 in 1932. . . . These are the threats to our democracy. These are our wars. We dare not permit other wars to wholly distract us from them."[10] Similarly, during the 1941 Lend-Lease hearings, Lindbergh testified: "We are strong enough in this nation and in this hemisphere to maintain our own way of life, regardless of . . . the attitude . . . on the other side. I do not believe we are strong enough to impose our way of life on Europe and on Asia."[11]

Some advocates of neutrality hated and feared communism more than fascism or Nazism, and they thought of Hitler as defending Europe against the godless "Red hordes" of Asia loosed by the Russian Revolution of 1917. They had little sympathy with the young American men who enlisted in the Abraham Lincoln brigade to fight in the Spanish civil war (1936–39) for the Spanish republic against the fascist forces of General Francisco Franco, who had the help of Germany and Italy. (For instance, James Lardner, a reporter for the New York *Herald Tribune*, before his death in action in the Spanish civil war in 1938 wrote his mother: "I believe that fascism is wrong and must be exterminated, and that liberal democracy or more probably Communism is right."[12])

The peace movement had flourished after World War I, led by the traditional peace churches (the Quakers, the Mennonites, and the Church of the Brethren), the War Resisters League, and the Women's International League for Peace and Freedom, and supported by organizations in other churches and by student peace societies on many campuses. They strongly opposed intervention, arguing primarily on the basis of the gospel or from socialist political philosophy. Unlike the America First Committee, however, pacifists opposed strengthening America's military defense.[13] Thus, the National Council for the Prevention of War, an umbrella organization of both pacifist and nonpacifist groups, sponsored *Peace Action,* an eight-page monthly bulletin edited by Quaker pacifist Frederick J. Libby. Libby in 1940 said that he would not participate in any war in which the United States might engage, anticipating the position taken by pacifist Congresswoman Jeannette Pickering Rankin.

Rankin was the first woman elected to the House of Representatives. In 1917 Montana had sent her to Congress, where she had joined 49 other representatives in voting against U.S. entry into World War I. She left politics in 1919, but in 1940 she campaigned again, as an isolationist Republican, with the support of other pacifists such as advertising executive Bruce Barton and Progressive Senator Robert La Follette, Jr. She took her seat in Congress on January 3, 1941, where she argued against the military draft and the Lend-Lease bill. The day after Pearl Harbor, refused permission to speak against U.S. entry into the war by Speaker Sam Rayburn, Rankin cast the only vote against declaring war on Japan, thereby ending her political career.[14]

In the isolationist-interventionist debate, American Communist Party members and sympathizers swung back and forth, synchronizing their changes of position with those of the USSR. During the Spanish civil war, they advocated fighting fascism whenever and wherever it might appear. After Stalin and Hitler signed their nonaggression pact in August 1939, American communists opposed U.S. intervention in Europe. Then when Hitler invaded the USSR on June 22, 1941, they ardently urged American support of the Allied nations—which by then of course included the Soviet Union.

Oddly enough in retrospect, the threat posed by Japanese expansion into Manchuria and then China was seldom mentioned in the debate between the isolationists and the interventionists. On August 11, 1941, the America First executive committee adopted a resolution against war with Japan except in case of attack. But like their opponents, the isolationists largely ignored Japan's actions in Asia.[15] The America First Committee never mounted a major campaign to prevent war with Japan.

Isolationist Organizations

Until the fall of 1940 (when the America First Committee was founded) the Keep America Out of War Committee (KAOWC) was the only national organization specifically created to lobby for strict neutrality and to denounce the president's foreign policy, which its members saw as leading the country into war. KAOWC was founded in March 1938 by Norman Thomas, a Socialist who argued that if America entered the next war it could not remain a democracy regardless of who won. The organization drew much of its support from

The German-American Bund, an American Nazi organization that opposes U.S. entry into the war, parades in New York City, October 30, 1939. *(Library of Congress, LC-USZ62-117148)*

socialists, pacifists, and civil libertarians.[16] An emergency peace conference of the major noninterventionist organizations meeting in Washington, D.C., in October 1940 founded the short-lived No Foreign War Committee, which achieved much publicity before disbanding in April 1941.

The student generation also entered the debate, most vigorously through the American Youth Congress, an organization that attracted young people whose aim was to build a more just and humane world but in which the leadership had been (to a great extent) seized by Communist Party members and sympathizers. The *Harvard Crimson* editorialized: "We are frankly determined to have peace at any price. We refuse to fight another balance of power war."[17] Chapters of a tongue-in-cheek organization called "Veterans of Future Wars" sprang up on numerous college campuses; its members were demanding their bonuses *before* the United States entered the next war—whenever and wherever that might be.

Despite competition from rival groups, from September 1940 to December 7, 1941, the well-financed America First Committee became the most powerful isolationist pressure group in the United States. Primarily, according to Anne Morrow Lindbergh, wife of Charles Lindbergh, "the movement was conservative, traditionalist, and Middle Western. . . ." Its 850,000 members included all varieties of isolationists. As biographer Ronald Steel writes, this committee linked "such diverse types as pro-Nazis like Father Coughlin and Gerald L. K. Smith; defeatists like Charles and Anne Morrow Lindbergh, who argued that fascism was the 'wave of the future'; old-style progressives like Senators Burton Wheeler and Gerald Nye, who saw the war as another chapter in the bloody volume of European rivalry; socialists like Norman Thomas; antiwar liberals like Robert Hutchins, Charles and Mary Beard, and Chester Bowles; and the Roosevelt-hating Hearst papers and the *Chicago Tribune.*"[18] These odd bedfellows joined together to keep the United States out of the war, urge a negotiated peace, and "permit Germany free economic control of western Europe."[19] The existence of the America First Committee encouraged Hitler to believe that the United States would not fight.

As the primary isolationist spokesperson, Lindbergh evoked bitter criticism. In the years from 1936 to 1939 his firsthand observation of the German air force deeply impressed him. In October 1938 he accepted the Service Cross of the German Eagle, a civilian decoration, from Field Marshal Hermann Goering. His reputation never recovered from the speech he made on September 11, 1941, in Des Moines, where he alleged that "the three most important groups who have been pressing this country toward war are the British, the Jewish and the Roosevelt Administration." In the same speech, he said that "no person with a sense of the dignity of mankind can condone the persecution of the Jewish race in Germany."[20] Nonetheless, the speech evoked accusations that he was a Nazi and an anti-Semite.

Interventionism

Unlike the isolationists with their many different reasons for opposing America's entry into the war, the interventionists had but two arguments. On moral grounds and for the security of the United States, they believed it necessary to oppose the spread of the evil empires of Germany under Hitler and Italy under Mussolini before these two dictators gained more territory and greater strength. This reasoning was powerful in terms of the country's self-image and self-defense. Nevertheless, many Americans did not take seriously the threat to the security of their country. The United States was then a continental nation that had not been attacked in its own territory for more than 100 years. Moreover, they believed, it would always be protected by the two great oceans that lay between it and the rest of the world. The country could feed itself and support itself, letting other nations quarrel and destroy each other, as they seemed eager to do. People wanted no repetition of the suffering and losses the United States had borne in World War I, seemingly to no purpose.

The great advantage of the interventionists was their powerful position in the executive branch of the federal government. Interventionism was advocated by the widely popular president of the United States, Franklin D. Roosevelt (FDR), who in 1936 had been elected to a second term in a landslide by a majority of almost 55 percent of the popular vote and almost 85 percent of the electoral vote.[21] A majority of the population trusted him, and many felt an almost personal relationship to him, an attitude that this master politician carefully cultivated by his fireside chats, in which he addressed the nation as "My Friends"—one neighbor to another. Although the Great Depression was to go on until a war economy ended it, most Americans felt both more secure and slightly better off in 1936 than they had in 1932, and they attributed the improvement to him.

This attitude was reinforced by his remarkable wife, Eleanor Roosevelt, who not only genuinely felt but also managed to convey a rare concern for every person she met, and in her extensive travels up and down the land she met hundreds of thousands. Americans who merely shook hands with her in reception lines felt her personal interest, as did others who encountered her

President Franklin D. Roosevelt addresses the nation in a "fireside chat." *(National Archives, NLR-PHOCO-A-4849311)*

casually on trains and on her visits to factories and institutions. Anecdotes abound of farmers and miners who looked up from their labors, unsurprised to find her approaching, and poured out their troubles to her. Thousands who never met her wrote her for help, and she seldom if ever failed to respond, often more wholeheartedly and thoroughly than they could have imagined.

With the isolationist mood of the country in the 1930s, however, and with Congress populated by so many isolationists, even President Roosevelt dared not openly speak his mind. By the terms of the Neutrality Act of 1935, with its subsequent extensions and amendments, the country was severely limited in what it could do to help England and France. As late as 1940, for example, the law forbade American ships to transport war materiel to any belligerent in a declared war—sales could be made only on a cash-and-carry basis. Other legislation prohibited extending credits to any nation in default of its World War I debts. Nonetheless, the president had a responsibility to think about what might happen to the United States were England forced to move its capital to Canada or, in the worst case, to capitulate. In 1940 during his campaign for a third term, political exigencies led Roosevelt to assure anxious parents that their boys would not be sent to fight in any foreign war.[22]

Meanwhile, however, FDR was working to bring the nation to an understanding of the dangers it and the rest of the world were facing. To help him get the American people to think of "conceivable consequences [of the war] without scaring the people into thinking that they are going to be dragged into this war,"[23] in the spring of 1940 he instigated the organization of the Committee to Defend America by Aiding the Allies. This group, chaired by the influential Kansas journalist William Allen White, remained active until after Pearl Harbor, although it attracted nothing like the publicity of the America First Committee.

Other organizations friendly to Britain, France, and the other Allies sprang up to support those embattled countries. Among them were several relief societies, including Bundles for Britain and a group of American recipients of the French Legion of Honor, who undertook in September 1939 to gather contributions of clothing for war-evacuated communities.

With each speech, fireside chat, and news conference, President Roosevelt strove to win the American people from isolationism, always emphasizing the threat to the United States presented by Hitler and Mussolini and stressing the advantages to the United States of utilizing the time won by the gallant persistence of the British to strengthen American defenses. Step by step he persuaded Congress to modernize the U.S. military and to help the increasingly desperate Allies opposing the Axis powers of Germany and Italy. To these ends, he used to the full the existing powers of the presidency and persuaded Congress to expand them. He created multiple agencies to shift the economy to a wartime basis. He employed existing civilian agencies to help the military. He enlisted the support of other interventionists, whether Republicans or Democrats. His hand was strengthened when in 1940 his Republican opponent for the presidency, Wendell Willkie, endorsed the first peacetime draft in the nation's history.

By a combination of oratory, reasoning, political astuteness, faits accomplis, clever euphemisms, and outright guile, Roosevelt altered public opinion and wrung from Congress the authority that he believed he must have to fulfill his oath of office. He took desperate chances, engaging in overtly pro-Ally actions that might have provoked a German attack and risking impeachment for violation of the Neutrality Acts. Much as he achieved, he never dared ask for a declaration of war.

Nonetheless, American sentiment was gradually swinging toward interventionism as the war situation and the actions of the interventionists in power began to speak more loudly than the propaganda of the isolationists. In June 1940, the National Association of Manufacturers pledged its knowledge and resources to the national defense. More congressmen and senators began to take seriously the dangers threatening the United States.

Reluctant as most Americans were to get into the war, they knew that they might not be able to escape involvement. As early as August 1939, just before World War II began, 60 percent of them recognized that if England and France went to war with Germany, the United States would be drawn into the conflict.[24] Their sympathies lay with the Allied cause. As time went on, they were stirred by the lonely, courageous stand that Great Britain was making against the Axis dictators. According to Gallup polls in May 1940, 64 percent of Americans thought it more important for the United States to stay out of war than that Germany be defeated; by the end of 1940, 60 percent thought the defeat of Germany more important. With their attention focused more on the European war than on the Japanese rampage through eastern Asia, Americans were willing to tolerate the risks of helping England even to an extent that might provoke the Axis into attacking the United States.

The nation continued in the same direction throughout 1941. Early in January Harry Hopkins, as FDR's personal representative, told British prime minister Winston Churchill, "I came here to see how we can beat that fellow Hitler." In his own words, Hopkins stated the president's conviction that "if England lost, America too would be encircled and beaten."[25] In May 1941 FDR declared an unlimited national emergency, a step that by law he could take only when he believed war imminent. Churchill and Roosevelt's historic Atlantic Charter meeting at sea in August 1941 trumpeted to the world what U.S. governmental actions had more quietly announced—the alliance of the United States with the aims of Great Britain. Even as they met, though, isolationist women were picketing the White House with signs reading "Impeach Roosevelt—Traitor to the United States" and "Drive the British from Washington Again."

On December 7, 1941, the Japanese attacked the U.S. Pacific fleet at Pearl Harbor, Hawaii, with devastating destruction. Germany immediately declared war on the United States. The isolationist-interventionist debate had become moot.[26] The America First Committee disbanded just four days after Pearl Harbor,[27] and most isolationists (except for some pacifists and the die-hard fascists) thenceforward firmly supported the war. They had argued up to the point of decision; thereafter they backed it. America First's chairman Gen. Robert Wood hastened to Washington to offer his services. Lindbergh supported the war effort, contributing his expertise to improve designs for aircraft and working on problems connected with high-altitude and long-distance flying. With the exception of one man who had been injured in an automobile accident, every founding member of the Veterans of Future Wars served in the U.S. armed forces.[28]

CHRONICLE OF EVENTS

1922
Mussolini's Fascists march on Rome and seize power in Italy.

1931
Japan occupies Manchuria.

1933
January 30: Adolf Hitler is appointed chancellor of Germany.

March 22: Dachau concentration camp opens.

April 1: Germans boycott Jewish shops and businesses.

April 26: The German Gestapo is established.

October: Germany leaves the League of Nations.

1934
August 2: Hitler proclaims himself *Führer und Reichskanzler* (leader and chancellor) of Germany. The armed forces must now swear allegiance to him.

1935
A Gallup poll shows that 70 percent of respondents believe that U.S. entry into World War I was a mistake.

August: The U.S. Neutrality Act bans shipping war material to combatants in any war and forbids American citizens to travel on belligerent vessels except at their own risk.

1936
February: Congress amends the Neutrality Act of 1935 to prohibit granting loans to belligerent nations.

March: The Veterans of Future Wars (VFW) organization is founded at Princeton University to satirize the decision to pay a bonus earlier than anticipated to veterans of World War I. As the organization spreads nationwide, it becomes in part a protest against war.

June: The national headquarters of the Veterans of Future Wars adopts a resolution calling upon Congress to declare that the United States will not enter a foreign war except by majority vote of the residents of three-fourths of the states of the Union.

July 4: The American Youth Congress issues a declaration of the rights of youth. Its leadership, which falls under Communist influence, follows the Communist line in regard to the war in Europe that breaks out in September 1939.

Fall: The Veterans of Future Wars suspend operations, which are never resumed.

1936–1939
Many idealistic young Americans enlist in the Abraham Lincoln brigade to fight in the Spanish civil war (1936–39) for the Spanish republic against the fascist forces of Gen. Francisco Franco, who has the help of Germany and Italy.

1937
Japan invades China. A Gallup poll shows that 94 percent of the American people support congressional acts intended to protect neutrality.

January and May: Congress extends the Neutrality Act of 1935 to cover civil wars.

1938
The isolationists in Congress introduce the Ludlow amendment to the constitution, which would necessitate a plebiscite for any involvement in war, except in the case of an invasion of the country. The amendment is defeated in the House of Representatives, but by a low margin of 21 votes.

March: Nazi Germany annexes Austria.

March: U.S. Socialist Norman Thomas founds the Keep America Out of War Committee.

September 30: Czechoslovakia is dismembered in the Munich Pact, signed by German dictator Adolf Hitler and by British prime minister Neville Chamberlain.

October: U.S. aviator hero Charles A. Lindbergh accepts the Service Cross of the German Eagle, a civilian decoration, from Nazi field marshal Hermann Goering.

1939
March 14: German troops invade what is left of Czechoslovakia.

August: Communist dictator Joseph Stalin of the USSR and Nazi dictator Adolf Hitler of Germany sign a nonaggression pact.

September 1: Germany invades Poland.

September 3: England declares war on Germany after Hitler fails to respond to Chamberlain's ultimatum to Germany to withdraw its troops from Poland.

September 5: U.S. president Franklin D. Roosevelt (FDR) formally declares U.S. neutrality and admonishes Americans to conform to the U.S. Neutrality Acts.

September 17: Republican senator Arthur Vandenberg insists that the United States is threatened not from without but by the policies of FDR.

1940

March: Congress denies a request for additional funding for expansion of military personnel, facilities, and equipment.

spring: FDR instigates the organization of the Committee to Defend America by Aiding the Allies, chaired by journalist William Allen White.

June: Henry Ford refuses, on isolationist principles, a government contract to build Rolls Royce engines for British Spitfire planes.

June 20: The U.S. Committee for the Care of European Children is established as an umbrella organization, with First Lady Eleanor Roosevelt as honorary chair, with goals of persuading the State Department to relax visa restrictions for these children and of constructing a network of families willing to receive the children.

summer: On FDR's order, Secretary of State Cordell Hull rules that visitor visas can be issued to British refugee children "upon a showing of intention they shall return home upon the termination of hostilities," and Congress amends the Neutrality Act to permit unarmed, unescorted American ships to sail to Britain to evacuate British children, provided that safe conduct is granted by all belligerents.

The USS *Arizona* burns after the Japanese attack on Pearl Harbor, December 7, 1941. *(National Archives, 080-G-32420)*

August 17: Wendell Willkie, in accepting the Republican nomination for president, endorses the draft.

September 5: The isolationist America First Committee is founded to propagandize against U.S. participation in the war in Europe.

October: An emergency peace conference of the major noninterventionist organizations meeting in Washington, D.C., founds the short-lived No Foreign War Committee.

November: FDR is reelected in a landslide victory.

December: Labor leader Walter Reuther's proposal that automobile plants be converted to the manufacture of airplanes is rejected by leaders of the auto industry.

1941

Charles A. Lindbergh resigns his air force commission. He is denied reinstatement after the Pearl Harbor attack on December 7, 1941.

January 3: Pacifist Jeanette Rankin takes her seat in the U.S. Congress, where she argues against the peacetime draft and Lend-Lease and casts the only vote against the U.S. declaration of war on Japan after the attack on Pearl Harbor.

January 23: Lindbergh testifies against Lend-Lease before the House Foreign Affairs Committee.

February 11: Defeated Republican presidential candidate Wendell Willkie testifies before Congress in support of Lend-Lease.

April: The No Foreign War Committee disbands.

June: Jackie Cochran becomes the first woman to ferry a bomber across the Atlantic.

June: Women are banned from participation in the Civilian Pilot Training Program.

June 20: Thousands of people attend a rally in the Hollywood Bowl sponsored by the isolationist America First Committee.

June 22: Germany invades the USSR.

August: Aviator Charles Lindbergh, the foremost noninterventionist in the country and the principal spokesperson for the America First Committee, summarizes the case against intervention in a speech given in Oklahoma City to a cheering audience estimated at 15,000.

August 3: As a conservation measure, 17 states order a gasoline curfew, closing gas stations from 7 P.M. to 7 A.M.

August 11: The America First executive committee adopts a resolution against war with Japan except in case of attack.

September 11: Charles A. Lindbergh alleges to an audience in Des Moines, Iowa, that the United States is being pushed into war by Franklin Roosevelt, the British, and the Jews.

December 7: The Japanese attack the U.S. naval base at Pearl Harbor, Hawaii.

December 11: The America First Committee is dissolved.

EYEWITNESS TESTIMONY

Isolationist Arguments

It's your crowd that's going to do the dying and bleeding, not the Wall Street flagwavers. . . . If there is another war I intend to make James Roosevelt go to the front line trenches. . . . I am not afraid! Let them shoot me! I'm all through. Let's get shot here at home if we're going to be shot."

> *Maj. Gen. Smedley Butler, retired Marine hero, in an address to a Veterans of Foreign Wars convention in Buffalo, New York, 1937, and in a statement two years later, quoted in Bill Kauffman,* America First, *197.*

Except in the event of an invasion of the United States or its Territorial possessions and attack upon its citizens residing therein, the authority of Congress to declare war shall not become effective until confirmed by a majority of all votes cast thereon in a nationwide referendum. Congress, when it deems a national crisis to exist, may by concurrent resolution refer the question of war or peace to the citizens of the States, the question to be voted on being, "Shall the United States declare war on _____?"

> *Resolution introduced by Representative Louis Ludlow, Indiana Democrat, quoted by Arthur Krock, "In the Nation,"* New York Times, *December 14, 1937, Section 4. This amendment was voted down in December 1937, by a vote of 209 to 188. In a 1938 Gallup poll, Ludlow won a popular vote of 68 percent.*

How horrible, fantastic, incredible it is that we should be digging trenches and trying on gas-masks here because of a quarrel in a far-away country between people of whom we know nothing. . . . [W]ar is a fearful thing, and we must be very clear, before we embark on it, that it is really the great issues that are at stake.

> *British prime minister Neville Chamberlain, radio speech, September 27, 1938, quoted in Parkinson,* Origins of World War Two, *93.*

To my attention was called today Spain by the factions in this country that favor one side or the other, folks here wanting to settle Spain's problem. If Europe gets into war, it will be because of folks like these— many of them fine folks, who nevertheless feel they know the way to solve the problems of the world. It would be better if some of these women stayed home and mended the socks of their husbands and cooked meals for them.

In these days my thoughts have been running to a thought of a program for democracy for America. We seem to have had no program here except to feed out money to the needy, a function which Cleveland said didn't belong to the federal government, and the demands are getting greater and greater. Where do we stop? The reason we don't seem to be getting anywhere, as I see it, is that we are losing faith in our political democracy. We are depending too much upon Washington.

I got to thinking about the consequences of war today. This menace constitutes the greatest danger to our free institutions. War would take away the functioning of our democratic processes. War means murder. No one can commit murder without demoralizing his mental storehouse. War means breaking down the democratic way and the means of doing business, running government and living. It means dictatorship. It means the exaltation of hatred and passion, development of suspicion, propaganda gone riot, spies everywhere putting the minds and thoughts of the people in a rut, despoiling the Constitution. America must not get into a war unless it be to repel the invasion of our own continent or to preserve the rights of mankind. It was said on March 15th, 1939. Perhaps in the field of sane thinking I am to make my contribution, talking the need of keeping the mind poised, maintaining a mental equilibrium.

> *1964 reminiscences of Senator Alexander Wiley about events of 1940, the Columbia University Oral History Research Office Collection (hereafter CUOHROC), 45–46.*

[The United States is not threatened by foreign invasion unless] American peoples bring it on through their own quarreling and meddling with affairs abroad. . . . [T]here are powerful elements in America who desire us to take part. They represent a small minority of the American people, but they control much of the machinery of influence and propaganda. They seize every opportunity to push us closer to the edge.

> *Col. Charles Lindbergh, speech of May 19, 1940, quoted in the* New York Times, *May 20, 1940, 8.*

The hypocrisy and subterfuge that surrounds us comes out in every statement of the war party. When we demand that our Government listen to the 80% of the people who oppose war, they shout that we are causing disunity. The same groups who call on us to defend democracy and freedom abroad, demand that we kill democracy and freedom at home by forcing four-fifths of our people into war against their will. The one-fifth who are for war call the four-fifths who are against the war the "fifth column."

Col. Charles Lindbergh, speech of August 9, 1941, in Cleveland, Ohio, quoted in Cole, Lindbergh, *190.*

It was in Little Falls [Minnesota] that I first heard my father's [Charles Lindbergh's] voice on tape in the Des Moines speech of 1941. . . . [H]e was telling the world that one of the greatest dangers to pre-World War II America was the influence of Jews in prominent positions.

It was not the first time I had come across this speech but it was the first time I had heard it spoken in my father's own voice. I was again transfixed and horrified, again ablaze with shame and fury—"Not you!" I cried out silently to myself, and to him— "No! You never said such things! You raised your children never to say, never even to *think* such things—this must be somebody else talking. . . ." I felt a global anguish—the horror of the Holocaust, the words of my own father ignoring the horror, but surely not condoning the horror, surely not dismissing, or diminishing it, surely not. But I also felt a piercingly personal rage. . . .

Reeve Lindbergh, Charles Lindbergh's daughter, speaking of an event of September 11, 1941, Under a Wing, *201.*

My first experience with the war situation that was developing between China and Japan came about— well, it was a more or less progressive situation that all of us were aware of, in our visits to the northern China ports in the summer during the various cruises that we took. We'd run across the Japanese armed forces—navy—quite often. . . .

[In 1937, harvest time,] we came in [to Shanghai] on the 12th, and the 13th was Bloody Saturday in Shanghai. Two Chinese planes accidentally dropped 500 pound bombs into the most crowded section of Shanghai. . . . Oh, it was the most bloody catastrophe. There were arms, legs, torsos. The streets were running with blood. You couldn't keep an equilibrium in your stomach when you saw the effects of those two bombs in Shanghai that night. It hit one of the most crowded places. . . .

I woke up one morning around September—I was sleeping below decks—looked out the porthole and there I saw, in the ebb of the tide, this [Chinese] woman. Evidently she'd been a guerrilla. Her legs were bound, her hands were bound behind her, she was entirely open in front—I couldn't tell whether she'd been really mutilated in that area or not, but it looked horrible, and her throat was open. It was just cut completely open, just like there were two mouths. I looked into that, just about 5 feet away. . . . I recall the callous way we started looking at the thing. It was so darn big for us, so much killing and so much brutality that we just took on a callous [attitude] and started laughing and joking about it to keep ourselves under control. We used to laugh about the corpses that would come floating by the gangway. They'd float up and down on the ebb and flow of the tide, lie there by the gangway. It was quite an experience for all of us. [In August 1937] We'd watch it at close range while the Japanese occupied Putung (?) Point, which was just across from us. . . . We watched all day while Japanese officers came and interrogated those poor characters [who had been tied to a post.] They were smoking cigars and they would thrust them in their forehead—I recall that and I recall the screams that would come. They were very close. I didn't watch this myself at dusk. I think I was someplace else on the ship, but some of my friends told me that they had watched the Japanese marines use them for bayonet practice after the day's torture. . . .

[After I joined the American Volunteer Group, which became the Flying Tigers,] We were on the Atlantic Coast at that time, convoying supplies between Bermuda and the Canary Islands. That was about between May and July of 1941. I got tired of that duty. It was so obvious that we were getting ready to go to war. I had no sympathy with any war at that time, for the United States to be against Germany, helping England, because at the time as I recall there was a good deal of sentiment against England involving us again in a war. I felt that way about it, too, and I wanted to get back to the Orient, anyway.

1962 reminiscences of Flying Tiger Thomas G. Trumble, who as a Navy yeoman in 1936 was assigned to the Augusta *in Chinese waters and subsequently witnessed the beginning of the Japanese invasion of China. His reminiscences here extend until the early summer of 1941 and are recounted in CUOHROC, 2, 5, 6, 7, 8, 26.*

Isolationist Organizations

In April 1940 the Southern Conference [for Human Welfare] had its second convention, in Chattanooga. The meeting was dominated by fighting between the people who wanted to go to war against Hitler and the ones who didn't. I was one of the ones who wanted to go to war. . . . In 1938 the conference had had the backing of the Roosevelts, but by the time we met in Chattanooga in 1940, Mr. Roosevelt had turned from Dr. New Deal to Dr. Win-the-War. . . . I'm sure he passed the word among the New Dealers not to involve themselves with the conference, because he wanted to keep the support of the Southern congressmen and senators. . . . John L. Lewis [president of the United Mine Workers] had become a complete isolationist; he had broken with Roosevelt. . . . [The miners] had gotten orders to come and they came. They formed an alliance with the few Communists there to try to get a resolution passed against the Allies. . . . But the miners were absolutely bored to death. They couldn't have been more bored with all the technicalities. . . . All the parliamentary folderol that goes on was just too much. Finally they all just drifted out, and the isolationist resolution lost.

Democratic activist Virginia Durr writing about events in April 1940, Autobiography, *132–133.*

Statement of Principles of the America First Committee, September 1940.

1. The United States must build an impregnable defense for America.
2. No foreign power, nor group of powers, can successfully attack America.
3. American democracy can be preserved only by keeping out of the European war.
4. "Aid short of war" weakens national defense at home and threatens to involve America in war abroad.

Statement of Principles of the America First Committee, adopted September 1940, quoted in Cole, Lindbergh, *117.*

I told our committee [America First] when I closed it up—some of them wanted to go on—I said, "Listen, we formed this committee to prevent our country from going to war, but it is in war, so our function is done. Now let's all go and do what we can to help our country."

But I still feel it was a great mistake. It started though—really—the original mistake was made in England. In '36. I was over there at that time, on a business trip, and Hitler had approached the British. He wanted to attack Russia then, and he wanted the British to stay neutral, to give him carte blanche to [attack].

Well, there were two parties—they weren't split along political lines, but the governing classes who then still ran England—half of them were in favor, on the theory that the Nazis and the Soviets would tear each other apart, and neither could lick the other. The Germans were far superior in size and technology, and on the other hand the Russians had that weapon of space which licked Napoleon and which eventually kicked him out of there. They thought that then both countries would be in such shape they'd be no menace to the world. I thought that was sound reasoning, and I still think so.

Churchill, on the other hand—I had lunch with him alone, in London, in 1936. He was the head of the opposition, but he was not in the government, and he said to me, "Germany is getting too strong. We've got to smash her."

I said, "Mr. Churchill, do you think you can smash her?"

"Oh," he said, "yes." I could see how weak England was. I'd been through her plants and there wasn't a single modern plant in England. . . .

I got into [America First] by accident. . . . A young idealistic college student by the name of Bobby Stuart, son of my next door neighbor, formed this chapter at Yale, and they came to me, and I helped them some financially. Then they couldn't get any man of any substance to head the movement, because it was not too popular with the so-called best people. I finally said, "I'll take the acting chairmanship." Well, they never did find anybody who'd bear the brickbats. But it wasn't my organization. I didn't start it. As I said, I was opposed to our getting into the war. . . .

FDR, with all his enormous influence, could never get a declaration of war on Germany from Congress. The people were opposed to the war. He finally got us in, through the back door, through Japan. He never could get that permission granted him, and he'd given his commitments to Churchill. The incredible hypocrisy, when he made that famous speech, "Fathers and mothers of America, I will never send your sons to die on foreign soil." He knew all the time he was lying. He'd given his commitments. He was crazy to get into the war. . . .

The majority of people who were in [America First] were young students who were very idealistic. They weren't pacifists. Bobby [Stewart, who formed the Yale chapter] served in the Army and had a good record.

[Yes, our idea was mostly to organize public opinion against war measures.] We had three or four Senators. Burton Wheeler, Errye from North Dakota, Vandenberg of Michigan, Governor Edison of New Jersey—Lindbergh was the most effective of all. He was the idol of the young people. Of course, he'd been over there. He knew the extent of the German preparations. . . .

That speech he [Charles Lindbergh] made in Des Moines, in September, 1941 [damaged him]—when he classed the Anglophiles and the Jewish people as two of the principal forces leading us into war. Well, he was telling the truth. He was telling the truth about both: The people, the society people who were drawn to England, and the Jewish people who had a great deal of excuse. If I'd been a Jew, I would have been strong for intervention—going after the Nazis. But he didn't blame the Jews. He simply said, "These are the forces."

That, I think, did us a good deal of harm, exposed the America First Committee to a good deal of criticism. On the other hand, of course, we had some anti-Semites join us, for no other reason, and as I say, I got rid of them wherever I saw them. I threw out the head of the chapter in San Francisco. But they were relatively few. As I say, any movement of that kind does attract extremists of every kind. But it was a very trying experience for me. I took the brickbats, and plenty of them. But the more I got, the madder I got. . . . I felt very sincerely that if men were afraid to stand up for what they believed in, it was a very bad thing for this country. As a matter or fact, it turned out all right. I was never harmed in business, I was never harmed by my friends. Even my Jewish friends stood by me—all the Rosenwalds did, and all the men I knew. . . .

1961 reminiscences of Gen. Robert E. Wood about events of 1936–41, in CUOHROC, 84–85, 87–88, 90–91. After the United States entered the war, Wood was sent around the world "trying to teach the ABCs of supply."

Interventionism

I have seen war. I have seen war on land and sea. I have seen blood running from the wounded. I have seen men coughing out their gassed lungs. I have seen the dead in the mud. I have seen cities destroyed. I have seen two hundred limping, exhausted men come out of line—the survivors of a regiment of one thousand that went forward forty hours before. I have seen children starving. I have seen the agony of mothers and wives. I hate war.

President Franklin D. Roosevelt, Chautauqua speech, August 14, 1936. Malaspina University, available online. URL: http://web.mala.bc.ca/davies/ H324War/FDR.Chautauqua Speech.Aug14.1936htm.

The present reign of terror and international lawlessness began a few years ago. It began through unjustified interference in the internal affairs of other nations or the invasion of alien territory in violation of treaties; and has now reached a stage where the very foundations of civilization are seriously threatened. . . .

Without a declaration of war, and without warning or justification of any kind, civilians, including vast numbers of women and children, are being ruthlessly murdered with bombs from the air. In times of so-called peace, ships are being attacked and sunk by submarines without cause or notice. Nations are fomenting and taking sides in civil warfare in nations that have never done them any harm. Nations claiming freedom for themselves deny it to others. . . .

If those things come to pass in other parts of the world, let no one imagine that America will escape, that America may expect mercy, that this Western Hemisphere will not be attacked, and that it will continue tranquilly and peacefully to carry on the ethics and the arts of civilization. . . .

When an epidemic of physical disease starts to spread, the community approves and joins in a quarantine of the patients in order to protect the health of the community against the spread of the disease. . . . War is a contagion, whether it be declared or undeclared. It can engulf states and peoples remote from the original scene of hostilities. We are determined to keep out of war, yet we cannot insure ourselves against the disastrous effects of war and the dangers of involvement. We are adopting such measures as will minimize our risk of involvement, but we cannot have complete protection in a world of disorder in which confidence and security have broken down.

President Franklin D. Roosevelt, "Quarantine speech," October 5, 1937, available online. University of Kansas, URL: www.ku.edu/carrie/does/texts/fdrquam.html.

When the draft went into effect, I registered as required. Later I got a message to see the man who headed the local draft review board. . . . He noted that I had indicated I was all ready for service but also saw that I had a dependent, my mother. . . .

Ulmer explained to me that the government was not bashful about telling men to go. Later on they would probably get around to me, but that in the meantime they were not ready to have me kiss my ma goodby. . . . I think he felt I could be more useful continuing my work [cartooning] at this time than I could be in the service. In fact, I felt that way too. So I was glad for the reprieve and the chance to continue coping with isolationism. . . .

[A senior editor at Scripps-Howard] gave me a little lecture . . . and told me that I should not be an "interventionist"—while I told him I was simply "anti-isolationist." . . . I should go out and see a good show and forget about all that stuff in Europe. He said, "Let them have their war," which he seemed to feel every generation was entitled to, but which was none of our business.

Cartoonist Herbert Block, whose drawings won him the Pulitzer Prize about the period from the fall of 1940 on, in Block, Herblock, 64–65, 65–66.

Today no one can honestly promise you peace at home or abroad. All any human being can do is to promise that he will do his utmost to prevent this country from being involved in war.

First Lady Eleanor Roosevelt, writing in her column "My Day," November 2, 1940, in Chadakoff, Eleanor Roosevelt's My Day, 182.

[T]oday's threat to our national security is not a matter of military weapons alone. We know of new methods of attack, the Trojan horse, the fifth column that betrays a nation unprepared for treachery. Spies, saboteurs and traitors are all the actors in the new strategy. With all that we must and will deal vigorously. . . .

President Franklin D. Roosevelt, in his May 26, 1940, Fireside Chats of Franklin D. Roosevelt, available online. URL: mhric.org/fdr/fdr.html.

First Lady Eleanor Roosevelt, who traveled the United States and the world during World War II as her husband's personal representative, and who after the war shepherded the Universal Declaration of Human Rights through the United Nations. *(Library of Congress, LC-Z62-25812)*

On this tenth day of June, 1940, the hand that held the dagger has struck it into the back of its neighbor [Italy has entered World War II]. . . . We will extend to the opponents of force [the Allies] the material resources of this nation. . . . We will harness and speed up those resources in order that we ourselves in the Americas may have the equipment and training equal to the task of any emergency and every defense. . . . We will not slow down or detour. Signs and signals call for speed: full speed ahead.

President Franklin D. Roosevelt, speaking at the commencement exercises of the University of Virginia on June 10, 1940, U.S. State Department International Information Program, available online. URL: http://usinfo.state.gov/usa/infousa/facts/democrac/52.htm.

Unless we can establish our ability to feed this Island, to import the munitions of all kinds which we need, we may fall by the way, and the time needed by the U.S. to complete her defensive preparations may not be forthcoming. . . . The moment approaches where we shall no longer be able to pay cash for shipping and other supplies. While we will do our utmost and shrink from no proper sacrifices to make payments across the exchange, I believe you will agree that it would be wrong in principle and mutually disadvantageous in effect if, at the height of this struggle Great Britain were to be divested of all saleable assets so that after the victory was won with our blood, civilization saved and the time gained for the United States to be fully armed against all eventualities, we should stand stripped to the bone. Such a course would not be in the moral or economic interests of either of our countries. . . .

You may be assured that we shall prove ourselves ready to suffer and sacrifice to the utmost for the Cause, and that we glory in being its champions. The rest we leave with confidence to you and to your people, being sure that ways and means will be found which future generations on both sides of the Atlantic will approve and admire.

British prime minister Winston Churchill, in a letter to FDR, December 1940, in Kimball, ed., Churchill & Roosevelt, *1:102–109.*

Well, let me give you an illustration: Suppose my neighbor's home catches on fire, and I have a length of garden hose four or five hundred feet away. If he can take my garden hose and connect it up with his hydrant, I may help to put out his fire. Now what do I do? I don't say to him before that operation, "Neighbor, my garden hose cost me $15; you have to pay me $15 for it." What is the transaction that goes on? I don't want $15—I want my garden hose back after the fire is over. All right. If it goes through the fire all right, intact, without any damage to it, he gives it back to me and thanks me very much for the use of it. [If it's damaged, he can replace it.]

President Franklin D. Roosevelt, speaking at a press conference, December 16, 1940, proposing Lend-Lease, New York Times, *December 18, 1940, 1.*

Many of us . . . believed at the time and still believe a quarter of a century later that Nazism was an ultimate threat to everything decent in our lives, an ideology and a practice of political domination so murderous, so degrading even to those who might survive, that the consequences of its final victory in World War II

were literally beyond calculation, immeasurably awful. We see it—and I don't use the phrase lightly—as evil objectified in the world, and in a form so potent and apparent that there could never have been anything to do but fight against it.

Historian Michael Walzer, speaking of the Nazi threat, in 1939–41, "World War II: Why This War Was Different," in Cohen et al., eds., War and Moral Responsibility, *86.*

Of course we are going to give all the aid we possibly can to Russia.

President Franklin D. Roosevelt, speaking to the press, June 24, 1941, against the advice of the U.S. military, after Hitler invaded Russia, quoted in Goodwin, No Ordinary Time, *256.*

No matter what it takes, no matter what it costs, we will keep open the line of legitimate commerce in these defensive waters. . . . Let this warning be clear. From now on, if German or Italian vessels of war enter the waters, the protection of which is necessary for American defense, they do so at their own peril. . . . When you see a rattlesnake poised to strike, you do not wait until he has struck before you crush him. These Nazi submarines and raiders are the rattlesnakes of the Atlantic.

President Franklin D. Roosevelt, September 11, 1941, in New York Times, *September 12, 1941, 4.*

[When Germany attacked Russia,] our own Army and Navy were impoverished. Congress and the American press were demanding more supplies for the Army then in training. [Only] little by little there came to be an understanding that Russia's ability to hold off the German hordes gave us greater time to train and equip an Army and Navy and build up military production. As that opinion grew, the Russian supply program grew.

Wayne Coy, the head of the program to fill Russian orders, writing in the New Republic, *April 15, 1946, 547.*

Interventionism and the Draft

Today we meet in a typical American town. The quiet streets, the pleasant fields that lie outside, the people going casually about their business, seem far removed from the shattered cities, the gutted buildings and stricken people of Europe. . . . [W]e know that we are not isolated from those suffering people. We live in the same world as they and we are created in the same image. . . . Try as we will, we cannot brush the pitiless pictures of their destruction from our eyes or escape the profound effects of it upon the world in which we live. . . . [I cannot ask the American people to put their faith in me] without recording my conviction that some form of selective service [the draft] is the only democratic way in which to assure the trained and competent manpower we need in our national defense.

Wendell Willkie, accepting the Republican nomination
for the presidency, August 17, 1940,
quoted in Goodwin, No Ordinary Time,
144–145.

This is the first lottery I ever won in my life.

Joke often made by the first men to be selected for the
draft, October 29, 1940, in Goodwin,
No Ordinary Time, *187.*

Very simply and honestly, I can give assurance to the mothers and to the fathers of America that each and every one of their boys in training will be well housed and well fed. . . . And while I am talking to you fathers and mothers I give one more assurance. I have said this before, but I shall say it again, and again, and again. Your boys are not going to be sent into any foreign wars.

President Franklin D. Roosevelt, in an October 30, 1940
speech, quoted in Goodwin, No Ordinary Time, *187.*
The president later tried to justify breaking this pledge by
saying that because the United States had been attacked at
Pearl Harbor, it was no longer a foreign war.

2

Gearing Up: National Defense, Military, and Economic Mobilization
1939–December 7, 1941

HISTORICAL CONTEXT

"Once the war in Europe had begun, the [U.S.] government began inching slowly away from a strict neutralist stance. Hitler's lightning war in the west leading to quick victories over Belgium, Holland, and France in the spring of 1940 was an important catalyst for speeding up industrial production in the United States intended to help Britain stave off defeat."[1]

Adolf Hitler invaded Poland on September 1, 1939, precipitating war between Germany and its satellites on the one hand and Great Britain and France on the other. On June 10, 1940, Italy declared war on England and France, thus implementing the Italo-German entente of 1936 that formed a Berlin-Rome axis.

President Franklin D. Roosevelt early on understood the global nature of the conflict and the improbability that the United States could stand aloof from it. Accordingly, over the loud protests of the isolationists, to protect the United States he undertook to bolster the Allies' resistance to Axis aggressions, to curb Japan's militaristic expansions, and at the same time to strengthen the United States's own military forces. His efforts were necessarily limited by the strong isolationist sentiment throughout the country, particularly in the Midwest, but he used every conceivable means at his command.

For example, in 1939 the Hungarian-born and German-educated physicist Leo Szilard, who had fled Nazi Germany in 1933, consulted with his former teacher and colleague Albert Einstein. Szilard, who had conceived the idea of a nuclear chain reaction, spoke of his concern about the possible German development of an atomic bomb. The two drafted a letter to FDR warning him of the possibility. The Advisory Committee on Uranium that the president then convoked eventually resulted in the decision to build such a bomb for the Allies. Two of these bombs, dropped on Japan in August 1945, ended World War II.

Aid to Great Britain and the Defense of the United States

On September 5, 1939, Roosevelt issued a proclamation of neutrality, and three days later he declared a "limited" national emergency under which he was able to make use of various emergency statutes, particularly those allowing him to expand the peacetime army and navy: He authorized an increase to 227,000 for the regular army and to 235,000 for the National Guard.[2] On September 21 he called Congress into special session to repeal the Neutrality Acts so that England and France could buy American arms. After a hot debate, Congress agreed to permit the export of all goods, including war materiel, to belligerents on a cash-and-carry basis.

As German troops stormed through Europe in a *blitzkrieg* (lightning war), the situation of the Allies deteriorated. In the late spring of 1940, between May 26 and June 4, Britain was driven out of continental Europe, its troops abandoning equipment and arms as they fought toward the ships and small boats summoned to Dunkirk, on the north coast of France, to take them back to England. Nevertheless, on June 4, 1940, British prime minister Winston Churchill defied the seemingly inevitable: "We shall not flag or fail. We shall go on to the end . . . We shall fight on the beaches, we shall fight on the landing grounds, we shall fight in the fields and in the streets, we shall fight in the hills; we shall never surrender, and even if, which I do not for a moment believe, this Island or a large part of it were subjugated and starving, then our Empire beyond the seas, armed and guarded by the British Fleet, would carry on the struggle, until, in God's good time, the new world, with all its power and might, steps forth to the rescue and liberation of the old."[3] France fell to Hitler on June 26, leaving Britain isolated, in imminent danger of invasion, and blockaded by German submarines. An agonized British cabinet was forced to contemplate surrender.[4] However, Hitler did not invade, and Britain fought on alone.

By August 1940 the British were finding it difficult to pay for the huge orders for arms and raw materials that they had placed in the United States. Roosevelt had to consider the possibility that England might be forced to negotiate with Hitler or move its government to Canada, bringing the war closer to the shores of North America.[5] On August 13, 1940, he wrote Churchill with a promise and a warning: "It is my belief that it may be possible to furnish to the British Government as immediate assistance at least fifty destroyers, the motor torpedo boats heretofore referred to, and . . . five planes each of the categories mentioned, the latter to be furnished for war-testing purposes. Such assistance, as I am sure you will understand, would only be furnished if the American people and the Congress frankly recognized that in return therefore the national defense and security of the United States would be enhanced."[6]

Throughout the rest of 1940, the British condition worsened. Moreover, in September Germany, Italy, and Japan strengthened the Axis by signing the Tripartite Treaty, whereby Japan recognized German and Italian leadership in creating a "New Order" in Europe, and Germany and Italy recognized Japan's leadership in organizing the "Greater East Asia Co-Prosperity Sphere."

Roosevelt provided as much aid to Britain as was possible legally and within the limits of public opinion. The fall of France and the desperate plight of Britain had shifted U.S. popular sentiment from absolute neutrality to efforts to aid Britain without becoming embroiled in the fighting. Insisting that the strongest defense of the United States was Britain's ability to hold out against the Germans, Roosevelt sought ways to keep ships and supplies flowing across the Atlantic. On September 3, 1940, he announced the transfer of 50 obsolete four-stack American destroyers to Britain, in return for 99-year leases on British naval and air bases in the Caribbean and Newfoundland. The destroyer-bases deal spelled, in the words of historian Warren F. Kimball, "the end of traditional American neutrality."[7] It was only the beginning of greater U.S. support for the Allies. President Roosevelt's reelection for an unprecedented third term in November 1940 enabled him to respond more freely to Churchill's anguished pleas for the ships, bombers, and munitions desperately needed for the defense of Britain.

Lend-Lease

While he labored to support England, Roosevelt tried to placate the isolationists and reassure the public. He declared his hatred for war and promised not to send American boys to fight in a foreign war. He spoke about American aid in homely terms that gained support for his policy among the people and in Congress. At a press conference on December 17, 1940, he outlined Britain's plight, telling a story about a man whose neighbor's house is on fire: Of course

The four freedoms are posted on the bulletin board of this social studies classroom in Schenectady, New York, June 1943. *(Library of Congress, LC-USW3-031440-C)*

Model for 30,000 prefabricated two-bedroom temporary emergency dwellings for Lend-Lease to Great Britain *(Library of Congress, LC-USW3-057425-C DLC)*

he lends his neighbor his garden hose to put out the fire—an action that saves his own house from burning. In this speech Roosevelt provided the rationale for what became Lend-Lease, a policy that enabled the United States to provide further aid to Britain and eventually to other Allied nations.

Twelve days later, after a devastating Nazi bomber attack on London, Roosevelt called for a massive production of war materiel to supply those nations under Nazi attack. "We must become the great arsenal of democracy. For us this is an emergency as serious as war itself. We must apply ourselves to our task with the same resolution, the same sense of urgency, the same spirit of patriotism and sacrifice as we would show were we at war. We have furnished the British great material support and we will furnish far more in the future. There will be no 'bottlenecks' in our determination to aid Great Britain. No dictator, no combination of dictators, will weaken that determination by threats of how they will construe that determination."[8] Again, in a speech to a joint session of Congress on January 6, 1941, the president urged support of those nations fighting in defense of what he called the "Four Freedoms": freedom of speech, freedom of religion, freedom from want, and freedom from fear.

Congress approved Lend-Lease in March 1941 and appropriated $7 billion to implement it. The measure, officially cited as "An Act to Promote the Defense of the United States," enabled Roosevelt to pursue the interventionist policy that he believed essential to defend the country. It authorized the president to "sell, transfer, exchange, lease, lend, or otherwise dispose of" war goods to "the government of any country whose defense the President deems vital to the defense of the United States." The act defined "defense articles" to include not only armaments, aircraft, and ships but also the materials and facilities necessary for their manufacture, production, processing, repair, servicing, and operation. Also included were component materials and equipment and any agricultural, industrial, or other commodity necessary for their production. The president was to set the terms for aid and repayment, which might be "in kind

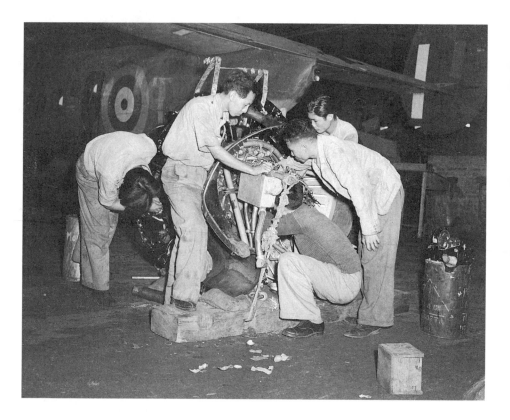

Chinese mechanics in eastern India work on an American Lend-Lease Cyclone motor for a Hudson bomber (also Lend-Lease). *(Library of Congress, LC-USW3-057131-C)*

or property, or any other direct or indirect benefit which the President deems satisfactory." Passage of Lend-Lease committed the United States to support Britain's war effort against Nazi Germany, subject only to two restrictions: "Nothing in this Act shall be construed to authorize or to permit the authorization of convoying vessels by naval vessels of the United States," and "Nothing in this Act shall be construed to authorize or to permit the authorization of the entry of any American vessel into a combat area in violation of section 3 of the Neutrality Act of 1939."

Initially intended to help Great Britain, the program was soon extended to include China and the Soviet Union after the latter was attacked by Nazi Germany in June 1941. By war's end Lend-Lease assistance was extended to more than 40 nations at a total cost of $50 billion, of which $31 billion went to countries of the British Commonwealth and over $11 billion to the Soviet Union.[9]

Lend-Lease was enacted into law over the vehement objections of isolationists in and out of Congress, who denounced the plan as a clear road to war, ridiculing the argument that it was "aid short of war." Churchill, on the other hand, hailed its passage before Parliament as "the most unsordid act in the history of any nation."

Cooperation with Britain

By the Lend-Lease Act the United States transformed itself from a friendly neutral to an active nonbelligerent, extending help to the Allied cause ever more widely.[10] In April 1941 U.S. troops went to Greenland, vital as the site of a cryolite mine needed to produce aluminum, as a base for aircraft flying antisubmarine patrols, and as a base for ferrying planes to Britain.[11] In the same month the navy broadened its patrols eastward and began reporting U-boat (German submarine) positions to the British. That month too, under the terms of the Pan-American Neutrality Act of 1939, the United States in cooperation with the Congress of American Republics began operating a "neutrality patrol" that effectively excluded U-boats from the Atlantic west of Bermuda.[12] On May 27 Roosevelt proclaimed an "unlimited" national emergency, which further enlarged his powers.[13] In July the United States occupied Iceland, an area considered critical in the battle against U-boats. That summer also Roosevelt ordered the navy to escort merchant convoys as far as Iceland—a move that resulted in an undeclared war between American destroyers and German submarines and led to the sinking of the U.S. destroyer *Reuben James* by the Germans on October 31. By the fall of 1941 British warships were being repaired in American shipyards, and pilots and air crews of the Royal Air Force were being trained in the United States. To help the British navy guard the sea lanes of the western Atlantic, the United States enlarged and reequipped its navy.[14]

By supporting the British war effort, the United States was buying time to build up its own military and defense industry. U.S. military and civilian specialists, especially technicians, moved back and forth across the Atlantic, informing the British about American methods, reporting British methods, and coordinating British and American efforts to defeat the Axis. British combat-testing of U.S. planes and weapons transferred to them under Lend-Lease enabled U.S. observers to recommend changes in their design.[15] Moreover, beginning in August 1940 the two countries were developing plans for military cooperation if and when the United States had to enter the war.[16] These discussions were nonbinding and subject to alteration or renunciation, but they enabled planning and prioritizing for the administration of Lend-Lease.[17] A U.S. military mission working from London offices scouted for potential bases and oversaw Lend-Lease deals.[18] At the United States–British Staff Conversations that began on March 27, 1941, the participants agreed that if and when the United States went to war, its army air force would collaborate with the Royal Air Force in attacking German military power at its sources. At this conference American representatives also agreed to the important decision, held to throughout the war, to set the defeat of Germany, rather than Japan, as the Allies' first priority.

In the United States scientist Vannevar Bush of the Carnegie Institution headed first the National Defense Research Committee and then its successor, the Office of Scientific Research and Development (OSRD). Well-funded, and ultimately commanding the services of 30,000 scientists and engineers, this agency developed radar, bomb sights, sonar to detect submarines, the proximity fuse to increase accuracy of artillery fire, an improved homing device for aerial bombs, and computers. Academic and industrial laboratories in Canada and England as well as the United States shared in this work. The OSRD sent Harvard president James Conant to England to facilitate the exchange of scientific information on all subjects, including atomic energy and radar.[19]

As 1941 drew to an end, the United States adopted an even more openly warlike stance. In September 1941 President Roosevelt announced that American ships would convoy British supplies and that the U.S. Navy would shoot on sight German raiders that came within the broad American defensive zones in the Atlantic. In November the U.S. Coast Guard was transferred from the Treasury Department, which controlled it during peacetime, to the navy. That month too Congress in a close vote lifted restrictions that forbade American ships to sail into combat zones and permitted the arming of American merchant ships.[20]

Cooperation with Britain benefited the United States vitally in the development of its security forces. In July 1941 Roosevelt created the office of the Coordinator of Information, the nation's first peacetime, freestanding intelligence organization, to

> collect and analyze all information and data, which may bear upon national security: to correlate such information and data, and to make such information and data available to the President and to such departments and officials of the Government as the President may determine; and to carry out, when requested by the President, such supplementary activities as may facilitate the securing of information important for national security not now available to the Government.[21]

This office was directed by William "Wild Bill" Donovan, who had military experience in World War I and thereafter worked as a civilian attorney. It functioned until June 1942, when it was succeeded by the Office of Strategic Services, which Donovan also headed. In its early days it relied heavily on the sophisticated and experienced British intelligence service in developing its methods and training its personnel. Moreover, to improve the detection and frustration of enemy espionage and sabotage activities in the Western Hemisphere, the British and U.S. security services began working out methods of cooperation. Together they thwarted attempted Nazi takeovers in Bolivia and Panama.[22]

In the 15 months between the outbreak of hostilities in Europe and the December 1941 Japanese attack that forced the United States into the war, President Roosevelt had to maintain a balance not only between support for Great Britain and isolationist sentiment in the United State but also between the demands for Lend-Lease and the needs of the U.S. military. U.S. naval officials warned that its Pacific fleet must not be stripped of equipment by the urgency of defending against U-boats in the Atlantic, and U.S. Army experts warned that both their ground and air forces were seriously short of equipment and weaponry, both in quantity and in quality.

Strengthening the U.S. Military

Getting money for adequate U.S. defense was not easy in the face of a Congress determined to keep the country out of foreign wars. Nonetheless, even before the outbreak of hostilities in Europe, Roosevelt found opportunities to strengthen the military. For example, during the Great Depression he had used Work Projects Administration (WPA) funds to make machine tools for the manufacture of small-arms ammunition—a move that advanced the production schedule for that ammunition by at least a year.[23] The WPA, instituted originally to furnish jobs to the unemployed, also accomplished a great deal in the construction of airports, highways, and bridges that later proved to have strategic importance, and the experience gained by army engineers in these endeavors served them well in wartime. In 1938 Gen. George Marshall discovered that the WPA and the Public Works Administration had spent about $250 million on war department projects; in its issue of May 1942 the *Army and Navy Register* reported: "In the years 1935 to 1939, when regular appropriations for the armed forces were so meager, it was the W.P.A. worker who saved many army posts and Naval stations from literal obsolescence."[24] Again, in September 1938 Roosevelt sent Harry Hopkins to the Pacific Coast to form some estimate of the prospects for expanding the aircraft industry for war production.[25] In spring 1939 Congress authorized the Civilian Pilot Training Program and the organization of a Coast Guard auxiliary of civilian small-boat owners to help in patrol work.

Nevertheless, after the outbreak of war in Europe in September 1939 most Americans were taken aback by the weakness of the country's military. In May 1940 the U.S. military force consisted of a small regular army of 75,000 men, a one-ocean navy, and an air force fewer than 24,000 men—a military force 19th in size worldwide.[26] It so lacked prestige that most officers wore civilian clothes to work; when on December 8, 1941, Secretary of War Henry Stimson ordered all officers in the department to wear uniforms to work, the place reeked of mothballs—"an odor," commented military historian Geoffrey Perret, "that suited the place. The department was a time-locked curiosity, an archaeological wonder, something like ancient Troy."[27]

In September 1940 the Congress enacted the country's first peacetime military draft (the Selective Training and Service Act), and Roosevelt ordered a partial mobilization of the National Guard. Although Selective Service was maintained only by the slimmest majority, administration efforts to build up America's military force were, in the main, acceptable even to many isolationists—so long as their purpose was to defend the country from attack. Traditional military wisdom envisaged mobilization as something that occurred *after* the need presented itself and thus was tied to the actual outbreak of hostilities. Modern war, however, required more lead time, both to produce the increasingly sophisticated tools of war and to train personnel to use them.[28]

Accordingly, beginning that fall the Selective Service system sent men into the military to be trained for a period of a year—a period that, when the United States entered the war, was extended to the duration of the war plus six months. The Selective Service system worked as well as it did in large part because it utilized local draft boards, volunteers who knew local conditions and sometimes were acquainted with the young men who were being called up—expertise that enabled them to make fair and compassionate decisions about whom to call up and whom to defer.

Responsibility for creating a mass army fell to Gen. George Marshall and the men he selected to command it. Getting the manpower was a problem solved by the draft, but these men had to be housed, fed, equipped, and trained. So neglected and starved was the U.S. military that at first the draftees had to train with wooden models of rifles and tanks. The greatest barrier to military preparedness was the lack of physical facilities, which required from several months to two years or even longer to create. To have delayed the construction of such facilities until the United States was actually involved in battle might have lost the war before it began.

Every branch of the armed services struggled to modernize its equipment and make its organization and tactics more efficient and effective. Serious problems of this order had to be worked out before the U.S. Army could meet Hitler's military power in combat—like the search for an effective tank and for an effective weapon against tanks. The Sherman tank was designed in haste in 1940; it proved maneuverable, reliable, and durable, but it lacked the armor of the German tanks it faced in battle. In early 1940 Capt. Leslie Skinner and Lt. David E. Uhl were assigned the task of devising a workable weapon powerful enough to knock out a tank. By May 1942 they produced a weapon officially designated "Launcher, Rocket, Anti-Tank, M1" but better known as a "bazooka." General Marshall, impressed by its performance at an Aberdeen Proving Ground demonstration, ordered 5,000 of these bazookas from General Electric, which contracted to produce them within 30 days. It took 22 days to design, test, and redesign them. Steel and gunstocks were transported to the factory by plane or in the trunks of racing police cars. The last bazooka left the factory only 89 minutes before the deadline.[29] To such industrial pushes the Allies owed much of their ultimate victory.

German military successes in the spring and summer of 1940 gave impetus to the demand for U.S. rearmament. Meeting this demand was another matter. First, the military services did not know exactly what they might need.[30] Early on they had supposed that they would be defending U.S. territory. As industrialist Donald Nelson wrote in 1940, "None of us—not one that I know of, except the President—saw that we might be fighting Germany and Japan all over the world."[31] Though the 1914–18 conflict has long been called a world war, in actuality it was largely confined to Europe, and it was as a European war that most Americans thought of the conflagration ignited in 1939. When in 1941 some military leaders began to glimpse its global nature, they recognized needs far exceeding their previous estimates.

Second, the Roosevelt administration and the military dared not request appropriations from the Congress for equipment like landing ships that they already knew would be vital should the United States have to fight, lest they be accused of dragging the nation into war. They had to proceed cautiously within the boundaries set by isolationist fervor and the reluctance of the nation to involve itself in a foreign war.

Third, many companies dragged their feet about making the change from peacetime to wartime production. Some of their executives were isolationists: For instance, in June 1940 automobile manufacturer Henry Ford refused a government contract to build Rolls Royce aircraft engines for England. But most industrialists were simply worried about the risks involved. The consumer goods they were manufacturing were selling fast. Distrusting Roosevelt, dreading government control, and made wary by the depth and length of the Great Depression, they feared to take on the expense of retooling and retraining their labor force for a war that might end soon in a German victory.

Mobilizing U.S. Industry

An Industrial Mobilization Plan had been prepared by the U.S. Army in 1931 and revised by the Army and Navy Munitions Board (ANMB) in 1933, 1936, and 1939.[32] During the 1930s this board compiled lists of critical materials and successfully appealed to Congress for modest funds to import and stockpile them. It also surveyed industrial capacities. In mid-1939, President Roosevelt assumed direct control of the ANMB by placing it in the executive office of the president.

The Industrial Mobilization Plan assumed that in wartime the president would create and staff temporary civilian agencies to direct industrial production.[33] It provided for a civilian superagency, a War Resources Administration (WRA), to oversee war finance, trade, labor, the procurement of strategic materials, and price-control organizations. The armed forces would see to their own procurement, but the WRA would balance their needs against those of the rest of the nation.[34] In actuality, things were never so tidy or so well defined. Instead production was managed—and often mismanaged—by a set of agencies whose responsibilities and powers overlapped and whose titles, duties, and personnel changed confusingly, especially as Roosevelt often sought to avoid problems by creating yet another agency.

The War Resources Board (WRB) was created August 4, 1939, to provide civilian oversight of production and distribution. Edward R. Stettinius, Jr., chairman of the board of the United States Steel Corporation, headed the WRB, which also included the president of the Massachusetts Institute of Technology, Karl T. Compton; the president of American Telephone & Telegraph, Walter S. Gifford; and a director of General Motors, John L. Pratt. It immediately came under attack both by reformers, who feared that its creation would undermine support for recent social legislation, and by labor and agriculture representatives angry about their omission from the board. It was dissolved November 24 of that year—only to be followed by a multitude of presidentially created boards and bureaus that regulated the nation's entire economic life throughout the war and that, despite false starts, mistakes, and prophecies of doom, somehow muddled into triumphs of production, research, and supply.

Persistently, the president nudged and cajoled, trying to shift the nation to a wartime economy. The beginning of the mobilization of civilian manpower for defense came in late May 1940 with the formation of the National Defense Advisory Commission (NDAC)—a superagency of the sort envisioned by the army's Industrial Mobilization Plan. It became, according to presidential speechwriter Robert Sherwood, "the parent of all the war production, food production, priorities and price control organizations."[35] Its members included William S. Knudsen of General Motors (industrial production), Sidney Hillman of the Congress of Industrial Organizations (labor), Edward Stettinius of U.S. Steel (industrial materials), economist Leon Henderson (price stabilization), railroad president Ralph Budd (transportation), farmer and banker Chester C. Davis (agriculture), and political scientist Harriet Elliott (consumer protection). Donald M. Nelson of Sears Roebuck was later added to coordinate national defense purchases. With no precedents to guide it, the NDAC assembled a staff to prepare the country for war.

High-powered industrialists became the men of the hour, many of them working for the federal government for $1 a year while they retained their corporate salaries. Given much authority, they undertook broadly defined tasks. For example, Donald Nelson summoned textile manufacturer Robert T. Stevens and told him, "Look around in the War and Navy Departments and find out what their requirements are in textiles and figure out a way to meet them."[36] These executives often proved effective, but to the disappointment of small businesses they tended to deal with people they already knew, and to award defense contracts to the largest corporations, whom they felt they could count on for speed and reliability.

To induce industry to build more war plants, Roosevelt secured the legislation of June 25, 1940, giving new powers to the Reconstruction Finance Corporation (RFC), an agency established in 1932 by Roosevelt's predecessor, Herbert Hoover. With its new authority the RFC could make loans to and buy stock in any corporation. By such means it could finance plant construction, expansion, and the purchase of equipment and help manufacturers to produce and acquire strategic and critical materials. Thus "[a]n RFC loan helped [Henry Kaiser] to erect a gigantic new steel mill at Fontana, in southern California, to keep [his ship]yards supplied with steel."[37] Again, a section of the Selective Service Act of August 1940 empowered the secretaries of war and navy to require any manufacturer to produce necessary war materials. Great Britain financed the construction of 61 war production plants in the United States at a cost of $171 million.[38] The U.S. government guaranteed profits for manufacturers by negotiating cost-plus contracts, by which manufacturers were paid whatever costs they incurred plus a given profit—an open invitation to high costs, but an effective means to persuade them to support the defense effort.

In 1941 Roosevelt moved to mobilize the work force. He created the Fair Employment Practices Commission, entrusting to it the double task of utilizing all available personnel in the fullest employment possible to achieve high production and of eliminating discrimination against workers.

Even after Pearl Harbor, industry continued to stall. Robert Sherwood described the "whole production imbroglio before Pearl Harbor and even after it" as a "story of endless tugging and hauling between the proponents of the total war effort and the protectors of the civilian economy." This struggle was sometimes known as the "Battle of 7-Up," in which "valuable trucks were being used to deliver the soft drink of that name to bobby soxers [teenagers] when they ought to be delivering ammunition to troops."[39]

Despite the bitter opposition of the isolationists and despite the skepticism of the American people about international involvement, the United States built its defenses in the years between the outbreak of the European war in September 1939 and the Japanese attack on Pearl Harbor in December 1941. All in all, by that time, some 35 separate agencies had been created to mobilize and organize the country for war.[40] Increasingly throughout this period Roosevelt succeeded in procuring congressional appropriations to build military and industrial muscle, so that the nation was far better prepared for global war in 1941 than it had been when it entered World War I in 1917. During 1941 defense production soared: For example, from January 1941 to December 1941, munitions production increased 225 percent. The military services numbered 2 million men by the end of 1941. Lend-Lease was flowing freely, supplying vitally needed goods to the Allies.[41]

Negotiations with Japan

Throughout these years of growing support for the Allied cause in Europe, Roosevelt also had to weigh the increasing gravity of Japanese aggression in

Asia. Japan's alliance with Germany threatened the security of the United States, confronting the country with the dread prospect of a two-ocean war. Roosevelt sought to counter Japan's expansionism by economic measures, such as embargoes on scrap iron and oil, by supporting the regime of Chiang Kai-shek in China, and by sending the Pacific fleet to Hawaii. He outlined the U.S. position to a congressional delegation in October 1940: "We pick no quarrels with Japan. We back down on no issue with her. We reserve the right to use economic pressure in the hope of bringing Japan to reason. The door, meanwhile, is to be left wide open for discussion and accommodation within the framework of our historic position in the Far East."[42] In that month's polls 96 percent of Americans expressing an opinion approved the total embargo on scrap iron against Japan, and those who thought that the country should chance a war with Japan to prevent its control of China had risen 17 percentage points to 29 percent.[43] In the spring of 1941 the State Department refused a Japanese proposal that the United States mediate an end to the Sino-Japanese war, lest the Japanese use the military forces so freed against the United States or the Allied cause. Negotiations with Japan continued throughout most of 1941, with Japan protesting ever more heatedly the economic measures imposed against it yet refusing to withdraw its army from China—a key issue for the United States.

The American people did not expect Pearl Harbor, but many among them by the time of the attack recognized that the question of the country's involvement in World War II had long since been answered.

CHRONICLE OF EVENTS

1939

April: Congress authorizes President Franklin D. Roosevelt to reorganize the government.

June: Congress authorizes the creation of a Coast Guard Auxiliary of civilian small-boat owners willing to serve in patrol work.

June: The Civilian Pilot Training Program is established, providing pilot training across the country and allowing one woman to be trained for every ten men.

August 2: Albert Einstein sends the first of three letters to FDR alerting the president to the possibility of the development of an atomic bomb. FDR then creates the Advisory Committee on Uranium.

August 9: The Navy and War Departments form the War Resources Board, but it lasts only until November 24, 1939.

September 8: FDR proclaims a limited national emergency.

October 2: The Pan-American Conference agrees on a 300-mile security zone off the American coast; any act of war therein will be considered a hostile act against the nearby country. The U.S. Navy is to enforce this declaration.

November 4: The Neutrality Act of 1935 is revised to allow the United States to furnish materiel to combatants on a cash-and-carry basis.

1940

The National Defense Research Committee is created, absorbing the Uranium Committee, and work on atomic fission is given highest priority and a substantial budget.

April: The U.S. Pacific fleet is based at Pearl Harbor to deter Japanese aggression.

May: The National Defense Act permits the president to keep at home all products that may be needed for defense, including oil.

May 10: Adolf Hitler launches a successful attack on France, Belgium, and the Netherlands.

May 16: FDR seeks appropriations to finance more men for the army, purchase guns and equipment, build modern tanks, construct naval ships, and support the capacity to build 50,000 planes a year.

May 25: FDR creates the Office of Emergency Management.

May 26–June 4: British and Allied troops are evacuated from Dunkirk on the French coast.

May 28: As a step toward industrial mobilization, FDR reactivates the National Defense Advisory Committee (predecessor of the Office of Production Management) under the Office of Emergency Management.

May 31: FDR introduces a billion-dollar defense program to build up American military strength.

June: The National Association of Manufacturers in a full-page advertisement pledges its knowledge, skill, and resources to the national defense.

June: FDR asks Vannevar Bush to organize and run the National Defense Research Committee, later superseded by the Office of Scientific Research and Development, which Bush also heads.

June 12: FDR sends Britain 93 bomber planes, 500,000 Enfield rifles, 184 tanks, 76,000 machine guns, 25,000 Browning automatic rifles, 895 75-mm guns, and 100 million rounds of ammunition.

June 14: FDR signs a naval expansion bill.

June 22: France surrenders to Germany.

Adolf Hitler stands in Paris on June 23, 1940, the day after he defeated France. *(National Archives, 242-HLB-5073-20)*

June 25: Congress authorizes negotiated contracts rather than competitive bidding and authorizes the Reconstruction Finance Corporation to create agencies to build metal and rubber supplies.

June 26: FDR refuses U.S. military advice to discontinue aid to Britain and transfer most of the American fleet to the Atlantic Ocean. Congress authorizes an army of 375,000.

June 28: Congress limits profits on defense production contracts to 8 percent.

July 10: The Battle of Britain begins.

July 19: FDR signs the "Two-Ocean Navy Expansion Act," authorizing an increase of about 70 percent in total tonnage of naval vessels.

July 28: The United States prohibits selling aviation fuel, scrap iron, and steel to countries outside the Americas.

August 14: A British scientific mission brings the United States details of Britain's research in vital military fields.

August 22: The Defense Plant Corporation is established to develop defense production capability.

August 27: Congress authorizes FDR to call the National Guard and reserves to active duty for 12 months for training.

August 29: The Defense Supplies Corporation is created to stockpile strategic materials not covered under other legislation.

September 3: Under his authority to increase the national security, FDR sends 50 destroyers to Britain in exchange for island bases for the U.S. military.

September 9: Congress votes $128 million for the construction of military bases and $100 million for defense housing.

September 16: The Selective Service Bill is enacted into law, the first U.S. peacetime draft.

October: Congress authorizes each state to establish a state guard in the absence of its National Guard.

October 14: Congress passes the Community Facilities Act (the Lanham Act) and appropriates $150 million for purchasing land and constructing housing, utilities, nursery schools, child care centers, transportation, and other community facilities.

November 11: The jeep makes its debut.

December 17: FDR in a press conference outlines a plan to provide aid to Britain that he describes as similar to lending a neighbor a hose to put out a fire. This plan becomes Lend-Lease.

December 23: The British Purchasing Mission is allowed to buy up to 40 percent of U.S. aircraft production.

December 29: FDR in a fireside chat proposes that the United States become the "arsenal of democracy" and give full aid to Britain.

1941

January 2: FDR announces a program to produce 200 7,500-ton "liberty ships."

January 3: FDR announces that he is sending Harry Hopkins to London "to maintain . . . personal relations between me and the British government." Hopkins tells Churchill, "I came here to see how we can beat that fellow Hitler."

January 6: FDR enunciates the Four Freedoms in his State of the Union message to Congress and again refers to the U.S. role as the "arsenal of democracy."

January 7: FDR creates the Office of Production Management, headed by William Knudsen of General Motors and Sidney Hillman of the Amalgamated Clothing Workers of America.

January 29–March 27: Secret staff talks between British and American military representatives in Washington produce agreement on joint policies in the event of war with Germany and Japan.

February: Congress creates the Coast Guard Temporary Reserve, members of which serve without pay.

February 18: FDR sends Averell Harriman as his personal representative to London to "recommend everything that we can do, short of war, to keep the British Isles afloat."

February 24: The Office of Production Management releases the first industry-wide priority schedule affecting aluminum and machine tools.

March: A U.S. delegation visits England to select sites for American air and naval bases in case the United States enters the war with Germany.

March: Steel workers at Bethlehem, Pennsylvania, strike over continued company support of a company union, violating a National Labor Relations Board order.

March 1: The U.S. Senate establishes a Special Committee to Investigate National Defense Programs, chaired by Senator Harry Truman.

March 11: Congress passes the first Lend-Lease Act, enabling Britain to borrow or lease any equipment the president deems vital for the defense of the United States.

March 19: FDR creates the National Defense Mediation Board to settle all labor disputes in defense industries.

March 27: In the ABC-1 Staff Agreement the United States and Great Britain agree that in the event that the United States enters the war, they will both focus first on defeating Germany.

April 4: FDR allows British navy ships on combat missions to be repaired and to refuel in the United States.

April 9: At the invitation of Denmark, the United States undertakes to protect Greenland.

April 11: The United States extends the American Defense Zone and declares the Red Sea no longer a "combat zone," thus permitting U.S. ships to carry cargo to ports in that area, including supplies for the British in Egypt.

April 11: FDR creates the Office of Price Administration and Civilian Supply under economist Leon Henderson to recommend price control measures.

April 14: Iceland agrees to allow U.S. occupation to replace British forces there.

April 17: The auto industry agrees to a 20 percent cut in the production of civilian automobiles beginning on August 1.

April 24: FDR orders U.S. warships to report to the British movements of German warships west of Iceland, making official what had been an unofficial practice.

May 1: U.S. Defense Savings Bonds and Stamps go on sale.

May 20: The Office of Civilian Defense (OCD) is created, with New York mayor Fiorello LaGuardia as director.

May 27: FDR declares an unlimited national emergency, a step that he can take only when he believes war to be imminent and that gives him the power to increase the size of the military, place compulsory defense orders in factories, and assign priority rating to producers and suppliers.

June: FDR uses his emergency powers to seize North American Aviation at Inglewood, California, after strikers violate their pledge to remain at work while negotiations with management continue.

June 6: Legislation allows the U.S. government to confiscate foreign ships in U.S. ports.

June 14: FDR freezes German and Italian assets in the United States.

June 15: FDR creates the Fair Employment Practices Committee.

June 16: FDR closes all German and Italian consulates in the United States.

June 22: Germany attacks the Soviet Union.

June 24: FDR announces that he will send aid to the Soviet Union.

June 25: FDR creates the Committee on Fair Employment Practice to prohibit racial discrimination in defense industries.

June 28: The Office of Scientific Research and Development is created to conduct research on weapons of war.

July: The Office of Production Management announces an aluminum scrap drive.

July 11: FDR names William J. "Wild Bill" Donovan "coordinator of information," thus creating the first U.S. central intelligence system. In 1942 this service becomes the Office of Strategic Services.

July 21: FDR asks Congress to extend the draft period from one year to 30 months. The bill barely passes.

July 24: The American Federation of Labor and the Office of Production Management sign a no-strike agreement for the duration of the national emergency.

July 26: FDR freezes all Japanese assets in the United States, notifies the Japanese that the Panama Canal will be closed for repairs, and cuts off shipments of high-octane gasoline to Japan.

August: FDR creates the Supply Priorities and Allocation Board as the policy-making and coordinating agency for the entire defense program. The new board works on allocation of materials until the creation of the War Production Board on January 16, 1942.

August 1: FDR bans exports of oil and aviation fuel except to Britain, the British Empire, and the Western Hemisphere.

August 2: Lend-Lease aid for the Soviet Union begins.

August 9–12: British prime minister Winston Churchill and FDR, meeting at sea, issue the Atlantic Charter.

September: The Ford Willow Run bomber plant near Detroit is completed with 3.5 million square feet of factory space, the largest in the world. On October 1, 1942, the first B-24 Liberator bomber rolls off the assembly line.

September 1: The U.S. Navy may now escort convoys in the Atlantic that include at least one U.S. merchant ship.

September 11: Using the incident of a clash at sea on September 4 between the USS *Greer* and a German submarine as provocation, FDR announces that American ships will convoy British supplies, and the navy will shoot on sight in waters "the protection of which is necessary for American defense."

September 19: The American cargo vessel *Pink Star* carrying food for Britain is sunk off Greenland.

October 2: The United States occupies Funafuti, Tuvalu, a tiny coral atoll in the South Pacific with a large lagoon.

October 17: A German torpedo strikes the U.S. destroyer *Kearney.*

October 31: A German torpedo hits and sinks the U.S. destroyer *Reuben James.*

November 1: The Coast Guard is transferred from the Treasury Department to the navy.

November 8: Revisions in the Neutrality Act enable the arming of American merchant ships.

November 20: Japan proposes that Japanese troops might be pulled back to the northern part of Indochina once Japan has gained control over the Chinese mainland, setting a deadline of midnight, November 30, for American acceptance. U.S. secretary of state Cordell Hull replies that Japan should withdraw from China (not Manchuria or Korea), but he leaves room for further negotiation.

November and December: Defense Special Trains tour the country with exhibits of 60,000 parts needed by the army and navy, so that small manufacturers can see what they can do to help defense production.

December: The Office of Scientific Research and Development is established.

EYEWITNESS TESTIMONY

Aid to Great Britain and the Defense of the United States

Some indeed still hold to the now somewhat obvious delusion that we of the United States can safely permit the United States to become a lone island in a world dominated by the philosophy of force. . . . Such an island represents to me and to the overwhelming majority of Americans today a helpless nightmare, the helpless nightmare of a people without freedom. Yes, the nightmare of a people lodged in prison, handcuffed, hungry and fed through the bars from day to day by the contemptuous, unpitying masters of other continents. . . .

Overwhelmingly we, as a nation, and this applies to all the other American nations, we are convinced that military and naval victory for the gods of force and hate would endanger the institutions of democracy in the Western World—and that equally, therefore, the whole of our sympathies lie with those nations that are giving their life blood in combat against those forces.

Franklin D. Roosevelt, speech at the University of Virginia, Charlottesville, June 10, 1940, available online. U.S. State Department, URL: http://usinfo.state.gov/usa/infousa/facts/democrac/52.htm.

The President [Roosevelt] will sell about 50 destroyers to the British. He will do this without submitting the matter to Congress. His lawyers are working on the ways and means of doing it legally. Politically, the President believes that the public will accept it, given the fact that the United States is getting the naval bases it desires. Strategically, the President believes that the Navy will now favor it, since the new naval bases are a greater asset to our defense than 50 old destroyers.

U.S. minister to Canada Jay Pierrepont Moffat, August–September 1940, relaying information he had received from Canadian prime minister Mackenzie King, quoted in Lash, Roosevelt and Churchill, 213.

No combination of dictator countries of Europe and Asia will stop the help we are giving to almost the last free people now fighting to hold them at bay. . . . We will continue to pile up our defenses and our armaments. We will continue to help those who resist aggression, and who now hold the oppressors far from our shores.

President Franklin D. Roosevelt, in response to the signing of the Tripartite Pact by Germany, Italy, and Japan, campaign speech on Columbus Day 1940, quoted in Lash, Roosevelt and Churchill, 227.

The experience of the past two years has proven beyond doubt that no nation can appease the Nazis. . . .

Thinking in terms of today and tomorrow . . . there is far less chance of the United States getting into war if we do all that we can now to support the nations now defending themselves against attack by the Axis than if we acquiesce in their defeat, submit tamely to an Axis victory, and wait our turn to be the object of attack. . . .

We must be the great arsenal of democracy. . . .

President Franklin D. Roosevelt, "Arsenal of Democracy" speech, December 29, 1940, available online. Temple University, URL: http://oll.temple.edu/hist249/course/Documents/arsenal of democracy.htm.

Lend-Lease

[With Lend-Lease] this country passes from large promises carried out slyly and partially by clever devices to substantial deeds openly and honestly avowed.

Journalist Walter Lippman, December 1940, quoted in Steel, Walter Lippman, 389.

I go back to the idea that one thing that is necessary for American national defense is additional productive facilities; and the more we increase those facilities—factories, shipbuilding ways, munitions plants, etc., and so on—the stronger American national defense is. Now orders from Great Britain are therefore a tremendous asset to American national defense, because they create, automatically, additional facilities. I am talking selfishly, from the American point of view—nothing else. . . .

Suppose my neighbor's home catches fire, and I have got a length of garden hose four or five hundred

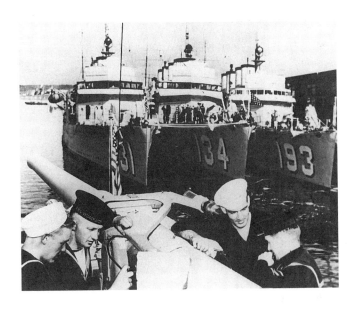

At a Canadian port, U.S. naval gunners instruct gunners from the British navy in the operation of a secret device that is part of the guns aboard the over-age destroyers turned over to Britain in exchange for naval and air bases, September 1940. *(National Archives, PHOCO-A-7420[283])*

feet away; but, my heaven, if he can take my garden hose and connect it up with his hydrant, I may help him to put out his fire. . . . I don't say to him before that operation, "Neighbor, my garden hose cost me $15; you have got to pay me $15 for it." . . . I don't want $15—I want my garden hose back after the fire is over.

President Franklin D. Roosevelt, speaking at a press conference, December 17, 1940, in Roosevelt, Public Papers and Addresses, 1940, *643.*

I find it, unhappily, necessary to report that the future and the safety of our country and of our democracy are overwhelmingly involved in events far beyond our borders.

Armed defense of democratic existence is now being gallantly waged in four continents. If that defense fails, all the population and all the resources of Europe, Asia, Africa, and Australasia will be dominated by the conquerors. Let us remember that the total of those populations and their resources in those four continents greatly exceeds the sum total of the population and the resources of the whole of the western hemisphere—many times over.

In times like these it is immature—and incidentally, untrue—for anybody to brag that an unprepared America, single-handed, and with one hand tied behind its back, can hold off the whole world.

No realistic American can expect from a dictator's peace international generosity, or return of true independence, or world disarmament, or freedom of expression, or freedom of religion—or even good business. . . .

There is much loose talk of our immunity from immediate and direct invasion from across the seas. . . .

The first phase of the invasion of this hemisphere would not be the landing of regular troops. The necessary strategic points would be occupied by secret agents and their dupes—and great numbers of them are already here, and in Latin America. . . .

Therefore, the immediate need is a swift and driving increase in our armament production. . . . I shall ask this Congress for greatly increased new appropriations and authorizations to carry on what we have begun.

I also ask this Congress for authority and for funds sufficient to manufacture additional munitions and war supplies of many kinds, to be turned over to those nations which are now in actual war with aggressor nations. . . . The time is near when they will not be able to pay for them all in ready cash. We cannot, and we will not, tell them that they must surrender, merely because of inability to pay for the weapons which we know they must have. . . . I recommend that we make it possible for those nations to continue to obtain war materials in the United States, fitting their orders into our own program. Nearly all their materiel would, if the time ever came, be useful for our own defense. . . .

For what we send abroad, we shall be repaid within a reasonable time following the close of hostilities, in similar materials, or, at our option, in other goods of many kinds, which they can produce and which we need. . . .

Such aid is not an act of war, even if a dictator should unilaterally proclaim it so to be. . . .

In the future days, which we seek to make secure, we look forward to a world founded upon four essential human freedoms.

The first is freedom of speech and expression—everywhere in the world.

The second is freedom of every person to worship God in his own way—everywhere in the world.

The third is freedom from want—which, translated into world terms, means economic understandings which will secure to every nation a healthy peacetime life for its inhabitants—everywhere in the world.

The fourth is freedom from fear—which, translated into world terms, means a world-wide reduction of armaments to such a point and in such a thorough fashion that no nation will be in a position to commit an act of physical aggression against any neighbor—anywhere in the world....

President Franklin D. Roosevelt, State of the Union address, January 6, 1941, quoted in the New York Times, *January 7, 1941, 5.*

Cooperation with Britain

The President has laid down the secret ruling for the closest possible marriage between the FBI and British Intelligence. The fact that this cooperation was agreed upon is striking evidence of President Roosevelt's clarity of vision. The fact that it has to be kept secret even from the State Department is a measure of the strength of American neutrality. It is an essential first step toward combating enemy operations but it is insufficient to meet the demands of the situation. The Nazis in America are already well organized and well entrenched. They realize the extent of British dependence on American material aid, and so direct their subversive propaganda toward buttressing the wall of traditional isolationism by which the President is encompassed.

William Stephenson, chief of British intelligence operations in the United States, to Prime Minister Winston Churchill, probably in spring 1940, quoted in Lash, Roosevelt and Churchill, *140.*

The function of your Committee [the National Defense Research Council] is of great importance in these times of national stress. The methods and mechanisms of warfare have altered radically in recent times, and they will alter still further in the future. This country is singularly fitted, by reason of the ingenuity of its people, the knowledge and skill of its scientists, the flexibility of its industrial structure, to excel in the arts of peace, and to excel in the arts of war if that be necessary. The scientists and engineers of the country, under the guidance of your Committee, and in close collaboration with the armed services, can be of substantial aid in the task which lies before us.

President Franklin D. Roosevelt, letter to Vannevar Bush, June 15, 1940, in Sherwood, Roosevelt and Hopkins, *156.*

We have declared Red Sea area no longer a combat zone. We propose sending all types of goods in unarmed American flagships to Egypt or any other non-belligerent port via Red Sea or Persian Gulf. We think we can work out sending wheat and other goods in American ships to Greenland or Iceland through the next six months. We hope to make available for direct haul to England a large amount of your present shipping which is now utilized for other purposes. We expect to make use of [recently seized] Danish ships very soon and Italian ships in two months.

President Franklin D. Roosevelt, cable to Winston Churchill, April 10, 1941, quoted in Lash, Roosevelt and Churchill, *299–300.*

[The U.S. Atlantic fleet] will protect all merchant ships—not only American ships but ships of any flag—engaged in commerce in our defensive waters.... From now on, if German or Italian vessels of war enter the waters, the protection of which is necessary for American defense, they do so at their own peril.

President Franklin D. Roosevelt, September 1941, after a German submarine attacked an American destroyer, quoted in Lash, Roosevelt and Churchill, *418.*

Strengthening the U.S. Military

On this tenth day of June, 1940, the hand that held the dagger has struck it into the back of its neighbor [Italy has attacked France].... In our American unity, we will pursue two obvious and simultaneous courses: we will extend to the opponents of force the material resources of this nation; and, at the same time, we will harness and speed up the use of these resources in order that we ourselves in the Americas may have equipment and training equal to the task of any emergency and every defense.

President Franklin D. Roosevelt, speaking on June 10, 1940, in Charlottesville, Virginia, quoted in Lash, Roosevelt and Churchill, *152.*

Prime Minister Winston Churchill of the United Kingdom (left), President Franklin D. Roosevelt (center), and Prime Minister of Canada Mackenzie King (right) meet at a press conference. *(Library of Congress)*

I simply have not got enough Navy to go round—and every little episode in the Pacific means fewer ships in the Atlantic.

> *President Franklin D. Roosevelt, letter to Secretary of the Interior Harold Ickes, July 1, 1941, quoted in Lash,* Roosevelt and Churchill, *456.*

Mobilizing U.S. Industry

[The 50,000 planes a year called for by President Roosevelt on May 16, 1940, seemed] like an utterly impossible goal; but it caught the imagination of Americans, who had always believed they could accomplish the impossible.

> *U.S. Steel chairman Edward Stettinius, writing in 1944 about an event of May 1940, in Goodwin,* No Ordinary Time, *45.*

I know that private business cannot be expected to make all of the capital investments required for expansion of plants and factories and personnel which this program calls for at once. It would be unfair to expect industrial corporations or their investors to do this, when there is a chance that a change in international affairs may stop or curtail orders a year or two hence. Therefore, the Government of the United States stands ready to advance the necessary money to help provide for the enlargement of factories, of necessary workers, the development of new sources of supply for the hundreds of raw materials required, the development of quick mass transportation of supplies. . . .

President Franklin D. Roosevelt, fireside chat, May 26, 1940, available online. Mid-Hudson Regional Information Center, URL: www.mhric.org/ fdr/chat15.html.

It seems to me intolerable to allow private people to use public capital in order to make a guaranteed profit for themselves. . . . If private citizens won't supply munitions of war at a reasonable profit and take pot luck with the rest of the citizens in the matter of taxation, then the government ought to build its own plants and conscript the necessary managers to run them.

Secretary of the Interior Harold Ickes, writing in his diary, summer of 1940, in Goodwin, No Ordinary Time, *157.*

I cannot escape the feeling that the tendency so far has been to say that labor must make sacrifices of wages and hours because of necessities of national defense. I have yet to see anywhere a statement that manufacturers and business concerns . . . shall make this same type of sacrifice by cutting profits and reducing the salaries of executives.

First Lady Eleanor Roosevelt, writing in her "My Day" column, December 9, 1940, Marist College Archives.

[In 1940 and 1941] with Marie Hayes . . . I made a shipyard survey of the whole East Coast. We watched as giant steam shovels dug out a building basin for Ugly Duckling cargo carriers at South Portland, Maine, and moved on up to the Bath Iron Works, which specialized in destroyers. Bill Newell, the boss of the Bath company, exuded a confidence that did not seem to consort with the bad news from the war zones of Europe. "We can build anything," he said, "just get us the orders." . . . We went on to places like the Bethlehem Ship Company's Sparrow Point yard in Maryland with a growing sense that if America were to be drawn into the war as an active participant, it would be capable of out-building—and outlasting—Hitler. Another enlightening assignment took

me through virtually every factory in Bridgeport, Connecticut, and its industrial environs. Bridgeport had 20,000 new people, many of them ex-anthracite miners from Pennsylvania; and its 50 machine shops had huge backlogs of work.

Journalist John Chamberlain, writing in 1982 of the events of 1940 and 1941, Life with the Printed Word, *75.*

The problem is to turn existing mass-production facilities as rapidly as possible to the production of armament. We are fumbling that problem, and we have no time to fumble.

Journalist I. F. Stone, in The Nation, *May 3, 1941, 519.*

Negotiations with Japan

A large part of my time [on a visit to the Pacific fleet in September 1940] was directed to inculcating all the officers and men I met with the imminence of war and the high likelihood that we would be involved before it was over. There was too little appreciation of how near war was in the Fleet as I found it.

Secretary of the Navy Frank Knox, writing on his inspection trip to the Pacific fleet in September 1940, quoted in Lash, Roosevelt and Churchill, *225–226.*

And so we go more and more—farther and farther along the road to war. But we are not ready to fight any war now—to say nothing of a war on two oceans at once—and that is what the Berlin-Rome-Tokyo agreement means. Nor will we be ready to fight any war for eighteen months in the future.

State Department Special Assistant Secretary Breckenridge Long, probably in October 1940, quoted in Lash, Roosevelt and Churchill, *224.*

We are opposed to [sending a National Guard division to Hawaii, as President Roosevelt wished], and the Secretary of War [Stimson] succeeded in stopping it. . . . I saw the Secretary when he returned from the White House and we decided that rather than appearing to disapprove all suggestions made by the President, we might send something [an antiaircraft regiment].

Gen. George Marshall, probably in October 1940, quoted in Lash, Roosevelt and Churchill, *224–225.*

Tell Former Naval Person [Churchill] . . . in great confidence that I have suggested to [Japanese Ambassador Kichisaburo] Nomura that Indochina be neutralized . . ., placing Indochina somewhat in status of Switzerland. Japan to get rice and fertilizer but all on condition that Japan withdraw armed forces from Indochina in toto. I have had no answer yet. When it comes in it will probably be unfavorable but we have made at least one more effort to avoid Japanese expansion in South Pacific.

President Franklin D. Roosevelt to his representative Harry Hopkins, cable, July 26, 1941, quoted in Lash, Roosevelt and Churchill, *381–382.*

[T]his Government [of the United States] now finds it necessary to say to the Government of Japan that if the Japanese Government takes any further steps in pursuance of a policy or program of military domination by force or threat of force of neighboring countries, the Government of the United States will be compelled to take immediately any and all steps which it may deem necessary toward safeguarding the legitimate rights and interests of the United States and American nationals and toward insuring the safety and security of the United States.

Warning issued by the U.S. government, August 1941, quoted in Lash, Roosevelt and Churchill, *408.*

Our policy was not to say "No" to the Japanese ultimatum of November 20 [1941]. It was not to remain silent even, it was to grab every straw in sight, in an effort to keep up the conversation and to give time to our armies and navies here, and among our future Allies to make further preparations, and also to show our continuing interest in peace.

Secretary of State Cordell Hull, testifying before Congress in July 1946 about the events of November and December 1941, quoted in Lash, Roosevelt and Churchill, *467.*

[The United States will] continue to be patient if Japan's courses of action permit continuance of such an attitude on our part. [But it cannot offer any] substantial relaxation in its economic restrictions unless Japan gives this country some clear manifestation of peaceful intent.

President Franklin D. Roosevelt to Japanese representatives in Washington, D. C., November 28, 1941, quoted in Lash, Roosevelt and Churchill, *474.*

3

Crisis Government
December 7, 1941– September 2, 1945

HISTORICAL CONTEXT

Government-Industry Relationships

After the Japanese attack on the U.S. naval base at Pearl Harbor, Hawaii, on December 7, 1941, American leaders set about mobilizing the economy to wage "total war" against the enemy. They faced two central questions.

First, who was to control the wartime economy: government or business? Proponents of the capitalistic free-enterprise system such as Sears Roebuck chairman Donald Nelson believed that the federal government should do no more than "show industry what had to be done, and . . . do everything in our power to enable industries to do it, placing our chief reliance on the limitless energy and skill of American manufacturers." For he said, the United States had to defeat the enemy "in our own way," to prove that . . . our system of political and economic freedom was in fact more efficient, more productive, more able to respond to the demands of a great emergency than the dictatorial system of our enemies." Whatever powers government assumed in the emergency, it should go no further than devices "for enabling industry to get what it had to get in order to do the job."[1] On the other hand, liberals feared that if power were handed over to conservative industrialists, many of whom hated President Franklin D. Roosevelt and all he had done, they would strike down New Deal social legislation enacted in the 1930s and cancel the gains labor had made as the nation struggled to recover from the Great Depression.

No matter how people felt, the demands of all-out, worldwide war against enemies far better prepared than the United States necessitated a lot of governmental intervention. For one thing, to do its job the military needed new, complicated, and precisely designed and manufactured equipment, weapons, and ammunition, and it needed them immediately. For another, there just were not enough resources to go around—in some cases not even enough to meet all military needs, let alone civilian desires.[2] Even weapons manufacturers had to fight desperately for the steel they needed. Someone—and who else but the government—had to allocate scarce materials. Someone had to force the production of goods that no one wanted to manufacture.

Despite disagreements that continued throughout World War II and after, practically speaking the federal government assumed control, although it exercised that control not dictatorially but with considerable respect for the existence and profits of corporations—especially large corporations—and for the civil liberties of individual workers.

Second, who was to have final authority over the economy: the military or civilians, particularly the civilians who ran the executive branch of the government and the agencies they created to run the economy? Thanks in large part to the president, civilians assumed this authority, although the military frequently challenged it.

The military's prewar plan of industrial mobilization as revised in 1939 called for it to control the whole economy in wartime. FDR, however, was both determined and able to keep that control firmly in civilian hands. A master politician, he not only fully exercised his powers as chief executive of the country and as commander in chief of the military, but he also persuaded Congress to increase those powers. His authority was broadened by the War Powers Acts passed by Congress in December 1941 and March 1942, which gave him control over all production of materials related to the war effort. He used this new power with restraint: "The government opened mines, took over some industries and services, and stockpiled raw materials of various kinds, yet it assumed direct management of few industries. Unlike the British government, it left the running of the railroads and the operation of manufacturing plants to private companies."[3]

The confusion in Washington and elsewhere as the nation scrambled to fight a war did not bother the president—indeed he seemed almost to welcome it, and sometimes deliberately to foment it as a tool to his own ends. He seldom micromanaged, but he was able to carry in his head an overview of the national and international situations so that he could balance conflicting needs and pressures. To control the economy, he set up agency after agency. Some of these he placed within existing departments and bureaus in the executive branch. Freestanding agencies he sometimes placed more directly under his oversight within the Office of Emergency Management in the White House.

Industrial Mobilization

Immediately after Pearl Harbor, all was confusion in Washington.[4] As thousands rushed to volunteer, the city was awash with people looking for jobs and seeking housing—from young hopefuls looking for ways to serve in the war; to businessmen seeking contracts and raw goods, offering their services to the government, or lobbying; to organizations seeking to do their part or advance their own interests.

The task of mobilizing industry for war was difficult by its very nature. As Gen. Brehon Somerville, head of the army's Services of Supply, testified before a congressional subcommittee: "We are asking contractors to produce articles which have never been produced before. We are asking other contractors to produce articles which they have never produced before. We are asking still other contractors, who have produced articles in small quantities, to produce them in vastly larger quantities. . . . Facilities must be converted, new facilities obtained, new personnel employed and trained to new methods, and new sources of supply developed."[5]

Moreover the task was complicated by greed and self-interest, both corporate and individual. The American generation that waged World War II was indeed a great one, to whom the nation still owes its life and much of its well-being, but it was far from perfect. Acrimonious struggles between industrial leaders and the military community, between labor unions and manufacturers' associations, and between New Dealers and Roosevelt haters in the corporate world often hindered efficient production. Despite massive propaganda efforts to stimulate patriotism and self-sacrifice, domestic and partisan politics intruded.

In January 1942 President Roosevelt moved to centralize control over economic mobilization by creating the War Production Board (WPB), with Donald M. Nelson as its head, an agency designed to convert the economy from civilian to war production.[6] Potentially a strong civilian agency, it suffered from Nelson's failure to control the vested interests, both civilian and military, that obstructed economic mobilization.[7] Naturally tending to go easy on those corporate officers with whom he had worked in earlier days, he also failed to deal firmly with the military.

The War Production Board circulated this poster in 1942. *(Library of Congress, LC-USZC4-1647)*

Critics of military officials condemned their inability even after the outbreak of war in Europe in September 1939 to comprehend the dimensions of the task that lay ahead and concluded that they should not be entrusted with military procurement.[8] Although Nelson recognized their inefficiency, acknowledging in his memoirs that "I had the facts, and could very easily have shown the mistakes the Army had made," he left procurement in their hands.[9]

They refused to prioritize their needs, insisting that any and all of these were more critical than civilian needs.[10] Allocation of any resources for civilian use caused them to charge bureaucrats with being too soft on civilians. Although the military perforce relied on civilians to produce war materiel, they ignored the nation's need to feed, clothe, and house those workers or even to furnish them the necessary tools, seeming to believe that the civilian economy could get along with the machinery and equipment it had when the war began. Thus the army opposed allocating materials for farm machinery, arguing that farmers should use their old equipment.[11] Similarly General Somervell denied the need for repair parts even for coal-mining machinery. "It was a mystery to me," Nelson commented in his memoirs, ". . . how we could hope to turn out a maximum volume of munitions unless we obtained enough coal to power the munitions-making plants."[12]

In September 1942 the Office of Price Administration operated this volunteer headquarters in Nyack, New York. *(Library of Congress, LC-USW3-055123-C)*

As a case in point, the military objection to WPB's allocating newsprint for comic strips verges on the absurd, particularly since this objection came from a department that endlessly and unnecessarily demanded multiple copies of everything. To his credit, Nelson recognized the free-speech issue that underlay this controversy: "If [a government] can stop the printing of comic strips it can—and inevitably *will*—forbid the publication of cartoons and other material, perhaps, ultimately, of certain classes of editorial matter which, in its opinion, represent a waste of newsprint."[13]

However, the WPB suffered in many other ways from Nelson's administrative hands-off policy that kept him from controlling military and civilian vested interests. For instance, he surrendered WPB control over the Office of Price Administration, which subsequently became an independent agency, and over the purchasing activities of the Maritime Commission and the Treasury Department. Even when on April 18, 1942, FDR created the War Manpower Commission (WMC), Nelson rejected the president's offer to place it under the WPB—a rejection that caused trouble later when all policies and programs related to labor were brought together under the WMC.[14] Other agencies created to deal with specific requirements such as food, rubber, aviation gasoline, coal, and transportation also competed with the WPB in their own areas.

In May 1943 FDR put James Byrnes in charge of a new Office of War Mobilization (OWM), which superseded the WPB. The OWM emerged as the closest the country came to acquiring an effective national agency to manage the noncombatant side of the war.

The WPB and the OWM that displaced it controlled industrial production primarily in three ways: (1) by allocating raw materials, (2) by prohibiting the manufacture of civilian goods, and (3) by offering inducements to industry.

Children near Norwich, Connecticut, collect scrap for victory, August 1942. *(Library of Congress, LC-USF34-083838-C)*

Allocating Raw Materials

In early 1942 the WPB was deluged with some 130,000 requests a week for allocations of raw materials,[15] for shortages were a continuing problem. In June of that year it made compulsory the Production Requirements Plan, already in use on a voluntary basis.[16] This plan required factories with government contracts to submit a production schedule and indicate what raw materials they needed. On the basis of these submissions the WPB assigned priority ratings to the manufacturers. The plan never worked well, for it did not prevent procurement agencies from contracting for more than their suppliers could possibly produce and businesspeople from overstating their needs in order to stockpile as much as possible. In the fall of 1942 the WPB abandoned it in favor of a new Controlled Materials Plan. This plan allocated scarce materials only for specific contracts, and it remained in effect until the end of the war.

The evolving techniques for dealing with shortages can be illustrated by the response to rubber shortage. The need for rubber became critical after the Japanese seized the Dutch East Indies and Malaya in early 1942, blocking off 90 percent of the U.S. crude rubber supply. Jesse Jones, head of the Rubber Reserve Corporation, had neither stockpiled rubber nor pushed for the development of a synthetic substitute, though every army tank took a ton of rubber and every battleship seventy-five tons. Research on a substitute had been blocked by a conflict between the oil companies, who wanted synthetic rubber derived from petroleum, and the farm bloc, who wanted it derived from grain alcohol. To resolve the issue, Roosevelt appointed a committee headed by financier Bernard Baruch. The committee's report, issued after five weeks of hearings and study, endorsed the petroleum process and recommended a gas-rationing program to curtail nonessential motoring and a maximum speed limit of 35 miles per hour to save tires.[17]

For a time government avoided rationing for rubber and other materials, instead using scrap drives as a more acceptable alternative and a means to increase popular involvement in the war effort. The petroleum industry managed the rubber drive, asking people to turn in their old tires, rubber raincoats, garden hoses, rubber shoes, and anything else made of rubber, paying the contributors a penny a pound, selling it to the government at $25 a ton, and contributing profits to charity.[18] More usefully, the government launched the synthetic rubber industry by spending $700 million to build 51 plants, which it leased to companies at low cost, awarding them cost-plus contracts.[19] One of the largest of these plants, covering 77 acres, built in West Virginia and run by the United States Rubber Company, could produce 90,000 tons a year or the equivalent of about 20 million rubber trees.[20] Rubber Administrator William "Bull" Jeffers, appointed in the fall of 1942, ably directed the synthetic rubber program.[21] As for the gas rationing recommended by the Baruch committee to conserve rubber by restricting driving, by the spring of 1942, 17 eastern states had adopted it, and by December it was imposed on the whole country.

Forbidding Manufacture of Nonessential Products

It soon became obvious that in wartime the U.S. economy could not meet all demand, particularly as that demand was not only national but international, with the nation's allies depending heavily on it to produce necessities of life as well as war materiel. Accordingly, soon after the United States entered the war, the WPB prohibited the production of certain civilian goods.

On February 10, 1942, the WPB stopped the production of civilian automobiles. The automobile industry converted to wartime production, in which it manufactured more than half the army's tanks and tank parts, half its diesel engines, and all of its trucks. It also produced some 27,000 airplanes and more than half of all aircraft engines, as well as airplane parts.[22]

Likewise, the WPB ordered the Singer Sewing Machine Company to stop making sewing machines, except for industrial machines used to produce such items as tents, tarpaulins, and parachute harnesses. By June 1942, the company's factories had been converted to the production of equipment needed by the military, such as airplane navigation equipment, gyro compasses, hydraulic electric motor control units for airplane control, gun turret castings, and parts for guns.[23] And the International Silver Company moved from manufacturing tableware to producing clips for machine-gun cartridge belts, magnesium bombs, and a host of other items required by the armed forces.[24]

Inducements for Industrial Production

As a rule, during the war the federal government preferred using the carrot to the stick, so it frequently offered manufacturers inducements to switch to wartime production. These included government financing of new plants, government financing of research, antitrust exemptions, cost-plus contracts, and tax

This owner of the Pierson Motor Company in Lititz, Pennsylvania, had lost his business of selling cars. Repairs in his garage earned only enough to pay taxes and mechanics, so he took a defense job at the Armstrong Cork Company and also volunteered as an air-raid warden and airplane spotter. *(Library of Congress, LC-USW3-011151D)*

relief. Such inducements guaranteed that manufacturers would not lose money, and in most cases gave them fat profits.

The nation faced the need to build new factories, as well as convert existing ones to war production. Even conversion was not simple or cost-free, as Charles E. Wilson, president of General Motors, explained to Nelson: "When you convert one of our factories, you move everything out and start with blank space. Out of a long row of intricate machines on the production line a certain percentage may be used in the manufacture of a war product, depending on what that war product is. But the production line will necessarily consist mainly of new, special-purpose machines along with any of the old machines that can be rebuilt for the new manufacturing process."[25] When manufacturers hesitated to invest in new factories, the U.S. government built them and leased them at low cost—ensuring that manufacturers would not be left at war's end with plants that they could not use.

Similarly, when manufacturers proved loath to invest in the scientific research necessary for the development of war goods, the government anted up almost a billion dollars, exclusive of money spent on atomic research. Large companies in particular profited. Not only were they saved the costs of research, but they also usually received the patents for discoveries made in their laboratories but paid for by government funds, with the government receiving a royalty-free license for its own use. These patents of course continued to benefit the companies long after the war.[26]

In the interests of encouraging among industries a free exchange of information that might increase efficiency of production, the government offered immunity from the antitrust laws for "firms which engaged in pooling and other cooperative arrangements, provided that they first obtained approval by demonstrating a link between increased efficiency and war needs." The government accepted some 600 such plans. Moreover, in March 1942 FDR suspended all antitrust suits that might impede essential production.[27] Given such leeway, industries readily exchanged industrial secrets with former competitors in order to solve problems, to increase production, to qualify for war contracts, and to stay up-to-speed on developments in technology.

Moreover, the government resorted to cost-plus contracts, agreeing to pay all costs incurred, plus a fixed fee—a guaranteed profit. This arrangement obviously invited waste of materials and the hoarding of labor, but it worked so well in encouraging production that it remained in force during most of the war.

Finally, the government offered industry important tax incentives. Early on, the WPB developed a plan allowing industry to amortize the cost of expansion within five years, a device that cut taxable income and increased earning capacity. Moreover, the government allowed a refund of excess-profits taxes should a business show a loss after the war.[28]

Transportation

In the 1940s the nation still relied mainly on railroads for the movement of goods. The end of automobile production, the rationing of gasoline and tires, and greatly increased demand strained rail resources. Between 1940 and 1943 the amount of freight doubled and the number of passengers more than tripled. Traffic destined for new military bases, defense plants, and coastal ports shifted demand over specific routes. In World War I the U.S. government had taken over operation of the railroads, but in World War II it relied instead on the cooperation of the industry, which voluntarily submitted to central direction.

The railroads worked together, combining their resources, permitting rerouting among competing companies, and increasing efficiency by running longer trains, loading the cars more heavily, and hauling them longer distances.[29] As German submarines sank the tankers that had previously carried oil to cities on the East Coast, the railroads took over a major part of that traffic, and by September 1942 they were carrying more than 70 percent of the total.[30] To relieve railroads of that burden, the WPB approved, and the U.S. government financed, the construction of two pipelines. By August 14, 1943, the Big Inch had been completed, a pipe 24 inches in diameter and 1,254 miles long that carried crude oil. The Little Big Inch, carrying refined products, 20 inches in diameter and running from Houston and Port Arthur, Texas, to Linden, New Jersey, was completed on March 2, 1944. Together the pipelines carried over 350 million barrels of crude oil and refined products to the East Coast before the war in Europe ended.[31]

Limitations on Agency Control of Industrial Production

The constitutional checks and balances at the heart of the U.S. democratic system of government provided a number of constraints on the bureaucracy that ran the economy. The executive branch exercised life-and-death control over wartime agencies by the president's authority to create and close them. The legislative branch scrutinized their activities and those of the industries subject to them through congressional committees; Congress also affected agency functioning by enacting laws and imposing taxes on industry. Agency interaction with the businesses they controlled inevitably affected their rulings, as did the frequent overlapping of one agency's powers and responsibilities with another's—so did the practice of bringing business executives into the government to administer these wartime agencies—the dollar-a-year men.

FDR experimented freely throughout his presidency. If an agency did not succeed in its mission, or if its personnel had too much difficulty in getting along with others, he might replace it or transfer some of its powers elsewhere—a practice that often caused hardship to the business representatives trying to find their way through the Washington labyrinth.

Of the congressional committees investigating the wartime economy, by far the most prominent and successful was the Truman Committee. Early in 1941 stories of mismanagement in war industries reached Senator Harry S. Truman of Missouri. He discovered that contractors were being paid a fixed profit no matter how inefficient their operations; he also found that a few large corporations (largely headquartered in the East) were receiving a disproportionate share of government contracts. At his instigation the Senate on March 1, 1941, created a special Committee to Investigate the National Defense Program. Under Truman's chairmanship this committee held hundreds of hearings, traveled thousands of miles to conduct field investigations, and saved the country huge sums—by some estimates as much as $15 billion.[32] It also enhanced Truman's reputation, easing his selection as FDR's running mate in the election of 1944 and his subsequent ascent into the presidency on FDR's death in 1945.

The committee conscientiously tackled the problem of waste from many angles, thereby not only reducing expense but also increasing efficiency. For example, the committee found that the navy wanted to order an inferior landing craft and instead prodded it into choosing the Higgins product, which could land troops not only in established harbors but also on many kinds of shallow beaches.[33] Truman also questioned the use of dollar-a-year men—businessmen loaned to the government while remaining on the payroll of their own corporations, thinking that their corporate incomes might influence their governmental decisions. On that issue, though, bureaucracy and Donald Nelson won out.

It was all too easy for government officials awarding millions of dollars in contracts to fall into the habit of relying on companies they already knew and whose ability to perform as promised they had already tested. Prompted by allegations of waste in the construction of new army camps and favoritism in the awarding of war contracts, Truman told his fellow senators: "The little manufacturer, the little contractor, and the little machine-shop have been left entirely out in the cold. The policy seems to make the big man bigger and to put the little man completely out of business. . . . I am reliably informed that from 70 to 90 per cent of the contracts let have been concentrated in an area smaller than England."[34] To counteract this tendency on June 11, 1942, Congress set up the Smaller War Plants Corporation to make direct loans to private entrepreneurs, encourage financial institutions to make credit available to small war plants, provide technical assistance, and advocate for small business to federal procurement agencies and big business.

Congress also influenced the wartime conduct of business by imposing the excess-profits tax in 1941, the rate on which ran as high as 90 percent.[35] It attempted to reduce abuses on cost-plus contracts by the Renegotiation Act of 1943. This act recognized the difficulties of estimating costs in advance. As General Somerville testified on March 31, 1942, both parties to a war contract knew that during the period of adjustment costs would be high, but no one knew how long that period would last. Therefore contracts made for army, navy, or maritime procurement were to include a renegotiation clause, requiring repricing after actual costs were figured out.

Finally, their interaction with the very people and businesses they were created to control inevitably modified the conduct of the wartime agencies. Take the bizarre case of Sewell Avery, president of Montgomery Ward. When for 18 months he had defied National War Labor Board orders to pay his unionized workers higher wages and to enforce a closed shop, in April 1944 on FDR's command U.S. soldiers picked up the chair on which Avery was sitting and carried him out of his Chicago office. The irate Avery flung at Attorney General Francis Biddle the worst epithet he could think of: "You New Dealer!"[36] Even after that he continued battling, bringing suit, and refusing to obey orders. Soon after Christmas 1944, the army took over and began to operate seven key Ward stores, which remained under army control until the end of the war. Of course affairs rarely came to such extremes, but equally companies did sometimes persuade agencies to modify their rulings.

The Wartime Civilian Economy

Among the many wartime agencies, the Office of Price Administration (OPA) had the most direct impact on the home-front consumer. Established in January 1942 to prevent inflation, it was vested with authority to regulate prices and residential rents, and to ration scarce consumer goods. In April 1942 the OPA froze prices for most commodities at the level charged the preceding month. It also imposed a ceiling on residential rents. Successive OPA administrators (Leon Henderson [1941–42], Prentiss H. Brown [1943], and Chester Bowles [1943–46]) modified and extended these regulations. In time some 90 percent of retail food prices were frozen. Despite complaints of unfairness, fraud, and black marketeering OPA managed to secure general compliance and keep consumer prices relatively stable.

The agency also instituted rationing of scarce consumer goods, including tires, automobiles, sugar, gasoline, fuel oil, coffee, meats, and processed foods. Over the course of the war price controls and rationing were gradually abolished, and the OPA was terminated in 1947.[37] Life in the OPA was no more peaceful than in the WPB. OPA administrators clashed with agencies whose authority overlapped theirs.

To settle these disputes the president created the Office of Economic Stabilization with James F. Byrnes as director. In this capacity he had authority to stabilize matters affecting civilian purchasing power. He also was empowered to be the "final judge of any jurisdictional disputes among the various wartime agencies." Byrnes set up his office in the White House, a meaningful status symbol in wartime Washington, and soon became known as the "assistant president."[38]

In comparison with its allies and enemies, the United States kept a higher percentage of its labor force out of the fighting services. Moreover, its gross national product (GNP) increased by 50 percent in constant dollars from 1939 to 1944, and war production represented only about 40 percent of the GNP—a smaller percentage of its GNP than any other major country at war.[39] Consequently during World War II the people of the United States were able to raise their living conditions and standards even while they turned their country into the arsenal of democracy.[40]

However, that happy fact did not satisfy all employers and all labor. Immediately after Pearl Harbor FDR negotiated an agreement with representatives of industry and labor that for the duration of the war there would be no strikes or lockouts. To adjust unsettled disputes between labor and management peacefully, in January 1942 he set up the National War Labor Board (WLB). In the War Labor Dispute Act, Congress confirmed and strengthened that board's authority to maintain the flow of war materials by settling labor disputes.

Many unions signed no-strike pledges, but these were not legally binding, and the period from 1941 to 1945 witnessed more strikes than any other in American history, though most lasted only a few days and many were wildcat strikes. Organized labor resisted wage controls and any moves to eliminate collective bargaining, while the WLB fought to control spiraling wages and the attendant threat of inflation. The workers were dissatisfied with wages and working conditions, resentful of industry's profits, and stirred up by internal strife between the Congress of Industrial Organizations (CIO) and the American Federation of Labor (AFL). Full employment made them more confident about striking than they had been in the lean years of the Great Depression. However, these strikes won them no kudos either among GIs or among Americans generally. In June 1943, after United Mine Workers president John L. Lewis had defied the WLB and taken the coal miners out on a long strike, polls identified him as the most hated public figure in the country, and Senator James Eastland of Mississippi "was disappointed to learn that Lewis could not be charged with treason."[41]

Labor unrest in 1943 caused state legislatures to restrict the right of unions to picket and strike. Then Congress passed over FDR's veto the Smith-Connally bill (the War Labor Disputes Act), authorizing the president to seize "plants useful in the war" and criminalizing the encouragement of strikes in such plants.[42] Denounced by both the CIO and the AFL as "the very essence of Fascism," the law in fact did not seriously weaken the trade unions. Most of the strikes came about as a result of rank-and-file pressure, often without approval of the union leaders; loopholes were found to enable the unions to achieve acceptable contracts with employers, wage hikes, and other gains.

As well as work stoppages, the government faced the necessity to find, classify, and often retrain labor for new kinds of work and recruit them for new factories in new places. For many people, in and out of government, the obvious solution to these problems was some form of civilian conscription, which FDR refused to support. He entrusted the responsibility to determine where workers were needed and how they should be divided between the military and industry to the War Manpower Commission (WMC), created in the spring of 1942, with former Indiana governor Paul V. McNutt at its head. With no power over deferments from the draft, no voice in labor relations, and no authority to bring workers and jobs together, McNutt had little choice but to try voluntary cooperation, which did not work. In December 1942 navy enlistments were stopped to keep skilled workers from leaving their jobs, and Selective Service was transferred to the War Manpower Commission. In January 1943 McNutt issued a "work or fight" order, ending deferments for men in nonessential work, even fathers, but Congress intervened and McNutt had to back off. Family values triumphed over national security when in December 1943 Congress insisted that childless men in essential jobs be drafted before fathers doing nonessential work.[43]

The ever-powerful farm bloc early on persuaded Congress to defer all "essential" farm workers and in 1943 got through the Senate—but not through the House of Representatives—a bill providing for the release of any serviceman who had worked on a farm. Moreover, farm lobbies for particular crops managed to get their workers into the essential class—including the tobacco interests, whose congressmen held that crop dear. These political moves made for inefficient use of farm labor while casting more than its share of the burden of providing draftees on the industrial labor force.[44]

Nonetheless, as armed forces manpower requirements rose and market forces lured many farm workers into higher-paying jobs in defense industries, the number of farm workers in the United States decreased from 1940 to 1943, even as demand for agricultural products rose both within the United States and among the country's allies. By 1943 the successful harvest of the nation's food supply was in jeopardy. On April 29 of that year the Congress approved the Farm Labor Supply Appropriation Act, to "assist farmers in producing vital food by making labor available at the time and place it was most needed."

State agricultural extension services assumed responsibility for the emergency labor programs thus created, primarily by coordinating and overseeing labor recruitment, training, and placement. Between 1943 and 1947 Oregon's Emergency Farm Labor Service assisted with more than 900,000 placements on the state's farms, trained thousands of workers of all ages, and managed nine farm labor camps. Farm laborers included urban youth and women, soldiers, white-collar professionals, displaced Japanese Americans, returning war veterans, workers from other states, migrant workers from Mexico and Jamaica, and even German prisoners of war.

Outcomes

To study the particulars, disagreements, and mistakes of any aspect of the U.S. war effort is to wonder how the Allies won the war. But wars are waged on both sides by human beings prone to error and waste. Whatever the conflicts attending the mobilization of U.S. resources, the end result was impressive. Production far exceeded all estimates and expectations. As President Roosevelt had asked, the country turned itself into the world's arsenal for democracy, supplying 60 percent of all combat munitions for the Allies in 1944;[45] as he had not foreseen, at the same time the nation raised its own standard of living.

The details are staggering. During its three-year existence the heavily flawed WPB supervised the production of $185 billion worth of weapons and supplies. "The mobilization gave an enormous impetus to aluminum and magnesium production, enlarged electricity output to nearly half again as much as in 1937, increased machine tool production sevenfold, and turned out more iron and steel than the whole world had produced a short time before. In 1939 America's airplane industry employed fewer than 47,000 people and produced fewer than 6,000 planes; in the peak year of 1944, the industry employed 2,102,000 workers and rolled out more than 96,000 planes. Medium tank production advanced so rapidly that it had to be cut back. By the beginning of 1944 the industrial output of America was twice that of all the Axis nations."[46]

Historians have long described this U.S. achievement as prodigious, a miracle of production. Recently revisionists have challenged that concept as a sentimental myth, arguing that the production is explained by "the American advantages of abundant raw materials, superb transportation and technological infrastructure, a large and skilled labor force, and, most importantly, two large ocean barriers to bar bombing of its industries."[47]

Whether or not they achieved a miracle, U.S. workers contributed critically to winning the war. They neither sacrificed nor suffered as did the people in the countries all over the world where the war was fought, or the servicemen who actually fought on the beaches of Iwo Jima and Normandy, endured the depredations of submarines and kamikaze attacks, or were brought down by antiaircraft fire. But they enabled the survival of millions in the warring countries, and they fed and clothed and housed the servicemen and furnished them with equipment, weapons, and ammunition with which to fight.

CHRONICLE OF EVENTS

1941

December 7: Japanese planes attack Pearl Harbor, Hawaii. About 19 U.S. naval ships are sunk or damaged, and 3,000 Americans lose their lives.

December 8: Congress declares war on Japan; Representative Jeannette Rankin casts the sole dissenting vote.

December 10: The Japanese invade the Philippines.

December 11: Germany and Italy declare war against the United States.

December 15: The American Federation of Labor executive committee adopts a no-strike policy in war industries. This is confirmed on December 23 by an industry-labor conference. All disputes are to be settled by peaceful means.

December 18: The Office of Defense Transportation (ODT) is established in the Office for Emergency Management to promote the maximum utilization of domestic transportation facilities to support the war effort. It is authorized to coordinate activities of federal agencies and private transportation groups to prevent congestion and make maximum use of available resources; it also investigates causes of shipping delays.

December 18: Congress passes the first War Powers Act, authorizing the president to create the agencies necessary to manage the war.

December 27: The Office of Price Administration announces the rationing of tires, the first rationing regulation for consumers.

1942

Thousands of civilians over the draft age pour into Washington, D.C., to find jobs in the many wartime agencies.

January 1: The Office of Production Management (OPM) bans the sale of new cars and trucks.

January 6: In his State of the Union address, Roosevelt calls for the production of an astronomical number of planes, tanks, merchant ships, and antiaircraft guns as indispensable, superseding all previous estimates.

January 12: Roosevelt creates the National War Labor Board (NWLB) in the Office for Emergency Management to replace the prewar National Defense Mediation Board. The NWLB is responsible for the settlement of labor disputes and adjustments in certain wages and salaries. It is superseded in December 1945 by the National Wage Stabilization Board.

January 16: The War Production Board (WPB) is established by executive order and put in charge of the entire war production program under Donald M. Nelson. It supersedes the OPM, which is subsequently abolished. The task of the WPB is to convert the economy from civilian to war production.

January 30: Roosevelt signs the Emergency Price Control bill giving the OPA the power to regulate consumer prices except those for farm products.

February 9: Daylight saving time (war time) becomes effective throughout the year to utilize better all the hours of daylight and cut consumption of electricity.

February 10: The last new civilian automobile is made for the duration of the war.

March 17: William Green (AFL) and Philip Murray (CIO) announce a no-strike agreement.

March 27: Congress passes the second War Powers Act, adding to the president's powers to act without congressional authority.

April 4: The War Manpower Commission is created within the Office for Emergency Management to control civilian employment by recruiting workers for essential industries, training labor for war jobs, increasing labor efficiency, and gathering data on the national labor market. It is also vested with authority to mobilize every adult in the country if necessary for the war effort.

April 28: The OPA stabilizes rents, affecting 86 million people in 301 areas.

May 5: Sugar rationing begins.

May 15: Gasoline rationing begins in 17 eastern states, setting a limit of three gallons a week for nonessential driving.

June: The liberty ship production program headed by Henry J. Kaiser achieves a record when one of his four West Coast shipyards builds and launches a 10,500 ton ship in four days.

June 11: The Small Business Act, popularly known as the Smaller War Plants Corporation, becomes law. Its purpose is to "mobilize aggressively the productive capacity of all small business concerns."

June 13: FDR establishes the Office of War Information (OWI) to control the dissemination of official news and propaganda. Journalist Elmer Davis is appointed head of the agency.

June 25: Congress passes the War Labor Disputes Act (Smith-Connally Act), giving the government the power to seize plants that can be used in the war effort, and restricting unions from making political contributions.

October 1: Robert Stanley, chief pilot for Bell Aircraft Corporation, tests the first American jet aircraft at Munroe Army Base, California.

November 2: The Controlled Materials Plan to improve the system for the allocation of scarce materials is officially announced.

November 29: Coffee rationing begins.

November 30: The first war bonds are offered for public sale.

December 1: Nationwide rationing of gasoline goes into effect.

December 2: Scientists in the Argonne Project at the University of Chicago demonstrate the first sustained nuclear reaction, the first step in the production of an atomic bomb.

December 2: The Petroleum Administration for War (PAW) is created by executive order and made responsible for the wartime conservation, use, marketing, and development of oil and other petroleum products. The PAW replaces the Office of Petroleum Coordinator for National Defense created in May 1941.

December 27: The food rationing program is announced.

1943

Prompted by labor shortages, the U.S. government negotiates an agreement with the Mexican government to supply temporary workers, known as *braceros*, for American agricultural work.

February 7: Shoe rationing begins, limiting civilians to three new pairs a year.

February 9: FDR orders a 48-hour minimum work week in war plants.

March 1: Rationing of canned goods begins.

March 25: Chester C. Davis is appointed U.S. food administrator to combat shortages.

March 29: Rationing of meat, fat, and cheese begins.

April 8: FDR's "hold the line" order freezes prices.

April 17: The War Manpower Commission freezes essential workers in war industries, preventing some 27 million workers from leaving their jobs.

May 1: The government seizes coal mines after about 530,000 striking miners, led by John L. Lewis, refuse to comply with a War Labor Board order to return to work.

May 5: Fuel Administrator Harold L. Ickes is authorized to seize coal stocks for use in war plants and civilian purposes in case of an emergency.

May 27: The Office of War Mobilization is created with James F. Byrnes as director; it is responsible for the conduct of the war on the home front.

June 10: FDR signs the Current Tax Payment Act, initiating the pay-as-you go income tax to finance the war.

June 20–21: Race riots in Detroit, Michigan, result in 35 deaths and more than 500 wounded (mostly African Americans). During the summer race riots also break out in Mobile, Alabama (May 25), Los Angeles (June 4), Beaumont, Texas (June 19), and Harlem, New York City (August 1). All are caused in part by housing shortages as black workers flood into the cities.

1944

January 19: Railroads seized by presidential order on December 27, 1943, to prevent a nationwide rail strike are returned to their owners after settlement of the wage dispute.

February 29: OPA director Chester A. Bowles reports that during 1943 black-market transactions cost consumers an estimated $1.2 billion.

April 19: The Lend-Lease program is extended to June 30, 1945, continuing the country's commitment to be the Allies' "arsenal of democracy."

April 26: Army troops seize Montgomery Ward property in Chicago after the company chairman, Sewell Avery, refuses to extend the company's contract with the CIO as ordered by the War Labor Board. After union elections, the seizure is terminated until December 27, 1944, when an executive order authorizes the secretary of war to seize all Ward's property to force compliance with War Labor Board orders. The seizure is finally terminated in 1945 by President Truman.

May 3: OPA ends rationing of all meats except for steak and choice cuts of beef.

June 6: D day—Allied forces successfully invade France on the coast of Normandy.

June 22: FDR signs the Servicemen's Readjustment Act (the GI Bill) that provides a wide range of

General Dwight D. Eisenhower urges men of the U.S. 101st Airborne Division to "Full victory—nothing else," during the invasion of Normandy, June 6, 1944. *(National Archives, III-SC-194399)*

benefits to returning veterans, including opportunities to go to college.

August 14: The WPB authorizes resumption of production of such consumer goods as pots and pans, vacuum cleaners, and electric ranges.

November 18: The cost of living is reported as 29–30 percent higher this year than in 1943; the report causes labor unrest.

1945

January 15: A national dimout is ordered to conserve energy resources.

February 26: A midnight curfew is ordered for all places of entertainment.

March 1: John L. Lewis, head of the United Mine Workers, demands a 10 percent royalty on all coal mined.

April 12: President Roosevelt dies; Vice President Harry Truman assumes the presidency.

April 30: Sugar rations are reduced by 25 percent because of diminishing reserves.

May 7–8: V-E Day: Germany surrenders unconditionally, and the war in Europe is officially ended.

May 8: The national dimout is lifted.

May 9: The midnight curfew for places of entertainment is lifted.

May 10: The War Production Board lifts the production ban on 77 consumer items.

May 25: Military aircraft production is reduced by 30 percent.

June 30: Congress extends the life of OPA by one year.

August 1: President Truman signs the McMahan Act, creating the Atomic Energy Commission.

August 14–15: V-J Day: Japan surrenders unconditionally and the war in the Pacific is over.

August 14: The War Manpower Commission suspends all manpower controls.

August 18: President Harry Truman moves to restore the civilian economy by ordering full restoration of civilian consumer goods production and collective bargaining.

August 20: WPA lifts controls over production of 210 consumer goods.

Sept. 2: Japanese representatives sign the official Instrument of Surrender aboard the USS *Missouri* in Tokyo Bay.

EYEWITNESS TESTIMONY

I ask that the Congress declare that since the unprovoked and dastardly attack by Japan on Sunday, December seventh, a state of war has existed between the United States and the Japanese empire.

> *FDR, Pearl Harbor speech to Congress, December 8, 1941,* BCN Government/Political Center, available online. URL: http://bcn.boulder.co.us/ government/national/speeches/spch2.html.

For months now, the knowledge that something of this kind [the attack on Pearl Harbor] might happen has been hanging over our heads. . . . That is all over now and there is no more uncertainty. We know what we have to face and we know we are ready to face it. . . . whatever is asked of us, I am sure we can accomplish it; we are the free and unconquerable people of the U.S.A.

> *First Lady Eleanor Roosevelt, December 7, 1941, radio broadcast, quoted in* New York Times, *December 8, 1941, 4.*

Government-Industry Relationships

We looked at each other and knew that any one of us might be picked for the czar [of the aircraft industry]. Nobody wanted to be czar and we didn't want anybody else as czar. We decided to offer the President an 8-president-soviet to regiment our part of the industry.

> *President Donald Douglas of Douglas Aircraft, quoted by Henry Taylor,* Saturday Evening Post, *November 22, 1942, quoted in Nelson,* Arsenal of Democracy, *232.*

We want aluminum, not excuses.

> *Senator Harry Truman, chair of the Truman Committee, summer 1943, speaking to Alcoa officials, quoted in McCullough,* Truman, *287–288.*

The news from New York is that the Sanitation Department had to sweep up twenty-two tons of confetti, ticker tape, and waste paper after the report of Italy's unconditional surrender. No such burden was imposed on the authorities here [in Washington, D.C.], where official celebration was restrained. At the State Department Wednesday noon the press room was jammed, and

we all felt happy and excited over the news. A bet was made that such an occasion could not fail to get a rise even from Secretary Hull, but your correspondent, who was one of the optimists, must report that he lost the wager. When the Secretary was asked whether he cared to comment on the surrender . . . he said—this is as nearly verbatim as the rules allow—that he had nothing to give us, that he had no comment to make, and that he had nothing to say at that time.

> *I. F. Stone, column of September 12, 1943, in Stone,* The War Years, *36.*

It appears certain that the pressure will be toward increasing the availability of landing craft by forcing an immediate increase in production. Inclination is to force production at the expense of the Maritime Commission, particularly cargo vessels. Be prepared to adjust radically upward the production of landing craft, especially larger sizes.

> *Adm. Ernest J. King, commander in chief of the U.S. Fleet, telegram to WPB, December 4, 1943, quoted in Nelson,* Arsenal of Democracy, *258.*

When my grandchildren ever ask me what I did during the Great War, I'm going to tell them it was too horrible to talk about.

> *Unidentified OPA official, December 1944, quoted in Bowles,* Promises to Keep, *82.*

Industrial Mobilization

As the threat of involvement in World War II brought an urgent need for American industry to shift to defense work in 1940, however, his company loaned [Wallace] Higgins to head Cleveland's War Production Board. For two years he complained bitterly about factory owners' lack of patriotism as one after another declined bids to accept war preparedness contracts.

> *Allied military governor Raymond Higgins writing in 1997 about events of 1940,* From Hiroshima with Love, *10.*

The present number of gainfully employed workers is inadequate to fill even the many requirements of the war production program. In many areas the lack of adequate housing and transportation facilities compels full use of the local labor supply. These considerations require that substantially increased numbers of women be employed in gainful occupations in war production and essential civilian employment. The recruitment and training of women workers must be greatly expanded and intensified.

War Manpower Commission, "Policy on Women"
October 17, 1942, in its Manual of Operation,
Record Group 86.

Looking back across the year [1942], the President has much with which to be pleased. The task of mobilizing a fairly prosperous and contented capitalist democracy for war is like trying to drive a team of twenty mules, each stubbornly intent on having its own way. Only by continual compromise with the ornery critters is it possible to move forward at all. Examined closely, by the myopic eye of the perfectionist, Mr. Roosevelt's performance in every sphere has been faulty. Regarded in the perspective of his limited freedom of choice and the temper of the country, which has never really been warlike, the year's achievements have been extraordinary.

Journalist I. F. Stone writing about events of 1942,
War Years, *134.*

I knew that we were going to win the war when I saw the big Willow Run aircraft factory outside Detroit. My God, but it was a big one.

A Canadian, probably late 1942 or early 1943,
quoted in Fussell, Wartime, *9.*

The other thing that I think we performed a good job on was narrowing the scope of orders and regulations to what was really necessary, making exceptions for unimportant transactions or small operators. The typical "dollar-a-year" businessman official of the WPB would propose an order speaking in terms of no one shall do this and everyone must do that. But when you pinned him down and asked, "Does it matter whether the guy with two employees and a total business of a few thousand dollars a year does this or that?" He'd say, "No, it doesn't." He just didn't think in those terms. He was thinking of the big businesses that he came from.

Another very interesting part of it to me was the philosophy of businessmen in Government. They tend to think in terms of the job to be done and they tend to be quite impatient with legal restrictions. I remember talking to one of these fellows. He was very impatient with what he considered nit-picking at the order

that he wanted to get out. I was concerned as to whether it exceeded our powers and, on the merits, as to whether it was really necessary to go this far. And his answer was, "Well, we shouldn't worry about whether it's in our powers. We've got a war to win," and so on. And I said, "Well, now look here. You are exactly the kind of businessman who has been griping for years about Government bureaucrats exceeding their powers, doing more than Congress meant them to do, and butting into the running of business. Now you are doing exactly the same thing yourself." He sort of grinned sheepishly, but it was true. This was also my experience way back, when I was with the SEC. The businessman in a Government position, once he gets on that side of the fence, is more ruthless towards other businessmen who are still in business than the professor of economics or the lawyer in Government whom the businessman who is still in business looks upon as the impractical, theoretical bureaucrat.

Isaac N. P. Stokes, lawyer for the Office of Production
Management, interview of July 3, 1973, regarding
events of 1942–44, conducted by Richard D. McKinzie,
in the Truman Library.

Allocating Raw Materials for Industrial Production

The nation waits anxiously these days for the definite report on rubber. That report may mean the end of auto driving for leisure for the duration and thus drastically change the pattern of American life; but it is believed here that the man in the street will accept the sacrifice once the facts are laid before him. The confidence is due in no small measure to the character and reputation of the man [Bernard Baruch] whom the President has named to head the special investigating committee.

W. H. Lawrence, "Dr. Facts Digs In," New York
Times, *August 16, 1942, VII: 5.*

Forbidding Manufacture of Nonessential Products

Today's papers carry the news that 206,000 workers in Michigan will lose their jobs in the next seven days because no steps have yet been taken to convert automobile factories to defense production. This inability of a great and rich country to gather up sufficient will to mobilize its full energies for war is characteristic of empires in their senility. . . . Solution of the problem has been hampered by a succession of complacencies in the capital. The first was the easy assumption that we were unbeatable because we had the greatest productive system in the world. When it began to be realized that this productive system was being largely devoted to a boom in consumer goods, it was assumed that it would transform itself automatically into a vast arsenal if we curtailed the output of automobiles, washing machines, refrigerators, and new houses. A few months ago, however, officials and others began to see that curtailment alone was no guaranty that facilities made idle by scarcity of materials would be converted to defense production. Smaller industries found it hard to obtain orders from the big business men running the OPM [Office of Production Management] and hard to interest the conventionally thinking army-navy procurement officers in the possibility of turning out armament in factories normally used to produce washing machines. . . . The attack on Pearl Harbor should have ended 'business as usual,' but it did not.

I. F. Stone, December 27, 1941, in
The War Years, 96–97.

The first step the [WPB] tackled was . . . the conversion of the auto industry, and we promptly issued our first order, which stopped production of all passenger cars and light trucks, effective February 1 [1942]. The order applied to the production of cars and light trucks, with or without tires, and regardless of the terms of any contract entered into by a producer prior to the issuance of the order. We had then a stock of 130,000 new passenger cars . . . and some 38,000 light trucks; and as far as the civilian side of the economy was concerned we had to make these answer until war production no longer needed the facilities of the automobile companies. Hence, these cars had to be doled out, in miserly fashion. . . .

Donald Nelson, WPB chair, writing in 1946 about
events of January and February 1942 in Arsenal of
Democracy, 203.

Inducements for Industrial Production

The [Automotive] Council [for War Production] established a pattern of industrial teamwork for victo-

ry. Its purpose was the fostering of complete interchange of mass-production information, time-saving techniques, product improvements, tooling shortcuts, and developments.

. . . Brought together on mutual problems, onetime competitors quickly discovered that they could plan together and work together. And immediately after the first service-functions began to operate smoothly, a big step toward even closer collaboration was taken in the organization of committees through which an actual sharing of productive "know-how" could take place.

Alvan Macauley, Packard's board chair, speaking of
events beginning in February 1942, quoted in Nelson,
Arsenal of Democracy, 228.

A manufacturer with a big contract for Hispano-Suiza cannon wanted the government to finance a $5,250,000 plant expansion. After consultation with the Army and OPM, he was informed that he could utilize the existing facilities of smaller neighbors—buildings, machine tools and other equipment, manpower—for the production of 118 of 121 parts. He could make the three most difficult parts and handle the whole job as prime contractor. . . . After a few experiences of this nature the Army and Navy began to see that it was foolish to finance expansions until the subcontracting possibilities of smaller firms had been fully explored.

Donald Nelson, WBP chair, writing of
events of 1943, Arsenal of
Democracy, 275.

Limitations on Agency Control of Industrial Production

First step in this struggle was a bitter scrap between the War Department and WPB over the extent of WPB's powers.

WPB controlled the distribution of raw materials through the exercise of its priorities authority. This control, originally, was incomplete; a good part of the priorities power had been vested in the Army and Navy Munitions Board, and there was a good deal of conflict.

Historian Brace Catton writing in 1948 of
events in early 1942, in War Lords of
Washington, 204.

The Wartime Civilian Economy

To build the factory, to buy the materials, to pay the labor, to provide the transportation, to equip and feed and house the soldiers and sailors and marines, and do all the thousands of things necessary in a war—all cost a lot of money, more money than has ever been spent by any nation at any time in the long history of the world. . . . As we sit here at home contemplating our own duties, let us think and think hard of the example which is being set for us by our fighting men.

President Franklin D. Roosevelt, fireside chat of April 28, 1942, announcing an economic program of heavier taxes, war bonds, wage and price controls, and comprehensive rationing, Mid-Hudson Regional Information Center, available online. URL: www.whric.org/ fdr/chat21.html.

So we were concerned about manpower shortages and the orderly organization of our labor market, for war production purposes, which was basically the purpose of the War Manpower Commission.

When the War Manpower Commission was organized . . ., those of us who had background and experience in it were asked to transfer over as war transferees. . . . We formulated what came to be known as management-labor programs, and devised a system of restricting the movement of labor between jobs through a certificate of availability procedure. That was basically manufactured out of whole cloth. It vested in a management the power to grant or deny a certificate of availability to an individual who left its labor force. The objective was the staffing and stabilization of the labor force in war production industries. . . .

Recognizing the potentiality for injustice in this program, we set up principles to govern good cause for leaving and management-labor appeal boards to hear appeals from denials of certificates of availability. On the other hand, we provided, in these programs, for unrestricted certificates of availability to workers in nonessential industries, in order to entice them away from those industries.

The other side of the program was an attempt to control the hiring practices of industry, through a provision that no employer may hire an individual except through the public employment offices or unless he had a direct referral from an employment office, in the shortage skills. . . .

Another activity of the War Manpower Commission was a much closer working relationship with the selective service system, again for the same purpose— to coordinate the selective service regulations governing occupational deferments. There were many who wanted to use the selective service system as an enforcement device for keeping critical workers in their jobs—in effect, inducting them into the army if they left their jobs. You remember that era? I'm not defending it. There were many aspects of it that troubled us, but it was a period of war crisis and our effort was to devise as many controls, and impartial bodies to hear complaints and review injuries to individuals, as possible. We were affecting the freedom of individuals.

Reminiscences of Social Security Administrator Bernice Lotwin Bernstein describing events beginning probably in the late spring or early summer of 1942, in the Columbia University Oral History Research Office Collection 1965, 99–101.

There are too many people in this country . . . who are not mature enough to realize that you can't take a piece of paper and draw a line down the middle of it and put the war abroad on one side and put the home front on the other, because after all it all ties in together. When we send an expedition to Sicily, where does it begin? Well it begins at two places practically; it begins on the farms of this country, and in the mines of this country. And then the next step in getting that army into Sicily is the processing of the food, and the processing of the raw material into steel, then the munitions plants that turn the steel into tanks and planes or the aluminum. . . . And then, a great many million people in this country are engaged in transporting it from the plant, or from the field, or the processing plant to the seaboard. And then it's put on ships that are made in this country . . . and you have to escort and convoy with a lot of other ships. . . . Finally, when they get to the other side, all these men go ashore. . . . But all through this we have to remember that there is just one front, which includes at home as well as abroad. It is all part of the picture of trying to win the war.

President Franklin D. Roosevelt speaking at a press conference, in the New York Times, *July 28, 1943, 9.*

President Roosevelt and Premier Joseph Stalin discuss the state of events at the Tehran Conference, 1943. *(Library of Congress)*

To American production, without which this war would have been lost.

> *Joseph Stalin, toast offered at Tehran Conference, late 1943, in Walker et al.,* Our Glorious Century, *219.*

The overwhelming majority of our people have met the demands of this war with magnificent courage and understanding. They have accepted inconveniences; they have accepted hardships; they have accepted tragic sacrifices. However, while the majority goes on about its great work without complaint, a noisy minority maintains an uproar of demands for special favors for special groups. There are pests who swarm through the lobbies of the Congress and the cocktail bars of Washington, representing these special groups as opposed to the basic interests of the nation as a whole. They have come to look at the war principally as a chance to make profits for themselves. . . .

It is our duty now to begin to lay plans . . . for the winning of a lasting peace. . . . We cannot be content, no matter how high the general standard of living may be, if some fraction of our people—whether it be one-half or one-third or one-tenth—is ill-fed, ill-housed and insecure. This Republic had its beginning under the protection of certain inalienable political rights—among them rights of free speech, free press, free worship, trial by jury, freedom from unreasonable searches and seizures. They were our rights to life and liberty.

As our nation has grown in size and stature, however—as our industrial economy expanded—these political rights proved inadequate to assure us equality in the pursuit of happiness. We have come to a clear realization of the fact that true individual freedom cannot exist without economic security and independence. "Necessitous men are not free men." People who are hungry and out of a job are the stuff of which dictatorships are made.

> *President Franklin D. Roosevelt's State of the Union message to Congress, January 11, 1944,* New York Times, *January 12, 1944, 3.*

But we of this generation chance to live in a day and hour when our nation has been attacked, and when its future existence and the future existence of our chosen method of government is at stake.

To win this war wholeheartedly, unequivocally and as quickly as we can is our task of the first importance. To win this war in such a way that there will be no further world wars in the foreseeable future is our second objective. To provide occupations and a decent standard of living for our men in the armed forces after the war, and for all Americans, are the final objectives.

Therefore, reluctantly, but as a good soldier, I repeat that I will accept and serve in this office if I am so ordered by the commander-in-chief of us all, the sovereign people of the United States.

> *President Franklin D. Roosevelt, letter to Robert E. Hannegan, chair of the Democratic National Committee, July 11, 1944, in Brinkley,* Washington, *257.*

4

Civilian Daily Life
1940–June 1945

HISTORICAL CONTEXT

"One front and one battle where everyone in the United States—every man, woman, and child—is in action. The front is right here at home, in our daily lives."

—President Franklin D. Roosevelt, April 1942

World War II transformed the lives, expectations, and prospects not only of the 16 million Americans who entered the military but also of the 116 million civilian men, women, and children. They were just emerging from one of the most dispiriting decades in the history of the United States. With its unemployment rate running up to 25 percent and people literally fainting in the streets from hunger, the Great Depression had sapped Americans' confidence in their political and economic system and in themselves. Family structure was threatened as teenagers left homes that could not feed them and young people had to postpone marriage and babies.

Moreover, the disillusionments of World War I had left Americans distrustful of international involvement. Largely committed to peace, the nation looked on apprehensively as the dictators Hitler, Mussolini, and Stalin seized power in Europe, and the Japanese raged through Asia. Regarding war as ignoble and futile, but fearing that they could not escape it, Americans gradually accepted preparations for defense, and, after the outbreak of the European war in September 1939, extension of help to the Allies. The attack on Pearl Harbor on December 7, 1941, instantaneously transformed the national mood. It infuriated Americans; it challenged them; it energized them. They began to act as one people, putting the demands of society ahead of their own desires.

The War-Centered Society

During the four years following Pearl Harbor, Americans focused their lives on the war, even as they dreamed of and saved for the day when it would end.

Early on, local defense activities absorbed much of their leisure time and effort. The Office of Civilian Defense was organized on May 20, 1941, under the direction of New York City mayor Fiorello LaGuardia. A year later it had involved more than 5 million Americans in its programs, a number that eventually doubled.[1] Volunteer air raid wardens passed out instructions for blackout curtains and supervised practice air-raid alerts, with wailing sirens, simulated injuries, and novices applying first aid. The Ground Observer Corps recruited spotters to learn to recognize and watch for enemy planes; eventually it recruited 11,000 volunteers, mostly women.[2] Most of these activities dwindled or died a natural death as soon as people realized the improbability of an air attack on the continental United States. However, on the coasts air wardens continued to patrol the streets, making sure that the brownout was maintained, so that lights from the shore would not illuminate Allied shipping as targets for submarines.

On December 1, 1941, LaGuardia organized the Civil Air Patrol (CAP). Its civilian crews flew more than 24 million miles on coastal patrols, summoning help for ships in distress and survivors of submarine attacks; spotting enemy submarines, dropping bombs and depth charges on them, and calling other planes and ships to attack them; airlifting people and light cargoes; towing targets and tracking flights for training antiaircraft gunners; patrolling powerlines, pipelines, and the Mexican border; checking for forest fires; and providing orientation flights to thousands of prospective aviation cadets and recruits. At its peak it numbered 40,000 pilots, and 20,000 cadets in training; each pilot bought his own uniform and operated his or her own plane.[3]

This notice on a bus window in Baltimore, Maryland, April 1943, reads: "Passengers and crews are now required by law to leave street cars, buses and trackless trolleys and seek shelter under penalty of fine, imprisonment or both. Conductors and operators will issue upon request special Air Raid Slips, good as fares on any vehicle up to one-half hour after the second 'Blue' signal." *(Library of Congress, LC-USW3-022097-E)*

A Red Cross volunteer paints the destination of boxes of supplies for American prisoners of war in Japan and elsewhere in the Far East, to be loaded on the neutral Swedish ship *Gripsholm. (Library of Congress, LC-USW33-042498)*

Civilians devoted even more time to supporting the morale of soldiers, sailors, and Marines. For those servicemen still in the United States the United Service Organizations (USO) of civilian volunteers provided recreation at service clubs. Movie stars entertained them and waited tables; carefully chaperoned young women jitterbugged and danced the Lindy Hop with them; and older women cooked and played games or music with them. Families arranged with the USO to invite soldiers and sailors to their homes for meals and a taste of home life. Local women fed servicemen passing through on trains at station canteens, or handed homemade food to them through the train windows; in some towns women battled with their neighbors to ensure that they served *all* in the military, blacks included.

American servicemen in England found a bit of home at the USO clubs, where they could snack, read, write letters, and dance with local young women. In London the Rainbow Corner run by the Red Cross offered full meals, theater tickets, and now and then a chance to send radio messages home. USO shows featuring performers from movie stars to struggling actors toured the theaters of war, enduring hardships, and approaching dangerously close to enemy lines. Comedian Bob Hope traveled constantly with Jerry Colonna and singer Frances Langford. Comedienne Martha Raye, who went to remote bases around the world with actresses Kaye Francis, Mitzie Mayfair, and Carol Landis, won the title of "Colonel Maggie of the Boondocks" and, in 1993, the Presidential Medal of Freedom for her service in World War II and successive wars.

Civilians endlessly wrote letters to their men in the service, often daily, and packed small gifts for them, stuffing the boxes of cookies and birthday cakes with popcorn to protect them. Some of their letters were written on V-mail, preprinted blue letter sheets that folded to make envelopes; these were then put on microfilm for transmission and printed out close to their destination about a quarter of the original size. Between June 15, 1942, and April 1, 1945, more than 556 million V-mails were sent to service people abroad, and many times that number of letters went by regular mail.[4]

Reminders of the war were everywhere. Radios played over and over the popular singer Kate Smith's rendering of "God Bless America," Frank Loesser's "Praise the Lord and Pass the Ammunition," the haunting German song "Lili Marlene," and the first four notes of Beethoven's fifth symphony to represent the Morse code for V (for victory): dot, dot, dot, dash. Radio news, which preempted about a third of network air time,[5] brought reports from such distinguished journalists as Elmer Davis and Edward R. Murrow, famed for his rooftop reports of London burning and for his broadcast live from a bomber as it dropped its bombs over Berlin. George Hicks described the D day invasion from a warship just off Omaha beach. Listeners at home moved pushpins on maps to follow troop movements.

The nation stopped to listen when President Franklin D. Roosevelt talked directly to the people in his homey fireside chats about government policy and the progress of the war. Novelist Saul Bellow recalled "walking eastward on the Chicago Midway on a summer evening. The light held after nine o'clock, and the ground was covered with clover, more than a mile of green between Cottage Grove and Stony Island. The blight had not yet carried off the elms, and under them drivers had pulled over, parking bumper to bumper, and turned on their radios to hear Roosevelt. They had rolled down the windows, and opened the car doors. Everywhere the same voice, its odd Eastern accent, which in anyone else would have irritated Midwesterners. You could follow without missing a single word as you strolled by. You felt joined to these unknown drivers, men and women smoking their cigarettes in silence, not so much considering the President's words as affirming the rightness of his tone and taking assurance from it."[6]

Even while newspapers put out abbreviated editions to save paper, circulation rose from 42 million daily in 1941 to 46 million in 1944.[7] Although no one had a television set, newsreels and magazines showed Americans what war looked like, from the rubble of bombed-out cities and the fires of London to the invasions of Pacific atolls and Sicily—although editors suppressed the most graphic photos of the havoc wrought on human bodies by high explosives. News magazines like *Life* and *Look* filled their pages with pictures taken by combat photographers and civilian photographers such as Joe Rosenthal, famed for his picture of the flag-raising on Iwo Jima. Margaret Bourke-White, the first woman accredited by the U.S. Army in World War II as a war correspondent, sent back pictures of the German attack on Moscow, Gen. George Patton's troops crossing the German border, and the unforgettable series *The Living Dead of Buchenwald*. Photograph after photograph of Winston Churchill showed him with index and third fingers upraised in a victory V.

The war news Americans heard was censored, in some part by groundless official optimism, in larger part by the determination of the press to present the war effort in the light best for morale. In the Pacific Gen. Douglas MacArthur fictionalized his press releases for his own aggrandizement, and the U.S. Navy suppressed bad news about its defeats, so that a journalist once wrote, "Seven of

Government employees labor in the News Bureau of the Office of War Information in November 1942. *(Library of Congress, LC-USZ62-090303)*

the two ships sunk at Pearl Harbor have now rejoined the fleet."[8] Information from the European theater clung closer to the truth, the air force early on reporting exact numbers of bombers lost.

Bookstores touted such books as William Shirer's *Berlin Diary;* Elliot Paul's *The Last Time I Saw Paris;* Marion Hargrove's comic *See Here, Private Hargrove;* Richard Tregaskis's *Guadalcanal Diary;* and William White's *They Were Expendable.* Movie theaters, where women "usherettes" had taken the place of male ushers, collected contributions for the USO and sold war bonds, showed short subjects explaining rationing or urging the audience to postpone buying a house, and featured such war films as Charlie Chaplin's satiric *The Great Dictator, Casablanca, Bataan, Song of Russia,* the realistic *The Story of G. I. Joe* (based on one of Ernie Pyle's stories), and *The Sullivans* (commemorating the five brothers who went down together in one ship). The Office of War Information encouraged producers to show a prettified world in which "Uncle Joe" Stalin ruled benignly over an admirable and gallant Union of Soviet Socialist Republics and American blacks and whites fought together as a band of brothers. Before theatrical performances and at the end of movies, audiences stood and sang the national anthem.

Despite the efforts of the War Advertising Council to tone them down, corporations advertised their contributions to the war effort to the point of absurdity. "Lucky Strike Green has gone to war!" (Their cigarettes now came in white packages.) The Coty perfume company let it be known that their "worldwide organization is in the service of the United States and the United Nations," furnishing facial makeup for camouflaged jungle fighters.[9] Air-conditioning manufacturers claimed credit for sulfa drugs because they were made in air-conditioned laboratories. The tasteless ad headline "Who's Afraid of the Big

Focke-Wulf?" (a German fighter plane) drew a response from an American bomber crew, who wrote "I am" and signed their names.[10]

Propaganda assaulted the public's ears and eyes from billboards and subway cards, newspapers and radios. "Buy a share in America!" "Zip your lip, save a ship!" "Hurry them back, join the WAC!" "Carry your packages!" "United we win." "Grow more in '44!" "When you ride alone, you ride with Hitler!" "Pay your taxes, Beat the Axis!" "Is this trip necessary?" Some cafeterias served butter pats stamped with "Keep 'em Flying" or "Remember Pearl Harbor," and they advised their customers: "Use less sugar and stir like hell. We don't mind the noise." Radio shows, feature films, and movie shorts incorporated war messages into their programs. The artist and illustrator N. C. Wyeth depicted farmers on tractors beneath the massed flags of the allied nations and named his picture "Soldiers of the Soil," extending FDR's metaphor of the home front. Posters hailed factory workers as "soldiers without guns."

Workers on assembly lines paused to clap their hands to the rhythms of the 1942 hit "Don't Sit Under the Apple Tree"—but fell silent when a death telegram was delivered to one of their number. Service flags hung in the windows of many homes—shields with a white background framed in red, with a blue star for each servicemember still alive, and a gold for each one killed.

People talked about the war constantly. They talked about the news from the various fronts and about the letters they had received from their servicemen—or the letters for which they were waiting in anguish. They talked about what they heard on the radio and saw in the newsreels. They said to each other, sardonically, "I'm in no hurry; I'm signed up for the duration [of the war] plus six [months]," the period for which their obligations to the government remained in force. Over and over, sales clerks and waitresses told their frustrated customers, "Don't you know there's a war on?"

Shortages and Rationing

Compared with the rest of the world, American civilians were flourishing. Unlike most of the world, they were safe. No bombs fell; no ships bombarded them. War did not ravage their homes or destroy their businesses. Their government remained stable and their freedoms protected. The United States was the only belligerent country that raised its civilian standard of living during the war.[11] Americans were making good money, much of which went into savings for want of consumer goods to buy. They were able to pay not only for the necessities but also for entertainment. They flocked to movie theaters, sports events, bars, and clubs.

They did not, of course, have everything they wanted. Americans who had done without during the Great Depression because they had no money now did without because little was available to buy, and that little often of poor quality. Even though from 1939 to 1945 the American output of textiles rose 50 percent and that of processed foodstuffs 40 percent, military needs forced the country to cut goods for civilians severely.[12] Dozens of small items such as paper clips became difficult to replace. A cartoonist showed one executive behind a big desk demanding of his secretary, "Where is my rubber band?" Lead coins replaced copper pennies, and the nickel disappeared from the five-cent piece. People who loaned their binoculars to the navy for the duration were rewarded with $1 in war savings stamps, as were those who donated old radios to the Signal Corps so that repairmen in training could practice on them.

But most people had most things they really needed. They ate well, though not always what they wanted. They could and did send food packages to the truly deprived English and supplied their own servicemen with food to take to their hosts around the world.

In the United States clothing was in short supply. In the summer of 1942, the government established regulations at the manufacturing level. To save cloth, men's suits no longer came with two pairs of pants, and if they had vests they could not be double-breasted. Men wore Victory suits, with narrow lapels, cuff-less trousers, and buttons instead of zippers on the flies—except for the young, mostly black and Hispanic zoot-suiters who until the War Production Board put a stop to it defiantly flaunted wide-brimmed fedora hats, oversized jackets, and baggy pants cuffed at the ankles. Women did not object to shorter skirts, skirts with no pleats, and two-piece bathing suits, but they raised an outcry when the rubber shortage threatened the manufacture of girdles, which all nice young women wore (older women still wore corsets). Hosiery made of silk or of the prized, newly invented nylon disappeared from the stores (to make parachutes), and women stood in line for ugly, ill-fitting stockings (held up by supporters on their girdles) made of rayon, lisle, or more mysterious threads that ran on first wearing. They dyed odd stockings to make them match and bought devices with which to reknit runs. Many younger women resorted to leg makeup that had to be scrubbed off each night to keep it from staining the sheets. The more imaginative used eyebrow pencil to draw seams down the backs of their legs. With shoes rationed, parents with growing children scrounged to keep up with changing sizes, and mothers of new babies looked for substitutes for rubber pants. Unusually tall or fat people had a hard time finding anything to wear. Service wives double-hung their clothes so they could send their newly inducted husbands enough wire coat hangers to satisfy the demands of drill sergeants and scoured stores for electric irons to meet sailors' requests.

Women with families to clothe, keep clean, and feed bore the brunt of food shortages and rationing—their tasks even more burdensome and complicated for the many women also working outside the home, in an era when stores did not stay open evenings or weekends. Keeping house had not been easy during the Great Depression. In 1941, a third of all households still cooked with wood or coal. Half of women washed by hand or in hand-cranked washing machines. Both farm and city women spent more than 50 hours a week on household responsibilities.[13] During the war many housewives took on tasks that they had hoped to leave behind, like sewing (although they had a hard time getting hooks and eyes, zippers, and metal buttons), and canning. Martha Wood remembered, "So I was canning until midnight, and later, night after night, and I frequently said, 'I wish I had Hitler in that pressure cooker.'"[14]

Piles of mending mounted, as women turned irreplaceable sheets (ripping them in two, putting the worn sections on the outside edges, and re-hemming them), reversed shirt collars to put the wear on the underside, and converted long sleeves into short, obeying the omnipresent propaganda to "Wear it out, use it up, make it do, or do without." Overworked physicians trying to combine their own work with the practices of the doctors called into the military cut back on house calls; so women had to get their children to doctors' offices. Familiar brands of soap disappeared (detergents had yet to become popular), and housewives struggled to wash clothes with brands that might as well have been made of ground rock for all their suds and cleansing properties, while laundries were swamped with work and unable to get enough help.

Shopping consumed endless hours and depended on both persistence and luck. Service wife Audrey Davis wrote her sailor husband in April 1945, "Honey, I'm a success. I got sheets! Such a time—went to four of the biggest stores first and was turned down cold. Finally ended up in the basement of J. C. Penney's . . . and saw some bedding so on the off-chance, I asked. The girl said, shhh, and sneaked into a back room and brought out some carefully wrapped—didn't even know what I had bought, until I got home. I felt like someone buying hooch during Prohibition."[15]

No new household appliances were available, for the factories that made them had converted to turning out military supplies. Household help left to take more lucrative jobs. Repairmen and handymen disappeared. One New Mexico housewife reported, "Almost everyone in town is doing their own furnace tending and I certainly am having a lesson in applied mechanics. . . . I am learning all about coal stokers, hot water heaters, wells and pumps, together with frozen pipes."[16] Daily milk deliveries dropped to a delivery every other day, and most grocery stores stopped delivering completely; department stores urged their customers to take with them as many packages as they could carry.

With gasoline rationed, women walked to the butcher and grocery store carrying the waste fats (to be used in making explosives) they had saved up to turn in at the meat counter (in return for a couple of extra ration points) and their empty toothpaste tubes (which had to be turned in with each toothpaste purchase). With ration books for each family member in hand, they lined up for food in scant supply, then doled out red stamps for meat, butter, fats, cheese, canned milk, and canned fish; and green, brown, or blue stamps for canned vegetables, juices, baby food, and dried fruit. If supplies ran out before they reached the counter, they either had to go to other stores or search for substitutes like saccharin (previously used mostly by diabetics and dieters) or adjust their recipes to use corn syrup instead of sugar. The makers of newly popular margarine, forced by the butter lobby to sell only a white product, first included little packages of dye with each pound, which housewives laboriously stirred into the margarine; later margarine was sold in plastic bags with a bubble of yellow dye inside, to be burst and worked in with the fingers. When on October 31, 1942, OPA cut the coffee ration to a cup a day for each person over 15, women used coffee grounds twice.

Their families complained most about the shortage of the meat they had hungered for during the Great Depression and now could afford. Most families did not like the liver, kidney, and tongue that were more easily available, and with cheese also rationed it was hard to find meat substitutes. Even with tobacco and alcohol also in short supply, the black market in meat was larger than that in any other product—a market that flourished in the cattle industry generally and to a lesser extent among local butchers.[17]

Shortages of meat changed eating habits, as people ate more vegetables, growing many themselves in their victory gardens. The department of agriculture estimated that these gardens produced 40 percent of the vegetables grown during the war.[18] Housewives canned the produce to carry the family through the winter. The government helped to improve nutrition by teaching its basics, beginning to issue nutritional standards, requiring fortification or enrichment of bread, margarine, and milk, and the addition of iron, thiamine, riboflavin, and niacin to white flour.

Eating out, in those days an infrequent practice by 21st-century standards, was seldom pure pleasure. One restaurant warned in an advertisement, "If you miss familiar Brass Rail faces. . . . If we sometimes fall short of the perfect service you have always enjoyed. . . . Please remember that about one-third of our crew have gone—with our blessing—into the service of our country."[19] Drinking soared at such a rate as to produce an unanticipated shortage: When the whiskey people converted to making industrial alcohol, they thought that they had a five-year supply of whiskey on hand, but consumption rose from 140 million gallons in 1941 to 190 million gallons in 1942.[20] Even though the British filled the returning Lend-Lease ships with scotch whiskey to reduce their unfavorable balance of trade, the shortage persisted. Cans of beer vanished, and bottled beer was sometimes hard to find.

Going anywhere was a problem—a problem created partly by troop movements from base to base, partly by the vast migrations of the civilian population: During the war 15 million civilians moved within the United States. Almost all Americans in their teens, 20s, and 30s moved at least once.[21] Service wives followed their husbands until they were shipped overseas, sometimes lugging their children along with them.

Consequently, public transportation was crowded to the bursting point. Passenger air travel, still in its early stages, was reserved almost entirely for those with high priorities in the war effort. It was always uncertain, for at the last minute a traveler could be bumped by someone with a higher priority. Those traveling for pleasure often found themselves stranded, unable to get back home. Neither railroads nor bus companies could replace equipment, and both were short on personnel, so as the war went on passengers lucky enough to get seats sat on worn upholstery in dirty trains and buses that shook, rattled, and rolled. Trains were jammed with people standing, sitting on suitcases, even sleeping in the aisles. Occasionally fatigue, overcrowding, and delays occasioned by breakdowns or by being sidetracked for troop trains snapped tempers, but most of the time people helped each other. One young service mother remembered how soldiers and sailors passed her baby over the heads of the crowd into the train window and then forced a passage for her onto the train, and how they got off at stops to get her some food.

Few could travel very far by car. A critical shortage of rubber, essential to the war effort, necessitated the rationing of tires. Restrictions began in December 1941, with an order forbidding the sale of new tires and multiplied thereafter. Most people were allowed five tires to an automobile; any extras had to be turned over to the government. Physicians, ministers, war workers, and public officials showing real need could buy one new set. Gasoline was rationed mostly to prevent people from driving and thereby save rubber. Rations of gas on an "A" (nonessential) card, the one most people received, varied throughout the war from five gallons a week down to two gallons—this at a time when gas mileage from 10 to 15 miles per gallon was considered acceptable. "B" cards allowed a bit more to people who needed gasoline for their work; "C" cards, larger amounts for such persons as physicians and law enforcement officers; and "X" cards, unlimited amounts for VIPs, like senators—until public outrage ended this privilege. The Victory speed limit was set at 35 miles an hour, with the penalty for exceeding it the loss of gas and tire rations. Driving for pleasure stopped abruptly, and people walked. People carpooled to work, often five or six to a car. Parties broke up early so that guests could catch the last bus. Some people decided that running a car was more trouble than it was worth and put it up on jacks for the duration or simply got rid of it. One used car company advertised: "OPA Bans Pleasure Driving. Now is the time to sell your car while our prices are extremely high. Describe your car and we'll buy it over the phone."[22]

Hotels, forced to shut down floors for want of help or to rent many of their rooms to the government, had more business than they could handle. Often they did not honor reservations. Guests were thankful for any room they could get, and if the sheets had not been changed they had to hope that the previous occupant had been clean. Tourist cabins and tourist rooms in private homes, the 1940s version of motels, had few traveling customers, but those near military bases or defense industries were sought out by servicemen's families and defense workers.

For the greatest shortage of all was housing. A large proportion of those 15 million Americans on the move were relocating to get better jobs. Despite governmental efforts to award contracts to small businesses across the continent, the large manufacturers who won most of them were concentrated in the Northeast, along the West Coast, and in midwestern cities. New or temporary residents vied to rent any shelter, paying high prices for converted garages, attics, chicken coops, tents, and shantytowns, or rooms shared with another family with only a sheet hung between. To the distress of neighbors, trailer camps sprang up, often with inadequate water, sewage, laundry facilities, and playgrounds. "Hot beds" cost 25 cents for eight hours.

Congress appropriated money, and contractors threw up public housing near industrial centers and military bases, but it was never enough or built soon enough. During 1942 and 1943 more than 1,000 of these emergency war-housing communities serving as many as 1.5 million people were built under the aegis of the National Housing Agency.[23] Some of these exemplified models of worker housing, especially the 450-unit complex of Atchison Village built in Richmond, California, in 1941, near the Kaiser shipyards. Adopting the principles of the "city beautiful" and "garden city" movements, its designers placed one- and two-story wood duplexes and fourplexes with spacious yards on winding streets and provided a community center and park. So severe was the competition for places in public housing that in some industrial centers racial tensions mounted; in Detroit in June 1943 workers rioted over public housing.[24]

Rationing of scarce goods worked reasonably well. Americans grumbled about it, of course, particularly about its nuisance and about the waste of rationed items in the military, but popular sentiment condemned hoarders (who nonetheless remained a problem throughout the war), and a majority felt that buying and selling on the black market was wrong. A Gallup poll in May 1945 found that 77 percent of women and 71 percent of men thought buying on the black market was never justified.[25] Meat proved to be the hardest commodity to control, partly because the cattle industry's methods lent themselves to cheating and partly because so many people wanted it so badly. Gasoline was also a problem, particularly as counterfeit ration stamps entered the economy. Gangsters ran a flourishing black market in cigarettes and alcohol, and an underworld character known as Waxey Gordon went to prison for trading in sugar, though black marketeers were seldom prosecuted. They sold nylon stockings for $5 a pair, cigarettes for 30 cents a pack, and boneless ham for double its ceiling price—but only a minority bought.[26] The gray market was another matter. The temptation was too much to resist when the local butcher reached under the display counter for a bit of steak he had saved for a special customer, and a plea of desperation sometimes persuaded a gas attendant to add an extra gallon of gas.

Although the combination of rationing and price controls burdened merchants, the price controls were a boon for customers and tenants. On March 2, 1942, the Office of Price Administration ordered landlords to roll back rental rates to those in effect on April 1, 1941. Landlords evaded these restrictions by improving the property so that higher rates were legal, or by selling the property to tenants with nominal down payments and monthly payments in excess of the controlled rent—a move that the government countered by requiring a minimum down payment of one-third of the purchase price. Homeowners around military bases who rented out below-standard housing to service families at exorbitant rates were hard to catch.

Economic Conditions

Nonetheless, price controls, the reduction of interest rates to an all-time low, and campaigns to encourage saving averted runaway inflation. With the 1935–39 period as a base of 100, by 1945 the cost-of-living index stood at 128.4, with most of the inflation occurring in 1941 and 1942. Price increases during the war years ran above average for food, clothing, and furniture, and below average for fuel, rent, and most other things. Wholesale prices increased more than retail.[27] Poverty stubbornly persisted, as FDR's New Deal programs gave way to the war effort,[28] but overall Americans raised their standard of living, although their higher incomes came more from long hours than from higher wages.

As the national debt soared, the federal government imposed higher taxes, so that many people for the first time in their lives had to pay income tax. In 1939 only some 4 million Americans paid this tax; in 1945, this had increased to 43 million.[29] The maximum individual tax rate reached its all-time high in 1944, at 94 percent.[30] In 1941 a family of four with the then-high income of $5,000 a year paid $271 in income tax; in 1943, $773.[31] The withholding system was instituted in 1943.[32]

Partly as a measure to control inflation, the government aggressively encouraged saving, particularly through the eight war loans, making it a patriotic duty. As University of Wisconsin professor Stanley K. Schultz phrased it, "The government used bonds to sell the war, not the war to sell bonds"—to help civilians feel that they were participating. War bond rallies sparkled with celebrities. Bonds were easy to buy, costing as little as $18.75 for a bond that in ten years would return $25. Twenty-five million workers signed up to buy bonds through payroll savings plans.[33] Those of lesser means could buy war stamps for as little as a dime to paste in a book bearing the pledge: "To every soldier, sailor, and marine who is fighting for my country. For you there can be no rest, for me there should be no vacation from the part I can play to help you win the war. I therefore solemnly promise to continue to buy United States War Savings Stamps and Bonds to the limit of my ability." When the book was filled with stamps, it could be exchanged for a bond.

Volunteering

Just as Americans were urged to support the war by saving, so also with volunteering. Some volunteer efforts were desperately needed; others were makework. The Office of Civilian Defense enrolled thousands of Americans as spotters for enemy airplanes that never came and thousands of others for emergency action in air raids that never happened. The Red Cross, which needed to maintain the support of well-off women, had them bandaging each other in first-aid classes and studying water safety, home nursing, and nutrition; and millions of them (including Eleanor Roosevelt) hand-knitting articles, some unneeded, others of which could have been turned out by mills better and faster. On the other hand, prisoners and teachers did vital work in the processing and distribution of ration books, and others chanced angering their neighbors by serving on local OPA and draft boards. Volunteer aides in hospitals and Red Cross blood banks eased the nursing shortage.

Man, woman, or child, it was the rare American who did not in some way at some time serve as a volunteer. Americans spontaneously formed dozens of war relief organizations. Bundles for Britain, founded in October 1940, signed up half a million members to collect money and supplies for the British. The wealthy women who in January 1940 founded the American Women's Volunteer Service enrolled about 350,000 of their friends and neighbors to serve as air raid wardens, sell war bonds, and serve food to the needy. Governmental agencies recruited people for groups like the Victory Speakers Bureau to explain the rationing system, and the Citizens Service Corps to conduct salvage campaigns, staff speakers' bureaus, and serve as block captains. Almost all existing clubs and other social organizations recruited volunteers in support of the war.

About a quarter of American women spent their leisure in volunteerism, large numbers of them middle-class housewives in their 30s and 40s with white-collar husbands and with some college education.[34] This group was experienced in organized social activities, through which most war-related volunteering was run. Even with their restricted time, working women wanted to help, and some of them managed to work full-time, raise their families singlehandedly, and still volunteer. Blacks and Hispanics were usually excluded, except in the American Women's Volunteer Services. Middle-class black women in the Alpha Kappa Alpha (AKA) sorority combined war service with demands for racial equality, and the National Council of Negro Women (NCNW) stressed racial solidarity and voter registration while urging its mem-

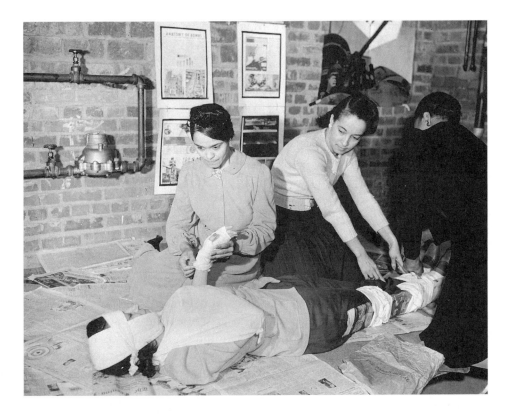

An air raid warden unit in Washington, D.C., learns first aid, November 1942. (*Library of Congress, LC-USW3-011412-C*)

bers to "hold your job." Pushed by Eleanor Roosevelt, the Red Cross in 1942 agreed in a high-level meeting with AKA, NCNW, and the National Association of Negro Nurses to hire blacks to run facilities for black soldiers, to appoint blacks to national and local staffs and steering committees, and to try to recruit black nurses—a promise little regarded.

At the same time women also stepped up their participation in politics, replacing men as party workers and local leaders. At the state level they made gains as officeholders. Several states called them for jury duty for the first time.[35]

Like their elders, schoolchildren from kindergarten to high school also volunteered. Dot Chastney Emer remembered: "Our teacher set aside a time in the school work—knitting time [to make afghans for the Red Cross to distribute]—and the girls taught the boys to knit. It was really fun because some of the boys couldn't get the hang of knitting. It gave us a little power over the boys. . . . They were good sports about it because everyone felt that we were doing this for the war effort."[36] At school pupils studied current events and drew maps reflecting changing world conditions and underwent air raid drills in which they huddled under their desks or sat down in the hallways. In New York City children received plastic dog tags stamped with their names, birth dates, and identification numbers.[37] Across the nation youngsters participated in scrap metal drives, collecting everything metal from old shovels and fences to empty lipstick tubes; paper drives, competing for the largest amount of wastepaper; and scrap rubber drives, throwing in their old rubber toys. Boy Scouts distributed posters and war information, collected musical instruments and razors for the troops, and built model airplanes for aircraft recognition classes. Girl Scouts volunteered in hospitals and babysat so mothers could work in defense industries. Young Minute Maids sold war stamps and bonds. With their elders young people picked cotton and lettuce at harvest time.

Education

The war transformed education at all levels. As teachers left their classrooms to take higher-paying jobs in defense factories, the quality of instruction dropped significantly. The numbers of high school dropouts multiplied, and many students took part-time and summer jobs. During the war, the teenage workforce grew from 1 million to 3 million, about 1 million of them high-school dropouts. In the emergency employers frequently ignored child labor laws.[38] Employers found that a couple of youngsters working at low-skilled tasks, for four-hour shifts each, could outperform an adult working an eight-hour shift.

College campuses teemed with activities related to the war. Students not only volunteered but also organized dances and parties to stimulate support and funds for the war effort. Male students and younger faculty left to join the military, to such an extent that on some campuses the student population dropped by half. Universities responded by running programs for 12 months a year, introducing accelerated academic programs, and stepping up the pace of Reserve Officer Training Corps (ROTC) classes to enable students to graduate and enlist in the military or the workforce sooner. Some lowered requirements. Institutions created compulsory physical education programs. They contracted with the military to train specialists, and marching soldiers and sailors clad in uniforms replaced the departed male students on many campuses. Smith and Mt. Holyoke provided sites for the training of women officers in the WAVES (Women Accepted for Volunteer Emergency Service).

Morale

Americans well knew how fortunate they were, compared with the rest of the world. In a poll taken in August 1943 asking, "Have you had to make any real sacrifice?" 69 percent said no. The others cited most of all as a sacrifice the absence of a near relative in the armed services. Fifteen percent spoke of financial sacrifices to buy war bonds. Twelve percent complained about less food, food of poorer quality, and less variety. No more than 10 percent identified any one other "sacrifice."[39]

Nonetheless, wartime for the folks at home is always a time of worry and anguish about their servicemen, and many a parent, wife, and sibling lay sleepless night after night, wondering, hoping against hope, and fearing. Uncertainty clouded the future. People were tired with overtime, volunteering, and coping with shortages and rationing; some were exhausted.

Family life underwent strains. Defense workers trying to get settled in crowded new locales short of housing and community amenities and far from all that was familiar had a hard time. The more than 5 million service families endured even more grueling experiences, especially if the war separated them.[40] Unless they had savings or the wife worked at a decently paid job, they had financial problems, for the government allowed service wives only $28 a month plus $12 for the first child and $10 for each additional child; enlisted men were also encouraged to allot $22 from their monthly pay of $50 to their wives.[41] Some desperate mothers had to put their children in orphanages.[42]

Marriage rates soared, and the median age of women at marriage dropped. In 1940, 48 percent of all women 14–34 were married; in 1946, 59 percent. In 1940 the median age for brides was 21.5 years, and in 1945, 20.3. The strong societal sanctions against sex outside of wedlock and the fear that death would part them without their ever having consummated their passion made couples turn to hasty marriages—a surprising number of which survived. Of all the new marriages in 1940, only one in six ended in divorce; in the late 1990s the figure had reached one in two.[43] Even though separation or financial inability to support themselves unless the wife worked forced many young couples to postpone having babies, birth rates increased. From 1927 to 1939 the annual number of births had ranged between 2.1 and 2.3 million yearly; in 1943 the number increased to 2.9 million, and in 1945 to 2.7 million. By the end of the war 41 percent of servicemen were husbands and 21 percent fathers. The number of service wives peaked at about 5 million.[44]

With so many of the principal crime-committing group—young men—in the military, crime rates dropped: murders fell from 8,329 in 1940 to 6,675 in 1944, and rose again as veterans returned. Suicides plummeted from 19,000 in 1940 to 13,000 in 1944.[45] What happened with illicit sex is hard to say. Cities launched campaigns against prostitution, trying to clear out red-light districts, particularly near military bases. The military attempted to scare servicemen by showing them graphic films on the dangers of venereal disease. However, as one medical officer observed, "The sex act cannot be made unpopular."[46] Sociologists of the time blamed the spread of venereal disease on "victory girls" (also called "khaki-wackies" and "cuddle-bunnies"), young amateurs who looked on sex with servicemen as an expression of patriotism. But the distinction between prostitutes and victory girls is blurred. Some scholars estimate that a third of married soldiers and one service wife in six engaged in extramarital affairs, but these figures are shaky.[47] Sexologist Alfred Kinsey, who relied on his subjects' own reports, found that during the 1940s about 26 percent of women were not virgins when they married.[48] Suffice it to say that by the standards of the early 1940s, when society still condemned extramarital and premarital sexual relationships, sexual conduct loosened.

Civilian morale rose and fell with the fortunes of war, which in the early years ran strongly against the Allies. On the whole, however, American morale remained strong. As military historian John Keegan remarks, Americans were "untainted by any fear of defeat."[49] They were sustained in large part by the optimism and strength of Franklin Delano Roosevelt and the trust they felt in him. Under his leadership they had survived the Great Depression and were back at work. Rightly or wrongly, they were infuriated by the perfidy of the Japanese attack at Pearl Harbor; they believed that they were fighting for a just cause. They were determined to win the war and they were sure they could—after all, the United States had never lost a war. The possibility of defeat seldom entered their heads. What was more, despite danger and discomfort, despite the terrible suffering and the evil abroad in the world, life was interesting, as millions of Americans moved to new locales, took new jobs, met new people, and adopted new lifestyles.

CHRONICLE OF EVENTS

1940

The first nylon stockings are marketed.

January: The American Women's Volunteer Service is founded.

June 20: The U.S. Committee for the Care of European Children is established as an umbrella organization, with First Lady Eleanor Roosevelt as honorary chair and goals of constructing a network of families willing to receive the children and of persuading the State Department to relax visa restrictions for these children.

October: Bundles for Britain is organized to collect money and supplies for the British.

October: The Lanham Act provides government funds for public housing, 3 percent to be used for community facilities.

1941

February: African-American Charles Richard Drew, medical director of the American Red Cross blood bank program and assistant director of blood procurement for the National Research Council (which is responsible for collecting blood for use by American troops), resigns to protest a military order to keep separate the blood of blacks and whites.

April 11: The Office of Price Administration (OPA) is established.

May 20: The Office of Civilian Defense (OCD) is organized, with New York mayor Fiorello LaGuardia as its director.

November: The War Advertising Council is formed to enlist advertisers, companies, and the government to put issues of the war before the public.

1942

January: Mystery writer Rex Stout organizes the Writers' War Board to put the talents of novelists, short-story specialists, and newspaper and magazine writers at the service of the government.

January 24: The OPA is authorized to ration goods.

January 30: The Emergency Price Control Act is enacted.

February 9: The United States changes to war time—now called daylight saving time.

February 10: The last new civilian car is manufactured.

March: The War Production Board rations the amount of fabric that can be used in men's suits.

March 2: The Office of Price Administration orders landlords to roll back rents to those in effect on April 1, 1941.

April: The Office of Price Administration announces that price controls will go into effect in May at levels that existed in March.

May 15: Gasoline rationing begins on the eastern seaboard and later is extended westward.

June: The Office of War Information establishes the Magazine Bureau, which publishes a bimonthly *Magazine War Guide* for publishers and editors.

mid-June: FDR initiates a scrap rubber drive, at a penny a pound.

July 22: Gasoline rationing begins for the whole country.

August: FDR mentions meatless days as a possibility.

September: The U.S. Office of Education creates the High School Victory Corps to study and do volunteer work within their choice among five divisions: air, land, sea, production, and community service.

October: Fuel oil is rationed in most parts of the country.

October: FDR is granted power to control wages and agricultural prices.

November: Coffee is rationed.

November 30: The first war loan drive begins.

December 27: A food rationing program is announced.

1943

January: Irving Wexler, known in the underworld as Waxey Gordon, is sentenced to a year in prison for black-market operations in sugar.

February: The first point-rationing books are distributed.

April 8: Prices are frozen.

April 12: The second war loan drive begins.

June 1: On orders of the Office of Defense Transportation, New York dairies cut milk deliveries to every other day.

July: Coffee rationing ends.

fall: Magazines conduct a major campaign for "Women in Necessary Services" in response to seri-

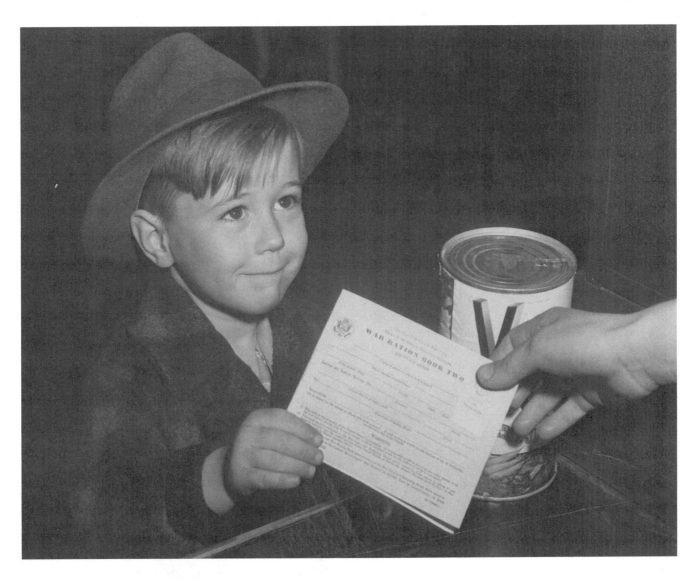

An eager schoolboy gets his first experience in using War Ration Book Two. Since many parents are engaged in war work, children are being taught the facts of point rationing for helping out with the family shopping, February 1943. (*National Archives, 208-AA-322H-1*)

ous labor shortages in service, trade, and supply industries.

September 9: The third war loan drive begins.

October: The standard "A" gasoline ration is reduced from four gallons a week to three.

1944

January 18: The fourth war loan drive begins.

spring: Magazines conduct a massive "Women in the War" campaign to recruit women for the military, get more workers into local economies, and keep women already working on the job.

March: The standard "A" gasoline ration is reduced from three gallons a week to two.

April: The U.S. Supreme Court rules that blacks cannot be barred from voting in the Texas Democratic party primaries.

May: Most meats are taken off the rationing list, prematurely.

June 12: The fifth war loan drive begins.

November 20: The sixth war loan drive begins.

December: All meat is again rationed.

December: Butter rationing ends.

1945

May 14: The seventh war loan drive begins.

June: The standard "A" gasoline ration is raised from two gallons a week to three.

Eyewitness Testimony

The War-Centered Society

Cliff [Clifford Durr, the liberal southern editor, Virginia Durr's husband] got a letter from Oxford, where he had been a Rhodes scholar, which said the University was trying to send all the dons and their wives over to America because Hitler was threatening to bomb Oxford and Cambridge. . . . The letter from Oxford asked Cliff to take a refugee, a lady named Mrs. Woozley, whose husband was the librarian of Queen's College. Cliff said he thought we had to take her. Then he found out she also would be bringing her baby with her. In my house at that time were Cliff, myself, Ann, Lucy, Tilla, [daughters], and Decca [Britisher Jessica Mitford], who was pregnant; also, my mother and father came to stay very often. . . . Well, ten people are quite a lot to feed, especially if we went on rations, but Cliff said we had to take her. Mrs. Woozley wrote me and said she didn't want to be any trouble, but she would need, of course, a private room and bath for herself and her baby, and also, would I engage a nanny for her? Can you imagine having to find a nanny? Well, I could see that Mrs. Woozley was going to be a pain in the neck and a lot of trouble and I didn't know if I could manage that or not, but I told Decca to stay until Mrs. Woozley came. Then Mrs. Woozley wrote and said the torpedoing had gotten so bad in the North Atlantic that she believed she would take her chances on staying in England with her husband and being bombed. . . . Since Mrs. Woozley wasn't coming, Decca said she would be our refugee. And she was, for almost three years. We had all become devoted to Decca by then and it was all a big joke about her being our refugee.

Democratic activist Virginia Durr writing about events, probably in 1940, Autobiography, *140.*

It is our hope that Ernst will be able to come to the U.S. quickly. He will stay in our house and go to school with [our son] Bob. With his knowledge of English, it should not take him long to adjust to life in the United States.

Looking beyond his expected arrival, we would also hope to assist you, your wife and Ernst's sister to join him eventually. I have been in touch with people in the Wilmington Jewish community who want to be of assistance. Our family prays for your well-being, and we hope that with God's help you can begin a new life in our country.

Herbert V. Lindsay of Wilmington, Delaware, in 1938, shortly before the outbreak of World War II, quoted in Michel, Promises to Keep, *21. On a trip in Germany Lindsay had been given directions by the German-Jewish boy Ernst Michel and had thereafter arranged a correspondence between Ernst and Bob Lindsay. Despite Lindsay's efforts, the U.S. State Department told Ernst that he could not leave for the United States until 1942. In 1939 he was sent to a concentration camp, from which he escaped just before the war ended and made his way to the United States.*

The [refugee] children are not immigrants. The parents of these children will recall them when the war is over. . . . Therefore, [they] should be classified as temporary visitors and not as immigrants. . . . Red tape must not be used to trip up little children on the way to safety.

First Lady Eleanor Roosevelt in a CBS radio address, June 1940, quoted in Goodwin, No Ordinary Time, *100.*

[I hope] the list [of Jewish socialists who have opposed fascism in Europe] can be put into the hands of our people in Europe with the request that they do everything they can to protect these refugees. I do not know what Congress will be willing to do, but they might be allowed to come here and be sent to a camp while we are waiting for legislation.

First Lady Eleanor Roosevelt, letter to Summer Welles in the State Department, June 24, 1940, quoted in Goodwin, No Ordinary Time, *104.*

In August 1941 I had come out to Whittier, California, from Oklahoma to join my boyfriend, who was in the Navy. George came home in September, but the news was a little bit touchy with Japan, so he was called back after a week. In December he was going to take a thirty-day leave and we were going to make arrangements to get married. The day that he left San Francisco to hitchhike down to Whittier, Pearl Harbor was attacked. When he and his buddy arrived at seven o'clock that night, there was a telegram waiting for them at George's mother's house asking them to come back. They left at seven the next morning. I saw him again for three days in June when the ship took on provisions in San Diego, then I didn't see him again until June of 1944.

Civilian Rachel Wray remembering events of 1941–44,
quoted in Harris, The Homefront, *25.*

From the news dispatches, however, one could hazard a grim guess. My father kept a map of Europe on a wall, with pins of different colors marking various armies' advances and retreats. In the summer of 1941, the black pins, representing the Russians, were retreating east toward Moscow. I remember that one day my father told my mother that he had just heard on the radio about a fierce battle fought in Shepetovka. . . . She knew of no close relatives still here, but the news brought tears to her eyes. If Shepetovka fell, the *shtetls* nearby would be overrun easily. We were reasonably sure that Shlomo and his family would be safe in Moscow, but what about Sam's sister Sura-Rivka Zvainboim and her husband and sons, and the Malamuds of Korets? If the stories of summary executions of Polish and Russian Jews were true, they wouldn't stand a chance. As despised as Hitler was in 1941, nobody could bring himself to believe the stories were absolutely true. Such total evil was impossible—beyond human invention or perception.

Author Burton Bernstein describing events of 1941,
in Family Matters, *97.*

It was 7:55 A.M. I was sitting on the veranda overlooking the ocean and Pearl Harbor, drinking morning coffee. When I heard the blasting going on, I assumed it was the Army Air Force out on the usual Sunday-morning maneuvers, and I paid no attention. Then the radio came on, and the alert started, and I heard them say over the radio, "Hawaii is under attack. The Japanese are attacking Hawaii. Take cover. Do not go into the streets. Pour as much water as you can into big pots and bathtubs. Do not go into the streets." . . . This was repeated over and over. . . .

I was sitting on the veranda of our house, about eight hundred feet above the ocean, and it commanded a view all the way from Diamond Head to Pearl Harbor. I saw the attack. I saw the bombs that were dropped in the ocean very, very vividly. In fact, as I first saw them, before I knew about the actual attack, I still thought that it must be the Army Air Force. Then I saw that they almost hit the Royal Hawaiian Hotel, and I said to myself, that was awfully close! The splashes were like plumes, going way up into the air, going splash,

splash, one after the other. Then, when I heard over the radio that Hawaii was under attack, I ran up the side of my property that had a slight elevation, and there I saw the most dreadful thing I ever saw in my life. The fire, the blasting of the ships, just one after the other, in flames! . . . A Japanese plane passed right in front of my yard, not more than forty feet from where I was sitting on the veranda. It was so vivid I could see the face, the profile, and the rising sun on the plane. By noon, we got our breath, the worst was over. But there was a rumor that they would come back, and they did come back. But by that time, our battleships were out in the harbor and ready, and the attack was nothing like the first one. But we underestimated the Japanese; they could have landed, they could have taken Hawaii that day. I don't think there is any question about that.

Navy wife Cornelia MacEwen Hurd describing events of
December 7, 1941, quoted in Hoopes,
Americans Remember, *7.*

In an incredibly short time [after we heard the news of Pearl Harbor]—it seemed to be almost a matter of moments—a wave of patriotism swept the country. As we drove home we felt, This is our country, and we're going to fight to defend it. When we got home that evening we were glued to the radio. "The Star-Spangled Banner" was played, and everyone in the room automatically rose. And we were disillusioned college students—the 1940s version of the 1960s kids. The outward show of patriotism was something that I had always sneered at, but we all stood and we all tingled. So the fervor started right off the bat. It was like a disease, and we all caught it.

College student Dellie Hahne describing events after
December 7, 1941, in Harris et al., Homefront, *27.*

Coming from the prairies of Montana, I had perhaps been rained on not more than six times in my life, so when I got to Juneau [to work for the weather bureau] and there was constant rain, I decided that this was one of the few places in the world where one could live under water. We even went on picnics during the rain as the forest areas abounded with covered shelters specifically built for that purpose. We even built our house in the rain, and when we would hit the nail into the board the water would splat on our faces.

Weather bureau worker Mary E. Coleman Haas
describing events probably occurring 1942–45,
Women in the Weather Bureau, *38.*

In Washington [D.C.] we saw the seamy side of the Good War. We saw greedy business executives opposing conversion to defense production, then joining the government to maneuver for postwar advantage. We saw the campaign by dollar-a-year men against "grade labeling" of canned products—the tactic OPA used to prevent the sale of diluted goods at the same price. We were informed that one in eight business establishments was in violation of the price ceilings. We saw what a little-known senator from Missouri called "rapacity, greed, fraud, and negligence" in the national defense program, and we applauded Harry Truman's committee for its work of investigation and exposure. The war called for equality of sacrifice. But everywhere one looked was the miasma of "chiseling," the term applied to those, and there were plenty of them, who were out to get more than their fair share. The home front was not a pretty sight at a time when young Americans were dying around the world.

Historian Arthur Schlesinger describing events occurring probably 1942–45, Life, *283–284.*

In 1942–43, when I was 13 or so, there was a ferrying base in Wilmington [Delaware] for planes, especially over the hump [the mountains, to China] as they called it, but also to England. The field, which would be bare one week, would slowly fill up with fighters and bombers, nose to tail, all camouflaged. And then they would take off, going over our house, which was on the river, and as one would disappear over the horizon another would appear; sometimes it would go on for three days. Once a guest said, "How can you stand that noise?" and my father said, "Oh, I find it very comforting."

Driving, we would go 45 miles an hour, which was a terrible bore. Sometimes my father would take a back way, crossing the railroad by the Chrysler plant, which was turning out tanks. Sometimes we would have to wait for trains of flatbed cars to go by, two tanks on every car—one day we counted 200 cars—but all I thought was, I'm going to be late for school.

We'd summer on [the island of] Nantucket, and of course the ferry over was blacked out and the streetlights were fixed to shine straight down. Everybody knew there were submarines out at sea. One day when we kids were riding our bikes, a woman with a German accent came out and berated us for being on

"her" beach. We went home and told our parents she was a spy, and we got the good liberal lecture—you mustn't judge people by an accent. It turned out she really was a spy—she was talking to those submarines and telling them about the convoys. A lot of people in the DuPont company were friends of my family; some of them were physicists, and they would disappear for months at a time. Little did I know that they were building the atomic bomb.

Civilian Anne Penniman describing events of 1942–45, author interview.

Ponta Vedra [off the coast of Florida] . . . had had German spies landed from submarines. I was there when that happened, and from then on, we couldn't leave the island without identity cards, which we all had to carry. To get into Jacksonville we had to take the bus and cross the bridge to get off the island, and when we boarded the bus, everybody had to take out his identity card and be checked out to leave. They did catch the spies, who got up, I believe, as far as Kingsland. It was in the early days of the war, and the spying technique was really amateurish. Someone heard them speaking German, I think, at a gas station, and they picked them up.

I can also remember tankers burning off the coast. We had oil slicks and debris all over the beaches. There were horse patrols on the beach every night. I used to ride for pleasure on and off, and I remember seeing the tracks of the horse patrol when I would come down in the morning. The lighthouse at Fernandino was extinguished, and the houses were strictly under blackout rules.

Floridian Celeste Cavanaugh describing events probably beginning in early 1942, in Hoopes, Americans Remember, *253.*

Robert R. Guthrie resigned [from the War Production Board] in March 1942 "charging that industry representatives were blocking war production and that the dollar-a-year men diverted materials necessary to the war to their own industries. He repeated his charges before the Truman committee. . . . Carefully read and considered, the Truman report on the Guthrie case is the key to the continued setbacks suffered by ourselves and our allies. The arsenal of democracy, as the Guthrie case and the reactions to the report show, is still being operated with one eye on the war and the other on the convenience of big business. The progress made on production so far is the fruit of necessity and improvisation rather than of foresight and planning, and the men running the program are not willing to fight business interests on behalf of military efficiency. . . . The Guthrie report shows that, months after Pearl Harbor, the men Nelson put in charge of converting the consumer durable-goods industries to war were still trying their best to postpone curtailment of civilian production. It shows that when it came to the test Nelson took his stand with the men of 'business as usual' against a business man who seemed only to be acting on the principles Nelson himself was expressing in his speeches. It shows that Nelson and his aides are still trying to palm off curtailment as the equivalent of conversion, although the former is only the first and negative step of the process. It shows that the big-business crowd is as powerfully entrenched under Nelson as it was under Knudsen. It shows that we are not going to get maximum utilization of our resources until there is a shakeup more fundamental than the adding of the new alphabetic alias.

Liberal journalist I. F. Stone describing events of spring 1942, War Years, *119–120.*

We sent the newspaper free to all the guys who were away in service. In the second year of the war we decided to do a special Christmas thing. This particular year we felt that the thing the ones who were away needed most was a picture of their hometown. So we asked the photographers in the six towns in the area [near Torrington, Connecticut] if they would do the work for free. And we asked the Legion and other patriotic organizations if they would do the mailing. We did the editing and split it up into eight pages of pictures of people and places, casual pictures, funny pictures, candid-camera shots everywhere. . . . One boy wrote back, "I've taken down all my pinup girls and put up the *Journal.*"

Lakeville, Connecticut, newspaper editor Ann Hoskins describing events of 1943, in Hoopes, Americans Remember, *129.*

The trip impressed me with the patriotism of the doctors who enlisted and the patriotism of those who stayed behind and worked to the limits of their endurance. It also impressed me with the complexity of the problem. The doctor shortage, the OWI investigation concluded, had not yet seriously harmed the nations's health, but the maldistribution of doctors was doing great harm in particular localities." Why not then simply move doctors from areas of relative oversupply to areas of acute need?"

Historian Arthur Schlesinger describing a trip probably in 1943, Life, *275–276.*

The train trip was a lot of fun. . . . Naturally we pulled our wedding pictures out at every opportunity and passed them around. . . . At one place in Nevada they had a USO at the station and served coffee, milk, sandwiches, cake, cookies, candy, ice cream, chicken to all of the servicemen and their wives.

Newlywed Peggy Sorrells Moore, letter to her in-laws, probably 1944, quoted in Astor, Operation Iceberg, *108.*

When my husband was going through basic training, I had followed him down to Camp Campbell, Kentucky, and gotten a stupid job with the army keeping totally inaccurate inventory sheets. We were lucky enough to get a trailer right on base, and whenever we both could get off duty we had fun. Then when he was shipping out someone tipped me off that his outfit would leave through Ft. Devens, Massachusetts, not far from where my folks were living in Gloucester, so I went there and we had a couple of days together before he sailed.

After that the days turned gray. I don't know why I didn't join the WAVES as an officer candidate. Instead I conventionally got a job as secretary to the personnel director in a war plant that made cotton filters for navy engines in South Boston. My boss was low on the management totem pole, so we had nasty little offices almost on the factory floor—dark, hot, windowless, and noisy.

I did like getting to know the people we hired, though. They had such hard lives. Especially the women—I can still hear them explaining that some relative was going to look after their five kids, or they and their husbands would work different shifts. We hired them anyway, knowing that they would be absent a lot and probably quit in a few weeks. We had to get someone to do that boring, unhealthy work with all those dangerous machines in huge rooms with cotton flying everywhere. The only part of the plant I liked visiting was the wrapping room, where a bunch of older women—probably only in their 50s, but that seemed aged to me then—in aprons sat around big tables in a relatively quiet room and laughed and chatted as they worked.

For a couple of years my life centered around that place, five and a half days a week, with lots of overtime. The commute took about two-and-a-half hours round trip, so I'd leave my folks' house about 6:30 A.M. and theoretically got home a little before seven that evening, but sometimes it was eleven, or even one. I hardly saw daylight, except through a train window or on the walk on the ugly streets between the subway station and the plant.

My mother was so good to me; she did my laundry, packed my lunches, and always had a hot dinner waiting, though she and my father had eaten earlier. As a minister's wife, she had lots to do without having her day stretched out that way, and of course she was coping with shortages and ration stamps. Naturally I paid room and board, but I couldn't begin to pay for all she did and for the way she kept my morale up, particularly during those stretches when I wouldn't hear from my husband for two or three weeks, even though he was writing regularly. Weekends she'd help me bake cookies and prepare food packages for him, and she'd always put a good spin on the war news.

Civilian Dorothy Taylor describing events of 1944–45, authors' interview.

Twice [my husband] came to Chicago AWOL to see me. Of course I was glad to see him, but I sure did fuss and fuss at him for doing it. . . . He cried and said I just wanted him to be in the Army. . . . I write him letters five or six pages long every day just to keep him cheerful. Goodness knows I try to build up his morale.

Service wife describing events probably in 1944–45, quoted in Campbell, Women at War, *194.*

God of the free, we pledge our hearts and lives today to the cause of all free mankind.

Grant us victory over the tyrants who would enslave all free men and nations.

Grant us faith and understanding to cherish all those who fight for freedom as if they were our brothers.

Grant us brotherhood in hope and union, not only for the space of this bitter war, but for the days to come which shall and must unite all the children of the earth.

We are all of us children of the earth—grant us that simple knowledge. If our brothers are oppressed, then we are oppressed. If they hunger, we hunger. If their freedom is taken away, our freedom is not secure.

Grant us a common faith that man shall know bread and peace—that he shall know justice and righteousness, freedom and security, an equal opportunity and an equal chance to do his best, not only in our own lands but throughout the world.

And in that faith let us march, toward the clean world our hands can make.

President Franklin D. Roosevelt's prayer, D day, June 6, 1944, in Harriman and Abel, Special Envoy, *443–444.*

I was intensely moved by the crowds of soldiers and sailors and wives in the [railroad] stations. The officers and wives moving together, tired and worn, insecure, and yet, setting up a kind of housekeeping, a kind of security in their sections, with their knitting, their papers, their sparse words of understanding. So different from those wistful tired women—suspended—back from seeing their husbands or going to join them, like me. I felt a kind of happiness in being one of them and a kind of pride. A secret joy in being ordinary, in being let in a door I have never been allowed in before. "Yes, my husband is in the South Pacific. Yes, I'm hoping to see him."

Anne Morrow Lindbergh, diary entry, October 8, 1944, in Lindbergh, War Within and Without, *441.*

Following enemy propaganda broadcast from Germany has been intercepted: "Dearest Dorothy I am all right sweetheart I didn't get a scratch or anything. Please tell Mom and Dad Write me often I have been treated good Don't worry about me We'll get married as soon as I come home again I love you and miss you terribly sweetheart and wish that I could be with you soon I have lots to tell you when I get back."

Pending further confirmation this report does not establish his status as a prisoner of war. Additional information received will be furnished.

—Larch, Provost Marshall General
Telegram received by Dorothy Owens, fiancée of bombardier-navigator James Dowling, December 27, 1944, in Brokaw, Greatest Generation, *49. After the war they married.*

I was out raking the yard, and the man that came and brought the telegram went next door to my neighbor, and he asked her if she would come over with him, because it was the third one he had delivered that day in our town. At the time he handed me the telegram, I looked at it, and he said: "It's bad news."

Michigan resident Betty Bryce recalling the notification of her son's death March 14, 1945, quoted in Hoopes,
Americans Remember, *310.*

Of course, everyone was conscious of the war. . . . And you were worried about the guys overseas, your friends. But there was an exhilaration, strangely enough. . . . You would follow the war and the argument about opening up the second front and how they were doing at Anzio, the Battle of Leningrad, beachheads, Normandy. . . .

It was a very congenial time. Everybody was popping drinks for the soldiers in a bar. And sometimes the house would pop. Chicago was a great liberty town. And do you remember the Liberty girls? The little girls; they had a certain way of walking. They'd go arm-in-arm, three of them. And their feet wouldn't come off the pavement. They'd kind of shuffle like. Made them look a little sexier, more challenging. They were young—fifteen, sixteen, maybe—but they would chase after the boys, and the boys would chase after them.

Journalist Studs Terkel describing events throughout World War II, in Hoopes,
Americans Remember, *128.*

During my third week of pure bliss [working in New York for William Shirer, CBS correspondent and author of *Berlin Diary*], when answering phones and discovering that the people on the other end were named "John Gunther [author]" or something equally posh, Paris was liberated. Mr. Shirer did a magnificent broadcast that night; and then he took me, my aunt, and his wife Tess to a sidewalk café on Second Avenue where French sailors and soldiers of the Free French persuasion were celebrating. You can imagine the emotion! I must have sung the *Marseillaise* a thousand times as I danced and wept. But I made the mistake of writing a glowing letter to my husband in New Guinea, who was being bombed by the Japanese and bitten by snakes and derided by Tokyo Rose. The net result: I was to return to my

grandmother's home in Millbourne, Pennsylvania. *Immediately.* I did.

Service wife Ruth Malone describing events before, during, and after September 12, 1944, unpublished memoir.

Shortages and Rationing

Choke the Japs with your girdles. We want rubber.

Sign chalked on a store window, probably in 1942, depicted in Harris, Homefront, *77.*

[One building in Leesville, Louisiana, condemned before the war, now has 14 families in rooms] no larger than the pig runs. There were twelve babies under a year—"all boys" as the mothers told me proudly.

Roving reporter Agnes Meyer describing the shortage of quarters for service wives, probably in 1942, quoted in Campbell, Women at War, *198.*

For sale—four almost new de luxe white wall tires and tubes for $450. Throw in '38 Lincoln convertible.

New York classified ad, probably 1942, quoted in Ambrose, Americans at War, *149.*

High school students were also conscientious about gasoline rationing. In January of 1943 the weekly column in The Homer Enterprise for Homer High School, "HCHS Tatler," highlighted the feelings of responsibility young people were espousing: "Worry! Worry! We cannot jump into the car and drive uptown for some small articles now. We will walk to the home basketball games and remember the good old days when we could [go] to the out of town ones. Neither will we ride to the movies or other entertainments. When you do drive, ask your friends to go with you. If you are asked to take a group in your car, forget your grievances, for the next time it will be the other fellows turn to take his. . . . Here's your chance students, help Uncle Sam!" . . .

. . ."SLAP THE JAPS WITH RUBBER SCRAP is nation's new motto," and instructed residents of what rubber articles they could deposit at the filling station for pick-up. They urged everyone to donate even the most minuscule items, including jar rings and rubber stoppers. Schoolchildren delighted in the Student Council's frugal purchase of a new mat for the hallway which was made of recycled rubber tires.

They proudly reported that the mat "cost $12.75 . . . and is guaranteed to last a lifetime."

Reporter Stacy Jones writing about the early war years (1942–43) "The Rural World War II Homefront in Homer, Illinois," 28–30.

Almost immediately, we were involved in administering the rationing program. A chairman was appointed, and we organized committees, made up mostly of businessmen in town and chamber-of-commerce members. Soon we were swamped and had to take over larger headquarters because we had thousands of volunteers working for us. Whole plants, their office staff, would come in for an evening. . . . [W]hat would you have done if you were a board member and received this letter: "Dear Sirs: This morning a card came to my home stating that my husband may have booklets for more gasoline. My husband does not need more gasoline. He takes the bus to work on his day shift. When he works nights, he uses the car only three times a week: on Tuesdays and Thursdays he drills at the armory and works days. You can figure out for yourself if three gallons a week is enough for twelve miles. The reason why he needs more gasoline is for pleasure. He likes to go out with women. I'm sorry to tell you this, but I'm sure you will help from breaking up my home. You can come to my home any time and talk to me personally. I am keeping the card. If he appears before the board, you can show him this letter. He will tell you I'm crazy. Sincerely, Mrs.———. P.S. I will probably get a beating for this, but it's the God's truth."

Alida Pierce, then secretary to the chamber of commerce in Dunkirk, New York, remembering 1942 and thereafter, in Hoopes, Americans Remember, 282–284.

[In Detroit] people [were] living in stores which had been remodeled, tool sheds, tents, cellars, unfinished houses–almost anything. Nine times out of ten, the toilets and sewage disposal were completely inadequate and the water supply questionable. It is something of a miracle that an epidemic of dysentery and typhoid has not broken out.

Detroit reporter describing the housing shortage, probably in 1943–44, quoted in Campbell, Women at War, 169.

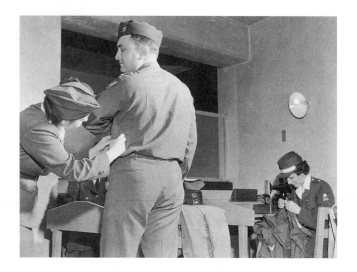

Members of the "Button Brigade" of the American Women's Volunteer Service (AWVS) unit at Glendale, California, do minor tailoring jobs for soldiers at the Army Air Force barracks, March 1943. *(Library of Congress, LC-USW3-055490-D)*

There was a tremendous black market in Hingham, no question about that—gasoline, tires, food stamps, et cetera. I think the Godfather and his people were involved and, of course, there were a lot of phony stamps around. The shipyard . . . was running three shifts with about ten thousand people to each shift, and lots of people seemed to be chiseling for more. They were all fighting for that dollar. They all wanted to get into the shipyard because the shipyard was paying more than anyplace else, and then, it gave the young people a draft status they wanted. . . . I used to get real provoked at some of these fellows in the yard and some of the civilians when I saw them chiseling and trying to get theirs. That bothered me, especially when I found fellows that wouldn't work properly. I transferred some of them the hell out.

Capt. Fred Kirkham describing his work after his navy ship was sunk and he was discharged from the navy in 1943 for medical reasons, quoted in Hoopes, Americans Remember, 89.

General Provisions

. . . The blue stamps in War Ration Book 2 are used for most canned goods . . . and for dried beans, peas and lentils, and for these frozen commodities: vegetables, fruits, berries and juices. The red stamps are used for meats, canned fish, butter, cheese, edible fats and oils, and condensed and evaporated canned milk. You have to give up more points when buying scarce foods than when buying the same quantity of a more plentiful kind. *The government urges housewives to use more fresh fruits and vegetables, spaghetti and other foods for which no ration stamps are required.*

Red Stamps J, K, and L may be redeemed through June 30. Blue stamps G, H, and J are valid through June 7. Blue Stamps K, L, and M are valid through July 7.

Ration stamps are not valid if detached from their appropriate ration books. . . .

Meats, Cheese, Butter, Fats, Canned Fish

Each person has a red stamp quota of 16 points a week for these foods. The same stamps will be used for all products in this group, with the proportions to be expended on the various items at the consumer's discretion. The point values of the different items and of cuts of meat permit an average of 2 pounds of meat a week per person, depending on how stamps are used for other items. . . .

Canned and Processed Vegetables, Fruits, Soups, Etc.

Each consumer has 48 points in blue stamps to expend from June 6 to July 3. . . . You may buy dried prunes, raisins, other dried fruits, blackeyed peas, dried and dehydrated soups, and some vegetables and vegetable juices without giving up any coupons. . . .

Shoes

Stamp 17 in War Ration Book 1 is good for one pair of shoes until June 15. Stamp 18 will become valid June 16 for one pair of shoes. Families may pool the coupons of all members living in the same household. . . .

Gasoline and Tires

All pleasure driving is banned to holders of A, B and C ration books.

All A coupons are valued at three gallons. B and C unit coupons are valued at 2-1/2 gallons. Coupon 5 in A book is good for 3 gallons through July 21. Under the cut in the basic ration the value of each coupon remains unchanged, but an A-book holder's eight No. 5 coupons must do him twice as long, thus cutting his average to 1-1/2 gallons a week. Motorists must write license number and State on back of each coupon before offering it to dealer. . . .

"Rationing Situation in the New York Area," New York Times, *June 6, 1943, 38.*

It was a very mixed group around Seminary Hill. . . . We all got to know each other well and to depend on one another because of the car pool. . . . We used to have square dances in the neighborhood because we couldn't get into Washington to do anything. We didn't have gas, so we were thrown on each other. And we all became extremely good friends. We were all caught in the same situation, worrying about closing the black shades at night because we thought the Germans were going to bomb us. You can imagine what trouble that was—every single night having to close all the shades. Every neighborhood had a warden. If he saw a crack of light, he warned you. And then we'd have trouble with ration stamps. If anybody got sick, everybody else helped. . . . If you live close that way, ideological differences don't mean so much. We were all trying to win the war. We were all united on that, but there were differences of opinion and lots of arguments.

Democratic activist Virginia Durr describing events throughout the war, Autobiography, *150–151.*

I remember using leg make-up because there were no "silk" stockings. Drawing on seams was a challenge, which most people gave up on. . . . I remember drawstring underpants because there was no elastic. I remember knitting 6" x 6" squares to be made into Afghans for soldiers. I remember pulling a wagon going house to house to collect cans of grease. I remember volunteering at the Court House to paste ration stamps into books (why, eludes me).

Civilian Carol Dasse remembering the war years, "Recollections," in Thoburn and Knapp, "Perspectives," 13.

You could get what we called reclaimed tires that were reprocessed rubber. The quality was very poor, and sometimes they didn't run over a hundred miles.

Iowan Vernon Sietmann remembering the war years, quoted in Harris, Homefront, *76.*

The thing that I have heard the most comment on is the fact that the country went along, heroically doing without coffee and then last week there was a news item saying that coffee had been dumped because there was no room for storage for it. . . . [My friends] don't mind doing anything, however hard, if they know what it is all about, but they do not like being made to feel that they have to be rationed unnecessarily to make them realize we are at war.

Housewife living in Taos, New Mexico, commenting on
wartime rationing, quoted in Campbell,
Women at War, *182.*

Economic Conditions

During one of my tours I visited the Kaiser Shipyards and Henry Kaiser himself showed me the large housing development near the shipyard that he'd built to attract workers from the East and from the southern states. He said, "It's difficult to recruit personnel for shipbuilding from those who proved ineligible for the draft or who have some handicap that prevents them from enlisting. We used up the supply in California, so many of our recruits are mountain folk or farmers, all 4-F, of course." Some couldn't even read or write; some had never seen a modern bathroom till they moved into the housing development. Mr. Kaiser told me, "One family we had built fires in the bathtub to cook over; they knew no other way to prepare a meal."

Former I.B.M. vice-president Ruth Amonette
reminiscing about events, probably in 1944 or 1945,
in Among Equals, *113.*

Red Cross workers in Washington, D.C., sort scraps of wool from tailors, manufacturers, and individuals and prepare the wool for reprocessing. *(Library of Congress, LC-USW3-004660-D)*

Volunteering

All the girls, including my wife, were in the Red Cross because, they said, "You got to be trained: the submarines are coming into Portsmouth." And they were taught how to give baths. The whole thing was great. Crazy. Everyone was frantic.

Newton Tolman reminiscing about early 1942, quoted in
Hoopes, Americans Remember, *208.*

Am waiting at the British War Relief headquarters for the last report on organizations selling 6th War Loan Bonds. After they come in the Potter boy at the book shop will inscribe seven prizes at the Grand Rally in John M. Greene this evening. They will then be put into frames and wrapped—my job. Over $400,000 in war bonds have been purchased. Orion and I are giving a dinner at the mess for the speakers and committee heads—fifteen in all. . . . We finished the last

surgical dressing yesterday and the rooms are being vacated today.

Letter of Grace Coolidge, former first lady,
December 1, 1944, in Ross, Grace Coolidge, *317.*

[At my modeling agency] they told us very definitely that they would prefer that we go one or two afternoons or evenings a week to this Stage Door Canteen. The atmosphere there was sheer desperation. I mean, people coming in, and it wasn't just our own servicemen, people from Australia, Canada, anyone who happened to be passing through. They wanted someone to talk to, and there was a desperate kind of quality about the thing—like here you are now, now sit down and be charming, sparkle—a very unnatural situation. I didn't like it at all; I wasn't good at it. I met some very nice Norwegian sailors, but we were not supposed to go out with them, which was great, because I didn't want to. Some of the girls did violate the club rules and go out with them. Why not, if they felt like it?

Fashion model Patricia Megargee reminiscing probably about events in 1944 and 1945, in Hoopes, Americans Remember, *92.*

My wife and I both gave a lot of blood and that kind of thing, but by and large we did not become involved in volunteer war work. I was busy all the time. Later in the war I was in the Coast Guard Auxiliary for about two years. I spent one day a week on San Francisco Bay patrolling what they called the degaussing area, where ships came in to get this anti-magnetic belt around the hull that would deflect magnetic mines. I was on a fifty-two-foot patrol boat manned entirely by volunteers. Our mission was to keep other boats out of the way—this was right in the middle of the bay. They had some rather delicate electronic gear in this area, and we just patrolled around it, keeping fishing boats out. I think there were cables on the floor of the bay, so they didn't want any risk of hooks. It was kind of fun—we ate well.

Coast Guard Auxiliary member Don Baldwin reminiscing about events, probably in 1944 and 1945, in Hoopes, Americans Remember, *137.*

When the second World War started I tried to go back to hospital work, but was refused . . . on account of age. The Orthopaedic took me to go over their

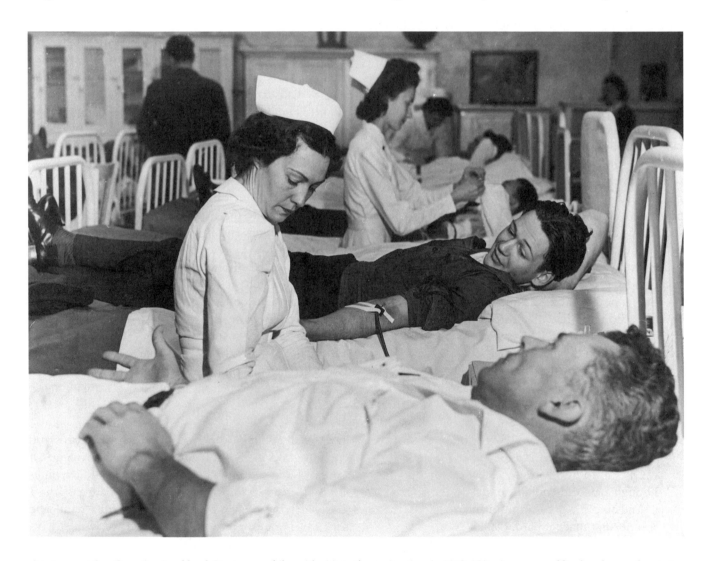

A prisoner at San Quentin gives blood. During a mobile unit's visit to the penitentiary in 1943, 150 prisoners gave blood, and more than twice that number volunteered but were unable to give because of lack of time and equipment. *(Library of Congress, LC-USW3-054809-D)*

case histories, and the Travellers Aid found me useful in their canteen at Grand Central Station three times a week, from midnight until four in the morning. They were rather strenuous hours, but I got used to them, and I always slept late the next day. . . .

My relationship with the young men in the armed services was very amusing. I delighted in serving the soldiers and sailors, and the M.P. who told me that my badly mixed coca-cola tasted like embalming fluid is my friend for life. I found that the Navy always went to bed with its shoes off, so it could swim if necessary. The Army went to bed with its shoes on, so it could march if necessary. I liked them very much. What I hated were the glamour girls who used to come before I did and were so apt to hang up coats and things on the wrong hooks. When a man tried to make his train, he might just as well miss it, because the glamour girl ahead of me had hung his coat on the wrong hook and he couldn't find it. . . .

At the Orthopaedic I kept the records, but the doctors got to using such grand words that it was very difficult for me really to get much amusement out of it. When I could understand what they were talking about, I used to like it very well. . . . At least I did keep the records in order. That I did twice a week, and three times a week I went to the Memorial. There I used to work in the bandage room, putting away the linen, and taking the most ignoble specimens of the human body down to the laboratory. I enjoyed that very well, except that I thought the nurses were rather untidy. They would take a uniform and try it on, and if it didn't fit they'd wad it up into a bundle and just put it back in the cupboard. I thought that if it didn't fit, the least they could have done would have been to put it back in its folds. *I* had to do that.

Finally they got so tiresome that when I was asked to give them a cake for some holiday, I wrote them beforehand:

Dear girls, here is a cake, but not
  Because I take a rosy view of you;
In point of fact, there is a lot
  Of fault to find with not a few of you.
Though I am old enough to kill,
  And all old work is uninspiring,
You needn't make it harder still
  By mussing gowns you're not requiring.
If I again behold your shelves
  In chaos as I did last Friday,

You just may do the job yourselves—
  I'm damned if I will keep you tidy!
And they were tidy for two weeks—two solid weeks!
Caroline King Duer, playwright, reminiscing about the war years, in Columbia Oral History Project, 67–70.

[Q]ualifying for the [volunteer] auxiliary police was not particularly rigorous. An example was the member of that elite corps who stopped an out-of-state car. Ever watchful for saboteurs and spies, he asked the driver where he was from. The driver replied, "Philadelphia." "Oho!" snarled the policeman, "then how come your car has Pennsylvania license plates?"
Shipyard worker Harry Benford reminiscing about the war years, in "The Lighter Side," in Thoburn and Knapp, "Perspectives," 62.

[A]t Lockheed I got off work 3:30, and then that [Civilian Defense Corps] duty was from 8:00 to midnight. . . . I'd get home between 12:30 and 1:00. . . . [T]hey had like a small station wagon and they'd drop us off. The idea of the thing was the danger of us being attacked by plane. We would help by being there, communicating. There was a huge hall under the police station with phones and switchboards. We had a certain section of the city, and in case of attack we had certain air raid wardens that we had to call and tell them what to do. There was eight of us on duty every night, and if we were tired, four would go and relax—there were bunk beds where we'd lie down for a while—and four would stay there. . . . We also had servicemen clubs. . . . We'd entertain servicemen; give them coffee, doughnuts, make them feel at home, especially men that were far away from home or lonesome. . . . And we'd visit Sawtelle Veterans' Hospital, a lot of little activities like that.
Lockheed aircraft worker Margarita Salazar McSweyn reminiscing about the war years, in Gluck,
Rosie, 87–88.

I was a member of the Red Cross Motor Corps and spent a good many thousands of hours convoying. Of course, I was working, but on weekends and evenings I would go into Chicago and spend whatever time I could driving convoys. The young recruits would be sent from one camp to the other, and we would drive them from the train, as they arrived, to Lake Bluff or into some of the other areas. We'd also drive the blood bank, entertainment buses, and things of that sort. Or we would pick up an admiral and take him wherever he wanted to go in the Chicago area. . . . Sometimes it was a little bit scary, but the uniform protected me. We drove all hours of the night. There were some black and white problems in the area at that time. Once, I knew someone was following me as I got off at the station in Evanston on my way home. Finally the person caught up with me—a young girl who said, "Oh Ma'am, you walk so fast, but I knew if I got close to your uniform, I'd be safe."

Pauline Christensen, who during the war was a widow with two young sons and her own publishing business, reminiscing about the war years, in Hoopes, Americans Remember, *304.*

Morale and Morality

All your letters which I got today are so sad and mournful of your midnight adventure [a brief infidelity]. Forget it—it's not going to change anything. Our life together has never had sex as its main and unfailing point of contact. We have evolved some relationship between ourselves which far transcends the mere physical contacts of sex. Sex, as we both agree, is a wonderful emotional background for marriage, but it is by no means the cornerstone of the foundation. . . . This, of course doesn't mean that I shall condone or even put up with any more nonsense like that, for the act of yours was, as far as I'm concerned, about the lowest anyone can pull. Because it was just giving in to promiscuity. If you thought or believed yourself dreadfully in love or something like that, I might understand it. But just leaping into bed with strangers is the business of some women, the pleasure of others, but my wife fits neither of these categories. Enough said!

Marine Capt. John David Hench to his wife, March 11, 1943, quoted in Carroll, War Letters, *216. A year later Captain Hench disappeared at sea, presumably drowned.*

We were an awful lot squarer in those days than eighteen-, nineteen-, twenty-year-old kids are now. When I was going out with my husband, who had been married previously, divorced, and was seven years older than I, I can remember my mother telling me that under no circumstances was I to get near Al's apartment. Now I was twenty-one, I had been work-

ing for three years, supporting myself. He had some records, and I wanted to hear them. . . . So he said let's go have a drink and listen to some records . . , which we did. It was perfectly fine—no passes, no nothing, and if there had been, I could have handled it. Mom was absolutely horrified!

Defense worker and fashion model Patricia Megargee reminiscing probably about 1944, in Hoopes, Americans Remember, *92.*

It is too bad that you and your husband have not been punished by some deadly disease. Maybe though you and your husband will have to look into the faces of the dead corpses of your four sons. . . . God always punishes the wicked in some way.

Letter to First Lady Eleanor Roosevelt from a woman whose favorite nephew had been killed while serving in the navy, My Day *column, January 6, 1944, quoted in Goodwin,* No Ordinary Time, *507.*

The tough times were when Western Union would call or send out a telegram with two red stars stamped on it. It would be telling you that your loved one was missing in action or taken prisoner or killed in action. My wife received two of these telegrams. One telling her I was missing in action and then another telling her I had been taken prisoner.

Infantryman "Johnnie," 106th Infantry Division, "My Thoughts on the Homefront," available online. Kingsbay.net news, URL:eagnet.com/edipage/user/joanie/news.htm.

Of course we [in Lakeville, Connecticut] had a little of that rumor kind of thing where somebody would suspect somebody of having German leanings. There was a restaurant up in Canaan . . . run by a German family. They were refugees, poor darlings, and I understand they had a really tough time. . . . [A] professor and his wife from Columbia University had a house in Salisbury. They had some Nisei friends and wanted to bring them up, so they wrote a letter to the paper asking how the community would react to it. One of the officers of the American Legion, whose son was in the Pacific, said, "Sure get any Japanese you can around here so I can knock them down." . . . Then John McChesney, a great Liberal, came out and said this is not what we are fighting the war for, this is exactly the kind of thinking that Hitler has. The fat was in the fire with everybody arguing about it back and forth, and the poor people who wanted to bring up their friends for the summer finally said to heck with it and brought them up anyway. And the people came and marketed and everything else, and nobody paid any attention to them.

Lakeville, Connecticut, newspaper editor Ann Hoskins, reminiscing about the war years, in Hoopes, Americans Remember, *130.*

My son was seventeen when he decided to go into the service. I didn't want him to quit school, because he had won a scholarship, but he wanted to join the marines. When he was at Pa[r]ris Island [a Marine base], two boys committed suicide during basic training because it was so rough. I remember him writing to tell me that he would never again do anything that I told him not to do, because he realized he didn't know as much about the military as he thought he did. He was assigned to ships going back and forth overseas and, of course, I was concerned. . . .

Airplane factory worker and later army nurse Margaret Oakham reminiscing about the war years, in Hoopes, Americans Remember, *318–319.*

There was a tremendous social change at the time to admit blacks and females to full citizenship, to accept them in terms of their own abilities, or inabilities, instead of in terms of the stereotypes we were accustomed to. We had no choice except to take anything that was alive and warm and see if we could use it. We learned a great deal. . . . And we found we had one hell of a reserve we hadn't been using.

Radio newsman Bill Gold reminiscing about the war years, in Hoopes, Americans Remember, *134.*

People feel good when they're making sacrifices and being cooperative, whereas in good times, in a prosperous country, the majority—and I always say "for the majority" because there's a minority that isn't having a happy time at all—begin to feel guilty, and get greedy and selfish.

I think, as in most wars, mental health for the majority of Americans improved. During wartime there is less suicide, less crime. People were friendlier; they took care of each other. It's a horrid thing to realize that during wartime people are mentally more healthy than they are during peacetime, especially in a country where so many people live relatively comfortable lives. This kept making me come back to the conclusion that our species is designed to cope with adversity rather than take it easy. In the depression, these same kinds of statistics prevailed: less crime, less suicide.

Pediatrician Dr. Benjamin Spock commenting on the war years, in Hoopes, Americans Remember, *178.*

5

Civilians at Work
September 1941–
September 2, 1945

"Like England's battles were won on the playing fields of Eton, America's
were won on the assembly lines of Detroit."

—*labor leader Walter Reuther[1]*

"Build'em fast, built to last, Build 'em right, fit to fight."

—*Cmdr. S. M. Alexander[2]*

By the time that the Japanese attack on Pearl Harbor precipitated the United
States into World War II, most Americans understood that an Allied victory
depended on the ships and tanks and weapons that the United States could
produce. Civilians responded energetically to President Franklin D. Roosevelt's
call to make the country the "arsenal of democracy." Emerging from the physical and psychological sufferings of the Great Depression, and elated by the
opportunity to work so long denied so many of them, they exceeded all pro-
jections.

With their ranks depleted by the 16 million able-bodied men and women
in uniform, American civilians confronted three tasks: to sustain the civilian
economy on the limited basis allowed by wartime restrictions; to grow the
food and manufacture the goods necessary for the conduct of the war; and to
provide the support services required by the war. They succeeded beyond
expectation, beyond hope. Through their production they actually raised their
own standard of living in the war years and avoided the necessity for severe
rationing. Even during the five years of the war, when the yearly output of
munitions rose from $8.4 billion to $57.8 billion—from 10 percent to 40 percent of the gross national product—they stepped up the production of consumer goods by 12 percent.[3] At the same time they produced weapons, tanks,
aircraft, and ships in sufficient quantities to equip their own fighting men and

to supply many of the needs of the other Allied nations. Finally, they built and manned the ships and airplanes to maintain supply lines to troops stationed around the world and on the seas, furnishing them not only with the tools of war and necessities of life but also with some comforts.

Industry

Sometimes with government help, sometimes despite bureaucratic red tape, industrial leaders established new manufacturing plants and converted existing ones to wartime production. Merry-go-round factories made gun mounts; corset factories made grenade belts; stove manufacturers produced lifeboats; toy manufacturers made compasses; pinball machine manufacturers made armor-piercing shells.

In June 1940 isolationist Henry Ford had refused a government contract to build Rolls Royce aircraft engines for England. But later that year German victories and atrocities persuaded him to plan a new factory to produce aircraft on an assembly line. By September 1941 construction was complete on the 3.5 million square feet of factory space at the Ford Willow Run B-24 Liberty Bomber plant, a space so huge that aviator Charles Lindbergh called it the Grand Canyon of the mechanized world. Initially difficulties beset it, and the wits punned "Will It Run?" But by August 1943 it was producing 231 planes a month; by December 1943, 365 a month; and by December 1944, 650 a month.[4]

In the Northwest industrialist Henry Kaiser set up seven shipyards that built about a third of the 3,000 Liberty ships that became the workhorses of the American merchant marine.[5] FDR called them "ugly ducklings," and they literally made their crews sick as they wallowed through the waves at low speeds, but they proved remarkably useful cargo carriers. Kaiser cut the time necessary to build one ship from 355 days in 1940 to 60 days in early 1942, and then to 25 days. By 1943, his yards were sending a ship down the ways every 10 hours.[6] Each ship was capable of carrying 2,840 jeeps, 440 light tanks, and three million C-rations.[7]

The government tried to spread its contracts around the country, partly to keep afloat small companies unable to get supplies to make consumer goods, and partly to take advantage of existing housing, schools, shops, and other community facilities. But most government contracts went to big companies like Ford and Kaiser, simply because it was easier and cheaper to negotiate with one company than with 20, and the military already knew and trusted the potential of big suppliers. Moreover, the dollar-a-year businessmen running government agencies naturally turned to the colleagues whom they knew well. In 1940 about 175,000 companies accounted for 70 percent of the manufacturing output of the country, and 100 companies produced the other 30 percent; by 1943 the 100 large companies had increased their share to 70 percent of all government contracts.[8] Some of these large companies as their contribution to the war effort did not charge the nation for a part of their work. For instance, Eli Lilly, which supplied the government with more than 200 different pharmaceuticals, including the newly developed penicillin, processed and delivered without charge more than 1 million quarts of blood plasma.[9]

The military "E for Excellence" banner floated over plants large and small across the nation. Among them all, war production soared. From 1940 through 1944, the gross national product rose 125 percent. Between 1940 and the end of 1945, the United States spent $183.1 billion for war materiel—a sum that almost equaled the spending of all the belligerents on both sides throughout World War I. In 1939 the country was producing fewer than 6,000 planes; in 1944 it turned out 96,369. Steel production increased 85 percent, copper 70 percent, and coal 55 percent. The production of synthetic rubber went from almost none to 900,000 tons. Workers turned out 1,200 new combat vessels; 64,546 landing craft; 12 million rifles, carbines, and machine guns; 47 million tons of artillery ammunition; and 3.5 million military vehicles.[10.] As the Southern Pacific railroad advertised, "It takes eight tons of freight to k.o. 1 Jap," and Americans stood ready to make as many tons as necessary. The impact of this enormous achievement echoes in the many anecdotes of German prisoners of war who—when they saw Allied stockpiles or looked out at the ships in the Normandy invasion—said, appalled, "We have lost the war."

Throughout the war the Allies depended on American food and manufactures. By November 1943 American factories were providing the Soviet Union with two-thirds of the vehicles and half the planes military used. The United States sent the USSR rails to rebuild railroads, communication equipment to control military movements, tires and oil for their trucks and planes, explosives to manufacture bombs and shells, millions of tons of food, and seeds to replant their devastated fields. America was clothing 13 million Soviet soldiers and supplying them with boots and blankets. In November 1943 at Tehran, Stalin publicly acknowledged: "I want to tell you, from the Russian point of view, what the President and the United States have done to win the war. The most important things in this war are machines. The United States has proven that it can turn out from 8,000 to 10,000 airplanes per month. Russia can only turn out, at most, 3,000 a month. England turns out 3,000 to 3,500. . . . The United States, therefore, is the country of machines. Without the use of these machines, through Lend-Lease, we would lose the war."[11.]

Agriculture

> "Those overalls are your Uniform, bud."
> —*Soldier to farmer wearing a "Food for Freedom" badge,*
> *depicted on a government poster*

Like American industry, American agriculture achieved beyond all expectations. During the Great Depression (1929–39) thousands of farmers had lost their farms and left the countryside. With the New Deal in 1933 and the outbreak of war in Europe in 1939, the agricultural economy gradually improved. World War II increased the demand for food grown in the United States, both from the Allied nations and from Americans now earning enough to put on the table not only their daily bread but also meat.

Agriculture rose to the challenge. The restrictions that the New Deal had placed on crops no longer applied, and farmers could plant as much of their land as they could tend. Even with so many of their former neighbors gone

and with so much of the remaining rural population moving into war factories—between 1940 and 1945 the farm population fell 17 percent[12]—farmers
increased production. As 7 million people left the formerly overpopulated rural
areas to join the military or work in defense factories, farming became prof-
itable.[13] The war accelerated the movement toward mechanization and toward
agribusiness. Farmers replaced mules with tractors, used more chemical fertiliz-
ers and insecticides, and abandoned the least-productive land. With machines
and more sophisticated practices, productivity per farm laborer soared, and
farm owners took over land they had previously rented out to tenants. All this
of course required capital of sizable amounts, inviting corporate investment in
farmlands.

Full Employment

Employers hired new workers by the millions: In a single day in June 1943 the
Willow Run aircraft plant hired more than 3,000 workers.[14] Manpower shortages forced industry to resort to groups they had formerly rejected: minorities,
women, oldsters, and youngsters. Employers still preferred white males and still
awarded them the best jobs, but they now needed whatever workers they could
find. Recruiters at the large industrial centers in the Midwest and on the West
Coast wooed southern workers. In some factories an ability to find the door
constituted the only requirement for hiring. Desperate managers even contracted with prisons for convicts to inspect bombs, cartridge clips, and gun
parts.[15] About 40,000 Native Americans aged 18 to 50 left their reservations to
work in defense industries.[16] On occasion, at the urgent request of the War
Manpower Commission, the military released men with particular expertise so
that they could return to their jobs in industry or furloughed them for 90 days
for industrial work. Factories added new shifts, and six- and seven-day work-
weeks became routine in war plants.

The unemployment rate plummeted from 19 percent in 1938 to 1.2 percent in 1944.[17] In 1944 18.7 million more Americans were employed than in
1939, of whom 2 million had recently become old enough to work.[18]
Although the government could legally draft men who left war production
jobs or went on strike, it seldom enforced its threats.

Farmers had a hard time competing with industry for labor. They picked
up help wherever they could. Sixty-thousand Mexicans were imported into
the United States as farmhands and 50,000 to work on railroads.[19] Another
26,000 farmhands came from Jamaica and the Bahamas. Later, prisoners of war
captured in the North African invasion were put to work on farms and in factories.[20] The army sometimes detailed soldiers to temporary duty to help in
the harvest. The authorities in charge of Japanese-American internees released
some of them temporarily to work with farmers. Officials detaining 1,000
European refugees behind barbed wire in Oswego, New York, yielded to the
pleas of upstate New York farmers to allow 50 of them to help gather crops.[21]
Some conscientious objectors were assigned to farm work. In May 1942 the
American Women's Volunteer Services recruited 1,500 women to work in the
fields between July and October at the standard pay, ranging from $4 to $8 a
day. The U.S. Agricultural Extension Service coordinated a program to train
750,000 women at agricultural colleges for a Women's Land Army; those

among them who wished wore a uniform of blue denim overalls, bright blue shirt, and a visored cap with a logo. The extension service also sponsored the Farm Cadet Victory Corps for high-school age Americans.[22]

Government too absorbed huge numbers of workers. Washington became a boomtown, its population nearly doubling between 1940 and 1943.[23.] Many of the newcomers were young women wanting to be among the GGs— government girls, whom the Office of War Information recruited as "secretaries of war." Their housing needs could not be met even with the huge dormitories built for them, and they tripled and quadrupled up wherever they could. Bureaucratic offices expanded into every available space, even gyms and skating rinks, and for a while some GGs spent their days typing perched in bathtubs.

White Male Workers

American civilian men made up the backbone of the labor force. They were the laborers with the expertise and the experience. Except for those with unusual skills, the younger and most able-bodied among them were off in the service, and the brunt of farming and manufacturing fell on those remaining. All during the war they worked long hours at a rate of pay not much higher than before, accommodating themselves, sometimes under protest, to changed conditions of labor and new, inexperienced coworkers. "Sure I'm working

A shipyard worker erects staging at the Bethlehem-Fairfield shipyards, Baltimore, Maryland, May 1943. *(Library of Congress, LC-USW3-023585-E)*

harder," declared a workman on a government poster, "Come on, Gang! We're building arms for victory!" "Everyday! Every Hour! Every Minute Counts! Only 278 Days Remain in this Year to Do the Job! Keep 'em Firing!"

It was not easy. For all workers, many factories were hazardous, what with exposure to spray painting and dangerous chemicals, welding, hanging from scaffolds, and shooting hot rivets into ships under construction. Whereas before the war an auto worker or an aircraft worker might expect to associate all his life on the assembly line with the neighbors with whom he had gone to grammar school, now he was side by side with people from different parts of the country and holding different sets of values; with youngsters; and even with women, blacks, and members of other ethnic groups.

Unemployed and underemployed southern job seekers traveled to the industrial North and Far West. Eight million moved in the largest western migration in American history.[24] Cars traveled from Oklahoma to the Northwest loaded with passengers seeking work, each of whom paid $6 or $8 for the trip and thought himself or herself lucky if the driver did not steal the luggage. High school youngsters dropped out or worked part-time and summers in such numbers that the steady prewar decline in child labor was temporarily reversed. In 1940 1.7 million persons between 14 and 17 were working; in 1944, 4.61 million, of whom 1.43 million were part-time students. Lockheed Aeronautics found that two boys could accomplish more in four hours each on a low-skilled job than an adult could during an eight-hour shift.[25]

Moreover, unless the experienced male laborer was in a low-wage industry like coal mining or textiles or on the swing (4 P.M.–midnight) or graveyard (midnight–8 A.M.) shift, he had little hope of increasing his wage rate after the government stabilized wages at 1942 rates in May 1942.[26] He knew that with profits soaring, wages controlled, and the government awarding cost-plus contracts, industry was making unprecedented profits. Still, he was happy to have a job, happy that wage rates had risen in the late 1930s and early 1940s, and glad to be able to work all the hours he wanted, thereby significantly increasing the amount in his pay envelope. He enjoyed the new benefits that industry was offering to attract workers, ranging from cafeteria meals, transportation, and recreation to fully paid pensions, paid vacations, and holidays—even in some cases Turkish baths, Florida vacations, and wristwatches at Christmas. All the same, a raise in wage rates would have been more to his liking.[27]

Despite his fears, the blue-collar male did not fare badly during the war. He preserved his freedom to accept, turn down, or switch jobs—although if he worked in a defense industry he could switch only to another defense industry. He could and did strike. Overtime at time-and-a-half or double-time rates so swelled his pay that his average weekly earnings nearly doubled, climbing from $25.20 in 1940 to $47.08 in 1944.[28] Only a bit more than a third of the 42 percent increase seen by the average American worker from 1939 to 1944 came from higher wage rates.[29]

Unions

The average worker, if he was a union man, feared that the war might cost him the powers and protections for which the unions had fought so hard in the recent past. He was glad to see union membership increase: It grew by more than 50 percent during the war.[30] However, he was not so sure about the new members, particularly the many women and minorities among them. (Indeed, most of those women who planned to work only for the duration of the war joined the union only reluctantly and begrudged the money for union dues.) Regarding them as transients who would not be around after the war, many a man did not see why his union should do anything special for them. After all, they had not sacrificed as he had for the union, but they were now enjoying the gains he and others like him had won.

He was uneasy about the pledge made by his union not to strike during the war. Pledges like this were repeatedly broken—14,000 times—usually in strikes provoked by fatigue, difficult managers, rises in the cost of living, restrictive government policies, union rivalries, worker suspicion of union leaders, and especially worker resentment of industry's fat profits.[31] Most were wildcat strikes unauthorized by the union; most were short; and most involved relatively few people, as when resentment at the disciplining of a friend prompted inexperienced workers simply to walk off the job.

Nevertheless several major union-sanctioned strikes so damaged war production as to necessitate government intervention ranging from presidential jawboning (talking tough) to mediation to actual commandeering of plants and mines. In some cases, to the rage of fighting troops, unions struck for more control or for higher wages. Notoriously, John L. Lewis, head of the United Mine Workers, who evoked complete loyalty from miners and fury from other Americans, repeatedly resorted to strikes. In 1943 he called out on strike more than 500,000 mine workers to secure wage increases. When the government ordered them back to work, only 15,000 returned. The miners closed down the steel mills for two weeks and threatened the war effort with power

Electrical workers of the Congress of Industrial Organizations "electrocute" someone posing as an effigy of Hitler in the Detroit Labor Day parade, September 1942. *(Library of Congress, LC-USW3-008470-C)*

shortages. The government finally put them back at work by taking over the mines, but ultimately they won portal-to-portal pay and other benefits.

Such work stoppages caused the United States to lose man-days it could ill afford. In 1942, 2,968 work stoppages cost 4.1 million man-days; in 1943, 3,752 work stoppages cost 13.5 million man-days; and in 1944, 4,950 work stoppages cost 8.7 million man-days.[32] Strikes provoked widespread public anger, intensified by the thought of the hardships, danger, and suffering that fighting men were undergoing. On the other hand, under a plan put forward by Donald Nelson of the War Production Board, labor-management committees worked throughout the war to reduce absenteeism, increase productivity, and involve workers in collecting scrap and buying war bonds.

Minority Workers

Early in the war President Roosevelt told the nation, "In some communities, employers dislike to employ women. In others, they are reluctant to hire Negroes. We can no longer afford to indulge such prejudices or practices."[33] The manpower shortage opened up unprecedented opportunities in the workplace to women, blacks, and other minority groups such as Native Americans, Mexican Americans, and Chinese Americans—but only when the supply of the preferred white males was depleted. The economy needed ethnic workers and eventually used them. FDR's Executive Order 8802 of June 25, 1941, prohibiting discrimination in defense and government jobs helped, even though it was issued only under threat by black leaders of a protest march on Washington.

The press seldom mentioned the contributions of minority workers. Many of their fellow workers did not welcome them, protested their presence, and often refused to work with them, especially if they were black. Often such protests could be silenced if management held firm; at other times they erupted into violent hate strikes. In Mobile, Alabama, in June 1943, in protest against the promotion of black welders to the same jobs as whites, whites attacked the blacks with bricks and clubs. Detroit suffered hate strikes over housing in 1941 and 1943.

Overall, however, minorities improved their economic status. By war's end blacks held almost 8 percent of all defense industry jobs—a number almost proportionate to their presence at that time in the population.[34] Seven hundred thousand blacks left the South, where most of them had worked in agricultural or unskilled occupations, for jobs in war plants in the North and West. From 1942 to 1945, nearly half a million blacks migrated to California alone.[35] In 1939, the earnings of black males averaged only 41 percent of the earnings of white males; in 1947, they came to 54 percent.[36] Thousands of minority cooks and maids abandoned domestic work for the assembly

The Liberty ship SS *Frederick Douglass* is shown in May 1943, a week after the hull was laid at a Baltimore, Maryland, shipyard. In the prior century, Douglass, a noted orator and abolitionist had worked near here shortly before he escaped from slavery. During World War II the yard employed more than 6,000 black workers. *(Library of Congress, LC-USW3-024169-C)*

line, multiplying their earnings from $3.50 a week to as much as $48 a week.[37] Their former employers circulated stories about the "Eleanor Clubs" inspired by Mrs. Roosevelt that had made the help difficult to manage and uppity. The first lady was not to blame; as one black woman said, "Hitler was the one that got us out of the white folks' kitchen." In fact, however, the numbers of black women in domestic service actually increased during the war, as whites left that occupation.[38]

On average, black urban workers more than doubled their pay, usually by shifting their occupations.[39] They were most likely to be hired in plants with federal contracts, which forced managers to obey antidiscrimination regulations, and in states like New York with strong fair-employment laws. Many black women for the first time found clerical jobs with government departments and the new emergency agencies. Moreover, the migrating blacks moved to places where they could vote, as they had found it almost impossible to do in the prewar South. Significantly, as blacks could afford to pay dues, the National Association for the Advancement of Colored People (NAACP) between 1940 and 1945 grew from 50,000 to 500,000 members, thereby enormously increasing its funds and power.[40]

Women Workers

"I think this is as good [a time] as any . . . to warn men that when the war is over, the going will be a lot tougher, because they will have to be compared with women whose eyes have been opened to their greatest economic potentialities."

—*Secretary of the Interior Harold Ickes*[41]

The presence of women changed the workplace most of all. From mid-1941 to mid-1945, the number of women over age 14 employed in nonagricultural jobs increased from 11.4 million to 16.5 million, and with the addition of those in agriculture, from 12.9 million to 18.8 million.[42] By contrast, throughout most of the war Germany promoted for women a policy of *"Kinder, Küche, Kirche"*—children, kitchen, and church—an ideology that after the war Nazi leader Hermann Goering bemoaned as a major error. American policymakers, on the other hand, believed it necessary to enlist as many people as possible in an economic "army" of workers. Now and then during the war they even contemplated conscripting women, as the military and first lady Eleanor Roosevelt advocated, but FDR never consented.

Instead, the Office of War Information (OWI) launched a huge campaign to entice women to enter the military or the paid workforce and to retain women already so engaged. It put out reams of special stories earmarked for the rural press, labor publications, foreign-language and black newspapers, business house organs, and the women's pages of local newspapers. It subsidized films to be shown at churches, schools, war plants, and clubs. It suggested plots and slants for Hollywood films. It sponsored special messages on the radio on 75 programs a week for two months, with each station carrying three announcements a day.[43]

At the request of the magazine industry, in the spring of 1942 the OWI created a bureau to publish a bimonthly *Magazine War Guide,* which supplied ideas for fiction writers. To confessions magazines it suggested, "A story . . . might show a seduced and despondent girl regenerated through observation of the good done by a nurse and her self-sacrifice," or "A seduced girl throws herself into [work], say physiotherapy, to forget. Working side by side with a crippled doctor, learns to love him. After crisis in their task which she helps him meet, she discovers that although he knows all about her past, he loves her."[44] Science fiction pulps, thought OWI, could usefully publish stories in which "an Amazonian economy might trace its inception to this war-enforced change in our mores [of having women in non-traditional jobs]. A story of the supernatural might be woven around a woman locomotive engineer, for instance, or a feminine bus driven meeting with eerie adventures in lonely streets. . . . [There might even be] stories of utopias in which public health setups [are] administered by the descendants of nurses of our day."[45]

Women who from the beginning of U.S. history had been told to stay at home after they married were buffeted by propaganda exhorting them to work outside the home. Suddenly everywhere in the nation working women were portrayed as patriots and heroines. Women were to remain selfless, but they were to direct their service to the country—while still, of course, fulfilling their responsibilities at home. Women were to put aside personal ambition and pleasures, work hard, never complain about fatigue or shortages, bring up model children, keep the home fires burning, and prop up soldier morale.

In the absence of products to tout, ad agencies eagerly cooperated. Newspapers, subway cards, films, billboards, popular songs, popular fiction, and commercial advertisements all tried to attract women into new roles and encourage public acceptance of them there. They endeavored to induce guilt in women about not doing their part in the war effort or inspire fears that the lack of their labor might cause the death of a serviceman. Alternatively, they told the girl he left behind that he might stop loving her if she did not take a job. As a 1943 Eureka vacuum cleaner ad put it, "When Jimmy joined the Air Corps, she thought the end of her world had come. But he set her straight . . . as always. 'This is something we can do together, kid. You make 'em. I'll fly 'em. It's still the firm of Us, Incorporated.'"[46] Only when victory neared did advice columns stop instructing married women to take paid jobs, even if their husbands disapproved. Throughout the war, propaganda emphasized the temporary nature of women's employment: Women, it said, were just pitching in for the emergency. They were not giving up their home responsibilities—frequently they were shown in coveralls caring for their children or cleaning the house—and they would of course gladly go back home when the men returned.

Recruiters for industry built up the image of a beaming "Rosie the Riveter," famously portrayed by the popular painter Norman Rockwell, who showed her in overalls with the sleeves of her blouse rolled up over her muscular arms, and hailed in song by bandleader Kay Kyser. Slogans like "She's a WOW (Woman Ordnance Worker)" encouraged these workers to wear the logo on the bandannas covering their hair while they operated heavy cranes and milling machines, bagged gunpowder, made weapons, and created ammunition.

Blacks and other minorities seldom appeared in the propaganda, although 600,000 black women worked in war production.[47] Ads and fiction portrayed mostly young, slim, pretty, white, middle-class women workers, whereas in reality most women who entered war production were working-class wives, widows, divorcées, and students, of disparate ages, figures, and appearance, and minorities were well represented among them.[48] The OWI inspired stories aimed at reassuring whites that blacks were patriots who would not infringe on white supremacy.

Industrialists and governmental and private agencies alike supplemented the propaganda by trying to recruit women directly. The New York City Junior League set up a clearinghouse to provide information about jobs for women. In Buffalo, New York, the Womanpower Commission built Cape Cod cottages in the center city to invite applicants for work with the "cheery warmth of a friendly neighbor." In Los Angeles Lockheed Aeronautics sent some of its women workers as "victory visitors" to recruit door-to-door.[49] In Akron, Ohio, the government interviewed 87,000 housewives but recruited only 630.[50]

Indeed, all these efforts had only limited success. Women did work in all sorts of jobs formerly closed to them, not only as welders and riveters, but also as gas station attendants, truck drivers, postal workers, and observers and forecasters in the national weather bureau. As historian David Kennedy remarked, however, "If you look at the whole distribution of what women were doing in wartime, you might say the typical woman war worker should be called Sally the Secretary, or, in fact, maybe even Molly the Mom, because most women persisted in their traditional functions during the war."[51] The 2 million women in defense plants never constituted more than about 10 percent of the total female work force.[52] Some housewives who had not done paid work after they married did enter or reenter the labor force; three-fourths of the new women workers were married. By war's end a quarter of married women were gainfully employed.[53] At the height of wartime employment women made up about a third of the civilian workforce, of whom about 5 million were new workers.[54]

But most of the more than 19 million women workers either were continuing their participation in the labor force or had recently come of age to enter it.[55] In 1944 the Women's Bureau reported that only 25 percent had less than two years' work experience; almost half had been in the labor force at least five years, and almost 30 percent at least 10. Only a third of the women in war manufacturing plants described themselves as previously housewives, and the census bureau survey of March 1944 reports that of the 30 million women at home with no paid employment in 1941, seven out of eight were still at home in 1944.[56] It was still a world in which a working woman writing her serviceman husband that she was pregnant could expect to receive back a letter saying, "I trust that you've already quit your job. If you haven't, you have, as of now."

However, demographics of working women changed. In 1940, 36 percent of them were married; in 1944, 46 percent.[57] The participation rate in the

Nan Hannegan recruits door-to-door for women to work in war plants, May 1943. She wears a War Manpower Commission (WMC) ribbon along with her plant button. This recruiting effort was organized by the WMC in cooperation with local war plants that had loaned 19 women workers as recruiters. *(Library of Congress, LC-USW3-023905-D)*

labor force of women 35–64 years of age grew from 25 percent in 1940 to 36 percent in 1945.[58]

Patriotism certainly played a part in women's decisions to work during the war, but other reasons also operated. Some women wanted to escape confinement to housework; some wanted to establish their independence from their husbands. Money and opportunities for the more challenging jobs formerly reserved for men powerfully motivated most.

Wages in munitions plants and aircraft factories averaged 40 percent higher than those in traditionally female fields, even though women were paid less than men on the same jobs.[59] In 1944 women in manufacturing averaged $31.21 per week and men $54.65[60]—a situation due in large part to women's working at lower-level jobs but also to higher rates for men. Opposition to equal pay for women in defense plants for the most part came not from their employers, who charged up wages to the federal government in cost-plus contracts, but from labor unions worried about postwar labor relations, although some unions argued for equal pay for women lest employers hire them in preference to men because they were cheaper. As women fled the traditional women's occupations, wages in those fields rose sharply: from 1939 to 1943 beauticians' pay rose 28 percent.[61] But everywhere, men were more highly paid for the same or comparable work as women. For instance, during the war, when banks for the first time hired women as cashiers, tellers, and loan officers, they paid the women so much less that after the war men would not take those jobs.[62]

Women invading traditionally male fields encountered both hostility and support. All the propaganda may have softened the reactions of laboring men, particularly the reassurance that the situation was temporary. Some men welcomed these new colleagues, treating them as comrades, sisters, or daughters, and helping them adjust to the new workplace.

However, society had long endorsed the idea that woman's place was in the home. Many men feared for their jobs. They worried about losing status and masculinity if women proved that they could do the same work. They resented employers' giving women privileges only later extended to men. They did not understand women's problems, needs, and emotions. They had been brought up believing that it was quite acceptable to comment critically on women's appearance, intelligence, and behavior and to put them down with generalizations and jokes. Sexual harassment was commonplace, with no laws to punish its perpetrators. Most women handled it by reporting it, threatening to quit if it continued, or dealing with it themselves, sometimes by menacing gestures with their blowtorches. "Oh," said one woman factory worker offhandedly, "when a fellow whistles at me, I whistle right back at him. He doesn't know what to do next."[63] Other women resorted to fluttering eyelashes and traditionally feminine wiles. Still others stoically accepted it, figuring it was their own fault, or just the way the world worked.

To their credit, many men helped to train new women workers, for with so many new hires the training provided by the companies was often scanty to nonexistent. Manufacturers did, however, break down tasks formerly performed by skilled workers into simpler steps and provide mechanical aids to help with the heavy lifting. Some companies hired matrons to fill women in on workplace practice. The women had lots to learn in their new workplaces. Just wearing the necessary clothing required a change in self-image for many. They had to learn the importance of covering their hair completely for safety's sake. The heavy clothing, some of it weighing as much as 60 pounds, weighed them down. (Welders wore leather gloves, leather pants, a big hood, and a leather jacket.) They could not find safety shoes small enough for a woman's foot. They complained that when their jobs required them to wear pants they did not receive the courtesies and respect that skirts evoked.

Women sustained fewer on-the-job accidents than men, but when they were injured they stayed at home longer. They were more vulnerable to dermatitis and back strain, and they were more likely to call in sick or to suffer from exhaustion. Their turnover rate was significantly higher than that of men, often because of home responsibilities, and sometimes because they were not used to the routines of working outside the home. They were reluctant to work overtime. A large proportion of them worked part-time, and they frequently moved in and out of the labor force, as caring for their children necessitated.[64] Their absentee rates were high.

Perhaps the greatest difficulty they faced was coping with both home and outside jobs. Society was not set up for working women. With her thorough knowledge of the country and her empathy with the problems of all sorts of Americans, Eleanor Roosevelt advocated measures to help working housewives: providing community laundries and family restaurants that would offer complete meals to take out; transporting children from home to school; staggering opening and closing times at factories; opening banks and department stores at night (Bloomingdale's set up defense plant branches, but most stores kept to their regular hours); asking butchers and grocers to save some rationed goods until 6 P.M. rather than dispensing them all to full-time housewives; and advising war plants to hire personal shoppers to take orders at the beginning of the shift and have groceries waiting at its end. Responsibilities as single parents weighed heavily on service wives whose husbands were overseas.

Most of all, the first lady believed, women workers needed care for their children. In early 1943 more than a third of them had children under 14.[65] The need for public child-care facilities was acute. Latchkey children were all too common, and some working mothers were locking young children in their houses or having their children sleep in cars parked close to the mothers' workplace windows. In 1941 Congress passed the Lanham Act (Community Facilities Act), which provided money for community facilities, including child care, for communities with their populations multiplied by the war, but these took care of only a fraction of the estimated 2 million children in need.[66]

Eleanor Roosevelt persuaded Henry Kaiser to set up model facilities at his Portland shipyards, with the U.S. Maritime Commission covering the construction costs and Kaiser the operating costs. More than half a century later the Swan Island Center is still held up as an example. Fifteen playrooms with pastel walls and banks of windows on two sides were clustered around a large inner court equipped with swings and seesaws. Indian, Mexican, black, and white children from 18 months to six years were tended by well-trained caregivers and teachers. The center kept its doors open day and night, providing cribs and cots for the children to sleep on; it also offered special isolated facilities for sick children. During school vacations it added a program for children aged 6 to 12. For all these services it charged for full-time care and food for one child only $0.75 per day, and for two in the same family only $1.25. To add to all this, it freed working mothers to spend a bit more time with their children in the evenings by offering them at cost fully cooked meals to take home at the end of their shifts. Not surprisingly, these services proved an effective recruiting tool, with mothers coming from as far away as Louisiana when they heard about them.

By the summer of 1945 more than 1.5 million children were in day care, public and private. The country spent about $50 million for that purpose, $3 million on construction, and $47 million on operating costs.[67] Many mothers, however, especially blue-collar women and black women, preferred to arrange for relatives to tend their children. Of the tens of thousands of new nursery schools only half the capacity was used, often by women who did not work at paid jobs.[68]

Millions of women in the workforce outside the war industries toiled to keep the home economy rolling, frequently in jobs vacated by men. Secretaries found themselves suddenly, if temporarily, promoted to their bosses' jobs, though seldom to their pay. Women worked as disk jockeys, movie ushers, sports editors, air traffic controllers, armed guards, fish and game wardens, and monorail operators. They delivered army trucks to bases for five cents a mile and bus fare back; they taught the Morse code to servicemen; they loaded trains; they identified fingerprints for the FBI. "Maisies"—women musicians—toured in hundreds of all-woman bands, many of them for the United Service Organizations (USO) entertaining soldiers: Phil Spitalny's All-Girl Orchestra, the Hormel Girls (whites), the International Sweethearts of Rhythm (lighter-skinned blacks and whites); and the Darlings of Rhythm (darker-skinned blacks).[69] The federal government in 1940 employed 1 million women and at war's end, four million, about a quarter of them in cleri-

Mrs. Trinidad Gutierrez (left) and Miss Molly Alcanto (right) work at the Atchison, Topeka, and Santa Fe Railroad roundhouse in San Bernardino, California, replacing lamps and oil cans on incoming locomotives, March 1943. Mrs. Gutierrez, whose husband was recovering in the hospital after an injury at the Kaiser Fontana steel mill, had four children. Miss Alcanto's boyfriend was in the army. *(Library of Congress, LC-USW3-022273-D)*

cal jobs. By the end of the war almost 38 percent of all civilian government employees were women.[70]

The new prominence of women in the workplace during the war changed the workplace and changed women. Women and men working side-by-side at the same jobs developed new relationships. Women who regarded themselves as temporary workers insisted on cleaner factory restrooms and brought in curtains and flowers for them. They were more concerned than men about safety. Overseers found that they had to change their tactics with women, who responded well to praise and badly to harsh criticism. At the same time women developed a new self-respect and self-confidence on finding they could do "men's jobs." They often compared making precise small parts to crocheting or needlework.

To all workers—men, women, the young, the middle-aged, and the old—the war brought new experiences. They lived in new areas of the country. They worked and often lived with people whose like they had never met—open homosexuals, blacks, Mexicans, Jamaicans, southerners and northerners, and recent immigrants—who challenged their assumptions and prejudices. The war sophisticated American workers.

The Merchant Marine

The members of the U.S. Merchant Marine were civilians, paid by their civilian employers, and had their own union of seamen to negotiate for better wages, bonuses, and overtime pay, but they experienced the war much as did the combat troops, amid hardship and danger: In the early years they had to confront enemy submarines (U-boats) in unarmed vessels. They sailed in the old ships owned by the Merchant Marine when the war started, in ships scrounged from other owners, and the Liberty and Victory ships that other American workers turned out by the thousands.[71] They ran the risk of death by high explosives, fire, drowning, freezing, and starving. They put U.S. armies and equipment on enemy territory and maintained them there, transporting across the seas the 7 to 15 tons of supplies it took to support one soldier for one year. On the run to Murmansk alone they supplied the USSR with 15,000 aircraft, 7,000 tanks, 350,000 tons of explosives, and 15 million pairs of boots.[72]

Moreover, the Merchant Marine participated in Allied invasions, both in the Atlantic and in the Pacific. In preparation for the Normandy landings, for instance, a thousand Merchant Marine volunteers sailed 22 obsolete merchant ships laden with explosives across the English Channel and under heavy fire set them in position for scuttling to form artificial harbors; on D day, 2,700 merchant ships landed troops and munitions under enemy fire on the beaches of Normandy. Thereafter during the battles for France and Germany, merchant ships shuttled 2.5 million troops, 17 million tons of munitions and supplies, and half a million trucks and tanks from England to France.[73]

During the war the numbers of merchant mariners swelled from 55,000 to 215,000, a growth enabled in part by the training programs of the U.S. Maritime Service. Among them were 24,000 African Americans, constituting almost 10 percent of the service, who labored in every capacity aboard the ships. Still, prejudice beset blacks. Captain Hugh Mulzac, a black man born in the British West Indies who had become a naturalized American citizen in 1918, earned his captain's rating that year, but prejudice denied him command except on a ship with an all-black crew. He refused to command a Jim-Crow ship. Finally, 22 years later, in World War II, he was put in command of the S.S. *Booker T. Washington* with an integrated crew of 18 nationalities. The ship made 22 round-trip voyages in five years, transporting 18,000 troops, but after the war Mulzac never again received a command.[74]

Attacks on merchant ships by submarines, armed raiders and destroyers, and aircraft—combined with encounters with mines and storms—killed almost 7,300 crew members at sea; wounded 12,000, of whom 1,100 died from their wounds; and made prisoners of 663 men and women. Sixty-six died in prison camps or aboard enemy ships.[75]

In the Atlantic in the early days of the war the unarmed or lightly armed merchant ships sailing without air cover were easy prey to enemy submarines, which often traveled in "wolf packs" and from 1940 until mid-1942 sank more ships than Americans built. Defense measures to protect them were too little and too late. In early 1942 navy gun crews designated as naval armed guards were assigned to merchant ships.[76] In late spring of 1942 the War Shipping Administration began to organize convoys with fighting escort ships to protect the merchantmen from the submarines lined up about 15 miles apart across convoy routes. The convoys could move only at the speed of the slowest ship among them—perhaps 7 knots, but U-boats averaged 17.5 knots on the surface and 7 knots submerged. Moreover, escort vessels could not simultaneously hunt submarines and pick up survivors. In June 1942 the government finally ordered a blackout of seacoast cities, so that at least the merchant ships would not be outlined against the lights, making them easier targets for submarines. In October 1942 when Allied bombing of enemy submarine pens began, the Germans had so heavily shielded them with reinforced concrete that not a single U-boat was damaged.[77]

In the Pacific, convoys were unnecessary except during invasions, because the Japanese did not target shipping. Although an occasional cargo ship was torpedoed, the heavy losses occurred during American attacks on Pacific beachheads. During those invasions kamikazes (suicide pilots who crashed their planes into targets), bombers, artillery, and torpedoes sank 44 merchant ships and damaged many others.[78] In the battle for the Philippines in October 1944, merchant mariners delivered 300,000 troops and 500,000 tons of supplies to Leyte, shot down at least 107 enemy planes with the help of their naval armed guards, and helped army doctors with the wounded. Gen. Douglas MacArthur testified: "I have ordered them off their ships and into foxholes when their ships became untenable under attack."

After V-J day the Merchant Marine kept busy carrying surrendering Japanese back to their native land, returning American troops and dead to the United States, and transporting forces and supplies for the occupations of Germany and Japan—operations during which 49 merchant ships were sunk or damaged.[79]

Despite their stellar record, only in 1988 after a long court battle did members of the Merchant Marine win a court decision for limited veteran status.[80]

CHRONICLE OF EVENTS

1941

September: Construction is completed on the 3.5 million square feet of factory space at the Ford Willow Run B-24 Liberty Bomber plant.

December 21: Representatives from labor and management pledge no strikes, no lockouts.

1942

At a Kaiser steel mill in southern California and at Kaiser shipyards in San Francisco and in Vancouver, Washington, Dr. Sidney Garfield establishes group-practice prepayment plans for workers and their families.

early 1942: Navy gun crews designated as naval armed guards are assigned to U.S. merchant ships.

spring: The Office of War Information creates a bureau to publish a bimonthly *Magazine War Guide* to help editors and writers insert propaganda into their publications to recruit women to the work force.

late spring: The War Shipping Administration begins to organize convoys with fighting escort ships to protect the merchantmen from German submarines along convoy routes.

May: The American Women's Volunteer Services recruit 1,500 women to help with the harvest between July and October.

May: The U.S. government stabilizes wage rates at the 1942 level.

June: The U.S. government finally orders a blackout of U.S. seacoast cities so that Allied shipping will not be outlined against the lights, making easier targets for submarines.

July 16: The War Labor Board approves a 15 percent increase for certain workers whose wages have not increased since January 1, 1941.

December 2: Enrico Fermi's laboratory achieves a nuclear chain reaction.

1943

A hundred large companies hold some 70 percent of all government contracts, whereas in 1940 these companies had produced only 30 percent of the manufacturing output of the country.

Henry Kaiser's seven shipyards are completing a Liberty ship every 10 hours.

Women, with hoe and rake in hand, model two types of uniforms worn by the Women's Land Army when planting and harvesting war food crops, 1942. *(Library of Congress, LC-USZ62-101577)*

Two Kaiser shipyards in Portland, Oregon, open model child-care centers. The population of Washington, D.C., has nearly doubled since 1940.

The pay of women beauticians has risen 28 percent since 1939.

early 1943: Seventy-five percent of women workers are married, 60 percent of them are over 35, and more than a third have children under 14.

March: The Manhattan Engineer District, controlled by the Office of Scientific Research and Development and the army, is tasked with developing the atom bomb.

late May: White shipyard workers in Mobile, Alabama, riot when black welders are assigned to work on the same job with white welders, forcing a return to segregation.

June: Over President Franklin D. Roosevelt's veto, Congress passes the Smith-Connally Act, giving the War Labor Board statutory powers in strikes, authorizing the president to seize war plants and mines where illegal strikes occur, banning strikes in war plants seized by the government, banning political contributions by labor unions, and requiring local unions to give 30-day notice of a strike followed by a cooling-off period of 30 days and then to put the strike to a vote among its membership.

June: In a single day the Willow Run bomber plant hires more than 3,000 workers.

early June: 25,000 Packard plant workers producing engines for bombers and PT (patrol torpedo) boats stop work to protest the promotion of three blacks; reportedly one of the protestors shouts, "I'd rather see Hitler and Hirohito win than work beside a nigger on the assembly line."

June 2: Coal miners strike for an increase of $2 a day, infuriating most of the nation; soon thereafter FDR issues instructions for the government to take over the mines and orders the miners back to work.

June 20: Race riots begin in Detroit.

June 25: FDR vetoes the Smith-Connally Act imposing drastic penalties and restrictions on any person encouraging a strike in government-owned plants, noting that in 1942 "99.95 percent of the work went forward without strikes. . . . That record has never been equaled in this country." The Congress overrides the veto.

August: Henry Ford's Willow Run B-24 Liberty bomber plant is producing 231 planes a month.

fall: At the request of the War Manpower Commission, the army releases 4,300 soldiers to return to the mines.

November: U.S. factories are providing the Soviet Union with two-thirds of the vehicles and half the planes their military are using.

November: At the Tehran Conference in Iran, Soviet dictator Joseph Stalin publicly acknowledges the major contributions to the war effort of the United States in supplying goods necessary to the conduct of the war.

December: Willow Run is producing 365 B-24 Liberty bombers a month.

1944

In this year the United States turns out 96,369 planes, whereas in 1939 it was producing fewer than 6,000.

Women workers in manufacturing average $31.21 per week and men $54.65.

Whereas in 1940, only 36 percent of employed women were married, in 1944 46 percent are.

The U.S. Women's Bureau reports that only 25 percent of women workers have less than 2 years' work experience; almost half have been in the labor force at least 5 years, and almost 30 percent at least 10.

The average wages of a blue-collar U.S. worker have nearly doubled since 1940 from $25.20 to $47.08.

The unemployment rate stands at 1.2 percent, having fallen from 19 percent in 1938.

March: A census bureau survey reports that of the 30 million women at home with no paid employment in 1941, seven out of eight are still at home in 1944.

second week in April: FDR sends in troops to quell the strike at Montgomery Ward in Chicago, evoking much criticism because Montgomery Ward is not doing war business, though 75 percent of its customers are farmers producing food vital to the war effort.

August 1: Ten thousand mass-transit employees in Philadelphia strike to protest the upgrading of eight black employees to motormen.

August 4: FDR issues an executive order calling upon the army to operate the mass-transit system of the Philadelphia Transportation Company.

August 5: Striking mass-transit workers in Philadelphia are arrested for violating the Smith-Connally Act.

August 7: Mass-transit strikers in Philadelphia return to work.

summer: The War Department begins propaganda to remove women from the workforce after the war, soon echoed in magazines, movies, and plays, despite polls showing that most women want to continue working.

October: In the battle for the Philippines, merchant mariners deliver 300,000 troops and 500,000 tons of supplies to Leyte, help army doctors with the wounded, and with their naval armed guards shoot down at least 107 enemy planes.

December: The Office of War Mobilization directs draft boards to reclassify and induct into the military all men between 18 and 38 years of age not engaged in war work.

December: Willow Run is producing 650 B-24 Liberty bombers a month.

1945

Since 1940 the U.S. farm population has fallen by 17 percent, yet farmers have increased their production.

The National Association for the Advancement of Colored People (NAACP) between 1940 and 1945 has grown from 50,000 to 500,000 members.

The participation rate in the labor force of women 35–64 years of age has grown from 25 percent in 1940 to 36 percent in 1945.

January: FDR asks for national service legislation to freeze male workers in their jobs and to include a "work or fight" clause that would also apply to women.

summer: By this time more than 1.5 million children are in day care, public and private.

July 16: The atom bomb is successfully tested in the New Mexico desert.

mid-1945: From mid-1941 to mid-1945, the number of women over 14 employed in nonagricultural jobs has increased from 11.4 million to 16.5 million, and with the addition of those in agriculture, from 12.9 million to 18.8 million.

Eyewitness Testimony

Industry

As far as you could see in every direction [from Omaha beach in Normandy] the ocean was infested with ships. . . . The wreckage was vast and startling. . . . There were trucks tipped half over and swamped . . . tanks that had only just made the beach before being knocked out . . . jeeps that had burned to a dull gray . . . boats stacked on top of each other. On the beach lay expended sufficient men and mechanism for a small war. They were gone forever now.

And yet, we could afford it. We could afford it because we were on, we had our toehold, and behind us there were such enormous replacements for this wreckage on the beach that you could hardly conceive of the sum total. Men and equipment were flowing from England in such a gigantic stream that it made the waste on the beachhead seem like nothing at all, really nothing at all. . . .

> *Ernie Pyle reporting three weeks after D day*
> *(June 6, 1944), in* Brave Men, *358.*

Agriculture

That's when the real boost came. The war . . . does something to your country. It does something to the individual. I had a neighbor just as the war was beginning. We had a boy ready to go to service. This neighbor told me what we needed was a damn good war, and we'd solve our agricultural problems. And I said, "Yes, but I'd hate to pay with the price of my son." Which we did.

> *Iowa farmer recalling a conversation probably*
> *in late 1941 or early 1942, quoted in Terkel,*
> Good War, *10.*

I was convinced that we were in a desperate situation and that anything we could do to hold up the English now and the Russians later so far as the question of food was concerned was for our sake. . . . Sure, we wanted to uphold the hand of democracy wherever we found it. However I have to admit that no one could say that we were doing that when we helped the Russians. . . .

We created the Joint Anglo-American Food Committee in order to make effective or to carry out the food responsibilities that came out of the Lend-Lease program. . . .

I didn't know that the consumers of this country were going to be given the buying power they were given. I didn't see the big inflation coming and the great big increase in payrolls that was coming. That created on the domestic front a demand which I couldn't anticipate. And surely I couldn't anticipate the Russian demand, and I didn't have any encouragement much from the British. . . .

[The Japanese attack at Pearl Harbor] meant the Department of Agriculture and I had a much graver responsibility, a much greater task, than we had thought about until that time. All our peacetime pro-

This 1943 U.S. Crop Corps poster recruits farm workers.
(Library of Congress, LC-USZC4-2683)

jects would have to be secondary entirely always to the war effort.

Reminiscences of Claude Wickard, secretary of agriculture, 1953, about the early years of the war, on pages 9:1991; 10:2274–75 in the Columbia University Oral History Research Office Collection.

Full Employment

So we were concerned about manpower shortages and the orderly organization of our labor market, for war production purposes, which was basically the purpose of the War Manpower Commission.

...We formulated what came to be known as management-labor programs, and devised a system of restricting the movement of labor between jobs through a certificate of availability procedure. . . . It vested in a management the power to grant or deny a certificate of availability to an individual who left its labor force. The objective was the staffing and stabilization of the labor force in war production industries. . . .

Recognizing the potentiality for injustice in this program, we set up principles to govern good cause of leaving and management-labor appeal boards to hear appeals from denials of certificates of availability. On the other hand, we provided, in these programs, for unrestricted certificates of availability to workers in nonessential industries, in order to entice them away from those industries.

The other side of the program was an attempt to control the hiring practices of industry, through a provision that no employer may hire an individual except through the public employment offices or unless he had a direct referral from an employment office, in the shortage skills. . . .

Another activity of the War Manpower Commission was a much closer working relationship with the selective service system, again for the same purpose—to coordinate selective service regulations governing occupational deferments. There were many who wanted to use the selective service system as an enforcement device for keeping critical workers in their jobs—in effect, inducting them into the army if they left their jobs. . . . There were many aspects of it that troubled us, but it was a period of war crisis and our effort was to devise as many controls, and impartial bodies to hear complaints and review injuries to

individuals, as possible. We were affecting the freedom of individuals.

Reminiscences of Bernice Lotwin Bernstein of the War Manpower Commission, 1965, speaking about wartime employment conditions, on pages 99–101, in the Columbia University Oral History Research Office Collection.

White Male Workers

One thing I was quite impressed with then and have been impressed with ever since in government organizations is the number of people working in the organizations who are very conscientious, very hard working, and who make only a negative contribution—who serve only as bottlenecks. . . . They were essentially people who were spending all their time on negatives, people who didn't have training enough to understand things but who, anytime anything new came along would insist it would have to be explained to them.

Reminiscences of scientist Norman Ramsey, 1960, speaking of wartime government employees, on pages 54–55, in the Columbia University Oral History Research Office Collection.

We [San Franciscan young men about to enter the military] were all able-bodied, the labor shortage was unbelievable, and the shipyards were anxious to hire

A high school boy eats lunch with coworkers at the plant where he works after school, October 1942. *(Library of Congress, LC-USW3-024618-C)*

any of us, even for a few months.... Many of us had short deferments until we could finish the current school terms. We preferred the swing shifts or graveyard shifts so we could attend daytime classes. When our shifts were over, we would adjourn to an all-night diner, talk about the war and then head off to late-night movies.

Bob Graydon, letter to the editor, New York Times, *October 23, 2000, speaking of an unidentified time during the war years.*

I went with my boss [at DuPont] on a cruise off Norfolk on the aircraft carrier *Ticonderoga.* A main gear box on one of the four propeller drive shafts had been replaced after a failure, and it was critically important to avoid another failure that would take the ship out of action again. We put our vibration measuring instruments on the huge drive shaft, about 20" diameter as I recall, and monitored the torsional vibration as it went through the full speed range. I remember being a bit awed by my own importance down in the bowels of the ship telling the captain up on the bridge at what speed to run the #3 propeller. We were able to tell him later—go ahead into operation, but to avoid a vibration build up don't let the shaft speed linger between 29 and 31 revolutions per minute. The ship went out to sea a few days later and operated well during the ensuing war years.

During the next four years I was assigned to the very difficult navy problem of the design and protection of shipboard electrical equipment from the damaging effect of mechanical shock....

Engineer Bob Wells reminiscing about his wartime assignments, unpublished memoir, n.p.

With the draft, the UP had trouble keeping its bureaus manned, and every week or so it lost another manager.... The UP moved me to its Nashville, Tennessee, bureau and appointed me manager. Surely a resounding title at the age of twenty-two, but less than it appeared. I would manage a one-man bureau, the one man being myself. And giving me the title simply was a way to evade the new wage-and-hour law and avoid paying me overtime.... so for a fifty-to seventy-hour week I was paid $42.50.

Newsman David Brinkley recalling events of 1942, in Brinkley, Memoir, *45.*

Andrew Higgins is the man who won the war for us. If Higgins had not designed and built those LCVPs (landing craft vehicle, personnel), we never could have landed on an open beach. The whole strategy of the war would have been different.

Gen. Dwight D. Eisenhower speaking of Higgins's adaptation of his Eureka boat to a landing craft, probably in 1942, quoted in Caraccilo, "Americans," 20.

[I observed] the near absence among the men I worked with . . . of any comprehension of what Nazism meant—we were fighting Germany essentially because she had allied herself with the Japanese who had attacked us at Pearl Harbor.

Playwright Arthur Miller reminiscing probably about 1942 and/or 1943, in "The Face in the Mirror," 3.

[Washington, D.C.] was then full of a lot of people running around not sure what they were doing. Although a lifelong Democrat, I had been quite disillusioned with FDR's ability to run anything, and I was terribly concerned about how the government was going to get organized to fight the war. However, when I went to work in OPA [the Office of Price Administration], I was overcome by the enthusiasm, the dedication, of everybody in that place. Working in a war agency was a hell of an experience. You just routinely worked till midnight; you worked Saturdays. You always had in mind the fact that all these guys were in foxholes someplace or sitting out on some cold deck somewhere.

Office of Price Administration worker Stephen Ailes speaking of events probably from 1942 to 1946, quoted in Hoopes, Americans Remember, *49.*

While these American boys are over here sweating, bleeding and dying to protect America and even the right to strike, those people [striking miners] back there have the gall to quit their jobs.

Pfc. John Adkins writing from North Africa, June 1943, in Meyer, Stars and Stripes, *60.*

[The FBI] wanted me to make sure every man [at the shipyard] did his job. In other words they were afraid of sabotage, and I think not without reason, because some of our cables were sabotaged. We never found out who did it.

I turned in two different fellows who were sort of drifters. They had hooked up some of the wires in the

The War Manpower Commission circulated this poster in 1943.
(Library of Congress, LC-USZ62-107842)

electronic equipment wrong. I asked them why, and they answered, "Oh, golly, I don't know." . . . After I turned them in, I asked the FBI fellows about it, and they said not to worry, that they were in the army now—drafted.

We had a bit of bribery. In fact, I got a lot of that myself because I was the one that promoted the men. First I had gas coupons offered to me and then meat coupons. I would lie if I didn't say I had a little piece of meat once in a while. . . . We also had "Rosie the Riveter." A lot of gals did welding work. As a whole, I'd say they did a pretty good job. Of course, some of the Rosies were conducting a little business on the side. The oldest profession. Some were doing it for promotion and some for actual dollars.

Capt. Fred Kirkham reminiscing about the Brooklyn Navy Yard during the period 1943–45, quoted in Hoopes, Americans Remember, *89.*

Carl Vinson put me on a subcommittee to go to Honolulu to hold hearings on defense housing in March of 1945. He said there were thousands of mechanics, engineers and electricians, and brick layers, carpenters, over at Pearl Harbor preparing those ships and they couldn't get any place to live. So we went over and . . . found out that the Chamber of Commerce, the fruit people, the pineapple people, and the army and the navy were all feuding . . . about where they were going to build defense housing. . . . So we went out and designated the land. . . . And two months after we got back around 250 defense houses were built. . . .

Congressman Roy Madden reminiscing about events of 1945, quoted in Hoopes, Americans Remember, *59–60.*

The opinions of our scientific colleagues on the initial use of these weapons [atomic bombs] are not unanimous: they range from the proposal of a purely technical demonstration to that of the military application best designed to induce surrender. Those who advocate a purely technical demonstration would wish to outlaw the use of atomic weapons, and have feared that if we use the weapons now our position in future negotiations will be prejudiced. Others emphasize the opportunity of saving American lives by immediate military use, and believe that such use will improve the international prospects, in that they are more concerned with the prevention of war than with the elimination of this specific weapon. We find ourselves closer to these latter views; we can propose no technical demonstration likely to bring an end to the war; we see no acceptable alternates to direct military use.

Report of the Interim Committee to advise President Truman on the use of atomic bombs, June 1945, quoted in McCullough, Truman, *394. Among the members were Henry Stimson, secretary of war; James F. Byrnes, director of war mobilization; James B. Conant, chair of the National Defense Research Committee; and others of similar experience and intelligence. They were advised by outstanding atomic scientists, including J. Robert Oppenheimer, Enrico Fermi, and Arthur H. Compton.*

Minority Workers

I got a job with the General Accounting Office as a clerk. . . . I stayed there about a year and went over to the Office of Price Administration [OPA], first as a clerk, and then got involved with several of the black employees who felt they were being underutilized. They were college graduates too. At that time, the OPA, under Leon Henderson, was a pretty progressive agency, probably way ahead of its time, as far as equal or fair employment practices were concerned. Finally they hired me as a junior economist. . . .

As I recall, it was the first time blacks in government got really top jobs. . . . Several of us blacks made a breakthrough because of OPA. We got professional experience there.

> *Government employee Al Sweeney recalling events from 1941 on, quoted in Hoopes,* Americans Remember, *51–52.*

"Go west," that was the theme. "Everything is great in California, all doors are open, no prejudice, good jobs, plenty of money."

> *Black Oklahoman Sybil Lewis recalling 1942, quoted in Harris,* Homefront, *29.*

When I first arrived in Los Angeles, . . . I decided I didn't want to do maid work anymore, so I got a job as a waitress in a small black restaurant. . . . Then I saw an ad in the newspaper offering to train women for defense work. I went to Lockheed Aircraft and applied. They said they'd call me, but I never got a response, so I went back and applied again. You had to be pretty persistent. Finally they accepted me. They gave me a short training program and taught me how to rivet. Then they put me to work in the plant riveting small airplane parts. . . .

I worked for a while as a riveter with this white girl, when the boss came around one day and said, "We've decided to make some changes." At this point he assigned her to do the riveting and me to do the bucking. I wanted to know why. He said, "Well, we just interchange once in a while." But I was never given the riveting job back. . . .

After I passed the trainee course, they employed me at the shipyards. That was a little different than working in aircraft, because in the shipyard you found mostly men. There I ran into another kind of discrimination: because I was a woman I was paid less than a man for doing the same job.

> *Black riveter and welder Sybil Lewis recalling events of 1942–43, quoted in Harris,* Homefront, *118–119.*

Every effort should be made to place applicants with a history of mental disease if . . . they will be able to perform satisfactorily, without hazard to themselves or others. . . . Applicants who have a history of mental instability are not to be instructed to report to Washington, D.C., for employment, inasmuch as they might have more difficulty in adjusting to conditions in Washington during wartime than would an individual with a perfectly stable nervous system.

> *1944 government manual for hiring officials, quoted in Campbell,* Women at War, *107.*

Women Workers

In the 1940s . . . [m]ost systems service employees were women whom IBM had recruited to replace the hundreds of men off serving their country in World War II. . . . Without the changes World War II created in the workforce and without the vision and foresight

This recruiting poster shows a woman working on a casing for a bomb, 1942. *(Library of Congress, LC-USZ62-111835)*

of Mr. Watson Sr. [CEO of IBM], I never would have penetrated the man's world at the top of corporate life, rising in four years from a typewriter demonstrator at the World's Fair to become one of five corporate vice presidents at IBM in 1943.

Ruth Amonette, a former vice-president of IBM, speaking of 1939 to 1943, in Amonette, Among Equals, *xiii.*

We, girls in our 20's mostly, . . . learned to make the vital weather observations that the pilots depended on. Mere girls decided when planes could take off or land. Sometimes the pilots would come in and try to get us to change our ceiling or visibility report. Handsome, glamorous pilots were pretty hard to resist but we stuck by the rules.

Dorothy Hurd Chambers remembering the war years, in Chambers, Women in the Weather Bureau, *18.*

[D]uring World War II, [my mother] left our small town in western Massachusetts to come down here to Washington and work for the Army Signal Corps. . . . [S]he saw an ad in a puzzle magazine that said, "Do you like to do puzzles? Write us for free puzzles." She sent for the puzzles and they came with a letter that said: "If you can solve these puzzles, we'll send you more free puzzles." She solved them and sent them in, but what came by return mail was not more puzzles—it was a letter from Uncle Sam offering her a job in the Army's code-breaking project.

Mary Ann Glendon, "What Would My Mother Have Thought of Women's Freedom Network," in The Women's Freedom Network Newsletter *no. 3, 1.*

[O]pen code . . . is extremely hard to find and requires people who have a keen knowledge of the idiom in a language. . . . [In our little counterespionage section of the Office of Censorship,] we had people who knew French very well and Spanish and other foreign languages and would be able to recognize . . . where the language was strained. It would be recognized that "Aunt Louise had pneumonia last week" would mean something else.

Office of Censorship employee Hilda O'Brien recalling the war years, quoted in Hoopes, Americans Remember, *63.*

When our daughter was six weeks old, we decided to go to California. . . . We had $25.00, but we had

canned some white beans and we took those and put flour, lard, pans, and the bed in the back of the pickup. We headed out and camped and cooked by the side of the road. . . . It was July and it sure was hot. We stopped at a service station on the desert for gas and were so thirsty for a cold drink, but water was ten cents a glass. Some servicemen out on maneuvers gave us a canteen of cold water for the baby's bottle and we filled her bottle and drank the rest.

Katie Grant, who during the war years found work at a fish cannery and then in the Richmond shipyards, in "Wartime Memories," 1.

I spent a great deal of time in bathing suits for pinups. Even that was part of the war effort. . . . [O]ur careers were built on the war-camp walls.

Movie star Evelyn Keyes recalling the war years, quoted in Hoopes, Americans Remember, *171.*

I'd never worked in my life. . . . I loved the look of welding, the smell of it. You'd look through really dark glass and all you'd see was the glow. You moved the welding rod in tiny, circular motions, making half-crescents. If you did it right, it was beautiful. It was like embroidery.

Phyllis McKey Gould, welder at the Kaiser shipyards, quoted in Brown, "'Rosie the Riveter' Honored in California Memorial," New York Times, *October 22, 2000, 76.*

"By golly," said C.M., "if I ever win the $1000 bond [in the Work-to-Win bond drawings held each month], I'm going to take it and say, 'Thank you, I'm terminating!'" . . . At that particular moment, I am ashamed to say, we had completely lost our enthusiasm for building bombers and winning the war. We found out later that all women workers felt the same way on their second aching night of work—and many of them did terminate. One girl who had come in with our own group quit after an hour and twenty minutes on the job.

Schoolteacher Constance Bowman, working for the summer (year unnamed) at an aircraft plant, Slacks and Callouses, *43.*

The second summer [that I worked at the plant, 1944] . . . there was a wildcat strike. The plants had gotten awards—you remember the "E" awards [from the military] for excellence if you met certain production schedules? We were proud of this in the plant, and we were concerned about the negotiations that were going on. . . . A lot of people did walk out, but I refused to. . . . I didn't think it was right. . . .

University of Wisconsin student Mary Dandouveris, who worked during wartime summers as a riveter in an airplane factory, quoted in Hoopes, Americans Remember, *103.*

Once [at the shipyard] I went down into a submarine and the power went off and you're walking just on beams, and I had to stay there for about two and a half hours and not move because of all the electrical equipment. A man had been electrocuted above decks, and that had caused the power outage. . . . These jobs during the war certainly broadened my view, my outlook on life. . . . I was a narrow-minded girl who lived in a cloistered community and now after the war, and all my experience and everything, I could see the other side.

Geraldine Amidon Berkey, electrical inspector, recalling experiences probably from 1942 to 1945, in Wise and Wise, Mouthful of Rivets, *8, 9.*

[On the seismic crew] I worked on the records and did the geology work. I really enjoyed that. I got to make maps [because] there was a guy on the crew who didn't like to make maps and I did.

Joy Hampton, who for three years—from 1942 to 1945—traveled through the Southwest testing for good oil drilling locations, in Wise and Wise, Mouthful of Rivets, *61.*

I was only there two weeks when they made me a woman counselor. They didn't call a woman a shop steward. Since the men didn't like having women in the shipyard, the girls had to come to me with problems and if I couldn't handle them, I had to take them to the north yard to have them cleared up.

Matilda Hoffman Becky Havers recollecting 1942, when she worked at General Electric in New Jersey, in Wise and Wise, Mouthful of Rivets, *35.*

I was either just eighteen or not quite eighteen. . . . [The managers at Pratt and Whitney] were desperate for people to work. They put me into a training program for about two months. . . . I got this certified machinist certificate. . . . I really wouldn't mind doing it again. . . .

I remember some of the older guys who had been there for years used to say, "Hey, kid, don't be in such a hurry!" But I'd get into the thing and geared up for it and I'd just keep plugging away, measuring and grinding, measuring and grinding, and they'd say, "Hey, kid, take it easy." They'd been doing it for fifteen or twenty years, and they didn't want me approaching what they had done at the end of the day because then they didn't look good, and of course they could do it with one hand tied behind their backs.

Machinist Patricia Megargee reminiscing about 1942, quoted in Hoopes, Americans Remember, *90–91.*

[T]he Los Angeles CIO asks equal rights for women so there will be no repetition of the blunders of 1918

Women war workers dance the Lindy Hop during a break. *(Collection of Penny Caccavo)*

when women were used to create a fluid labor market and to beat down wage scales.

> CIO News, *quoted in Campbell,* Women at War, *147, citing Office of War Information, Bureau of Intelligence, "Women and the War," Media Division Report 62, August 6, 1942, 6.*

I never did anything more mechanical than replace a blown-out fuse. But after the war broke out I wasn't satisfied with keeping house and playing bridge. . . . The foreman [at Consolidated in Fort Worth, Texas] asked if I could run a lathe. I said, "I can, if you'll show me how." He did, and I've been at it ever since.

> War worker Frances DeWitt, in the Saturday Evening Post, *May 30, 1942, 31.*

What are you doing to prevent the spread of the day nursery system which I regard as a most unfortunate reaction to the hysterical propaganda about recruiting women workers?

> Secretary of Labor Frances Perkins to Katherine Lenroot, June 26, 1942, chief of the Children's Bureau, in Children's Bureau, Department of Labor Records, National Archives, Record Group 102.2, 1942.

May we suggest that care be observed not to create the impression that women engaged in any phase of war work, whether with the military services, in civilian war agencies or in war industry, are more tempted or more susceptible to extra-marital dalliance than others? War service, rather, should be depicted as a regenerative influence, by example.

> Magazine Bureau's War Guide Supplement for Confession Magazines, *September 11, 1942, quoted in Honey,* Creating Rosie the Riveter, *154.*

[In Connecticut] a woman in the graveyard shift drives her car close to the windows of the place where she is employed and her four children sleep in the automobile. . . . First let it be understood that this country has long had a serious child care problem never adequately met. Now the industrial upheaval of war is blowing up the child care problem to the proportions of an enormous and thinly stretched balloon.

> "Eight-Hour Orphans," Saturday Evening Post, *October 10, 1942, 20.*

[These "government girls"] were young, eager, believing they were helping to win the war, as no doubt they were, feeling that as young women they were for the first time in their lives being taken seriously as individuals and allowed some responsibility. And [their pay of] $1,440 a year was more than most of them had ever made in their lives.

> Newsman David Brinkley recalling 1943, *in Brinkley,* Memoir, *52.*

We now have about $780 in the bank and 5 bonds, which sho looks good to me and as soon as I can get the buggie [baby boy] in good shape we can really pile it away.

> Polly Crow, swing shift worker at the Jefferson Boat Company, letter to her husband, probably in 1943, *quoted in Ambrose,* Americans at War, *141.*

The real situation is that unless industry draws 2.8 million more [women] away from household or school duties in 1943 . . . production quotas will have to be revised down.

> "Labor, Women — Now!" Business Week, *January 9, 1943, 72.*

Women who maintain jobs outside their homes . . . weaken family life, endanger their own marital happiness, rob themselves of man's protective capabilities, and by consequence decrease the number of children. The principal evil in women's work is that it alienates the life of the wife from the life of the husband and gives marriage as much permanence as the room sharing of two freshmen at boarding school.

> Winifred Hayes, "Woman's Place in the Future World Order," in Catholic World, *August 1943, 482–486.*

I'm glad you haven't turned the old house into just a headquarters, Mom; I'm glad you're keeping it our home, the way it was. That's the way I feel about it out here, that is also part of a woman's war job—keeping up the home, the homes we're fighting for, that some day we want to come back to.

> Soldier in Office of War Information film, *released December 30, 1943, quoted in Honey,* Creating Rosie the Riveter, *133.*

The Merchant Marine

In expanding our shipping, we have had to enlist many thousands of men for our Merchant Marine. These men are serving magnificently. They are risking their lives every hour so that guns and tanks and planes and ammunitions and food may be carried to the heroic defenders of Stalingrad and to all the United Nations' forces all over the world.

President Franklin D. Roosevelt, fireside chat, Columbus Day, 1942, available online. Mid-Hudson Regional Information Center URL: www.mhric.org/fdr/fdr.html.

In behalf of the men in my command, I thank the men of the Merchant Marine for their pledge of full cooperation in our common effort to destroy the forces of tyranny and darkness. The huge quantities of supplies that have been brought across the Atlantic are a testimonial to the job that has already been done.

Gen. Dwight D. Eisenhower, cable to War Shipping Administration, June 28, 1944, available online. "Quotes about American Merchant Marine." URL: www.usmm.org/quotes.html/#anchor.2778810.

The men and ships of the Merchant Marine have participated in every landing operation by the United States Marine Corps from Guadalcanal to Iwo Jima—and we know they will be at hand with supplies and equipment when American amphibious forces hit the beaches of Japan itself.

Lt. Gen. Alexander A. Vandegrift, U.S. Marine Corps commandant, speaking probably in 1944 or 1945, quoted in "U.S. Merchant Marine in World War II," 7, available online. URL: www.usmm.org/ww2.html.

6
Military Life: The U.S. Army and the European Theater of Operations
September 3, 1939–May 8, 1945

HISTORICAL CONTEXT

"There are really two wars and they haven't much to do with each other. There is the war of maps and logistics, of campaigns, of ballistics, armies, divisions and regiments—and that is General [George] Marshall's war. Then there is the war of the homesick, weary, funny, violent, common men who wash their socks in their helmets, complain about the food, whistle at the Arab girls, or any girls for that matter, and bring themselves through as dirty a business as the world has ever seen and do it with humor and dignity and courage."

—John Steinbeck[1]

On December 7, 1941, the Japanese attacked the U.S. naval base at Pearl Harbor, Hawaii, destroying much of the U.S. Pacific Fleet. Immediately Americans of all ethnicities rallied to the war effort, whether in industry or in the military. Young men rushed to enlist in the army, navy, and Marine Corps in such numbers that no conscription was needed for most of 1942. Prominent among them were American Indians, so many of whom volunteered that conscription would have been unnecessary had the rest of the population joined up in the same proportions.[2]

These volunteers swelled the ranks of servicemen who, thanks to the foresight of President Franklin D. Roosevelt, had been drafted and trained after the outbreak of the European war in September 1939. Ultimately the Axis powers—Germany, Italy, and Japan—would face 16.3 million American servicemen and servicewomen of a bewildering diversity: whites, blacks, Jews and gentiles,

121

Native Americans, Asian Americans, Latinos, and Filipinos, rich and poor, educated and little more than illiterate.[3] In the course of the war Germans would come to dread the Black Panthers who in their tanks spearheaded Patton's drive through France and would name the Tuskegee Airmen "Black Birdmen." Inmates of German concentration camps would be bewildered at being liberated by Japanese-American soldiers. The Japanese could not break American codes based on Native American languages.

According to the U.S. Department of Defense, the total number of American military personnel mobilized during World War II from 1941 to 1946 was 16,112,566. Of these 11,260,000 served in the army; 4,183,466 in the navy; and 669,100 in the marines, in 57 different countries. A total of 291,557 were killed in combat; 113,842 died of other causes; and 671,846 suffered wounds that were not mortal.[4] The USSR mobilized 22 million people, and Great Britain 12 million.[5]

The Army: The Draft and Volunteering

In September 1939, the U.S. Army consisted of fewer than 188,000 men.[6] Ranking 17th in the world, the institution was as outmoded in its thinking as in its numbers and equipment. Some diehards among its planners wanted to keep the cavalry; on the other hand, some fantasized that precision bombing from safe altitudes could win the war.[7]

On September 16, 1940, with war raging in Europe and U.S.-Japanese relations worsening, the U.S. Congress first passed Selective Service legislation, authorizing a draft of no more than 900,000 men to be inducted into the military for a year, but forbidding their use outside the Western Hemisphere.

The Ephrata, Lancaster County, Pennsylvania, Draft Board No. 5 meets in November 1942. *Left to right:* W. E. Buchholder (chairman), justice of the peace, and insurance and real estate man; Harold Shirker, full-time clerk; George C. Ballman, secretary, hat manufacturer; John L. Bowman, attorney. *(Library of Congress, LC-USW3-011765-D)*

Accordingly, on October 16, 16,500,000 men registered, and on October 29 the first lottery was held to determine who among them would serve. By the time the first draftees were actually called to duty, the world situation had deteriorated, and Americans had begun to see war as inevitable. So many men had volunteered that the navy had all it needed. On December 20, 1941, after the attack on Pearl Harbor, a new law required all males 18–65 to register and made those 20–45 eligible for military service. By the spring of 1943 the army had expanded to 4.3 million.[8] By the end of the war in 1945, 31 million men had registered, of whom just over 10 million were drafted.[9] Throughout the war regulations about deferments and age limitations shifted. Eventually the Marine Corps and the navy took 17-year-olds, but the army set its lower limit at 18.

The military drew its officer corps from older, better-educated people. In addition to graduates of the service academies, the military provided several other ways to become an officer: Officer Candidate Schools operated by the separate branches; the Reserve Officer Training Corps (ROTC) at colleges and universities; the navy's V-5 (for aviation cadets) and V-12 programs (for surface line officers) initiated during the war at 131 colleges and universities across the nation; the accelerated Marine Corps Platoon Leaders programs; direct commissions, awarded early in the war to civilians who had skills that the military needed; and battlefield commissions, awarded to enlisted men who displayed extraordinary valor and leadership in combat.

The influx of servicemen from November 1940 onward created huge problems of training, equipment, and supply. Tiny cadres of noncommissioned officers from the small U.S. regular army suddenly were tasked with training hundreds of thousands of men. The weapons and equipment given the draftees and the volunteers were outmoded; some of them were issued wooden models of guns with which to drill. With isolationism still strong within the United States and the nation still far from persuaded that it must enter the war, the draftees of course griped and grumbled and wrote to First Lady Eleanor Roosevelt to complain. Gradually American industry began to supply better equipment and the army began to respond to the need for modernization. Military observers returning from Europe introduced new methods of training. Morale improved. As the United States gained combat experience, the army would bring back combat veterans to teach what they had learned.

The gradual flow of volunteers throughout 1941 spurted into a torrent after Pearl Harbor. They had mixed motives: patriotism; a craving for adventure; anger at what most Americans regarded as a sneak attack by the Japanese; fury at the losses inflicted on the navy; a sense that the world could not afford to allow the Germans, Italians, and Japanese to succeed in their aggressions; a feeling that the evil abroad in the world must be stopped. Many recognized this war as the event of their generation and did not want to be left out.

The Great Depression of the 1930s had deadened their hopes and spirits, starving and stunting them. The war invigorated them, offering opportunity for effective action. Moreover, for some victims of the depression, the war brought bounties, as for Kansan Charles McCauley. Forced to drop out of high school after a year, he studied on his own to pass the entrance examinations for pilots. As a trainee he marveled, "Just imagine what I was getting for free. It cost the government seventeen dollars an hour for a plane to be in the air. I also got my living quarters, food and pay of seventy-five dollars per month!" As an officer he rejoiced: "I have been told that I will need to pay ninety dollars in income tax for 1944. This is the first time I have ever heard of this tax. I guess I am making too much money now. We draw $246 per month, pay for food at thirty-five dollars, and my War Bond is seventy-five dollars, leaving $129. I still think Uncle Sam has been pretty good to me."[10]

Army Assignments

Only a relatively small proportion of American soldiers made the invasions and fought on the front lines. Of the 11 million men in the U.S. Army in 1945, only 2 million were in combat divisions, of whom fewer than 700,000 were in the infantry—the "grunts" who did the fighting and most of the dying: They suffered 70 percent of the casualties.[11] Every man in combat required 10 men in support.[12] Young single men constituted a majority of these ground combat troops.

Most soldiers were assigned to the service and technical forces: the Chemical Warfare Service, the Corps of Engineers, the Medical Department, the Ordnance Department, the Quartermaster Corps, the Signal Corps, and the Transportation Corps. They supported the combat troops by training them; planning the battles the combat troops fought; transporting them; supplying them with food, shelter, clothing, weapons, and ammunition; buying and servicing their equipment; caring for the sick and wounded; operating the postal and financial services and the chaplaincy; running newspapers (*The Stars and Stripes* and base newspapers) and magazines (*Yank* and various unit publications); keeping records on them; getting them paid; running stores for them; and providing them with entertainment and rest-and-recreation facilities—all the multifarious tasks required to operate a modern military. Although they faced enemy guns only in unusual crisis situations, the millions who went

American servicemen relax at the bar at the United Services Organization in Oswego, New York, June 1943. *(Library of Congress, LC-USW3-031516-D)*

overseas in support capacities were still at substantial risk—of accidents, submarines, the V-1 and V-2 bombs that the Germans rained on England, or the kamikaze planes in the Pacific.

Army Strategy

After Pearl Harbor, with the U.S. declaration of war on Japan and the German and Italian declarations of war on the United States that immediately followed that attack, the United States was a full-fledged member of the Allied powers. By that time the Allied leaders—Roosevelt, Churchill, and Stalin—had already agreed on targeting Germany and Italy before Japan, and on concentrating planes and armaments in the European theater of operations (ETO) first. At the same time the United States had to rebuild and supply its navy to fight Japan in the Pacific.

Although the Allied nations shared the common goal of defeating the Axis nations, jealousies and differences on strategy arose among them. Their leaders had to take into account political as well as military realities. President Roosevelt was far more hopeful about the Soviet premier Joseph Stalin's good faith than was the British prime minister Winston Churchill. Hitler had sent his armies to invade the Soviet Union on June 22, 1941, and the fighting that developed on that front was prolonged, bloody, and bitter, costing millions of lives. Consequently Stalin pressed his allies to invade France as soon as possible, to gain some relief for the embattled Soviet army. Worried about a possible defeat, Churchill dragged his heels, insisting on invading first North Africa, Sicily, and Italy. Roosevelt's personal friendship with Churchill was stronger than with Stalin, just as the ties between Great Britain and the United States were stronger than those between the Americans and the Soviets. Nonetheless Roosevelt favored an earlier invasion of France. He mediated between Stalin and Churchill, conciliating first one, then the other. On the next lower level, the American general Dwight Eisenhower as supreme commander in the ETO had to reconcile differences between British and American generals.

Roosevelt also had to handle interservice rivalries among the U.S. Army, the U.S. Navy, and the Marine Corps, which persisted throughout the war. Commanders competed for men, equipment, and supplies—all too scanty in the early days of the war. Cocky young marines taunted infantrymen with accusations of cowardice, failing to recognize that they were older, wiser, and more experienced. Ultimately, however, the services had no choice but to depend on one another, and some men recognized the valor of other services. For instance, Cpl. William Preston wrote his father after the invasion of Normandy: "I cannot say enough for the Navy for the way they brought us in, for the firepower they brought to bear on the beach. Whenever any of us fired a burst of tracer at a target, the destroyers, standing in so close they were almost ashore, fired a shot immediately after us, each time hitting what we were firing at on the nose."[13]

Confronted with a two-ocean war, the United States assigned major responsibility for fighting in the ETO to its army. Nonetheless, even though the army operated a larger number of ships and watercraft (troop ships, cargo ships, hospital ships, repair boats, tankers, coastal freighters, tugboats, launches, amphibious assault craft, barges, and pontoon sections) than the navy,[14] the army relied on the navy to battle the German submarines that infested the Atlantic, to transport troops across the Atlantic to battlefields in North Africa and Europe, and to back up every invasion with bombardments. The army also depended on the civilian merchant marine to transport supplies, under conditions of great hazard. Similarly, the country entrusted to the navy and the Marine Corps the brunt of the war in the Pacific, but army infantrymen fought side by side with marines in the agonizing battles to retake Pacific islands, and army troops under the command of Gen. Douglas MacArthur warred in the China-Burma-India theater.

The navy also had to evolve a method of combating the Axis submarines that wreaked so much havoc on shipping in the Atlantic. At British and American naval insistence, in January 1943 the Casablanca conference of Allied leaders gave priority to antisubmarine warfare. Early in the war the British and Canadians developed antisubmarine tactics and escort vessels more effective than those of the United States. By 1944, however, the U.S. Navy had worked out the hunter-killer groups built around escort carriers that eventually defeated the submarine menace and enabled the enormous lift of men, supplies, and equipment necessary for the invasion of Normandy that spring.

The Enemy

During World War II up until the discovery of the concentration camps in which the Nazis interned, tortured, starved, and murdered Jews, gypsies, homosexuals, and those they considered their political enemies, Americans directed their enmity toward the Nazi party and its leaders—particularly Adolf Hitler—not the German people as a whole. For one thing, millions of Americans had German ancestors and relatives. Many admired German culture, particularly German music, and German military skills.[15] American soldiers made a distinction between the German SS—elite, fanatical Nazi troops, whom they hated as ruthless—and other German soldiers. Generally speaking, they trusted Germans to play by the rules.

In fact, of course, no nation played by the rules all the time. Every army had its sadists. Exhausted soldiers who had just seen their friends killed or suffering took their own revenge. Armies moving fast did not want to bother with prisoners or spare the men to guard them. The longer the war went on, the more violations there were. Germans did their worst at Malmédy in France in December 1944, when SS officers and men killed 107 American prisoners of war in cold blood; 43 others escaped by feigning death.[16] Nevertheless, most of the time in most places American and German troops maintained some sort of mutual understanding of the rules of war.[17]

The North Africa Campaign—Operation Torch (November 8, 1942–May 12, 1943)

Because the Italians, French, and British had empires in North Africa, the Axis and Allied powers had been battling in that region since 1939.[18] Even though many Americans sympathized with African desires for liberation from European domination, as an Ally the United States was drawn into this conflict. Moreover, it was vital to secure the Suez Canal and thus control access to India. American engagement began in cooperation with the British in Operation Torch, the invasion of Northwest Africa, on November 8, 1942. American forces under the command of Gen. Dwight D. Eisenhower and British forces under Gen. Bernard Montgomery opposed German troops commanded by Field Marshal Erwin Rommel, whose strategic successes had earned him the nickname "The Desert Fox." At the outset, power struggles among the French and inadequate Allied communications with them caused some, known as "Vichy French," to scuttle their fleet, which the Allies had hoped to acquire. Others, however, known as the "Free French," fought on the side of the Allies.

The Allies succeeded in dominating the coastline in Libya, Algeria, and Morocco, but the arrival of more German forces from Europe beginning on November 16 changed the course of events. The Germans were deployed to hold the eastern Atlas mountains against Eisenhower's advance and resist attacks by the British and French on Tunis and Bizerte.

In the early days of the North Africa campaign, Americans made a poor showing, not for lack of courage, but for lack of good training and military skills. In the words of Gen. Omar N. Bradley, "[I]t was fortunate . . . that the U.S. Army first met the enemy on the periphery, in Africa rather than on the beaches of France. In Africa we learned to crawl, then walk—then run. Had the learning process been launched in France, it would surely have . . . resulted in an unthinkable disaster."[19]

These Americans were inexperienced soldiers and sailors facing an enemy already hardened by years of battle. Even the best training cannot demonstrate the actualities of war, and in the early days the men's training had been pitiably insufficient. Their officers had not yet learned to coordinate combined operations of airplanes, infantry, artillery, and armor. Commanders had yet to learn to allow time for caring for the wounded, handling enemy prisoners, rearming and refueling, and gathering and analyzing intelligence. Enlisted men had not yet learned to move forward under fire and to move out from underneath shell fire; infantrymen had to generate more small-arms firepower, and artillerymen more heavy-weapons firepower. Men coming under fire had to learn to restrain their impulse to bunch up, to avoid presenting too easy a target. Armor leaders had to adapt deployment of their tanks to the terrain. Bombardiers and artillerymen had to learn how to maneuver and to keep to a minimum deaths from "friendly fire"—their own. Fighting men on land had to learn how to detect, disarm, and clear mines and booby traps, and both on land and at sea they had to learn how to identify enemy planes and vehicles and to evaluate the capabilities of enemy weapons, as well as how to maintain themselves, their equipment, and their weapons.

The Americans suffered humiliation at the Kasserine Pass in mid-February 1943 when only British intervention enabled the defeat of a German effort to dislodge them. But they rallied under Gen. George Patton to cooperate with British general Bernard Montgomery's troops to skirt the German line and ultimately defeat the German forces in Tunisia, who suffered from a lack of supplies caused by successful Allied attacks on Axis shipping.

All in all, for the Americans in particular and the Allies in general, North Africa was a learning experience. But learn they did, and thanks to the bravery and persistence of British, American, and Free-French fighting men, thanks to the flow of weapons and equipment that American factories were already turning out, and thanks to the British and American sailors and merchantmen who despite German submarines transported supplies, the Allies conquered. The turning point came in early March with Montgomery's victory at the battle of Medenine. In mid-May 275,000 Germans and Italians, the remainder of the Axis forces, surrendered in Tunisia.[20]

The Sicily Campaign—Operation Husky (July 10, 1943–August 17, 1943)

After the Allied victory in North Africa, an invasion of Sicily seemed an obvious next step for the Allies to control the Mediterranean Sea and possibly to secure a foothold for an attack on Europe itself. In what became standard operating procedure, Allied ships shelled and Allied planes bombed ports in preparation, and Allied paratroopers were dropped to seize enemy airfields. To deceive the enemy the Allies intimated an attack on Sardinia, planting bogus plans on a dead body that washed up in Spain.

The invasion itself began in force on July 10, 1943, with powerful air and naval cover. The 230,000 Italian troops on Sicily offered only light resistance, and naval gunfire soon helped overcome their counterattacks. The U.S. Third Army under the command of Gen. George Patton swiftly cut a path across the center of the island to the north coast and thence eastward toward Messina. Heavy resistance from some of the 80,000 German troops on the island slowed Allied advances, particularly that of the British commanded by Montgomery, delaying their joining up with the Americans.[21] However, the Allies overcame by resorting to a series of amphibious attacks to dislodge the enemy. The British and Americans reached Messina on August 17, but meanwhile the Axis powers had evacuated most of their troops and equipment.

Operation Husky, as the attack on Sicily was known, contributed to the downfall of the Italian dictator Benito Mussolini, whose resignation the Fascist Grand Council requested on July 25, and soon thereafter he was arrested and then killed by mob action. In his place the Italian king Victor Emmanuel appointed as prime minister Marshal Pietro Badoglio, who secretly began negotiations with the Allies. Left with only a shadow army, the Italians signed an unconditional surrender on September 3. But the Germans fought on in Italy, formidably opposing Allied troops.

The Campaigns in Italy and the Balkans (September 8, 1943–December 31, 1944)

In the disagreements over strategy among the Allies, the Soviet Union and the United States usually favored concentrating on invading France as soon as practicable, while Great Britain argued, more often than not successfully, for a series of smaller invasions elsewhere—North Africa, the Mediterranean, and Italy. After Sicily, the British encountered defeat in some of their incursions into Italy. The Allies who landed at Salerno on September 8, 1943, ran into stiff

German resistance but managed to stay ashore and began to slog their way northward in bloody fighting. Month after month Allied troops drawn from the United States, the United Kingdom, Canada, India, New Zealand, French Morocco, Poland, and eventually South Africa and Brazil struggled against the Germans, with heavy losses. Sometimes they bogged down. At the Garigliano River, the American engineer commander charged with clearing mines and bridging the river warned that "an attack through a muddy valley that was without suitable approach routes and exit roads and that was blocked by organised [sic] defences behind an unfordable river [would] create an impossible situation and result in a great loss of life."[22] The attempt failed at the cost of 1,000 American lives.

Partly to circumvent such barriers, partly to secure a base for future amphibious operations, on January 24, 1944, the Allies landed at Anzio, north of the German line. The Americans and British got ashore with large numbers of men and vehicles but they were pinned down for the next four months.

In yet another attempt to fight northward toward Rome, Allied troops with heavy air support assaulted Monte Cassino four times between February 12 and May 17, 1944, succeeding only in the last attempt. Promptly thereafter, on May 23, American infantry and British armor surged northward and the Allies stranded at Anzio at last broke through the German lines. Rome was declared an open city, and the Germans retreated—but in a fighting withdrawal, not in a rout. In August 1944 they established yet another line of defense that ran across the boot of Italy a little north of Florence.

Meanwhile the Allies withdrew some of their troops from Italy for Operation Anvil, a landing in the south of France between Cannes and Toulon on August 15. Though on a reduced scale, fighting continued in Italy, inflicting heavy losses on both sides. In December 1944 the Allied campaign dragged to a halt. The heroic engineers who rebuilt blown bridges, dismantled demolition charges and booby traps, bulldozed a way through ruined towns, and cleared harbors choked with sunken ships, and the equally heroic infantry who renewed their assaults repeatedly against well-nigh impregnable mountains and rivers knew all too well that after the invasion of Normandy on June 6, 1944, they were fighting a marginal campaign. Military resources and the attention of the world were concentrated on the battles to reach and crush Germany through France.

Meanwhile after the surrender of Italy the Yugoslav communist guerrillas under Josip Broz, Marshal Tito, began to pose a real threat to Germany's domination of the Balkans, important to the Axis particularly because of the Romanian oil fields. At the same time the threatened and actual defections of the Balkan states from the Axis with the approach of the Soviet armies further weakened the German grasp of the area.

Men of the 370th Infantry Regiment move up through Prato, Italy, April 9, 1945. *(National Archives, 111-SC-205289)*

The Normandy Invasion—Operation Overlord—and the Battle for France (June 6, 1944–September 15, 1944)

In September 1942 Hitler told five of his most important officials that if an Allied invasion could be delayed beyond the spring of 1943, "Nothing can happen to us any longer. . . . We have got over the worst of our foodstuffs shortage. By increased production of anti-aircraft guns and ammunition the home base will be protected against air raids. In the spring we shall march with our finest divisions down into Mesopotamia and then one day we shall force our enemies to make peace where and as we want."[23] To the Allies also the invasion of France seemed almost impossible. The Germans had taken advantage of their mastery over much of Europe to fortify the coast heavily. *Festung Europa*—Fortress Europe—looked impregnable. Yet to win unconditional surrender the Allies had no choice. Even as the first forces landed on the beaches of Normandy on the long-awaited D day, June 6, 1944, General Eisenhower, supreme Allied commander of the ETO, had in his pocket a press release that he had composed in case they failed. He had been warned that the Germans might defend against the invasion by establishing a lethal radioactive barrier on the beaches, or by exploding an atomic bomb.[24]

Preparations had been long and complicated for this, the greatest invasion and one of the most daring in the history of the world. It involved 5,000 vessels; 200,000 men in the initial assault; 2 million men landed over 109 days; 500,000 vehicles; and 17 million ship tons of supplies.[25] Both Eisenhower and Montgomery, who would command the landing force, checked the planning and insisted on strengthening all elements of the forces involved. To divert Ger-

Yankee soldiers crouch in a Coast Guard landing barge crossing the English Channel to Normandy, June 1944. *(Library of Congress, LC-USZ62-92432)*

man troops from the real landing site in Normandy, the Allies plotted to persuade the Germans that they would land in the Pas-de-Calais, developing a fictitious American army group in England opposite Calais, making false radio transmissions from its site, mentioning the firebrand American general George S. Patton as its commander, scattering wooden models of military vehicles in the area to deceive spy planes, and heavily bombing the fictitious landing region in France.

To prepare for D day, Allied planes attacked German fortifications and transportation systems. Minesweepers cleared channels for the ships. For the actual invasion, the Allies constructed two artificial floating harbors, which would be towed in once the beaches were secured. Airborne troops transported in planes and gliders would drop inland. Paratroopers would jump from 1,000 planes; frail steel-frame canvas-and-wood engineless gliders filled with infantry, artillery, and engineers would be cut loose from their tow planes and piloted to earth. Most soldiers and equipment, however, would come from the sea, carried across the English Channel by an armada of ships and boats and nearer to the beaches in landing craft. The seven naval forces, composed of 6,483 vessels that constituted the armada, would meet in mid-Atlantic and proceed in parallel columns to the five beaches, known by code names, on which the infantry and amphibious tanks would debark: Utah on the west, then Omaha, Gold, Juno, and on the east Sword. Seven battleships, 23 cruisers, and 104 destroyers would bombard the coastal batteries in Europe, assisted by rocket-firing landing craft that could go closer in. Infantry would land first, followed immediately by beach parties to set up traffic control and signal stations, organize obstacle clearance, and evacuate casualties; and air controllers to call in rocket, bomb, and machine-gun strikes from the air. The planners knew that the Allies would control the sea and the air: 5,000 Allied fighter planes would overwhelm the 169 the Germans could put up on the Channel coast; and German naval defenses were equally insignificant. The problem was getting onto the strongly fortified beaches.[26]

Eisenhower made an agonizing decision to invade on June 6, 1944, despite bad weather and a rough sea. He had already postponed the invasion by one day, and if he postponed further, weather experts warned, favorable conditions of time, weather, and moonlight could not be expected for some time. Moreover, the risks of German discovery of the true landing sites constantly increased, and the Allied servicemen had already screwed their courage to the sticking point twice.

The invasion began before dawn with the dropping of the paratroopers and gliders. The British made a good drop and proceeded immediately to their task of blowing up or holding designated bridges. The Americans, dropped by inexperienced pilots, were separated; some drowned in areas that had been defensively flooded; others were lost as far as 25 miles from their objectives. Yet even this foul-up added to the confusion of the Germans. One group of wandering Americans captured a German general who did not know that the invasion had begun.

The German defenders above Omaha beach awoke that morning to an awesome sight. They stood with their machine guns and rockets in their concrete bunkers atop the cliffs overlooking the landing sites, where the beaches were mined, covered with obstacles, and strung with barbed wire, and the sea beyond mined and filled with obstacles. Yet that morning they gazed at an armada that covered the ocean to the horizon.

Things went smoothly for the Americans on Utah beach, who took only 197 casualties among the 23,000 men landed.[27] The British and Canadians who hit Sword and Juno beaches met more resistance but were able to get ashore and moved inland with dispatch. On Gold, also assigned to British and Canadians, one brigade proceeded apace, but the other took heavy casualties when it ran into fortifications untouched by the bombardment; nonetheless the division by nightfall had advanced almost to Bayeux. But the Americans assigned to Omaha beach, most efficiently defended by terrain, fortifications, and well-trained German troops, underwent a terrible ordeal. They took most of the 4,649 casualties inflicted on Americans that day.[28] The seasick men had endured a rough channel crossing. The landing craft could not approach as near the shore as planned and debarked the men in water too deep for wading. In their heavy clothing and equipment, some drowned. Their Sherman tanks foundered, depriving them of fire support. Nevertheless, some of the troops got ashore, braved the dash across the sand and shale to the steep cliffs, scaled them under direct enemy fire, destroyed the concrete pillboxes atop them, and began to press inland and toward the port of Cherbourg. Against the odds, by miracles of coordination and the courage and self-sacrifice of the men who fought, the Allies had won the day.

In the next few days, while thousands of men and tons of equipment surged on to the beaches to reinforce them, the Allies from the several beaches linked up. As they pushed inland, they encountered a new problem—fighting through the ten-foot-thick hedgerows that bounded the French fields and offered cover for German gun emplacements. As American general Norman D. Cota commented, "[W]e originally were organized to assault the beach, suffered a lot of casualties among key men, then hit another kind of warfare for which we were not organized. We had to assemble replacements and reorganize."[29] They also had to improvise. For a while they relied on paratroopers to jump behind the Germans, but eventually they figured out how to alter tanks so that they could cut a way through the hedgerows.

For weeks, however, the Allies could not break out of the Contentin peninsula, even with the new technique of carpet-bombing, by which bombardiers prepared the ground for a battle by bombing every inch of it, and followed up by direct bombing attacks on enemy troops. Finally on July 25, with yet more carpet bombings and an assault by a tank force commanded by General Patton, the Germans retreated and the Allies rapidly advanced in a confusion that caused one artilleryman to exclaim: "The boss done f——ed up, he has got us here ahead of the infantry."[30] Patton put it differently: "We passed through the corridor [at Avranches] 2 infantry and 2 armored divisions in less than 24 hours. There was no plan because it was impossible to make a plan."[31] This breakthrough not only enabled the Allies to push toward Paris but also helped them to trap Germans in the "Falaise Pocket," from which they escaped only by abandoning 200,000 prisoners, 50,000 dead, and masses of wrecked equipment.[32] All in all, the battle of Normandy cost the Allies 209,671 casualties and 39,976 dead; two-thirds of the losses were American. It cost the Germans about 450,000 men, 240,000 of them killed or wounded and the others prisoners of war.[33]

Meanwhile, on August 15 in Operation Anvil, another Allied army had invaded southern France and raced up the Rhone valley. Its men joined with the forces that had invaded Normandy and with Free-French general Charles de Gaulle and the inhabitants of Paris itself to liberate that city. By August 25, 1944, German resistance there had ceased.

The Battle for France (September 1, 1944–March 1, 1945)

By mid-September the Allies had freed Belgium, Luxembourg, and part of Holland, and were preparing to cross the Meuse River. In their haste to penetrate Germany, they did not take all of the Channel ports, an omission that caused them supply problems and permitted Germans to continue to launch V-2 unmanned missile-rockets against London from Antwerp. German troops fought ever more fiercely as they fell back toward their homeland. As winter set in the Allies were stalled in the Huertgen Forest, before the Saar River, and in Strasbourg. Helped by snowstorms that prevented the Allies from using planes, on December 16 Hitler launched a winter offensive in the Ardennes Forest in France near Bastogne, an action that became known as the Battle of the Bulge. Some of the Allied defenders were inexperienced; some were exhausted men who had been sent to this portion of the line to recover. All of them suffered in the intense cold and waist-deep snow. Their khaki uniforms stood out against the snow until they borrowed sheets from local residents for camouflage. Nonetheless they fought indomitably, in a spirit expressed by Gen. Anthony C. McAuliffe when, his troops surrounded within Bastogne, he rejected a German demand for surrender with the word, "Nuts." Soon after Christmas the weather cleared, allowing air support and supply, and Patton's tanks broke through to relieve the beleaguered troops. Montgomery launched a counterattack, and by January 16 the German offensive had failed. In the month it lasted the Germans killed 19,000 Americans and took 15,000 prisoners, but at the cost of 100,000 of their own men killed, wounded, or captured and 800 tanks and 1,000 aircraft lost—this at a point when, with their industries and transportation systems staggering under bombing and their manpower depleted, they had little hope of replacing personnel or equipment. The dangers of the Bulge met, the Allies pressed on until by the first week in March British, Canadian, Free French, and American troops stood ready to cross the Rhine into Germany.

The Battle for Germany (January 1945–May 7, 1945)

While their allies battled in the Ardennes, Soviet troops were breaking into Germany from the east, raging to avenge the suffering that Germany had inflicted on their country. By mid-January they were already deep into Germany, terrorizing the inhabitants, who fled before their advance. Meanwhile on the western front Eisenhower, with 4 million Allied troops at his command, planned to cross the Rhine at several points, directing his heaviest attacks at encircling the industrial Ruhr River basin. On March 7, by chance, an American armored division found an unguarded intact railroad bridge across the Rhine at Remagen and captured it. Two weeks later Patton sneaked troops across near Oppenheim; they rushed into southern Germany in a thrust that by the beginning of May carried them within 30 miles of both Prague, Czechoslovakia, and Vienna, Austria. In early

The first U.S. Army men and equipment pour across the Remagen bridge, March 11, 1945. *(National Archives, 111-SC-201973)*

April other Allied troops reached the Elbe River, where they were stopped, not by the enemy, but by orders from Eisenhower. An inter-Allied agreement dictated that they must stay where they were, just 50 miles from Berlin, while the British and Canadians cleared northern Germany, the French and other American troops occupied Bavaria, and the Soviet army took Berlin. Hitler's refusal to surrender in the face of certain defeat condemned Germans to an unnecessary prolongation of the war. He finally killed himself on April 30. The terrible Soviet siege of Berlin ended on May 2, and German forces all over Europe surrendered one by one. On May 7 Gen. Alfried Jodl signed a general surrender of German forces at Eisenhower's headquarters. The war in Europe was over. The Nazis, who had tortured and murdered and caused so many to suffer unspeakably, left behind 10 million Axis prisoners of war, 8 million German refugees, 3 million Balkan fugitives, 2 million Soviet prisoners of war, unknown numbers of concentration camp victims, and uncountable millions of slave and forced laborers in the wreckage of Europe.[34]

Servicemen's Identity

The U.S. Army was above all a citizens' army, most of whose members thought of themselves as civilians and hooted at the idea of making a career of soldiering. Most American servicemen regarded their wartime work as a disagreeable but unavoidable interruption to their real lives. Few wanted to go where they were sent. They were often frightened, bored, and lonely. Almost everyone longed for the end of the war and a return to private life. As historian Lee Kennett wrote, the GI was "suspended between two ways of life. . . . Physically he left civilian life, yet mentally he never joined the Army; he was in the service but not of it."[35]

In the military the people of the United States mingled as never before. Ph.D.s shipped out with laborers from the Chicago stockyards; Mormons and Seventh-Day Adventists served with Jews, Protestants, and Roman Catholics; Americans met their countrymen from Maine and California, North Dakota and Louisiana. No one bought his way out or hired a substitute, as in the Civil War. Civilian rank and status counted for little: in a famous cartoon by G.I. Bill Mauldin, after the war a former enlisted man hails an elevator operator: "Ah, Captain Smith! Back in uniform, I see." Almost every family had not just one but several servicemen relatives and close friends.

The servicemen learned more about their own country and their fellow citizens, as in their training they moved from one base to another within the United States. When they were shipped overseas, they learned more about the world—and the more they saw of other places, the more these homesick men idealized "God's country."[36] By contrast to the bombed-out cities and the jungles in which they fought, the United States represented a haven of safety, comfort, and peace. Egged on by media talk of "mom's apple pie," they indulged in an orgy of sentimentality.

That was their point of vulnerability. Otherwise, in contrast to the soldiers of World War I, those of World War II were a skeptical lot, wary of being lured into a European conflict, cynical about slogans like "Make the world safe for democracy." Angered by the Japanese attack at Pearl Harbor, they were grimly determined that fascists like the German leader Adolf Hitler and the Italian Benito Mussolini must be stopped. Those among them who knew or thought much about world affairs aimed to halt the efforts of Germany, Italy, and Japan to dominate the world. In the words of gunner George Odenwaller: "We wanted to get those Japanese bastards and stop that Nazi SOB."[37] But many resembled navigator Dan Villani: "I can't say I had any sense of world affairs. I cannot remember ever having conversations with my male friends in high school about the war. It was just something happening elsewhere and we were not concerned until Pearl Harbor. I don't even remember teachers ever talking about the war. It was a case of being swept up by events after Pearl Harbor. From then on, as the draft took hold, we all talked about what branch of the military we wanted to enter."[38] Most of the time most of them believed firmly in the invincibility of the United States; it simply never occurred to most Americans that they might lose the war.

All these millions of American soldiers, of course, had their own faults, and among them in both the officer and the enlisted ranks were cowards, malingerers, sadists, bigots, thieves, rapists, and murderers, some of whom took advantage of opportunities to harass and kill and torture, and some of whom evaded their duty. But most of them were decent men who did their best among all the horrors of war.

War matured some of them, like marine rifleman Earl Rice: "I think I became a man because Lieutenant Cook treated me like one. He made me a squad leader with a corporal under me. I had been the biggest s——-bird of the company and he talked of me being a sergeant. . . . I learned what discipline and responsibility were all about."[39] Others even found war redemptive, like communications specialist Ernest Schlichter: "I believe fighting for your country in the infantry in battle is the most purifying experience known to man. These men who trained hard together and fought for extended periods together became so completely unselfish, so absorbed with the welfare of the group that you could believe that their principal concern was for the 'other guy.' I've never wished to die before or since, nor did I wish to die in battle then. But I thought there was a good chance that I would, and I thought then that there was no better way to die, and no better men to be buried with."[40]

To win, Americans submitted to military discipline, but most of them were far too independent to be comfortable with it. Although in basic training and in garrison the army maintained strict obedience and formality, in the field the soldiers' independence asserted itself in ways that sometimes approached insubordination. To avoid making targets of themselves, officers wore the same uniforms as enlisted men, and in heavy fighting those men with the most energy and initiative sometimes led regardless of rank. Doubtless soldiers' accounts sometimes exaggerate their own defiance, as when Sergeant George Pope said: "I stopped the colonel right there and said, "What's the big f---ing rush? Where the f--- you think you are at, Louisiana on maneuvers? This ain't maneuvers, this is real s---, and I'm going out there, not you. . . . I didn't give a c--- about nothing."[41] But enlisted men and officers alike were capable of resisting orders that they thought violated common sense and endangered them, as when flier John Truluck told a base engineering officer: "Major, when you're flying that airplane you can put that [oxygen] regulator anywhere you damn please. But as long as my ass is up there being shot at, the oxygen regulator is going to be where I want it. I don't give a damn what you, fighter command or Wright Patterson Field [headquarters for aircraft design and engineering] says about it."[42] When in March 1945 Americans were trying to seize the bridge across the Rhine at

In 1943 in its first big raid, the Eighth Air Force attacks a Focke Wulf plant at Marienburg, Germany, at the cost of at least 80 planes and 800 men. *(National Archives, 208-YE-7)*

Remagen, Germany, one GI refused to cross, saying, "I tell you, I'm not going out there and get blown up. No sir, . . . you can court-martial and shoot me, but I ain't going out there on that bridge." Yet when 2nd Lt. Karl Timmerman led the way across, he followed.[43]

American technology, ingenuity, and adaptability helped when soldiers had to throw the book away. They knew about engines and vehicles; they had built with Erector and Meccano sets as children and constructed model airplanes and tinkered with old cars as teenagers. American military practice in the field allowed for individual improvisation. In Normandy enlisted men in armored units equipped their tanks with hedgerow cutters constructed of salvaged railroad tracks and materials from German beach obstacles. They improvised visual signals and standard operating procedures as they faced new situations. This process continued throughout the war. In the Ardennes mortarmen kept their powder rings warm by stuffing them inside their shirts, medics put drops of liquor in their canteens to keep the water from freezing, and infantry protected their rifles from moisture by slipping condoms over the barrels.

All through the ETO, the army had to develop successively new techniques as it moved from landing on the beaches to hedgerow fighting to taking towns and cities to fighting in the forests to crossing the rivers. The Eighth Air Force engineering officers arranged for local contractors to pave nose compartment floors of Liberators with boiler plate to protect the navigator and bombardier and added sheet steel plates to the sides to protect the pilot.[44] In the Pacific, where soldiers and marines had to protect against Japanese who made human bombs of themselves, they welded two-inch U-channels to tanks and bolted lumber to them, so that magnetic mines would not stick and the air space so created would dissipate the effect of a blast. They also draped extra tracks around tank turrets or over the front slope plate, fastened sandbags over the engine compartment, and welded four-inch wire bird cages over each hatch. For the foot soldiers they welded 25-gallon cans of water with spigots onto the tanks to refill canteens and placed telephones outside so that infantrymen could communicate with those inside.[45]

Men bore the stresses and strains of war as best they could. Most solaced themselves with tobacco—servicemen smoked on average two packs of cigarettes a day.[46] Many drank whatever they could get: In the European theater between October 1944 and June 1945 more soldiers died from alcohol poisoning than from acute communicable diseases.[47] They prayed fervently and asked their families and friends to pray for them.[48] They carried lucky charms. The folks at home, though far from fully informed about the realities of war, sent letters and packages to remind their soldiers of home and their love. The Red Cross and the United Service Organizations (USO) provided recreation and entertainment. The military distributed manuals on fear. The *Officer's Guide* alleged that what keeps the soldier from giving away to fear is "his desire to retain the good opinion of his friends and associates. . . . [H]is pride smothers his fear." A manual instructed the enlisted man: "Don't be too scared. Everybody is afraid, but you can learn to control your fear. And, as non-coms point out, '[Y]ou have a good chance of getting through if you don't lose your head. Being too scared is harmful to you.' Remember that a lot of noise you hear is ours, and not dangerous. It may surprise you that on the whole, many more are pulled out for sickness or accident than become battle casualties."[49]

As a group, Americans would not go blindly to certain death: Their commanders sometimes had to threaten to shoot them to get an attack going. But they did want to get the war over with; as machine gunner Gordon Larkins put it, "We saw [the fighting] as a way to get home." Despite their fears, they landed on the beaches and endured the jungle rot of the Pacific atolls and the bitter cold of Bastogne and faced death in its most horrible forms. Many of them were heroes of startling courage, sometimes unsung. Among those who won the Congressional Medal of Honor, the nation's highest award to military personnel, was Clarence Craft. His citation read in part:

With 5 comrades, Pfc. Craft was dispatched in advance of Company G to feel out the enemy resistance. The group had proceeded only a short distance up the slope when rifle and machinegun fire, coupled with a terrific barrage of grenades, wounded 3 and pinned down the others. Against odds that appeared suicidal, Pfc. Craft launched a remarkable 1-man attack. He stood up in full view of the enemy and began shooting with deadly marksmanship whenever he saw a hostile movement. He steadily advanced up the hill, killing Japanese soldiers with rapid fire, driving others to cover in their strongly disposed trenches, unhesitatingly facing alone the strength that had previously beaten back attacks in battalion strength. He reached the crest of the hill, where he stood silhouetted against the sky while quickly throwing grenades at extremely short range into the enemy positions. His extraordinary assault lifted the pressure from his company for the moment, allowing members of his platoon to comply with his motions to advance and pass him more grenades. With a chain of his comrades supplying him while he stood atop the hill, he furiously hurled a total of 2 cases of grenades into a main trench and other positions on the reverse slope of Hen Hill, meanwhile directing the aim of his fellow soldiers who threw grenades from the slope below him. He left his position, where grenades from both sides were passing over his head and bursting on either slope, to attack the main enemy trench as confusion and panic seized the defenders. Straddling the excavation, he pumped rifle fire into the Japanese at pointblank range, killing many and causing the others to flee down the trench. Pursuing them, he came upon a heavy machinegun which was still creating havoc in the American ranks. With rifle fire and a grenade he wiped out this position. By this time the Japanese were in complete rout and American forces were swarming over the hill. Pfc. Craft continued down the central trench to the mouth of a cave where many of the enemy had taken cover. A satchel charge was brought to him, and he tossed it into the cave. It failed to explode. With great daring, the intrepid fighter retrieved the charge from the cave, relighted the fuse and threw it back, sealing up the Japs in a tomb. In the local action, against tremendously superior forces heavily armed with rifles, machineguns, mortars, and grenades, Pfc. Craft killed at least 25 of the enemy; but his contribution to the campaign on Okinawa was of much more far-reaching consequence[,] for Hen Hill was the key to the entire defense line, which rapidly crumbled after his utterly fearless and heroic attack.[50]

The Airmen

In World War II airplanes, crews, and the paratroopers and gliders that they transported proved of incalculable importance. In 1940 Great Britain's Royal Air Force (RAF) saved the nation in its heroic resistance to German attacks on London, causing Churchill to remark, "Never have so many owed so much to so few." In the dark days after Pearl Harbor, an attack on Tokyo, Japan, by a small force of American planes led by Gen. Jimmy Doolittle raised American morale. On D day in June 1944, Allied control of the skies may well have made the difference between the success and failure of the Normandy invasion.

In the European theater the Allied air forces operated both independently of and in cooperation with ground and sea forces. Independently they attacked the enemy's communication and supply systems. They machine-gunned trains and bombed bridges, ports, and railroad tracks and yards. They bombed industrial targets supplying the German military in an effort to cut off such supplies as oil, roller bearings, and electrical power.

As the war dragged on they extended their attacks on factories to the areas around them where their workers lived; thereby, Allied leaders theorized, they would destroy working-class morale. Thus they justified bombing cities, a practice earlier forsworn by both the Allies and the Axis. This promise was first violated by Germany in repeated attacks on Warsaw, Poland, in 1939; Rotterdam in the Netherlands in 1940; and such British cities as London and the industrial city of Coventry in 1940. In fact in the ETO, bombing of cities proved not to be cost-effective, inflicting extremely heavy losses on the raiders and failing to destroy enemy morale; it also deprived the Allies of the high moral ground important to their own understanding of why they were fighting.

While the British bombed at night, the Americans conducted daylight raids. These were enabled by the accuracy of the Norden bombsight and the heavier armament that protected American bombers, theoretically allowing them to make their raids in daytime even before fighter escorts had the range to accompany them all the way to the targets. However, the American fliers took such heavy losses that these raids were called off in August 1943 until long-range escort fighters could be manufactured to protect the bombers. By the spring of 1944 these were ready, and raids resumed with considerably more effect. During the autumn, winter, and spring of 1944–45, between them the RAF and the U.S. Army Air Force, strengthened by the development of new fighters, paralyzed German economic life.[51]

Besides these independent operations, Allied airmen cooperated with the other services. With naval forces they attacked enemy ships. For ground forces they mapped areas to reveal enemy presence and fortifications; acted as spotters to direct artillery fire; attacked communications centers and ammunition dumps; and responded to calls from the ground to destroy machine-gun nests. One infantryman after another has attested to the value of air support and protection.

Most airmen recognized their own good fortune in living comfortably at their bases while the infantry trudged and battled through fair weather and foul, often without the comfort of hot food, warm dry clothing, and bathing facilities. On the other hand, the terrible flak (antiaircraft ground fire, or ack-ack) along the European coasts and over the cities they bombed and the enemy fighters that attacked them on missions early in the war subjected them to levels of stress that could not be sustained indefinitely. Accordingly, a system was worked out to send those who flew in the bombers back to the United States after a certain number of missions, although the need for air personnel more than once raised the prescribed number, from 25 to 30 to 35 to 50.[52] Thereafter they were assigned in North America on noncombat duty.

Medics, Doctors, and Nurses

In World War II the U.S. Army provided medical care unprecedented in the history of warfare. To conserve the fighting strength of the armed forces, the military not only had to treat the wounded but also prevent and cure disease. It started with men and women in good physical condition, rejecting one out of three potential inductees, enlisting those in better health. Training and nutritious food further improved their condition. On the other hand, crowded living quarters, stress, and exposure to new germs made them vulnerable to disease. In the field combat troops endured tropical heat, intense cold, hard living, dirt, lice, flies, and mosquitoes—as well as the terrible wounds inflicted by modern weapons.

Yet fewer than 4 percent of the American soldiers treated in the field or evacuated died from wounds or disease.[53] This excellent record originated in part in the usually good condition of men when they were wounded, thanks to the supply system that kept them well nourished and well clothed and provided adequate medical supplies for them, including the medications designed to prevent malaria. The success rate owed much also to the evacuation system, with comfort of facilities, sophistication of service, and distance from the front lines increasing from the battlefield aid stations to the evacuation hospitals to the general hospitals. With this system the medical corps could begin to treat a man soon after he was wounded—and speed was of the essence—limiting the shock and preventing the development of gangrene, which had so horribly killed so many in World War I.

A wounded man was usually treated first by a battlefield medic, trained to give first aid, stop the bleeding, prevent infection, prevent shock, and ease pain under fire. These efficient, dedicated enlisted men, some of them conscientious objectors, inspired an almost blind faith among GIs, who often believed that if a medic reached them they would live. Many a medic took enormous risks to reach a wounded man and heroically sheltered him with his own body. Many a GI called the medic who saved him "Doc" and described him as "the bravest man I ever saw." To preserve their noncombatant status under the Geneva Convention, the medics in the ETO did not carry arms and did not receive combat pay. Enemy respect for them caused them to try to make their red cross armbands more visible, and to paint a red cross on a white square on their helmets.

Medics saved thousands of lives with their prompt treatment, even though their supplies were limited mainly to bandages, morphine (which they sometimes carried next to their bodies to keep it from freezing), sulfa powder, and sulfa pills. (Each GI also carried sulfa powder and was taught to sprinkle it in any open wound.) Thanks to the pioneering work on blood plasma of African-American Dr. Charles Drew and the Red Cross blood banks he organized, medics also could give plasma in the field, thus reducing shock. The small doses

Pvt. Roy Humphrey is given blood plasma by army medic Pfc. Harvey White after being wounded by shrapnel on August 9, 1943, in Sicily. *(National Archives, 111-SC-178198)*

of morphine they administered often combined with exhaustion to render the wounded unconscious until they reached a field hospital, sparing them the agonies that World War I wounded endured during transport.

Litter bearers were then sent out from the forward aid stations located 300 to 1,000 yards from the front; they transported the wounded man to the nearest point to which a jeep could travel, and the jeep took him to an aid station one to three miles behind the lines, where a physician diagnosed his condition, applied a more permanent bandage, and gave other emergency care. This doctor was but the first among the many who would ultimately treat a seriously wounded soldier.

In addition to those who were drafted, about 56,000 doctors volunteered in the course of the war.[54] They ranged from newly trained men and a few women to highly skilled and experienced physicians[55] who served as consultants, instructing in their specialties and checking on standards. Many brought with them from civilian life not only medical expertise but also administrative skills that they could employ to find hospital sites and organize personnel and supplies in remote places. They had to learn to deal with the medical problems that accompanied jungle fighting and to teach troops preventive techniques, such as carrying dry socks to prevent trench foot. They also had to develop new specialties, such as aviation medicine, with its unique problems that called for new solutions, such as the development of the pressure suit to prevent blackouts in dive-bombing, and extensive training of the flight crews in first aid. The military doctors had first call on the newest drugs available, just as they did with plasma and whole blood. For instance, the penicillin discovered by bacteriologist Alexander Fleming in 1928 saved thousands of lives, as during the course of the war, scientists found superior mold strains from which to make it and improved the drug itself. The public health expert Fred L. Soper pioneered the use of DDT to kill lice and combat typhus and other insect-carried diseases. Department of Agriculture scientist Herald R. Cox enabled the manufacture of a typhus vaccine.[56]

Physicians in the field were assisted by a prestigious civilian Armed Forces Epidemiological Board formed in 1942 to predict and counter epidemic outbreaks and direct research, as well as by a number of other private and government agencies that sponsored research.[57] The American Medical Association ran a Procurement and Assignment Service as a clearinghouse to match available doctors, dentists, and veterinarians with civilian and military needs, under the Office for Emergency Management (later the War Manpower Commission). During the course of the war, as civilian viewpoints changed the military, more and more lay officers served in the Medical Administrative Corps, freeing more doctors to practice.

From the aid station an ambulance took the wounded man to a well-staffed and well-equipped field hospital, still farther to the rear, where if necessary he underwent an emergency operation. After that he went to an evacuation hospital even farther back, thoroughly equipped to give him the treatment and care he needed. If his wound was so severe that he would not soon recover, he was shipped back even farther to a station hospital, a general hospital, and eventually to the United States. Station and general hospitals were usually housed in more or less permanent locations, in buildings with running water and electricity. Station hospitals did surgery and administered specialized treatments. General hospitals offered facilities for diagnosis, specialized laboratory tests, therapy, and long recuperations.

When the wounded reached the field hospitals, nurses began to participate in their care. More than 59,000 women served in the Army Nurse Corps (ANC) during World War II, often under fire, in field and evacuation hospitals, on hospital trains and hospital ships, and as flight nurses on medical transport planes.[58] On December 7, 1941, when the Japanese attacked Pearl Harbor, the Army Nurse Corps numbered fewer than 1,000. Six months later its rolls had soared to 12,000.

At first the nurses were plunged at once from civilian service into military duty; finally, in July 1943 the military instituted a four-week training course for all newly commissioned army nurses, teaching them army organization; military customs and courtesies; field sanitation; defense against air, chemical, and mechanized attack; personnel administration; military requisitions and correspondence; and property responsibility. To fill shortages, the army also instituted a course to train nurse anesthetists and another to train psychiatric nurses. At the beginning of the war, the nurses' lack of officer status complicated their work and undermined their authority over corpsmen. In June 1944 the army granted them commissions and full officers' benefits and pay.

To increase the numbers of nurses available for both military and civilian service, from 1943 to 1948 the government offered free education to nursing students through the Cadet Nurse Corps (CNC) established in June 1943. Students had only to promise that they would render essential military or civilian service for the duration of the war. Their practical training in the last six months of their program in government hospitals relieved the nurse shortage.

Ultimately the CNC graduated more than 150,000 nurses.[59] Schools subsidized by the federal government also accelerated their programs to graduate nurses within two and a half years. Army miscalculation of the number of military nurses needed caused a halt in recruiting from December 1943 to the spring of 1944, and the resulting shortfall prompted a 1945 bill in Congress to draft nurses. The American Nursing Association reluctantly supported this measure, while labor, peace, and feminist groups opposed it.[60] The proposal was abandoned when Germany surrendered on May 8, 1945.

As with the rest of its personnel, the army followed a racist practice in its nurse corps. Despite obvious needs, the ANC turned down black nurses eager to enroll, insisting that they be allowed to care for only black troops. A public outcry in 1944 forced the army to abandon its racial quota system, but even at war's end the 50,000 nurses in the corps included only 479 black women.[61]

ANC nurses on duty in the Pacific served with distinction beginning with the attack on Pearl Harbor. In the Atlantic their colleagues proved their abilities and professionalism when on November 8, 1942, 60 of them waded ashore in the invasion of North Africa and, under fire, cared for the American wounded there under primitive conditions and with pitiably insufficient supplies.[62] With other members of the Medical Department they learned to transport their patients out of danger and to set up a new hospital within 12 hours. Subsequently army nurses served in Sicily and throughout the ETO.

The wounded usually first encountered them in the field hospitals, each of which had 18 nurses assigned to handle 75 to 150 patients. There with army doctors they performed triage to determine which patients should be treated first, assisted in operations, cared for patients in shock, and stabilized patients for transport to the evacuation hospitals. At each evacuation hospital 53 nurses could care for up to 750 patients until they were well enough to be evacuated by air or by hospital ship to station and general hospitals. Nurses assigned to set up station and general hospitals in preparation for a new offensive scrubbed their new sites in abandoned or bombed-out hospitals, schools, and factories, and scavenged for equipment.

Army nurses on hospital trains watched over their patients for stress and complications, dispensed medication and food to them, and made them as comfortable as possible. One nurse could care for one car with some 32 patients on litters, or for several cars of ambulatory patients. Flight nurses, who received special training, had to be in excellent physical condition, both because of their arduous duties and because of the possibility of crash landings. Hospital ships were theoretically immune from attack under the Geneva Convention,[63] but planes carrying wounded did not enjoy such protection because they were also used to transport cargo. The C-46s often used for patient transport had a design flaw that sometimes caused heaters to explode during flight, so many pilots refused to turn the heaters on; the nurses had to try to keep their critically ill patients warm with blankets and hot drinks. A single nurse aided by a corpsman bore responsibility for patients in flight—up to 25 of them on litters suspended in tiers. Sometimes her patients included combat-fatigue victims under restraint in "locked litters." The planes lacked emergency equipment, so nurses had to improvise. Nonetheless the 500 army nurses in the 31 medical air evacuation transport squadrons operating worldwide kept alive all but 46 of the 1,176,048 patients they tended. Seventeen of the nurses in this service lost their lives.[64]

At Anzio in Italy, for four months nurses lived in "Hell's Half Acre" as "part of a front that had no back. The beachhead was 15 miles wide and 7 miles deep and allowed no retreat from enemy fire."[65] Nurses landed on the beachhead in Normandy only four days after D day and followed the troops through France, moving at short intervals. Some were taken prisoner. In Germany, one nurse reported, civilians looked at her and her colleagues "with actual hatred in their eyes—and children threw stones at ambulances and spit at jeeps."[66] On Easter Sunday 1945, Germans ambushed a hospital convoy with 10 nurses, firing at it with machine guns; when the Americans surrendered, the Germans confiscated their vehicles and equipment and ordered them to set up a hospital for German wounded; nine hours later American troops liberated them.[67] That was far from the only time American army nurses looked after Germans, for among the thousands of surrendering Germans in the last days of the European war were many ill and wounded. In those times too nurses cared for the newly liberated starved, tortured, and diseased concentration camp victims.

Army nurses served in all the theaters of war, in the Pacific and the China-Burma-India theater as well as in the European theater. They earned 1,619 medals, citations, and commendations—and the eternal gratitude of most of their patients. During the war 201 ANC nurses died, at least 16 of them as a result of enemy fire.[68] More than 75,000 registered nurses served in the military during the war.[69]

Spies, Codes, and Secret Operations

When the United States entered World War II, the nation had no central intelligence system. On June 11, 1941, President Roosevelt issued a military order establishing the office of Coordinator of Information—the agency that would on June 13, 1942, become the Office of Strategic Services (OSS). Officially it was under the supervision of the Joint Chiefs of Staff, but in most ways it operated independently. Eventually it had five branches: Secret Intelligence, for the procurement of information by clandestine means; Secret Operations, for work behind the lines and encouraging resistance movements; Research and Analysis, for using available information like the price of oranges to guide military strategy; Morale Operations, for psychological warfare, which sponsored radio stations purportedly operated by German anti-Nazis inside Germany and distributed propaganda encouraging the enemy to defect or not to fight; and X-2, counterintelligence—spying on spies. Its head, William J. "Wild Bill" Donovan, recruited a group of 15,000 elite, well-off men and women—an adventurous, often unconventional lot.

OSS personnel were elaborately trained, at first in British and Canadian camps, and later under the supervision of social psychologist Kenneth Baker at "The Farm" in Maryland, about 20 miles from Washington, D.C. Agents who were to go abroad were taught to recruit local subagents to assist them in their work, to choose cover identities to account for their presence in a particular place and explain their source of income, to disguise themselves by drastic changes in their appearance, to use codes and secret inks, to recognize aircraft, and to kill quickly and silently. At another base on Long Island, New York, playwright and presidential speechwriter Robert Sherwood trained agents for foreign-propaganda broadcasting.

The OSS sent about 200 spies inside Germany, mostly foreign nationals and German prisoners of war, whom the OSS called "deserter-volunteers," but almost all of them were soon captured. During the Battle of the Bulge, for instance, the OSS had only three active agents there.[70] The organization also sent agents to assist the resistance movements in the countries occupied by Germany. Spain was a hotbed of spies and refugees where Allied and Axis agents eavesdropped on each other. Americans there painstakingly gathered information about conditions inside Germany from gossip and from Spanish and Portuguese newspapers. Support personnel known as backup agents searched the bodies of dead Germans to obtain papers that their expert forgers could alter or imitate. Others in the United States collected information from European refugees and bought European clothes from them to be used for disguises.

Perhaps the greatest success in Allied espionage came from the cryptographers, who not only taught agents to encode their messages but also toiled in offices in Great Britain and the United States decoding intercepted messages broadcast by the enemy. Throughout most of the war the Allies enjoyed the advantage of being able to read "secret" German documents and transmissions, thanks in part to the capture of enemy codebooks and a German Enigma encoding machine, and in part to the brilliant work of Allied cryptographers, particularly the Polish and the British.

The Women's Army Corps (WAC)

Servicewomen constituted at most 2.3 percent of the military.[71] Their numbers peaked at 271,600; altogether 350,000 entered at some point.[72] More women were so urgently required that the army seriously considered asking Congress to draft them. Meanwhile, potential volunteers held back in the belief that if they were really needed they would be drafted. Moreover, the War Manpower Commission, faced with the demands of agriculture and manufacturing for womanpower, restricted military recruitment.

The women's military services came into being partly because of the leadership of women like Congresswoman Edith Nourse Rogers, and partly because of a demand for their services from such high-ranking officers as Gen. George Marshall, Adm. Ernest J. King, and Gen. Hap Arnold, head of the Army Air Corps. These men profited from the example of the women who served in the navy in World War I. Their reasoning was expressed by Arnold: "[I]n the fields for which a woman's civilian training best fits her, a woman can do the job of two men. . . . As we ship men to the theatres of operation in increasing numbers, it becomes . . . essential to recognize and use the skill and training of women to the maximum extent possible."[73]

The American public, after an initial hesitation, generally accepted the creation of these services. Some Roman Catholic leaders actively opposed the idea, but later they too applauded it, because, said one chaplain, in the military women would learn "respect for authority, discipline, scrupulous regard for promptness and exactness and execution of detail" and later transmit it to their children, thus producing a "much better disciplined generation."[74]

In May 1942 Congress passed a bill introduced by Congresswoman Rogers establishing the Women's Auxiliary Army Corps (WAAC)—*auxiliary* because the army was wary of accepting women as full-fledged members. Women officers were not to command men and received less pay than their male counterparts. Women were assigned ranks different from though comparable to those of men. The army did not offer WAACs overseas pay, government life insurance, veterans' medical coverage, or death benefits. If they were captured, they had no protection under the Geneva Convention. By the spring of 1943, in the midst of plans for the invasion of Europe with a corresponding increase in the size of the military, the army realized that these provisions were unworkable, and on July 3, 1943, President Roosevelt signed into law a bill converting the WAAC into the Women's Army Corps (WAC). Members of the WAAC were given their choice of returning to civilian life or joining the WAC. Twenty-five percent of them left.[75]

This mass exit was but one example of the difficulties that the WAAC and WAC encountered in recruitment and retention. The corps was by far the largest of the women's services, with an authorized strength of 150,000. Although more than 150,000 women eventually served in it, including more than 300 Japanese Americans, it consistently was under strength.[76] At peak it reached about 100,000 members.[77] Eventually the corps had to lower standards for admission, although throughout the war they remained higher than those for men.

When the corps was formed, women rushed to join—35,000 of them for fewer than 1,000 places.[78] But enthusiasm among the public plummeted, largely because of the attitudes of male military personnel other than top officers. Their opposition to accepting women as colleagues expressed itself in skepticism about women's courage and skills, resentment of their success and their very presence in the man's world of war, fear that women's taking over their work might send them into combat, sexual harassment, and nasty gossip and innuendoes attacking servicewomen's reputations. These attitudes have since diminished, but they persist. During World War II they were virulent. Men wrote home alleging that the WACs were there to "keep the men happy"; that contraceptives were issued to all WACs in expectation of their sexual activity; that 40 percent of them were pregnant; that 90 percent of them were prostitutes; that many were lesbians. They forbade their wives, fiancées, and sisters to join up, sometimes under threat of divorce or disinheritance.[79] They did incalculable harm, both to the WAC and to the women who constituted it. Those among them who eventually met WACs often changed their minds—too late for the good of the corps and for the good of the country.

Other factors added to the difficulties of recruiting. Secretary of War Henry Stimson appointed as director of the WAAC Oveta Culp Hobby, an experienced Texas newspaper editor and politician, a good administrator, and a popular choice. Eager to reassure anxious parents about the safety and reputation of servicewomen and tell the public that the WAAC would not disrupt the traditional way of life, she said: "The gaps our women will fill are in those noncombatant jobs where women's hands and women's hearts fit naturally. WAACs will do the same type of work which women do in civilian life. They will bear the same relation to men of the Army that they bear to the men of the civilian organizations in which they work." To some potential recruits and new WAACs this statement meant, in the words of a WAAC trainee: "The WAAC mission is the same old women's mission, to hold the home front steadfast, and send men to battle warmed and fed and comforted; to stand by and do dull routine work while the men are gone."[80] Moreover Hobby substituted a policy resembling parental supervision for military discipline. Such a practice was unattractive to women in their twenties and thirties, quite capable of looking after themselves.

Wives and mothers were not welcome in the corps, and the pay of military women did not include dependency allowances. The WAC allowed blacks to serve only in segregated units, setting a quota of 10 percent, but in fact blacks never represented more than 6 percent.[81] The services at first refused wives of service husbands; later they accepted women in different branches of service than their husbands. If a woman married a serviceman, she had to resign. If she became pregnant, she had to resign, even if the pregnancy ended. Seventy percent of WACs were single, 15 percent married, and 15 percent divorced, widowed, or separated.[82] A majority of them came from northern rural areas and small towns. Many had significant work experience.

Women volunteered for the corps for much the same reasons that men volunteered—first and foremost out of patriotism and a desire to get the war over as soon as possible and bring the men back home. Some wanted adventure. Others seized a chance to better themselves economically. In the military enlisted women earned about what they had in civilian life, and officers about twice as much as before, whereas servicemen were paid less in the military than in their previous occupations.[83]

Like male soldiers, servicewomen were often assigned to jobs far below their experience and skills: For instance, women trained as medical technicians were used as charwomen. The military would not allow women in combat jobs, even after a 1942 experiment in which 400 of them had proved their capabilities in antiaircraft batteries around five cities.[84] On bases within the United States WACs might be assigned to the same work as civilians—who received higher pay, lived as they wished, and wore nicer clothes than the unattractive khaki WAC uniforms that made the worst of women's bodies. Many a WAC spent the war on a remote army base amid an unwelcoming civilian populace doing dull, unnecessary work, bossed by a temporary major (promoted for the duration from sergeant) much less intelligent than she. In 1945 the military announced a plan to send large numbers of civilian women abroad to perform tasks similar to those the WACs had been doing, wearing WAC uniforms, but with officers' privileges, not subject to military discipline or supervision, and much better paid. Yes, the army said, once discharged WACs could also have these jobs, but of the 8,000 WACs then in Europe, only 126 accepted.[85]

WAC officers had a hard time, especially at the start. Typically they knew little about the military. Their male colleagues often denigrated them. They had no mentors and had to figure things out for themselves. Promotions were slow, and the top ranks unattainable. WAC officers, from Oveta Culp Hobby on down, encountered difficulties because from a strictly military point of view they were not needed. Military agencies already existed to feed, clothe, house, and discipline the servicewomen, had they been really integrated into their services. Hence the women officers could hardly help invading someone else's turf, no matter what they did. They had responsibilities without authority or policy control. Women officers much preferred other tasks to those specific to the women's services, which they saw as babysitting a group of women who neither wanted nor needed babysitting.

Social life for all WACs was difficult to nonexistent. The women recruited were on average significantly older and better educated than the men, for the military wanted youthful zest in its men, maturity in its women. Women were not accepted until age 20: the median age for WACs was 25, with their officers a few years older, though women over 35 were usually rejected, except for the top spots. Enlisted women had little interest in dating young GIs, yet military policy forbade fraternization between these servicewomen and male officers. In the Southwest Pacific one commander, fearing encounters between the large numbers of soldiers in the area and the relatively few women, actually kept army women behind barbed wire except when they were working and assigned armed guards to march them to work.[86]

The Army Air Force, more flexible and innovative than the rest of the army, wanted women from the outset and treated them well. They employed 40 percent of all WACs.[87] They offered women opportunities as weather observers and forecasters, cryptographers, radio operators and repairers, sheet-metal workers, parachute riggers, Link trainer (machines to train pilots) instructors, bombsight maintenance specialists, aerial photograph analysts, and control tower operators. They allowed a few to fly in the course of their duties, among them radio operators, mechanics, and photographers. A WAC won the air medal for her work in mapping "the Hump" in India for pilots ferrying Lend-Lease supplies to the Chinese. Nonetheless half of the WACs in the air force worked in traditional "women's" jobs.

Another 40 percent of WACs went to the Army Service Forces, working in ordnance, transportation, chemical warfare, the quartermaster corps, the signal corps, and the medical department. Eventually WAC women were assigned to hospital ships as secretaries, clerks, and radio operators. In the corps of engineers a few WACs served on the Manhattan Project, creating the atomic bomb. M. Sgt. Elizabeth Wilson of the Chemistry Division at Los Alamos, New Mexico, ran the cyclotron; other WACs at Oak Ridge, Tennessee, maintained the top secret files related to the project, working 12-hour shifts seven days a week. Three WACs on the project were assigned to the Corps of Engineers in London to help coordinate the flow of information between English and American scientists.

At the outset the Army Ground Forces did not want women and assigned three-quarters of the 20 percent of WACs it received to training centers to sit out the war doing routine clerical work and another 10 percent to motor pools, with little or no opportunity for specialist training.

The WACs highly prized the opportunities given them to go overseas, so much so that some enlisted women turned down the chance to become officers instead, even though abroad they were usually assigned to routine work. WACs served in North Africa, the Mediterranean, Europe, the Southwest Pacific, China, India, Burma, and the Middle East. By V-E Day 7,600 WACs were stationed across England, France, and Germany.[88] An additional 5,500 WACs worked in the Southwest Pacific Area at Hollandia and Oro Bay, New Guinea, and at Leyte and Manila in the Philippines; there they suffered disproportionately from malaria, dermatitis, and pneumonia because in those tropical climates the army issued them wool uniforms and failed to provide them with lightweight clothing that would protect them against insect bites and overheating.

Naturally, the more challenging the women's jobs, the better they liked them, and in fact more interesting jobs did open up as the war went on. Commanders who originally had not wanted them in the army began to clamor for them, and noncommissioned male officers who had insisted "Not in *my* army" actually became protective of them.

Although relatively few worked in interesting jobs, it must be remembered that millions of men also toiled at dull work in dull places where they did not want to be, and many of them were exposed to more danger and discomfort than most women. What was more, many WACs who performed routine work could see that they were contributing to the war effort and to the health and morale of the servicemen. The WAC postal units, for instance, knew how important the mountains of mail they handled were to soldiers and sailors everywhere. Even working as a stenographer or typist could be exciting in an office that was planning for D day, or if one's duties consisted of recording and translating broadcasts from the French underground. Some WACs found as much or more adventure as they could have wanted, as when five WAAC officers were torpedoed en route from Great Britain to Algiers to work in General Eisenhower's headquarters as executive secretaries. Two of them were rescued from the deck of their sinking ship; the other three drifted in a lifeboat, pulling seamen into the boat with them, and eventually being picked up by a destroyer. What mattered most, however, to the nation and to the servicewomen, was the respect they earned from their commanders and colleagues. Most telling of all was the army's request in 1946 that the WAC be made a permanent part of the regular army.

The Women's Auxiliary Flying Squadron, the Women's Flying Training Detachment, and the Women Airforce Service Pilots

The U.S. Army never accepted women as pilots in World War II, but women pilots were not to be denied participation in the war. Early in 1942 the pilot and cosmetics manufacturer Jacqueline Cochran recruited a few women with pilots' licenses to go to England to ferry planes for the RAF in the British Air Transport Auxiliary. In September of that year flying school operator Nancy Love organized others into the Women's Auxiliary Flying Squadron (WAFS), which delivered planes in the United States. After Cochran complained to air force Gen. Hap Arnold that he had promised her the top position in any organization of women in the Army Air Force, a compromise was reached by which she became the director of the Women's Flying Training Detachment (WFTD), assigned to train women pilots for Love's outfit. In August 1943 the WAFS and the WFTD merged to form the Women Airforce Service Pilots (WASP), with Cochran as director and Love in charge of the ferrying branch.

The WASP numbered about 1,000. They ferried military aircraft, towed air gunnery targets at considerable risk from gunners just learning to shoot,

Jacqueline Cochran discusses her plans to organize the 3,258 licensed American woman fliers to ferry aircraft to Great Britain with Capt. Norman Edgar, British Transport Auxiliary Service representative, 1942. *(Library of Congress, LC-USZ62-111981)*

and taught flying to Army Air Force cadets. Thirty-eight of them died in the course of duty.[89] Bright, merry, and intrepid, they accepted such challenges as this: "We don't know anything about these planes except that you'll have to refuel them often. Plan on doing it every hour until you find out how far they can go on a full tank. They're fast—take off fast because you have a heavy load on board. Land fast—you'll probably come in over the airport fence at 100 miles per hour or better. But we really don't know. . . . Fly them to March Field. . . . And when you get back here, give me a full report on what you learned about how the things fly. These PQ-8's are an important deal. Top secret. Good Luck."[90]

In 1944, as former male combat pilots returned home after completing the prescribed number of missions, the WASP were summarily dismissed. They had more than answered Hap Arnold's doubts about "whether a slip of a young girl could fight the controls of a B-17 in the heavy weather they would naturally encounter in operational flying," for they flew everything from the army's smallest trainers and hottest fighters to its biggest bombers, holding their accident rate a little lower than the men's.[91] Nevertheless, although they wore uniforms and took military orders, having never been formally recognized as part of the military they could be dropped at any time. Only more than 30 years later, on November 23, 1977, did the U.S. Congress finally grant them status and benefits as military veterans.

GIs (American Soldiers) Abroad

Almost 425,000 GIs arrived in Britain in the 30 months before the invasion of France in June 1944, crowding the British Isles and straining their facilities.[92] They were received at first as saviors and liked for their amiability and liberality. But there were too many of them with too little to do while they waited. British soldiers, paid much less than the Americans and much worse clad, envied their money and their success with the British women: the British quipped about a new brand of women's panties, "One Yank and they're off." The GIs, the British accused, were "oversexed, overpaid, overfed, and over here." In reply the Americans taunted the "Limeys" as "undersexed, underpaid, underfed, and under Eisenhower."

Some American troops behaved badly, drinking, brawling, and harassing and even raping British women. They bought up scarce British goods and drank the pubs dry. They littered the landscape with used condoms, even poking them through mail slots in people's houses. The situation was aggravated by British prostitutes, known as "Piccadilly Commandos" and "Hyde Park Rangers," who gave naïve GIs a false impression of British women. In August 1948, *Life* magazine estimated that in wartime Britain white U.S. soldiers fathered 22,000 children out of wedlock, and black U.S. soldiers 1,200–1,700 more.[93] Clashes between black and white GIs also disturbed and upset the British.

The U.S. military tried to educate American soldiers about the British and their customs. They beefed up the military police, restricted the sale of bottled alcoholic beverages, and imposed curfews. They paid the GIs twice a month rather than once, to reduce the cash available at any one time, and urged them to buy war bonds. They encouraged them to take American goods to the

British as hostess gifts—gifts most welcome to the severely rationed British. Sometimes these efforts had odd results, as when a GI told a British officer asking him how he liked the country, "Sir, we like you and you like us and that's our orders, sir."[94]

What most advanced British-American relations, however, were the friendships that sprang up as individual GIs and British got to know one another. Many generous British families virtually adopted American soldiers, giving them a home away from home. Many GIs married British women. General Eisenhower's headquarters estimated in February 1944 that 4,093 U.S. military personnel were married to individuals residing in the United Kingdom, and Anglo-American marriages surged thereafter, as victory approached and GIs began to look forward to the end of the war.[95]

The American forces that invaded France, Belgium, and even Italy often were hailed as liberators and heroes. Their easy informality, their generosity with cigarettes and candy, and their fondness for children soon won them friends. In Germany they met a sterner, more resistant enemy than in Italy. In the last days of the war even German lads of 14 and 15, uniformed soldiers in Hitler's army, fought viciously. Cartoonist Bill Mauldin depicted GIs occupying a confiscated German home. In a room filled with signs saying "Welcome to our home; please respect it," and "God bless our home," one GI warns another, "Be careful: the toilet's booby-trapped." Yet even in conquered Germany many GIs made friends, holding no grudges, indeed liking the Germans. However, few of the GIs who had liberated the concentration camps shared these sentiments, for in these camps they had found sickening evidence of the tortures, suffering, and death that official Nazi policy and individual Germans' sadism inflicted on Jews, Gypsies (Romany), and homosexuals, in an effort to wipe from the face of the earth those whom they hated.

GI Combat Fatigue

In any war humans have to deal with the psychological devastation caused by war's violation of moral standards—specifically, with killing. The writer William Manchester described his reaction when, terrified, he burst into a hut and found an enemy sniper who would certainly kill him if he did not shoot first: "I shot him with a .45 and I felt remorse and shame. I can remember whispering foolishly, 'I'm sorry' and then just throwing up. . . . I threw up all over myself. It was a betrayal of what I'd been taught since a child."[96]

Moreover, World War II exceeded in extent, in the numbers of people involved, and in horrors all other wars. As Paul Fussell writes, "Unthinkable [in World War I] would have been the Second War's unsurrendering Japanese, its suicides and *kamikazes,* its public hanging of innocent hostages, its calm, efficient gassing of Jews and Slavs and homosexuals, its unbelievable conclusion in atomic radiation."[97] Some men were haunted all their lives with the nightmares of being struck by the severed legs or heads of their comrades flying through the air, of seeing men disemboweled. Prisoners of war of the Japanese suffered torments that approached those of the victims in the German concentration camps. Long-sustained, unrelieved fear drove men mad on the ammunition-carrying merchant ships trailed by German submarines and on the American submarines assaulted by depth charges. Downed pilots floated on tiny rafts at sea, sometimes dreadfully burned, so consumed with thirst that they drank their own urine. Everyone in combat underwent prolonged suspense and fears of cowardice, madness, death, crippling, capture, torture, and at times of ultimate defeat.

These terrors and traumas often proved more than men could bear. Combat exhaustion could afflict even the bravest soldiers, a fact that military psychologists and the Veterans Administration were slow to recognize. They were horrified by the experience of World War I, in which "shell-shocked" soldiers not only endangered their own combat units but also continued to suffer for years after the war, sometimes for all their lives. Consequently, at the outset of World War II psychologists tried to screen out the psychologically vulnerable.

However, in early 1943, after the heavy psychiatric casualties inflicted on American servicemen on Guadalcanal in the Pacific and at the Kasserine Pass in North Africa, psychologists began to understand that the terrible experiences the men had to endure—not their psychological makeup—caused their breakdowns. Even experienced veterans could collapse after four months in combat, and such casualties came sooner and occurred more frequently among replacements not integrated into their units.

This psychological state manifested itself in more than one way. The approach of the "old sergeant syndrome" was signaled by irritability, apathy, inefficiency, and carelessness, posing dangers to other troops.[98] Some soldiers turned into zombies, failing to recognize even their closest friends. Some got physically sick. Some shook; some had heart palpitations or nightmares or insomnia—or all of these. Some cried, screamed, and ran about in confusion.

Gradually psychologists and psychiatrists learned methods of prevention and treatment. The best way to protect a man against combat fatigue was to put him in a supportive unit, where he cared for his comrades, respected his immediate leader, was concerned about the unit's reputation, and wanted to contribute to its success. In ideal circumstances, he was not so much fighting against an enemy as fighting for his unit. (Consequently, the soldier sent as a replacement to a decimated unit suffered a sense of isolation that endangered his psychological health.) Moreover, any fighting man must be removed from combat before physical and psychological exhaustion set in. Servicemen found reassuring this recognition that "Every Man Has His Breaking Point," which became an official army slogan.

At the start of the war doctors had treated combat fatigue by shipping its victims back to the United States. They later learned that they could treat such patients better and more successfully on site in a remarkably short time. They had to act promptly, keep the men close to the front, and reassure them that their condition was temporary and treatable, terming it "exhaustion." In some cases a couple of days not far behind the lines loading trucks would restore a man to fitness for combat duty. In other cases psychiatrists used group therapy and encouraged the men to relive their traumatic experiences. This was a win-win treatment for both the military and the serviceman. The military saved the soldier to fight another day, and a quick recovery was the soldier's best protection against permanent disability.

Not that these servicemen who recovered their mental balance escaped scot-free. Veterans telling their stories 50 years later still weep, still mourn their catastrophic discoveries of the power of evil and the limits of human endurance. Moreover, other men experienced such severe cases of combat exhaustion that they had to be sent to hospitals in restraints. One out of every 12 patients in army hospitals was admitted for psychiatric care.[99]

GI Prisoners of War (POWs)

During World War II 130,201 American servicemen and servicewomen were taken prisoner, of whom 14,072 died, most of them as prisoners of the Japanese.[100] As in all wars, injustices occurred both in the taking and the treatment of prisoners of war. On both sides, men trying to surrender were shot; both sides shot enemies discovered between the lines. Sometimes advancing armies simply could not provide for large numbers of surrendering men, and they died from exposure and starvation, as in the Rhine Meadows camps (open fields surrounded by concertina wire [rolls of twisted barbed wire]) of April and May 1945, when the Allied forces had to deal with hundreds of thousands of newly taken German POWs. The rage of American soldiers who had just discovered the Nazi concentration camps contributed to the ill-treatment of the Germans.

To a degree, however, in the ETO both sides observed the Geneva Convention of 1929, which provided that POWs "must at all times be humanely treated and protected, particularly against acts of violence, insults and public curiosity," prohibited measures of reprisal against them, and spelled out proper treatment, including the right of inspection by a representative of a neutral power.

Some enemy POWs taken in Europe and shipped to the United States were not only safe and well fed but also comfortable doing farmwork, able to

Shortly after black troops entered this town of Enterprise, Alabama, townspeople rioted, August 1941. *(Library of Congress, LC-USF34-080410-E)*

take college courses, and well treated by sympathetic bosses—bosses often of German or Italian descent. Certainly they were better treated than some American blacks: Black soldiers were refused meals in U.S. restaurants where enemy POWs ate, and black farmworkers in the cotton fields had a daily quota of 250 pounds against the POWs' 100 pounds.[101] At least one German in the 1950s was still describing his time as a POW in the United States as "the happiest years of my life."[102]

No American would so describe his experience as a POW in Europe. American POWs might find themselves living in barracks that included a washroom and an indoor toilet and were heated by small stoves, and sleeping on crude double- or triple-decker beds. Most of them were ill-fed, particularly as the war wore on and German supplies dwindled, and many did not receive the Red Cross packages to which they were entitled weekly. Bombardier Bill Topping remembered, "We caught some cats and ate them. The Germans put up signs saying it's *verboten* [forbidden] to eat the Pomeranian long-tailed rabbits. They didn't have to worry because we'd already eaten all of their cats and were trying to catch their dogs next. We all lost weight, with starving conditions. . . . I volunteered to work in the German kitchen. We would grind up horsemeat, making hamburgers for the German troops. I stole some of the meat, packed it around my stomach and sides, patted it down underneath my shirt. When I'd come home from work detail, I'd unbotton my shirt, pull out all the meat and the eighteen guys in my room would eat pretty good with what I was stealing. If they'd have caught me, they would have shot me."[103]

The Geneva Convention allowed that enlisted men be required to work, but noncommissioned officers were to be employed only in a supervisory capacity, unless they requested remunerative work, and commissioned officers were to work only if they volunteered.

The POWs organized, for entertainment, for sports, for trading, and most especially for escape. Escaping was a dangerous course, particularly when the escapee was caught out of uniform and could be treated as a spy, but many POWs considered attempting it a duty. Although few actually escaped, the possibility necessitated that the enemy assign more guards, diverting them from battlefield duty. For this purpose, and to communicate useful information to the Allies, the POWs utilized the many skills among them, building clandestine radios, forging identification papers, preparing "escape food," tailoring civilian clothes or German uniforms, and engineering escape tunnels. Bombardier Marshall Draper of the Eighth Air Corps reminisced, "I was part of a small group that conveyed information [by radio to the Allies] on strategic targets, aircraft equipment failures or malfunctions, information on concentration camps, requests for escape supplies and other equipment. . . . Information of this kind was elicited by 'goon sprechers,' individuals designated to cultivate 'pet goons'"—guards.[104] The prisoners traded with and through some of their guards, who then became vulnerable to blackmail.

Some POWs, especially airmen, underwent stringent questioning when they were captured, in which the Germans used isolation, beatings, and psychological torture to persuade them to divulge more than the prescribed name, rank, and military serial number. The POWs found the Germans disconcertingly well informed about them, with extensive knowledge of their units and even of their hometowns. Pilot Jim McCubbin found that they knew his roommate's name and had recorded radio communication between the two in which the Americans exulted over shooting down a Messerschmitt plane.[105]

In September 1943, when Italy surrendered, thousands of Allied POWs it had held were liberated, only to be recaptured by the German troops rushed into Italy. Many of them finally were rescued only when in June 1944 American troops marched into Rome. In the spring of 1945, as the Soviet army advanced toward Berlin and German defenses crumbled, some camp commandants turned over authority to the POWs and others decamped with their staffs, leaving the POWs to their own devices. However, some diehards tried to take the POWs with them, on brutal forced marches or crammed into railroad boxcars—trips on which some Americans died on the verge of liberation. Navigator Lu Cox told of marching away from Sagan, Germany, in February 1945: "It was so cold that our bread and margarine froze. Our clothes froze. Worst of all our shoes froze. To start up again after a ten or fifteen minute rest was sheer agony. I felt as though I was wearing iron shoes with loose gravel inside. My shoes had frozen so solidly that both of them broke in half at the balls of my feet."[106] At the same time the POWs knew that they might be bombed or strafed by American planes. However, as German morale sagged, some of the POWs began to assume more authority, promising decent German guards that if they cooperated they would receive better treatment when American forces arrived, even putting some of these guards into American uniforms to protect them. Eventually, as Germans acknowledged defeat, they began surrendering to the POWs, literally seeking their protection.

When, one way or another, the POWs were finally liberated, they were deloused, given hot baths and new uniforms, and offered vitamins and as much food as their debilitated bodies could endure. Best of all, they were given priority for a ticket home.

CHRONICLE OF EVENTS

1939

September 3: Great Britain declares war on Germany after Hitler's invasion of Poland on September 1.

September 17–October 10: The Union of Soviet Socialist Republics (USSR) invades Poland, Estonia, Latvia, and Lithuania, forcing these countries to accept Soviet bases on their territory.

1940

March 12: The USSR forces Finland to cede territory.

April 9: German forces overrun Denmark and Norway.

May 6: Great Britain occupies Iceland.

May 10: Germany invades the Netherlands, Belgium, and France.

May 15: The Dutch surrender to Germany.

May 26: German forces reach the English Channel near Dunkirk in France.

May 28: Belgium surrenders to Germany.

May 30: A makeshift English fleet of large ships and small boats begins the rescue of 380,000 trapped Allied troops from Dunkirk in France.

June 10: Benito Mussolini takes Italy into World War II in alliance with Germany.

June 14: German troops enter Paris and raise the German swastika over the Eiffel Tower.

A Frenchman weeps as German soldiers march into Paris after the Allied armies have been driven back across France, June 14, 1940. *(National Archives, 208-PP-10A-3)*

June 20: The U.S. secretary of war creates the U.S. Army Air Forces, incorporating into the army the air corps established by Congress in 1926.

June 22: France capitulates to Germany, signing an armistice at Compiègne, France.

June 28: Romania hands over Bessarabia to the Soviet Union.

July: German planes attack British coastal towns and shipping in the English Channel, and the Royal Air Force (RAF) mounts a defense.

July 3: The British attack the French fleet at Mers el Kébir, Algeria.

August 4: Italy invades British and French Somaliland.

August 13: In the Battle of Britain, the Germans, armed with more than 2,000 fighters and bombers, attack Royal Air Force ground installations; the British have only 700 first-line fighters and some older craft, but maintain a two-to-one ratio in downing enemy planes.

August 24: German planes accidentally bomb London, and England retaliates on Berlin.

September 7: German planes begin a blitz (short for *blitzkrieg,* or "lightning warfare") against British cities, especially London, sustained for 57 nights.

September 14: Italy invades Egypt.

September 26: Germany, Italy, and Japan sign the Tripartite Pact for the alliance that becomes known as the Axis, in which Japan recognizes Germany and Italy's leadership in establishing a new order in Europe; Germany and Italy recognize Japan's leadership in establishing a new order in Asia; the three countries agree to assist each other when one is attacked by an outside entity not involved in the European war or the Chinese-Japanese conflict; and all three nations agree that the terms established do not bear on the relations of any of them with the USSR.

October 28: Italy invades Greece.

October 29: President Franklin D. Roosevelt (FDR) draws the first number in the draft lottery.

November 8: The U.S. War Department announces that the wearing of the saber by officers on duty with troops will be discontinued.

November 20: Hungary, Romania, and Slovakia join the Tripartite Pact.

December 9: The British defeat the Italians in Egypt.

1941

February 1: The U.S. Atlantic fleet is reactivated under Adm. Ernest J. King.

March 1: Bulgaria joins the Tripartite Pact.

March 11: Congress passes the Lend-Lease Act to assist countries whose defense is necessary to the security of the United States.

March 27: Official United States–British military staff conversations begin.

April 3–4: A German submarine wolf pack sinks 10 out of 22 ships in a slow transatlantic convoy, prompting the decision that the United States must help escort ships transporting Lend-Lease supplies.

April 6: Germany invades Greece and Yugoslavia.

April 17: Yugoslavia surrenders to Germany.

April 18: In Operation Plan 3-41 Admiral King orders that any belligerent warship or aircraft approaching within 25 miles of the Western Hemisphere be "viewed as actuated by an intention immediately to attack such territory."

April 24: FDR authorizes the U.S. Navy to patrol the North Atlantic and report the movements of German vessels but not to shoot unless attacked.

May 2: The British invade Iraq.

May 10–11: The London blitz ends with a raid that kills 1,212 people.

June: U.S. embassy officials supervise the closing of the surviving American consulates in Germany, the repatriation of their personnel, and the transfer of their responsibilities to the embassy in Berlin.

June 8: Vichy French forces in Syria and Lebanon surrender to the British.

June 22: Germany invades the USSR, and the USSR becomes an ally with Great Britain and the United States. British prime minister Winston Churchill comments in Parliament, "If Hitler invaded Hell, I would make at least a favourable reference to the Devil in the House of Commons."

July 8: At the country's invitation, the U.S. Marines occupy Iceland.

July 11: FDR appoints Gen. William "Wild Bill" Donovan as coordinator of information, the agency that was transformed a year later into the Office of Strategic Services.

July 23: Japan occupies southern Indochina.

August 10: Churchill and Roosevelt meet in the Atlantic and issue the Atlantic Charter.

August 25: Great Britain and the USSR invade Iran.

German troops engage in battle in Russia, 1941. *(National Archives, 242-GAP-286B-4)*

September 4: FDR issues orders to shoot on sight any ship interfering with American shipping.

September 16: The U.S. Navy begins to escort convoys to a mid-Atlantic point, where the British navy takes over.

September 19: The American cargo vessel *Pink Star* carrying food for Britain is sunk off Greenland.

October: The American destroyers *Kearney* and *Reuben James* are sunk in the Atlantic.

December 1: The U.S. Civil Air Patrol (CAP) is organized. Later in the month CAP pilots harass German submarines off the east coast of the United States and sink two.

December 7: Japan attacks the U.S. naval base at Pearl Harbor, Hawaii.

December 8: The United States declares war on Japan.

December 8: So many American men volunteer to join the military that the draft is suspended for almost a year.

December 8: The Iroquois Confederacy, never having made peace with Germany after World War I, renews its declaration of war against Germany and extends it to Italy and Japan.

December 11: Germany and Italy declare war on the United States, and FDR asks the Congress to recognize a state of war with those nations.

1942

January: German submarines sink 58 Allied and neutral merchant ships in the North Atlantic, only three of which are in transatlantic convoys.

January 10: The first American troop convoy sails from Halifax, Nova Scotia, to the United Kingdom.

January 12–26: German U-boats sink 13 Allied vessels near the U.S. Atlantic coast.

January 28: Aviation machinist's mate Donald Francis Mason sends the message "Sighted sub, sank same" in the belief that he has sunk a German U-boat off the coast of Newfoundland.

January 29: The U.S. Coast Guard cutter *Alexander Hamilton* on escort duty is torpedoed and sunk.

February: The American Red Cross (ARC) and the U.S. military agree that the army will take care of soldier welfare on base, the ARC off base.

February 9: The luxury liner *Normandie,* waiting to be converted into a troop transport, burns and capsizes in New York Harbor.

February 22–24: In a U.S. Atlantic convoy, 24 ships are torpedoed and sunk.

March: Iceland and Greenland give the United States air bases from which to fly cover over sea routes to England in exchange for the United States's assuming responsibility for their defense.

March: Jackie Cochran takes 25 American women pilots to Britain to ferry planes for the British Air Transport Auxiliary.

March 1: FDR signs into law the establishment of the Women's Auxiliary Army Corps (WAAC).

March 1: Naval pilot William Tepuni sinks a U-boat off Newfoundland.

March 9: The U.S. Army is restructured into the Army Ground Forces, the Services of Supply (later Army Service Forces), and the Army Air Force (usually called the Air Corps).

April 1: As a stopgap effort to protect merchant shipping from German submarines, a "bucket brigade" is established at places without harbors, like Cape Hatteras and Cape Fear, North Carolina, so that small craft can escort merchant ships by daylight from one harbor to another.

April 1: The Anti-Submarine Warfare Operations Research Group (ASWORG) is organized to invent, develop, and test new weapons (like sonar and microwave radar) and advise on their best use: e.g., "What pattern of depth charges at what settings has the best chance of killing a submarine?"

April 15: A U.S. naval destroyer sinks a U-boat near Cape Hatteras off North Carolina.

April 18: The navy orders a brown-out in which U.S. Atlantic coast waterfront lights and sky signs are to be extinguished to prevent the silhouetting of Allied ships in American coastal waters (the Eastern Sea Frontier).

April 18: The military newspaper *The Stars and Stripes* begins printing a weekly edition in London.

May–June: A U-boat blitz sinks many Allied ships.

May 9: The Coast Guard cutter *Icarus* sinks a U-boat off Cape Lookout, North Carolina.

May 11: The first American flying personnel arrive in England.

May 29: USSR foreign minister Vyacheslav Molotov visits FDR to urge a second front, to which FDR agrees in principle.

June: The Manhattan Project is launched to develop an atomic bomb.

June: Base pay for privates in the U.S. Army is increased to $50 a month.

June 1: African-American leader Mary McLeod Bethune endorses the WAAC and urges black women to join, but she repudiates the policy of segregation.

June 8: The U.S. War Department reinstates an old marriage rule for troops overseas, forbidding them to marry without the approval of their commanding officer. (See entries for July 28 and October 22 below.)

June 18: Churchill visits FDR to argue against an assault on Europe; FDR promises that the United States will take responsibility for the development of the atomic bomb; they agree on an invasion of French North Africa.

June 21: The British stop the German advance on Cairo at El Alamein in North Africa.

June 21: The British garrison of 30,000 men at Tobruk in Libya surrenders to the Germans.

July: British-American Convoy PQ-17 to Soviet ports Murmansk and Archangel loses 22 out of 33 ships to German U-boats and dive bombers.

July 28: Gen. Dwight D. Eisenhower issues a directive that officers and men may marry only with their commander's permission, which is to be given only when the marriage is in the interests of the military service, and after written notice of three months, denying citizenship or any other privileges to wives in such marriages.

August: A complete interlocking convoy system has been organized along the American Atlantic coast, with local branch lines from all important points on the east coast of the United States, the Gulf, the Caribbean, and Brazil.

August: The military begins to issue Eric Knight's *A Short Guide to Great Britain* to GIs arriving there.

August: The American Joint Chiefs of Staff set up the Joint Security Council to protect the security of information and to implement and coordinate deception operations.

August 6: Passage of the U.S. Visiting Forces Act by the British Parliament provides the American military with exclusive jurisdiction over its soldiers, even when those soldiers break British law.

August 19: A mismanaged Canadian-British raid on Dieppe, France, costs more than 3,000 Allied lives and achieves nothing.

August 31: The battle of Alam el-Halfa halts German progress in Egypt.

September 10: The Women's Auxiliary Ferrying Squadron (WAFS) is organized under Nancy Love to deliver planes within the United States.

September 15: The Women's Flying Training Detachment (WFTD) is created to train women pilots for the WAFS, with Jacqueline Cochran as director.

October: In London an inter-Allied conference agrees that the British will handle Europe, the Mediterranean, the Middle East, and India-Burma, and the American Joint Security Council the Western Hemisphere, the Pacific, and China.

October: German submarines sink 88 merchant ships in the Atlantic.

October 22: The U.S. Army softens its policy on marriage, reducing the waiting period to two months and allowing commanders to authorize marriages that will not bring discredit on the military service; entitling wives in such marriages to allotments, insurance, and other benefits; and entitling them to speedier naturalization and exemption from immigration quotas.

October 23–November 5: The Battle of El Alamein in North Africa results in the first and the decisive land victory for the Allies.

November: The U.S. draft age is lowered to 18.

November: Sinkings in the Atlantic from U-boat attacks for one month reach an all-time high, at 106 ships.

November: Congress extends the draft law and amends the Neutrality Act to permit arming of merchant vessels.

November 2: The Stars and Stripes printed in London becomes a daily newspaper.

November 4: In North Africa the British under Gen. Bernard Law Montgomery force the Germans to withdraw toward Tunisia.

November 7: Marine Corps Commandant Gen. Thomas Holcomb approves the establishment of a women's reserve.

November 8: American and British troops under General Eisenhower land in French North Africa at Casablanca, Oran, and Algiers.

November 8: Yank magazine begins its London edition.

November 11: French forces in North Africa cease fire, and in the next few days Admiral Darlan becomes head of the civil government and Gen. Henri Honoré Giraud head of the French armed forces there.

November 11: Germany occupies southern France.

November 13: The British recapture Tobruk, Libya.

mid-November: FDR announces that "It would seem that the turning-point in this war has at last been reached"; and Churchill speaks of "the end of the beginning."

November 19: Soviet forces counterattack against the Germans at Stalingrad.

November 23: The Women's Reserve of the Coast Guard (SPARS, derived from the Coast Guard motto, "Semper Paratus," is established.

November 27: The Vichy French scuttle their fleet.

December: The army and navy take over the Civilian Pilot Training Program begun in 1939 and rename it the War Training Service.

December–January: At the Arcadia Conference in Washington, D.C., the British and Americans debate how to beat Germany.

December 5: Voluntary enlistment in the military is replaced by conscription, and the Selective Service Office is transferred to the War Manpower Commission.

1943

Standards are lowered to boost enlistments into the WAAC.

January 14–24: FDR and Churchill meet at Casablanca, Morocco, and agree to postpone the cross-channel invasion of Europe until 1944, to invade Sicily in July 1943, and to accept from the Axis nothing less than unconditional surrender. They give priority to a major bombing offensive against Germany.

January 27: U.S. Flying Fortresses and Liberators for the first time bomb Germany; they fly in daylight, and no fighters escort them.

January 31: German forces at Stalingrad surrender to the Soviets.

February 20: Inexperienced U.S. forces at Kasserine Pass in Tunisia are defeated in a German blitzkrieg (lightning war) commanded by Gen. Erwin Rommel, the "Desert Fox."

March: U-boats sink 108 Allied ships.

March 6: British troops under General Montgomery defeat the Germans under General Rommel in North Africa; shortly thereafter 275,000 German and Italian troops there surrender.

April: Higher standards for enlistment into the WAAC are imposed.

April 28–May 6: British sinking of U-boats marks a turning point in the North Atlantic struggle.

May: Improved detection devices and more warships and planes to shield convoys enable the Allies to lower dramatically the number of ships lost to German submarines. In this Battle of the North Atlantic, the Allies lose 2,778 ships, 2,603 of them merchantmen; the Germans lose 780 of their 1,162 U-boats.

May 9: Axis forces in Tunisia surrender to the Allies.

May 11: Churchill arrives in Washington for the "Trident Conference," where he and FDR form a general resolution calling on U.S. general George Marshall to draft a plan "to eliminate Italy from the war and to contain the maximum number of German forces."

May 17: The first Allied trans-Mediterranean convoy since 1941 leaves Gibraltar, reaching Alexandria, Egypt, on May 26 without loss, thus reopening the Suez lifeline.

Summer: The British War Office establishes a subcommittee to review relations between British and U.S. troops in all theaters.

June: Operation Pointblank, aimed at undermining the Luftwaffe by bombing the German aircraft industry, is approved.

June: British and American authorities agree that in the winter of 1943–44 GIs will be billeted in British homes, an arrangement that, despite official fears, leads to improved relations.

June 15: Through the Bolton Act Congress establishes the Cadet Nurse Corps, providing free nursing education to students who promise to render essential military or civilian service for the duration of the war.

July: The first Women's Army Corps battalion arrives in Britain.

July 1: The Women's Auxiliary Army Corps (WAAC) becomes the Women's Army Corps (WAC).

July 1: Direct commissions as officers are discontinued except for medical personnel, chaplains, and a few other highly specialized personnel.

July 4: The American Forces Network radio begins operations in Britain.

July 10: American, Canadian, and British troops invade Sicily in Operation Husky.

July 22: Forces led by Gen. George S. Patton enter Palermo in Sicily.

July 27: Palermo harbor is opened to Allied shipping.

July 28: Italian dictator Benito Mussolini is ousted and arrested.

August: The Women's Auxiliary Flying Squadron and the Women's Flying Training Detachment are combined into the Women Airforce Service Pilots (WASPs) with Jacqueline Cochran as director and Nancy Love in charge of the ferrying division.

August 17: U.S. Flying Fortresses hit the rail yards at Rouen in occupied France.

August 17: FDR and Churchill confer in Quebec to set the date for the invasion of France (Operation Overlord) and agree to appoint an American commander for it.

August 17: Sicily is under Allied control.

August 22: A State Department memo states that Churchill and FDR agree that "all possible steps should be taken to promote fraternization between the U.S. and British forces in the British Isles."

September: The Council on Books in Wartime publishes the first paperback of the Armed Services Editions.

September 3: The defeated Italians sign a secret armistice.

September 8–15: Allied forces invade Italy at Salerno, in the face of severe German resistance.

October 1: The U.S. Fifth Army enters Naples, Italy.

October 13: Italy declares war on Germany.

October 14: On this "Black Thursday" Americans attacking the ball-bearing factories at Schweinfurt, Germany, lose 60 aircraft.

November 28–30: FDR, Churchill, and USSR premier Joseph Stalin confer at Tehran.

December 9: FDR tells General Eisenhower that he is to command Operation Overlord, the Allied invasion of Normandy in France.

December 11: U.S. P-51 Mustang fighters begin to escort bombers to and from Germany.

1944

January 8: The British Ministry of Information forms an American Forces Liaison Division, with regional information officers to coordinate British hospitality committees of community leaders and representatives of voluntary organizations.

January 12: Allied forces land at Anzio, Italy, where they are pinned down until early May.

February 19: General Eisenhower warns GIs against drinking, bad language, and discourtesy to British civilians.

February 20: The British Bomber Command and the American Eighth and Fifteenth Air Forces begin "Big Week," a massive assault on German industry in which the U.S. Eighth Air Force drops nearly 10,000 tons of bombs, damaging or destroying more than 70 percent of the German factories involved in aircraft production, and breaks the back of the Luftwaffe (German air force) by downing more than 600 German fighters.

February 26: FDR signs legislation awarding commissions to navy nurses (rather than equivalent rank).

March: At his own request Patrick Hitler, German dictator Adolf Hitler's nephew, is inducted into the U.S. Navy.

March 1: The British Ministry of Information secures a budget to support British hospitality toward GIs.

March 3: A British-American Liaison Board is formed to deal with relations between GIs and British civilians.

April: General Marshall warns General Eisenhower of possible nuclear dangers in the invasion of Normandy, France.

April: A quarter of GI letters written in Normandy are addressed to British homes.

April: 100,000 members of the Army Specialized Training Program on college campuses and 30,000 air cadets are transferred to troop duty, primarily infantry divisions, to relieve the manpower shortage.

June 6: On this "D day," Allied forces invade Normandy, France.

June 7–18: Allied forces consolidate the beachheads in France and begin a massive buildup.

June 10: The first U.S. nurses enter France.

June 12: The Germans begin V-1 rocket attacks on England.

June 18–20: A great storm hits the Allied beachheads in France, temporarily halting unloading and underlining the necessity to capture the port of Cherbourg, France.

June 22: Allied forces liberate the port of Cherbourg.

June 22: FDR signs legislation awarding commissions to army nurses (rather than equivalent rank).

July 6: General de Gaulle visits the White House.

July 9: The Allies take Caen, France.

July 20: A German attempt on the life of Hitler fails.

July 25–27: In Operation Cobra, U.S. troops break out of hedgerow fighting in Normandy, uncovering the German left wing and enabling Patton's Third Army tanks to exploit the breakthrough.

August 7: Allied forces under General Patton trap Germans in a pocket near Falaise, France, but fail to prevent their escape.

August 15: American and Free French troops land in the south of France and drive up the Rhone valley in the Champagne Campaign.

August 24: Allied forces enter Paris.

August 26–September 30: The Allied Expeditionary Force sweeps through France to the Siegfried Line.

August 28: Toulon and Marseilles in France surrender to the Allies.

September 2: German national Jupp Kappius, the first U.S. agent to parachute into Germany, lands near Sogel, Germany.

September 3: Allied forces enter Brussels, Belgium.

September 8: The first V-2 rockets, launched by Germans from Holland, hit London.

September 11: Patton's Fourth Division, First Army, breaks through the German Siegfried Line.

September 13: Churchill and Roosevelt confer at Quebec, plan strategy in the Pacific, and sign a memo calling for "converting Germany into a country primarily agricultural and pastoral in its character" by "eliminating the war making industries in the Ruhr and the Saar," a decision that is soon abandoned.

September 16–December 15: Allies fight a bitter war of attrition in their effort to move through Germany.

September 17: U.S. forces fail to break into the Reich from the Netherlands, leaving the British isolated at Arnheim, Holland.

October: The Eighth Air Force, bombing industries deep within Germany by daylight without fighter escort, suffers losses of 26.7 percent.

November 1944–May 1945: The German U-boats make a comeback, to be defeated only at the end of the war in Europe.

U.S. troops of the 28th Infantry Division march down the Champs Elysées, in Paris, in a victory parade, August 29, 1944. *(National Archives, 111-SC-193197)*

November: The American Red Cross creates a Home Hospitality Division in London to bring together Britons offering hospitality and GIs seeking it.

December: The U.S. Office of War Mobilization directs draft boards to reclassify and induct into the military all men between 18 and 38 years of age not engaged in war work.

December 16: Germans begin the Battle of the Bulge in a massive counteroffensive in the Ardennes Forest in France, which is defeated only in late January 1945.

December 16: During the Battle of the Bulge General Eisenhower promises that black servicemen volunteering for frontline duty will be integrated into combat units; after the crisis they are sent back to their segregated labor units, but their combat performance forces senior military officers to question the wisdom of barring them from combat units.

December 17: In the Malmédy massacre Germans shoot U.S. prisoners of war. This action follows Hitler's directive for "a wave of terror and fright [in the battle of the Ardennes in which] . . . no human inhibitions should be shown."

December 22: To a German demand to surrender at Bastogne, France, Gen. Anthony McAuliffe sends the one-word answer "Nuts."

December 26: Bastogne, France, is liberated.

Late 1944: WAC standards for enlistment are lowered again but always exceed those for men.

1945

January 6: FDR calls for drafting nurses.

February 1–March 6: Allied soldiers in Europe fight their way to the Rhine.

February 4–11: At the Yalta conference on the Soviet Black Sea coast, FDR, Churchill, and Stalin agree to divide Germany into four zones of occupation, one for each of their countries, and one for France; Stalin promises Soviet assistance in the Pacific.

February 8–March 28: Allied troops struggle to take the Rhineland.

February 13–14: Allied bombing of Dresden, Germany, creates a firestorm.

March 23: General Patton informs Gen. Omar Bradley that a division of his troops has crossed the Rhine.

April 11: The U.S. Ninth Army reaches the Elbe River, 53 miles west of Berlin; on General Eisenhower's orders it stops there.

April 12: FDR dies.

Mid-April: 325,000 German troops surrender in the Ruhr pocket; in effect the Wehrmacht gives up, leaving the SS, the Volkssturm, and the Hitler Youth still fighting, inspiring fears that Nazi leaders will hole up in the Austrian Alps and call on small armed bands to continue the struggle.

April 14: British troops enter the Bergen-Belsen concentration camp.

April 23: Advanced U.S. operatives discover a cave near Hechingen, Germany, that contains the chief German atomic pile; they remove the equipment and dynamite the cave.

April 26: U.S. and Soviet troops meet at several places near the Elbe, cutting Germany in two.

April 28: Benito Mussolini is killed.

April 28–May 2: USSR forces take Berlin.

April 30: Hitler commits suicide in Berlin.

May 7: The Germans sign a document of unconditional surrender.

May 8: V-E (Victory in Europe) Day—the Allies have won the war in Europe.

EYEWITNESS TESTIMONY

The Draft and Volunteering

"Since when has it been necessary for Blackfeet [Indians] to draw lots to fight?"

> *Query by members of the Blackfeet tribe near the beginning of World War II, quoted in Morgan, "Native Americans in World War II," 23.*

I was young, in good shape, and they were not going to have a war without me.

> *Sgt. Harry Bare speaking of 1942, when he enlisted as an infantryman, in Drez,* D-Day, *8.*

[P]eople of my age wanted to be in the service because all of our friends were there.

> *Combat engineer Robert Healey speaking of 1942, in Drez,* D-Day, *9.*

I was, like many draftees, quite unhappy with my situation at the time. A city boy, separated from his young bride and a widowed mother, and outrageously out of shape.

> *Pfc. Harry Parley speaking of his training perhaps in 1942 or 1943, in Drez,* D-Day, *37.*

General [Hubert R.] Harmon, commanding the Gulf Coast Flight Training Command, came to Washington to see me. He said he had now at all times 20,000 to 30,000 "of the finest young men in America" getting their flying training at our numerous fields in Texas, Oklahoma and New Mexico and that the government provided ample funds to give them three square meals a day. However, General Harmon said these boys were almost literally starving because the food service was scarcely organized at all in that area; and he didn't have competent mess officers or cooks, and that he felt we must find for him someone who could correct that condition.

> *Air Force Col. Carlton G. Ketchum writing about events in the summer of 1942, in* The Recollections of Colonel Retread, *37.*

By 1943, after a series of defense industry deferments, and with a constant reminder from mothers who had sons in the army saying to me, "How come you're still around here?—my son has been in for so many years," I was anxious to join them.

> *Naval signalman Martin Fred Gutekunst remembering 1943, in Drez,* D-Day, *10.*

The Army Assignments

I am not proud of having been a member of a combat division whose mission was to kill other human beings, even though in those days, they were just "Japs" or "Jerries."

On the other hand, I have reflected many times on the hapless human beings that we rescued. I have wondered who would have released the Jews, the slaves, the gypsies, the religious and political dissenters, and the elderly if we had not. Who would have saved the hundreds of thousands of prisoners of war who were so mistreated while in captivity? And how else would the decent Germans and Japanese who wanted to rid themselves of Nazism and Imperialism have been able to do so?

> *Combat infantryman H. Stanley Huff writing in 2001 of his wartime experiences, in* Unforgettable Journey, *243.*

Why don't they talk about the guy who is just a soldier? Why doesn't anybody ever mention the poor bastard who got dragged into the Army, got stuck out here in one of these God-forsaken holes, and is doing nothing but his job? . . . The guys [truckdrivers, mechanics, cooks, clerks] whose jobs have become so regulated and monotonous . . . are the real heroes of this war.

> *Capt. Earl Nelson, "Heroes Don't Win Wars," writing in 1944, quoted in Linderman,* World within War, *52.*

We don't give a damn about not going to college [in the Army Special Training Program]. But we hate the idea of sitting in some broken-down camp all this war, and marching. . . . We won't even be sent overseas—because it takes at least 10 months' training before you're sent. . . . We've been told that we can't transfer out of the infantry. . . . There are guys here with three years of college as engineers, mechanics, radio men or with knowledge of languages, medical training and photography, as I am. You know, we were supposed to be the cream of the crop. Our I.Q. had to be higher than that of Officers Training School. . . . Then what is the reason of taking 100,000 best guys in the country and dumping them in infantry camps to wallow in the mud?

Aleck Hovsepian of the Army Special Training Program, March 6, 1944, in Hovsepian, later that month he was transferred to Intelligence. Your Son and Mine, *35.*

The Enemy

We thought the Krauts were evil; but we were evil too. . . . Should it be right for me to kill a middle-aged Kraut who loved his family and believed in God, not in Hitler, but who was drafted by the Third Reich to serve his country? I could not stop to think it out.

Infantryman John Bassett in Italy remembering 1943 and 1944, in Innocent Soldier, *43.*

[A wounded GI] kept calling for someone to help him. Isn't anybody going to take care of me? He was saying . . . and then he'd cry. [Medic] Pico . . . grabbed a Red Cross flag and ran across the snow waving it. . . . He was kneeling by the wounded man; he had just given him a shot and was putting on a dressing when the machine gun cut him in two. The German was clearly having a lot of fun because he kept on firing long bursts into the wounded man and into Pico, keeping the bodies jumping and spreading red all over the snow. He's used the wounded man for bait, an old SS trick.

Dr. Brendon Phibbs describing an event of January 11, 1945, in Other Side of Time, *137–138.*

Pulling on his Red Cross bib, Doc [William Mellon, a medic] stood in the open to make sure the Germans spotted him. He then walked slowly toward the river [and the wounded G.I. After treating him, Doc returned to the American lines to find a wheelbarrow and started back.] Men yelled across the river to the Germans, "Okay, hold it, hold it," and the Germans hollered back, "Okay." . . . [Doc loaded the wounded man on the wheelbarrow and trundled it a quarter of a mile.] As he finally pushed the wheelbarrow into an alley behind a ruined house . . . a cheer went up from every man in K company.

Oral historians Harold P. Leinbaugh and John D. Campbell using eyewitness accounts of men in the 84th Division to reconstruct events of January 1945, in Men of Company K, *212–213, 225–226.*

Finally the [German] revealed that he had lived many years in America. He stated he knew how Negroes were treated in the United States, but couldn't understand why Negroes were so faithful to such a country. I asked him why [the Germans] were so hard on the Jews. . . . He responded that the Jews had sold Germany out after the last war, and that they had hoarded all the capital of Germany. I inquired as to why [the Germans] attacked Poland and occupied all the smaller countries of Europe. He maintained that the Germans were the underdogs of Europe, that they were allowed to travel through only one street of Poland to get to Danzig, and the Poles, backed up by France and Britain, made fun of them.

Tuskegee Airman Lieutenant Long speaking of his POW experience, Spring 1945, quoted in Francis, Tuskegee Airmen, *156.*

The North Africa Campaign—Operation Torch (November 8, 1942–May 12, 1943)

You hear of casualties, see casualties, and read of casualties, but you believe it will never happen to you.

Member of an ordnance unit in North Africa speaking of 1943, quoted in Linderman, World within War, *7.*

We then moved up along the Spanish-Moroccan border to a desert village, where part of the French Foreign Legion was stationed—a wild bunch! The local Arab sheik put on a cous-cous dinner for officers of both groups. He whispered to me in French, "When are you going to kick the French out of Morocco and make us one of your states?" I whispered, "Jamais!" ["Never."]

Staff officer Stephen J. Rogers speaking probably of early 1943, "From Casablanca to Berchtesgaden," in Thoburn and Knapp, "Perspectives," 58.

In February [1943], I was told I was to accompany Assistant Secretary of War John J. McCloy on an important mission to North Africa. I was to serve as an intelligence advisor and as interpreter for the group. . . . Despite his fluent French, on formal occasions the Sultan spoke only in Arabic; so that [his] Minister then put it into French and I translated it into English. This four-way conversation proceeded for one-half hour and as a result of it we all knew the

Moroccans and French were glad to have us there and we were indeed happy to be there.

Intelligence officer Edmund Delaney writing of February 1943, in Me Voilà, *63–64.*

In this war no units in the line get relief. We just go on and on. I believe that the very fierceness of this fighting means that later resistance will be softened.

Brig. Gen. Theodore Roosevelt, letter in March 1943, quoted in Tapert, Lines of Battle, *80.*

The Sicily Campaign—Operation Husky (July 10, 1943–August 17, 1943)

It is a world no civilian can ever know. Civilians can hide from the storm and wait and pray for its passing. We must go into the hell and finish the job. With sickened souls, despairing hearts and hate in our minds we must stick it out to our finish (in one way or another) or the war's finish. There must be a hell hereafter for men who willfully make such hells here for us.

Infantryman Orval Faubus, Summer 1943, in In This Faraway Land, *157.*

In July 1943 we landed on the south coast of Sicily. I remember a peasant coming down a dirt road leading a donkey with a load of melons. I asked, "Quanto lire por melone?" He replied, "Oh, give me a dime. I'm from Brooklyn."

Staff officer Stephen J. Rogers remembering July 1943, "From Casablanca to Berchtesgaden," in Thoburn and Knapp, "Perspectives," 58.

I got through the campaign [in Sicily] without a scratch, save for those on my hands from crawling through bushes, scouting. . . . I enjoyed the campaign immensely. It's a fascinating game, particularly when you're the first element out front. And the fact that the stakes are high make it all the more engrossing.

Morton Eustis writing of events from July 27 to late August 1943, quoted in Eustis, Letters, *132.*

TAKE CALCULATED RISKS. That is quite different from being rash. My personal belief is that if you have a 50% chance take it because the superior fighting qualities of American soldiers lead [sic] by me will surely give you the extra 1% necessary.

In Sicaly [sic] I decided as a result of my information, observations and a sixth sense that I have that the enemy did not have another large scale attack in his system. I bet my shirt on that and I was right. You cannot make war safely. . . .

Gen. George S. Patton, June 6, 1944, in Carroll, War Letters, *239.*

The Campaigns in Italy and the Balkans (September 8, 1943–December 31, 1944)

[In combat] the ductless glands pour their fluids into the system to make it able to stand up to the great demand on it. Fear and ferocity are products of the same fluid. Fatigue toxins poison the system. Hunger followed by wolfed food distorts the metabolic pattern already distorted by the adrenalin and fatigue. The body and the mind so disturbed are really ill and fevered. . . . Under extended bombardment or bombing the nerve ends are literally beaten. The ear drums are tortured by blast and the eyes ache from the constant hammering. . . . [A]ll your other senses become dull, too. . . . In the dullness all kinds of emphases change. . . . The whole world becomes unreal.

Correspondent John Steinbeck, November 5, 1943, dispatch from Italy, in Once There Was a War, *199–201.*

For weeks we would be halted before one of these old cities [in Italy], and we would shell it without pause until it was rubble. Why? The shelling killed only a very few of the enemy, it wasted countless tons of supplies, and yet in almost every case it was only through the final attack by armor and infantry that the Germans were routed from the rubble, which proved better protection for them than the buildings and which merely impeded the movement of our own vehicles. . . . Frequently one stood with an artilleryman and listened to remarks like this: "I'm getting tired of seeing that big white building there. Knock the goddamn thing down." He did not know, and would not have cared, whether it was an enemy headquarters, a family home, or a famous museum. It had become a kind of obsession to destroy, to fire for the sake of firing.

Correspondent Eric Sevareid writing of events of late 1943 and 1944, in Not So Wild a Dream, *419–420.*

The Normandy Campaign (June 6, 1944–August 6, 1944)

In late February, 1944, a huge package had arrived in the Western European branch [of Army Military Intelligence], to be opened personally by myself. These were three heavy volumes containing the basic intelligence data for the Normandy Invasion. The maps of the French coast showed the precise landing spots and the beach defenses. Other maps gave the radius of artillery fire from German coastal defenses from LeHavre to Cherbourg. I was somewhat horrified by the responsibility of being the guardian of these documents. They were securely placed . . . within our branch safe and were rarely withdrawn. More than once, in the middle of the night, I would awaken with worry about the security of these papers and get in my car and go to the Pentagon and check that the combinations on the safes were properly set.

American intelligence officer Edmund Delaney writing about February to June 1944, in Me Voilà, *72–73.*

[T]he report we received was discouraging. Low clouds, high winds, and formidable wave action were predicted. . . . The meteorologists said that air support would be impossible, naval gunfire would be inefficient, and even the handling of small boats would be rendered difficult. . . . [The other commanders differed from each other, and] I decided that the attack would have to be postponed. . . .

At three-thirty the next morning [June 5] . . . the first report given us . . . was that the bad conditions predicted the day before for the coast of France were actually prevailing there and that if we had persisted in the attempt to land on June 5 a major disaster would almost surely have resulted.

Gen. Dwight Eisenhower writing about June 4–5, 1944, in Crusade in Europe, *249–250.*

I looked at my watch. It was 10 P.M., 5 June 1944. D-Day minus 1. For men of the 82nd Airborne Division, twelve hours before H-Hour, the battle for Normandy had begun.

We flew in a V or Vs, like a gigantic spearhead without a shaft. England was on double daylight-saving time, and it was still full light, but eastward, over the Channel, the skies were darkening. Two hours later night had fallen, and below us we could see the glints of yellow flame from the German anti-aircraft guns on the Channel Islands. . . . In the plane the men sat quietly, deep in their own thoughts. They joked a little and broke, now and then, into ribald laughter. Nervousness and tension, and the cold that blasted through the open door, had its effect upon us all. Now and then a paratrooper would rise, lumber heavily to the little bathroom in the tail of the plane, find he could not push through the narrow doorway in his bulky gear, and come back, mumbling his profane opinion of the designers of the C-47 airplane. Soon the crew chief passed a bucket around, but this did not entirely solve our problem. A man strapped and buckled into full combat gear finds it extremely difficult to reach certain essential portions of his anatomy, and his efforts are not made easier by the fact that his comrades are watching him, jeering derisively and offering gratuitous advice.

Gen. Matthew B. Ridgway writing about June 5, 1944, in "D-Day Minus One," 1.

There were four rolls [of barbed wire] laid down the [Easy Red section of Omaha] beach, and someone yelled for bangalore torpedoes, and we started handing bangalore torpedoes, laying on our backs, shoveling them down toward one area and started putting them together—males one end, females at the other—and started screwing them together. Each was about five feet long, and we got enough fellows to push these heavy bangalore torpedoes under the barbed wire through the entire four or five rows of wire. Then someone yelled "Fire," and they blew the wire. Everyone rushed through the wire and started running for the bluffs, and there was a good path to climb, which we did. I looked back momentarily and it was unbelievable the amount of fellows that were killed and wounded.

Tech. Sgt. Theodore Aufort recalling June 6, 1944, in Drez, D-Day, *241.*

I started up the bluff, with four or five men behind me, and about half to two-thirds of the way up, a machine gun opened up on us from the right front. Everyone hugged the ground. I scurried and scratched along until I got within ten meters of the gun position. Then I unloaded all four of my fragmentation grenades, and when the last one went off, I made a dash for the top. The other kids were right behind me, and we all made it. I don't know if I knocked out that gun crew or if they bugged out [retreated]. In any event, those grenades were all the

U.S. soldiers leave a Coast Guard landing boat off the coast of France under heavy machine gun fire, June 6, 1944. *(National Archives, 26-G-2343)*

return fire that I provided coming off the beach. I didn't fire a round from either my rifle or my pistol.

John Ellery recollecting June 6, 1944,
in Drez, D-Day,
249–250.

Oh, that hillside [at Omaha Beach] was loaded with mines, and a unit of sappers had gone first, to find where the mines were. A number of those guys were lying on the hillside, their legs shattered by the explosions. They'd shot themselves up with morphine and they were telling where it was now safe to step. They were about twenty-five yards apart, our guys, calmly telling us how to get up the hill.

Veteran Gino Merli of Wilkes-Barre, Pennsylvania,
remembering June 6, 1944, in Brokaw, Greatest
Generation, *xxi–xxiii.*

[The cliffs on the land between Omaha and Utah Beaches] were 115 to 125 feet high. We fired our rockets [carrying grappling hooks] up the cliff and onto French soil. As we were getting ready to climb the ropes, the German machine guns strafed the area from three hundred yards away on our left. A battleship was called to strike the machine guns. We free climbed—since we were unable to touch the cliff—up the ropes. Germans were shooting, bullets flying, and as the men came up to join me, I told them, "Boys, keep your heads down. Headquarters has

fouled up again and issued the enemy live ammunition."

Ranger Sgt. Gene E. Elder speaking about
June 6, 1944, in Drez, D-Day, *262.*

I . . . became fascinated with a duel going on between a destroyer, which was running parallel with the beach, and a bunker, which was firing on us from up on the left bluff. The destroyer was at full speed and almost up on the beach, and he was throwing five-inch shells into that thing just as fast as he could pump them in.

Master Sgt. Paul Ritter speaking of June 6, 1944,
in Drez, D-Day, *285.*

[O]ur job was to blow the underwater obstacles. [In training] we had photos taken every twenty-four hours by P-38s . . . to see if there were any changes on [Utah] beach, on which there were Belgian Gates, which is what they called the steel obstacles which were made of rails. There were Belgian Gates, "hedge-hogs," and a variety of other obstacles. . . . [A]s we hit the beach, we started out and jumped into the water; some was to the waist or higher, and each man going ashore carried a sixty-five-pound pack of demolitions. I happened to be the one who carried, in addition to explosives, the reel of primer cord. And Lieutenant Grant had all the detonating fuses, and he had them taped to his helmet.

Sgt. Al Pikasiewicz recalling June 6, 1944, in Drez,
D-Day, *177–178.*

When we caught sight of [the beach], I could see the exploding shells churning up the sand. My feet were soaking wet. My rifle was still wrapped in plastic, which I ripped off before the ramp went down. Because of many beach obstacles, our boat couldn't move in close to shore. When the ramp went down, a boy in my squad started crying and yelling that he couldn't leave the boat, and begged to be left on. I inflated my life jacket and grabbed his arm and pulled him into the water with me. A shell came in close, and we ducked into the murky water with just our heads showing. Another shell came in, and by now he had stopped crying and was facing up to trying to get to shore. I was so exhausted and weighed down that I lost my fear of becoming a casualty on the beach.

Reginald Galdonick recalling his experience with the
90th Division on June 6, 1944, in Drez, D-Day, *183.*

When I reached the first [enemy] gun position again, Lieutenant Winters was still there, but the breech of the gun was blown out like a half-peeled banana. . . . He said he dropped a block of TNT down the barrel, and since TNT requires a percussion cap or some kind of heavy force to detonate, Bill Guarnere had dropped a German "potato-masher" grenade down the barrel with it and that had done it.

Parachute infantryman Carwood Lipton speaking of June 6, 1944, in Drez, D-Day, *193.*

The heat drew the nylon chutes toward the fire [in a haybarn in Sainte-Mere-Eglise, near Utah Beach]. The air to feed the fire was actually drawing us toward the fire One guy, I heard him scream, I saw him land in the fire. I heard him scream one more time before he hit the fire, and he didn't scream any more. [I jerked my suspension lines to avoid the fire and came down on the roof of the church; my chute caught on a steeple, and I was hanging there when] John Steele came down, and his chute caught too. [Sergeant John Ray] hit in front of the church. A Nazi soldier, billeted on the next street behind the church, came around from behind, a red-haired German soldier. He came to shoot Steele and myself, hanging there. As he came around, he shot Ray in the stomach. John being a sergeant, he had a forty-five pistol and while he was dying in agony, he got his forty-five out and when this German soldier turned around to kill us, John shot the German in the back of the head and killed him.

Parachutist Ken Russell, then 17 years old, remembering his Normandy landing in June 1944, in Ambrose, Americans at War, *81–82.*

One persistent memory . . . of a bone-sagging weariness, possibly a result of long-standing strain or of feeling that on the basis of having to fight for every hedgerow, the war would go on forever. Whatever the causes, it seemed to affect us all—I noted young men around me take on the look and movements of middle age. This physical weariness was accompanied by unrest that made sleep fitful. The effect was that of a motor racing to move a sluggish machine or of trying to run in a nightmare with much effort and little progress. Also affected was my boasted ability to maintain outward emotional control.

Capt. Charles R., battalion surgeon, remembering the summer of 1944, in Cawthon, "St. Lo," 714–715.

[In hedgerow fighting, typically] a machine gun [is] knocked out here, a man or two [is] killed or wounded there. Eventually the leader of the stronger force, usually the attackers, may decide that he has weakened his opponents enough to warrant a large concerted assault, preceded by a concentration of all the mortar and artillery support he can get. Or the leader of the weaker force may see that he will be overwhelmed by such an attack and pull back. Thus goes the battle—a rush, a pause, some creeping, a few isolated shots, some artillery fire, some mortars, some smoke, more creeping, another pause, dead silence, more firing, a great concentration of fire followed by a concerted rush. Then the whole process starts all over again.

Maj. G. S. Johns, Jr., describing a typical infantry assault in Normandy, summer 1944, in Ellis, On the Front Lines, *93–94.*

[In an artillery bombardment] the best thing to do is to drop to the ground and crawl into your steel helmet. One's body tends to shrink a great deal when shells come in. I am sure I have gotten as much as eighty percent of my body under my helmet when caught under shellfire. . . . [Once] I had to push through a hedgerow. A submachine-gun emitted a long burst right in front of my face. . . . The bullets went over my head. I fell backward and passed out cold from fright.

Capt. John Colby recalling summer 1944, quoted in Ambrose, Victors, *200.*

[When the 120th Infantry relieved the 82nd Airborne in Normandy,] the green, unblooded newcomers gazed in shock and awe at the paratroopers they were to succeed. We asked them, "Where are your officers?" and they answered, "All dead." We asked, "Who's in charge, then?," and some sergeant said, "I am."

Infantry Lieutenant Sidney Eichen speaking of events of July 1944, in Hastings, Overlord, *156.*

The Germans [who called us Roosevelt's butchers] thought we were all ex-cons emptied out of San Quentin and Sing Sing to practice on the Germans the same savagery we had committed against our own countrymen. We were cannon fodder in their eyes, desperate men with nothing to lose and no reason to fear death. Fine, . . . [l]et them think it. Nothing is as terrifying as a man who doesn't mind dying. As long as they thought that of the 4th Armored, we would have a considerable psychological advantage. . . .

Nat Frankel of the 4th Armored Division, recalling fall 1944, in Frankel and Smith, Patton's Best, *5.*

In fact, there is one cartoon by [Bill] Mauldin . . . that I can't help but think of when I think of Patton. Joe and Willie [Mauldin's battle-weary GIs] are in a trench, their guns peeking out over the top. Some young stalwart officer is standing atop the trench, his eyes steadfastly gazing upward and outward. Joe looks up and says, "Excuse me, lootenant, but do you think you can try to inspire us without drawing fire?"

Nat Frankel of the 4th Armored Division, reminiscing about fall 1944, in Frankel and Smith, Patton's Best, *54.*

Paratroops land in Holland during operations by the First Allied Airborne Army, September 1944. *(National Archives, 111-SC-354702)*

The Battle for France (September 1, 1944–March 1, 1945)

[In August, 1944] one dark night we pulled off the road. One of our guys lay down to sleep beside an already sleeping German soldier who had become separated from his comrades and had lain down for the night. When the German awoke the next morning he shook the American to arouse him and then surrendered to him.

Capt. John Colby recalling August 1944, in Ambrose, Citizen Soldiers, *100.*

We commandeered the [two] cows and hung our mortars and equipment on them. They were very docile and plodded right along with us. As we neared Nijmegen, the Dutch people welcomed us. But while pleased and happy to be liberated, they were quite shocked to see paratroopers leading two cows. The first questions were, "Where are your tanks?" We were not their idea of American military invincibility, mobility and power. We could only tell them, "The tanks are coming." We hoped it was true.

Sgt. D. Zane Shlemmer recalling late August and September, 1944, in Ambrose, Citizen Soldiers, *122.*

Get off your fanny as fast as you can and move on until your engines run dry, then get out and walk.

Gen. George S. Patton to his leading tank corps commander, fall 1944, in Ryan, A Bridge Too Far, *71.*

[T]here was a redneck, a Sergeant Luther, who never went to grammar school. His mind *was* a map and his estimates of probable enemy positions and numbers were uncanny. Indeed, Luther received a field commission. . . . After the war, however, he couldn't keep it, since he couldn't read. . . . He stayed in the army for the rest of his career, but only as the highest ranking noncom.

Nat Frankel of the 4th Armored Division, remembering the fall 1944 push toward Bastogne, in Frankel and Smith, Patton's Best, *89.*

[The sergeant] sort of smiled and said . . . he had just pissed his pants. He always pissed them, he said, when things started and then he was okay . . . and then I realized . . . [t]here was something warm down there and it seemed to be running down my leg. . . . I said, "Sarge, I've pissed too," or something like that and he grinned and said, "Welcome to the war."

Replacement soldier, probably fall 1944, quoted in Fussell, Wartime, *278.*

It was there in that green forest [overlooking the Siegfried Line] that we ran into the most frightening weapon of the war, the one that made us almost sick with fear: *antipersonnel mines.* By now I had gone through aerial bombing, artillery and mortar shelling, open combat, direct rifle and machine-gun firing,

Cpl. Charles H. Johnson of the 783rd Military Police Battalion waves on a "Red Ball Express" motor convoy rushing priority materiel to forward areas, near Alençon, France, September 5, 1944. *(National Archives, 111-SC-195512)*

night patrolling, and ambush. Against all of this we had some kind of chance; against mines we had none. They were viciously, deadly, inhuman. They churned our guts.

Lt. George Wilson recalling fall 1944,
in If You Survive, *111–112.*

They then told us to get the boats and go across the river. The boat was like a canvass material with a wood frame to it and it held about twelve men in a boat. We had to paddle to get it across. We took the boats and came from behind the factory (where the Krauts I don't think knew we were there). We started down across the sandy shore which was maybe 50 yards long till we got to the water. We were running with these boats and our weapons and what not. In addition to all that crap the old man said you lay a telephone line across the river so . . . we can talk back to them, if we need support fire or something. We weren't sure that the radios would work that distance

with the one's we had. So I had a kid from the communications section join us with a roll of wire on a spindle-like thing.

We got into the damn boats and thought . . . at first it looked like rain in the water. Then we realized it was lead coming from the Krauts on the other side. And away we went. I'll tell you we were paddling like mad to get across. Quite a few of the boats were overturned; guys in a lot of them were killed in the getting across the thing.

Thomas F. Pitt, Jr., of the 504th Parachute Regiment
describing events of September 20, 1944, in "The Waal
River Crossing," available online. URL: www.
thedropzone.org/europe/Holland/pitt.html.

Now the fight for Huertgen was at its wildest. We dashed, struggled from one building to another shooting, bayoneting, clubbing. Hand grenades roared, rifles cracked—buildings to the left and right burned with acrid smoke. . . . The wounded and the dead—men in the uniforms of both sides—lay in grotesque positions at every turn. From many the blood still flowed.

Infantryman Paul Boesch remembering the fall and
winter of 1944, in Road to Huertgen, *226–227.*

Every day more men are falling out due to trench foot. Some men are so bad they can't wear shoes and are wearing overshoes over their socks. These men can't walk and are being carried from sheltered pillbox positions at night to firing positions in the day time.

Col. Ken Reimers of the 90th Division, December
1944, quoted in Ambrose, Victors, *300.*

So they got us surrounded again, the poor bastards!
GI Constant Klinga speaking in the winter of
1944–45, quoted in Frankel and Smith,
Patton's Best, *108.*

The Battle for Germany (January 1945– May 7, 1945)

[Our] demolition squad crawled up with TNT on their backs and blew the door in. And the infantry guys took a beating while they did it. Even the tanks had pulled back after their firing point-blank at the pillboxes had failed. But this one company of guys with just rifles had to stick it out. You figure it out. We can't.

Medic William Tsuchida recalling early 1945, in Wear It Proudly, *49.*

The Germans were on our transmissions as well as Axis Sally, who was telling us about rioting in Cleveland, Ohio, and telling us to go home and doing all she could to break our morale. . . . [T]hen [she] played Louis Armstrong's recording of "I Can't Give You Anything but Love, Baby." . . . We did not move fifty yards before we were hit! It sounded like heavy plate glass bursting into a million ear-splitting pieces. Concussion blew me out of the tank. Had my hatch not been open, all of us would have been killed by the concussion alone. I got up and ran, for I was in a state of hysteria. . . . My clothing was cut to shreds. [I was] bleeding profusely. . . . The area was now drawing enemy fire. I ran until I was exhausted. I remember stopping at a monastery. The Germans began shelling this also, so I took off again. In my delirium, I made my way to an aid station about three kilometers from the scene of a battle, running through wooded areas infested with German snipers. . . . I collapsed. . . . When I came to my senses, I was on a litter. I was evacuated at night in a convoy of ambulances which slowly moved through mine fields and booby-trapped roads.

African-American GI Walter Lewis, 761st Tank Battalion, describing the action of January 4, 1945, quoted in Potter, Liberators, *194–5.*

With the exception of the great tank battle at El Alamein, probably no tank engagement in World War II will be remembered longer than the dashing coup which first put the American Army across the Rhine at Remagen.

It was accomplished by the U. S. Ninth Armored Division.

It is no exaggeration to say that the speedy fording of the Rhine at a comparatively undefended point by tanks and infantrymen and engineers who knew there was strong likelihood the dynamite-laden bridge would blow up under them at any moment has saved the American nation 5,000 dead and 10,000 wounded.

Hal Boyle of the Associated Press reporting on the events of March 7–8, 1945, in Toland, Last 100 Days, *219. Soldiers who crossed the bridge later passed a sign reading, "Cross the Rhine with dry feet, Courtesy of the 9th Arm'd Division."*

The bridge was built in parts, with four groups working simultaneously on four boat rafts, mostly by feel in the dark. By 0400 the next morning, fourteen four-boat rafts had been completed and were ready to be assembled together as a bridge. When the rafts were in place they were reinforced with pneumatic floats between the steel pontoons so the bridge could take the weight of thirty- six-ton Sherman tanks. . . .

[Ten LCVPs (landing craft vehicle and personnel)] were able to hold the bridge against the current until we could install a 1" steel cable across the Rhine immediately upstream of the bridge, to which the anchors for each pontoon were attached. . . . The remaining four-boat rafts were connected to the anchor cable, eased into position and connected to the ever-extending bridge until the far shore was reached.

Finally, at 1900 March 11, 27 hours after starting construction, the 9769-ft. heavy pontoon bridge was

U.S. POWs captured by the Germans during the Battle of the Bulge march along a road somewhere on the western front, December 1944. *(National Archives, 111-SC-198240)*

completed. It was the longest floating bridge ever constructed by the Corps of Engineers under fire.

Maj. Jack Barnes of the 51st Engineer Combat Battalion remembering March 11, 1945, in Ambrose, "The Last Barrier," 541.

[The CO sent a German-speaking Jewish private with a white flag to encourage the German teenage boys to surrender.] They shot him up so bad that after it was over the medics had to slide a blanket under his body to take him away. [Then eight of the Germans came out waving a white flag and with their hands up.] They were very cocky. They were about 20 feet from me when I saw the leader suddenly realize he still had a pistol in his shoulder holster. He reached into his jacket with two fingers to pull it out and throw it away. One of our guys yelled, "Watch it! He's got a gun!" and came running up shooting and there were eight Krauts on the ground shot up but not dead. They wanted water but no one gave them any. I never felt bad about it although I'm sure civilians would be horrified. But these guys asked for it. If we had not been so tired and frustrated and keyed up and mad about our boys they shot up, it never would have happened. But a lot of things happen in war and both sides know the penalties.

Cpl. James Pemberton of the 103rd Division describing events in Germany in the spring of 1945, quoted in Ambrose, Victors, 331.

U.S. troops cross the Rhine under enemy fire in an assault boat at St. Goar, Germany, March 1945. "We all tried to crawl under each other because the lead was flying around like hail," one of them reported. *(National Archives, 208-YE-132)*

Personnel Identity

We did everything we could to please [Lady Luck]: we showed her trinkets, crucifixes, St. Christopher medals, the foot of a rabbit, vials of holy water, small pieces of paper with prayers written on them, lucky coins, sacred photographs in gold lockets, a pair of loaded dice, a pressed flower from a girl, a picture of a child in an embossed leather case, and many other beloved charms.

B-17 pilot John Muirhead writing about practices common among servicemen throughout the war, in Those Who Fall, 122–123.

[In] our innocence we [soldiers] knew almost nothing about homosexuality. We had never heard of lesbians, and while we were aware that male homosexuals existed—they were regarded as degenerates and called "sex perverts," or simply "perverts"—most of us had never, to our knowledge, encountered one.

Author William Manchester writing of his wartime service as a marine, in Goodbye, Darkness, 100.

[S]train and tension wear away at the leader's endurance, his judgment and his confidence. The pressure becomes more acute because of the duty of a staff constantly to present to the commander the worst side of an eventuality. [It is up to the commander to] preserve optimism in himself and in his command. Without confidence, enthusiasm and optimism in the command, victory is scarcely obtainable. . . . [A cheerful, hopeful attitude in the commander] tends to minimize potentialities within the individual himself to become demoralized . . . [and] has a most extraordinary effect upon all with whom he comes in contact. With this clear realization, I firmly determined that my mannerisms and speech in public would always reflect the cheerful certainty of victory—that any pessimism and discouragement I might ever feel would be reserved for my pillow.

Gen. Dwight D. Eisenhower, about the problems of leadership in wartime in his draft introduction to his memoirs (later discarded), quoted in Ambrose, Victors, 41.

They send you to Tunisia, and then they send you to Sicily, and they send you to Italy. God knows where they'll send you after that. Maybe we'll be in France next year. . . . Then we work our way east. Yugoslavia.

Greece. . . . All I know is, in 1958, we're going to fight the Battle of Tibet.

Pvt. Archimbeau Brown speaking probably in 1943,
in Walk in the Sun, *27–28.*

[Scores of women who wrote "Dear John" letters explaining that they no longer loved the recipients were] guilty of murder. These were our private letter-writing Fifth Column [traitors to their own country] who knocked the guts out of the fighting men. . . . If you must write, for God's sake write cheerfully. I know of six murderers of that sort.

Infantryman R. M. Wingfield remembering the campaign
of August 1944 to February 1945, in The Only Way
Out, *174.*

But what we had together was something awfully damned good, something I don't think we'll ever have again as long as we live. Nobody in his senses wants war, but maybe it takes war to make men feel as close to each other as we have felt.

Combat engineer Henry Giles, July 12, 1945, in Giles,
G. I. Journal, *377.*

What was worse than death was the indignation of your buddies. You couldn't let 'em down. It was stronger than flag and country.

Marine E. B. Sledge remembering his service in the
Pacific from fall 1944 to summer 1945,
in
With the Old Breed, *60.*

[O]ut stepped John Wayne, wearing a cowboy outfit. . . . He grinned his aw-shucks grin . . . and said, "Hi ya, guys!" He was greeted by a stony silence. Then somebody booed. Suddenly everyone was booing. This man was a symbol of the fake machismo we had come to hate, and we weren't going to listen to him.

Author William Manchester watching the movie star
with other wounded in a naval hospital, probably in
1945, in "The Bloodiest Battle," 84.

["Ninety-day wonder" replacement officer John Toole:] Why don't you aim your rifle?
[Pvt. John Orr:] You damn fool! You think I want a hole in my head like Davis there? Why don't you fire *your* carbine? You ain't doin' anything else. . . .
[Toole, later, to himself]: I think of all the rules of the Infantry School at Ft. Benning which we had violated.

We had dug in on the reverse slope of a hill. We conducted an unauthorized withdrawal. An enlisted man had deliberately disobeyed the orders of a commissioned officer. A Sergeant gives orders to a Lieutenant.

Officer John Toole and Pvt. John Orr, probably in early
1945, in Toole, Battle Diary, *38–39.*

[The men in the 99th Infantry are] a bunch of soda jerks and grocery clerks. . . . [T]hat's what all these American soldiers are. They're not professional military men but just a bunch of guys over here doing a job, and a darn good one, and proving themselves much the superior soldier to the German, who has spent the better part of his life pursuing military training.

Lt. Robert Bass, letter of January 5, 1945, quoted in
Tapert, Lines of Battle, *215–216.*

[W]hen we got to the front and the 1st Sgt. told me my lieutenant wanted me to lay out and roll up his bedroll for sleeping, my response was that I was not Lt. Zahora's servant, and [I] refused to do it. I could tell that the 1st Sgt. liked my reply and I was not gigged for it.

Cpl. Rev Ehrgott, date unknown, World War II Survey,
Historical Services Division, U.S. Army Historical
Institute, Carlisle Baracks, Pennyslvania.

The ubiquitous Kilroy, his long pathetic nose hanging over the wall with the two peering eyes above it, always the spectator, never inside. 'Kilroy was here.' It was marked on the standing walls of ruined buildings, on latrine walls and other places from Seattle to Miami and from Italy to Australia. No one ever knew who started it. Everybody understood it. If something bad had happened, Kilroy was responsible. If something good had happened, Kilroy had been outside looking in.

James Jones, quoted in "Glider Pilot Humor," no date,
available online. URL: www.pointvista.com/
WW2GliderPilots/GliderPilotHumor.htm. Kilroy
turned up everywhere American servicemen went all over
the world, his head bald except for one hair, his hands
grasping the top of a fence, his eyes enormous just above
the fence, and his long nose drooping down over the
fence, nothing more of him visible. Servicemen claimed
that wherever they landed, wherever they fought, Kilroy
had always preceded them, welcoming them
even from enemy buildings.

The Airmen

Cut the size of your office to a five-foot cube—engulf it in the roar of four 1,000-horsepower engines—increase your height above the ground to four or five miles—reduce the atmospheric pressure by one-half to two-thirds—lower the outside temperature to 40 or 50 below zero. . . . That will give you an idea of the *normal* conditions under which the pilots, navigators, and bombardiers must work out the higher mathematical relationships of engine revolutions, manifold and fuel pressure, aerodynamics, barometric pressure, wind drift, air speed, ground speed, position, direction, and plane altitude. . . . As the final touch to this bizarre picture of intense concentration amid intense distraction, add the *fear of death.*

Air surgeon Maj. Gen. David N.W. Grant describing the conditions of wartime flying, in "Work of the Flight Surgeon," 131–135 passim.

[In 1943 and early 1944] it was seldom that more than ten percent of the squadrons flying from England would complete the twenty-five missions necessary for the Lucky Bastard Ribbon (Distinguished Flying Cross) and return to the States.

Bomber pilot John Vietor describing 1943 and early 1944, in Time Out, *130.*

Snow White, a B-24 bomber of the U.S. Army Ninth Air Force, arrived at a forward bomber base in the Libyan desert, April 1943. *(Library of Congress, LC-USW3-033190-E)*

We were under [antiaircraft] fire for twelve minutes that time. It is the most terrible experience you can have. It is just like going "over the top" into an artillery barrage.

B-24 gunner James McMahon, letter of March 10, 1944, in Tapert, Lines of Battle, *144.*

We watched in awe . . . as [our P-39s and P-47s] delivered huge demolition bombs, smaller fragmentation bombs, machine-gun fire, and Napalm bombs which exploded in a great, spectacular gush of flaming oil. The planes zoomed low over our heads as they streaked for Jerry's [German] lines to support our attacking units.
. . . Just as we were shouting the airmen's praises without restriction, a pair of [American] Thunderbolts roared out of the sky. To our horror we could see their bombs release and come screaming straight at us. . . . I had no sooner scrambled shakily to my feet and checked my platoon . . . when the P-47s returned to strafe. . . . We stood up, brushed off and hardly had time to cuss before two others roared out of the sky on a bombing run. Again we hugged the earth.

Lt. Paul Boesch remembering the fall and winter of 1944, in Road to Huertgen, *54–55.*

Medics, Doctors, and Nurses

I saw them, the man with the deep hole in the front of the skull, his nose gone, whose mind would eventually come back to normal, whose face would be restored by plastic surgery; the man who could neither talk nor register words, whose brain was now . . . at the mental level of a rabbit. He, too, with neurological care, should be able to climb back to normal, although he would have to progress through all the steps of evolution—from rabbit to horse to dog to ape, and so on.

Journalist Richard Tregaskis, entry for January 13, 1944, in Invasion Diary, *241.*

It has been a hellish bit of night duty. Admitting critically wounded patients on the double, getting them cleaned up, starting I.V.s, changing dressings, getting them something to eat (if they could), and giving medications. . . . To compound the misery, it started to pour and the tents leak. They were filled to over capacity and there is no place to put the poor soldiers to keep them dry. We're high up in the mountains and it gets bitter cold, noisy too. The big guns boom all night long and shake the ground. . . .

The Germans bombed and strafed a hospital on the beachhead a few days ago. Latest reports listed 23 dead and 68 wounded. The dead included two nurses, six patients, 14 of the hospital personnel, and a Red Cross worker.

Combat nurse June Wandrey, February 9, 1944, from "Somewhere in Italy," in Carroll, War Letters, *247.*

The low, low point of my time in England has affected my relationships with people: A soldier wounded in North Africa and sent to 30th General to be readied for return to the States died. He died a day or two after asking me, "Why am I fighting the white man's war when there are race riots in Detroit?" I, as a Southern woman, learned much from his question.

Army nurse Mary M. Sexton, "June 6, 1944," in Thoburn and Knapp, "Perspectives," 33–34.

Direct hits with 20-mm shells are no problem because the victim is dead. Most men felled with penetrating head wounds from machine-gun bullets are also dead. Shrapnel from 88s and "Nebelwerfers" [rockets] or screaming meemies is disabling, but many victims will survive if their wounds are in the extremities.

Army surgeon Klaus Huebner, July 1944, in Long Walk Through War, *110.*

The pre-op tent is full to overflowing. I have seen life and death and am thoroughly distressed by the futility of it all. It is hard for me to draw a picture in words of the dingily littered tent, the grassy-mud floor, the rows of litters filled with their uncomplaining bundles of humanity. Some lie quietly; some groan softly; some lean up on one elbow and talk—almost whisper. There is no sterile white which some might expect to see here. It is all brown, a dirty brown from the doctors to the nurses to the soldiers and wounded. The poor lighting accentuates the brownness of everything. The shadows deepen into blocks of darkness. The standards supporting the plasma and blood throw sharp brown shadows. The sudden opening of a stove top momentarily transforms the brownness to red umber. The litter bearers keep bringing in more wounded.

Surgeon Capt. Sydney W. Stringer, letter of October 21, 1944, describing his evacuation hospital, quoted in Cowdrey, Fighting for Life, *262.*

These field hospital nurses arrived in France via England and Egypt, August 12, 1944. *(National Archives, 112-SGA-44-10842)*

To all Army nurses overseas: We men were not given the choice of working in the battlefield or the home front. We cannot take any credit for being here. We are here because we have to be. You are here because you felt you were needed. So, when an injured man opens his eyes to see one of you . . . concerned with his welfare, he can't but be overcome by the very thought that you are doing it because you want to. . . . [Y]ou endure whatever hardships you must to be where you can do us the most good.

Letter signed by hundreds of GIs, Stars and Stripes, *European edition, October 21, 1944.*

One trained oneself to think with a cold, steely, ferocious concentration on each specific motion; . . . and every skill one had focused on sponging the blood and torn tissue, finding the ripped end of the artery and sealing it with as much care as if one had all day in the finest operating room in the United States. This kind of savage exclusion of the terror and pain around us meant speed, and our speed meant men's lives.

Army surgeon Brendan Phibbs remembering Christmas 1944, in Other Side of Time, *110.*

The field hospital was a depressing experience. We were all put in a waiting room upon arrival. It was wall-to-wall litter cases. The walking wounded had to stand because there wasn't room for a lot of benches.

Some of the wounded were moaning, some were crying and one GI was calling for his mother. Those who couldn't fit in the waiting room were set up in ward tents and told not to wander off. . . .

Father Le Clerc, the chaplain, came around. I spoke to him for about fifteen minutes and asked him to write a letter to my parents and explain that my wound was not life threatening. He agreed. I mentioned that I heard a couple of medics bitching about how much work they had to do, and could Father arrange to have complainers sent to the front? He smiled and said complainers didn't realize how well off they were. Don't misunderstand me. I give the U.S. Army medics very high marks for the care they gave me, and the company aid men and litter bearers are the unsung heroes of the war.

> *Len Lazarick describing his movements back from*
> *the front after being wounded, on May 12, 1945,*
> *in Astor,* Operation Iceberg,
> *344–346.*

If I had only known before I joined what I know now they could have shot me before I would have ever joined. Your people at the recruiting office show a beautiful film that shows the girls at work really doing things for the boys. . . . We scrub walls, floors, make beds, dust, sweep, and such only. . . . They should stop this farce of recruiting "medical technicians" and ask for "mop commandos."

> *WAC medical technician, undated quote in Campbell,*
> Women at War, *32.*

Spies, Codes, and Secret Operations

If you can pass the training, you'll be the employee of a brand-new service, the Office of Strategic Services, and we're accountable to only one guy—General Wild Bill Donovan. No government department has jurisdiction over our operations—except the President. The FBI is responsible for intelligence gathered within our borders—and right now they're also helping us out in South America. We can't train recruits fast enough. That leaves us the rest of the globe to cover—and it's plenty. OSS has five sections. MO, Mobile Operations, coordinates agent activities behind enemy lines. There's the propaganda section. R&A, Research and Analysis, collects and sifts strategic war data. CE, Counterespionage, deals with gathering foreign intelligence while overseas. And SI, Secret Intelligence, handles agents assigned special missions in countries abroad.

> *Initial briefing of OSS agents, 1942 or 1943, in Aline,*
> *Countess of Romanones,* The Spy Wore Red, *23.*

At the Farm [where I was trained as an OSS agent] I had been taught to form a chain by finding one reliable woman who would recruit another who in turn would find another, until fifteen formed the group. Some would be secretaries, others charwomen, cooks, dressmakers, laundresses. I would only know the one woman I recruited; the others would each know two, except the last woman. In this manner if one part of the chain was caught, the whole group would not be exposed at once. . . . It occurred to me to ask the *portera* to recommend a female teacher to help me improve my Castilian [Spanish]. . . . Pilar Hernandez was plain, gray-haired, bespectacled. . . . From the first lesson I realized she was efficient and capable. Nevertheless, I observed her for a few weeks during our daily sessions. . . . Two weeks later I proposed to Pilar the job of forming a women's chain and she accepted.

> *OSS agent Aline, Countess of Romanones, speaking*
> *probably of 1943, in* The Spy Wore Red, *108–109.*

A man should not have too many ideals, should work with his intelligence rather than his heart.

> *OSS manual on recruiting, probably 1944, in Persico,*
> Piercing the Reich, *38.*

We were dealing with an unusual type of individual. Many had natures that fed on danger and excitement. Their appetite for the unconventional and the spectacular was far beyond the ordinary. It was not unusual to find a good measure of temperament thrown in.

> *American officer describing OSS agent recruits in 1944,*
> *in Persico,* Piercing the Reich, *38.*

The German military often dressed their own men in various Allied uniforms and bailed them out over territory they held. The purpose was so these men who spoke whatever language was necessary for the ruse might be picked up by underground members and thus later be able to give away the identities and locations of underground participants and residences to the Gestapo.

> *Pilot Howard Snyder remembering his experiences after*
> *being shot down in February 1944, in Astor,*
> Mighty Eighth, *239–240.*

All I wanted to know was what lay around the next bend of the road [in Brittany in France], or whether that enemy machine gun in that clump of trees could cover the road to my left, or how soon it would be before I could stop and rest. Could I trust this Resistance leader? That barn we were hiding in, what was the best escape route if a German patrol came, and could we fight our way out? Most of the questions were like that, basic and uncomplicated. . . . The answers often were not easy, but you got them fast enough. You were not dealing with a lot of trivial matters, or if some of them were trivial, they did not seem that way.

American infantry officer William Dreux, volunteer for OSS missions, July 1944, in No Bridges Blown, *314–315.*

On the north side of the RR railroad line MUNICH-STRAUBING agent saw a single continuous underground factory 12 kms long extending from a point at (map coordinate) Y-711581 west to a point at (map coordinate) Y-624588 between the road and the RR tracks. Six individual bunker entrances set at 2 km intervals. . . . [T]racks join the entrances to the main RR line. . . . [A]gent was told by a Salzburg Hauptquartier employee that the factory was used for manufacture of poison gas, and V-1 type shells as containers for the gas. Name of the gas is "Influensia Inzitus Eukalyptus." It was said at Hauptquartier [headquarters] that Hitler would use gas at the time of the last great breakthrough.

Undated Report of OSS agent "Vacuum" indicating targets after a "tourist mission" into Germany, in Persico, Piercing the Reich, *115.*

Women's Services: The Women's (Auxiliary) Army Corps

There were always homosexuals throughout the military. Some of them were extremely competent military personnel who either were known or were not known to be so. In the cases of some that I knew or knew of, they were so competent that their commanding officers closed their eyes to the fact that they were gay.

African-American WAC Dorothy Jones remembering the war years, quoted in Moore, To Serve My Country, *137.*

I was nearing the end of my fourth year as a teacher when the invitation . . . to apply for the Women's Army Auxiliary Corps arrived. . . . I had been recommended by the Dean of Women of Wilberforce University. The letter also emphasized career and leadership opportunities. . . .

Because we had some difficulty getting uniforms in the correct sizes for our troops, sometimes the company made a strange appearance. . . . Every woman in the service was issued an enlisted man's overcoat. We soon found out what was meant by the saying that GI clothing came in two sizes—too large and too small. I was five feet, eight inches, and although my coat reached my knees, the sleeves struggled to approach my wrists. The small people were completely lost in their coats, which reached the ankles and covered the hands.

African-American WAC Lt.-Col. Charity Adams Earley probably speaking of 1942, in One Woman's Army, *10, 44, 57.*

Had I stayed in New York, I could see no advancement for me in any field. I was working in the garment district, and at one time I was working on a specialized machine where you did one little thing over and over and over all day long. . . . I wasn't really satisfied with how my life was progressing at that time, and I felt that women in the military were going to have a better opportunity when everything was over and there would be more jobs opening up, particularly for black women.

Single-parent African-American WAC Bernice Thomas speaking probably of 1942 or 1943, quoted in Moore, To Serve My Country, *10.*

Are you a girl with a Star-Spangled heart? Join the WAC now!

1943 Recruiting poster for the Women's Army Corps, Library of Congress Collection POS-WWII-US. J22 1943. Available online. URL: http://lcweb2. loc.gov//pp/pphome.html.

I moved my WACs forward early after occupation of recaptured territory because they were needed and they were soldiers in the same manner that my men were soldiers. Furthermore, if I had not moved my WACs when I did, I would have had mutiny . . . as they were so eager to carry on where needed.

Gen. Douglas MacArthur, October 10, 1945, quoted in Treadwell, Women's Army Corps, *423.*

Women's Services: Pilots

But the British system was a little bit different from ours, when I came back here and joined the WASPs. The United States policy was, if in doubt, if you get into any trouble, jump. Well, we had parachutes in England too, had to carry them, and use them all the time. Their policy was, get the airplane down in as few pieces as possible. Nobody would even think of jumping there, because, you know, they could always replace pilots, I guess, but the machines were expensive. . . . I was flabbergasted when I joined the WASP and they said, any slight bit of trouble, why, jump. I wouldn't jump anyway. . . .

   The British are a great people when they just take everything in their stride. It would drive you crazy. Sometimes you'd go to a factory to get an airplane, and you maybe had three to deliver, so time was of the essence. You wanted to get your job done. It would be tea time or coffee break time, and, "Well, just a minute, dearie. You know, it's tea time." . . . [T]he American feeling was, we've got this to do, and, you know, we rush. We're there, we're at the factory, the plane is ready, give it to me. But you got it when they jolly well got finished with their tea break. . . .

   Up in England, for instance, I'd maybe ferry three. . . . Spitfires each ten or fifteen minutes. Well, the British Isles aren't very big, at two hundred miles an hour. . . . If you were in . . . a Fairchild-24, where you could cruise maybe seventy miles an hour, why, you know, was one thing, you didn't mind, and, of course, it had such a good glide and everything, and the high wing, why, you'd feel fairly comfortable in much less visibility than where you were flying a fighter, where you had, of course, two hundred miles an hour. That's nothing nowadays, but it was then, and when you're flying over the treetops, they go by kind of quickly. [On average our altitude was] like four or five hundred feet. Maybe you'd get up to a thousand on a decent day.

   Pilot Emily Chapin remembering her experiences in the
   British Air Transport Auxiliary after the winter of 1940,
   in the Columbia Oral History Collection, 24, 32–33.

None of us can put into words why we fly. It is something different for each of us. I can't *say* exactly why I fly but I *know* why as I've never known anything in my life. . . . I know it in dignity and self-sufficiency and in the pride of skill. I know it in the satisfaction of usefulness. . . . I, for one, am profoundly grateful that my one talent, my only knowledge, flying[,] hap-

pens to be of use to my country when it is needed. That's all the luck I ever hope to have.

   Pilot Cornelia Fort, "At the Twilight's Last Gleaming,"
   Women's Home Companion, July 1943,
   U.S. Air Force Museum, Women Pilots History
   Gallery available online. URL: www.wpafb.af.mil/
   museum/history/wasp17.htm. Fort was killed on
   March 21, 1943, when a male pilot flying near her
   rolled his plane over hers, miscalculated, and sliced
   his wing through her cockpit.

GIs Abroad

When I was stationed in England the Lavenders made me a member of the family. They'd leave the key under the mat so that I could take a shower or just be alone in a comfortable place for a while. They put me up overnight. They invited me to their holiday celebrations. And Eric used to take me with him on business trips or to Rotary meetings.

   Army clerk Charles Taylor, stationed in England
   1944–46, quoted from a personal interview
   with the authors.

One of the pleasantest sights on Paris streets and park walks these afternoons of warm spring sun is that of eager GIs and dark-eyed demoiselles attacking the problems of language. . . .
The Stars and Stripes and the French newspaper *Resistance* . . . [e]ach publishes daily one or more useful phrases [such as] . . . "French girls are wonderful" . . . [and] "What are you doing tonight?" These conversational gambits are considerably more useful to the GI in Paris than the ones suggested in Army handbooks, which include phonetical French for "I am lost," "I want insecticide," and "Give my horse water."

   Life *journalist John Neill, Spring 1945, quoted in*
   Shukert and Scibetta, War Brides, *111–112.*

A British soldier would take a girl for a drink, bore her to death talking about cars or sport, etc. If he saw any "mates" he abandoned the girl except to buy her a drink now and then until it was time to go home. With the GIs it was very different. The GI would buy me a drink and entertain me as though I were the only person in the room.

   Teenage British aircraft factory worker, undated wartime
   recollection in Reynolds, Rich Relations, *265.*

GI Combat Fatigue

Some of them do [break down]. But you can see it comin' on, and sometimes the other guys can help out. . . . Why, first they get trigger happy. They go running all over the place lookin' for something to shoot at. Then, the next thing you know they got the battle jitters. They jump if you light a match and go diving for cover if someone bounces a tin hat off a rock. Any kind of sudden noise and you can just about see them let out a mental scream. . . . [Y]ou can kind of cover up for a guy like that before he's completely gone. He can be sent back to get ammo or something. . . . Then he can pretend to himself he's got a reason for being back there and he still has his pride.

19-year-old corporal in North Africa speaking probably in 1943, quoted in Cooke, All But Thee and Me, *150.*

[H]appily, someone a lot smarter than me had thought of a very sensible remedy [for combat fatigue]. It was to take a man in question and send him back to a rear service area. There he would work on loading cases of ammo, supplies, and rations that were destined for the front lines. After several days, the individual would accompany the supplies to the front. And then later he would be returned to his unit. . . . I actually had men who went through this process and returned to duty. They all performed well on their return.

Marine company commander Martin (Stormy) Sexton, probably in May 1944, in Astor, Operation Iceberg, *363–364.*

My mind blanked itself for my body's sake.

Combat artist Tom Lea, September 1944, in Peleliu Landing, *12.*

I'm not badly injured . . . but I guess I am hurt, Pop. Hurt inside—in my brain . . . I'm scared of memories. You see, as soon as I'm left with them at night, the little bastards begin to crawl in my brain. . . . I don't care if they cut my letters to pieces. I don't care even if you don't get them at all. All I want is to get them off my mind and out of my system so I could maybe sleep. . . .

I happened to look at one of the dead krauts. I could see him open his eyes and look at Pat, and I'd never seen so much hate in anybody's eyes before. I stood there paralyzed. So, that's what we were going to get in this damn country [Germany]—even the dead hated us. Then, I saw his hand move to his pocket and pull out a luger [German pistol]. That brought me back to life. I fell on him, pulled back his head and broke his neck like they taught us in jujitsu. Pat was on top of me, pulling me away. "You're nuts—let go that damn stiff." I got up and saw that the man was dead all right—all cold and rigid. Must have been dead at least ten-twelve hours. I was so scared I didn't tell Pat anything. . . . We drove on. Ahead was Germany. Eighty million people—each ready to kill me. . . .

We just got two snipers in a bombed-out church and were combing the graveyard behind it, when one guy called to us to come over and take a look. He'd got a tall Jerry covered, his gun on the ground, and his hands up in the air. And there were two of our boys on the ground, dead. They were prisoners and the son-of-a-bitch murdered them—they were still warm.

Well, Pop, one of them was Lou. His shirt was torn in front and there was his dog tag and a six-pointed star of David. . . . I never knew Lou had one, but there it was, all in blood, because a bayonet had been driven right through it. I knelt and took it, and my hand was full of blood and I looked at the fellows standing around me. "Look," I said and I pulled out the gold cross from my shirt. "This is what my mother gave me—and that is what his mother gave him. They both have the same faith in the same God who is supposed to protect His children." . . . I was pretty shot, I guess. I wanted to say that it wasn't just another GI lying in the dirt dead—that it was my buddy, my friend, a part of my life, that we went to school together and that I knew his mother and dad. . . . "Look, guys," I kept saying. "Look . . . it isn't right . . . it is not right . . . it isn't. . . ."

Combat-fatigue victim Alec Hovsepian, letter to his father March 18, 1945, in Hovsepian, Your Son and Mine, *165, 168–169.*

GI Prisoners of War (POWs)

Even though the son of a bitch is a member of the Nazi party and has killed . . . your best friend, you're supposed to pat him on the head, hand him a ration of Texas steak, and give him a free ride to a stockade way out of range of his own artillery. Next thing you know he's in Louisiana cutting cane or in Illinois picking sweet corn. Then when the war is over, he applies for American citizenship, grabs our own girls, has a family, and enjoys the beer. All the time your friends are six feet under and missing all the fun.

A marine's view of treatment of German POWs, probably voiced in April 1943, quoted in McCormick, The Right Kind of War, *83.*

[The German POWs who picked potatoes on our farms] were like our own boys. My brothers were over there fighting. We just hoped they were being treated as well as we were treating those boys.

Maine resident Catherine Bell speaking probably of 1944 or 1945, quoted in "Town's Fond Memories," New York Times, *March 17, 2002, 37.*

I was treated better by the American Army than by my own Italian Army. I suffered while in the Italian Army. There were various times when I had to beg for food from civilians in order to stay alive.

. . . It was later that the girl I met in Salt Lake City came over to Italy and our marriage followed. I loved Italy and wanted to stay there, but my wife wanted to return to the United States. I remember how humane my treatment was here as a prisoner of war. Otherwise I would never have returned to live in this country.

Italian POW Ruggerio Purin, probably 1944 or 1945, quoted in Buxco and Adler, "German and Italian Prisoners of War." 64.

One day, after I had been [held in a German prisoner-of-war camp] about a year, two American brothers named Wowczuk, Michael and Peter, and a third American whose name I forget, spoke to me about conditions in the Russian compound. . . . [The Americans] were from Chicago, workers in the stockyards. . . . [They] proposed a plot by which the Americans would smuggle food to the Russians. They told me that not only the three of them, but many others of the Americans were willing to participate. . . . Oh, of course [it was dangerous]! . . . We would have been shot if they had caught us. Merely to be found outside the barracks at night was a shooting offense, and many men were executed in that camp for much less! . . . They waited until the sentry had passed at night and threw parcels over the fence. The fence was only eight meters high. Those Americans were strong! . . . I organized a group

on our side to rush out to the fence and retrieve the packages. In one night, we received 1,350 parcels in this way. . . . Do you realize what I am saying? This was nearly seven thousand kilos of food in one night! Do you understand what this food meant on our side of the wire, where men were dying every night of starvation? This went on at least one night a week for many months. At least one night a week, the Americans, many different ones, risked their lives to collect food parcels and dash out at night to throw them to us.

Dr. Nikita Zakaravich, former Russian prisoner of war of the Germans, speaking probably of 1944 or 1945, in Kuralt, A Life on the Road, *229–230.*

The [German] officer said to me, "Mr. Kilmer, you've been very stubborn. You haven't told us what we want to know, so we're going to tell you what we know about you [information that included the activities of Kilmer's bomber squadron, its bombing reports, and biographies of the crews]. . . . You think we're pretty smart, don't you? We know ninety-five percent of what's going on in the AMERICAN armed forces. However, your government knows *ninety-seven* percent of what's going on in the German armed forces.

Pilot Lloyd Kilmer of Rochester, Minnesota, interrogated after solitary confinement after he crashed on June 29, 1944, in Brokaw, Greatest Generation, *64.*

In our convoy we had eleven German paratroop prisoners. When we stopped once, somebody said that they hadn't been searched. When we got through searching them, we found fifty boxes of our K-rations on them. We stacked them in the road. Then we told the French kids that the K-rations were theirs.

Yank correspondent Sgt. Saul Levitt, "Down and Go," in Yank, *July 2, 1944, 5.*

Upon arrival in this sector we were told no prisoners. They didn't say, "Shoot any German who surrenders," but there was no alternative. Our forces were spread thin. We had no one to take care of those who surrendered or were wounded. Few people back home were aware of or could understand the necessity of the thing.

Pvt. Phillip Stark remembering December 24, 1944, during the Battle of the Bulge, in Ambrose, Citizen Soldiers, *240.*

The good news here [at a prison camp in Nuremberg] was that the soup had more peas. The bad news was that over half the peas had worms in them. We soon eliminated the foolishness of discarding the worst ones, to just squeezing out the worms, to finally just enjoying the badly needed protein. We slept on a hard floor in groups to conserve body heat and to share the one five-square-foot blanket issued each.... We became so weak that we rationed trips to the latrine. You had to be careful rising to the standing position to avoid blacking out.

Pilot Jim McCubbin speaking probably of the period after January 1945, in Astor, Mighty Eighth, *415.*

[On] the forced march from Stalag Luft [German prison camp] III . . . [w]e marched a distance of about 85 kilometers in bitter cold weather. We were guarded by Volksturm guards made up of old men. There was about two and a half feet of snow on the ground and the temperature was about ten degrees below zero. I saw four guards fall out from exhaustion. No one seemed to pay much attention to them and they probably froze to death. Fortunately for us, when we got ready to move the Red Cross gave us new shoes, heavy socks, gloves, scarfs, and new overcoats.... [We] ended up in Moosburg . . . at Stalag 7-A.... We lived in tents about 40 feet wide and 100 feet long. We slept on the ground as comfortably as possible, but had one faucet for approximately 400 men. . . . The intense sweating out what the Germans were eventually going to do with us was torture. . . . We knew the Americans were coming, and feared the Germans might shoot us rather than let us be rescued by the allies. We also feared that we would be caught in the midst of a battle between the Americans and the Nazi guards. We watched B-17s bomb Munich. It was really a wonderful sight, but after that we feared that we would be victims of such a raid.

Tuskegee Airman Lt. Alexander Jefferson quoted in the spring of 1945, in Francis, Tuskegee Airmen, *255–256.*

Soldiers of the British Commonwealth!
Soldiers of the United States of America!
The great Bolshevik offensive has now crossed the frontiers of Germany. The men in the Moscow Kremlin believe the way is open for the conquest of the Western world. This will certainly be the decisive battle for us. But it will also be the decisive battle for England, for the United States and for the maintenance of Western civilization. . . . Therefore we are now addressing you as white men to other white men.... WE ARE SURE THAT MANY OF YOU SEE WHAT THE CONSEQUENCES OF THE DESTRUCTION OF EUROPE—NOT JUST OF GERMANY BUT OF EUROPE—WILL MEAN TO YOUR OWN COUNTRY....

We think that our fight has also become your fight.... We invite you to join our ranks and the tens of thousands of volunteers from the communist crushed and conquered nations of eastern Europe, which have had to choose between submission under a most brutal Asiatic rule—or a national existence in the future under European ideals, many of which, of course are your own ideals....

ARE YOU FOR THE CULTURE OF [THE] WEST OR THE BARBARIC ASIATIC EAST? MAKE YOUR DECISION NOW.

German pamphlet distributed to American and British prisoners of war in the spring of 1945, in Toland, Last 100 Days, *18.*

Shortly after the German surrender in 1945, one of those German POW's [whom we had gotten to know] stopped at our farm again, this time just before dawn. . . . In broken English he told my parents he had escaped from the camp. He did not want to go back to Germany. He wanted to stay in the United States. He slept that day in our barn. Mother packed him some food, and he left sometime during the night.

Marlene Downing Silliman remembering an event of Spring 1945, "World War II: The Home Front," in Thoburn and Knapp, "Perspectives," 69.

You never saw such a sight in your life. The Russians came in, tore the gates down, drove cattle in. The guys went crazy; there was a training school for girls nearby and all the guys wanted to go over and see the girls but they'd been moved out. Some men just took off, trying to get to the British and American lines. I rode a little distance with Russians in a tank who said they were going to go to Berlin. I'd been taught a little bit of Russian. There were women in the tank as part of the crew and I decided, this is crazy. Let's get out and get back to camp.

Bombardier Bill Topping recalling a time probably in March or April 1945, in Astor, Mighty Eighth, *418–419.*

Yesterday at 12:40 the American Flag was raised over Moosburg [prison camp]. The battle for the area started at 9:00 and continued until then. It was a tense three hours for us [prisoners-of-war], but we had few casualties. . . . To be free once again and to describe it is far beyond my ability. It [freedom] is a man's greatest possession and without it, he finds he is only half alive. I find my entire nature has changed already. . . . We are supposed to be flown to LeHavre and then from there home, which should be soon. . . .

It was indeed a spectacle that I'll never be able to fully describe—to be one of 175,000 prisoners in this camp and see them all, English Poles, Indians, Russians, Senegales, French, and Americans, fall to their knees to pray as they watched the American Flag raised over this "hellhole."

We are to receive liver shots and a bland diet for about two weeks, then will be on our way toward home.

2nd Lt. Richard Wellbrock, April 30, 1945, quoted in Carroll, War Letters, *278–279.*

And . . . Kilroy

Kilroy was everywhere. He appeared on shattered earthen walls in the Loire River Valley, *inside* the paper-foil containers of Meals, Ready to Eat. ". . . When found in inaccessible areas, the logo could only have been put there by the assemblers. How many of these (which are still being discoverd today as WWII vehicles are restored at the hands of enthusiastic collectors) were put there by Rosie the Riveter? . . .

By the time our troops arrived in Europe, Kilroy had come there with them, and the little "peeking over the top" graphic that represented Kilroy soon began to accompany the rapidly-scrawled graffiti. This simple, but charming little graphic was important in the global spread of Kilroy because it could be quickly and easily drawn by virtually anyone. . . .

And, not only did he go there with our soldiers, he got there first! Navy Seal divers found Kilroy scrawled on the sea-facing surfaces of concrete enemy pillboxes—on the beaches of Japan! At the Potsdam conference, Stalin excused himself to go to the restroom. Roosevelt and Churchhill would later hear him ask an aid[e], "Who's Kilroy?"

LaMar Stonecypher, "Kilroy Was Here," Kudzu Monthly, *available online. URL: http://www. kudzumonthly.com/kudzu/jul01/kilroy.html. Downloaded February 25, 2003.*

7

Military Life: The Navy, the Marine Corps, the Coast Guard, and the War in the Pacific
September 3, 1939–September 9, 1945

HISTORICAL CONTEXT[1]

The Navy, the Marine Corps, and the Coast Guard

In wartime the sailors who man the ships of the U.S. Navy fight enemy ships, submarines, and aircraft; transport troops, equipment, and supplies; and back up amphibious operations. Those on aircraft carriers provide a base for navy planes, maintenance crews, and pilots.

The navy works closely with the U.S. Marine Corps, which has two primary functions: first, to protect the security of the ships to which the marines are assigned by maintaining order and fighting against enemy attack, and second, to make amphibious landings. In wartime the navy takes over the Coast Guard. In peacetime until 1967 it was under the Treasury Department. As an arm of the navy, the Coast Guard escorts convoys to protect them against submarines, conducts amphibious landings and search-and-rescue operations, provides port security, and patrols beaches. The navy also of course cooperates with the U.S. Army.

Of the 16 million men and women in the U.S. armed forces during World War II, most were in the army; only about a quarter were in the three sea-borne forces.[2] At the navy's height in 1945, it enrolled 3,405,525 personnel.[3] The Marine Corps peaked in 1944 at 475,604 men and women.[4] The Coast Guard at its height numbered 175,000.[5]

When World War II broke out in Europe in 1939, the U.S. Navy, though superior in naval aviation and submarines, lagged behind in antisubmarine warfare—a deficiency that was to cost the nation dearly. Improvement began with the passage of the Two-Ocean Navy (Naval Expansion) Act of 1940 and progressed with the Lend-Lease Act of 1941, which sent much outdated equipment to the Allies, allowing the U.S. Navy to build modern replacements.

Many volunteers preferred the navy to the army because it was smaller, older, and to some ways of thinking more elite and more romantic. Although its men faced the additional danger of drowning, their daily life appealed to some as more comfortable than that in the army; it even had a reputation for better food. Accordingly, the proportion of volunteers to draftees was considerably higher than in the army. The Marine Corps, noted for the hardihood and courage of its men, challenged other volunteers. The Coast Guard, best known for its search-and-rescue operations, appealed to others.

A naval recruit might be assigned to shore duty or put on a naval ship—an aircraft carrier, a battleship, a destroyer, a submarine, a submarine chaser (sometimes made of wood in the early days of the war), a mine hunter, a patrol torpedo boat (PT boat), an amphibious assault ship, or one of the many small vessels that maintained and supplied the larger ships and their crews. Or he might be sent to a unit of the Seabees, the "Build and fight!" construction battalions that on six continents built airstrips, bridges, roads, warehouses, hospitals, gasoline storage tanks, and housing.

Strategy and Tactics

At a meeting on March 27, 1941, the U.S. and British Joint Chiefs of Staff agreed that if and when the United States entered World War II, even if it were at war with Japan, it would exert its major effort first in the European theater of operations (ETO). They reasoned that Germany, with its greater military potential than that of Japan and its control of almost the entire Atlantic coast of Europe, more immediately threatened North and South America. Germany also was more likely than Japan to invent an unbeatable weapon. Finally, the United States could more effectively help England in its fight against Germany than China in its fight against Japan.[6]

After the Japanese attack on the U.S. naval base at Pearl Harbor, Hawaii, on December 7, 1941, Adm. Ernest J. King, chief of U.S. naval operations, interpreted this agreement to allow sufficiently aggressive operations in the Pacific to prevent the Japanese from consolidating their gains. He insisted in 1942 that enough battleships and carriers be transferred from the Atlantic to the Pacific Fleet to keep Japan off balance and to ensure that the Pacific Fleet get a share of new construction. This interpretation enabled the victory at Midway in June 1942 that reversed the course of the war in the Pacific. It was supported moreover by President Franklin D. Roosevelt (FDR), who even when the army and Atlantic Fleet were preparing for the invasion of North Africa insisted on reinforcing Guadalcanal. The victory there in early 1943 made possible the beginning of the series of island invasions ever closer to Japan that finally ended the war in the Pacific.

In the Pacific as in the Atlantic the Allies created "notional" (fake) divisions, corps, and armies. In the North Pacific, for instance, notional American landing forces in Alaska and the Aleutians deceived the Japanese into keeping 80,000 troops in the Kurile Islands.[7]

Throughout the war the navy, like the army, quickly profited by experience. It learned to use its aircraft carriers not only to strike into enemy territory but also, and with more effect, to provide cover for amphibious landings and for battles at sea. It learned the importance of air power—that it is more effective to use battleships to protect aircraft carriers than air strikes to protect battleships. It learned to prepare for amphibious landings both with air bombings and with bombardments from ships. Perhaps most valuably, it learned that it could leapfrog some enemy-fortified islands to attack others closer to Japan, thereby ending the war several years before its own estimates. This strategy both confused the Japanese about where the Americans might land next and cut off supply lines to the islands skipped over. In some cases harassment by U.S. aircraft reduced Japanese garrisons on the leapfrogged islands to farming and fishing to sustain themselves.

Between the two world wars, the marines had hit on the idea that landings must be tactically managed: that is, that ships must not simply put troops ashore in small boats but must also cover them with heavy fire during the landings, and that the men must immediately push inland, beginning the fight in or beyond the enemy's first defensive line. For a successful invasion, the men had to be specially trained. They had to be equipped with special landing craft designed to move across the water and onto the beaches at high speed and back off without waiting for tides. They had to be supported by air power, particularly dive-bombers.

When marine troops took heavy casualties, their commanders learned to change their tactics, on one occasion even having exact copies of enemy defenses built so that marines could practice the best ways to overcome them.

This landing craft was used during the occupation as a ferry between Okinawa and Ieshima. *(Collection of Mildred Corey)*

On Tarawa Maj. Michael P. Ryan developed a winning technique for island invasions where the enemy was deeply dug in: "Sherman tanks covered by infantry, improvised assault squads of flamethrowers and demolition experts, and a shore fire-control party with a working radio to call in naval fire."[8]

Learning was equally important to the individual servicemen. More experienced men told replacements and reinforcements: "Training saves lives, so pay attention. Instant obedience to orders. Don't have time to explain things in the field. Learn Japanese weapons, language and tactics. Learn all of our weapons. Learn patrols in brush, roads, trails and jungle, night and day. Learning is a constant necessity."[9]

During most of the war in the Pacific, the navy landed relatively small groups of marines on remote atolls and transported the army on shorter jumps in larger numbers to larger areas. In 1945 the army and the marines were able to undertake large-scale invasions in tandem against the islands nearest Japan itself.

The Enemy

Except in California, where some envied their modest economic success, few Americans knew any people of Japanese descent. The Japanese attack on Pearl Harbor transmuted the vague endemic racism against them into active hatred. Henceforth many Americans thought of these Asians as despicable, unethical, untrustworthy fanatics. The contrasts between Japanese Americans and European Americans in skin color, facial characteristics, size, religion, and political philosophy all reinforced this antagonism. In the European theater, Americans directed their hatred mainly toward German leaders; in the Pacific theater, Americans turned their hatred toward the Japanese people themselves.

For their part, the Japanese ardently returned it, hating the United States for its demands that they withdraw their conquering troops from Indochina and China, and for its economic policies that, they believed, were designed to crush their nation. Lacking natural resources, they needed oil, so in their eyes the American threat of an oil embargo endangered their national survival, leaving them with no alternative but war. To get raw materials they planned to seize territories in Southeast Asia. To succeed in this undertaking, they first had to immobilize the U.S. fleet. Consequently they saw the surprise attack on Pearl Harbor simply as an intelligent military maneuver, for which they had been planning and practicing since October 1940. Its success contributed to the domination in the Pacific that Premier Hideki Tojo presented to them as the will of their emperor and the manifest destiny of their nation. Like the United States, Japan had never been vanquished—not in 3,000 years. Moreover, having been warring in China for years, they had built an army and navy stronger than those of the United States at the time.

As the war advanced, the conduct of the Japanese troops further persuaded Americans that Japanese soldiers were vicious animals who deserved only to be killed.[10] U.S. troops could not understand Japanese refusal to surrender in the face of a hopeless situation. They did not know that Japanese troops were sworn not to surrender, any more than they knew that Japanese schoolchildren were required to repeat every day the imperial rescript, "Should any emergency arise offer yourself courageously to the State."[11] Any who might try to surrender could expect to be killed by their comrades.[12] On Guadalcanal, wrote intelligence officer William H. Whyte, Japanese officers never surrendered, and the few enlisted men who did were often in a state of shock, pleading to be killed.[13]

Above all, the Japanese concept of suicide as a matter of honor puzzled Americans. As engineer officer Bob MacArthur commented, "It was the damnedest thing. I watched them up on a ridge, taking their grenades—they had a button that detonated them—bang them on their helmets and hold them to their chest while they went off. I couldn't fathom it."[14] Many Americans considered these suicides evidence of insanity. Yet for the Japanese this form of refusal to surrender was both official military policy and a societal code of honor. Their military used not only kamikaze planes that their pilots deliberately crashed into targets, but also suicidal massed banzai attacks, rocket-propelled flying bombs with pilots to guide them, suicide motor boats, and suicide swimmers with mines.[15] In some places, particularly late in the war, the Japanese persuaded local civilians to commit mass suicide, terrifying them with accounts of what the Americans would do to them otherwise. Toward the end of the war militaristic leaders in Japan glorified death for civilians in the service of the emperor, propagandizing for "One Hundred Million Die Together."[16]

As the war wore on, as GIs and marines observed the Japanese treatment of native populations—using other Asians as slave laborers and starving, beating, and beheading them for small infractions—and as U.S. servicemen found other American fighting men tortured to death when caught by themselves or in small groups, abhorrence of the Japanese mounted. Experience taught the Americans that the Japanese code of honor had nothing to do with fair play on the battlefield or with mercy toward the wounded. They began to think of the Japanese as inhuman, as jungle animals—monkeys, snakes—furtive, sneaky, and poisonous, and accordingly they became ruthless in their treatment of the Japanese. The difference in the barbarities committed by the two nations was one of Japanese official policy versus individual American fury. As Japanese expert Donald Keene remarks, "When I speak of the terrible things that the Japanese have done, I am not saying that individual Americans are not capable of acts of wickedness themselves. . . . If you want to know if Americans haven't done the same things of which I have accused the Japanese, I will say that they have indeed committed some of these atrocities, but always individually and not as part of an organized program of immorality."[17]

Equally, Japanese troops hated and despised Americans. They understood surrender as cowardice and considered prisoners of war undeserving of treatment as human beings. Japanese and Americans fought a war without rules, governed only by mutual contempt and loathing. Most tragic of all, for some men in combat, was the change in themselves. As marine William Manchester put it, "[We] came to hate the things we had to do, even when convinced that doing them was absolutely necessary; [we] had never understood the bestial, monstrous and vile means required to reach the objective."[18]

Pearl Harbor and Japanese Expansion (December 7, 1941– May 31, 1942)

On Sunday, December 7, 1941, the Japanese attacked the naval base at Pearl Harbor, Hawaii, where 90 U.S. ships lay at anchor. In an assault by air and sea · that lasted only about two hours, they sank or damaged 21 ships, including 8 battleships, 3 cruisers, and 4 destroyers. They also demolished 188 aircraft and damaged 159 others, most of them still on the ground.[19]

To Americans both at Pearl Harbor and at home, the deed was unbelievable. Pharmacist's Mate Lee Soucy, crewman aboard the battleship *Utah,* reported: "[E]ven after I saw a huge fireball and cloud of black smoke rise from the hangers [sic] on Ford Island and heard explosions, it did not occur to me that these were enemy planes. It was too incredible! Simply beyond imagination![6] What a SNAFU [situation normal, all f---ed up],' I moaned."[20]

The attack outraged most Americans, violating their sense of invulnerability, fostered in part by the nation's confidence in its own strength, in part by the protection afforded by two oceans. Now another nation, a small nation, had sneaked an attack without a declaration of war, even as Japanese diplomats were negotiating in Washington. In his speech to Congress on December 8, President Roosevelt emphasized the national sense of betrayal, calling the day before "a date that will live in infamy."

For the next six months the Japanese raged through the Pacific, scoring victory after victory. Almost simultaneously with the attack on Pearl Harbor, they also assaulted Malaya, Thailand, Burma, the Philippines, Guam and Wake Islands (destined to be used as part of the Japanese plan to fashion an extended island shield for their country), the British colony of Hong Kong, and the atolls of Tarawa and Makin in the British Gilbert archipelago.

They succeeded everywhere. On December 10 they sank two of Great Britain's largest warships, the new battleship *Prince of Wales* and the battle cruiser *Repulse,* which had been sent to the defense of Malaya. Guam fell at once, and Wake on December 23. Tarawa and Makin were also captured in Decem-

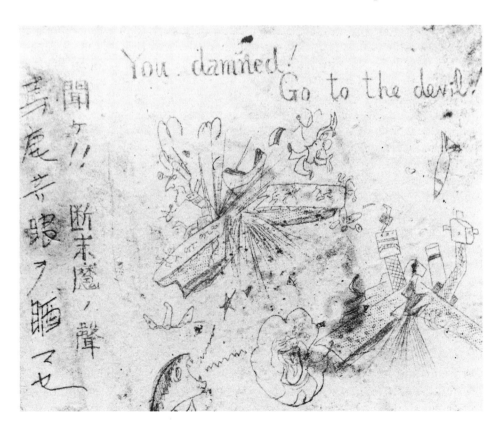

This cartoon was found in a crashed Japanese Navy plane following the attack on Pearl Harbor. The Japanese inscription on the left reads: "Hear! The voice of the moment of death. Wake up, you fools!" *(U.S. Naval Historical Center, 80-G-32891)*

ber. Hong Kong capitulated on Christmas Day 1941. Singapore did not fall until February 15, 1942. From mid-January on they assaulted the Dutch East Indies (Borneo, Celebes, Timor, Sumatra, and Java), completing their conquest on March 12, 1942. The Allies withdrew from Burma into India on May 19. Additionally by May the Japanese had bombed Darwin in northern Australia and assaulted the British Eastern Fleet in Ceylon, chasing its battleships into East African ports.

The Philippines, recently granted provisional independence, had been since 1898 an American protectorate with a democratic form of government. The Filipinos and Americans there under Gen. Douglas MacArthur resisted long and hard after the Japanese strike on December 8, 1941, at last withdrawing onto the Bataan peninsula, along with many civilians. On March 12, 1942, under orders, MacArthur left, vowing to return. On April 8 his successor, Gen. Edward King, defied orders and surrendered his starving, diseased troops. The tiny offshore island of Corregidor, to which a few survivors of Bataan had fled, submitted on May 6 after weeks of heavy shelling.

Japan was building a power bloc, which it called the "Greater East Asia Co-Prosperity Sphere." The Allies saw this plan as a mask for Japanese imperial ambition, but many Asians understood it as the Japanese leading other Asians to freedom from foreign rule. The Filipinos, however, trusted the declared American intention of giving them independence, and they continued their resistance in guerrilla groups and in individual undertakings.

The Japanese had made all these territorial gains with their fleet intact. They had denied the United States the use of all its battleships and many of its cruisers and destroyers in the Pacific fleet; they had demolished the British and Dutch Far Eastern fleets; and they had driven the Royal Australian Navy back to port. To oppose their 11 battleships, 10 aircraft carriers, and 38 cruisers, the United States had only its 3 carriers. Moreover, the Japanese Zero fighter plane had showed itself top-notch, and Japanese bombers, though relatively slow, could carry heavy loads over long ranges.

After the Doolittle air raid on Tokyo in April 1942 (see below, "Air Attacks on the Japanese Homeland," p. 196), horrified Japanese generals and admirals reacted to the threat to the safety of their emperor by deciding to attack Port Moresby in New Guinea and then Midway Island.

Battles of the Coral Sea and Midway (May 7, June 3–4, 1942)

Thanks to the Allied ability to read Japanese military code, U.S. carriers *Lexington* and *Yorktown* intercepted the Japanese invasion fleet in the battle of the Coral Sea on May 7.[21] Japanese carrier-based aircraft sank the *Lexington,* and American planes sank the carrier *Shoho,* but the Japanese impetus had been slowed.

A month later Americans again intercepted the Japanese at Midway. The United States pitted three carriers with 180 aircraft against four Japanese carriers with 272 planes, but the Americans could also call on land-based planes on Midway. Furthermore, the Japanese were at first distracted from the carrier battle by their determination to destroy Midway's defenses. On the other hand, the superiority of the Japanese Zeros and the seamanship of Adm. Chuichi Nagumo worked to their advantage.

On June 4, after Nagumo had fought off attack after attack on his carriers and was preparing to launch his own assault on the U.S. carrier force, a dive-bomber group from the *Enterprise* caught the Japanese by surprise, their decks cluttered with piles of bombs interlaced with high-octane hoses. The dive-bombers sank the carriers *Akagi* and *Kaga* and disabled the *Soyu,* which was then sunk by an American submarine. That afternoon other *Enterprise* dive-bombers caught up with and demolished the fleeing carrier *Hiryu.* These feats reversed the course of the Pacific war, putting the Japanese on the defensive.

Guadalcanal and Santa Cruz (August 7, 1942–February 9, 1943)

The battle for Guadalcanal, the first stage in the American drive toward Japan, was long and bloody. For months on land and sea the Japanese and Americans struggled, one gaining the advantage only to lose it soon after. After the marines invaded on August 7, 1942, the Japanese strongly reinforced their troops by sea while simultaneously attacking the U.S. ships supporting the landings. On August 24 the naval Battle of the Eastern Solomons resulted in an American victory, but Japanese land forces fought furiously. Meanwhile every night Japanese destroyers ran equipment and supplies to Guadalcanal on the "Tokyo Express," passing through "the Slot," a channel surrounded on three sides by other islands in the Solomons. In one of their efforts to stop this traffic, U.S. ships engaged a Japanese cruiser force on the night of October 11 in the Battle of Cape Esperance. They bested the Japanese, but on October 26 in the Battle of Santa Cruz the Japanese triumphed, sinking the carrier *Hornet.* From October 23 to 26, the Japanese counterattacked on the island, but the marines held out. In the Slot, Japanese and U.S. battleships clashed from November 12 to 15, the Americans finally emerging victorious, but in the Battle of Tassafaronga on November 30 the Japanese came off better.

Gradually, however, with both sides on land suffering from leeches, wasps, and malarial mosquitoes, U.S. ships so shattered the enemy supply chain as to reduce the Japanese to near starvation. In January 1943, the Japanese commander moved to Bougainville and in early February began to withdraw his forces. The marines, who had endured so much for so long, lost just above 1,000 dead—the Japanese, 22,000 killed or missing.[22] Moreover, the navy had confirmed by experience the best tactical method of island invasion, landing elite troops supported by ground-attack aircraft and naval gunfire. Japanese and Americans alike were valiant, but the Americans had more firepower.

Meanwhile, elsewhere in the Pacific, the Allies were also making progress. In May 1943 the U.S. Navy dislodged a Japanese force on Attu, and in August other U.S. ships retook Kiska, the other of the

U.S. Marine "Raiders" and their dogs, which are used for scouting and running messages, start off for the jungle front lines on Bougainville, November/December 1943. *(National Archives, 127-GR-84-68407)*

two Aleutian Islands that the Japanese had occupied in June 1942. In New Guinea, after long hard fighting, Australian troops supported by Americans forced Japanese who had landed at Buna and Gona in July 1942 to surrender in December 1942 and early January 1943.

New Guinea (Operation Cartwheel, March 2, 1943– July 30, 1944)

In Allied efforts to dislodge the Japanese from New Guinea, U.S. aircraft sank Japanese transports and destroyers in the Battle of the Bismarck Sea in early March 1943. In April the new U.S. P-38 Lightning fighters attacked Japanese naval forces, sinking none but soon after shooting down a plane carrying the brilliant Japanese strategist Adm. Isoroku Yamamoto. In June the Allies launched a double attack, in which General MacArthur was to envelop Rabaul, New Britain, from the south and drive the Japanese from New Guinea and the southern Bismarck Islands, while Adm. William F. Halsey, Jr., advanced toward Rabaul along the Solomons to Bougainville. Lae in New Guinea fell on September 16. Late in October 1943 Halsey made an amphibious assault on the Treasury Islands and on November 1 another on Bougainville. In December Americans seized Arawe and Saidor on New Britain. Halsey took the Russel Islands in February 1944 and the New Georgia group and Vella Lavella during the summer.

Meanwhile Adm. Chester Nimitz prepared to invade the Gilberts, with landings in the Marshalls to follow. Accordingly U.S. Marines and GIs took Makin and on November 21, 1943, landed on Tarawa, where stiff Japanese resistance inflicted terrible casualties, but by noon the next day U.S. forces had prevailed. Leapfrogging several other islands, they then attacked the westernmost of the Marshalls—Kwajalein and Eniwetok—in early February

First Lady Eleanor Roosevelt visits an American Red Cross installation in New Zealand, 1943. "She visited every Red Cross installation there," says Red Cross Club and Recreation Supervisor Mildred Corey. "The New Zealand men were angry at G.I.s for taking their girls, and used to treat us badly, force us off the sidewalks, that kind of thing. But then Mrs. Roosevelt came and spoke to an audience of 4,000, saying, 'I bring you greetings from my husband, the president of the United States.' And after that the New Zealanders' attitude changed completely."
(Collection of Mildred Corey)

A battery of U.S. Coast Guardsmen on a boat with an antiaircraft gun do their part in the invasion of Tarawa in the Gilbert Islands, 1943. *(Drawing by Coast Guard combat artist Ken Riley, Library of Congress, LC-USZ62-98332)*

1944 and the more remote atoll of Truk the same month. The fall of the Marshalls opened a passage to the Marianas.

Impatient to move on, the Allies decided to attack Rabaul only by air. Between February 29 and March 18, 1944, MacArthur secured the Admiralty Islands and then in a long leap surprised the Japanese at Hollandia on New Guinea's north coast, causing them, for once, to flee. On July 30, having subdued the off-coast islands of Wakde and Biak, he seized the Vogelkop peninsula at the northern tip of New Guinea.

The Marianas (June 15–August 11, 1944)

After heavy naval and air bombardments, 20,000 U.S. marines and soldiers landed on Saipan in the Marianas on June 15, 1944. While the Japanese on the island fought bitterly, 9 Japanese aircraft carriers rushed to attack the 15 American carriers supporting the landing. It was no contest. On June 19, with the new Hellcat fighters and more accurate radar, the Americans shot down 243 out of 373 Japanese aircraft, with the loss of just 29 U.S. planes, and U.S. submarines sank two of the Japanese carriers. The next day, in the Battle of the Philippine Sea, U.S. forces sank another carrier and damaged two others and two heavy cruisers. The defenders on the island, out of ammunition, committed suicide. Saipan fell on July 9, 1944. After an overwhelming bombardment and a desperate defense, Guam fell on August 11.

In the summer of 1944, with victory in the Marianas, the Allies had an air base from which the new U.S. B-29 Superfortresses could attack the home islands of Japan. The U.S. Pacific Fleet now threatened Japanese control of the South China Sea.

The China-Burma-India Theater (July 7, 1937–September 3, 1945)

The spectacular Japanese gains of the first six months of the war had trumped the previous efforts of other nations—the Spanish, Dutch, British, French, and Russians—to dominate the Pacific. Even in mid-1944 the Japanese controlled 6 million square miles, whereas Hitler never controlled more than 4 million. Yet their strategic situation presented problems, with difficulties in communication among their holdings and a draining war in China.

The war in China, which began with the Japanese invasion on July 7, 1937, dragged on interminably. Even supplied and equipped by the United States and aided by the U.S. general Claire Chennault's Flying Tigers, by the U.S. regiment "Merill's Marauders,"[23] and by the advice of U.S. General "Vinegar Joe" Stilwell, Chinese generalissimo Chiang Kai-shek could not end this war, nor could the Chinese Communist leader Mao Zedong, but both armies tied up numerous Japanese troops.[24] After the Japanese took Burma and closed the Burma Road in early 1942, supplies were flown to Chiang over the Himalayan "Hump," and Chinese troops were trained in India. Between November 1942 and February 1943, the Japanese turned back Allied efforts to retake Burma. On March 6, 1944, they launched the Ichi-Go offensive. Their push went well in China, endangering the very existence of Chiang's army. But the attempt to invade India from Burma proved disastrous: Only 20,000 of the 85,000 Japanese troops who had started out were still standing by the time they were allowed to retreat in late June. Japanese attention was then diverted by the Allied capture of Morotai, between New Guinea and Mindanao in the Philippines, on September 15, 1944.

A U.S. convoy operates between Chen-Yi and Kweiyang, China, ascending the famous 21 curves at Annan, China, March 26, 1945. *(National Archives, 111-SC-208807)*

The Philippines (September 14, 1944–End of February 1945)

The capture of Peleliu in the Palau Islands in mid-September 1944 prepared a way for MacArthur to land on Leyte in the Philippines on October 20, backed by a naval air force three times larger than the Japanese had ever had. By then Allied depredations on the Japanese merchant fleet had so shrunk their oil supply that they had to use destroyers to transport troops and equipment. After Americans downed more than 500 Japanese aircraft in pre-Leyte air offensives from October 10 to 17, the Japanese undertook a naval strike to divert U.S. ships from support of the landings. In the huge Battle of Leyte Gulf from October 23 to 25, the Japanese did indeed lure U.S. ships dangerously far from Leyte, jeopardizing the invasion. They also deployed numbers of kamikaze ("divine wind") planes packed with high explosives but with only enough fuel to reach their targets, onto which their pilots were to crash—a maneuver almost impossible to defend against. In the end, however, the Americans

Veteran artillery men of the "C" Battery, 90th Field Artillery, lay down a barrage on Japanese artillery positions in Balete Pass, Luzon, Philippines, April 19, 1945. *(National Archives, 111-SC-205918)*

triumphed, inflicting a quarter of the losses the Japanese navy had suffered since Pearl Harbor.

On Leyte itself the Japanese fought desperately. The struggle ended only when on December 6 the Americans repelled an attack on their main airfield complex. In the prolonged struggle the Japanese lost 70,000 and the Americans 15,500.[25] On January 9, 1945, the Americans invaded Luzon, seat of the Philippine capital city, Manila, encountering fierce resistance. In Manila the building-to-building fighting ended only in late February.

By this time the military situation had changed in favor of the Allies in the China-Burma-India theater. U.S.-supported Chinese troops progressed into Burma and turned back the Ichi-Go offensive in China. Chinese forces joined up in Burma from the north and south, reopening the Burma Road on January 27, 1945.

Iwo Jima (February 19, 1945– March 26, 1945)

The U.S. Joint Chiefs of Staff planned to take Iwo Jima in the Bonin Islands as an emergency landing field for bombers on their way to and from mainland Japan and a staging post for the invasion of Okinawa. To defend Iwo Jima, the Japanese had tunnels everywhere, protecting both their troops and their guns, so that the heaviest preparatory U.S. bombardment to date had almost no effect.

In the battles that ensued after the invasion on February 19, 1945, the Japanese were helped by the heavy layer of volcanic dust that covered the island, in which the U.S. Marines' amphibious vehicles could get no traction and ground to a halt, and the trenches the attackers dug collapsed, leaving them exposed. The terrible fighting, which some thought the worst of the war, lasted 36 days before the U.S. victory. Among the more than 26,000 American casualties, 6,800 died, while all but 1,083 of the 20,000 Japanese defending the island died. "Among the Americans who served on Iwo Island," said Adm. Chester W. Nimitz in tribute, "uncommon valor was a common virtue."[26]

Okinawa (April 1, 1945–June 30, 1945)

The experience in Iwo Jima caused changes in the plans of both sides for the invasion of Okinawa, a large island in the Ryukyus, at the southern tip of Japan itself. For a week U.S. ships bombarded Okinawa more heavily than any other island, firing almost 30,000 heavy-caliber shells, in preparation for attacking the waist of the island on April 1. The Japanese, instead of defending the beaches in their usual fashion, allowed the U.S. forces to land unopposed and instead fought them at heavily defended lines inland. If possible, they intended to resist more desperately than ever before, knowing that the next American invasion must be against their home islands.

On April 6, the formidable *Yamato,* the largest and most heavily armed and armored battleship ever built, sailed from Japan—a 72,000-ton ship with nine guns that could fire 3,200-pound armor-piercing shells. Reputedly, so critical was the Japanese shortage of oil that the *Yamato* sailed for Okinawa without enough fuel to return to base. The next day U.S. aircraft sank it and several of its escort ships.

Much more effectively, the Japanese launched unprecedented *kikusui* ("floating chrysanthemum") attacks of massed kamikaze planes—the air equivalent of the banzai charges on land. They were effective and terrifying: Even if a plane was shot down, the pilot often maneuvered it to crash onto its target. The kamikazes killed more than 5,000 American sailors and sank many U.S. ships, but they did not succeed in repelling the U.S. fleet. The Americans found no adequate defense against them; the kamikaze attacks stopped only as the Japanese ran short of pilots and airplanes.

Meanwhile ashore, marines and soldiers slogged from one heavily defended ridge to the next. The Japanese frightened some Okinawan civilians into fighting with them and others into committing suicide by telling them horror stories of what the Americans would do to them. By the time some 4,000 Japanese finally surrendered in the last days of June, some 4,000 U.S. soldiers and 2,938 marines had died, along with 70,000–160,000 Okinawans, and about 110,000 Japanese.[27] The slaughter on Okinawa, the fierceness of the Japanese resistance, and the participation of civilians in the fighting figured largely in the U.S. decision to use their ultimate weapon, the atomic bomb.

A landing ship medium, rocket (LSM[r]) fires rockets at the shores of Pokishi Shima, near Okinawa, Ryukyu Islands, five days before invasion, May 21, 1945. *(Library of Congress, LC-USZ62-92435)*

Air Attacks on the Japanese Homeland

During most of the war in the Pacific, the U.S. services used their planes to attack Japanese ships, to defend American ships, to shoot down enemy aircraft, and to support Allied invasions by bombing and dive-bombing. An exception was the Doolittle raid early in the war, aimed to throw fear of the United States into the enemy and to raise morale on the American home front. On April 2, 1942, the American aircraft carrier *Hornet* left San Francisco with 16 medium-range bombers under the command of Col. James Doolittle. On April 18, the planes took off from the flight deck and bombed Tokyo and three other targets in the Japanese homeland. Remarkably, of the 80 airmen involved, 71 survived to return to the United States. Lacking enough fuel to return to the *Hornet,* these men had landed in or parachuted into the Soviet Union or China, according to plan. Few Japanese civilians even realized that the Americans had attacked, but their generals and admirals were horrified by the threat to the safety of the emperor.

With the capture of the Marianas in the summer of 1944, the Americans won an airbase from which their bombers could attack the home islands of Japan. The Japanese had already dispersed their large war industries away from the main centers, making them difficult to find. Accordingly, the Americans resorted to high-level precision attacks against the cities, where piecework was done in homes and small-scale shadow manufacturers operated factories hidden among dwellings.[28] In February 1945 Gen. Curtis LeMay, newly arrived in the Marianas, changed tactics to dropping thousands of incendiary bombs in low-altitude night attacks. Japanese cities, where most of the buildings were made of wood and paper, experienced firestorms so strong that the water in their canals boiled. On March 9, for instance, such a raid destroyed 16 square miles of Tokyo, burning down 267,000 buildings and killing 89,000 people, with small loss to the attacking aircraft. LeMay continued these raids remorselessly on Nagoya, Kobe, Osaka, Yokohama, and Kawasaki, rendering homeless some 9–13 million people.[29] The pledges not to bomb cities made at the beginning of the war had vanished in a welter of rubble and retaliation.

The situation of both the Japanese military and of Japanese civilians was by any logical standard impossible. Their navy and their planes were demolished. They had little oil. Their steel and chemical industries and their railroads could not continue to operate. Their people were hungry and homeless. Yet they ignored American efforts to negotiate presented by Alan Dulles to the Japanese legation in Switzerland in May, and they disregarded the Potsdam Declaration threatening "the utter destruction of the Japanese homeland" that was broadcast to Japan on July 26.[30]

A Corsair fighter looses its load of rocket projectiles against a Japanese stronghold on Okinawa, ca. June 1945. *(National Archives, 127-GR-97-126420)*

A wartime hedgehopper is used during the occupation to commute between Okinawa and Ieshima. *(Collection of Mildred Corey)*

The Atom Bomb

The physicists Leo Szilard and Albert Einstein in August 1939 had warned President Franklin D. Roosevelt about the possibility that the Germans might create a bomb of unprecedented force from a new source of energy, uranium. The Advisory Committee on Uranium that Roosevelt then convoked finally reached a decision to build an atomic bomb for the Allies.

For this purpose, the Manhattan Project began in June 1942 under the supervision of Gen. Leslie R. Groves, deputy chief of construction for the U.S. Army Corps of Engineers. He set up three widely separated production centers: the Clinton Engineer Works at Oak Ridge, Tennessee; the Hanford Engineer Works in the state of Washington; and Project Y at Los Alamos, New Mexico. Other work was conducted at the University of Chicago, where Italian refugee physicist Enrico Fermi on December 2, 1942, produced the first controlled nuclear chain reaction, opening the way to develop nuclear fuel for atomic weapons. Scientists at Oak Ridge worked on uranium and others at Hanford on plutonium. Physicist J. Robert Oppenheimer collected distinguished scientists and engineers to join under his direction at Los Alamos to produce the atomic weapons themselves.

Groves and Oppenheimer labored mightily, although not always peaceably, to keep all these independent-minded scientists working harmoniously and productively. After many false starts, some errors, and at least one serious accident, they tested the first atomic bomb in the New Mexican desert on July 16, 1945. It produced a human-made explosion of unprecedented strength. Samuel Morse is said to have asked about the telegraph he invented, "What hath God wrought?" The atomic scientists instead looked at each other, appalled, and asked, "What have we done?" Most of them were relieved that the decision of whether or not to use this terrible weapon rested on President Harry S. Truman.

His advisers differed among themselves. Chief of Staff Gen. George Marshall represented the majority opinion among the military—that dropping the bomb was the only way to avoid the tens of thousands or even hundreds of thousands of deaths on both sides they foresaw if the Allies had to invade Japan. They pointed to the terrible losses both sides had suffered on Okinawa, knowing that the next battle could only be worse. The scientists were divided. Szilard and others petitioned against using the bomb. Some suggested that the Japanese be warned beforehand of the power of the atomic bomb, and others argued that Japanese representatives should be invited to a demonstration of the bomb's power. Other scientists cautioned that the next atomic bomb might fail to explode and that only two more bombs were immediately available. The military said that given a warning, Japan might shoot down the plane carrying the atomic bomb and/or move American prisoners of war to the site. Physicist Edward Teller's proposal to explode a bomb high over Tokyo Bay at night without warning was rejected because of doubts that such a demonstration would adequately impress the Japanese. In the end, the formal panel of scientists advised the president's committee considering the question that they saw "no acceptable alternative to direct military use."

Thanks to the cracking of the Japanese diplomatic code in 1940, the Americans knew that in the fall of 1944 and again in April 1945 the Japanese had approached the Soviet Union, with whom they were not yet at war, in the hopes of negotiating a conditional surrender. However, the intercepts also showed that the Japanese still held out for significant Allied concessions. Moreover, in the summer of 1945 intercepted military dispatches revealed that the Japanese had built up a huge force in southern Japan, the site of the prospective invasion, and the conduct of Japanese troops throughout the war had repeatedly demonstrated the national determination to fight to the death rather than to surrender. Indeed, history has shown that Japanese militarists were urging a mass immolation of the populace, in an effort to impose the ancient samurai code of honor developed for warriors on civilian men and women. The god-emperor Hirohito took no decisive action until after the dropping of the atomic bombs.

Japanese expert Joseph Grew, U.S. acting secretary of state, raised the possibility of assuring the Japanese that if they surrendered their emperor would be allowed to remain. Only the emperor, said Grew, could make his armed forces accept surrender. Yet anything that modified the demand for unconditional surrender would raise difficulties among the Allies, for Hirohito symbolized the evil system in Japan in the same way that Hitler symbolized it in Germany.

The planned American invasion, "Operation Downfall," had two parts. In the first, about November 1, 1945, 767,000 marines and soldiers would begin landing, backed by an invasion fleet larger than that of the landings in Normandy in June 1944. If the Japanese still held out after the occupation of the southern half of the island of Kyushu, the second part of the operation, about March 1, 1946, would send twice as many men as the first onto the main island, Honshu. Some experts estimated that the war so conducted would not cease until the end of 1946. Adm. William Leahy told the president that the United States would have to expect the same 35 percent casualties suffered on Okinawa.[31]

Believing that an invasion could cost a quarter of a million or even a million American casualties, Truman decided to drop the atomic bomb. He wrote in his diary, "I have told the Sec. of War, Mr. Stimson to use it so that military objectives and soldiers and sailors are the target and not women and children. Even if the Japs are savages, ruthless, merciless and fanatic, we as the leader of the world for the common welfare cannot drop that terrible bomb on the old capital or the new. He and I are in accord. The target will be a purely military one and we will issue a warning statement asking the Japs to surrender and save lives. I'm sure they will not do that, but we will have given them the chance. It is certainly a good thing for the world that Hitler's crowd or Stalin's did not discover this atomic bomb. It seems to be the most terrible thing ever discovered, but it can be made the most useful."[32] In a letter to Professor James Cate on January 12, 1953, Truman wrote, "I asked Secretary [of War] Stimson which sites in Japan were devoted to war production. He promptly named Hiroshima and Nagasaki, among others."[33]

On August 6, 1945, Col. Paul W. Tibbetts piloted the *Enola Gay* to the city of Hiroshima, carrying the "Little Boy" atomic bomb, fueled by uranium. When they dropped it, it destroyed the center of the city, killing some 66,000 Japanese instantly, and inflicting on some 69,000 others radiation that was to have devastating aftereffects. The Japanese still did not surrender, despite another warning from the White House that otherwise they might "expect a rain of ruin from the air," and on August 9 the "Fat Man" bomb, fueled by plutonium, was dropped on Nagasaki, killing 39,000 and injuring and exposing to radiation 25,000 more. The same day the USSR, having finally declared war on Japan, invaded Manchuria, where fighting continued until August 20. Meanwhile, on August 14 the Japanese agreed to an unconditional surrender, and the next day Hirohito without ever mentioning surrender told his people that his government was negotiating with the enemy and called upon them to accept the coming of peace. Even then, die-hard militarists in Japan tried to destroy all the copies of Hirohito's recorded announcement of war's end to keep the news from the people, and they came near to bringing off a coup.[35] On September 2 Japanese representatives signed the surrender document aboard the USS *Missouri* in Tokyo Bay—despite MacArthur's fears that a kamikaze attack might interfere.

Since then, the morality of using atomic bombs has been widely debated. No such debate occurred on the ships headed for Japan carrying war-weary U.S. soldiers from Europe; they cheered as their ships turned around in mid-ocean when Japan sued for peace. No such debate occurred among the U.S. sailors and marines on the navy ships that had fought their way island by bloody island across the Pacific. No such debate occurred among the U.S. soldiers and nurses who had been prisoners of war of the Japanese ever since the occupation of the Philippines. No such debate occurred among American families awaiting the return of brothers and sisters, husbands and sons, some of whom had been overseas for three years or more. No such debate occurred among the Australian soldiers who had fought around the world, knowing that their homeland was threatened with Japanese occupation, nor among the Chinese and Filipinos and Koreans who had known the terrors and tortures of Japanese occupation. Thousands of veterans who had already been assigned to the invasion of Japan when the bombs were dropped still say at the beginning of the 21st century, with infantry sergeant Don Dencker, "God bless the atomic bomb. It probably saved my life."[36] In the final reckoning it must be remembered that, according to the best estimates available, more people died in the

Gen. Douglas MacArthur signs as supreme allied commander during formal surrender ceremonies on the USS *Missouri* in Tokyo Bay, September 2, 1945. Behind General MacArthur are Lt. Gen. Jonathan Wainwright and Lt. Gen. A. E. Percival. *(National Archives, NA 80-G-348366)*

battle for Okinawa than were killed as a result of the atomic bombs on Hiroshima and Nagasaki combined.[37]

At the most basic level, Japanese and American cultures and values clashed, and neither country understood the other. Americans did not understand the concept of the god-emperor as the focal point of Japan's political and social system. It was one thing for Germans to envision life without Hitler, who had seized power only in 1933. It was another for Japanese to imagine their nation without a hereditary ruler whose authority had descended to him over a span of 1,000 years. Equally, the Japanese, who had made themselves hated all over Asia in the countries they conquered, could not anticipate the way in which the United States would help its former enemies rebuild their countries—indeed, in 1945 Americans themselves did not know how they would behave in victory.

Medics, Doctors, and Nurses

The naval medical system in most ways resembled that of the army. Navy corpsmen, doctors, and nurses went ashore with the invading marines and soldiers, and marine band members became combat medics. Because the Japanese often targeted red crosses, in the Pacific the medics tried to make their insignia inconspicuous and went armed. The evacuation system was primitive compared with that of the army in the ETO: The wounded walked, were carried on litters, were dragged by water buffalo, or were trucked to aid stations and hospitals on land or transferred to shipboard, often by landing vessels such as LSVPs (Landing Ships Vehicles or Personnel). Later in the war, cargo ships with doctors and beds helped evacuate after the battles. Wounded sailors were first treated on their ships. The more seriously wounded were then either airlifted out or transferred to hospital ships, which had sophisticated medical facilities.

They were painted white, lighted, and marked with red crosses, in the hope—often vain in the Pacific—that their status as noncombatant vessels might be respected.

On other ships naval personnel, both officers and enlisted men, were trained extensively in first aid, since in battle it might be impossible for medical personnel to reach parts of the ships. Medical supplies were stashed all over the ships, and medical personnel carried supplies. On small ships and submarines, which carried no doctor, the pharmacist's mates had to undertake duties ordinarily reserved to physicians.

Troops in the Pacific were more vulnerable to disease than elsewhere. From November 1942 to February 1943, so many contracted malaria—often because of their reluctance to take the preventive atabrine—that doctors refused to excuse from combat duty those with temperatures lower than 104.[38] Skin diseases and parasites made personnel miserable. Flies caused gastroenteritis, and mosquitoes brought dengue. Allied victories owed much to the fact that the Japanese suffered the same afflictions but without the preventive measures, medical supplies, food, nursing care, and evacuation system that saved the lives of so many Americans. As the U.S. medical corps learned how to cope with jungle conditions, they ordered the Seabees to drain swamps and spray pools. To protect troops against insects and parasites, the medical services provided them with mosquito-proof jungle hammocks and aerosol bombs to fend off mosquitoes and taught them to wear long shirts and trousers despite the heat, which sometimes reached 115 degrees.

Navy nurses compiled a distinguished record. These women served, not only on hospital ships and as flight nurses, but also in the island fighting and

Wounded servicemen are transferred from USS *Bunker Hill* to USS *Wilkes Barre;* the men were injured during a fire aboard the carrier following a Japanese suicide dive-bombing attack off Okinawa, May 11, 1945. *(National Archives, 80-G-328610)*

even in the Japanese prison camps, where so far as they were allowed they continued to practice, thereby saving not only the lives of many of their fellow prisoners but also preserving their own sanity.

Prisoners of War (POWs) and Civilian Internees

To be an American POW in the ETO was to experience loss of freedom, boredom, hardship, often hunger, injustice, and occasional brutality. To be a POW in the Pacific was infinitely worse. In some part, the contrast arose from cultural differences in diet and standard of living. But the real horrors experienced by prisoners of the Japanese, whether military POWs or civilian internees, arose from ethical and cultural clashes.

The Japanese regarded American POWs as cowards who deserved only contempt: Nothing was too bad for them. Moreover, these POWs had got in the way of Japanese empire building, which throughout the 1930s had been proceeding apace, so resentment was added to scorn. Additionally, the U.S. incarceration of civilian Japanese Americans inspired retaliation. The Geneva Convention did not protect prisoners of the Japanese: On February 4, 1942, the Swiss minister in Tokyo telegraphed his government that the Japanese had informed him: "Although not bound by the [Geneva] convention relative [to] treatment of prisoners of war, Japan will apply *mutatis mutandis* [after necessary changes] provisions of that convention to American prisoners of war in its power"—a promise that amounted to little more than lip service.[39] Because the Japanese were convinced that they would win, the fear of postwar judgment of war criminals did not deter them until the last days of the war.

U.S. POWs await orders on the Bataan Death March, their hands tied behind their backs, May 1942. *(National Archives, 127-N-114541)*

On the Bataan Death March, the Japanese herded 70,000 emaciated, exhausted, and ill Filipino and American survivors of the battle for the Bataan peninsula in the Philippines over 55 excruciating miles. They routinely tortured and beheaded downed airmen: Of about 5,000 B-29 crewmen of the 20th Air Force shot down, only a few more than 200 were found alive in Japanese camps after the war.[40] They punished male POWs by forcing water through a victim's nose and mouth into the lungs until he lost consciousness and then jumping on his abdomen; burning; electric shock; removing fingernails; suspending him by his wrists, arms, legs, or neck; forcing him to kneel on a sharp edge, heightening the pain by making him hold a heavy object in his hands; and applying the knee spread—forcing the victim, hands tied behind his back, to kneel with a pole about three inches in diameter inserted behind both knees, and then applying pressure to his thighs to separate his knee joints. Although they concentrated their worst tortures on males, they held all their prisoners in unspeakable conditions—starving, diseased, and denied medicine.

In defiance of the Geneva Convention, the Japanese transported POWs through battle zones from the Philippines to Japan. The horrors on those ships can be likened only to those on the ships that carried slaves from Africa to the New World in the 17th, 18th, and 19th centuries. The Japanese also ignored the Geneva Convention in forcing all their captives to hard labor regardless of rank or gender: POWs; women nurses, whom they refused to recognize as military personnel; and both male and female civilian internees.

Allied prisoners of war at Aomori camp in northern Japan cheer rescuers from the U.S. Navy, waving flags of the United States, Great Britain, and Holland, August 29, 1945. *(National Archives, 80-G490444)*

Japanese instructions to commandants of POW camps issued early in the war justified this practice: "Although the imposition of labor upon Prisoner of War officers and non-commissioned officers is prohibited under Article I of the Prisoner of War Labor Regulations (Army Note #139, September 10, 1904,) it is the policy of the Central Authorities, in view of the present condition of this country which does not allow anyone to lie idle and eat freely, and also with a view to maintaining the health of Prisoners of War, to have them volunteer to work in accordance with their respective status, intelligence, physical strength, etc."[41] Moreover, on average, prisoners in the Pacific theater were held for 1,148 days versus 347 days for a POW in Europe.[42] "Of the 93,941 U.S. Army and Air Corps members held prisoner in the ETO, 1,121 (almost 1.2 percent) died while prisoners of war. Of the 27,465 U.S. Army and Air Corps members held prisoner in the Pacific theater, 11,107 (40.4 percent) died while POWs."[43]

Even in such conditions, the POWs and internees in most camps managed to organize, but in the Pacific theater they had to focus on survival rather than escape. Their own physical weakness, the distance from friendly territory, and the Japanese practice of torturing recaptured prisoners and shooting ten POWs whenever one escaped discouraged attempts. Under duress and facing harsh reprisals, Allied officers and enlisted men signed "no escape" documents swearing loyalty and obedience to all orders given by the Japanese army.[44]

Those prisoners of the Japanese who survived the war were saved by their faith in the eventual triumph of the United States, work, personal pride, and refusal to cringe before the enemy. Outside Japan itself, many survived thanks only to the assistance of the local populace, particularly in the Philippines.

Some 14,000 U.S. civilians, including women and children, spent the war as prisoners of the Japanese, most of them in the Philippines, but others in China and Borneo and on the island of Celebes.[45] Many of them had long resided in these areas, supported by government or industrial jobs or working as missionaries. The Japanese called them "internees," thus placing them outside the protection of the 1929 Geneva Convention then in force, and claimed to be protecting them from local populations.

Unwilling to spend money on the internees, the Japanese provided only the most minimal food and facilities for them. To supplement their diets and clothe themselves, the internees had to spend their own money, arrange loans, rely on outside gifts, and barter clandestinely with indigenous civilians. Often these devices did not suffice, and they stole and ate raw roots as they worked to grow food for the Japanese, or they scrounged banana peels from the Japanese garbage with which to make soup. The women among them had feared rape— a rational inference from the treatment the Japanese inflicted on women in the countries throughout their sphere of influence—but as far as the records show, few American women fell victim to it.

A few Americans escaped internment by hiding out in the mountains. When the Japanese invaded the Philippines, a number of missionary families on Negros fled the island of Negros and, with the help of Filipinos who risked their own lives, survived long enough to be rescued by U.S. submarines. One such family—Jim McKinley, his tubercular wife, Virginia, and their three children—moved frequently, lived from hand to mouth in primitive conditions, and depended on the succor of Filipino converts and friends. Sometimes the Japanese were so close that they had to gag their baby daughter to escape discovery. When at last they stood on the submarine deck, Jim said, "Thank God we're safe." In fact they were in enemy waters and in great danger, but now they had the protection of the American navy.[46]

Among those who evaded capture by the Japanese were people with one American parent and one of another nationality. One of them, Dorothy Dore, worked for a while with the U.S. armed forces as a nurse's aide and was later inducted into the Philippine army as a second lieutenant. She then joined with Filipino guerrillas and married an American, who was killed by a local tribesman and left her pregnant. Eventually she got herself and her daughter to the United States.

Some American women remained free because they were married to Axis nationals or citizens of neutral nations. A few other Americans procured forged documents showing them to be citizens of an Axis or neutral nation. Masquerading as an Italian, entertainer Claire Phillips, nicknamed "High Pockets" because she hid information in her brassiere, organized aid for POWs and internees, passed information to the Allies, and sent supplies and information to Filipino guerrillas. In May 1944 the Japanese arrested, beat, and tortured her and sentenced her to hard labor; American troops liberated her in February 1945.[47]

Americans took almost no Japanese prisoners. True enough, many of them did not want to. Conditions often made it difficult to transport POWs. As officer Dick Thom observed, "My regiment never turned in a prisoner on Leyte. You couldn't get your own wounded back from the jungle there, and we sure as hell wouldn't waste time on one of their wounded." In another place he commented, "My regiment took only one prisoner. We never turned any others in. We had another exit for them, particularly since quite a few of them held up their hands to surrender while carrying a grenade. We thought of the Japs as just monkeys. You could sit on a dead Japanese and eat your lunch." And Tom Walker reported that on Okinawa, "We were told to take prisoners if we could, mainly for intelligence purposes. We had a Japanese-language man with recon[aissance]. Civilians were to be sent to the rear for Military Government to handle. We took very few prisoners; I can remember only one. Our men were not angels and they killed civilians on occasion. Japanese soldiers were killed on sight." Signs of Japanese torture of American prisoners made other Americans vow never to take a prisoner—as when a group on Saipan came across a five-man patrol of their comrades with legs bound with wire, hands tied behind their backs to bend them over, and bullet holes in the backs of their heads.[48] Mostly, however, Japanese troops simply would not surrender.

Spies, Codes, Saboteurs, and Secret Operations

The Office of Strategic Services (OSS) operated in several countries in the Pacific theater, including China. In Burma, for instance, an OSS group led by former Los Angeles police officer Carl Eifler taught the Kachin, members of a hill tribe, to operate radios and encode messages while learning survival skills in jungle warfare from them.[49]

Additionally, a few Americans who had successfully hidden when the Japanese invaded the Philippines or had escaped from Japanese prisoner-of-war camps joined with indigenous guerrillas in resistance movements. Almost all the "coastwatchers" who hid in the jungles to observe and report Japanese naval movements were Australian, but at least one American, Cpl. Benjamin Franklin Nash, did that dangerous work. In the summer of 1943 he was alone on Kolombangara in the Solomon Islands, sending reports of barge sightings by walkie-talkie to an Australian naval officer who then relayed them to call in Allied air strikes. When the Japanese pulled out of the area that fall, Nash managed to join up with invading Americans and land with them on Bougainville.[50]

The 375 to 420 Navajo Code Talkers in the Pacific theater participated in every U.S. Marine assault there from 1942 to 1945.[51] They served in Marine Raider battalions and parachute units, almost instantaneously transmitting information from one unit to another in a code the Japanese never broke. Even other Navajo could not understand the Code Talkers because under the leadership of Philip Johnson, son of a missionary to their tribe, a group of Navajo created a sophisticated alphabet and code dictionary. The alphabet used as many as three Navajo words for each letter of the English alphabet: For example, the letter *a* could be represented by the Navajo words for *ant, apple,* or *axe.* To encode a message, the Code Talkers spelled out English or Japanese words with strings of Navajo words—a meaningless jumble to their tribespeople. For commonly used terms, place names, and military terms they used Navajo words and phrases: *wola-chi-a-moffa-gahn* (a bout) for *about; beshlo* (iron fish) for *submarine; cha-yes-desi* (rolled hat) for *Australia.* The Code Talkers memorized the alphabet and the code dictionary so thoroughly that they could work at lightning speed: It was said that they could encode, transmit, and decode a three-line English message in 20 seconds.[52]

Women's Services

Throughout its history the navy has been the most conservative and elitist of all the military services. Despite the women who served as yeomen (female) in World War I, the navy refused a 1941 army request for support of a joint congressional bill to create women's auxiliaries. However, naval leaders had already seen a manpower shortage on the horizon, which loomed closer in the months after the Japanese attack on Pearl Harbor. Accordingly in early 1942 they persuaded Congress to establish not an auxiliary but a Navy Women's Reserve, to be called WAVES (Women Accepted for Volunteer Emergency Services), and a Marine Corps Women's Reserve, members of which were to be called Women Marines. President Roosevelt signed the enabling legislation on July 30. In late November the Coast Guard Women's Reserve was approved, to be known as SPAR, a name created from the Coast Guard motto "Semper Paratus—Always Ready." The military establishment saw these services as well as the WAC as means of freeing men for combat—an idea that did not always sit well with the men so freed.

Sp(G)3/c (Specialist [Gunnery] 3rd Class) Florence Johnson and Sp(G)3/c Rosamund Small are the first WAVES to qualify as instructors on electrically operated 50-caliber machine gun turrets, Naval Air Gunners School, Hollywood, Florida, April 11, 1944. *(National Archives, 80-G-45240)*

Barnard College dean Virginia Gildersleeve chaired an advisory council that guided policy in the WAVES, and Wellesley College president Mildred McAfee headed a highly qualified group of experienced women commissioned as officers. McAfee and these officers worked out an efficient and traditionally feminine mode of operation: After consulting among themselves about what they needed to get done, each of them returned to her office and tried to persuade the man in charge that he had thought up a brilliant solution to whatever problem the women were dealing with.

The navy set realistic, achievable goals for recruitment at 75,000 enlisted women and 12,000 officers.[53] They commissioned the top fashion designer Mainbocher to create attractive uniforms for both officers and enlisted women. Their officers trained at Smith College in Northampton, Massachusetts, and their enlisted women at Hunter College in New York City.

Both the SPARs and the Women Marines followed WAVES' practice closely and even recruited some of their core personnel from the WAVES. For leadership of the SPAR, the Coast Guard, the first service to train women officers at its academy, turned to Dorothy C. Stratton, dean of women at Purdue University in Indiana. SPARs wore the same uniforms and did the same work as navy women. The Coast Guard was asked to recruit 1,000 officers and 10,000 enlisted women.

Marine Corps leaders, although the corps had had women members in World War I, could hardly bear the idea of admitting them again. However, in August 1942 experience at Guadalcanal made it clear that more marines would be needed in combat, so they resigned themselves to recruiting 1,000 women officers and 18,000 enlisted women. The Women Marines director was Ruth Cheney Streeter, a licensed pilot, and at the time of the appointment the first woman president of the Morris County, New Jersey, Welfare Board.

All the women's naval services resisted admitting black women. Only in 1944 at the demand of President Roosevelt did the navy accept two black women officers and 72 black enlisted women. The SPARs took four and the marines none.[54]

As in the army, the naval aviation branches welcomed women and integrated them. Twenty-three thousand WAVES, more than a quarter of all WAVES, served in naval aviation, not only in clerical jobs but also as noncombat crew members, control-tower operators, and instructors of aircraft gunnery, instrument flying, and celestial navigation. Almost a third of Women Marines worked in aviation.

Most of the women in the naval services were assigned to administration and communication: WAVES handled navy mail, worked in the nerve center of the navy's communications system, and constituted 70 percent of the workers in the Bureau of Naval Personnel. Still, WAVES also instructed in instrument flying, did calculations at the Indian Head rocket-powder plant, and flew as navigators.[55] Both the navy and the Coast Guard employed women in LORAN, the most sophisticated navigation system of the time. Women Marines took over all Link trainer plane instruction, most of the photography department and film library, 90 percent of parachute packing, and 80 percent of control-tower operations.[56]

The 1942 legislation that established the naval women's services prohibited them from going overseas. However, on September 27, 1944, at the request of the navy, Congress enabled women to volunteer for Hawaii, Alaska, the Caribbean, and Panama, and in December 213 WAVES sailed for Hawaii.[57] Commanders in the Pacific clamored for more, but the war ended before significant numbers could be sent. That summer of 1945 the WAVES comprised more than 73,000 enlisted women and almost 8,400 officers.[58]

CHRONICLE OF EVENTS

1939
September 3: World War II breaks out in Europe.

1940
March 30: The Wang Ching-wei puppet government controlled by the Japanese is set up at Nanking, China.

May: The U.S. Pacific Fleet is stationed in Hawaii to deter Japanese aggression and to place the fleet in a better position to defend U.S. territories.

June 14: U.S. president Franklin D. Roosevelt signs the Two-Ocean Navy (Naval Expansion) Act.

June 20: FDR invokes the Espionage Act of 1917, which governs the anchorage and movement of all ships in U.S. waters and protects American ships, harbors, and waters.

June 26: Gen. George Marshall and Adm. James R. Stark urge FDR to discontinue aid to Britain; FDR refuses.

fall: Americans break the top Japanese naval code.

September 23: Japan occupies northern Indochina.

September 26: Germany, Italy, and Japan sign the Tripartite Pact for the alliance that becomes known as the Axis, in which Japan recognizes Germany and Italy's leadership in establishing a new order in Europe; Germany and Italy recognize Japan's leadership in establishing a new order in Asia; the three countries agree to assist each other when one is attacked by an outside entity not involved in the European war or the Chinese-Japanese conflict; and all three nations agree that the terms established do not bear on the relations of any of them with the USSR.

October 9: The Dangerous Cargo Act gives the U.S. Coast Guard jurisdiction over ships carrying dangerous cargoes.

1941–42
The Japanese carry out a "kill all, burn all, destroy all" campaign in parts of northern China.

1941
March: The U.S. Coast Guard seizes 28 Italian, 2 German, and 35 Danish merchant ships.

March: Ten modern U.S. Coast Guard cutters are transferred to Great Britain.

March 27: The British and American Joint Chiefs of Staff agree that if and when the United States enters the war, it will exert its principal military effort in the European theater, even if the country is at war with Japan.

spring: Some individual U.S. Coast Guard cutters and units are transferred from the Treasury Department to the U.S. Navy.

April: Greenland is incorporated into a western hemispheric defense system.

April 13: Japan and the Soviet Union sign a nonaggression pact.

September 6: The Japanese plan (1) the destruction of the U.S. Pacific Fleet and the British and American air forces on the Malay Peninsula and Luzon, prior to a declaration of war; (2) a quick conquest of the Philippines, Guam, Wake, Hong Kong, Borneo, British Malaya, and Sumatra; (3) the conquest of Java and the rest of the Dutch islands; (4) development of Malayan and Indonesian resources in oil and rubber, and establishment of a defensive perimeter to protect these and cut all lines of communication between Australia, New Zealand, and the Anglo-American powers; and (5) the subjugation of China.

September 12: The U.S. Coast Guard takes into protective custody the Norwegian trawler *Boskoe* and captures three German radiomen ashore in the United States.

October 2: The United States occupies Funafuti, Tuvalu, in the West Pacific.

November 1: The remainder of the U.S. Coast Guard is ordered to operate as part of the U.S. Navy.

November 10: British prime minister Winston Churchill promises that "if the United States should become involved in war with Japan, a British declaration would follow within the hour."

November 20: Japanese premier Hideki Tojo issues an ultimatum requiring the United States to concede Japan a free hand in Indochina and China, to refuse all aid to China, to restore trading relations with Japan, and to send no more military forces to the South Pacific or the Far East, in return for which the Japanese would send no more armed forces into Southeast Asia and would evacuate French Indochina after peace had been imposed on China.

December: Adm. Francis W. Rockwell establishes a new U.S. headquarters in a tunnel on Corregidor, off Luzon in the Philippines.

December 1: Adm. Husband E. Kimmel orders a squadron of marine fighter planes to be delivered to Wake Island in the North Pacific.

December 5: The U.S. aircraft carrier *Lexington* sails to convey a squadron of fighter planes to Midway.

December 6: The Japanese lay a mine field in British territorial waters near Singapore. A U.S. destroyer sinks a midget Japanese submarine near Pearl Harbor, Hawaii.

December 7: At 7 A.M. a U.S. destroyer sinks a second midget Japanese submarine. Soon thereafter Japanese planes attack the U.S. naval base at Pearl Harbor, destroying 188 planes on the ground; sinking or capsizing four battleships and heavily damaging four others, as well as three destroyers, three cruisers, and four auxiliary vessels; and killing 2,403 Americans and wounding 1,178.

December 8: The United States declares war on Japan.

December 8: Japanese planes attack Clark Field in the Philippines, Guam, Wake Island, and Midway Island.

December 8: The U.S. Coast Guard sustains its first casualties of World War II when Japanese aircraft bomb the *Leonard Wood* at Singapore.

December 10: Japanese bombers sink the British battleship *Prince of Wales* and the British battle cruiser *Repulse.*

December 10: Japanese troops land on Luzon in the Philippines. The Japanese take Guam.

December 21: The Japanese land in the Philippines at Lingayen Gulf.

December 23: The Japanese take Wake Island.

December 24: Gen. Douglas MacArthur decides to evacuate Manila in the Philippines and deploy his army on the Bataan Peninsula.

December 25: Hong Kong falls to the Japanese.

December 27: General MacArthur declares Manila an open city.

December 28: Naval construction battalions called Seabees are created.

December 31: Adm. Ernest J. King becomes naval commander in chief in Washington, and Adm. Chester Nimitz takes over as commander in chief for the Pacific Fleet.

1942

Japan cuts off China's last land route to its allies by seizing Burma and closing the Burma Road, but within three months the Chinese build a new transportation route from Burma to China.

January 3: Manila falls to the Japanese.

January 6: Japanese troops land on Brunei in the South China Sea.

January 12: The Japanese invade the East Indies.

January 20: At the Battle of Balikpapan, American destroyers sink four Japanese transports and a patrol ship.

January 23: Japanese troops land on Sarawak in Borneo.

January 23–24: Japanese troops take Rabaul in New Guinea.

January 31–February: Japanese troops take Amboina, a small island east of Celebes.

February 1: Admiral Halsey's *Enterprise* group raids the Marshall Islands, sinks a transport, and badly damages nine other Japanese ships.

February 8: Rangoon, Burma, falls to the Japanese.

February 14: The Japanese land on the island of Bangka, off the east coast of Sumatra, and on Palembang in Sumatra.

February 15: Singapore falls to the Japanese.

February 17: The Dutch abandon Sumatra to the Japanese.

February 20: Adm. Wilson Brown's *Lexington* group raids Rabaul and an air battle ensues.

February 20–25: British troops withdraw from Java.

February 23: A Japanese submarine fires at an oil field in Santa Barbara, California, causing neither damage nor injury.

February 25: An unidentified plane, rumored to be an enemy, is fired on by Los Angeles antiaircraft.

February 27–March 1: In the battle of the Java Sea, Japanese forces rout British, American, and Dutch forces, dooming the Dutch colonial empire.

March 1: The Japanese sink two U.S. cruisers, the *Houston* and the *Perth.*

March 2: Japan captures Batavia.

March 8: Allied forces on Java surrender to the Japanese.

March 8: Japanese troops land unopposed at Salamau and Lae, New Guinea.

March 11: General MacArthur, withdrawing from Bataan on FDR's orders, announces, "I shall return."

March 30: FDR appoints General MacArthur supreme commander, Southwest Pacific.

April 2: The U.S. aircraft carrier *Hornet* leaves San Francisco with 16 medium-range bombers under the command of Col. James Doolittle, with the intention of bombing mainland Japan.

April 9: Gen. Jonathan M. Wainwright evacuates troops from Bataan to Corregidor. American and Philippine forces on Bataan surrender to the Japanese, who herd them on a 55-mile death march to San Fernando, whence they are taken by rail to Capas and marched the six miles from there to Camp O'Donnell.

April 18: From the U.S. aircraft carrier *Hornet,* Lt.-Col. James Doolittle leads a bombing mission against Tokyo, Nagoya, Osaka, and Kobe, raising American morale, but the Japanese execute three of the eight airmen who crash in their territory.

April 26: The Japanese occupy Tulagi in the Solomon Islands.

May: The Japanese occupy Burma, cutting the Burma Road, a major supply route into China. For nearly three years thereafter, Allied planes supply China by flying over the "Hump" of the Himalayas.

May 4–8: The battle of the Coral Sea prevents a complete Japanese takeover of New Guinea, but the U.S. aircraft carrier *Lexington* is sunk.

May 6: On Corregidor, where they have retreated from Bataan, U.S. and Philippine forces surrender to the Japanese.

June 3–6: Admiral Nimitz defeats a Japanese fleet at the Battle of Midway, destroying four Japanese carriers, one heavy cruiser, three battleships, and 372 aircraft. This battle, decisively won by U.S. forces against the odds, turns the tide of battle in the Pacific.

July 2: The U.S. military services agree on a strategy by which, first, the navy will capture Guadalcanal; second, the army will advance into New Guinea and New Britain; and third, the army will assail Rabaul in New Britain.

July 21: Japanese troops begin landing at Buna and Gona on Papua New Guinea, preparatory to attacking Port Moresby.

July 30: The naval reserve force for women is established, titled Women Accepted for Volunteer Emergency Service (WAVES).

August 7–8: U.S. Army and Navy forces and U.S. Marines attack Guadalcanal and Tulagi in the Solomon Islands.

August 9: The Japanese defeat U.S. and Australian naval forces in the battle of Savo Island, winning control over the seas around Guadalcanal.

This Red Cross officer's club was built in New Caledonia, 1944. *(Collection of Mildred Corey)*

August 25: U.S. forces win a victory of sorts in the battle of the eastern Solomons.

August 29: Australian forces defeat a Japanese effort to attack Port Moresby, thus securing southeastern New Guinea.

September: A Japanese pilot releases incendiary devices over the Oregon woods; they sputter out harmlessly.

September 16: The Japanese take Ioribaiwa, New Guinea.

September 25: Australian troops retake Ioribaiwa.

October: A London Allied conference assigns the British responsibility for Europe, the Mediterranean, the Middle East, and India-Burma, and the American Joint Security Council responsibility for the Western Hemisphere, the Pacific, and China.

October: U.S. Marines raid Makin on Butaritari Island in the Gilbert Islands.

October: U.S. Marines occupy Funafuti Atoll in the Ellice Islands, from which land-based bombers can strike Tarawa in the Gilbert Islands.

October 8: American ships destroy most of a Japanese naval force sent to cover troop landings on Guadalcanal.

October 8: Australian troops capture Kokoda, New Guinea.

October 10: The Battle of Burma begins; it eliminates at least four Japanese army divisions and gives the Allies control in that region.

October 11–12: Japanese and U.S. forces battle at Cape Esperance in an attempt to control the seas near Guadalcanal.

October 26–27: Japanese and U.S. naval forces clash near Guadalcanal in the battle of the Santa Cruz Islands. The Japanese sink the carrier *Hornet* and damage the carrier *Enterprise,* in the process losing 100 planes.

November 12–15: The naval battle of Guadalcanal inflicts heavy losses on both sides, but at its end the United States is able to move onto the offensive.

November 30–December 1: Japanese destroyers inflict heavy damage on a U.S. cruiser force in the Battle of Tassafaronga off Guadalcanal.

December 2: At the University of Chicago, Italian refugee physicist Enrico Fermi produces the first controlled nuclear chain reaction, thus opening the way to develop nuclear fuel for atomic weapons.

December 9: After leading his Australian and U.S. troops through a malarial jungle in the Papuan campaign, Gen. John George Eichelberger captures Gona.

December 15: Work begins on the Ledo Road, later known as the Stillwell Road, linking India and China.

1943

early January: Japanese troops land at Lae and Salamaua, New Guinea.

January 2: After a battle of 45 days, General Eichelberger captures Buna, New Guinea.

January 18: After a lengthy and costly battle, General Eichelberger captures Sanananda, Papua.

January 23–February 7: The Japanese evacuate their remaining troops from Guadalcanal.

January 30: In the battle of Rennell Island the Japanese sink the U.S. heavy cruiser *Chicago.*

February 8–9: U.S. forces complete the conquest of Guadalcanal, begun on August 7, 1942.

February 13: The U.S. Marine Corps Women's Reserve (Women Marines) is established.

February 21: U.S. infantry and marines land unopposed on the Russell Islands.

March: Allied pilots introduce skip bombing, dropping bombs from such a low altitude that they slide along the surface of the water, on a Japanese troop convoy in the Bismarck Sea.

March 1–15: U.S. ships and planes sink eight Japanese transports and four destroyers in the battle of the Bismarck Sea.

March 22: A U.S. Navy flotilla prevents the reinforcement of Japanese holdings on Attu and Kiska in the Aleutian Islands.

March 26: In the battle of the Kormandorski Islands, Rear Adm. Charles H. McMorris fights a successful retiring action against a Japanese force twice the size of his.

April: U.S. military services agree on Operation Cartwheel, making Admiral Nimitz commander for the whole Pacific, leaving General MacArthur in charge of the Southwest Pacific and assigning Admiral William Halsey to operate in the South Pacific.

April 18: U.S. fighter planes shoot down a Japanese plane carrying Adm. Isoroku Yamamoto, but only after the U.S. secretary of the navy has consulted leading churchmen on the morality of killing enemy leaders.

May 11: Eleven thousand U.S. troops land on Attu in the Aleutians; after 18 days of bitter fighting, the remaining 1,000 of the 2,300 defending Japanese engage in a suicidal attack, leaving only 28 to surrender.

June 21–July 20: An Allied offensive on New Georgia fails.

June 22 and June 26: Allied troops land on Woodlark and Kirwana Islands in the Trobriands, preparing to gain control over the Huon Gulf area.

June 30: The three-month-long Central Solomons campaign begins with an attack by air, land, and sea to breach further the Bismarck barrier (the New Guinea–Minanao axis to the Philippines) as part of Operation Watchtower.

July 25: A second Allied offensive is launched in the New Georgia campaign, which ends in September with the capture of the airfield at Munda and of Arundel Island.

August: At the Quebec conference Rear Adm. Charles M. Cook, Jr., recommends leapfrogging—bypassing the strongest Japanese citadels in the Pacific, in thousand-mile leaps—a strategy that radically shortens the war.

August 15: Thirty-four thousand U.S. and Canadian troops invade Kiska in the Aleutians, only to find that the Japanese have evacuated, but 25 Americans are killed by "friendly fire."

mid-August: FDR sends First Lady Eleanor Roosevelt to the South Pacific.

September: The first Victory ship is launched.

September 4: Allied forces begin a successful effort to take Lae and Salamaua, New Guinea.

October: U.S. submarine commanders, now supplied with new submarines with improved sonar systems and torpedoes, begin using the wolf-pack tactics earlier employed by German submarines.

October 2: The Allied landing on Vella Lavella in the Solomon Islands forces the Japanese to evacuate Kolombangara.

November 1: Despite heavy Japanese air attacks, 14,000 U.S. Marines successfully land at Cape Torokina, Empress Augusta Bay, in Bougainville in the Solomon Islands.

November 8: Allied forces on Bougainville repel a Japanese counterattack.

November 11: U.S. air attacks on Rabaul in New Guinea inflict extensive damage on Japanese planes.

November 18: U.S. Marines on Bougainville initiate an engagement that in a week destroys most Japanese strong points, enabling the beginning of work on two airfields.

November 19–23: U.S. forces take Tarawa in the Gilbert Islands at the cost of the lives of over 1,000 marines and sailors.

November 22: U.S. Army forces take Makin in the Gilbert Islands.

November 24–27: FDR, Churchill, and Chinese generalissimo Chiang Kai-shek confer at Cairo.

November 25: In the last of 15 naval battles in the Solomon Islands, U.S. naval forces sink two Japanese escort ships and one destroyer transport. These naval battles and air engagements eliminate Rabaul, New Guinea, as a significant threat to Allied plans.

December 26: U.S. Marines land at Cape Gloucester, New Britain.

1944

January–February: Allied forces on Bougainville patrol trails and valleys, striking at Japanese positions in advance of the Allied perimeter.

January 1: This date is set by the Japanese as the time after which any Americans in the Philippines who have not surrendered will be executed.

January 2: Allied troops seize a Japanese airfield at Saidor, New Guinea.

February 1–2: U.S. forces take Roi and Namur at the tip of the coral atoll Kwajalein in the Marshall Islands. In the same period the southern part of the atoll is attacked.

February 5: U.S. forces secure the southern part of Kwajalein.

February 8: The submarine USS *Narwhal* evacuates from the Philippines some of the U.S. civilians who have been in hiding.

February 14: New Zealand troops occupy the Green Islands and construct an airstrip there.

February 17–18: U.S. air power subdues Truk in Micronesia.

February 18: U.S. Marines capture Eniwetok in the Marshall Islands.

February 23: U.S. forces begin bombing the Mariana Islands.

February 29: Allied troops land on Los Negros in the Admiralty Islands.

February 29–April 3: In the final move of Operation Watchtower, U.S. forces establish bases in the Admiralty Islands, leapfrogging Rabaul, New Guinea.

March 9–23: Allied forces on Bougainville in the Solomon Islands repel Japanese attacks and effectively destroy Japanese capabilities on the island.

March 13: Allied troops occupy Hauwei in the Admiralty Islands.

April 17: The Japanese attack three provinces in south central China, continuing to fight there until February 6, 1945.

April 22: Leapfrogging Wewak, U.S. forces land at Tanahmerah Bay and Humboldt Bay in the Hollandia area of New Guinea and on Aitape Island, 125 miles southeast.

end of April: By this time, U.S. Marines occupy more than 20 islands in the Marshalls.

May: The submarine USS *Crevalle* evacuates from the Philippines more U.S. civilians who have been in hiding.

May 1–June 29: U.S. forces capture Biak in New Guinea.

May 17: Allied forces land near Arare, New Guinea.

May 18: Allied forces land on Wakde Island, opposite Arare, New Guinea, and soon control the airfield there.

May 27: Allied forces land on Biak Island, east of New Guinea, where Japanese resistance continues until mid-August.

June 15: U.S. Marines invade Saipan in the Mariana Islands; fighting continues until early October.

July 1: Allied forces land on Noemfoor Island off New Guinea, where savage fighting continues until the Allied victory on August 31.

July 6: The fall of Saipan leads to the replacement of the Tojo cabinet by that of Gen. Kuniaki Koiso.

July 21: U.S. troops land on Guam; after savage fighting, they gain victory on August 10.

The officers club at Camp Barnes at New Caledonia *(Collection of Mildred Corey)*

July 24: U.S. forces land on Tinian in the Marianas; by August 1, organized Japanese resistance ceases, although banzai charges continue, and five months are required to clear out individual Japanese soldiers.

July 30: Allied forces land at Mar, New Guinea, and on the offshore islands of Middleburg and Amsterdam without opposition.

July 31: Allied forces take Sansapor in New Guinea.

August 12: U.S. forces invade Guam in the Marianas.

fall: Under Gen. Curtis LeMay, U.S. bombers based in the Marianas begin high-altitude raids on industrial targets in Japan.

September: At the Quebec Conference, the Allied Combined Chiefs of Staff predict that it will take 18 months after the defeat of Germany to force Japan to surrender unconditionally.

September 10: In a bloody debacle, a U.S. amphibious force attacks Peleliu in the Caroline Islands; fighting does not end until November 27.

September 15: U.S. forces land unopposed on Morotai on the way to the Philippines. In this operation General MacArthur allocates 28,000 combat troops, supported by six light carriers, to overcome fewer than 500 Japanese.

September 16: A U.S. amphibious force attacks Angaur in the Caroline Islands.

September 21–23: U.S. forces take the Ulithi Atoll on the way to the Philippines.

October 10: U.S. naval planes strike Okinawa in the Ryukyu Islands.

October 12: U.S. ships and planes bombard Formosa (Taiwan) to knock out Japanese air strength.

October 15: Rear Adm. Masbomi Arima aims his plane at a U.S. aircraft carrier. He is shot down, but the suicidal kamikaze program develops soon thereafter and rages for the last months of the war.

October 17–20: U.S. forces land on Leyte in the Philippines, beginning a struggle that ends in victory only in mid-February 1945.

October 23–25: In the battles of Leyte Gulf and Surigao Strait and off Samar and off Cape Engano, U.S. naval forces destroy the Japanese fleet as an effective fighting force.

October 25: The Japanese launch the first organized kamikaze attacks during the battle off Samar.

October 26–December 25: U.S. forces secure their hold on Leyte.

December 13–27: U.S. forces take Mindoro, just 15 miles south of central Luzon in the Philippines, to provide an air base for striking Luzon. In the attack U.S. ships undergo severely damaging kamikaze attacks.

1945

January: The Burma Road is reopened.

early January: The U.S. Navy imposes a veritable blockade of Japan.

January 1–6: Kamikaze planes wreak havoc on U.S. ships sailing toward Luzon in the Philippines.

January 7: The Japanese commanding officer at Cabanatuan prisoner-of-war camp in the Philippines tells the Allies that they are no longer prisoners of war.

January 9–12: U.S. forces land almost unopposed at Lingayen on Luzon in the Philippines.

January 13–June 30: U.S. soldiers slowly fight their way through Luzon.

January 29: The U.S. Navy lands forces on beaches at San Narciso, 45 miles across the mountains from San Fernando on Luzon.

January 29: U.S.-Filipino forces rescue the prisoners of war at Cabanatuan on Luzon, still under Japanese control.

January 31: U.S. forces land well south of Manila on Luzon.

February 1–3: The U.S. First Cavalry Division spearheads a dash to Manila, which is not completely liberated until March 4.

February 8: With the U.S. capture of the Novaliches Dam, a water source for Manila, the battle for that city begins. It ends only on March 6, after bitter fighting that destroys most of the city and causes the death of an estimated 100,000 Filipinos.

February 15: A U.S. amphibious operation takes Mariveles on the Bataan peninsula in the Philippines.

February 16–26: U.S. troops retake Corregidor, off the coast of Luzon in the Philippines.

February 19–March 26: U.S. troops take Iwo Jima in the Bonin Islands against deeply dug-in and armored opposition.

February 23: The 28th Marine Regiment raises the U.S. flag on Mount Suribachi on Iwo Jima, an event commemorated in a famed photograph taken by Associated Press photographer Joe Rosenthal.

February 25: U.S. planes assault Tokyo in a raid in which high-explosive bombs cause relatively little damage while incendiaries destroy a large area. As a result General LeMay decides to strip bombers of guns and ammunition, load them with oil and napalm incendiaries, and send them on low altitude bombing raids at night.

February 28–July 22: U.S. forces liberate the central and southern Philippines.

March 9: 300 U.S. B-29s shower Tokyo with incendiary bombs, igniting a fire storm that destroys about 16 square miles and in which more than 80,000 Japanese die.

April: Australian forces invade Borneo.

April 1–July 31: U.S. and British forces take Okinawa, with the Allies heavily bombarding the island and the Japanese defending it with *kikusui* (massed kamikaze) attacks on Allied ships. The land fighting is similarly prolonged and intense.

April 7: U.S. forces destroy the *Yamato,* the largest battleship afloat, which has previously been kept in reserve to oppose the invasion of Japan.

April 12: The first official statements about the kamikaze tactic are issued in the United States.

April 18: Columnist Ernie Pyle, who lived with GIs in both the European and the Pacific theaters of war and chronicled their stories, is killed by Japanese fire on Ie island off Okinawa.

May 3: British forces enter Rangoon, Burma.

May 5: One of several bombs carried by balloons launched by the Japanese explodes on Gearheart

President Harry Truman broadcasts to the armed forces, April 17, 1945. *(Library of Congress, 20268-Z62-44221)*

Mountain, Oregon, killing a woman and five children on a picnic.

May 10: Wewak in New Guinea falls to Australian troops.

June 17–August 14: With few viable targets remaining in Japan's largest cities, U.S. bombers attack secondary cities, destroying 54 percent of Tsu, 64 percent of Aomori, 75 percent of Ichinomiya, and 99.5 percent of Toyama.

July 1–August 14: U.S. ships bombard industries in Japan, halting production at the ironworks at Kamaishi, damaging the iron and steel complex at Wanishi, and destroying much of the radar and electronics center at Hitachi. U.S. naval planes attack Japanese targets, hitting airfields on the Tokyo plain and the Kure and Koba naval bases; bombing northern Honshu and southern Hokkaido; sinking coal-carrying ferries and colliers and the battleships *Haruna, Ise,* and *Hyuga;* and destroying 250 suicide bombers on the ground in northern Honshu.

July 7: With U.S. help, China stages a national counteroffense against the Japanese.

July 10: U.S. planes bomb Tokyo, encountering no opposition from the air, because the Japanese are saving their aircraft to be used in mass kamikaze attacks should the United States invade.

July 14–15: U.S. planes strike new Japanese targets in Honshu and Hokkaido, disrupting the coal trade. Simultaneously a U.S. naval force bombards the ironworks at Kamaishi.

July 16: A U.S. naval force bombards the Nihon Steel Company and the Wanishi Ironworks at Muroran, Hokkaido, in Japan.

July 16: In the New Mexican desert, U.S. scientists explode the first atom bomb at Alamogordo.

July 26: From the Potsdam Conference, Truman, Churchill, and Stalin warn the Japanese to surrender all armed forces unconditionally or suffer "complete and utter destruction."

July 29: Japanese premier Suzuki rejects the warning of July 26 as "nothing of important value."

August 6: The *Enola Gay,* piloted by Col. Paul Tibbetts, Jr., drops the first atomic bomb, named "Little Boy," on Hiroshima, Japan.

August 8: The Soviet Union declares war on Japan.

August 9: Major Charles Sweeney, flying a plane borrowed from Captain Fred Bock and called *Bock's Car,* drops the second atomic bomb, named "Fat Man," on Nagasaki, Japan.

August 10: The emperor of Japan at last decides provisionally to surrender according to the terms of the Potsdam Declaration.

August 14: V-J Day—Japan surrenders. On that day at an Imperial Conference, Navy Chief of Staff Admiral Toyoda, Army Chief of Staff General Umezu, and War Minister General Anami urge the emperor to fight a last battle to defend Japan and save national honor, but the emperor announces to the Japanese people his desire to end the war.

August 15: General Yamashita surrenders from his stronghold in the mountains of Luzon in the Philippines.

September 2: Japanese foreign minister Mamoru Shigemitsu signs the surrender on the battleship *Missouri,* anchored in Tokyo bay. World War II ends after the slaughter of more than 55 million people.

September 9: The Japanese Imperial Army in China formally surrenders in Nanjing after having killed more than 35 million Chinese.

Eyewitness Testimony

"I never wanted to have to fight this war on two fronts. We haven't got the Navy to fight in both the Atlantic and the Pacific . . . so we will have to build up the Navy and the Air Force and that will mean that we will have to take a good many defeats before we can have a victory."

President Franklin D. Roosevelt to First Lady Eleanor Roosevelt, December 7, 1941, quoted in Goodwin, No Ordinary Time, 289–290.

Navy Draft and Volunteering

[At the navy recruiting office the guy in charge said,] "Well, you've got to go to a doctor and get a release on [your hay fever and asthma]." . . . I called some guy in Boston, some specialist in allergies, and went to see him. He could see I wanted to get in the war, so he took a lot of scratchings and stuff like this and wrote a nice letter saying I'm totally cured. I paid fifty dollars for that. . . . That's hard money. I went back to New York, presented my papers, and the guy says, "You know bureaucracy, now you have to get an industrial release. Your employer, General Electric Company, has to release you." I said, "You could have told me that to begin with." So I went to the man who had hired me and said, "I want to leave. I've got all my papers and am all set." He said, "I'm sorry, but I won't release you." And that was the end of that.

General Electric employee David Soergal remembering 1944 or 1945, quoted in Hoopes, Americans Remember, 98.

Navy Jobs and Assignments

This responsibility [as a naval officer] was more educating than Harvard, more exciting, more meaningful than anything I'd ever done. This is why I had such a wonderful time in the war. I just plain loved it. Loved the excitement, even loved being a little bit scared. Loved the sense of achievement . . ., loved the camaraderie, even if the odd asshole reared his ugly head every so often. For years I was embarrassed to admit all this, given the horrors and sadness visited upon so many during the years I was thriving. But news of those horrors was so removed in time and distance.

Correspondents interview Japanese-American "Tokyo Rose" Iva Toguri, September 1945. *(National Archives, 80-G-490488)*

[On shipboard] no newspapers, no radio even, except Tokyo Rose, and of course there were none of television's stimulating jolts. I found that I liked making decisions. I liked sizing up men and picking the ones who could best do the job. Most of all I liked the responsibility, the knowledge that people were counting on me, that I wouldn't let them down.

Naval officer Ben Bradlee writing of the years 1942 to 1945, in Bradlee, Good Life, 76.

As with most wars, the men who fought World War II were very young. On my ship, they ranged from barely 17 to a few salty chief petty officers, maybe 40. Our first skipper was 35, the second only 30. Most of us were also "feather merchants," or what historian Stephen Ambrose called "citizen soldiers." My ship was a brand new high-speed destroyer-minelayer.

We went to Hawaii as part of a convoy escort and after a month's training at Pearl Harbor on to Saipan by way of Eniwetok. On the *Shannon*, 330 men were crammed into a very confined space, some 50,000 square feet in which to work, eat, sleep, and store all the stuff needed to live and to fight the enemy . . . and still be able to drive this virtual city through often inhospitable seas at up to 35 miles an hour. A ship has to be self-sufficient, except for food and fuel. We distilled our drinking and boiler-feed water from seawater. We also generated our electricity, and baked our own bread. We had laundry, sundries store, barbershop, pharmacy, hospital (called a sickbay), fire department, jail (the brig), machine shop, carpenter shop, newspaper and radio, and even a church organ about the size of a suitcase. The crew included all the skills needed to run this mini-city. Most of us also had collateral jobs: master-at-arms, recreation and movie officer, lay chaplain, coding officer, censors of outgoing mail, and many others.

Mail, however infrequent, was precious (except of course the "dear John" variety). So were other little things, like: Hot cinnamon buns when the bakers were in a good mood. Coffee, always available almost everywhere. And movies: they were shown on most nights not preempted by the Japanese. We got movies by trading with other ships, which usually drove hard bargains: five gallons of ice cream for a western film, 10 for Betty Grable [a blonde star known for her beautiful legs]. During one bad period, we saw Roy Rogers in "The Lights of Old Santa Fe" *seven* times. One of our enterprising projectionists helped break the monotony: whenever we got a good film, he edited out some choice scenes featuring pin-up girls and spliced them into a half-hour "thriller," which became a regular short subject [a short movie shown alongside a feature film].

Everyone stood watches, four hours on and eight off when we weren't at general quarters [on alert in expectation of an encounter with the enemy]. Training was continuous. And everyone had a battle station. For example, I was the link between the combat information center [CIC] and the fire control officer, who directed the guns. CIC contains all the radars, sonar and other devices used to detect and plot enemy movements.

Naval officer John Noyes speaking of his experiences from 1943 to 1945, unpublished memoir.

From the repo-depo [replacement depot], where they put all the spare guys until someone got killed, I was assigned to the *U.S.S. Nevada*, a World War I battleship, which had survived getting hit at Pearl Harbor, where it was then retrofitted. When you get on a battleship, you know you're going in harm's way. On the other hand if you're going into combat a battleship is a pretty good place to be, because it's surrounded constantly with ships that are going to interfere with its being attacked. The destroyers are supposed to hunt down the submarines. The cruisers are supposed to intercept the torpedoes. At the time I went out in a whaleboat to get on the *Nevada*, and I knew I was going in harm's way, I subconsciously put my life in parentheses: it was one day at a time. Get through the day; there's another day coming. Sooner or later it's going to get over, and you're going to go home—maybe. It was four hours on watch and eight hours off watch and God, isn't there anything else to read on this bloody ship? I read, and I worked to become a petty officer.

Sailor Larry Reeves remembering 1943, quoted from a personal interview with the authors.

The Enemy

In the beginning, we could not kill even a man. But we managed to kill him. Then we hesitated to kill a woman. But we managed to kill her, too. Then we could kill children. We came to think as if we were just killing insects.

Jintaro Ishida, reporting the words of an anonymous Japanese veteran, quoted in Mydans, "Japanese Veteran Writes of Brutal Philippine War," International New York Times, *September 2, 2001, 3.*

Early in the war I made a trip through the South Sea Islands to see conditions with my own eyes. . . . The Japanese were thoroughly enjoying the lush life. They had parties continually and were drinking all the liquor they had captured. I asked them why they did not prepare fortifications . . ., but they said that the Americans would never come, that they could not fight in the jungle and that they were not the kind of people who stand warfare in the south. . . . [H]ere in Japan it was very difficult because of the corruption on every hand and the continual fighting for position. Anything would be done to get power during the war. Sometimes very good men were kept at their work only a few weeks or months because someone else would get the job through corruption.

Vice Adm. Paul Weneker, German naval attaché in Tokyo, speaking probably of 1942, quoted in Bergerud, Fire in the Sky, *18.*

[On Bataan] when the Japs captured Filipino [soldiers], they stripped them naked and sent them to the rear without any guard. They did not take individual American prisoners, although they did apparently send some groups of captured Americans to the rear. Where a single American fought until surrounded he wasn't given any chance to give up.

Col. Paul Thompson speaking of early 1942, in Thompson, How the Jap Army Fights, *149.*

Kill the Bastards!
Down this road marched one of the regiments
of the United States Army
Knights serving the Queen
of Battles.
Twenty of their wounded in litters were
Bayoneted, shot and clubbed
by the Yellow Bellies.
Kill the Bastards!

Sign on Guadalcanal, in Life *magazine, September 27, 1943, 37.*

In 1945 we flew into Clark Field in the Philippines. One of our work details was to help clear the hundreds of Japanese planes . . . scattered all over the base. . . . [M]ost of them had something like a spark plug missing, or a wheel was off. But the Japanese didn't seem to have a coordinated salvage effort. . . . [T]hey never had the coordinated effort to pool the parts and get the maximum number of planes up. When we raided the place their planes were so dispersed they couldn't get their flights in the air fast enough to do serious damage. Some were a mile or so from the runway.

Ground crewman Fred Hitchcock speaking of 1945, quoted in Bergerud, Fire in the Sky, *23.*

[On Okinawa we] found this emaciated Japanese in [a] bunk of what may have been a field hospital. . . . About ninety pounds. Pitiful. This buddy of mine picked him up and carried him out. . . . We were sittin' on our helmets waitin' for the . . . corpsman to check him out. He was very docile. Suddenly he pulled a . . . grenade out of his G-string. . . . He was gonna make hamburger of me and my buddy and himself. I yelled, "Look out!" So my buddy said, "You son of a bitch, if that's how you feel about it—" He pulled out his .45 and shot him right between the eyes.

War correspondent Jim Lucas writing of an incident sometime in April, May, or June 1945, in Lucas, Combat Correspondent, *102.*

A jeep is stuck along a jungle road made impassable by rain, Guadalcanal, Solomon Islands, 1942. *(Library of Congress, LC-USZ62-106359)*

Pearl Harbor and Japanese Expansion (December 7, 1941–May 31, 1942)

At about 0800 this morning, Sunday, December 7, 1941, I was on the deck of my flagship [the *Oglala*], and saw the first enemy bomb fall on the seaward end of Ford Island close to the water. . . . Another fell immediately afterwards in the same vicinity and caused fires near the water. . . . The next bombs fell alongside or on board the seven battleships moored on the east side of Ford Island.

Japanese planes flew within fifty and one hundred feet of the water and dropped three torpedoes or mines. . . . A torpedo hit *Oglala* and *Helena*, which were moored abreast at Ten Ten Dock with *Oglala* outboard of *Helena*. Fire was opened by *Oglala* and *Helena* anti-aircraft battery. . . .

I then hailed two small contractor tugs, which were working with dredges across the channel from *Oglala*, to give assistance to haul *Oglala* aft of the *Helena* in order that *Helena* could sortie. I obtained submersible pumps from the *Helena* but then discovered that there was no power in the *Oglala* because of the hit which flooded the fireroom, and she could not use her pumps.

Rear Adm. William R. Furlong speaking of December 7, 1941, quoted in Karig et al., Battle Report, *44–45.*

Some of the planes were flying so low, strafing the barracks, we could make out the Japanese pilots in the cockpit. Our car, bedroom windows, and lawn furniture were shot up, and our home was shaking so badly we feared it would collapse.

My dad came and told us we were being evacuated back to the States on a rubber freighter. The smell on the ship was unbelievable—not just the rubber, but the smell of badly burned men.

> *Jean Elizabeth Williams Hynes describing her experiences on December 7, 1941, as a 10-year-old living on an Army Air Corps base in Hawaii, in Hynes, "Pearl Harbor," in* Modern Maturity, *available online.*

My gun crew fired on a Japanese plane as it came around the stern of the *Curtiss*. Apparently the pilot was hit, and he dove the plane onto our boat deck. We later found that there was also a man in civilian clothes in the plane. We found a map in his pocket that showed the exact location of every U.S. Navy ship in Pearl Harbor.

> *Robert T. Soper describing his experience while commanding a machine-gun crew on the USS* Curtiss, *December 7, 1941, in Soper, "Pearl Harbor," in* Modern Maturity, *available online.*

The Japs had cut our water supply and we had no water to cool that gun . . . so, we ran to a Coke machine, grabbed enough bottles of Coca Cola to fill the water tank reservoir of that machine gun and started firing away.

> *Pfc. Wilfred J. Toczko, Sr., recalling events at Hickam Field, December 7, 1941, "Pearl Harbor,"* Modern Maturity, *available online.*

My most vivid memory is standing on the fantail of the *Honolulu* overlooking the devastation in the harbor and wondering how long it would take to recover from the shock. I never doubted that the U.S. would wind up victorious, but I thought I might spend the rest of my life in the effort.

> *Naval member or marine James C. Hardwick recalling events aboard the USS* Honolulu, *December 7, 1941, "Pearl Harbor," in* Modern Maturity, *available online.*

[During each raid on Wake Island marine platoon sergeant Johnalson "Big" Wright yelled,] "Don't you worry, Godwin! I'm squeezing my lucky dollar for you!" Then the Japs were gone, and Big Wright stood up, dusting off the sand. He put his dollar back in his pocket. The men came crawling out of the shelter and somebody said the lucky dollar had worked again. . . . Men could argue endlessly whether there could be such a thing as a good-luck charm, a magic talisman. Most of them said it was a lot of bunk, but when the bombers came, even the scoffers felt easier being near Big Wright as he squatted in the . . . pit and squeezed his lucky dollar. . . . [T]here was one argument nobody could answer—they were still alive and how could anybody prove it wasn't the dollar that did it.

> *Marine colonel James P. S. Devereux writing of the period immediately after December 7, 1941, in Devereux,* Story of Wake Island, *127.*

Bataan was sort of another Alamo, with certain variations to it. You put men out here to do battle with a far superior enemy. And you don't support them. When that happens you're throwing men's lives away. We were told, "Hang on, hold out, help is on the way!" And after a while we began to give up on these little propaganda sheets that told us these things. We're stuck out here. We have an Uncle Sam somewhere. We just don't see him—in any form.

> *Maj. Richard Gordon speaking of the period December 8, 1941 to April 1942, quoted in Clarke, "Sons of Pearl,"* Modern Maturity, *available online.*

Battles of the Coral Sea and Midway (May 7, June 3–4, 1942)

We have history in the palm of our hands during the next week or so. If we are able to keep our presence unknown to the enemy and surprise them with a vicious attack on their carriers, the U.S. Navy should once more be supreme in the Pacific. But if the Japs see us first and attack us with their overwhelming number of planes, knock us out of the picture, and then walk in to take Midway, Pearl [Harbor naval base] will be almost neutralized and in dire danger—I can say no more—there is too much tension within me—the fate of our nation is in our hands.

> *Lt. Burdick Brittin on the destroyer* Aylwin *on the eve of the Battle of Midway, May 30, 1942, in Lord,* Incredible Victory, *58.*

[The old Buffaloes (U.S. planes)] looked like they were tied to a string while the [Japanese] Zeros made passes at them.

> *Lt. Charles Hughes remarking on the inferiority of American planes to the Japanese Zeros, June 1942, in Lord,* Incredible Victory, *102.*

Guadalcanal and Santa Cruz (August 7, 1942–February 1943)

[The attack comes] so fast, without warning! But then it always does in the jungle—the stinking jungle. God, how [the marine] hates this closed-in, stealthy, dirty kind of fighting in a terrain where there is no freedom of movement and practically zero visibility! Here all is cramped, narrow, turned in upon itself; an inward-spiraling darkness. Here a man hasn't a chance to brace himself against shock, no time to choose between different . . . responses to fatal challenges, and the decision goes not to the fairest and bravest and strongest but to the liar, the sneak, the cheat.

> *A hypothetical marine fighting in 1942 on Guadalcanal, in an account based on eyewitness marine captain Herbert C. L. Merillat's book* The Island, *in Davis,* Experience of War, *308.*

G Battery was in reserve and put to work unloading supplies. Now I got my first sight of the enemy. The body of a young Japanese was thrown into a ditch and garbage tossed over him and passing Marines used the trench as a latrine. I was sickened, but not as disgusted as I should have been . . . or as I am now.

A ship lies scuttled off Guadalcanal. *(Collection of Mildred Corey)*

At midmorning the pace of unloading really speeded up. A Jap task force had been spotted heading in our direction from Rabaul and since we were protected by only a few destroyers and cruisers, the success of our invasion was deemed very uncertain. In the afternoon, Jap torpedo bombers arrived and sank a transport about 100 yards away from the *Jackson.* Our fantail gunners shot one torpedo bomber into the sea as it skimmed toward us. It was only a few hundred feet from the ship when it crashed into the channel. . . .

The battle of Savo Island was another naval disaster for us. Four heavy cruisers were sunk. . . . Jap torpedo bombers attacked both days and sank one supply ship and damaged two troop transports. The carrier *Yorktown* had been sunk during the battle of Midway in early June; most of our battleships were resting at the bottom of Pearl Harbor; and now we had lost a good percentage of our remaining fleet. These were dark days for the swabbies as well as the Marines.

All hands worked through the night in a frenzied attempt to get everything possible unloaded before the whole convoy was sunk. Unknown to us, the decision had been made to pull out of the Solomons with whatever ships were still afloat. It was a dismaying sight for the Marines on Tulagi when daylight came and they discovered that all the ships had fled during the night. . . .

Tactically, the retreat of the navy was probably the correct decision. However, released accounts of the Solomon Islands campaign cite documents showing inter-service rivalries, fuzzy, expedient decisions, high-brass ego trips, and apparent callous disregard for the troops involved. It seems there was a panic situation. The Japs had control of the entire western Pacific. We had suffered two major naval disasters, Pearl Harbor and Savo, so why risk the loss of any more warships to support a tenuous beach-head that was doomed anyway? Naturally, we felt betrayed. Ghormley and Turner were the admirals commanding the task forces; "Gutless Ghormley" and "Timid Turner" were fervently cursed.

> *Marine captain William Trewhella Paull describing the landing on Tulagi and the Battle of Savo Island in the Solomon Islands, August 7–10, 1942, in Paull, "From Butte to Iwo Jima," chap. 8, available online.*

A Doughboy's [GI's] weapon is broken or worn out—so . . . ordnance is no good; he is short of food—so the [Quartermaster Corps] is a bunch of

Men of the U.S. 7th Division use flamethrowers to smoke out Japanese soldiers from a blockhouse on Kwajalein Island, backed up by others waiting with rifles ready in case any Japanese come out, February 4, 1944. *(National Archives, 111-SC-212770)*

fat-butted, useless deadheads; his head is tight and buzzing with fever, so the Medical Corps—other than his own Infantry medics—is an aggregation of military drones. The soldier sees himself the victim of a huge conspiracy, with the enemy, the elements, and even his own countrymen allied against him. If he lives through his ordeal of combat without becoming a confirmed cynic, he is lucky.

> *GI John George on Guadalcanal, sometime between*
> *August 1942 and February 1943, in George,*
> Shots Fired in Anger, *x–xi.*

We were outnumbered five to one and were soon hand to hand. After about thirty minutes, I was hit and dropped to the ground. Russ stood over me and fought like a madman. I asked him to leave me and he only said, "Go to hell Shep!!"

Things began to quiet down. . . . Russ worked over me about an hour trying to stop the blood flow. . . . We found ourselves behind the jap lines. . . . Moving along a narrow trail, we ran on into a jap patrol, and Russ instead of getting away, chose to die fighting to save my life. He dropped me to the ground and stood with a knife in hand and the three japs charged him with bayonets. With the cool art of a true Marine he used certain tricks . . . to kill the first two and the third one stabbed him in the back with a bayonet. He fell and the jap ran. He put a finishing touch on the two japs and lay down beside me. . . . I swear by God to avenge the death of the best pal I ever had. . . .

> *Marine private first class Edgar Shepard, letter to the*
> *parents of his best friend, who died protecting him on*
> *Guadalcanal in September 1942, in Carroll,*
> War Letters, *198.*

I was a US Navy Lieutenant in the Pacific Amphibious Force assigned as Commanding Officer of LCI 1056 (Landing Craft Infantry). . . . On September 11, 1942, we departed Pearl in convoy for Eniwetok Atoll, Marshall Islands, pursuant to the operation order for the invasion of Yap, a Japanese-held island in the Caroline Islands. . . . The 1056 was the lead vessel in a column of perhaps six LCI's [leaving Eniwetok] in the late afternoon of September 26. . . . However, the convoy [we were to join] was not to be seen. Awaiting further orders, the column slowly proceeded as the daylight was fading. Finally our signalman with binoculars sighted some vessels faintly appearing on our portside horizon. Although regulations forbade showing our signal light in such darkness, I had the signalman flash toward the vessels the letter "I" meaning "Identify." Shortly a signal light replied with the letter "P" meaning "Take Position." On our radar we picked up the image of the unidentified vessels, which we joined after midnight.

At daylight it was recognized as our convoy, which was proceeding on a course other than Yap. . . . Much later it was learned that on September 15 the decision was made to cancel the Moratai, Yap, and Mindanao operations. The tempo of the Pacific war had advanced because it was found that the Japanese were weaker in those areas than was formerly believed. . . . It had long been the cause of my wonderment as to when the Navy would have discovered the absence of our LCI column had our signalman failed to sight those vessels.

> *Navy lieutenant Douglas K. Reading remembering*
> *September 1942, "The Non-Assault on Yap," in*
> *Thoburn and Knapp, "Perspectives," 42.*

In the ordnance shack, just below the flight deck [of the carrier *Hornet*] we could see nothing. . . . [During the Battle of Santa Cruz] a bomb went off with a great flat bang that shook the ship deep in her bowels. . . . Then another, and the elevators jumped up in the air and came down, locked, with great bangs. Then, just up the passageway, past the dive-bomber ready rooms, . . . there was a huge explosion. . . . A Japanese plane, hit, had suicidally crashed the signal bridge and then ricocheted into and through the flight deck just forward of the area where we were sitting. . . . We got up and ran to the other, after, end of the passageway and by a ladder there up onto the flight deck at the after end of the island. There the one-point-one gun crews were down in a bloody mess. . . . We rushed back down the ladder and stood there hesitating whether to go back up on the flight deck or take our chance below. Two great heavy thuds raised and then dropped the entire ship, torpedoes going home one after another on the starboard side, below the waterline—the death wounds of the ship, though we did not know it at the time. . . . [T]he Japanese torpedoes were real killers, in contrast to our own inept weapons. . . .

Navy petty officer Alvin Kernan writing about October 26, 1942, in Kernan, "The Day the Hornet *Sank," 203, 206.*

U.S. Marines in a landing on Tarawa beach in the Gilbert Islands creep up on Japanese pillboxes (reinforced gun emplacements), 1943. *(Library of Congress, LC-USZ62-93438)*

New Guinea (Operation Cartwheel, March 2, 1943–July 30, 1944)

So I would just shoot them and bayonet them, shoot them and bayonet them. I was completely an insane man. To think that a human being would do that [to] another human being, what I did.

David Rubitsky, who according to a U.S. Army estimate killed 500 Japanese soldiers during the fighting in New Guinea some time between July 1942 and July 1944, in Schmidt, Ann Arbor News, *B9.*

A Marine jumped over the seawall (on Tarawa) and began throwing blocks of TNT into a coconut-log pillbox. Two more Marines scaled the seawall [with a flamethrower]. As another charge of TNT boomed inside the pillbox, causing smoke and dust to billow out, a khaki-clad figure ran out from the side entrance. The flamethrower, waiting for him, caught him in its withering flame of intense fire. As soon as it touched him the Japanese flared up like a piece of celluloid. He was dead instantly but the bullets in his cartridge belt exploded for a full sixty seconds after he had been charred almost to nothingness.

Correspondent Robert Sherrod speaking of November 1943, quoted in Keegan, Second World War, *303.*

Since the planes had not yet arrived [on Eniwetok], some of us were assigned to burial duty. . . . It was difficult to dig holes in coral, and it wasn't easy to carry a dead Marine in a stretcher to a boat that would take him to the next island, where the cemetery was located. I didn't know any of the men I was burying, and I tried to think of something else when I was carrying them. The corpses were heavy and the flies were everywhere. Our burial detail was frightened and angry.

"Watch out where you're going."

"Don't worry about me, just worry about yourself."

"You're going to drop the son of a bitch."

"I don't need you to tell me I'm going to drop the SOB."

"You men shut the hell up and put that body on the boat. The chaplain has to say prayers and get back to his ship." It went like this all day long.

"Dead Marine coming through."

"This guy has no dog tags."

"Put him over there. You others look for his dog tags. I'm not burying any unidentified Marines. Washington goes ape when we can't identify the dead." . . .

Occasionally, I cried as I was carrying a body, as much because he was my age as because he was a Marine. Also he was so damned far from home.

Marine Art Buchwald writing of early 1944, in Buchwald, Memoir, *165–166.*

The Marianas (June–July 1944)

Naturally everyone is pretty tense the night before the invasion [of Saipan]. The mess hall was jam packed and I was at the most sacred moment of the service when I hold up the chalice and say "This is the new covenant in my blood. . . ." Just then the ship's public address system came on with a loud nasal voice saying, "Now hear this, now hear this, garbage detail report to the fantail, garbage detail report to the fantail." It was a little difficult to restore the deep reverential mood after that. . . .

Early in the battle for Saipan our regiment covered a front line stretching from the Pacific shore up into the mountains. I spent the day going from foxhole to foxhole, beginning with the ones by the beach and going on up into the mountains. In each foxhole I would do whatever seemed to be appropriate: talk, kid, pray, counsel, answer questions, comfort, encourage.

I was about to get to the last of our regiment's foxholes when some "out-going mail" [our own artillery shells headed for the enemy] exploded behind our line down the mountainside. Some army outfit had started firing its shells without any forward observation of where our own troops were. In such situations there is one man with each group who has colored flares to fire indicating to the artillery that they are hitting their own troops. Boom, boom, boom, the shells kept marching up the mountainside headed straight for us. The poor fellow who was to

Chaplain Edward Brubaker, here shown in the Marine cemetery on Saipan, was awarded the Bronze Star for making "almost daily trips to the front line units, rendering religious services, assurance and confidence to the men. His cheerful presence and courageous composure under fire and disregard for personal safety . . . did much to enhance the high morale and fighting spirit of the men." *(picture and citation from Collection of Edward Brubaker)*

fire the warning flares was so nervous he fired the wrong color flare. Boom, boom, the shells came closer. The next one would hit where we were, but the flare shooter finally got the right color off just in time. Whew!

Marine chaplain Ed Brubaker speaking of
June 1944, unpublished memoir.

Behind the enemy assault formations moved a weird, almost unbelievable procession: the lame, the halt and the blind, literally. The [Japanese] sick and wounded from the hospitals had come forth to die. Bandage-swathed men, amputees, men on crutches, walking wounded helping each other along. Some were armed, some carried only a bayonet lashed to a

The bar in the "slopchute" (servicemen's club) on Saipan was regularly used as an altar. Here it is dressed for Easter. *(Collection of Marine chaplain Edward Brubaker)*

long pole or a few grenades, many had no weapons of any sort. . . . The carnage [was] ghastly beyond belief.

> *Marine major Frank O. Hough describing a banzai charge of the kind marines encountered in the Marianas in the summer of 1944 and throughout the war, in Hough,* The Island War, *81.*

[At Guam] we had to go over what is generally considered the greatest barrier reef in the Pacific. Our landing craft couldn't go over it, so we had to walk over it. We lost a lot of men before we ever got close enough for the Japanese to shoot at us. Everybody was carrying a helluva lot of weight. It was a helluva long distance from the boats to the beach. Some of the men were too seasick to keep themselves upright, some of them stepped into holes in the reef and just disappeared from sight.

The first worry we had, in the boats and after we got out of them, was that our own planes would aim

Chaplain Ed Brubaker serves at World Wide Communion on Saipan, October 1944. The kneeling benches are captured Japanese boxes for mortar shells. *(Collection of Ed Brubaker)*

short and hit us. . . . But when we saw the first guys go down in the water without a sound, and we reached for them and they weren't there, we realized that our biggest worry was just making it to the beach without drowning.

> *Dick Forse, a crewman on an armored, self-propelled amphibious vehicle, recalling events of July 1944, in Astor,* Operation Iceberg, *33.*

China-Burma-India Theater (July 7, 1937–September 3, 1945)

Basic tactics adopted with P-40s against Japanese fighters of superior maneuverability: 1.) *Never Use Climbing Maneuvers* unless you have excess speed from a dive because the Jap plane can outclimb you. 2.) Use the P-40s best characteristics; namely— speed, diving and fire power (head-on runs). Never use maneuverability. Avoid aerobatics because the Jap planes can do them faster and in much less space. *Never Dogfight Them.* 3.) Altitude is good life insurance. If the enemy has two or three thousand feet altitude advantage on you, turn at right angles to his course, or even directly away from him and avoid him until you have enough distance to climb safely at least to his altitude. Climbing straight up into an enemy formation at 150 MPH is almost a sure way to lose pilots and equipment. 4.) If you have to bail out while the enemy is in the vicinity, wait as long as possible before opening your chute, because if a Jap sees you, he will machine-gun you. 5.) Be patient; use the clouds and sun, and wait until you have an altitude advantage before attacking. If you have to dive away from the attack, it will take you twenty minutes to get back into it again. If you have an initial altitude advantage, you can dive, fire and climb again and repeat at very close intervals, thus doing more damage.

> *Combat techniques developed by the Flying Tigers in China, Summer 1941–Summer 1942, quoted in Bergerud,* Fire in the Sky, *450–451.*

I don't know just what it is, but when I get up there in that fighter and feel all that power responding to the touch of my hands, I almost go out of my mind. Sometimes I just yell out loud in the cockpit. I lose all

A Chinese soldier guards a line of American P-40 fighter planes, painted with the shark-face emblem of the "Flying Tigers," at a field somewhere in China, 1942. *(National Archives, 208-AA-12X-21)*

fear. I feel I can do anything. I just want to speed, smash fight. I guess I go mad for a while.

> *Flying Tiger pilot who stayed on in China after the group was disbanded, interviewed by war correspondent Eric Sevareid 1943–44, quoted in Sevareid,* Not So Wild A Dream, *335.*

The Philippines (September 14, 1944– End of February 1945)

In combat, cleanliness for the infantryman was all but impossible. Our filth added to our general misery. Fear and filth went hand in hand. . . .

> *Marine Eugene Sledge writing about his service in 1944–45, in Sledge,* With the Old Breed, *92.*

The almost constant rain also caused the skin on my fingers to develop a strange shrunken and wrinkled appearance. My nails softened. Sores developed on the knuckles and backs of both hands. These grew a little larger each day and hurt whenever I moved my fingers. I was always knocking the scabs off against ammo boxes and the like. Similar sores had tormented combat troops in the South Pacific campaigns and were called jungle rot or jungle sores.

> *Marine Eugene Sledge writing about experiences of 1944 or 1945, in Sledge,* With the Old Breed, *265–266.*

[T]hese Marines had been mutilated hideously by the enemy. One man had been decapitated. His head lay on his chest; his hands had been severed from his wrists and also lay on his chest near his chin. In disbelief I stared at the face as I realized that the Japanese had cut off the dead Marine's penis and stuffed it into his mouth. The corpse next to him had been treated similarly. The third had been butchered, chopped up like a carcass torn by some predatory animal.

My emotions solidified into rage and a hatred for the Japanese beyond anything I ever had experienced. From that moment on I never felt the least pity or compassion for them. . . . My comrades would field strip their packs and pockets for souvenirs and take gold teeth, but I never saw a Marine commit the kind of barbaric mutilation the Japanese committed if they had access to our dead.

> *Marine Eugene Sledge writing about an event of 1944 or 1945, in Sledge,* With the Old Breed, *148.*

While I was removing a bayonet and scabbard from a dead Japanese, I noticed a Marine near me. . . . He came up to me dragging what I assumed to be a corpse. But the Japanese wasn't dead. He had been wounded severely in the back and couldn't move his arms. . . .

The Japanese's mouth glowed with huge gold-crowned teeth, and his captor wanted them. He put the point of his kabar [knife] on the base of a tooth and hit the handle with the palm of his hand. Because the Japanese was kicking his feet and thrashing about, the knife point glanced off the tooth and sank deeply into the victim's mouth. The Marine cursed him and with a slash cut his cheeks open to each ear. He put his foot on the sufferer's lower jaw and tried again. Blood poured out of the soldier's mouth. He made a gurgling noise and thrashed wildly. I shouted, "Put the man out of his misery." All I got for an answer was a cussing out. Another Marine ran up, put a bullet in the enemy soldier's brain, and ended his agony. The scavenger grumbled and continued extracting his prizes undisturbed.

> *Marine Eugene Sledge writing about events of 1944 or 1945, in Sledge,* With the Old Breed, *120.*

On patrol through jungle trails where you are liable to meet Japs head-on, where they wait in ambush, where they bivouac, you can feel when they are near. A sharp, prickling sensation runs up your back; you slow down your patrol and approach with infinite caution and silence.

Marine company commander George Hunt on the battle for Peleliu, which began September 15, 1944, in Hunt, Coral Comes High, *99–100.*

During prolonged shelling, I often had to restrain myself and fight back a wild, inexorable urge to scream, to sob, and to cry. As Peleliu dragged on, I feared that if I ever lost control of myself under shell fire my mind would be shattered. I hated shells as much for their damage to the mind as to the body. To be under heavy shell fire was to me by far the most terrifying of combat experiences. Each time it left me feeling more forlorn and helpless, more fatalistic, and with less confidence that I could escape the dreadful law of averages that inexorably reduced our numbers. Fear is many faceted and has many subtle nuances, but the terror and desperation endured under heavy shelling are by far the most unbearable.

Marine Eugene Sledge on Peleliu, September 1944, in Sledge, With the Old Breed, *74.*

We had a fog generator on each side on the stern and when we came under attack they would fire up an engine on them and pour a light oil through it, which would put out a fog. Everyone made fog to hide the ship behind them. It was an eerie feeling being in the fog with the battle raging. It was worse than seeing them coming at you. I never saw anyone panic while we were in combat. I did see people who couldn't stop firing until they ran out of ammunition. The first time I fired at a plane with my 50 caliber on my tank lighter, I held the trigger down until the magazine was empty.

Coxswain David R. Friederich describing the invasion of Leyte, which began October 17, 1944, in Friederich, "World War II Memoir, War in the Central Pacific," available online.

Shortly after the landing [on Corregidor, Japanese-American] Specialist [Harry] Akune was able to extract timely and valuable intelligence from the few prisoners taken and documents he translated. This included the fact that the enemy commander had been killed just before the airborne landing, that severe damage had been done to the Japanese communication system, that the strength of the opposition was 5,000 and not the 850 previously estimated

and that the nature of the enemy force included a number of highly-motivated Japanese Imperial Marines who would not hesitate to give their lives while taking ours. These findings enabled our land forces to design the most effective offensive. Specialist Akune also discovered that there were 100 enemy motor boats packed with explosives in hidden caves around the island ready to destroy Allied shipping, thereby allowing the Navy to take timely countermeasures to avoid losses. Specialist Akune demonstrated that a human intelligence capability is essential for success in a wide variety of combat situations. The 503[r]d After Action Report recommended that an intelligence specialist be permanently assigned to every combat operation.

Citation from the induction of nisei Specialist Harry Akune of the 503rd Regimental Combat Team into the Military Intelligence Hall of Fame for his valor on Corregidor in February 1945, available online.

Iwo Jima (February 19, 1945– March 16, 1945)

[On Iwo Jima] the entire operation was directed by Navajo code. Our corps command post was on a battleship from which orders went to the three division command posts on the beachhead, and on down to the lower echelons. I was signal officer of the Fifth Division. During the first forty-eight hours, while we were landing and consolidating our shore positions, I had six Navajo radio nets operating around the clock. In that period alone they sent and received over eight hundred messages without an error.

Weeks later, when our flag was raised over Mount Suribachi, word of that event came in Navajo code. The commanding general was amazed. How, he wanted to know, could a Japanese name be sent in Navajo code?

Maj. Howard M. Conner speaking of February and March 1945, in Paul, Navajo Code Talkers, *73.*

At Iwo Jima there was one time our battleship moved closer to the island so that we could conserve powder. When the invasion started, we were feeling pretty blasé. There was not a lot of damage to navy vessels at Iwo Jima, except landing craft. There was not much coming from Japan. They had no place to come from, because they'd shut down their airfield on Iwo Jima and they were what? 600 miles from Okinawa and Okinawa was 300 and something miles from southern Kyushu [in Japan]. We were feeling fairly cocky. We were doing a good job. We were pretty brave; we were moving in closer. Then the invasion started, and an LCI—landing craft, infantry, a relatively small vessel—came up and tied up to us and landed its troops, because we had a doctor and a little place called a hospital. On the LCI there was a small crew, three or four, and a gunner right up in front. A couple of their crew members were badly wounded, and they brought them aboard our vessel. This gunner was dead, and he was still strapped into this gun, head was down, had the earphones on, and he was staring at nothing. And that brought it home. That was the first time we were actually exposed to the ultimate purpose of war, which was to kill the enemy. And the enemy had killed us. It was sobering—because he was a kid. Looked like he didn't have to shave. Wars are fought by kids. By teenagers.

Sailor Larry Reeves, speaking of his experiences as a 19-year-old in the invasion of Iwo Jima, which began on February 19, 1945, author interview.

Dad, a friend here at the hospital is going to the states tomorrow & says he'll take this letter & mail it there. It'll miss the censors, so I can tell you about my

Navajo Indian communications men (right) have landed with the first assault wave of marines on Saipan, June 1944. *(National Archives, 127-N-82619)*

"company." Out of 252 officers & men, only 12 men came through the campaign without being killed or wounded. None of these 12 were officers or sergeants. . . . It was awful to watch steel crash into human flesh & rip it apart. I saw a lot of good men die & I never want to see it again.

It seemed that every Nip had a mortar. One fellow said every one he saw carried a mortar but one, & that one had a requisition slip to get one. . . .

In the northern part of the island we had to take one cliff after another, all full of caves. A lot of caves were hidden & facing backwards. We got their fire in our backs as we advanced. . . . Our outfit was machine-gunned by our L.V.Ts [landing vehicle, tanks], hit by our own mortars, bombed by our rockets, shelled by our naval gunboats, and was hit hard by our artillery as we began an attack.

Marine private first class Bill Madden, April 22, 1945, quoted in Carroll, War Letters, *299.*

Okinawa (April 1–June 30, 1945)

Another ever-present threat was suicide boats, small craft about 30 feet long, built of plywood, powered by a Chevrolet engine, and loaded with enough impact-explosive to sink a ship. We destroyed a number of them during the campaign. We also attacked a "submarine" that turned out to be a large whale.

Navy officer John Noyes writing of his experiences from 1943 to 1945, unpublished memoir.

Straight [the kamikaze] dives for the ponderous old *Nevada*, rugged veteran of World War I, which has survived Pearl Harbor to perform brilliant services at Normandy and now here. Streams of tracers speed from her many guns. The plane is hit, smoke follows him down. The kamikaze staggers, pulls partly out, but then resumes the dive. Just above the ship it bursts into flames! The pilot must now be finished—but so is his work. His burning coffin carries on to its mark and smashes, in livid incandescence, straight into the main deck, just where the great barbette of Number Three, fourteen-inch turret rises and nearly under the guns themselves!

Vice-Adm. Morton L. Deyo writing of the late March 1945 naval preparations for the Okinawa campaign, quoted in Astor, Operation Iceberg, *156.*

April 1 began for us about three-forty-five in the morning. Reveille, then breakfast, as the LSTs [landing ship tanks] slowly crept forward. Last-minute checks on equipment, ammunition, weapons. As gray dawn broke, you could see huge hulks of battleships way ahead, belching occasional balls of fire, with the roar of the guns reaching us seconds later.

H-hour was set for 0830 and as it grew lighter, we went below and piled into our landing craft, LVTs [landing vehicle tanks]. One of the most uncomfortable moments of making an invasion is when they turn on the motors of all fifteen or sixteen LVTs in the tank deck of an LST. There is no outlet down there until they open the front and release the smaller craft. When all LVT motors are on, the fumes are unbearable. . . .

I was in the Zero boat that hit the beach between the second and third waves. We scrambled over the shattered sea wall and soon were looking for cover in the open potato, tomato and cabbage fields. . . . [I]f the Japs had chosen to defend the beach . . . they could have made life miserable for us. We had landed on the wrong beach, a half mile from the correct one, and it took two hours for the battalion to reassemble.

Pfc. Ellis Moore of the 383rd Regiment of the 96th Division, speaking of April 1945, in Astor, Operation Iceberg, *130–131.*

Soon after, all able bodies were called topside and told to stand along the rail on the port side because of the ship's list. A destroyer passed by us up close, trying to hose down fires on our ship. But the sea was too choppy. First the hose would point toward the sky and then down into the ocean. Later they tried to shoot a line to us so we could be towed . . . but the line missed. . . . The rest of the convoy continued on after the kamikaze attack. Soon we were alone, out in the ocean. I looked out on the horizon and could see two ships burning. Then the moon came up. It was the biggest moon I have ever seen, a full moon that could silhouette the *Henrico* for the Jap ships. My morale was not very high at this point. But no subs attacked us and we were later towed by another APA [attack transport] into the Kerama Retto anchorage. It was loaded with ships crippled by kamikazes.

Crewman Dick Forse, April 1945, in Astor, Operation Iceberg, *159.*

This monument on Ieshima near Okinawa commemorates journalist Ernie Pyle, who was killed by Japanese machine-gun fire on April 8, 1945. *(Collection of Mildred Corey)*

This second time up [Kakazu Ridge] we had a rash of self-inflicted weapon wounds, all in the foot. At least twenty men in the battalion shot themselves, all of them either new men or old-timers who still were in a daze after [the first assault on] Kakazu. There was a big fuss over these shootings, with orders that all who did it be court-martialed. It was difficult to pin it on a man unless he was actually seen shooting himself. I think most of them got away with it and ended up back in the States.

GI Ellis Moore of the 38th Regiment of the 96th Division, speaking of April 1945, in Astor, Operation Iceberg, *286.*

We sat in our foxholes the rest of the night, shamed and stricken with remorse as we listened to the cries and wails of the wounded and dying. At first light, corpsmen were out tending the ones that could be helped. . . . I stood, tears streaking my cheeks. . . . The hand that had dangled [into my foxhole] belonged to an old man, his thin arm disappearing into a Japanese soldier's jacket. Three or four feet away lay an old woman beside a little girl of five, their hands clinched together. In the next foxhole Hare was vomiting convulsively and Bens stared vacantly into space. Hill, next to me, just looked at his hands and cried.

Marine Nolen Marbrey describing the aftermath of a night operation in April 1945 in which the Japanese had driven Okinawan civilians, including children, toward the marine lines where the marines, supposing the civilians to be Japanese troops, shot them; quoted in Astor, Operation Iceberg, *214.*

Air War

Out there, the enemy first had to be found—a cluster of ships somewhere in all that space; and after the attack the planes had to find their way home, to another cluster somewhere over the horizon, and reach their own carrier while they still had enough fuel to land—if the carrier was still afloat after the enemy's attack. It was a flying war of intense insecurity and uncertainty, as fearful as the European bombers' war, but different—emptier, more remote from any familiar, comfortable thing, and with its own special kind of fear: where is safety, in all this space? Why fly one way rather than another? What will happen to me if I don't find the ship? There ought to be a psychological name for this sense of a self astray in vastness—the speck-in-space syndrome—will that do?

Aviator Samuel Hynes, The Soldiers' Tale, *describing the air war in the Pacific, 1941 to 1945, quoted in Dunne, "The Hardest War," 50–51.*

[In 1942 at Port Moresby, New Guinea, during the Battle of the Coral Sea] our positions were around Seven Mile or Jackson drome. We called it "Death Valley." The problem was that our fighters had a poor rate of climb and our radar gave them very little warning when an air raid was on the way. However, if Coast Watchers got the word to us soon enough, our fighters would get as high as they could, dive through the Japanese formation, keep right on going until they came into Death Valley with the Zeros on their tail. There we'd work over the Japs that followed them down. I can't say it was much of a killing zone but it did scare the hell out of the enemy and we did get a few.

Sgt. Lindsay Henderson, working with machine-gun crews, 1942, quoted in Bergerud, Fire in the Sky, *63.*

In 1941 my father, who was general manager of the explosives division of the Atlas Power Company, a spin-off from DuPont, literally became a war casualty. The demands were so tremendous on people like him to turn out more munitions, and they couldn't get steel.

The war to me became real when I was at boarding school. My last year at boarding school, I ran away and tried to enlist in the air force—and they snapped me back. I graduated in June of 1943 and went in the air force in July. I was 18, just about to be 19. I'm col-orblind, so I couldn't get pilot training, even though every chance I got I would apply. So I volunteered for gunnery school. After school I met my crew at March Field, and we shipped out to the Pacific together in October '44. We flew to New Guinea to a repple-depple [replacement depot], joined the squadron, and flew out to various islands. I was an engineer-gunner on a B-24 bomber.

Why did I enlist? It wasn't so much saving the world for democracy. It wasn't an act of heroism. Everyone was in it, and by God I was going to be in it too. I'm glad I did, actually.

I was coming off a very bad patch. I had been seriously depressed at boarding school; my father had died. I was sort of submerged, and my identity was lost. In the air force I grew tremendously and I got my self-respect back and I was proud of what I was doing. I was never a better person than I was during that period. Yes, part of it was my relationship with my crew. That was a tight little island, the crew. There were 10 of us. My assignment was the top turret. After all, in a crew, everybody's going to go down together, the good guys with the bad guys. So there's this marvelous thought, which you never talk about—this unspoken reliability.

I missed some of the things that I should have been doing at my age, when I was away doing this other thing. There I was 18 years old—I might have been down in someone's rec room listening to Benny Goodman and dancing. Nothing important. But I'm not so sure, now that I'm back down in one piece, that I would have traded anything in the world for that period of my life. Yes, mainly because of the bonding with the crew, but how many people in their lifetime go through anything like that? It's an experience that you could never fabricate, you couldn't teach it. You had to be there. You came back a rung up, higher. . . .

Things were highly structured in Europe, where my brother flew—officers and men ate in different places, and they saluted. In the Pacific we used to fly in shorts and a T-shirt and G.I. boots. In our area, which was just a cleared place on an island, you never saluted anybody. Our pilot, co-pilot, navigator, and bombardier were all officers; the rest were enlisted men. But there wasn't any division. The navigator—just a year older than I—and I got along well together, because we both had educated backgrounds; we talked a lot because we had so much in common. . . .

When we would take off, we knew that the enemy knew the minute we were airborne. We only owned a little part of the island: we had a perimeter, and the Japanese were up there and the airfield was down here. When Douglas MacArthur was given the go-ahead to implement his "island hopping" strategy, the game plan called for taking those islands which could best offer a strategic advantage as bases for carrying out air strikes to vital enemy targets. Therefore on most of the islands the Allies took, they simply set up a perimeter to contain the Japanese while the air strips were constructed. On Morotai, where we were based for many months, . . . the Japanese held at least three-quarters of the island. Every night we could hear the shooting of firefights. On at least one occasion several enemy soldiers broke through to the strip and messed up some airplanes. They never made it back to their own lines.

Of course we flew over water, so fuel was a problem. We usually flew with forward bomb-bay tanks, which meant that you would transfer fuel from them into the main tanks as you went along, because we would fly for nine hours over water sometimes. We sweated the fuel and we sweated the target. You never get used to that kind of fear. On one night mission, I had a cigar somebody had given me. When we left the target I thought I was going to be airsick. I never had been before. But I found out that I had chewed the damned cigar up and swallowed it. I was so afraid.

At the briefings they talk about flak and they talk about fighters and the escape-and-evasion officer talks. We were all given escape-and-evasion kits, which had maps and buckshot for the 45s so you could shoot parrots. And we had had three days in the jungle in New Guinea to learn how to survive. On this trip to Surabaya in Java the escape-and-evasion officer said, "If you go down in Java, the most important thing you've got are fishhooks. But there are a lot of dogs down there, and the idea of doing anything stealthily—forget it. And if you are discovered and caught, the Japanese will have you immediately. I think if you go down here, head toward here [pointing to the map]." Somebody said, "But that's open water." And he said, "Yes. Get on your rafts, and go that way." . . .

You come back, and after interrogation you go to the flight surgeon, and he gives you two ounces of whiskey. I didn't want the drink—I was so tired and chewed up. So I'd save it up, and after about ten mis-

sions we would have a whale of a time. But we would go back about six miles from the strip to where we lived, with real beds and sheets and a stable community. Then the days we flew we would have real eggs. I would hate to have been up on the perimeter, where those poor guys. . . . I never saw but one dead man, the whole time, and that was what was left of a kamikaze pilot. Our casualty rate was high—though nothing like the casualty rate they had in Europe. I think the German flak was much more intense, and the German fighters were so good. But somehow you weren't that aware of the casualty rate.

When we first got down there, the Japanese fighters were very good, but you could see as you went along they became less good. In fact on one strike we had terrible fighter activity. They chewed us up pretty badly, and then they ran out of ammunition, and they rammed two of our planes—they kamikaze'd them. But my point is the pilots became less good, ammunition became scarcer, and they resorted to other things. There's no way you can get a B-24 out of the way of a fighter that wants to ram you. . . .

We were all on alert for three days while they were watching a Japanese task force in Brunei Bay, in Borneo. They wanted to catch them dead in the water. They shut down all the other strikes, all the other missions, waiting. Then we were pulled from our sacks very early one morning and our two squadrons, joined by several from another group, headed up to Borneo to catch this task force when we thought they were refueling and dead in the water.

It was a terrible, terrible mission. We were jumped by fighters about fifty miles out. I was in the Martin (top) turret, numb from fear and mute from fright. I remember looking at the harbor, at that point maybe 30 miles away, and suddenly a single shell went up from a battleship, and it was exactly at our altitude. Flying over any kind of war ship was much worse than flying over the flak that was protecting a city. I almost threw up. I was monitoring strike frequency, and heard the Group Leader say something to the effect that they were hit, and that the Deputy Group Leader was to take over. . . . In what seemed like a bare instant later, I saw the Deputy Group Leader begin to smoke and go into a spin. No parachutes. . . . Since we were quite a bit forward of the other planes, and following a single plane ahead, we flew on.

Brunei Bay is one of those classically perfect harbors, a lovely crescent. Very impressive from 9,000

[feet]. As I remember, there were about 18 to 20 ships, including two heavy cruisers. Having received word that we were on our way, . . . each was frantically trying to get underway. . . . Each vessel was loaded with firepower (all major league stuff) since each must be responsible for its own defense.

By this time it seemed that every ship below was shooting at us alone, and with uncanny accuracy. At that point the sky was just black with anti-aircraft fire. Then it blossomed into a sickening blue and red (at times Japanese flak took on different colors). We pressed on behind the only B-24 we could see. Ordinarily, the enemy fighters shoot the hell out of you until they get to the target; then they leave you. They don't want to get shot down by their own flak. Remarkably, because I had never seen it happen before, on this mission the fighters kept after us over the target. Flying through their own flak!

Just short of the IP [initial point, that point at which a bomber turns onto the bombing run] our tail gunner told the flight deck that all the planes from our own squadrons following us had turned off course and were apparently heading for the secondary target. On hearing this bit of news, our pilot told the bombardier to "PULL THE F---ING RED HANDLE! (salvo the bombs—get rid of them regardless of where they fall) so we can get the f--- out of here." I suspect that Walt Gango, our bombardier, was fast coming to this conclusion all by himself. In fact, most of us sensed that Walt actually "pulled the red handle" a tad before our pilot suggested that it might be a good idea to do so. As soon as he did, we took monumental evasive action to get away.

Parenthetically, the "F-word" then, as now, was a remarkably versatile word. . . . It was routinely used as a modifier when asking for the bread to be passed in a messhall, but just as appropriate when indicating an honest respect and praise when shown a picture of a GI's wife or his girl back home.

Anyway, the glorious thing about the red handle saga was that 9,000 [feet] below one of the cruisers (heavy) exploded, listed heavily, and then slowly began to capsize. We knew that she was ours alone because the only other B-24 left in the fracas was the one we were following, and his bombs hung up. . . .

Several days later someone came by our tent and threw a bunch of small blue boxes on one of the cots. Inside each box was an oak leaf cluster for our Air Medals (the officers received Distinguished Flying

Crosses). In spite of the lack of flourishes & ruffles, the cluster was important. Each cluster meant five additional points toward the total we needed to go home. If I remember, each five missions counted as one point. I had an Air Medal with five clusters and a whole lot of other stuff which also counted. . . .

One day we were on what the briefing people told us would be a milk run, "just a little flak and no fighters." Wrong! We were jumped by a bunch of very good Japanese fighter pilots. By the time they were through with us, we were in very serious straits from a fuel standpoint, so we endeavored to lighten the plane by throwing out everything we could. I remember thinking at the time that dropping things from the plane would be sort of fun, if I were not so scared. We deep-sixed all the guns [threw them into the ocean]. Fortunately when we reached our airstrip the tower gave us permission to land immediately after any returning plane with wounded aboard. No sooner were we down than the engines cut out because of fuel starvation; we couldn't even taxi off the strip.

Other crews faced with a hairy landing sometimes resorted to lashing parachutes to the waist-gun mounts and popping them as they hit the strip—a scheme that reputedly worked quite well.

There were always natives in our living areas bent on selling something: shells, carvings, Japanese hand grenades, etc. Transactions were noisy, heated, and lengthy. The cigarette was the currency of choice. As I remember, every week we were able to buy a mixed carton from the PX. "Mixed" because for each pack of a familiar brand there were three of Raleighs. It took no time at all for the natives to realize there were more Raleighs than other brands turning up in every negotiation. Soon they began every bargaining session with "Two pack, no Raleighs." . . .

Air gunner Caleb Penniman writing about his service from 1943 to 1945, unpublished memoir.

[In late 1943] we were escorting B-24s hitting Wewak [New Guinea]. . . . Way out I saw some ships on the horizon. . . . When we got back they started loading the bombers and picked up some extra B-25s for a quick return trip. It was a convoy laying out waiting for us to do our normal "high noon" raid and then come in behind us. And sure enough, when we got back there about four o'clock . . . there was the convoy about ten miles offshore. The B-25s started

U.S. Marines on Saipan try to soothe a crying child by offering a shiny rations tin, July 1944. Island families were sheltered in a camp set up for refugees from battle areas by U.S. Marine Civil Affairs authorities. *(National Archives, 26-G-2528)*

skip-bombing these transports and sinking them right and left. The water was absolutely full of soldiers and sailors. They looked like cornflakes in milk. The B-25s and B-24s flew across the water dropping 500- and 1,000-lb. bombs into the water, killing the men swimming. We strafed them, too. This was a resupply into Wewak and those supplies would be used to shoot us down.

> *Fighter pilot Joel Paris, late 1943, quoted in Bergerud,*
> Fire in the Sky, *47.*

The new policy is to go in lower and lower. The object—as it should be—is to wipe out targets. But the terrific underlining of our complete expendability . . . doesn't help much. . . . I'm frankly afraid of these lowered-altitude runs. And I'm frankly afraid that Wing's refusal to tell us how many missions we're to fly means that we're here to be used up.

> *Air gunner John Ciardi speaking of June 1944,*
> *in Ciardi,* Saipan, *90–91.*

These incendiary bombs [that the Allies dropped on Japanese cities] and the fires they caused created such intense heat that inevitably after a heavy bombing raid we would have a tremendous rain. These rains—almost daily occurrences—saturated the land to such an extent that after the rainy season in the summer of 1945 the land could absorb no more moisture and huge landslides descended from the hills. Our home [in Kobe], which was spared the bombings, was destroyed by such a landslide in early October of 1945.

> *Japanese war bride Hertha Rogers speaking of the*
> *firebombing of Japanese cities in 1945, quoted in*
> *Shukert and Scibetta,* War Brides, *189.*

The Atom Bomb

About 40 seconds after the explosion [in the first test of an atomic bomb] the air blast reached me. I tried to estimate its strength by dropping from about six feet small pieces of paper before, during, and after the passage of the blast wave. Since, at the time, there was no wind[,] I could observe very distinctly and actually measure the displacement of the pieces of paper that were in the process of falling while the blast was passing. The shift was about 2 1/2 meters, which, at the time, I estimated to correspond to the blast that would be produced by ten thousand tons of T.N.T.

> *Physicist Enrico Fermi, "Eyewitness Report,"*
> *July 16, 1945, available online."*

[If invaded] the Japanese planned to coordinate Kamikaze strikes with attacks by 40 submarines from the Japanese Navy. In addition, they had 300 two-man suicide subs, each carrying a 1,320-pound bomb in its nose. They also were prepared to use human torpedoes over 60 feet long, carrying a warhead of 3,500 pounds and capable of sinking our latest ships. . . .

In addition to all of this, the Japanese were experimenting with poison gas and bacteriological warfare. The national slogan was "One hundred million will die for the Emperor and Nation." . . .

The atom bombs made these further horrors unnecessary. By concentrating the casualties in two cities, they spared millions of other Japanese, as well as their American opponents. . . .

The American invasion was to take place November 1, 1945, but in early October, out of season, a gigantic typhoon had sprung to life. Winds over 150 miles per hour hit Okinawa, completely devastating the island. Tent cities housing 150,000 American troops ceased to exist. . . . Over 250 [ships] were sunk or damaged beyond repair. . . .

Few people . . . have realized that an American invasion fleet of thousands of ships and planes and hundreds of thousands of men might have been in that exact spot had the war not ended in August. . . .

Today, some criticize the dropping of atom bombs in Hiroshima and Nagasaki. Yes, 140,000 casualties are horrible, but compare that to the millions that might have died had an invasion taken place.

> *Combat infantryman H. Stanley Huff speaking of conditions in fall 1945, in Huff,* Unforgettable Journey, *182–183.*

Personnel: Medics, Doctors, and Nurses

In the hospital corps you can fill a man's job and still do a woman's work.

> *Rear Adm. Ross T. McIntire, surgeon general of the navy, probably in 1942 or 1943, quoted in Campbell,* Women at War, *43.*

Now I don't make these rules [about disease prevention] but I sure as hell enforce them—and I enjoy doing it. Are there any questions?

> *First sergeant, quoted probably in 1944 or 1945, in Smith,* Approach to the Philippines, *446.*

[On Peleliu] my heart pounded from fear and fatigue each time we lifted a wounded man onto a stretcher . . . [while] bullets snapped through the air and ricochets whined and pinged off the rocks.

> *Stretcher bearer speaking of September 1944, quoted in Cowdrey,* Fighting for Life, *211–212.*

I knew there was only one thing to do and that was to give him [a man going into shock] some serum albumin. I opened a can and finally rigged it without the aid of light. With a tourniquet tied on the upper portion of his arm I tried to hit his vein with the needle as I crouched under a poncho and used the light of a match. Finally, after several attempts, I felt the needle enter the vein and could feel the blood stroking the needle point. I loosened the tourniquet and let the albumin run into the blood stream. I wait-

Pvt. W. D. Fuhlrodt is removed from the tank that carried him from the front lines on Okinawa, 1945. Japanese artillery and small arms fire made it impossible for ambulances to carry the wounded to the rear. *(National Archives, 127-N-126599)*

ed a couple of minutes and checked his arm to see if a bulge had formed. It was perfect. Shortly afterward he began to revive.

> *Pharmacist's mate Ray Crowder speaking of February or March 1945, in Crowder,* Iwo Jima Corpsman, *78.*

DOSS, DESMOND T.

Rank and organization: Private First Class, U.S. Army, Medical Detachment, 307th Infantry, 77th Infantry Division. Place and date: Near Urasoe Mura, Okinawa. . . . Citation: He was a company aid man when the 1st Battalion assaulted a jagged escarpment 400 feet high. As our troops gained the summit, a heavy concentration of artillery, mortar and machinegun fire crashed into them, inflicting approximately 75 casualties and driving the others back. Pfc. Doss refused to seek cover and remained in the fire-swept area with the many stricken, carrying them 1 by 1 to the edge of the escarpment and there lowering them on a rope-supported litter down the face of a cliff to friendly hands. On 2 May, he exposed himself to heavy rifle and mortar fire in rescuing a wounded man 200 yards forward of the lines on the same escarpment; and 2 days later he treated 4 men who had been cut down while assaulting a strongly defended cave, advancing through a shower of grenades to within 8 yards of enemy forces in a cave's mouth, where he dressed his comrades' wounds before making 4 separate trips under fire to evacuate them to safety. On 5 May, he unhesitatingly braved enemy shelling and small arms fire to assist an artillery officer. He applied bandages, moved his patient to a spot that offered protection from small arms fire and, while artillery and mortar shells fell close by, painstakingly administered plasma. Later that day, when an American was severely wounded by fire from a cave, Pfc. Doss crawled to him where he had fallen 25 feet from the enemy position, rendered aid, and carried him 100 yards to safety while continually exposed to enemy fire. On 21 May, in a night attack on high ground near Shuri, he remained in exposed territory while the rest of his company took cover, fearlessly risking the chance that he would be mistaken for an infiltrating Japanese and giving aid to the injured until he was himself seriously wounded in the legs by the explosion of a grenade. Rather than call another aid man from cover, he cared for his own injuries and waited 5 hours before litter bearers reached him and started carrying him to cover. The trio was caught in an enemy tank attack and Pfc. Doss, seeing a more critically wounded man nearby, crawled off the litter; and directed the bearers to give their first attention to the other man. Awaiting the litter bearers' return, he was again struck, this time suffering a compound fracture of 1 arm. With magnificent fortitude he bound a rifle stock to his shattered arm as a splint and then crawled 300 yards over rough terrain to the aid station. Through his outstanding bravery and unflinching determination in the face of desperately dangerous conditions Pfc. Doss saved the lives of many soldiers. His name became a symbol throughout the 77th Infantry Division for outstanding gallantry far above and beyond the call of duty.

Congressional Medal of Honor Citation for Seventh-Day Adventist and conscientious objector Desmond Doss, who refused to carry a rifle, for his actions in May 1945, Center for Military History, available online.

Prisoners of War and Civilian Internees

At breakfast on 8 December (which was 7 December in America) we had the radio on listening to the news, when suddenly we heard: "Pearl Harbor in the Hawaiian Islands has been bombed by the Japanese. . . . America is at war. We are no longer nonpartisan, but enemy aliens. Americans, please stay off the streets in Shanghai."

We looked up, and there at our window stood a Japanese soldier with a rifle and fixed bayonet. . . . We were confined to I-chi-shan 8 December 1941 until March 1942, three months during which it was our job to close the hospitals and send home all the patients, well or dying, so that the Japanese could use it as a military hospital. . . .

About the middle of April we Americans were confined to St. Lioba, Sister Constance's compound. . . . When the Japanese ordered the American flag that flew over St. Lioba's gate taken down, Sister Constance sawed down the flagpole herself so they couldn't run up their own flag in its place. . . . [In August] we were taken down to Shanghai under guard by train. . . . We were permitted to go about the streets because all exits from the city were carefully watched, but we had to wear a red flannel armband with an A on it for American, and our individual number. We were all supposed to be very much ashamed of that letter A. . . . I found clinic work and chased about on a bicycle. [In February 1943] I was assigned to the internment camp on the campus of a Chinese university in Chapei, a camp for women, children and sick people. . . . There were 1500 of us, the majority Americans, but also some British and Dutch, all living in two large university buildings. . . . I lived in a classroom with twenty-seven roommates. Our camp wasn't too bad. . . . We had plenty of water, with showers and plumbing. Nor were we treated as badly as were the prisoners in the Philippines, or in Hong Kong, which was the worst. . . . But it wasn't a picnic. . . .

Medical missionary Hyla S. Watters describing her confinement in China from December 8, 1941, to October 1943, in Landstrom, Hyla Doc, *223, 225–227, 231–233.*

The guards made me kneel in front of the desk. That is the routine position you assume for questioning—and I was stripped naked. You kneel on a metal plate with your hands at your sides. If you lean more than a few inches forward you lose your balance and instinctively throw your hands out in front to save you from falling. That is a signal for the guards to beat you.

Cmdr. C. D. Smith, captured December 8, 1941, and kept prisoner in Shanghai in a Japanese military police jail, in Reynolds, Officially Dead, *61.*

Daily I saw myself becoming hard, bitter, and mean. . . . My disposition and nerves were becoming unbearable. I was speaking to [my three-year-old son] George with a hysterical violence which I hated, but could not control. I did not have the food to give him when he asked for it; if I did I was so hungry I could not sit with him when he ate it. . . .

I wept in despair for what I could not give to him. Not for material things alone, food, playthings, comforts, but for the gentle, loving mother that I could not be to him. I was the only living thing that stood between George and destruction. I was not a mother, I was the whole force of circumstances in his world. My body was worn, my nerves torn, my energies flagging; because of this I could only show him a stern woman struggling grimly to get his food.

Agnes Keith, civilian American captive of the Japanese in Borneo, was imprisoned at the beginning of the war. She and her son George survived more than three years of captivity under conditions of extreme hardship and cruelty. The passage quoted is from *Keith,* Three Came Home, *149.*

[At Santo Tomas in the Philippines] gonorrhea was a serious problem among the guards, and those infected with venereal diseases would be severely punished before they were treated. Consequently they would gladly pay the corpsmen five pesos each for sulfathiazole tablets. . . . [T]he corpsmen made molds and combined chalk, kaolin, and sugar to create lookalike [sic] . . . sulfathiazole tablets, complete with the familiar groove across the center. Business went along very well until a dubious young Japanese officer wanted the tablets checked out by the [Japanese] laboratory. To pass their inept tests, one of the doctors suggested adding a little sulfanilamide powder. Thus business continued to flourish as nicely as the customers' social diseases.

Navy nurse Dorothy Danner, POW from December 8, 1941, to early 1945, in Danner, What a Way to Spend a War, *113.*

ANTRIM, RICHARD NOTT

Rank and organization: Commander, U.S. Navy. Place and date: Makassar, Celebes, Netherlands East Indies, April 1942. . . . Citation: For conspicuous gallantry and intrepidity at the risk of his life above and beyond the call of duty while interned as a prisoner of war of the enemy Japanese in the city of Makassar, Celebes, Netherlands East Indies, in April 1942. Acting instantly on behalf of a naval officer who was subjected to a vicious clubbing by a frenzied Japanese guard venting his insane wrath upon the helpless prisoner, Comdr. (then Lt.) Antrim boldly intervened, attempting to quiet the guard and finally persuading him to discuss the charges against the officer. With the entire Japanese force assembled and making extraordinary preparations for the threatened beating, and with the tension heightened by 2,700 Allied prisoners rapidly closing in, Comdr. Antrim courageously appealed to the fanatic enemy, risking his own life in a desperate effort to mitigate the punishment. When the other had been beaten unconscious by 15 blows of a hawser and was repeatedly kicked by 3 soldiers to a point beyond which he could not survive, Comdr. Antrim gallantly stepped forward and indicated to the perplexed guards that he would take the remainder of the punishment, throwing the Japanese completely off balance in their amazement and eliciting a roar of acclaim from the suddenly inspired Allied prisoners. By his fearless leadership and valiant concern for the welfare of another, he not only saved the life of a fellow officer and stunned the Japanese into sparing his own life but also brought about a new respect for American officers and men and a great improvement in camp living conditions.

Cmdr. Richard Antrim's Congressional Medal of Honor citation for his actions in April 1942, available online.

When food is denied, the sensation of hunger takes over. But this passes quickly. . . . However, when certain elements are withheld, a craving of the most painful kind will persist. . . . This state lasts a long time and some people never overcome the symptoms. Most often it is a craving for sweets—sugar is hard to do without. I have been through long sugar denials which were hellish, not only because my taste demanded it, but physiologically the old human machine was missing. Our blood sugar gets so low that we often fall asleep while eating or at work. It's during this phase of food denial that one becomes conscious of physical inefficiency, mental dullness, and the inability to concentrate.

Cmdr. Thomas Hayes, diary entry of July 1942, quoted in Haber, From Hardtack to Homefries, *151–52.*

On the day Pearl Harbor was bombed, my mother, younger brother (12 years old) and I (17) were in the Philippines. By the end of the month, my mother, brother, and I were interned by the Japanese and spent the next year and nine months in internment.

. . . There were two exchanges of civilian prisoners between the United States and Japan during the war, one in 1942 and the other in 1943, each involving about 1500 people on each side. Both the Japanese and the Americans were chosen by name by the Japanese. In the summer of 1943 approximately 50 people in the Philippines were notified of their selection for this exchange, out of a population of about 5,000 Americans. On September 24, my mother, brother, and I boarded the Teia Maru, a small, tired Japanese passenger ship with space for about 500 people but at that time carrying 1500. Passengers doubled up in the cabins and in addition the Japanese built forms six feet wide and about two feet deep, placed on legs, and stretching across the enclosed promenade deck in the forward part of the ship with space between for one person to walk alone. Two-foot wide rolls of cloth-covered tatami matting were placed side by side in the forms with no dividers between. This was your bunk, your cabin, and your space for three weeks. The food was atrocious and the crew was surly. About two weeks into the trip, we entered Sunday Strait between Sumatra and Java. We noticed that the Japanese cruiser that had been following us was turning around and going back east! It dawned on us that we were no longer in Japanese waters: we were in free territory. . . . After that, we got a little more cocky and the crew gave fewer peremptory orders.

A couple of days later we transferred to the Gripsholm, a beautiful Swedish liner, painted shining white with large green crosses on the sides and double or triple the size of the Teia Maru. . . . Freedom from constant fear made the mood on ship almost euphoric. We spent the first few days reading mail from home that had been brought on the ship and catching up on the world . . . through back copies of *Life, Time, Colliers,* and *Look* magazines. Everything on the ship was free—movies, used clothing for those who had no winter clothes, lots and lots of food—and those chocolate bars. . . .

As we sailed into Rio de Janeiro, our next port of call, we passed a freighter outbound. It had seen better days but it flew an American flag, the first we had seen since our internment started. We went wild, waving and hollering.

Missionary's daughter Barbara H. Ambler, recalling her return to the United States, September–October 1943, unpublished manuscript.

If I could only have been killed in action, its so useless to die here from Disentry with no medicin. . . . Bombed twice from 2 ships; on the 3rd now. Use my money to buy Turkey Ranch so you will always have some place to always go. . . . Write: Mary Robertson at Houtzdale, Penn. Her son died of disentry on the 17th of Jan. with his head on my shoulder. We were like brothers. . . . Tell Patty I'm sorry, guess we just weren't meant to be happy together. I weigh about 90 lbs now so you can see how we are. . . .

Farewell letter to his parents, January 1945, from Lt. Thomas R. Kennedy, who died that month on a Japanese prison ship, in Carroll, War Letters, *195.*

The Japanese Army is now going to release all the prisoners-of-war and internees here on its own accord.

1. We are assigned to another duty and shall be here no more.

2. You are at liberty to act as free persons, but you must be aware of probable dangers if you go out.

3. We shall leave here foodstuffs, medicines, and other necessities of which you may avail yourselves for the time being.

4. We have arranged to put up signboard at the front gate, bearing the following content: "Lawfully released Prisoners-of-War and Internees are quartered here. Please do not molest them unless they make positive resistance."

Notice posted by the departing Japanese at Bilibid Prison in Manila, February 4, 1945, in Kerr, Surrender and Survival, *250.*

For careful planning, daring execution, and brilliant results, this war offers few parallels to the rescue of 2,200 American, British and other Allied internees from Los Banos concentration camp last week. . . . As American paratroopers dropped from the skies to annihilate the Jap [sic] Garrison in the camp, huge amphibious tractors came roaring out of Laguna de Bay and smashed their way into the camp grounds. The internees and the paratroopers were loaded into the tractors which rolled back through enemy machine gun fire to the edge of Laguna de Bay, plunged into the water and carried their cargo safely behind American lines. . . . [T]he operation was carried out with total military casualties of two dead and two wounded, while two internees were slightly wounded.

Manila Free Philippines *(newspaper) February 27, 1945, quoted in Danner,* What a Way to Spend a War, *203.*

At one time we saw some Japanese soldiers walking toward us, hands behind their backs as though surrendering. We set up a horseshoe stance and let them walk into the mouth of it. One of our men went over to the side and saw something strapped to their backs. We found they had satchel charges of machine guns on their backs. We shot all of them before they got too close. It was unpleasant but just something we had to do.

Orders came down later that we could not take prisoners if they were surrendering for no apparent reason. "Just shoot them" was the word we got. I don't think it meant take no prisoners but it was interpreted that way.

We dug in that night outside the village in a place that overlooked a meadow. There was a problem of "civilians" coming back through the lines, and some were enemy soldiers dressed as civilians. So we were ordered to shoot some of these people. Some Americans, I'm sorry to say, shot kids.

Rifleman Herman Buffington speaking about April to June 1945 on Okinawa, in Astor, Operation Iceberg, *268.*

Navy of the Great Japanese Empire
Regulations for Prisoners
1. The Prisoners disobeying the following orders will be punished with immediate death:

(a) Those disobeying orders and instructions.

(b) Those showing a motion of antagonism and raising a sign of opposition.

(c) Those disordering the regulations by individualism, egoism, thinking only about yourself, rushing for your own goods.

Japanese POWs at Guam bow their heads as they hear Emperor Hirohito announce the end of the war. August 15, 1945. *(Library of Congress, LC-USZ6-1882)*

(d) Those talking without permission and raising loud voices.

(e) Those walking and moving without order. Those carrying unnecessary baggage in embarking.

(f) Those resisting mutually.

(g) Those touching the boat's materials, wires, electric lights, tools, switches, etc.

(h) Those climbing ladder without order.

(i) Those showing action of running away from the room or boat.

(j) Those trying to take more meal than given to them.

(k) Those using more than two blankets.

Notice posted on the day in the summer of 1945 before American POWs on Wake Island were to leave, in Kerr, Surrender and Survival, *40–41.*

Spies, Codes, Saboteurs, and Secret Operations

Ah doan kyar whut yo' gonna do, but sonofabitch if Ah'm gonna let no bunch of slant-eyed yellow bastards put mah ass in no jail.

Soldier who refused to surrender on Mindanao, December 1941, in Keats, They Fought Alone, *164.*

I am called on to lead a resistance movement against an implacable enemy under conditions that make victory barely possible even under the best circumstances. . . . I do not envision failure; it is obvious that the odds are against us and we will not consistently win, but if we are to win only part of the time and gain a little each time, in the end we will be successful.

Mining engineer Wendell Fertig ignored the command to surrender and with a handful of other Americans led Filipinos against the Japanese; by the time Americans returned to the Philippines, they found him commanding an army of 35,000 and heading a civil government with its own post office, law courts, factories, and money. Fertig, 1942 diary entry, Mindanao, quoted in Keats, They Fought Alone, *104.*

We know where you are . . . about to try to take [Cape] Gloucester. But back home the 4-F's are lying easy and having a good time with your sweethearts . . . your loved ones that you left at home. People are having a great time in the city of Los Angeles, Denver, Kansas City, *your* city. They're praying and they're hoping and they're saying, "Please, God, let this war go on four more years at least. We're getting rich; we're making good money; we're having such a good time." Your very sweethearts that you trust—your wives—they're in bed in the state of Utah, Arizona, Ohio, Texas, Pennsylvania. Think about

that, First Marine. Think about that. You're about to hit the beach. Think about that!

Report on broadcast of one of the women called "Tokyo Rose," probably December, 1943, in Paul, Navajo Code Talkers, *68–69.*

WAVES

If the Navy could possibly have used dogs or ducks or monkeys, certain of the older admirals would probably have greatly preferred them to women.

Dean Virginia Gildersleeve of Barnard College, probably in 1942 or 1943, quoted in Campbell, Women at War, *37.*

There is an unwholesomely large number of girls who refrain from even contemplating enlistment because of male opinion. An educative program needs to be done among the male population to overcome this problem. Men—both civilian and military personnel—should be more specifically informed that it is fitting for girls to be in service. This would call for copy . . . which shows that the services increase, rather than detract from, desirable feminine characteristics.

Office of Emergency Management memo, probably 1942 or 1943, about recruitment of WAVES and SPARs, quoted in Honey, Creating Rosie the Riveter, *113.*

People would come up to you in the street and say nice things to you. If you were on the street in uniform at 11:30 a.m. and had to be at work at noon, a dozen people would stop and offer you a ride to work. At bus stops, people always stopped their cars and offered rides. On the trolley cars they even wanted to give you their seats. . . . [First lady] Eleanor [Roosevelt] came to encourage us. She even took some of the girls over to the White House and gave them a private tour.

WAVES member Vivian Ronca speaking probably of 1942 or 1943, in Brinkley, Washington Goes to War, *239.*

U.S. Marines cross a Cape Gloucester, New Britain, stream looking for Japanese snipers, January 1944. *(Library of Congress, LC-USZ62-106483)*

I sent one [WAVES officer] down to Officer Personnel [on an errand]. . . . She was very pretty, she was an Ensign, and she never came back. . . . They just kept her down there. And that was fine, because we should have had a WAVE in Officer Personnel.

Lt. Jean Palmer speaking probably about summer 1942, in Treadwell, Women's Army Corps, *15–16.*

Can't imagine why anyone would want women [in the navy], but my women are marvelous.

Male chief petty officer, probably in 1943, quoted in Ebbert and Hall, Crossed Currents, *73.*

The male corpsmen looked at us with some misgivings when we ventured out through the hospital grounds. We were quartered in the first deck of a new square building, and corpsmen had to double up topside. Worse yet, a few were moved to neat rows of tents a few feet to the rear of the building. Maybe that is what the WAVE song means when sailors will "find ashore their man-sized chore was done by a Navy WAVE." And they did not like it a bit. First we took their jobs, which surely meant they would be "shipping out" soon, then we shoved them from their quarters. Things were pretty touchy for a few days, but after classes began and we were assigned our duty on the wards the situation eased considerably.

Hospital Corpsman Marie Bennett speaking probably of 1943, in Navy Department, Bureau of Naval Personnel, U.S. Naval Administration in World War II: Women's Reserve, *1:12–13.*

[When she and I spurned the sailors' advances,] one of them sought out the MP riding the train and demanded that we be forcefully compelled to carry out our military assignment [as G.I. concubines]. When the MP attempted to correct the obvious misconception the old sailors were crestfallen and incredulous.

WAVES member speaking probably of 1943, quoted in Campbell, Women at War, *39–40.*

If the work wasn't done, and it was dinner time, you stayed there. I slept nights on a desk to see if my [computer] program [for the Mark I] was going to get running.

Adm. Grace Murray Hopper, commissioned a navy lieutenant in 1944, who described her pioneering work during World War II as "chaperoning these two damned computers," in Slater, Portraits in Silicon, *222.*

[After FDR in 1944 ordered the WAVES to admit blacks] it was announced quickly that we would accept officers and we wanted officers particularly to help supervise the women—the Negro women—at Hunter [College] in the basic training school, where there was to be no segregation except that there would be a company of 250 [Negro] women, and they would have all the privileges of the station, they would eat in the same mess, everything there, which was a simply incredible achievement from the point of view of where we'd been in the Navy. . . . The 250 women to be taken into the company at Hunter were way short—I think that there were only 25. . . . The Negro girls simply went in and took their places with everyone else. . . . Captain Amsden said, "The only episode that we remember was when one white girl went down to the mate of the deck in the apartment house and said, 'I think there must be some mistake because I find that my roommate is going to be a Negro girl,' and the officer of the deck said, 'Well, we're in the Navy now, and we're all citizens.'" So, Captain Amsden said, "the white girl went upstairs and helped her roommate make her bunk."

Capt. Mildred McAfee Horton, director of the WAVES, speaking about 1944, quoted in Moore, To Serve My Country, *3.*

Commanding officers where WAVES are already at work [in Hawaii] have the highest praise for the work which the girls [sic] are doing. As the tempo in the Pacific increases and the pressure on these naval activities continues they feel that ComFourteen should have every priority on getting WAVES speedily and in large numbers. The internal Navy problems of volunteers for overseas duty and of replacements for these WAVES do not impress them as much as the urgency of the work to be done in the Fourteenth Naval District.

Memo from Louise Wilde to Capt. Mildred McAfee Horton, February 23, 1945, Fourteenth Naval District (1943–53), Navy Operational Archives.

Eventually in 1945 Congress approved our going overseas and I volunteered. My orders came through for Pearl Harbor, so Memorial Day weekend I set sail with a group of other WAVES on an attack transport ship, the USS *Leon.* The moment we cleared San Francisco's Golden Gate the ground swell made me sick. However, all officers were expected to take watch duty, even at 4 A.M., so the going was rough for me the first few days. VE day had occurred in Europe just before we left, but in the Pacific there were blackout regulations. We always wore life preservers and had abandon-ship drills.

WAVES officer Jane Lyons speaking of 1945, unpublished memoir.

I was proud of my service in the Coast Guard Women's Reserve, and was appreciative of the [veteran's] benefits. I remember feeling vaguely apologetic about it—at some point there is a distinct impression that our service was not considered really "military" because there was no front line activity—never mind that some of us did go overseas (Alaska), and that there were millions of men who performed vital services behind the lines also. Like our sister Rosie the Riveter—and I was that too—there was a distinct message that we should now let the men take over the real world and we should silently return to the kitchens.

A SPAR member speaking of the early postwar years, quoted in Willenz, Women Veterans, *200.*

Women Marines

[In 1935 I was working for retired Marine colonel, Acting Secretary of the Navy Henry Roosevelt, who was reviewing Claude Bloch's proposal for a new Naval Reserve Act.] After looking it over the Secretary said, "Claude, you don't have any women in this Act." Adm. Bloch replied, "No, Mr. Secretary, we won't have any women in the Navy or Marine Corps in the next war." "You will so," said Col. Roosevelt, "and here's one sitting right here." (Me.) Later when

the war came and the WAVES started up, I was asked to join them, but I felt I'd already been spoken for [by the Marines].

Marine officer Helen O'Neill speaking about 1935 and 1942, quoted in Ebbert and Hall, Crossed Currents, *52.*

[T]here's hardly any work at our Marine stations that women can't do as well as men. They do some work far better than men.

Gen. Thomas Holcomb, commandant of the Marine Corps, speaking probably of the years 1942 to 1945, quoted in Campbell, Women at War, *21.*

The Women's Auxiliary Service Pilots (WASP)

So it was that in May of 1944, Col. Tibbetts enlisted the help of two women pilots, members of the Women's Auxiliary Service Pilots (W.A.S.P.). With the use of two B-29s and two crews, Dora Daughtery and D. D. Moorman, the only women to fly the B-29, were put through an intensive training period of a few weeks that qualified them to fly the Superfortress. There was a special purpose for training these two women to fly the B-29. Their mission was to perform demonstration flights at air bases where B-29 crews were being trained, in an effort to reduce the mishaps that were occurring, which resulted in the loss of planes and crew members.

Air Force mechanic Wade H. Wolfe speaking about May 1944, "Why I Volunteered to Help Refurbish 'Fi Fi'," available online. URL: http://www.wwc.edu/about-us/publications/westwind.

8

Civil Liberties and "Military Necessity"
June 8, 1938– December 23, 2000

HISTORICAL CONTEXT

Any nation at war must balance preserving civil liberties against protecting itself from enemy spies, saboteurs, and terrorists. As Chief Justice William H. Rehnquist of the U.S. Supreme Court remarked in a speech of November 17, 1999, "Franklin Roosevelt felt the great task of his wartime administration was to win World War II, and, . . . if forced to choose between a necessary war measure and obeying the Constitution, he would opt for the former. This is not necessarily a condemnation. Sometimes the notion that more civil liberties protections are better is simply not possible to implement during wartime."[1] The attacks on the United States of September 11, 2001, have posed the same dilemma.

In some respects, the World War II years (1939–45) look harshly repressive. Yet significant progress had been made since World War I (1914–18), less than 25 years earlier.

The General Populace

The American population experienced some curtailments of civil liberties during World War II. Overseas mail and news reporting were censored, both by the bureaucracy and by reporters' self-censorship. The government put out reams of propaganda—on posters, on the radio, and in the newspapers—designed to modify American behavior. Indirectly it curtailed the travel of public citizens by gasoline rationing and by preempting space on public transportation for military travel. Americans of course were not free to enter the war zones at will: Except for such privileged people as the wife of Gen. Douglas MacArthur, spouses could not enter the same theater of operations as their husbands or wives. The Smith Act of June 1940 limited freedom of speech for all Americans by making it a crime to encourage insubordination in the military, to advocate the forceful overthrow of the U.S. government, and to join any organization that so advocated. The Selective Service Act of September 1940 carried penalties for urging resistance to the draft. The Nationality Act of October 1940 facilitated divesting naturalized immigrants of their citizenship for radical political beliefs. On the other hand, in 1944 the American Civil Liberties Union reported "an almost complete absence of repressive tendencies," noting that only about 130 persons had been prosecuted for speaking or writing in such ways as to obstruct the war, in contrast to the 1,500 so prosecuted in World War I.[2]

For the people of the U.S. territory of Hawaii, it was a much more difficult period. On December 7, 1941, immediately after the bombing of Pearl Harbor, Hawaiian governor Joseph B. Poindexter declared martial law, suspending the right of habeas corpus and transferring to the local commanding general all his own powers as governor and "all the powers normally exercised by the judicial officers . . . of this territory . . . during the present emergency and until the danger of invasion is removed." Martial law in Hawaii ended only on October 24, 1944, although earlier some strictures had been abated. Ironically, under this regime, although 2,000 were arrested and shipped to relocation centers in the continental United States, of them Japanese Americans as a group were not subjected to mass evacuation as they were on the mainland. Indeed, such an evacuation would have brought the island economy to an abrupt halt, for 40 percent of the residents were of Japanese ancestry. However, the movement of workers from neighbor islands to Oahu, the arrival of thousands of soldiers and civilian war workers, and the departure of thousands of locally recruited servicemen altered the demographics of the island.

Moreover, martial law subjected Hawaiians to rules and regulations—rationing, curfews, blackouts, and censorship—that limited formerly routine activities. Residents were required to carry gas masks, to get a permit to develop a roll of film, to obey curfews, and not to smoke outside after dark. Armed sentries and machine-gun nests studded Honolulu. Newspapers and radio broadcasts were censored, as was personal mail. Phone calls were monitored. Civilians were jailed for failing to comply with military authority, and for a period the civilian courts gave way to military tribunals. According to the *Honolulu Advertiser,* from 1942 to 1943, 22,000 criminal military provost court trials were conducted on Oahu, with 99 percent resulting in verdicts of guilty.[3] The military government confiscated all currency, burning more than $200 million to avert the possibility of its capture by invading Japanese and issuing in its place a special currency good only in Hawaii; even so no citizen could possess more than $200 of the Hawaiian currency. The government stockpiled food in auditoriums, theaters, and churches across Oahu, with plans to destroy it in case of a Japanese invasion.

The case of *Duncan v. Kahanamoku* (1946) raised the question of whether the president's imposition of martial law in Hawaii could justify trying civilians for criminal offenses in military courts rather than civilian courts. Duncan, a civilian shipfitter who worked for the navy yard, brawled with two marine guards there; he was tried and convicted in a military court for assault and sentenced to six months. He sought a writ of habeas corpus on the grounds that the military court lacked the authority to try him. On February 25, 1946, the U.S. Supreme Court agreed with him, holding that when Congress enacted the Hawaiian Organic Act of 1900, it did intend to make martial law possible but did not intend that martial law should give the military the power to try civilians for criminal offenses.[4]

Other groups of Americans besides residents of Hawaii experienced restrictions of their civil liberties, notably absolutist conscientious objectors, enemy aliens, and citizens of Japanese ancestry.[5] African Americans continued to suffer the deprivation of their rights that had been their lot in peacetime.

Conscientious Objectors

In World War I self-appointed moralists handed out white feathers to apparently able-bodied young men not in uniform and painted the gates and doors of their homes yellow. The U.S. government recognized only those conscientious objectors (COs) who belonged to the historic peace churches (HPC)—Friends (Quakers), Mennonites, and Church of the Brethren—and treated even them harshly. Of these, it court-martialed 504 men for refusing noncombatant military service, sentencing 450 of them to penalties ranging from death for 17 men to imprisonment lasting on average 16 1/2 years. (In the end, no one was executed and the last military prisoner was released in 1920.) Some men who refused to cooperate with the army "were beaten; they had their eyes gouged to the point of severe injury; they were stripped and scrubbed with brooms; . . . they were prodded with bayonets; they were dragged through latrines; they were chained, in solitary confinement, to the doors of their cells for nine hours a day; they were subjected to a stream of water from a firehose held directly against their faces for two hours at a time."[6] Finally after a board of inquiry that worked from June 1918 to January 1919 had vouched for the sincerity of most COs, about 1,500 of them were given "agricultural furloughs" and another 88 were assigned to the European reconstruction unit of the American Friends Service Committee.[7]

In World War II the general populace understood and accepted conscientious objection much more readily, but diehards still attacked young men out of uniform, often by anonymous hate letters, and many soldiers and their families resented the exemptions granted to COs. The government extended the right of conscientious objection to young men of all religious backgrounds who refused to fight on religious grounds and provided alternative service for them both within the military, in noncombatant roles, and without, in Civilian Public Service (CPS).[8] Some estimates put the number of conscientious objectors as high as 100,000, although something under 50,000 is probably a more reliable figure.[9]

On the whole, COs within the military experienced little hostility from combat troops. They were not readily identifiable, for many soldiers who were not COs had the same duties as those who were. Those among them who refused weapons training were instead assigned to KP (kitchen police). Indeed, COs who were combat medics in the field won the highest respect from the men they were treating, who saw the medics day after day risking their own

Dan Wilson, director of the CPS
camp No. 59 at Elkton, Oregon,
stands before his headquarters.
(Collection of Rosalie and Dan Wilson)

lives to reach wounded men and shielding their patients' bodies with their own. Many a combat soldier believed that if he were wounded, he would live if the medic could reach him before he died. In the course of World War II some 25,000 men served as what the Selective Service called "conscientious cooperators within the armed forces."[10]

Provisions for Civilian Public Service evolved from the careful planning of the historic peace churches in conjunction with the U.S. military. The HPCs participated because they wanted to avoid such injustices as those imposed on the COs of World War I, and the military cooperated because they did not want resisters within their ranks. With the aid of the military, particularly Maj. Lewis Hershey, later a general and head of the Selective Service System, the HPCs successfully lobbied for a compromise clause in the Selective Service Act that provided for most COs.[11]

The act did not completely satisfy the historic peace churches. It excluded "absolutist" COs—those who refused any service that might in any way contribute to the war effort, leaving them no alternative but prison. It did not give the HPCs the power to determine the validity of a claim to be a CO; instead, that power was assigned to local draft boards, and appeals went to the Department of Justice. However, this assignment did mean that such a claim was judged by the claimant's "friends and neighbors" who made up the local draft board, and the would-be CO was protected against induction into the military and court-martial and given the alternative of Civilian Public Service.

The act gave ultimate power over Civilian Public Service to the military, who regarded these COs as draftees with different assignments than fighting men, rather than to the historic peace churches, who regarded them as civilians. In the words of Selective Service officer Lt. Col. McLean: "The [Civilian Public Service] program is not carried out for the education of an individual, to train groups for foreign service or future activities in the postwar period, or for the furtherance of any particular movement. Assignees can no more expect choice of location or job than can men in the service. From the time an assignee reports to camp until he is finally released he is under the control of the Director of Selective Service. He ceases to be a free agent and is accountable for all of his time, in camp and out, 24 hours a day. His movements, actions and conduct are subject to control and regulation. He ceases to have certain rights and is granted privileges. These privileges can be restricted or withdrawn without his consent as punishment, during emergency, or as a matter of policy. He may be told when and how to work, what to wear, and where to sleep. He can be required to submit to medical examinations and treatment, and to practice rules of health and sanitation. He may be moved from place to place and from job to job, even to foreign countries, for the convenience of the government regardless of his personal feelings or desires."

Despite their reservations, the historic peace churches agreed to finance the operation of the Civilian Public Service system set up for those COs who objected to doing noncombatant work within the army but were willing to do work "of national importance under civilian direction," for which they received no pay. To this end the HPCs established the National Council for Religious Conscientious Objectors, later known as the National Service Board for Religious Objectors. The CPS was a joint effort of the government and the HPCs, which Hershey described as an "experiment in democracy to find out whether our democracy is big enough to preserve minority rights in a time of national emergency."[12] Camps within this service were assigned to different denominations. The first camp, supported and administered by the Friends, opened at Patapsco State Park near Baltimore, Maryland, on May 15, 1941; a week later, a Mennonite camp opened at Grottoes, Virginia, and a Brethren camp at Lagro, Indiana. The COs signed up for a year, a term first extended by 18 months and then for the duration of the war.

For all its complexities and division of authority, the Civilian Public Service worked reasonably well. The Camp Operations Division of Selective Service had ultimate authority, approving all projects as requests for manpower came in from soil conservation and forestry government agencies, and later from mental hospitals, farms, and other sources. The National Service Board for Religious Objectors handled CPS matters in Washington, D.C., for the historic peace churches, assigning the men to their tasks, receiving complaints from would-be COs refused that status, and selecting camps and arranging with church agencies for their operation. The historic peace churches' CPS directorates administered the operation of the camps, appointing the staff overseeing the establishment of routines; setting up educational, religious, and recreational programs; and raising and disbursing funds to operate the camps.

The strong belief of most COs that they were witnessing against war often caused discontent with their assignments, some of which they regarded as makework, and some as contributing to the enrichment of individual farmers rather than to the national welfare. One research chemist had to discontinue his penicillin research and dig ditches.[13] Others were disappointed in their hopes of doing reconstruction work in the war-torn countries when, in January 1943, Congress refused to fund sending COs overseas. Eventually the supporting churches overcame governmental fears of public reaction if COs were taken out of isolation to expand their work beyond conservation and forestry to hospitals and training schools, university laboratories, agricultural experiment stations and farms, and government surveying. COs not only built roads and

Dan Wilson, director of the CPS camp No. 59 at Elkton, Oregon, holds his son Mickey. Mickey helped in keeping up morale among the conscientious objectors. *(Collection of Rosalie and Dan Wilson)*

Civilian Public Service conducts a tree-planting project near Elkton, Oregon. *(Collection of Rosalie and Dan Wilson)*

dams, fought forest fires, planted trees, and built contour strips on farms, but they also cared for the mentally ill and juvenile delinquents.

Relatively few African Americans were among the COs of World War II; the "My History Is America's History" millennial project of the National Endowment for the Humanities estimates that there were only about 400. Selective Service System records indicate that of the 2,208 black violators of the Selective Service Act, 166 were classed as conscientious objectors, although others may have failed to appear before their draft boards as a matter of conscience.[14] In January 1941, black labor organizer and civil rights leader Ernest Calloway set a precedent by refusing to be inducted because he objected to the U.S. Army's racist segregation policy; his case was never officially settled, but he never served in the military. He belonged to the Conscientious Objectors against Jim Crow, which claimed that African Americans should be exempt from military service because of discrimination, but the group disbanded early in 1941. Twenty-three CPS members, some of them white, joined in the fight against Jim Crow by striking in their work at the prison in Danbury, Connecticut, and thus ending segregation there on December 23, 1943. About half the CPSers at Cheltenham training school in Maryland were black; with the support of the CPS members there, black staff members integrated the staff dining room. The musician Sun Ra (Herman Blount) worked in Civilian Public Service. The Nation of Islam did not support the war, and some of its members refused induction on religious grounds. African-American William Lynn was among those who refused to serve because the practices of the armed forces contradicted the antidiscrimination clauses of the September 1940 Selective Service and Training Act. The civil rights leader Bayard Rustin served a prison sentence for refusing to cooperate with the draft.

Women too "witnessed" against war by their actions, though they were not subject to the draft. In 1943 the activist Roman Catholic Dorothy Day spoke out against women's being "enslaved" to make the weapons of war. U.S. congresswoman Jeannette Rankin cast the only vote against the entry of the United States into the war. Mildred Scott Olmsted and Dorothy Detzer of the Women's International League for Peace and Freedom continued their work. Many pacifist women were members of the historic peace churches who registered their protests by supporting male COs either financially or by working in the CPS camps as matrons, nurses, nutritionists, or secretaries. Some women attended the HPC-run relief training schools organized when COs had hopes of going overseas to do relief work.[15] Doctoral student Edna Ramseyer suggested that pacifist college women join COs assigned as aides at state mental hospitals; some of the 300 or so who served in this way at eight psychiatric institutions adopted this suggestion, identifying themselves as "C.O. Girls."[16]

Intelligent and well-educated, the COs brought to their work convictions and creativity that made lasting differences. In Washington County, Maryland, at the suggestion of the local soil conservation agent, they set up experimental farms as possible models for demobilized soldiers. Small groups lived on each of five farms, two or three of them running the farm and the others working on soil conservation projects nearby and in the evenings helping to repair farm buildings, garden, and care for the livestock. Others straightened the Pocomoke River to convert swamps into agricultural fields. At a soil conservation station at Cochocton, Ohio, another group researched relationships among soil type, humidity, and plants, studying plant life and taking soil samples from all over Ohio. In North Dakota and Montana CPSers undertook farm reclamation and development; built irrigation dams, canals, and ditches; and constructed new farmsteads that were allocated to farmers who had lost their land during the droughts of the 1930s. In 1943 county agents contracted for the COs to fill the urgent need for dairy-farm labor, their wages to be paid to the National Service Board for Religious Objectors or to the U.S. Treasury. The COs kept milk records to increase efficiency, worked as technicians for artificial breeding associations, managed experimental herds of dairy cows, and experimented with grasses and seeds for feed.

Conscientious objectors eat lunch at a Civilian Public Service tree-planting project near Elkton, Oregon. *(Collection of Rosalie and Dan Wilson)*

Beginning in the summer of 1942, COs volunteered to work in mental hospitals, some of which, desperate for staff, were warehousing patients in filth. At the Philadelphia State Hospital, 10 COs took over the worst ward, where 350 incontinent patients lived; they cleaned and painted the entire building and transformed the lives of their patients with their kind and empathetic care. Even when shortages of personnel restricted what they could do, the COs improved the care significantly. At Duke University Hospital, Civilian Public Service men under doctors' directions administered advanced methods of therapy; at Asheville, North Carolina, they assisted with new deep-shock insulin treatments. Other units taught classes and acted as headmasters of cottages at training schools for the mentally ill in the hope that patients might eventually sustain themselves. Most COs tried to avoid violence even in dealing with violent patients. Out of their work came the Mental Health Hygiene Program, which later became the National Mental Health Foundation, to develop long-range reform programs; and a magazine called *The Attendant,* which later became the professional journal *The Psychiatric Aide.* A survey conducted by COs resulted in a book, *Out of Sight—Out of Mind,* by Frank L. Wright, Jr. In his 1994 book *The Turning Point: How Men of Conscience Brought About Major Change in the Care of America's Mentally Ill,* Alex Sareyan writes, "Many of the concepts of mental illness that we take for granted today began with the crusade spearheaded by the conscientious objectors and their wives. They have the right to be proud of their legacy as agents for social change."

Other Civilian Public Service programs focused on physical health. In five Florida counties where up to 80 percent of the population suffered from hookworm, COs checked the spread of the larvae by building and installing 4,200 privies, digging wells, and installing septic tanks. In Puerto Rico COs built and staffed hospitals and initiated immunization programs against smallpox, typhoid, and diphtheria. They established milk stations for children and encouraged the growing of soybeans to improve nutrition.

COs volunteered for scientific and medical experiments, subjecting themselves to discomfort and danger. Men building roads wore lice-infested clothing for three weeks in an experiment to discover which powder most effectively killed the lice that caused typhus. Others were inoculated with plasma suspected of being infectious, swallowed nose and throat washings and body wastes of infected patients, and drank contaminated water in a successful effort to determine the ways in which infectious hepatitis is spread. Some caught cold by inhaling or drinking throat washings taken from sick soldiers to prove that colds are caused by a virus and not by bacteria. Others allowed themselves to be bitten by bacteria-carrying mosquitoes in a search for an alternative to quinine in the treatment of malaria. Still others experimented to see whether they could survive on a diet of pelleted grass, spent two weeks on a life raft in salt water, or sat in temperatures of 20 degrees below zero and in pressure chambers simulating high altitudes.

Every Civilian Public Service man underwent hardships. He received no pay—in contrast to German POWs in the United States, who received $0.80 a day for their labor. The HPCs provided his food and an allowance of $2.50 a month. This pittance often reduced the CO to wearing used clothing donated by churches and getting his haircuts from an amateur barber among his colleagues. Just as he received no pay, he received no benefits and did not qualify for the GI Bill of Rights. He was often subjected to hostility. So severe was the feeling against the COs in some communities that even their caroling at Christmas was resented. Thirty of the men in CPS died, and 1,500 were discharged for physical disabilities.

Some wives did not agree with their husbands' position; others had to live with families who disapproved; some felt guilt because their husbands were not at risk. On the other hand, some COs' wives worked alongside their husbands. Other wives found work to support themselves at whatever jobs were available—usually menial—near where the COs were stationed, although this process was often complicated by community feeling against the conscientious objectors. Housing was tight, for them as for the soldiers' wives who followed their husbands from post to post, and many of the CO wives had little money. Mennonite Aganetha Fast, who visited many camps, sympathized with the dependents: "[The wives] had left homes and home environment to be near their husbands. As they move close to the camp they live in primitive homes and surroundings. . . . In most cases I found them living in only one tiny room: on the third story, in a dark basement, a barn or in tourist cabins." Families with children had a particularly hard time, though the churches struggled to provide $25 a month for each needy wife and $10 a month for each needy child.

Almost 12,000 men served in the Civilian Public Service, of whom almost half were in the Mennonite program. The Brethren numbered 1,353 and the Friends 951. The other 3,862 came from some 200 denominations or were unaffiliated. Together they contributed more than 8 million man-days of service to the country. They worked in 152 camps, units, and projects, in the United States, the Virgin Islands, Puerto Rico, and China.[17]

For such an assortment of idealists, ranging from Appalachians, Hoosiers, and rural laborers to Boston Brahmins, Main Line Philadelphians, and southern aristocrats, each of them with strong convictions, the men of the Civilian Public Service got along reasonably well, although they argued passionately about matters great and small, about how to deal with Hitler without violence and about smoking, card-playing, and pinups. As one of them remembered, "I had some of the most enjoyable fights in my life . . . with pacifists."[18] They had little money, energy, or leisure for recreation, many of them were isolated, and they were often bored and sometimes resentful about their lack of pay and the lack of opportunity to use their talents.

Nevertheless, by the time they were released in 1946, most of them acknowledged value received from the experience, especially in heightened understanding of other people's points of view. After the war some of them banded together in projects like alternative radio stations. Some of them suffered professionally because of their CO status, but others benefited by it. Those who had risked their lives as smoke jumpers to fight forest fires and as subjects in dangerous medical experiments knew that they had dramatically demonstrated their courage, but the rest too could pride themselves that for years they had accepted hardship and hostility for their principles.

Absolutist COs, who refused to participate in any way in the system, were imprisoned. Given their refusal to do any alternative work or in many cases even to register for the draft, it is hard to see how else the government could have treated them, except to give them complete exemption, as the historic peace churches wished. Popular sentiment opposed such an exemption; indeed, feelings ran high against these absolutists. To let them go scot-free while others sacrificed and risked so much would have been asking a lot. The Selective Service Act provided maximum five-year terms for failure to register for the draft and refusal to serve. Under this law about 6,000 went to prison.[19] Most of them were Jehovah's Witnesses, all of whom, like every other Jehovah's Witness, considered themselves ministers, but their draft boards refused them ministerial exemptions. About 1,000 of the absolutists were radical pacifists affiliated with the War Resisters League, the Catholic Worker Movement, or the Socialist Party.

With the exception of these absolutists, history has treated the COs well. The differences between most of those in the military and their fellow soldiers and sailors has all but vanished. The combat medics among them, however, are universally honored as among the war's greatest heroes. The COs constituted only a tiny minority: Only 15 COs were recorded for every 10,000 inductions into the military, although they may have been undercounted, since potential COs exempted from the military for other reasons were not included. Nonetheless, as Lewis Hershey observed, they established the principle that a democracy can respect the consciences of individuals even in wartime, a principle incorporated by the year 2000 into the draft laws of 31 countries.

Japanese Americans

In both world wars the United States felt itself particularly vulnerable because of its large numbers of residents—some American citizens and some aliens—who had immigrated fairly recently from the very countries that the United States was fighting. On the West Coast, prejudice against Japanese Americans had been virulent since the 1890s. The U.S. government limited their immigration with stringent quotas, and state laws limited their right to hold property. To many Americans the surprise attack by the Japanese on Pearl Harbor, Hawaii, on December 7, 1941, confirmed suspicions of Japanese Americans as underhanded neighbors who might betray their adopted country. The Federal Bureau of Investigation (FBI) at once began to round up citizens of enemy nations—Japan, Germany, and Italy—and to search their homes for weapons, explosives, and short-wave radios. Members of the Japanese American Citizens League (JACL), all American citizens by virtue of their birth in the United States, frantically tried to demonstrate their loyalty, while some Asian Americans began wearing signs, "Chinese, not Jap." Feeling threatened by a possible Japanese invasion, West Coast whites were in no mood to protect the civil rights of their Japanese-American neighbors.

The military, not the top command but that West Coast segment commanded by Gen. John DeWitt, pushed the Department of Justice to take measures against possible sabotage by Japanese Americans, threatening otherwise to take over that responsibility. Accordingly, the Department of Justice agreed to register Japanese Americans, to have the FBI conduct spot raids, and to establish restricted areas around sensitive West Coast military installations. These actions worried Secretary of Agriculture Claude Wickard, who feared that interning Japanese Americans would disrupt food production, and who came to believe that the propaganda against them sprang from a conspiracy to eliminate their economic competition. At the end of January 1942, the Department of Justice announced plans to remove enemy aliens from restricted areas but still opposed interning them. Several government departments and the top military command were trying to moderate anti–Japanese-American sentiment in Congress, while powerful West Coast figures such as congressmen, the governor of California, and General DeWitt were insisting on internment. California attorney general Earl Warren fanned the mass hysteria by warning that nisei—Japanese Americans born in the United States and hence American citizens—posed a greater threat than the issei, their parents born in Japan, because they were younger and more daring. The very absence of sabotage, he asserted, suggested that the Japanese Americans were getting ready for a massive attack. The JACL sought to prove loyalty by agreeing to internment, and several thousand Japanese Americans tried to relocate voluntarily but could find no place in the U.S. interior willing to receive them.

One restriction on Japanese Americans after another followed in dizzying succession. On February 4, 1942, the U.S. Army defined 12 restricted areas, within which Japanese Americans had to obey a curfew and could travel only to and from their places of employment, and not more than five miles from their places of residence. On February 14, the U.S. Navy decreed that all Japanese on Terminal Island, San Pedro, California, must leave by March 14, and then moved the date back to February 27. On February 19, despite an army intelligence report that it considered mass evacuation unnecessary, President Franklin D. Roosevelt signed Executive Order No. 9066, requiring the removal of all people of Japanese descent, including American citizens, from any area designated as a military zone. On March 2, General DeWitt designated military areas in the states of Washington, Oregon, California, and Arizona and excluded enemy aliens and persons of Japanese ancestry from living in some of them. On March 6, the Federal Reserve Bank was charged with helping evacuees dispose of their property; later the Farm Security Administration was similarly given responsibility for helping with agricultural property. On March 16, General DeWitt set up more military areas in Idaho, Montana, Nevada, and Utah, and on March 18, the War Relocation Authority (WRA) was established.

Ultimately, the operation of the evacuation was divided between the army and the WRA, the army to transport the evacuees and furnish guards for the relocation centers, and the WRA to run the centers and help relocate the internees once again at the end of the war. On March 21, 1942, the mass evacuation began when the first Japanese Americans voluntarily moved to assembly centers manned by the army, whence they were to be transported to relocation centers. On March 24, General DeWitt set in motion the first of 107 evacuations, forcing a few hundred Japanese families living on Bainbridge Island in Puget Sound to move to a reception center at the Puyallup, Washington, fairgrounds—though relocation centers had yet to be found. By the end of 1942 some 112,000 Japanese-American men, women, and children were interned, almost two-thirds of them American-born and 77.4 percent of them under 25. Almost 6,000 babies were born in the camps.[20]

Milton Eisenhower, first director of the WRA, found governors unwilling to permit relocation centers in their states. (Eisenhower quickly resigned, on June 17, 1942, asserting his belief that the "great majority" of the Japanese

Americans were loyal; he was replaced by Dillon S. Myer.) Finally 10 relocation centers were placed in remote areas in deserts and swamps on land that no one else wanted. Two each were sited in Arizona, Arkansas, and California; and one each in Colorado, Idaho, Wyoming, and Utah. There the Japanese-American families, deprived of liberty and property, were thrust into miserable, crowded quarters, in which the lack of privacy made the continuation of normal family life impossible—particularly when the parents were enemy aliens and their children American citizens.

At first some families lived in horse stables reeking of urine and manure, their linoleum floors covered with dust and wood shavings, their walls white-washed over insects, and they ate their meals in mess halls with wet cement floors. Later bleak and grim one-story barracks were built, some with open dormitories, others partitioned to allot a space 20 x 20 to a family of four or two couples. In the early days the internees were cold, they had to eat bad food, and they suffered from lack of water for washing. Gradually they improved their quarters with whatever materials they could scavenge and organized camp life into some semblance of order. They could earn up to $19 a month by performing necessary functions around the camp.

Kate Hobbie, who taught at the Tule Lake relocation center, believes that the Buddhist tradition *Shikata ga nai* (It can't be helped) sustained them. As Jerry Enomoto remarked, "You don't spend your time moping around won-

Albert Saijo, *Echoes* editor, looks over copy being cut on a mimeograph stencil by Shizu Yamaguchi, typist, at Heart Mountain Relocation Center in Wyoming, June 1943. *(National Archives, 210-G-B559)*

dering why you're there, or saying, 'This is a terrible injustice.'"[21] In an April 1943 trip to Gila River internment camp, Eleanor Roosevelt found that internees had created behind the barbed wire a productive community where they raised livestock and produced enough vegetables to feed the entire camp; set up barber shops, dental offices, newspapers, adult-education courses, schools, movie theaters, and their own government; and were producing camouflage nets in a factory.[22]

The internees were sharply divided among themselves. Those among them most resentful of their treatment pitted themselves against the JACL, whom they regarded as collaborators and informers. Many of the first group were *kibei*, born American but educated in Japan. Tensions between the two groups escalated throughout the war, exacerbated by having to live cheek-to-jowl with each other in a prison camp guarded by armed soldiers.

Early on it became apparent that the able-bodied among them were needed elsewhere. On May 21, 1942, a group of them left an assembly center to do agricultural work in eastern Oregon; on June 29, 1,600 of them were released to relieve a labor shortage in the sugar-beet producing areas of Oregon, Utah, Idaho, and Montana; and by October 24, more than 8,000 were working in agricultural harvests in the western states. Meanwhile some universities and the Society of Friends were working to free Japanese-American college students to return to their studies, where they would be supported by church groups; ultimately 4,300 were released for that purpose.[23] In time some found jobs with private employers and successfully relocated. During 1943, 17,000 evacuees were allowed to reenter civilian life through "leave clearance procedures" by which they passed a loyalty check and proved themselves capable of self-support in a receptive community.

That year too, beginning in mid-January, the army decided to recruit an all-nisei 5,000-man combat team drawn from Hawaii and the U.S. relocation centers. To this end the WRA, moving in its own mysterious ways, distributed a loyalty test to everyone over 17 in the camps—a test that included the critical questions No. 27 "Are you willing to serve in the armed forces of the United States on combat duty, wherever ordered?" and No. 28 "Will you swear unqualified allegiance to the United States of America and faithfully defend the United States from any or all attack by foreign or domestic forces, and forswear any form of allegiance or obedience to the Japanese emperor, to any other foreign government, power, or organization?" These questions posed dilemmas. For the older issei women and men born in Japan and disqualified by U.S. law for American citizenship, affirmative answers would have rendered them stateless. (Later they were required to answer instead the question "Will you swear to abide by the laws of the United States and to take no action which would in any way interfere with the war effort of the United States?") The nisei, on the other hand, feared that forswearing allegiance to Japan might be taken as a confession that they had once been loyal to that country, which many of them had never seen. Angry at the treatment they had received at the hands of the U.S. government, some of them answered negatively; others said, "Yes, if my rights are restored." Of the 75,000 people who filled out the questionnaires, most responded to question No. 28 positively and only 6,700 negatively; nearly 2,000 qualified their answers; and a few hundred left the question blank.

More than 1,200 volunteered for combat, of whom about two-thirds were accepted.[24] They fought in the European theater, where they distinguished themselves by their courage. Japanese-American soldiers of the 442nd Regimental Combat Team, in which future senator Daniel Inouye fought, famously rescued 140 members of a Texas outfit caught in a German trap in the French Vosges mountains. Nisei troops were among those who liberated German concentration camps, to the confusion of the inmates, who of course thought of Japanese as allies of Germany.

The questionnaire did a great deal of harm, causing distrust among WRA officials and cynicism and suspicion among the internees, many of whom saw question No. 28 as a Catch-22. The WRA with questionable wisdom decided to isolate at Tule Lake, California, those Japanese Americans whom it judged disloyal, often on the basis of their negative answers to question No. 28. Eventually about 18,000 Japanese Americans were sent there; of these 7,222, almost two-thirds of them American born, asked for repatriation to Japan, many because they feared that American society had no place for them.[25] (This fear was shared by some internees who were adjudged loyal but who had come to regard the relocation camps as the only safe place for them in the United States.) This transfer of "disloyal" internees to Tule Lake, which began in July 1943, not only concentrated all the "troublemakers" in one camp, but also failed in its objective of making the other relocation centers more peaceful, since it aggravated the internees' sense of injustice.

The WRA and the JACL had long urged that Japanese Americans be subject to the draft, and on January 20, 1944, Secretary of War Henry Stimson so announced. Though a large majority of the young men submitted to the draft, some of the internees had no stomach for being drafted from behind barbed wire. Some refused to show up for their physicals, and one or two tried just

Members of the 442nd Combat Team, a Japanese-American fighting unit, salute their country's flag at Camp Shelby, Mississippi, June 1943. *(Library of Congress, LC-USZ62-127108)*

walking out the gate to emphasize their lack of freedom. The U.S. government began initiating cases against Japanese-American draft resisters. On May 10 a federal grand jury in Cheyenne, Wyoming, indicted 63, who were found guilty and sentenced to three years' imprisonment; the appeals court rejected their appeal, and the U.S. Supreme Court refused to hear them. On July 21, 1944, eight evacuees were arrested on a charge of conspiracy to counsel, aid, and abet draft violations. They were subsequently convicted and sentenced to prison but freed on appeal.

As the Allies moved toward victory in 1944 and apprehensions about a Japanese invasion of the West Coast vanished, General George Marshall advised that no military objections to the return of the Japanese Americans existed, except for the possibility that whites prejudiced against them might attack them. Such action, he warned, might endanger American prisoners in the hands of the Japanese. On December 17, 1944, Major General Henry C. Pratt, the new head of the Western Defense Command, announced the termination of total exclusion of loyal Japanese-American civilians, effective January 2, 1945, and on September 4, 1945, revoked all restrictions against Japanese and Japanese Americans. By December 15, all WRA camps were closed, except Tule Lake, which closed on March 10, 1946. Each internee leaving the camps was given $25 and train fare. Thanks to the planning of such groups as the Quakers and the Pacific Coast Fair Play Committee for the harmonious integration of the Japanese Americans into community life, not to mention the hard work of the internees themselves, most of them remaining in the relocation centers returned to their communities and successfully began life anew. Some of them, however, suffered attacks on their persons and property.

Throughout the internment process, a few Japanese Americans had turned to the courts, for the most part unsuccessfully. On August 13, 1942, nisei Mary Asaba Ventura lost her suit against the imposition of a curfew. On June 21, 1943, the U.S. Supreme Court unanimously upheld the conviction of nisei Gordon Kiyoshi Hirabayashi for curfew violation and failure to report for evacuation (*Hirabayashi* v. *United States*) and, on December 18, 1944, the conviction of Fred Korematsu for failing to report (*Korematsu* v. *United States*).[26] Only on December 18, 1944, did Mitsuye Endo win her release from her relocation center, by means of a writ of habeas corpus that she had filed on July 13, 1942.

After the war Japanese Americans worked effectively through the executive, legislative, and judicial branches of the U.S. government for redress of the injustices done them. On November 10, 1983, Fred Korematsu's conviction was vacated. Some Japanese Americans who had renounced their American citizenship sued successfully for redress. It was a long process, for the courts ruled that each case must be heard individually, but the last case was settled in 1968.[27] On July 2, 1948, Congress enacted a Japanese-American Evacuee Claims Act, and over the next 15 years some 30,000 individual claims were adjudicated on an average of 10 percent of the value of the property lost, for a total restitution of about $30 million.[28] That December, President Harry Truman pardoned 282 Japanese Americans convicted of Selective Service violations and restored their civil rights. On February 19, 1976, President Gerald Ford officially admitted the mistake of the United States in incarcerating Japanese Americans. Seven years later, on June 23, 1983, the Congressional

Commission on Wartime Relocation and Internment of Civilians concluded that the evacuation was caused by "race prejudice, war hysteria, and a failure of political leadership," and recommended that each surviving victim be compensated $20,000, a recommendation enacted into law on November 2, 1989. Payments began in October 1990.

During World War II the U.S. government also pressured Latin American governments to round up people of Japanese, German, and Italian ancestry and hand them over for transport to the United States, where they were interned and later exchanged for U.S. civilian prisoners in enemy hands. According to Lawson Fusao Inada, 800 Latin American Japanese were so exchanged.[29] In 1996 a class action lawsuit, *Mochizuki et al.* v. *United States,* was filed, resulting in a settlement in which the U.S. government acknowledged that it had erred in evacuating Latin American Japanese and paid each of them $5,000.

Italian Americans, German Americans, and Aleut

In World War I mass hysteria and unjustified suspicions of loyal German Americans resulted in such silly actions as closing down German classes in schools and universities—actions that 25 years later embarrassed most Americans. The American people avoided such a reaction during World War II, but unknown to them, their government used a similar principle of discrimination against people of German and Italian ancestry as against people of Japanese ancestry, in some cases regardless of American citizenship. About half of the allegedly dangerous enemy aliens rounded up immediately after the United States entered the war were German or Italian.[30]

The actions focused on enemy aliens: To control them, the government used curfews, individual exclusion and evacuation from federally designated restricted areas, selective internment, exchanges for Americans held by enemy nations, repatriation, denaturalization, deportation, registration requirements, travel restrictions, and property confiscation. However, some German-American and Italian-American citizens were affected, as when enemy-alien parents were interned or exchanged and took their American-born children with them. The United States also pressured Latin American governments to arrest German and Italian Latinos and hand them over for shipment to the United States, where they were interned and in some cases later exchanged for American civilians in enemy custody. However, actions and attitudes toward German Americans and Italian Americans contrasted with the treatment of Japanese Americans, almost all of whom, citizens and aliens alike, were interned. The U.S. German and Italian alien population totaled nearly 900,000, of whom fewer than 1 percent were interned.[31] Thousands of German Americans and Italian Americans worked in defense industries and served in the armed forces.

Among the detainees were Italian sailors whose ships after the outbreak of war in Europe were held in U.S. waters. When the sailors allegedly began trashing these ships so that they could not be confiscated and transferred to Great Britain, American authorities interned them, along with a few Italians admitted on temporary visas to work at the 1939 World's Fair. They were eventually sent to Fort Missoula, Montana, which they called "Bella Vista." There they passed the time amusing themselves and later on working for U.S. farmers; they complained chiefly about the quality of the olive oil served them. Local residents readily accepted them, and eventually they visited Missoula unaccompanied. Soon after the Italian surrender in September 1943, most of them were sent back to Italy, though a few chose instead to join the U.S. Army and thus earn citizenship.[32]

Late in the 20th century, Italian Americans successfully lobbied Congress for redress. Public Law No. 106-451, signed on November 7, 2000, acknowledged that the civil liberties of some Italian Americans were infringed during World War II. Some German Americans are still working for a similar acknowledgement.

After the Japanese invaded Attu Island in the Aleutians on June 7, 1942, U.S. authorities evacuated 881 Aleut from nine villages, set their villages afire to prevent their falling to the Japanese, and sent them by sea to crowded "duration villages." Despite miserable conditions there with inadequate living and medical facilities, and despite the death of 74 of their number, the Aleut remained loyal to the United States. In August 1988 in Public Law 100-383 the Congress authorized an apology and formal compensation to the Aleut.

African Americans

"Hitler jammed our white people into their logically untenable position. Forced to oppose him for the sake of the life of the nation, they were jockeyed into declaiming against his racial theories, publicly."
—*Roy Wilkins, executive secretary, National Association for the Advancement of Colored People*[33]

In World War II the nation treated blacks no better than it had in World War I, demanding that they bear the responsibilities of citizens at the same time that both the U.S. government and their white fellow citizens deprived them of their constitutional rights. In the interval between the two wars, blacks as a group had learned to defend themselves somewhat better under the leadership of such men as A. Philip Randolph, president of the Brotherhood of Pullman Porters, and Thurgood Marshall of the American Civil Liberties Union (ACLU), but they still lacked the political strength to enforce their rights. Moreover, they chose to act as loyal citizens, as Americans first and blacks only secondarily, placing the duty of helping to win the war before their own welfare, even as they suffered humiliation and injustice. Although they were to make many gains during the 1960s, 1970s, and beyond, the nation never has admitted its guilt in the wrongs it inflicted on them during World War II.

It is hard even for Americans alive during World War II to remember how racist the country then was—racist against everyone but Caucasians, but particularly against blacks. The annual report of a single branch of the ACLU for June 1, 1944, to June 1, 1945, illustrates the point in its list of incidents in which the organization intervened:

1. Three whites beat to death black garbage-collector Homer Turner of Richmond, California; only the intervention of the ACLU brought them to a trial, in which they were acquitted.
2. In the case of *Joseph James* v. *Marinship Corporation,* the court restrained the company from firing blacks for failure to pay dues because the boilermakers

union restricted the rights and privileges of collective bargaining to whites. It ordered the union either to take blacks into the union with full privileges or give up its closed shop contract with the employer.

3. The ACLU tried, ultimately without success, to obtain a fair trial for the 50 survivors of the Port Chicago, California, disaster who refused to resume loading explosives after an explosion had killed 320 black sailors. In this case the U.S. Navy held that blacks were incapable of understanding how to handle explosives safely but ordered them to continue loading anyway.

4. The Richmond, California, housing authority operated dormitories for single white women but refused accommodations to single black women; when the ACLU intervened, the authority opened a separate 67-room dormitory for two black women. The ACLU also accused the housing authority of overcharging blacks and of simply padlocking a black tenant's apartment rather than following prescribed eviction routines.

5. The ACLU branch also intervened in several cases of harsh treatment of blacks by police officers and discrimination against blacks by several restaurants, hotels, and other places catering to the general public.

Throughout World War II, as in the years before and immediately afterward, black Americans, military and civilian alike, were consistently abused, discriminated against, and deprived of their civil liberties and often of their lives throughout the United States, although more harshly and openly in the Deep South. Civilians in the South and increasingly in the North mistreated blacks, often violently, as blacks seeking better jobs and better living conditions migrated northward and competed for employment and scarce housing.

Steward's mates stand at their battle stations as a gun crew aboard a Coast Guard–manned frigate in the Southwest Pacific. *Left to right:* James L. Wesley, standing with a clip of shells; L. S. Haywood, firing; William Watson, reporting to bridge by phone from his gun captain's post; William Morton, loading a full clip, assisted by Odis Lane, facing camera across gun barrel. *(National Archives, 26-G-3797)*

Well before the beginning of World War II, blacks were lobbying for the inclusion of more blacks both in industry and in the military, and for the integration of the armed forces. In June 1941, to avert a march on Washington threatened by A. Philip Randolph, president of the Brotherhood of Sleeping Car Porters, FDR signed Executive Order 8802, calling upon employers and labor unions "to provide for the full and equitable participation of all workers in defense industries" and setting up the Fair Employment Practices Commission (FEPC) to investigate grievances and monitor compliances. Lacking the support of white management and unions, the FEPC had little clout at first but gradually gained strength. The American Federation of Labor (AFL) did not welcome minorities, but the Congress of Industrial Organizations (CIO) from its inception in 1937 had adopted a policy of nondiscrimination. The U.S. Employment Service continued to discriminate against blacks until September 3, 1943, when discrimination was redefined to include the refusal to classify workers properly or hire workers of a particular color or race.[34] Nonetheless, blacks gained 1 million jobs during the war, mainly because the need for more workers forced industry and unions—especially in war industries—to crack open their doors, particularly after 1942.[35] Blacks also made significant gains within government agencies, jumping from 40,000 to 300,000 by war's end.[36]

Black pressure succeeded in getting antidiscrimination clauses into the Selective Service Act of 1940, though another clause awarding the War Department full control over acceptance into the military roused fears in the black community, fears that later proved justified, as the military dragged its heels on inducting blacks, segregated black servicepeople, and as long as it could confined them to labor and supply units.

The military turned down many African Americans because of the illiteracy that resulted from inferior black schools; allegedly, however, the authorities were willing to accept illiterate whites but not illiterate blacks.[37] As for the antidiscrimination clause, the military took the position that it was not a social agency and had no responsibility for changing the society. Moreover, it held fast to its established practice of segregating black and white troops.

Black leaders kept up the pressure, even though they were betrayed and denied time after time. Educator and reformer Mary McLeod Bethune lobbied Eleanor Roosevelt for the inclusion of black advisers in the office of the director of Selective Service and in the War Department. On September 27, 1940, Walter White, executive secretary of the NAACP; T. Arnold Hill, former industrial secretary of the Urban League; and A. Philip Randolph met with FDR to demand integration of all existing military units, acceptance of African Americans into the all-white U.S. Army Air Corps, expanded training of black officers in all service branches, integration of the navy, and assignment of black sailors to positions other than menial. Two days later the White House announced that "the services of Negroes [in the military] will be utilized on a fair and equitable basis. . . . [But] it is the policy of the War Department not to intermingle colored and white enlisted personnel in the same regimental organizations."[38] Moreover, this press release implied that White, Hill, and Randolph approved of segregation, an implication that sent them on a speaking tour to solidify black support against it. Black demands during the presidential campaign of 1940 resulted in the appointment of African-Americans Maj. Campbell C. Johnson as assistant to the Selective Service director and of Judge

William D. Hastie as assistant secretary in the War Department, and the promotion of African-American Benjamin O. Davis, Sr., to brigadier general. Not only black leaders but also black servicepeople struggled to improve conditions for blacks by striving for excellence and by protesting against discrimination to military and civilian black leaders, to civil rights organizations, to the White House (particularly to Eleanor Roosevelt), and to newspapers sympathetic to their wrongs.

The military gave ground only inch by inch. Not only did it fail to protect the civil rights and safety of its black troops from civilian violence, but it officially practiced blatant discrimination. It segregated black personnel, forcing them to live separately and use separate facilities. It officered black military units with whites and refused to give black officers authority over whites. It neglected promotions for blacks: In August 1942 the army still had only 817 black officers among its 100,000 black members, though officers constituted 7 percent of the whole army.[39] The army expected black troops to maintain morale and learn to fight in the face of humiliation and mistreatment from civilians and military alike. Although, as African-American Brig. Gen. Benjamin O. Davis, Sr., pointed out, black soldiers received better treatment in the northern states than in the South, the army introduced southern treatment of blacks into the North.[40]

The army relegated most black troops to service units and menial jobs, even though they were trained to fight. In 1942 half of all black soldiers were assigned to service units; by 1945 three-quarters were. Most of the 500,000 black soldiers who went overseas were employed in such work as loading supplies and burying the dead. But 22 black combat units, including nine field artillery battalions and two tank battalions, fought in the European theater, and a combat team of the 93rd Infantry Division won distinction at Bougainville.[41]

Racism infested every branch of the military. The army air corps, holding that blacks were too unintelligent and cowardly to fly, refused them training until early 1942, when Howard University student Yancey Williams sued the government for acceptance as an aviation cadet; the next day the War Department announced that it would form a black flying unit. Although African-American Walter Robinson was 13th in his class of 300 in the Civil Aeronautics Authority flight-training program at the University of Minnesota, the air corps turned him down. Reportedly, the air corps expected the experiment with a black flying unit to fail, but in fact the group developed into the famed Tuskegee Airmen. After being kept out of combat until April 1943 because no overseas commander wanted the squadron, they performed so brilliantly that bombing crews requested their presence as escorts on missions. Known as "Redtail Angels" because they painted the tails of their planes bright red, they were the only escort fighters never to lose a bomber to enemy fighters.[42] By war's end 82 black pilots had been awarded the Distinguished Flying Cross.[43]

Thanks to the heroism of black messman Dorie Miller at Pearl Harbor and pressure from the black community and the Roosevelts, in April 1942 the navy agreed to enlist blacks as gunners, clerks, signalmen, radio operators, and ammunition handlers, but they kept these men in segregated units and at shore installations and on harbor craft. On seagoing combat ships they were allowed to serve only as stewards or laborers. However, in 1944 two ships, the USS *Mason* and the submarine chaser PC 1264, were manned entirely by African

Americans. Later that year, the navy integrated the crews of 25 vessels and finally those of the whole auxiliary fleet. In 1945 Secretary of the Navy James Forrestal appointed African-American Lester B. Granger, head of the National Urban League, an adviser on racial policies.[44] The U.S. Marine Corps did not begin admitting blacks until June 1, 1942, and then assigned them primarily to defense battalions and combat support companies or as stewards.

The military was not above using blacks in integrated units in combat when they were needed and then sending them back to all-black service units. For instance, in May 1942 black troops fought in the Pacific, but soon thereafter they were reorganized into a service unit; only in 1944 were they again allowed into combat, in the Marianas. Similarly, in the ETO at the height of the Battle of the Bulge the army asked for black volunteers to be sent as replacements to units shredded in combat—one of the most disliked and dangerous assignments in battle. Four thousand of them volunteered, helped to win the victory, and were then again relegated to service units.[45]

Most black servicewomen were in the Women's Army Auxiliary Corps or, later, the Women's Army Corps (WAC) because the other services refused to admit them. The navy women's service excluded them until two and one-half years after its founding, explaining that there were no black men on sea duty for them to replace; it took a direct order from FDR in October 1944 to admit them to the WAVES. The Marine Corps accepted its first black women only after the war, in September 1949.

By the end of the war in 1945, conditions for African Americans both in the society at large and in the military had somewhat improved. Nonetheless in 1946 the military still had not accepted the idea of integrated armed forces. On July 26, 1948, President Harry Truman signed Executive Order 9981, providing for equal treatment and opportunity for black service personnel. But the military, arguing that segregation did not constitute discrimination, dragged its heels in the implementation of that order. Only on October 30, 1954, did the secretary of defense announce that the last racially segregated unit in the armed forces had been abolished.[46]

The history of civil rights in the United States during World War II demonstrates once again the truth of the saying, *Inter arma silent leges* (during hostilities laws are silent). As Chief Justice William H. Rehnquist concluded,

> There are obviously conflicting principles or public policies at work in this area of civil liberty in wartime. There may be some who think that here, as elsewhere, the more civil liberty the better. But neither presidents nor courts have ever operated on this principle. Wartime presidents are inclined to prefer claims based on military necessity to claims of individual liberty, and courts come to the rescue of civil liberty only after the war is over. There is a certain irony in this last fact, but the history of our nation suggests that both the nation and civil liberty have survived pretty well, if not totally unscathed, under it. Whether this is because of the actions of the Presidents and the courts, or in spite of them, I am not prepared to say.[47]

In one World War II case, however, the U.S. Supreme Court did protect a challenged civil liberty. In 1940 the case of *Minersville School District* v. *Gobitis* tested whether a school board might force a child to salute the flag, even though the child's religious beliefs as a Jehovah's Witness forbade him to. The court sustained the school board requirement, but the Witnesses refused to abandon their beliefs. As a result they were persecuted, even by physical assaults on the children. Finally in 1943 the Supreme Court agreed to hear another flag-salute case, *West Virginia Board of Education* v. *Barnette.* This time it held for the Jehovah's Witness child, finding that the Witnesses' refusal to salute the flag harmed no one, did not violate anyone else's rights, and posed no danger to public order. Justice Jackson delivered the opinion of the court, saying,

> To believe that patriotism will not flourish if patriotic ceremonies are voluntary and spontaneous instead of a compulsory routine is to make an unflattering estimate of the appeal of our institutions to free minds. . . .
>
> If there is any fixed star in our constitutional constellation, it is that no official, high or petty, can prescribe what shall be orthodox in politics, nationalism, religion, or other matters of opinion or force citizens to confess by word or act their faith therein. . . .
>
> We think the action of the local authorities in compelling the flag salute and pledge transcends constitutional limitations on their power and invades the sphere of intellect and spirit which it is the purpose of the First Amendment to our Constitution to reserve from all official control.

Arguably, military necessity may mitigate if it does not excuse the violation of the civil rights of conscientious objectors; citizens of Japanese, German, and Italian ancestry; and enemy aliens. It had nothing to do with the treatment of African Americans. As David K. Shipler writes, "[D]eep character flaws in nations, as in individuals, do not always disappear. They can lie dormant, mutate and emerge in crisis."[48] In the crisis of World War II the deep character flaw of racial prejudice that had existed in the United States since its birth manifested itself in the abuse of the African-American citizens who were fighting in its defense.

CHRONICLE OF EVENTS

1938

June 8: The Foreign Agents Registration Act is enacted, providing penalties for anyone whom the U.S. government deems a foreign agent who fails to register as such.

1939

May: The Committee for the Participation of Negroes in National Defense helps to get nondiscrimination clauses inserted into what would be the Selective Service Act of September 1940.

August: The Hatch Act restricts the political freedom of government employees and prohibits Communists from working for the national government.

September: The National Association for the Advancement of Colored People asks President Franklin D. Roosevelt (FDR) to create an interracial commission to investigate alleged discriminatory practices in the military.

1940

January: Earl Browder, general secretary of the U.S. Communist Party, is convicted of passport fraud, sentenced to four years, and fined $2,000.

January 10: Representatives of the Historic Peace Churches (Friends, Mennonites, and Church of the Brethren) present to FDR their goals for conscientious objectors.

March: An amendment to the World War I Espionage Act increases the penalties for spying, neutrality violations, and other infractions that apply during peacetime.

spring: FDR transfers the Immigration and Naturalization Service from the Department of Labor to the Department of Justice.

June: Congress passes the Smith Act (Alien Registration Act), requiring aliens 14 and older to register, to be fingerprinted, and to carry identification. The Smith Act also sets penalties for encouraging insubordination in the military, for advocating the forceful overthrow of the U.S. government, or for joining any organization that so advocates.

September: FDR announces the promotion of African-American Col. Benjamin Davis to brigadier general and the appointment to the War Department of African-American William Hastie, dean of Howard University law school.

September 16: The Selective Training and Service Act stipulates that "there shall be no discrimination against any person on account of race and color." It also extends eligibility for conscientious objector status to those who "by reason of religious training and belief" are "conscientiously opposed to participation in war in any form" and allows those opposed to noncombatant military service to do "work of national importance under civilian direction." But it provides no protection for absolutist objectors; it carries penalties for urging resistance to the draft; and it gives the War Department final authority to decide who will be accepted in the military.

September 27: Walter White, executive secretary of the NAACP; T. Arnold Hill, former industrial secretary of the Urban League; and A. Philip Randolph, president of the Brotherhood of Sleeping Car Porters, meet with FDR to demand integration of all existing military units, admission of blacks into the U.S. Army Air Corps, expanded training of black officers, integration of the navy, and assignment of black sailors to positions "other than the menial ones to which they are now restricted."

September 29: The White House announces that "the services of Negroes [in the military] will be utilized on a fair and equitable basis. . . . It is the policy of the War Department not to intermingle colored and white enlisted personnel in the same regimental organizations."

October: The Voorhis Act requires that every member of a group that advocates the overthrow of the U.S. government by force register with the Justice Department.

October 14: The Nationality Act of 1940 facilitates divesting naturalized citizens of their citizenship for radical political beliefs.

December 16: On this first day of draft registration, the War Resisters League, the Youth Committee Against War, and other small groups protest. In New York a few divinity students from Union Theological Seminary proclaim their refusal to register on grounds of conscience. In Florida, young Seminole men disappear without registering, on the grounds that they have never recognized the sovereignty of the United States.

late 1940: The First Army Headquarters sends secret orders to its draft boards requesting that no blacks be inducted in the first draft; the order is rescinded for Connecticut when that state's governor threatens to expose it.

1941

January: Labor organizer and civil rights leader Ernest Calloway becomes the first black to refuse induction because he objects to the army's racist policies.

January 13: The U.S. Army establishes the 78th Tank Battalion, the first black armored unit, later redesignated the 758th Tank Battalion (Light).

March: A training program for black combat pilots is established at Tuskegee Air Field in response to a legal suit filed by black pilot Yancey Williams, denied admission to the Army Air Corps.

April: The body of black Private Felix Hall is discovered at Fort Benning, Georgia, hanging from a tree, with his hands bound behind his back.

April 11: The Office of Production Management (OPM) sends a letter to all holders of defense contracts asking for the removal of all bans on the employment of blacks, and creates the Negro Employment and Training Branch and the Minority Groups Branch in its Labor Division.

May: Labor leader Sidney Hillman and auto executive William Knudsen agree to get manufacturers to hire more blacks for defense work.

May 15: Civilian Public Service begins for conscientious objectors at Patapsco State Park near Baltimore, Maryland.

June 25: The congressional Truman Committee holds a preliminary conference on racial discrimination.

June 25: Threatened with a march of 100,000 African Americans on Washington on July 1, FDR signs Executive Order 8802, calling upon employers and labor unions "to provide for the full and equitable participation of all workers in defense industries, without discrimination because of race, creed, color or national origin"; and setting up the Fair Employment Practices Commission to investigate grievances, monitor compliance, and publicize its findings.

June 28: Federal marshals raid the headquarters of the Socialist Workers Party; 29 leaders are indicted, of whom 18 are convicted and jailed.

July: The army opens its first integrated officers candidate schools.

August 6: Black and white servicemen battle in Fayetteville, North Carolina, in a dispute over seats on a bus bound for Fort Bragg; in the aftermath hundreds of black soldiers are herded into the base stockade, and many are beaten by their guards

August 11: 300 black troops from the 94th Engineer Battalion on maneuvers are attacked by a mob near Gurdon, Arkansas.

September 16: FDR requires that government departments must be able to assure him "that in the Federal Service the doors of employment are open to all loyal and qualified workers regardless of creed, race or national origin."

December: An amendment to the Espionage Act makes sabotage a national crime during peacetime as well as during wartime.

December 7: Under Presidential Proclamation 2525 the FBI begins a roundup of enemy aliens considered dangerous. The Department of Justice seals off the Mexican and Canadian borders to "all persons of Japanese ancestry" and begins roundups of some 3,000 "dangerous" enemy aliens, about half of them Japanese Americans. Within a year most of the Germans and Italians are released, usually with restrictions on movement and occupation.

December 7: Japanese attack Pearl Harbor, Hawaii.

December 7: Martial law is declared in Hawaii.

December 8: The Treasury Department seizes all banks and businesses owned by people of Japanese descent.

December 11: The FBI detains 1,370 Japanese classified as "dangerous enemy aliens."

December 16: By this date the Los Angeles nisei have set up a Committee on Intelligence and established regular liaison with the FBI.

December 19: The new Office of Censorship is authorized to censor all communications entering or leaving the United States by whatever medium.

December 27: FDR authorizes the censorship office to establish "voluntary censorship" of radio and press.

December 29: All enemy aliens in California, Oregon, Washington, Montana, Idaho, Utah, and Nevada are ordered to surrender all "contraband," including radios with shortwave bands, cameras, binoculars, and a variety of weapons.

December 30: Attorney General Francis Biddle authorizes the issuance of search warrants for any house in which an enemy alien lives, on the basis merely of a suspicion that there is contraband on the premises.

1942

January: By agreement with the Office of Censorship, the domestic news media agree not to report information of use to the enemy.

January 1: The U.S. attorney general freezes travel by all suspected enemy aliens and orders surrender of weapons.

January 5: All Japanese-American Selective Service registrants are placed in Class IV-C along with enemy aliens. Many Japanese Americans already in military service are discharged or put on kitchen police or other menial tasks.

January 9: FDR orders the navy and Marine Corps to enlist blacks into their regular military units.

January 14: FDR orders reregistration of suspected enemy aliens in the West.

January 25: An official committee of inquiry on the Pearl Harbor attack alleges that it was abetted by Japanese spies.

January 28: The California State Personnel Board votes to bar descendants of natives of countries against whom the United States is warring from all civil service positions, but it enforces the rule only against persons of Japanese ancestry.

January 29: The Justice Department announces a mass evacuation of enemy aliens from restricted areas near sensitive installations, to be effective February 25, and the appointment of a coordinator of the Alien Enemy Control Program within the Western Defense Command.

February: California attorney general Earl Warren warns that the very absence of fifth-column activity among Japanese Americans is ominous.

February: Secretary of War Henry L. Stimson issues a memorandum to commanding generals warning that "[T]he use of any epithet deemed insulting to a racial group should be carefully avoided."

February 4: The U.S. Army defines 12 "restricted areas" within which enemy aliens must observe a curfew, may travel only to and from their place of employment, and may travel no more than five miles from their place of residence.

February 19: Executive Order 9066 requires the removal of all people of Japanese descent, including American citizens, from any area designated as a military zone. The order also theoretically applies to Italian Americans and German Americans.

February 28: A mob of 1,200 whites blocks black families' attempts to move into the Sojourner Truth Housing Project in Detroit, Michigan.

March: The War Department orders the internment of all Japanese remaining in the prohibited zones, herding them into temporary holding cen-ters—stadiums, fairgrounds, and tent colonies—and then to permanent internment camps. Ultimately 112,000 men, women, and children are interned.

March 2: Gen. John De Witt issues Public Proclamation No. 1 designating military areas in the states of Washington, Oregon, California, and portions of Arizona and barring Japanese, German, and Italian aliens and any person of Japanese ancestry from living in Military Areas No. 1 and No. 2.

March 16: Four more military areas from which enemy aliens are to be barred are set up, covering Idaho, Montana, Nevada, and Utah.

March 18: An executive order establishes the War Relocation Authority, responsible for relocation centers and the later return of Japanese Americans into American life.

March 24: General De Witt issues Public Proclamation No. 3, extending travel restrictions, curfew, and contraband regulations to Japanese Americans, regardless of citizenship.

March 27: General De Witt issues Public Proclamation No. 4, prohibiting voluntary evacuation from Military Area No. 1 by Japanese aliens.

April: The War Department decides that black officers may on rare occasions command white enlisted men but not white officers.

April 7: The navy agrees to enlist blacks as gunners, clerks, signalmen, radio operators, ammunition handlers, etc. but only in segregated units at shore installations and on harbor craft; on seagoing combat ships they may serve only as stewards or laborers.

May: The Coast Guard begins accepting blacks to serve in capacities other than messmen.

May 7: The American Friends Service Committee organizes the National Japanese American Student Relocation Council to help evacuee college students continue their education outside the proscribed military areas.

June: African-American Winfred W. Lynn refuses to report for military service on the grounds that his induction violates the antidiscrimination clause of the Selective Service Act. He is arrested and indicted for draft evasion.

June: The U.S. Navy begins accepting black inductees from the Selective Service Board for the first time.

June 1: The U.S. Marine Corps begins admitting black recruits.

A Japanese-American family in Los Angeles awaits an evacuation train for Owens Valley, California, April 1942. *(Library of Congress, LC-USF33-013296-M3)*

June 13: FDR creates the Office of War Information, giving it powers to oversee the news and information output of all civilian government departments and bureaus and to disseminate propaganda through the media.

June 17: Milton Eisenhower resigns as head of the Wartime Relocation Authority, noting that the "great majority" of the Japanese evacuees are loyal. Dillon S. Myer succeeds him.

July: The first indictment for sedition is handed down by a grand jury in Washington, D.C., beginning the dismantlement of such organizations as the German-American Bund; the Silver Shirts; and We, the Mothers Mobilize for America, Inc.

July 13: Mitsuye Endo files a writ of habeas corpus seeking her release from her relocation center.

July 20: The first 40 black recruits begin attending the first Women's Auxiliary Army Corps (WAAC) officer candidate training at Fort Des Moines, Iowa, during which they eat and train with the 400 white women but live and play separately.

August 13: Nisei Mary Asaba Ventura loses her suit against the imposition of a curfew on Japanese Americans.

August 22: General De Witt orders commanders within the Western Defense Command to disregard court orders, including writs of habeas corpus, unless his headquarters authorizes them to obey.

September: Sixty-three Black Muslims are charged with sedition; they are convicted on a charge of draft evasion and jailed for three years (their leader Elijah Muhammed for five).

October 1: The War Relocation Authority establishes leave clearance procedures that enable some nisei to reenter civilian life.

1943

January: Congress prohibits the use of government funds to send COs overseas.

January 15: A segregated officer candidate school to train black ground officers for the air force opens at Jefferson Barracks, Missouri.

January 28: Secretary of War Stimson announces the decision to form an all-nisei combat team. Over 2,500 Japanese-American evacuees volunteer.

February 10: A questionnaire titled "Application for Leave Clearance" is distributed to all Japanese-American internees over 17, asking whether they are willing to serve in combat units and whether they will swear unqualified allegiance to the United States.

February 28: Violence erupts at the Sojourner Truth housing project in Detroit as whites attempt to prevent blacks with signed leases and rent paid from moving in. Officials postpone the move of the black tenants.

March: The director of training of black pilots at Tuskegee complains to First Lady Eleanor Roosevelt that the 99th Pursuit Squadron trained there has sat idle for more than a year; the president of Liberia becomes the first black to stay overnight at the White House and the first black since Reconstruction to address the Senate, which fails to welcome him.

March 10: The War Department forbids the designation by race of any recreational facilities on military bases.

April: FDR sends his wife to tour the Gila River Japanese internment camp in Arizona, where morale is deteriorating.

April 1: The army's adjutant general circulates a confidential letter stating that black WAAC personnel will be allocated on the basis of the number of blacks recruited from each service command and the needs of the service commands.

April 15: The all-black 99th Pursuit Squadron of the Army Air Corps sails for North Africa.

end of April: Black families move into the Sojourner Truth housing project in Detroit under a guard of Detroit police and state troops.

May 27: Executive Order 9346 transfers the Fair Employment Practices Committee to the Office of Emergency Management of the Executive Office and gives it powers to conduct hearings, make findings, and recommend measures to the War Manpower Commission. The federal government bars war contractors from discriminating on the basis of race.

June: The British War Office agrees with U.S. authorities that no black GIs shall be billeted in British homes.

June: The U.S. Coast Guard cutter *Seacloud,* the first integrated ship in the armed forces, is commissioned.

June: Ohio congresswoman Frances Payne Bolton amends the Nurses Training Bill to bar racial discrimination. Consequently, more than 2,000 African-American women enroll in the Cadet Nurses Corps.

Early June: 25,000 Packard plant workers producing engines for bombers and PT boats stop work to protest the promotion of three blacks; reportedly one of the protestors shouts, "I'd rather see Hitler and Hirohito win than work beside a n----- on the assembly line."

June 3: The Zoot-Suit Riots break out in Los Angeles between servicemen on shore leave and Mexican-American youths, during which servicemen often strip the zoot-suiters to their underwear.

June 9: Rioting breaks out between black soldiers and military police at Camp Stewart, Georgia, soon to be followed by disturbances at Fort Bliss and Clark Field in Texas, Camp Van Dorn in Mississippi, Camp Breckenridge in Kentucky, March Field in California, and Fort Huachuca in Arizona.

June 20: Whites and blacks riot for four days on Detroit's black east side.

June 21: The Supreme Court unanimously upholds the conviction of nisei Gordon Kiyoshi Hirabayashi for curfew violation and failure to report for evacuation.

July: The War Department's Advisory Committee on Special Troop Policies (Negro Troops) urges Gen. George Marshall to dispatch black combat troops "to an active theater of operations" as a means of reducing tension among them.

July: The War Relocation Authority begins segregating Japanese-American evacuees adjudged disloyal from those thought loyal.

August 1: A policeman's rough treatment in arresting a disorderly black woman sets off a riot in Harlem in New York City.

September 1: British Foreign Secretary Anthony Eden tells U.S. Ambassador John Winant that "our climate is badly suited to Negroes."

September 3: The War Manpower Commission redefines discrimination to include the refusal to classify workers properly or hire workers of a particular color or race.

September 15: The Fair Employment Practices Committee sends cease-and-desist orders to seven unions and 16 companies, ordering them to end discriminatory hiring practices and upgrade blacks on an equal basis; 16 of these companies and three unions, all southern, refuse to comply.

late 1943: Many Japanese-American internees are encouraged to leave relocation camps provided they can find employment in the interior of the United States; about 30,000 eventually do, and some 1,500 nisei join the armed services.

1944

January: An indictment for sedition accuses leaders of the Silver Shirts; We, The Mothers Mobilize for America, Inc.; and the German-American Bund of links with the Nazi Ministry of Propaganda.

January 20: Secretary of War Stimson announces that Japanese Americans will be subject to the draft.

February 23: The publication of Secretary of War Henry Stimson's letter alleging that "a relatively large percentage of the Negroes inducted in the Army have fallen within the lower educational classifications, and many of the Negro units have accordingly been unable to master the techniques of modern weapons" forces the assignment of black combat troops to Italy and the Pacific.

May 10: A federal grand jury indicts 63 Japanese-American draft resisters, who are found guilty and sentenced to three years' imprisonment.

May 20: Secretary of the Navy James Forrestal recommends that blacks make up 10 percent of the crews of 25 large auxiliary ships, and FDR approves.

May 25: Black GI Leroy Henry allegedly rapes a woman in Bath, England; he says that she is a prostitute whom he has earlier patronized, but that on this occasion she doubled her price, and that the MPs have beaten a confession of rape out of him; he is convicted and sentenced to death.

June: The nisei 442nd Regimental Combat Team arrives in Italy and fights there and in France until the end of World War II, becoming the most decorated unit in the army and suffering almost 10,000 casualties and the death of 600.

June: A unit of 63 black nurses is sent to England to care for German POWs. Black nurses have previously served in Australia and Africa.

June 6: When 185,000 Allied troops invade Normandy, only 500 black Americans, members of the 320th Barrage Balloon Battalion, are allowed to participate.

June 19: After public protests, Gen. Dwight D. Eisenhower throws out the conviction of rape for black GI Leroy Henry on the grounds of insufficient evidence.

July 8: The War Department orders that all "buses, trucks or other transportation owned and operated either by the government or by government instrumentality will be available to all military personnel regardless of race. Restricting personnel to certain sections of such transportation because of race will not be permitted. . . ."

August 1–5: Philadelphia transport workers strike to protest a Fair Employment Practices Committee antidiscrimination order, but they return to work when FDR threatens an army takeover, loss of their jobs, and cancellation of their draft deferments.

August 9: On the West Coast, 328 black sailors refuse to return to the docks to resume loading bombs and shells after an explosion on July 17, 1944, at Port Chicago, California, has killed 320 sailors, 202 of whom were black, and the finding thereafter of a naval court of inquiry that "colored enlisted personnel are neither temperamentally nor intellectually capable of handling high explosives." Some of the strikers

later agree to work after being threatened with prison terms or the death penalty.

October 19: The U.S. Navy opens the WAVES to blacks but recruits fewer than 100.

October 20: SPAR, the Coast Guard's women's auxiliary, begins enlisting blacks.

October 24: Martial law ends in Hawaii.

October 24: Fifty black sailors who refused to return to work after the Port Chicago explosion are sentenced to 15 years in prison and dishonorable discharges.

December 18: The Supreme Court upholds the conviction of Fred Korematsu for failing to report for evacuation.

December 18: The War Relocation Authority announces that all relocation camps will be closed before the end of 1945 and its entire program liquidated on June 30, 1946.

December 18: The Supreme Court unanimously rules that Mitsuye Endo was entitled to the release from a relocation center she procured through a writ of habeas corpus, concluding that, "whatever power the War Relocation Authority may have to detain other classes of citizens, it has no authority to subject citizens who are concededly loyal to its leave procedure."

December 25: Inflamed by repeated racial incidents, two truckloads of armed black sailors invade a marine camp on Guam, and a riot ensues.

December 26: The U.S. Army asks black servicemen to fight in the Battle of the Bulge.

1945

January 23: The National Association of Colored Nursing forces the army nurse corps to drop its racial restrictions on nurses.

January 25: The navy begins allowing black nurses to enroll.

February 3: The 688th Central Postal Battalion, the only black WAC unit to serve overseas, sails for England.

April 5: Authorities arrest 104 Tuskegee Airmen after they enter the officers club at Freemen Field, Indiana. Three of these black officers are court martialed. The others are reprimanded.

June: The Office of War Information (OWI) is closed.

June: African-American Wesley A. Brown receives an appointment to the naval academy.

November: Second Lt. Frederick C. Branch becomes the first black officer commissioned in the Marine Corps.

1946

Congress ends funding for the Fair Employment Practices Committee.

1947

March 31: Civilian Public Service for conscientious objectors ends.

December 13: President Harry S. Truman pardons 1,523 of 15,805 draft resisters, including 282 Japanese Americans.

1948

July: President Harry Truman's Executive Order 9981 integrates the armed forces.

July 2: Congress enacts a Japanese-American Evacuee Claims Act; in the next 15 years some 30,000 claims are settled on an average of 10 cents to the dollar for a total of about $30 million.

1950

September: Congress passes the Emergency Detention Act, giving civilian officials the right to set up camps for "The detention of persons who there is reasonable grounds to believe will commit or conspire to commit espionage or sabotage" after a presidential proclamation of an internal security emergency, created by invasion, declaration of war, or insurrection within the United States.

February 2: The Marine Corps admits black women.

1976

February 19: President Gerald Ford's Proclamation 4417 admits the mistake of the United States in incarcerating Japanese Americans.

1983

November 10: Fred Korematsu's conviction for failing to report for evacuation is vacated.

1989

November 2: President George H. W. Bush signs Public Law 101-162 guaranteeing funds for reparation payments to the World War II Japanese-American evacuee survivors beginning in October 1990.

1995

The U.S. Air Force reviews a racial incident involving Tuskegee Airmen, sets aside the conviction of 2nd Lt. Roger Terry for assault of a superior officer, and begins removing by request the reprimands in the files of 101 other Tuskegee Airmen.

1997

January: Seven black veterans are awarded the Medal of Honor for their actions in World War II—six of them posthumously.

1998

June 11: A class action lawsuit, *Mochizuki et al. v. United States,* is filed, resulting in a settlement in which the U.S. government acknowledges its error in evacuating Latin-American Japanese and pays $5,000 to each.

2000

November 7: Public Law 106-451 acknowledges that the civil liberties of Italian Americans were infringed during World War II.

December 23: President William Clinton pardons Freddie Meeks, one of the Port Chicago Fifty. Efforts continue to pardon the other 49, although some of them prefer that the full death benefits of $5,000 each, which were reduced to $3,000, be paid to the survivors of those killed in the explosion.

Eyewitness Testimony

The General Populace

I fought and killed so that the enemy might not invade our land, and I ask is it all for naught when red, white and blue fascists drive Nisei about like coyotes and plague the fathers, mothers, and relatives of our colored comrades that fight by our side.

Pvt. Herrett Wilson, letter of unknown date to his mother from the Pacific, quoted in Ambrose, Americans at War, *148.*

We [war correspondents] were all part of the war effort. We went along with it, and not only that, we abetted. . . . I don't mean that the correspondents were liars. . . . It is in the things not mentioned that the untruth lies. . . . The foolish reporter who broke the rules would not be printed at home, and in addition would be put out of the theater by the command.

War correspondent and author John Steinbeck, reminiscing about his experiences throughout the war, in Steinbeck, Once There Was a War, *viii–xii.*

Conscientious Objectors

Religion played no part in motivating my position [as a CO]. What did play an important role was my understanding and appreciation of Jewish life as it was lived in the ghetto and as it was reflected by my parents, my father particularly. The emphasis on education, as against material things in life, the emphasis on social justice. . . . Everything I knew about Judaism emphasized values which were and which are completely inconsistent with the use of war, violence, in the solution of problems.

Jewish conscientious objector Max Kleinbaum, interview coordinated by Murray Polner, no date given, in the Swarthmore College Peace Collection, quoted in Eller, Conscientious Objectors, *102.*

No skunks allowed! So you conscientious objectors Keep to H--- out of this Shop.

Sign on window, probably either in New Hampshire or California, depicted in an undated photograph taken by conscientious objector John Abbott, in Harris, Homefront, *114.*

I was in a reformatory. And I was in what was considered the most violent prison where the Jehovah's Witnesses spent time during the war. . . . [T]here were young people there who were easily agitated. They had their high emotions . . . and we had a good many mob acts against us. Very violent. As for myself, in one of these mob occasions, I walked outside the door of the building to attend one of our meetings, and I was knocked down and hit in the side of my head with a round point shovel and severely beaten. And I thought my head would never come back in shape.

Absolutist CO Fred Barnes, who was incarcerated in the El Reno Federal Reformatory in Oklahoma for a period during the war years, telephone interview with Cynthia Eller, May 13, 1987, in Eller, Conscientious Objectors, *76.*

Now one thing that might enter into [my reasons for being a CO] is that when I was little, my dad used to be horribly brutal. And I remember one time he just totally lost his temper, and he kicked me until I was down in the mud, and then kept on kicking me. . . . I was talking to a fella who also went through CPS, and I mentioned this as a possibility, that we were rebelling against the government because we were rebelling against our parents. And he said, yeah, that occurred to him also. That we figured we'd taken

Two conscientious objector couples relax near the headquarters of the Civilian Public Service camp near Elkton, Oregon, formerly a Civilian Conservation Corps camp. *(Collection of Rosalie and Dan Wilson)*

enough crap from our parents and we weren't going to take any crap off the government.

Conscientious objector Howard Ten Brink, September 24, 1986, reminiscing about his experience in Civilian Public Service during the war years, in Eller, Conscientious Objectors, *60.*

Generally speaking, the major Jewish organizations found it very difficult, didn't know quite how to handle this. Rabbi Hoffman at Columbia—when I was first going over that maybe I was a CO, I had a long talk with him, got the feeling of how I related to being Jewish, the Jewish religion. He and several other fellows, graduate students mostly at Columbia, started something called the Jewish Peace Fellowship, which still exists, still a tiny organization.... So that was the only one that was specifically a Jewish pacifist organization. Very limited resources, but [it] was helpful to various people who were Jewish, who were COs, who were needful of sympathetic support.

Nathaniel Hoffman, who served in CPS for almost three years during the war, volunteering for medical experiments and as an attendant in a mental hospital, in an interview conducted some time between the late 1970s and 1996 by Heather T. Frazer and John O'Sullivan, in Frazer and O'Sullivan, We Have Just Begun, *86.*

[My CPS experience was] a period of intense frustration, anguish, anger, and impotence.... Much of the work was merely a part of a boondoggle and effort by the government to keep conscientious objectors out of sight and out of mind. Fire suppression duties . . . provided some opportunity for plainly worthwhile service and work.... Massive tree-planting efforts also were seen as an effective contribution.... Only in late years did I come to a realization of my good fortune at being in a safe and productive environment during the horrible violence and destruction of World War II.

Conscientious objector "John," no last name given, who served in CPS during the war years, responding to a 1989 questionnaire sent out by Richard C. Anderson, quoted in Anderson, Peace, *60.*

At New Hampshire we had medical experiments too. There was a great interest in dealing with the needs of the people of Europe at war's end who were suffering tremendously from lack of proper food. The Harvard fatigue laboratory people joined in with an experiment to see what lack of vitamin C and lack of proteins would do to one and then how to reverse that quickly, because they felt that this was going to be an affliction to a whole generation of people. And so we went on an experiment in which I was on vitamin C; some were on protein. All of our food had to be weighed. It was very poor food there, we were almost like refugees ourselves. Once a week this Dr. Johnson would come down and give us a pack test. We would step up, as if we were walking up a mountain with a heavy weight on our backs, and he'd measure the decrease in our flow of blood and take blood samples to see how we were doing when we were deprived of these things. I remember my gums getting to be awfully soft....

Nathaniel Hoffman, who served in CPS for almost three years during the war, recalling his service as a volunteer in medical experiments and as an attendant in a mental hospital, in an interview conducted some time between the late 1970s and 1996 by Heather T. Frazer and John O'Sullivan, in Frazer and O'Sullivan, We Have Just Begun, *86.*

These conscientious objectors work at a Civilian Public Service camp in Gatlinburg, Tennessee, in fall 1943. *(Collection of Barbara Ambler)*

I stayed on at the [mental] hospital [in Williamsburg] for a couple of weeks because the woman who was supposed to come back on the ward, her husband was going overseas and she wanted two weeks off to be with him.... By that time, I was working on a tuberculosis ward all by myself.... [The doctor] gave [me] pep pills to be able to stay on the wards and tranquilizers to go to sleep afterwards.... [I was paid] fifty-eight dollars [per month], or something like that.

Anyway, when I finally did find a room . . ., it was in a house that this woman rented, and I had to room with her. I was kicked out of there when the landlord found out she'd rented a room to the wife of a conscientious objector. . . .

Wilma Ludlow, wife of CO William Ludlow, speaking of the war years in an interview conducted some time between the late 1970s and 1996 by Heather T. Frazer and John O'Sullivan, in Frazer and O'Sullivan, We Have Just Begun, *188–189.*

[In the CPS] I began to question whether I really was doing what was right. . . . What I was concerned about was the making of a stand against conscription. . . . And also, I really felt that in the South we needed to begin the process of working on race relations, and I wanted to dedicate my life to that. . . . [After I decided to leave CPS] I wrote to the attorney general, and I wrote to my draft board and told them what I was doing and where I was going and sent them back my draft card. . . . The judge . . . sentenced me to three years. I was sent to Federal Correctional Institution in Tallahassee, Florida. . . . I was exceedingly fortunate, because I had an opportunity to work in the prison hospital. . . . I had problems with officers but not with prisoners. . . . I asked to live in a black dormitory and, of course, was refused. But I made friends and later wrote letters for a lot of them. . . . I had to stay until August of 1945.

CO Edward Burrows, who voluntarily left CPS and accepted incarceration until his release in summer 1945, in an interview conducted some time between the late 1970s and 1996 by Heather T. Frazer and John O'Sullivan, in Frazer and O'Sullivan, We Have Just Begun, *130–134.*

Our daily work projects [as COs] were 1. building park roads from 7 a.m. to 5:30 p.m. by pickaxe and shovel, 2. digging trenches about two and a half feet wide and 6 feet deep and about 15 feet long in a 9-hour day in Maryland's clay soil for water mains, and 3. fighting forest fires all over Maryland with no protective clothing or fire masks. . . .

In looking back on my experience in World War II, I thank God I am an American. In Nazi Germany, I read recently through research, all C.O.'s were either hanged or shot.

God bless all veterans, and God bless America, the land of liberty *in law.*

Conscientious objector Robert R. Brewster, who received his draft notice in spring 1941, served in Civilian Public Service beginning in August 1941 and was medically discharged in March 1943, reminiscing in "My Experiences in World War II," *in Thoburn and Knapp,* "Perspectives," *40–41.*

I believed that opposition to all war and all killing was not only mandated by a Supreme Being but also by my conscience. Were I not opposed to all war on principle, there was simply no way I could, in conscience, enter the United States' racially segregated armed forces to fight for freedom, liberty and equality in other parts of the globe.

African American James Farmer, founder of the Congress of Racial Equality, who in 1942 was refused conscientious objector status but was deferred from the draft on the grounds that he held a divinity school degree, quoted in Potter, Liberators, *53.*

I came to the conclusion that I would rather be guilty of taking part in war through noncombatant work of mercy and education than see something I consider far worse than war take over this nation. In other words I believe our enemies represent something far worse than total war with all that implies and I do not think I have fallen for propaganda. While I cannot kill or join this part of the service I can aid those doing a dirty job which I now believe must be done.

John Ripley Forbes, who transferred from CPS to serve as a noncombatant in the military, letter of July 21, 1942, quoted in Eller, Conscientious Objectors, *170.*

I am a graduate nurse and am interested in some type of nursing in place of army nursing. I believe that my peace principles could be carried out more effectively outside the army or navy.

Letter, Mennonite woman to CPS officials, fall 1942, quoted in Goossen, Women against the Good War, *74.*

When the call was made for all males between 18 and 44, I refused (NOT EVADED) on the grounds that, first, I was a Muslim and would not take part in war and especially not on the side with the infidels. . . .

Second, I was 45 years of age and was NOT, according to the law, required to register.

Elijah Muhammad, Message to the Blackman, *quoted in "An historical look at The Honorable Elijah Muhammad," available online. Elijah Muhammad was also suspected of having taught that African Americans were related to the Japanese and that it did not make sense for African Americans to fight against the Japanese because both groups were victimized by white hatred and prejudice.*

For eight years I have believed war to be impractical and a denial of our Hebrew Christian tradition. The social teachings of Jesus Christ are (1) Respect for personality: (2) Service is the "summum bonum"; (3) Overcoming evil with good; and (4) The brotherhood of man. These principles as I see it are violated by participation in war.

Believing this, and having before me Jesus' continued resistance to that which he considered evil, I was compelled to resist war by registering as a Conscientious Objector in October, 1940.

However, a year later, in September 1941, I became convinced that conscription as well as war equally is inconsistent with the teachings of Jesus. I must resist conscription also.

On Saturday, November 13, 1943, I received from you an order to report for a physical examination to be taken Tuesday, November 16, at eight o'clock in the evening. I wish to inform you that I cannot voluntarily submit to an order springing from the Selective Service Training Act for War.

African-American activist Bayard Rustin, letter to his draft board, November 16, 1943, collection of Walter Naegle.

While we were working at Byberry [mental hospital] we had a group of 125 conscientious objectors who were doing their Civilian Public Service. We often had joint group meetings to discuss our experiences and our frustrations. We all were outraged that these conditions were allowed to exist. The big question was "What can we do to create change?" We had agreed that we needed the world to know how these sick people, through no fault of their own, were forced to live in these wretched institutions. But that was not easy. Security was tight. Going underground was the only solution. Furthermore, what did we have to lose? Being fired was certainly no threat and the

CO's could *not* be fired. We knew we had to expose these conditions to the public. I talked at length with one of the CO's, Charlie Lord, a professional photographer, to devise a strategy to get him with his camera on Building 11. . . . After weeks of careful planning we accomplished the deed. [After months of maneuvering,] there appeared in *Life* magazine a spread of our pictures. Directly out of that article a strong enough concern grew among the public and some government officials that the mental health movement was finally launched.

Charlotte Bartlett remembering her American Friends Service Committee summer job as ward attendant in 1944 or 1945, when she was a sophomore in college, unpublished memoir, June 15, 2001.

[On Leyte] I came across [Pvt.] David Kellner, [a devout Jewish man,] sitting down with his back to the attack, calmly firing his rifle into the air. I hollered at him and jerked him to his feet, . . . demanding to know what he was doing. He explained that he didn't want to kill anyone. I informed him that this was a kill or be killed situation and he had better hop to it.

As part of our field equipment, we carried a canteen on each hip and a large "Jungle Aid Kit" on the back of the cartridge belt. As Kellner stood up, with enemy rifle fire whipping around us, he yelled, "I'm hit." . . . I discovered that he had been shot through the canteen on his right hip and the "blood" he felt running down his leg was water. As he showed me this, he was shot through the canteen on his left hip. As he showed this to me, he got shot through the Jungle Aid pouch.

At this moment, David said to me, "Lieutenant, you're right. They are trying to kill me." As he turned to face the advancing Japanese and raised his rifle to his shoulder, a bullet went through his rifle stock. I've never seen so many close ones on only one person.

Lt. Buckner Creel, reminiscing about the Leyte invasion of October 1944, quoted in Astor, Operation Iceberg, *337.*

As a Christian I cannot cooperate with Selective Service's prison program of punishment, "correction", "rehabilitation", or of using me for the purpose of building war morale or of deterrence to the conscientious objectors.

I will not accept my criminal status.

I will not subject myself to prison rules or regulations.

I will not submit to the authority of prison guards or officials.

I have never stood in the way of any conscientious soldier or war worker in the following of his conscientious convictions. I give every man the right to his opinions—and I expect the right to mine; and when any individual or group attempts to cram their opinions down my throat, I do not intend to let threats, intimidation, or punishment deter me from obeying God.

Absolutist conscientious objector John Hampton, inmate at McNeil Federal Penitentiary, in The Absolutist, *June 19, 1945, quoted in Anderson,* Peace, *145–146.*

Japanese Americans

When [Eleanor Roosevelt] starts bemoaning the plight of the treacherous snakes we call Japanese, with apologies to all snakes, she has reached the point where she should be forced to retire from public life.

Editorial from an unidentified Los Angeles newspaper of unidentified date, in Hareven, Eleanor Roosevelt, *167.*

Before the war came . . . we'd be working at Hickam Field. That was with all local boys, but when I went to (Fort) Shafter, then I was in sort of a Haole [Caucasian] environment, so to speak. . . . Because civil service is you take the test and they grade you and all that. They don't discriminate [against] you for color line, see. That was the big difference. . . . Not like before the war when we were on separate strata, so to speak.

Hawaiian resident Etsuo Sayama speaking about his work experiences before and during the war, interview by Warren Nishimoto, An Era of Change: Oral Histories of Civilians in World War II Hawaii, *III: 976.*

I am proud that I am an American citizen of Japanese ancestry, for my very background makes me appreciate more fully the wonderful advantages of this nation. I believe in her institutions, ideals and traditions; I glory in her heritage; I boast of her history; I trust in her future. She has granted me liberties and opportunities such as no individual enjoys in this world today. She has given me an education befitting kings. She has permitted me to build a home, to earn a livelihood, to worship, think, speak and act as I please—as a free man equal to every other man.

Although some individuals may discriminate against me, I shall never become bitter or lose faith, for I know that such persons are not representative of the majority of the American people. True, I shall do all in my power to discourage such practices, but I shall do it in the American way—above board, in the open, through courts of law, by education, by proving myself to be worthy of equal treatment and consideration. I am firm in my belief that American sportsmanship and attitude of fair play will judge citizenship and patriotism on the basis of action and achievement, and not on the basis of physical characteristics. Because I believe in America, and I trust she believes in me, and because I have received innumerable benefits from her, I pledge myself to do honor to her at all times and all places; to support her constitution; to obey her laws; to respect her flag; to defend her against all enemies, foreign and domestic; to actively assume my duties and obligations as a citizen, cheerfully and without any reservations whatsoever, in the hope that I may become a better American in a greater America.

Creed of the Japanese American Citizens League, 1940, quoted in Daniels, Concentration Camps USA, *24–25.*

As Americans we now function as counterespionage. Any act or word prejudicial to the United States committed by any Japanese must be warned and reported to the F.B.I., Naval Intelligence, Sheriff's Office, and local police.

Broadcast by Editor Togo Tanaka of the Japanese American Citizens League, December 7, 1941, quoted in Daniels, Concentration Camps, USA, *41.*

Both [my husband, Karl, and I] were known activists in labor, civil rights, and antifascist organizations. About 7:45 A.M. on December 8, 1941, three FBI agents . . . searched our small upper four-room flat, taking nothing, and made snide remarks as they looked through some Chinese War Relief cards I was addressing for our Christmas . . . messages. They called them "a good cover for pro-Japan activity." . . .

Karl heard undercurrents in Japantown that volunteer Japanese American construction workers for a camp to be built in Manzanar were being recruited by Los Angeles Maryknoll priests. They were the liaison to the U.S. Army. Without any further questions we decided to move to Los Angeles. There my children and I could live with my parents while I got war-related work and Karl volunteered for a construction job. . . .

[N]othing must be done by us to impede the war effort. The immediate task was to defeat the enemy— the fascist Axis (Germany-Italy-Japan), for if they won the war, there would not be a shred of democracy left in this country or anywhere on this earth. We could thrash out the question of rights after victory.

> *Elaine Black Yoneda, the white wife of a Japanese American, reminiscing about events that began December 8, 1941, in her 1981 statement to the Commission on Wartime Relocation and Internment of Civilians. Ms. Yoneda insisted on accompanying her husband and her three-year-old son, who, because he had more than 1/16th Japanese blood, had to be evacuated. Statement quoted in Inada,* Only What We Could Carry, *154–155.*

Those [Japanese Americans] who attempted to cross [from the West Coast states] into the interior states ran into all kinds of trouble. Some were turned back by armed posses at the border of Nevada; others were clapped into jail and held overnight by panicky local police officers; nearly all had difficulty in buying gasoline; many were greeted by "No Japs Wanted" signs on the main streets of interior communities; and a few were threatened, or felt that they were threatened, with possibilities of mob violence.

> *1946 report of the War Relocation Authority, describing the situation as the war began, quoted in Daniels,* Concentration Camps USA, *84.*

I'm very doubtful that it would be common sense procedure to try and intern 117,000 Japanese in this theater. . . . An American citizen, after all, is an American citizen. And while they all may not be loyal, I think we can weed the disloyal out of the loyal and lock them up if necessary. . . . It would be better if [control over enemy aliens] worked through the civil channels.

> *Lt. Gen. John L. DeWitt, December 26, 1941, quoted in Daniels,* Concentration Camps USA, *40.*

In the course of our reading, the French and Indian War was mentioned. The children expressed surprise upon hearing that there had been French people in our country. I took a moment to review briefly the various waves of immigration from Europe and later from Asia and apparently made it clear that the Native Americans had been driven from their homes by the Europeans. Jimmie, who had been pushed from California to Arkansas and back said to us all, "Gee whiz, poor Indians, feel sad."

> *Dr. Kate Hobbie, reminiscing about her experiences beginning in 1942 teaching fourth-graders at Tule Lake internment center, manuscript for Japanese-American publication "Grains of Rice," Dr. Hobbie's private collection.*

A dust storm hits a War Relocation Authority center where evacuees of Japanese ancestry are held, at Manzanar, California, July 3, 1942. *(National Archives, 210-G-10C-839)*

Woodrow Wilson Higashi, a nisei, owned a small but prosperous drugstore in Los Angeles. He was unable to dispose of his stock and fixtures before being taken to the holding center of the Santa Anita race track, preliminary to internment. He was visited there by one "Edwards," a white acquaintance, who said he could dispose of the store's fixtures and Mr. Higashi's seven-year-old automobile for approximately $500, and he also offered to store his friend's household goods and personal possessions. The offer was gratefully accepted, and "Edwards" requested and was given a power of attorney to handle Higashi's affairs. That was the last Higashi saw of "Edwards."

After a few weeks at Santa Anita, Higashi was transferred to the Granada relocation center in Colorado. In October 1943, after he had been interned for more than a year, he persuaded the WRA [War Relocation Authority] to demand from "Edwards" an accounting of his stewardship. Months later, WRA reported that all of the property, including household and personal possessions, which had been placed in "Edwards" care had simply vanished; that "Edwards" had no assets which could be attached to recover the value of the store fixtures and automobile, and that, furthermore, the Los Angeles district attorney was not inclined to bring any charges against "Edwards."

> Impounded People, *official record of the War Relocation Authority, 1946, about events of 1942, quoted in abridged form in Phillips,* The 1940s, *112–113.*

One day I came home from school to find the two F.B.I. men at our front door. They asked permission to search the house. One man looked through the front rooms, while the other searched the back rooms. Trembling with fright, I followed and watched each of the men look around. The investigators examined the mattresses, and the dresser and looked under the beds. The gas range, piano and sofa were thoroughly inspected. Since I was the only one at home, the F.B.I. questioned me, but did not procure sufficient evidence of Fifth Columnists in our house.

> *Fifteen-year-old nisei California girl writing in a letter, probably January or February 1942, quoted in Daniels,* Concentration Camps USA, *44.*

This is our country. We were born and raised here . . . have made our homes here . . . [and] we are ready to give our lives, if necessary, to defend the United States. . . . [The nisei are] ready to stand as protective custodians over our parent generation to guard against danger to the United States arising from their midst.

> *Nisei leader James Y. Sakomoto of the Japanese American Citizen League, letter of January 21, 1942, protesting against Representative John Ford's proposal for internment, quoted in Daniels,* Concentration Camps USA, *48–49.*

A viper is nonetheless a viper wherever the egg is hatched—so a Japanese-American, born of Japanese parents—grows up to be a Japanese, not an American.

> *Editorial,* Los Angeles Times, *early February 1942, quoted in Daniels,* Concentration Camps USA, *62.*

[T]he Pacific Coast is in imminent danger of a combined attack from within and without. . . . It is a fact that the Japanese navy has been reconnoitering the coast more or less continuously. . . . There is an assumption [in Washington, D.C.,] that a citizen may not be interfered with unless he has committed an overt act. . . . The Pacific Coast is officially a combat zone: Some part of it may at any moment be a battlefield. And nobody ought to be on a battlefield who has no good reason for being there. There is plenty of room elsewhere for him to exercise his rights.

> *Walter Lippman, column of February 12, 1942, quoted in Daniels,* Concentration Camps USA, *68.*

[T]here must be a point beyond which there may be no abridgement of civil liberties and we feel that whatever the emergency, that persons must be judged, so long as we have a Bill of Rights, because of what they do as persons. . . . We feel that treating persons, because they are members of a race, constitutes illegal discrimination, which is forbidden by the fourteenth amendment whether we are at war or peace.

> *A. L. Wirin, American Civil Liberties lawyer, probably March 1942, quoted in Daniels,* Concentration Camps USA, *78.*

I feel most deeply that when the war is over and we consider calmly this unprecedented migration of 120,000 people, we as Americans are going to regret the avoidable injustices that may have been done.

> *War Relocation Authority head Milton S. Eisenhower, letter to Secretary of Agriculture Claude Wickard, April 1, 1942, quoted in Daniels,* Concentration Camps USA, *91.*

[In] April, 1942, . . . I was sent to the Federal Women's Penitentiary in Seagoville, Texas, where many Japanese ladies and their children from Peru and the Panama Canal Zone were already interned. A little later, a group of ladies from Hawaii joined us. Most of the ladies were schoolteachers and the educated wives of influential businessmen engaged in business with Japan. I was interned in Seagoville for about two years, but in May 1944 transferred to a family internment camp in Crystal City, Texas. About a month before our transfer to Crystal City, I was joined by my husband, who had been interned at Fort Sill, Oklahoma, and Camp Livingston, Louisiana. In Seagoville and Crystal City, I helped with camp affairs as an interpreter and counselor because most of the internees from Panama and Peru spoke only Japanese and Spanish.

Japanese American Take Uchida describing her experiences that began in April 1942, quoted in Daniels et al., Japanese Americans, 31.

Then in June [1942], with gathering momentum, the next phase of the forced migration got under way. At the former migratory labor camp doing duty near Sacramento as an assembly center, trains were loaded with men, women, children and babies and moved northward to unload their cargo near the little town of Tule Lake, California. Here the rough barracks of one of the first relocation centers were still under construction. Farmers from the rich Salinas Valley were transported to the Arizona desert. San Francisco businessmen were sent from the Tanforan race track to the bare, intermountain valleys of central Utah. From the fertile central valley of California to the sandy flats of eastern Colorado, from southern California to the plains of Wyoming, from the moist coastland of the Northwest to the sagebrush plains of southern Idaho, from the San Joaquin Valley to the woodlands of Arkansas, the trains moved during the spring, early summer and fall.

For the involuntary travelers, the break with the accustomed and usual was now complete. In the assembly centers behind fences and under guard by military police, the evacuees had suddenly found themselves, although looking out at familiar hills and highways, in a strange new world of social relationships. They were outcast but still in their own country. Now the world of human relations was matched by an equally strange physical world. It was clear, as the trains moved over the wastelands of the mountain states, that they were to be exiled in desert and wilderness.

Official United States government report on the events of June 1942, in Phillips, The 1940s, 111.

I think almost the biggest obligation we have today is to prove that in a time of stress we can still live up to our beliefs and maintain the civil liberties we have established as the rights of human beings everywhere.

First Lady Eleanor Roosevelt, "My Day," December 17, 1942, Marist College Archives.

[My nisei students] relished mimicking for me the idiosyncrasies of the various teachers, how one would twitch her eyes, how another would squeakingly exclaim in her high pitched voice "how sorry she was for the Japanese," or how she would bore them stiff by relating her experiences in Japan. "My goodness," they said, "we know that things aren't perfect for us, but we don't want anyone to make us feel sorry for ourselves." But they were even more disgusted with the other teacher who assured them, "Oh, but you do have freedom and self-government here. They're guaranteed to you in the Constitution."

Nisei internee Bob Sakai, who later enlisted in the U.S. Army, probably speaking of 1943, quoted in Daniels, Concentration Camps USA, 47.

I was very happy when I read your announcement that Nisei Americans would be given the chance to volunteer for active combat duty. But at the same time I am sad—sad because under your present laws I am an enemy alien. I am 22 years old, American in thought, American in act, as American as any other citizen. I was born in Japan. My parents brought me to America when I was only two years old. . . . Please give me a chance to serve in the armed forces. How can a democratic nation allow a technicality of birthplace to stand in the way when the nation is fighting to preserve the rights of free men?

Japanese American Henry Ebihara to Secretary of War Henry Stimson, about January 1943, quoted in Goodwin, No Ordinary Time, 430.

Information has come to me from several sources that the situation in at least some of the Japanese internment camps is bad and is becoming worse rapidly. Native-born Japanese who at first accepted with philosophical understanding the decision of their government to round up and take far inland all of the Japanese along the Pacific Coast, regardless of their degree of loyalty, have pretty generally been disappointed with the treatment they have been accorded. . . . The result has been the gradual turning of thousands of well-meaning and loyal Japanese into angry prisoners. . . . I am unwilling to believe that a better job in general could not have been done. Neither do I believe that we can't do better from here out, especially if we tackle the job in a different spirit and with real determination without further delay.

Secretary of the Interior Harold Ickes, letter to President Franklin D. Roosevelt, April 13, 1943, quoted in Daniels, Concentration Camps USA, 149.

Because racial discriminations are in most circumstances irrelevant and therefore prohibited, it by no means follows that, in dealing with the perils of war, Congress and the Executive are wholly prevented from taking into account those facts . . . which may in fact place citizens of one ancestry in a different category. . . .

The adoption by Government, in the crisis of war and of threatened invasion, of measures for the public safety, based upon the recognition of facts and circumstances which indicate that a group of one national extraction may menace that safety more than others, is not wholly beyond the limits of the Constitution. . . .

Supreme Court chief justice Harlan Fiske Stone in his June 1943 majority opinion in the case of nisei Gordon Kiyoshi Hirabayashi, convicted of violating the curfew and failing to report for evacuation, quoted in Daniels, Concentration Camps USA, *133.*

The broad provisions of the Bill of Rights . . . are [not] suspended by the mere existence of a state of war. . . . Distinctions based on color and ancestry are utterly inconsistent with our traditions and ideals. . . .

Today is the first time, so far I am aware, that we have sustained a substantial restriction of the personal liberty of citizens of the United States based on the accident of race or ancestry. . . . It bears a melancholy resemblance to the treatment accorded to members of the Jewish race in Germany. . . . This goes to the very brink of constitutional power.

Supreme Court justice Frank Murphy in his June 1943 concurring opinion in the case of nisei Gordon Kiyoshi Hirabayashi, quoted in Daniels, Concentration Camps USA, *135.*

I joined the 27th Division at Schofield Barracks in Hawaii in June 1943, and worked with ten other linguists as a team. There was no discrimination against us and we were accepted by the troops. . . . I had my first combat experience on Makin in the Gilberts. We came under fire as I participated in the beachhead landing. Through captured documents we passed along information on the units and order of battle for the Japanese on the island. We received a commendation from the G-2 [intelligence] colonel for this work after the campaign.

Japanese-American serviceman Nobuo D. Kishiue speaking of his experiences beginning in June 1943, in Astor, Operation Iceberg, *225–256.*

We are at war, and *these people* are our enemies.

University of Arizona president Alfred Atkinson, probably in 1944, refusing the request of Japanese-American internees at Gila River for library books and faculty lectures, in McWilliams, Prejudice, *160.*

Hundreds of Japanese Americans are employed in occupations which were denied to them on the Pacific Coast. They have, for the first time, found occupational outlets, and I do feel for that reason a great many of them will not return to the Pacific Coast. As you well know a great many Japanese Americans graduated from institutions of higher learning but were pigeon-holed into narrow employment channels because the doors were closed to them in California. Now that they have found they can express themselves [elsewhere], I do feel that a great many of them are quite happy, despite what they have undergone.

Japanese-American graduate of the University of California, letter to president of the University Robert Gordon Sproul from Chicago, October 9, 1944, in Daniels, Concentration Camps USA, *111.*

I saw [the soldier] and I thought, Oh, now the Japanese are going to kill us. And I didn't care anymore. I said, "Just kill us, get it over with." He tried to convince me that he was an American and wouldn't kill me. I said, "Oh, no, you are a Japanese and you're going to kill us." We went back and forth, and finally he landed on his knees, crying, with his hands over his face, and he said, "You are free now. We are American Japanese. You are free."

Former Dachau inmate Peggy Orenstein describing her liberation from that German concentration camp, probably in early 1945, in The New Yorker, *November 11, 1991, quoted in Inada,* Only What We Could Carry, *377.*

My best friend was Roland, a young Japanese child, the same age. I would never forget, Mr. Chairman, never forget, because the moment is burned indelibly upon this child's memory, six years of age, the day the . . . . trucks came to pick up my friend. I would never forget the vision of fear in the eyes of Roland, my friend, and the pain of leaving home.

My mother, bright as she was, try as she may, could not explain to me why my friend was being taken away, as he screamed not to go, and this six-year-old black American child screamed back, "Don't take my friend.". . .

So I would say to my colleagues, this is not just compensation for being interned. How do you compensate Roland, six years of age, who felt the fear that he was leaving his home, his community, his friend, Ron, the black American, who later became a Member of Congress; Roland, the Japanese American, who later became a doctor, a great healer.

This meager $20,000 is also compensation for the pain and the agony that he felt and that his family felt.

California Congressman Ron Dellums, September 17, 1987, speaking in support of the bill to compensate evacuees, quoted in Inada, Only What We Could Carry, *33–34.*

American Indians

They called my name [to be a Code Talker] and I said, "I'm not a full-blooded Indian; I can talk the language but you can find better people—I'm supposed to be a pilot." The guy said to me, "Hey, Apaches don't become pilots. They're not smart enough."

Spanish-Apache Louis Armijo reminiscing about 1942, in Brokaw, Greatest Generation, *206.*

African Americans

[Black pilots could not be used] since this would result in having Negro officers serving over white enlisted men. This would create an impossible social problem.

Air Corps general H. H. "Hap" Arnold, 1940, quoted in Potter, Liberators, *89.*

Our main reason for writing is to let all our colored mothers and fathers know how their sons are treated after taking an oath pledging allegiance and loyalty to their flag and country. . . . We sincerely hope to discourage any other colored boys who might have planned to join the Navy and make the same mistake we did. All they would become is seagoing bell hops, chambermaids and dishwashers. We take it upon ourselves to write this letter regardless of any action the Navy authorities may take. We know it could not

possibly surpass the mental cruelty inflicted upon us on this ship.

Fifteen sailors aboard the USS Philadelphia, *including Byron Johnson, Floyd Owens, Otto Robinson, and Shannon Goodwin, all 15 of whom were later dishonorably discharged for "unfitness," in an open letter to the* Pittsburgh Courier, *mid-September 1940.*

We must not place too much responsibility on a race [African Americans] which is not showing initiative. [First Lady] Mrs. Roosevelt engages in impulsive and impudent folly in her criticism of our policies. The foolish leaders of the colored race are seeking, at bottom, social equality.

Secretary of War Henry L. Stimson, diary entry of October 25, 1940, quoted in Potter, Liberators, *66.*

What happens when a Negro who has had excellent training at one of NYC's technical or trade schools applies for one of the thousands of new jobs opening up? He finds the jobs segregated even in New York City. "Wanted—white Mechanics, tool and die makers, sheet metal workers." Far less frequently he finds, "Wanted—colored. Porters, cleaners, janitors.". . . . [Or perhaps] the colored applicant is told that he can get a job only if he is a member of the AFL aeronautical workers union, chartered by the International Association of Machinists, whose constitution bans all but white persons from membership.

African-American leader Walter White, letter to the New York Post, *March 6, 1941.*

Probably no single factor has contributed so greatly to the lowering of morale of the colored soldier as his relationship to the Military Policeman. Bullying, abuse and physical violence on the part of white Military Policemen are a continuing source of complaints. The recent killings at Fort Bragg appear . . . to have been the result of extreme tension between colored troops and bullying and abusive white Military Policemen. . . . In the Army the Negro is taught to be a man, a fighting man; in brief, a soldier. It is impossible to create a dual personality which will be on one hand a fighting man toward a foreign enemy, and on the other, a craven who will accept treatment as less than a man at home. One hears with increasing frequency from colored soldiers the sentiment that since they have been called to fight, they might just as well do their fighting here and now.

Report on fact-finding mission by Judge William H. Hastie, September 22, 1941, quoted in Potter, Liberators, 70.

[A policy of integration] would be tantamount to solving a social problem which has perplexed the American people throughout the history of this nation. The Army cannot accomplish such a solution, and should not be charged with the undertaking. . . . [To do so would] complicate the tremendous task of the War Department and thereby jeopardize discipline and morale.

Gen. George Marshall memorandum, December 1, 1941, George C. Marshall Foundation.

During the period 1861–1865, many of the slave owners left their families in the care of slaves to go forth to fight for a cause they believed was right. There is no record of these slaves having violated this confidence imposed on them by their owners. Many of the colored men wearing the uniform of the United States are the descendants of those slaves. It is right and honorable that the white soldiers, descendants of the slave owners, accord the descendants of those slave fair play and the rights and privileges of citizenship earned by the fidelity of their ancestors.

African-American Gen. Benjamin O. Davis, Jr., 1942, quoted in Potter, Liberators, 76.

Two of us were told by officers to go into a little town [in rural Louisiana in 1942] and pick up supplies. I got out of the truck and went into the store, and I was ordering. I started out, and the storekeeper said, "Don't go back there!" I crowded under the porch, and I saw my comrade being dragged up and down the street until he died. It was about four o'clock, so I stayed under the porch until after dark, and then they took me out and back to camp. There was a big upheaval about it, and they moved us black troops out of the area immediately.

Paul Parks of the 183rd Combat Engineers speaking about rural Louisiana in 1942, in Potter, Liberators, 69.

You're filling too many colored troops up on the West coast. . . . [T]here will be a great deal of public reaction out here due to the Jap situation. They feel they've got enough black skinned people around them as it is. Filipinos and Japanese. . . . I'd rather have a white regiment.

Lt. Gen. John L. DeWitt, protesting to the U.S. Army's chief of classification and assignment, January 31, 1942, quoted in Daniels, Concentration Camps USA, 36.

The Army has adopted rigid requirements for literacy mainly to keep down the number of colored troops and this is reacting badly in preventing us from getting some very good illiterate [white] recruits from the southern mountain states.

Secretary of War Henry Stimson, diary entry for March 12, 1942, quoted in Putney, Nation in Need, 121.

Gentlemen: I am in receipt of my draft-reclassification notice. Please be informed that I am ready to serve in any unit of the armed forces of my country which is not segregated by race. Unless I am assured that I can serve in a mixed regiment and that I will not be compelled to serve in a unit undemocratically selected as a Negro group, I will refuse to report for induction.

African-American Winfred W. Lynn, letter to draft board, June 1942, quoted in McGuire, Taps for a Jim Crow Army, xiii.

I realize I'm a stranger to you, I have heard lots of people speak of what a nice lady you are and what I can hear is that you believe in helping the poor. . . . I was raised in Virginia on a farm. I never had a chance to make anything not even a good living. I always worked hard but I couldn't get anything out of it. I raised some wheat with a man named Oscar Davis and he took all of the wheat and I tried to get my share of it he wouldn't let me have the wheat. We got in a quarrel. And I shot him to keep him from hurting me not meaning to kill him. He carried a gun and I was afraid of him. . . . Please write to the Governor and get him to have mercy on me and allow me a chance. You will never regret it.

Odell Waller, convicted of murder by a jury of white male poll-taxpayers, letter to First Lady Eleanor Roosevelt, June 8, 1942, who tried to help but could not prevent Waller's execution. Waller's case became a cause célèbre in the black community. Letter quoted in Goodwin, No Ordinary Time, 351–352.

"Too many of your nationality over here," a white [British] sailor cried [to a black GI with a local white woman]. When the Negro protested, "I'm an American," he was told: "For me you're a nigger and always will be a nigger."

Incident reported by Adm. Harold L. Stark to Secretary of the Navy Frank Knox, July 1, 1942, quoted in Reynolds, Rich Relations, *219.*

I drew a book from the Service Club Library to read. The title of the book is *Negro Poets and Their Poems,* by Kerlin. I had the book with me at the motor pool where I work. . . . I had finished up my work (Records) for the day . . . when the Company Executive Officer walked in the office. . . . [H]e picked up the book and began looking through it; finally he came to this poem: "Mulatto" by Langston Hughes. He cursed and used all kinds of vile language about the author. . . . [He told me:] "Take that damn book where you got it and I don't want to ever see anything like that around the co. The wrong person might get a hold of it and it might cause some trouble."

African American Clarence E. Adams, letter to the black civilian aide to the secretary of war, July 8, 1942, quoted in McGuire, Taps for a Jim Crow Army, *101–102.*

The Negro problem has been very poorly handled here by our officers. . . . Rather than lessen the friction between the white and colored troops our officers have, through their actions & statements, definitely increased the friction . . . [and] have managed to give official sanction to the anti-Negro group in my outfit. This has tended to make others (who normally might have accepted working & associating with Negroes) equally as antagonistic. In my outfit [it] is now "The thing" to hate the negros [sic]. . . . Actually what is taking place in our army today is nothing more disgraceful than what Hitler is doing to minorities in Germany. I joined the American Army to fight against the persecution of minorities. I resent that our Army actually practices the same kind of persecution.

Response to a questionnaire given to GIs near Cheltenham, England, in September 1942, quoted in Reynolds, Rich Relations, *313.*

[In Britain] we have a very thickly populated country that is devoid of racial consciousness. They know nothing at all about the conventions and habits of polite society that have been developed in the U.S. in order to preserve a segregation in social activity with-

out making the matter one of official or public notice. To most English people, including the village girls—even those of perfectly fine character—the Negro soldier is just another man, rather fascinating because he is unique in their experience, a jolly good fellow and with money to spend. Our own white soldiers, seeing a girl walk down the street with a Negro, frequently see themselves as protectors of the weaker sex and believe it necessary to intervene even to the extent of using force, to let her know what she's doing.

Letter to Washington from Gen. Dwight D. Eisenhower, September 10, 1942, quoted in Reynolds, Rich Relations, *218.*

The Carolina Special, of the Southern Railway system, was segregated, as were all trains and other accommodations in the South. There were sometimes provisions made, such as they were, for Negro passen-

Members of the 34th Construction Battalion at Halavo Seaplane Base, Florida, in the Solomon Islands, construct a prefabricated steel storage warehouse, September 19, 1943. *(National Archives, 80-G-89138)*

gers to eat in the dining car in a small curtained-off section. I had boarded the train at night in Cincinnati, and the following morning I went to the dining car and joined the line of people waiting for a seat. . . . I finally made it to the door of the dining car when the steward put his arm across the door and announced that the car was full. I stood there in front of the line and waited. After a rather long time the steward called, "All persons in uniform first." I stepped forward. He thrust his arm across the door again and said, angrily, "I said all persons in uniform first." Before I could answer, I heard a voice behind me.

"Well, what in the hell do you think that is that she has on? Get your —— arm down before I break it off for you."

The voice was so obviously southern that I turned around in surprise. That voice belonged to a very tall, very blond second lieutenant, and he was so angry that his face was quite red. He continued to talk, and loudly. "What in the world are we fighting this damned war for? She's giving her service, too, and can eat anywhere I can. And, by Jesus, I am going to eat with her in this diner." . . .

There was the time I was returning to Des Moines from a southern city when I went to the dining car for dinner, and the steward met me at the door only to inform me that the places were all taken and that I could not be served. Looking over his shoulder, I could see that there were several empty tables in the car. The steward turned back toward the dining car and discovered that all the waiters (all Negroes, of course) had put down their trays and had started moving toward the pantry area of the car. He got the point, for he turned back to me and said, "I see I have one space left." The waiters all picked up their trays to continue service as I was seated at one of the empty tables.

Lt.-Col. Charity Adams Earley speaking probably about 1943 or 1944, in Earley, One Woman's Army, *62, 105.*

"I don't mind the Yanks, but I don't much care for the white fellows they've brought with them."

Unidentified Englishman speaking probably in 1943, quoted in Reynolds, Rich Relations, *303.*

Everybody here adores the Negro troops, all the girls go to their dances, but nobody likes the white Americans. They swagger about as if they were the only people fighting this war, they all get so drunk and look so untidy while the Negroes are very polite, much smarter and everybody's pets.

A British woman in Marlborough, Wiltshire, letter to a friend, March 1943, quoted in Reynolds, Rich Relations, *303.*

[A]n American airman walked in [to a canteen for Allied troops], and seeing the coloured airman quietly sitting at a table, strolled up to him and slashed [slapped] him across the face! Of course everyone jumped up ready for a fight but the proprietress managed to stop it. Someone said "send for the U.S. police" but the Americans tried to pass it off, and said that if the coloured man would go, everything would be all right. The British said if anyone ought to go, it was the American [assailant]. A schoolmistress who was helping at the back, dashed out and slashed the American's face, and her language was very choice! Anyway, they smuggled him [the American] out, but our men said if they saw him again they'd kill him and all the rest of it. . . . It seems amazing that the Americans are fighting on our side, when you hear things like that.

Letter from a young British woman student to a friend, April 1943, quoted in Reynolds, Rich Relations, *302.*

This two-star general came through the [100th General Hospital in Bardelieu, France]. I was the only black on the ward. He asked every soldier, "What unit were you in, So-and-so? How do you feel today? What did you do?" Those are the questions he put to the white troops. He came all the way to me, and in the next bed was my buddy, a cast all the way up his body. The general looked over at me, and I had my head all wrapped up from being hit by the shrapnel. He said, "What's wrong with you, boy? Got the clap?" God, did that sink a dagger into me! . . . I was dumbfounded; I couldn't say anything. This kid in his cast looks up and says, "If he got it, General, he got it from your mother, you m-----f---er!"

African-American sergeant E. G. McConnell, probably in 1944, quoted in Potter, Liberators, *177.*

When I heard about it, I said I'd be damned if I'd wear the same patch [that black soldiers] did. After that first day when we saw how they fought I changed my mind. They're just like any of the other boys to us.

> *White South Carolina platoon sergeant, probably in 1944, in Byers, "Negro in Military Service," 174.*

Don't mention my name in the paper please. For they would lynch me if they knew I was writing to a newspaper about this.

> *Black soldier, letter to* The Chicago Defender, *January 9, 1944, quoted in McGuire,* Taps for a Jim Crow Army, *89.*

It was to my amazement, a short time ago, when I had the opportunity of visiting the German . . . [POW] camp here at [Camp] Barkeley [Texas] to observe a sign in the latrine, actually segregating a section of the latrine for Negro soldiers, the other being used by the German prisoners and the white soldiers.

> *African-American private Bert B. Babero, February 13, 1944, letter to the civilian aide to the secretary of war, quoted in McGuire,* Taps for a Jim Crow Army, *51.*

Throughout the area, military authorities have intervened to see that business places, such a beer gardens[,] serve either white or Negro soldiers, and have used their "Off Limits" rule to enforce the Edict. The result? In each town one might find one or two Negro owned "joints" where Negro soldiers and officers must go after hours for recreation. In every other place if a Negro goes in he's told, "We don't serve colored." Throughout the large town of San Bernardino, California, up to a few weeks ago, signs were posted on the window of many business places "WE CATER TO WHITE TRADE ONLY." Those signs were removed at the request of a Priest, a Rabbi, and a Negro clergyman. The army never once attempted to remove this public insult.

> *"Negro Soldier," letter of June 2, 1944, to African-American Dr. Adam Clayton Powell, Jr., quoted in McGuire,* Taps for a Jim Crow Army, *54–55.*

Two [white] paratroopers came into the barracks last night, down stairs where I sleep. When we woke up he was between my bed and another girls [sic]. He woke her up kissing her. She screamed and I jumped out of bed. The rest of them did the same. He and his buddy ran out so fast it was impossible to do anything about it. . . . Well last night about 25 paratroopers came in our area and grabbed two colored boys and started dragging them down the road. The girls all ran out with broomsticks, rocks and bottles and ran after them through the woods but they never did turn the two boys loose. So they called the boys company. So the whole company came racing over in trucks, jeeps and what not. . . . They searched the woods high and low. I didn't know if they found the boys or not. After that 4 car loads of M.P.'s came over to guard, as they said, but only stayed about one hour. Well about 2 A.M. the paratroopers came back in taxes [sic] or, got out and made a rush on our barracks again. This time we came out with knives and sticks, beat them off and alarmed the whole camp. . . . Well after that round we stayed up all night, piled our foot-lockers to the door and stood guard until morning.

> *African-American WAC, letter of ca. July 1944, quoted in McGuire,* Taps for a Jim Crow Army, *25–26.*

I interviewed once a wonderful man named William Barber, who was the first black motorman in the history of the Philadelphia transit system. He told me that when he got the chance through the FEPC to take the exam, he was so proud, he scored a 95; he knew he was going to be a pioneer for his race. But the first morning when he went out to train to become a motorman there were no buses running, no cars, no trolleys, the whole system was paralyzed. He put the radio on and discovered that all 10,000 white workers had gone on strike that day because he, the first black man, was joining the force. So for three or four days all of Philadelphia's mass transit was shut down, people couldn't get to the war production centers. But Roosevelt had extraordinary powers when war production was being interrupted. He moved brilliantly and simply at this moment. He sent a telegram to each one of the striking workers and told them that if they were not back to work on Monday they would all be drafted on Tuesday morning. They came back to work on Monday. William Barber became the first black motorman in the history of Philadelphia's mass transit system.

> *Doris Kearns Goodwin, Landon Lecture, Kansas State University, April 22, 1997. Available online.*

If this could happen here, it could happen anywhere. It could happen to me. It could happen to black folks in America. . . . I often wonder what I would have done if, in 1939, my family and I had been caught up in this and for all those years nobody, but nobody, would help us. I would have been a bitter man . . . and

I thought about how many times my people were lynched and mistreated across this country and nobody raised a voice.

African American Leon Bass of the 18th Battalion of Combat Engineers describing his participation in the liberation of Buchenwald, April 1945, quoted in Potter, Liberators, *219.*

When we reached Steyr [in early May 1945], we started cleaning our tanks because we heard that the war was just about over. And these Germans or Austrians were coming across the bridge in droves. It was like the closer the Russians were getting, the more people were coming across. And then, all of a sudden, we had orders to stop them. No more Germans could come across. And that's when the Russians finally came. And I'll never forget: a big Russian broad shouting, "America! America! America!" Damn near broke my ribs hugging on me. And I have never seen it written anywhere that blacks were there when our soldiers met the Russians.

African-American staff sergeant Leonard "Smitty" Smith, May 1945, quoted in Potter, Liberators, 252–253.

When the thing broke up, we were forming up a convoy to go, and one of our sergeants didn't form up with us. We sent somebody back to get him. He came out, and there was this big Russian sergeant—a woman—all over him. And I was yelling, "For Christ's sake, speed it up! What's the matter with you!" And he came over to me and he says, "Colonel, you have no idea what I did for my country tonight."

Lt. Col. Paul Bates, commander of the black 761st Tank Battalion, describing the American meeting with the Russians in early May 1945, quoted in Potter, Liberators, 255.

When the United States Army War College published its report in 1925 that purported to be an analysis of the "physical, mental, psychological qualities and characteristics of the Negro as a subspecies of the human family" and concluded that Negroes are inferior,

Members of the 99th Fighter Squadron of the Army Air Forces, an all-black unit, are at the Anzio, Italy, beachhead, ca. February 1944. *(National Archives, 80-G-54413)*

ignorant, and immoral, promiscuous, deceitful, and thievish. And so on, ad nauseam.

When I was ordered to leave the officers club at Selfridge Field in Michigan.

When 101 African American officers were placed under arrest only because they attempted to enter the officers club at Freeman Field in Indiana.

When German prisoners of war, soldiers of America's enemy, could use all the facilities at the post exchange at Walterboro, South Carolina, and I, an American citizen who had fought the Nazis to defend America, could not, C-o-u-l-d n-o-t. COULD NOT!

When a U.S. Army Air Corps major general told me, and hundreds of American troops under his command, that because of our color, our ethnic ancestry, we were not ready to fight and fly for our country.

African-American Tuskegee Airman Lt. Col. Charles W. Dryden, USAF (Retired), answering the question "When was America not lovely to you?" on his experiences from 1925 through the war years, in Dryden, A-Train, *392.*

9

Victory: The Enemy
January 13, 1942–
April 28, 1952

The Occupation of Germany

Whereas the other Allies left the occupation of Japan almost entirely to the United States, they quarreled over the occupation of Germany. They agreed that Germany must be demilitarized and punished for the suffering it had inflicted on millions of Europeans, including its own Jewish citizens and dissidents. They agreed that it must never again be allowed to threaten the peace of the world. But they did not agree on how to achieve these goals. They left hanging such basic questions as reparations and the economic recovery of Germany.

Indeed, the government and people of the United States themselves could not agree on these matters. The Morgenthau plan developed by the secretary of the treasury in 1944 called for harsh treatment: the internationalization of the heavily industrial Ruhr, Bremen, Kiel, and Frankfurt; the forced labor of German personnel outside Germany by way of reparations; and the dismantling of all industrial and mining equipment so as to transform Germany into a pastoral country. Opponents of the plan argued that such treatment would not only evoke the kind of bitterness that had caused World War II but also cripple the economic recovery of all of western Europe. Although the Morgenthau plan was never a part of Anglo-American policy and was disavowed by President Harry S. Truman in July 1945, it influenced both international agreements and basic U.S. policy in Germany, as embodied in JCS 1067, the directive of the Joint Chiefs of Staff to the military governor of the American zone of Germany. The plan contributed to the decision to dismantle German industries, decentralize large business cartels, abolish the military, and divide Germany into four occupation zones.[1]

Wartime planning among Great Britain, the Union of Soviet Socialist Republics (USSR), and the United States had divided Germany into three zones of occupation, a plan modified in February 1945 to include a French zone. Berlin, located in the Soviet zone, was also divided into zones occupied by the same four powers. Theoretically an Allied Control Commission constituted of the commanders of the four zones would control all Germany, molding it into one economic unit, but in fact the zones came to resemble independent countries, blocking the passage of goods and people from one zone to another.

Technically, command of the U.S. zone was given first to Gen. Dwight D. Eisenhower and then in October 1945 to Gen. Joseph T. McNarney, but both delegated the work and the responsibility to Gen. Lucius D. Clay. He faced an awesome task. The zone comprised Hesse, Bavaria, the northern half of Baden-Württemberg, and the southern part of Greater Berlin. War's end had left it in chaos. Allied bombing had inflicted heavy damage on German cities, and Hitler's scorched-earth policy had destroyed not only viaducts and large bridges but even footbridges over streams. The food supply, transport, and mail systems had all broken down, and the government had collapsed. In the latter half of 1945, millions of people of German descent expelled from the countries of central and eastern Europe were flooding in. Millions of slave laborers from other countries had to be repatriated.

Moreover, Clay had personnel problems, both military and civilian. The eagerness of Americans to have the men who had served in wartime back home had caused U.S. military forces to deteriorate to the point, Clay said, that "they were nothing but young high school boys not wanting to be there." He found that Treasury Department occupation teams included communists or sympathizers who proved hard to get rid of.[2]

Clay recognized at once that JCS 1067 was unworkable: "If you followed it literally you couldn't have done anything to restore the German economy. If you couldn't restore the German economy you could never hope to get paid for the food they had to have. By virtue of these sorts of things it was modified constantly; not officially, but by allowing this deviation and that deviation."[3] For instance, by December 1945 the State Department had stopped dismantling industry in the U.S. zone.[4] Again, the practicalities forced Clay to seek authority, granted in 1946, to bring food into Germany and sell it for German marks, which he could then use at his discretion to help pay the costs of the occupation or to aid the Germany economy. Similarly, efforts to "denazify" Germany by forbidding Nazis to hold either public office or important private jobs stumbled over actualities. Millions of Germans had belonged to Nazi organizations, even if only for leisure-time activities. Among these were many of the people best qualified by training and experience to run government and industry.

With a promptness that startled even liberal political scientists, Clay turned responsibility over to Germans. "We created their little German governments," he said. "We had local elections the first year, in September. Everybody said they would be failures. They weren't failures. They got out, voted and elected their own officials. We turned the government of those towns, villages and cities back to the Germans right away. At this level we would have had no control over our own [administrators]. We had much better control over the German officials than we would over the type of people that we could get to stay there to run a town or city."[5]

At the same time that he was trying to bring some semblance of order into chaos, to get the zone up and running again, Clay was dealing with the malfunctioning of the Allied Control Commission and of the agreements it had made. For example the commission, in recognition of the enormous losses suffered by the USSR, had promised that nation reparations from the western zones in return for 15 percent of the agricultural products of the Russian zone. However, the USSR was secretly removing industrial equipment from its own zone and still demanding reparations from the western zones even as it refused to give West Germany food. Clay accordingly refused in the spring of 1946 to ship more factories and equipment to the USSR.

Facing such conflicts, the United States moved to hasten German economic recovery and political restoration. Speaking in Stuttgart on September 6, 1946, Secretary of State James Byrnes gave Germans new hope when he said that "Germany must be given a chance to export goods in order to import enough to make her economy self-sustaining. Germany is a part of Europe and recovery in Europe, and particularly in the states adjoining Germany, will be slow indeed if Germany with her great resources of iron and coal is turned into a poorhouse."[6] In May 1949 the German Federal Republic was formed—but it included only the three western zones. That month the Russian zone became the communist German Democratic Republic. For by then the wartime Allies were waging a full-blown "cold war"—a political and economic war—among themselves.

The Cold War: The Truman Doctrine, the Marshall Plan, and NATO

At the end of World War II, the fragile alliance between the Communists and the other Allies broke down, and East and West became enemies. This conflict began on February 9, 1946, with USSR premier Joseph Stalin's declaration that communism and capitalism were incompatible and that another war was inevitable. A month later British prime minister Winston Churchill in a speech at Westminster College in Fulton, Missouri, declared, "[A]n iron curtain has descended across the Continent. Behind that line lie all the capitals of the ancient states of Central and Eastern Europe. Warsaw, Berlin, Prague, Vienna, Budapest, Belgrade, Bucharest and Sofia; all these famous cities and the populations around them lie in what I must call the Soviet sphere," and warned, "Except in the British Commonwealth and in the United States where Communism is in its infancy, the Communist parties or fifth columns constitute a growing challenge and peril to Christian civilization."[7]

From then on for almost half a century the Western powers strove to block the spread of communism, while the USSR seized every opportunity to extend its dominion over satellite states and to encourage communism wherever it could—with notable success in China in 1949. On March 12, 1947, Truman initiated what became known as the Truman Doctrine—the policy of extending U.S. aid to countries in danger of falling under Soviet domination—by asking Congress to help Greece and Turkey. Their governments were deeply flawed, he acknowledged, but their survival was necessary to the security of the

United States. Greece must be protected against communist-led terrorist activities that defied its government's authority. Turkey's national integrity was essential to the preservation of order in the Middle East.

Later that spring in a speech at Harvard University on June 5, Secretary of State General George C. Marshall laid forth an even more extensive program of aid, the European Recovery Program, which became known as the Marshall Plan. "It is logical," he told his audience and the world, "that the United States should do whatever it is able to do to assist in the return of normal economic health in the world, without which there can be no political stability and no assured peace. Our policy is directed not against any country or doctrine but against hunger, poverty, desperation, chaos. Its purpose should be the revival of a working economy in the world so as to permit the emergence of political and social conditions in which free institutions can exist." He proposed offering up to $20 billion for relief, with the proviso that each European nation agree on a rational plan on how to use the money and goods. The money was to be spent on American goods to be shipped on American merchant vessels. (Marshall also proposed offering aid to the communist nations of Europe, but—perhaps fortunately for the acceptance of the plan in the United States—Stalin refused.) Working in close cooperation with Truman, Marshall laid on the line the enormous prestige that had accrued to him during the war to lobby this program through Congress.

The Marshall Plan, which by 1953 had cost the United States $13 billion,[8] turned out to be the most successful foreign aid program in U.S. history, not only as a humanitarian achievement, but also as a means of restoring Western Europe as a U.S. customer and as a bulwark against USSR imperialism and communist subversion. By demanding that the European nations agree on how to spend the aid, the plan encouraged European economic unification. It also speeded up the reintegration into the European community of West Germany, which the plan included.

In 1948 the USSR challenged the presence of the western powers in Berlin by blockading the city, a move that the United States defeated by an airlift of supplies so intensive that for more than 300 days a plane landed every three minutes around the clock.[9] In a further move against European instability and Soviet expansionism, Belgium, Canada, Denmark, France, Iceland, Italy, Luxembourg, the Netherlands, Norway, Portugal, the United Kingdom, and the United States created the North Atlantic Treaty Organization (NATO). In this treaty, signed on April 4, 1949, they pledged to strive to establish a just and lasting peaceful European order, and together to resist attack against any member. Greece and Turkey joined in 1952, the Federal Republic of Germany in 1955, and Spain in 1982. Originally NATO had no military force, but the outbreak of the Korean War provoked its formation.

In the context of the cold war, President Truman saw the invasion of South Korea by North Korea on June, 25, 1950, as not only a violation of a treaty that set the dividing point between the communist North and the more-or-less democratic South but also part of a worldwide communist offensive. Believing it was the duty of the United States as a member of the United Nations to resist, he sent troops to join in the defense of South Korea. This war dragged on for years, narrowly escaping escalating into a major conflict with China, but in the end the dividing line of 1950 was maintained with only slight modifications, and both the United Nations and NATO were strengthened. The armistice was finally signed on July 27, 1953.

The Occupation of Japan

The U.S. occupation of Japan seethed with contradictions. First and foremost, the proclaimed American aim of democratizing and demilitarizing the country conflicted with the perceived need to limit the spread of communism. Second, the job of democratizing and demilitarizing was put in the hands of Gen. Douglas MacArthur, a soldier of authoritarian temperament, who was committed to keeping the Japanese emperor and exonerating him from blame for Japanese war crimes. Third, democracy was imposed on the country in a kind of forced revolution. Fourth, efforts to democratize and demilitarize got in the way of economically stabilizing the country. As a result, beginning in 1947 the democratic reforms achieved during the early part of the occupation gradually gave way to efforts to stabilize the country economically, to integrate it into world markets, and to rearm it as an ally of the United States.

Inevitably in this paradoxical situation one American effort undermined and limited the other. The Japanese, particularly the old industrial establishment, seized the opportunities this confusion offered to replicate elements of the old order. In the end the Americans and the Japanese between them created a hybrid society, far more peace-valuing and less authoritarian than before the war, but also far more conservative and less democratic than the United States had envisioned at war's end.

Both faced a formidable task, for the war had left almost nine million Japanese homeless[10] and millions more near starvation. Probably about a quarter of the country's wealth had been destroyed. Rural living standards were estimated to have fallen to 65 percent of prewar levels and nonrural to about 35 percent.[11] A black market flourished with the assistance of corrupt officials. From 1945 until 1948 more than 650,000 people contracted cholera, dysentery, typhoid, paratyphoid, smallpox, epidemic typhus, scarlet fever, diphtheria, epidemic meningitis, polio, or encephalitis, of whom 99,654 reportedly died.[12]

A Red Cross clubmobile stands ready to serve on Okinawa.
(Collection of Mildred Corey)

The thousands of Koreans and other Asians the Japanese had held prisoner needed repatriation, and in the other direction so did some 6.5 million Japanese, both military and civilian, who had been employed in the occupation of other Asian countries.[13]

Japan was ill-prepared to handle the problems of its own and alien populations, for it had little tolerance for aliens and no strong tradition of responsibility toward strangers and victims of misfortune. Wrapped in their own misery, shocked and despondent over losing the war, many Japanese did not welcome their own returning veterans outside their own group, especially if the veterans were disabled. Equally, they had little sympathy to spare for the victims of the atom bombs, for war orphans, and for homeless children.

The United States, to which the other Allies left the job of occupation, established a Supreme Command of Allied Powers (SCAP) embodied in Gen. Douglas MacArthur. Allegedly fancying himself as a candidate for the U.S. presidency and determined to prove himself fit to run a country, he set about fashioning an antiwar Japanese democracy.

The United States did not intend to finance the rebuilding of the Japanese economy; the $2 billion of aid it furnished took the form of necessities to keep people alive. Nonetheless SCAP instituted economic reforms. It distributed land ownership, limiting the size of holdings and making the land thus freed available on easy terms. It designated some 1,100 Japanese enterprises for reparations to other Asian countries.[14] It tried, with little success, to break up the *Zaibatsu,* the oligarchy that had controlled finance and industry. And it encouraged unions, even for government employees, until union activity began to threaten law and order.

Red Cross Club and Recreation Supervisor Mildred Corey (left) talks with other workers on Okinawa, 1945. *(Collection of Mildred Corey)*

Red Cross supervisor Mildred Corey
had her quarters here on Okinawa.
(*Collection of Mildred Corey*)

Politically, SCAP persuaded the Japanese Diet (parliament) to adopt a constitution providing for a parliamentary system in which the emperor would be transformed from a demigod into a symbol of national unity. It included guarantees of due process and equality under the law with no discrimination because of race, creed, sex, social status, or family origin; universal suffrage; freedom of religion,[15] assembly, association, and speech; and equal opportunity for education "correspondent to ability." In the constitution the Japanese renounced "war as a sovereign right of the nation and the threat or use of force as means of settling international disputes," promising that "land, sea, and air forces, as well as other war potential, will never be maintained," though Japanese modifications of wording made these pledges ambiguous. The Japanese also eliminated equal protection under the law for resident aliens.

Progress toward democratization and demilitarization was soon undermined, partly by the machinations of Japanese conservatives, partly by a conflict between the principles of democracy and the methods (censorship, denial of the right to strike) employed by SCAP, but mainly by a shift in U.S. policy brought about by the cold war. American fears of the Soviet Union and of communism were mounting, particularly after the Communist Chinese drove out the Chinese Nationalist government of Gen. Chiang Kai-shek to Formosa (Taiwan). The State Department Policy Planning Staff came to believe that Japan must be made the dominant nation in Asia and a trading partner of the United States. Accordingly, beginning in 1947, SCAP was instructed to shift the emphasis from reform to economic recovery, and bank president Joseph Dodge was sent to Japan to stabilize the economy by such methods as curbing inflation and domestic spending, forcing the Japanese government to budget for a surplus, and promoting exports. In the process the labor movement was weakened and many employees lost their jobs.

The trend toward the right accelerated with the outbreak of the Korean War. The United States was now set on making Japan an ally in the cold war and a bulwark in the Pacific not only economically but also militarily. In July 1950, far from urging demilitarization, SCAP authorized and trained a Japanese National Police Reserve—in effect a little army with artillery, tanks, and aircraft—whose numbers were limited to 75,000 only at the insistence of the Japanese. Thereafter the Japanese resisted U.S. requests for a 300,000–325,000-man force.[16]

In September 1951 the peace treaty was signed at San Francisco between Japan on the one had and the United States and 47 other Allied nations on the other—but not by the communist countries. At the same time the United States demanded that Japan sign a bilateral treaty agreeing to many more U.S. military bases than the Japanese had anticipated, as well as a promise by Japan to rearm further. The Japanese acceded reluctantly. The peace treaty took effect on April 28, 1952, ending the occupation and restoring full independence to Japan.

The War Crimes Trials

Throughout the war, the Allies had warned Germany and Japan repeatedly that at its end they would punish those guilty of war crimes—such as the German genocide of the Jews, the torture and massacre of conquered civilians, and the enslaving of foreign workers, and such as the Japanese cruelties to other Asian peoples and to prisoners of war. Never again could those countries be allowed to inflict suffering on so many or to hurl the world into war by their aggressions. But among the Allies and within the United States, people disagreed on whom to punish and how. The political and industrial leaders bore ultimate responsibility, some said, and making them bear the brunt would ensure that they could not again militarize their countries. But, others argued, the people who obeyed their orders to commit atrocities shared the guilt, as, indeed, did their country people who had tolerated them and the sickening crimes they had committed.

Some would have the Allied military execute the guilty as soon as they were captured, after drumhead courts-martial. Others wanted full-fledged formal trials that would establish new international law. Robert Jackson, the American lead prosecutor, argued that the Kellogg-Briand Pact of August 17, 1928, had outlawed war: "The thing that led us to take sides in this war was that we regarded Germany's resort to war as illegal from its outset, as an illegitimate attack on the international peace and order."[17]

Ultimately in both Germany and Japan much-publicized trials were held of the Axis leaders, and thereafter a series of trials of those in less influential positions. Sheer numbers made these expensive to conduct and difficult to staff. Interest in punishment waned as people strove to forget the war and get on with their lives. Military governments found that to ensure a rapid recovery they needed the help of some of the Germans and Japanese who were guilty of war crimes as defined in the indictments. In the end, some who had opposed the Nazis and the militarist Japanese lost their positions and livelihoods, while many who were undoubtedly guilty escaped punishment. Yet if it was to any extent true, as most Germans claimed, that they had not known of the horrors committed by their government, the trials presented them with irrefutable evidence. Moreover, the trials took another step toward the goal of outlawing aggressive war.

GERMANY

The London Conference of August 8, 1945, among the Allies who had warred against Germany chartered an International Military Tribunal to try citizens of the enemy nations for crimes against peace, war crimes, and crimes against humanity. The conference named as defendants 24 men and six organizations who were tried at Nuremberg, Germany, from November 20, 1945, to October 1, 1946, before a tribunal of eight, two each from France, Great Britain, the USSR, and the United States. The accused included the highest-ranking Nazi officials who had not followed Hitler's example by killing themselves or otherwise evaded capture, an anti-Semitic journalist, a financier, two generals, and two admirals.

Those who conducted the trials endeavored to make them fair, though many worried about holding the accused guilty for acts that had not specifically been forbidden before they were committed. Germans protested the concept of collective guilt; they argued that members of other nations had also committed atrocities; and they claimed it unjust to be tried in a court where the judges and prosecutors were all Allies while the defense lawyers were German. The defense lawyers did indeed face a formidable-to-impossible task, handicapped by their lack of knowledge of Anglo-American law, lack of access to Allied files, lack of experience in cross-examination as practiced in the United States, and difficulties in getting affidavits from witnesses scattered across Europe. Yet an outraged world that had never conceived of any government's committing such sadistic tortures and mass murders demanded punishment. Flawed though they were, the trials certainly were far more fair than those conducted by the Nazis.

One defendant hanged himself while awaiting trial; 11 were sentenced to death and others to imprisonment; and Nazi vice-chancellor Franz von Papen, the sole defendant found not guilty, was later tried and sentenced to imprisonment by a German court. Of the organizations on trial, the General Staff and High Command was found not guilty, on the grounds that it was not a group or organization, but the court adjudged its members responsible for the misery and suffering of millions. Similarly the Nazi cabinet was termed not an organization after 1937, and the SA (Sturmabteilung)—party activists of the early days of Nazism—was shown to have lost significance after 1934. The guilty verdicts for the other organizations made membership in them a criminal offense, though members could try to show that they had joined involuntarily. The rolls of the organizations found guilty included a quarter to a half of the German population.

Thousands of other Germans were tried by courts in many different Allied countries, by the military governments of the occupying powers, and by Germany itself. Trial after trial resulted in yet more indictments, as the terrible evidence accumulated.

Enemy civilians are forced to remove the bodies of concentration camp victims for decent burial at Gusen Concentration Camp near Linz, Austria, May 12, 1945. The prisoners had been forced to labor in nearby stone quarries until they were too weak to work and then were killed. *(National Archives, 111-SC-204811)*

JAPAN

In Tokyo an 11-nation tribunal tried 28 defendants. The trial centered on charges of conspiracy to wage aggressive war, for this tribunal had jurisdiction only over defendants accused of offenses that included crimes against peace, although some of them were also charged with conventional war crimes (such as the execution of prisoners of war) and/or crimes against humanity. The emperor was never indicted, not because he was thought innocent but because MacArthur firmly believed him necessary to the preservation of order. Indeed, although many precautions were taken to ensure a fair trial, the testimony against the accused may have been skewed by loyalty to the emperor and by MacArthur's determination to protect him.

One of the defendants in the Tokyo trial deteriorated mentally to the point that he could not stand trial, two died during the trial, seven were executed, and the rest received prison terms.

As in Germany, other trials followed—in civilian courts, by courts-martial, and by military commissions. The latter allowed the defendants counsel and the production of evidence for the defense but denied them the protection of the procedural rules and safeguards provided in civil trials and courts-martial; military officers, usually with no legal training, sat as judges. Such a commission condemned to death Gen. Tomoyuki Yamashita, appalling many military officers, for he was hanged solely because as a commander he tolerated unspeakable conduct, including murder, whether knowingly or not.

In all the war crimes trials conducted by the United States, Great Britain, Australia, the Netherlands, France, the Philippines, and China, some 5,600 Japanese were prosecuted, of whom 4,400 were convicted and about 1,000 executed.[18]

Although most observers found the trials of the Japanese fair, the Japanese, unlike the Germans, never as a people confronted their aggressive past and the war crimes their leaders and soldiers had committed. Just as their emperor evaded saying that Japan had lost the war, just as MacArthur circumvented the question of the emperor's guilt, so the Japanese as a nation have avoided thinking about their responsibility for the anguish that millions suffered in Word War II.

CHRONICLE OF EVENTS

1942

January 13: Representatives of nine German-occupied countries denounce the German "regime of terror" and declare that they will punish war criminals.

mid-1942: The U.S. War Department establishes a school of military government.

October 7: Fifteen Allied nations establish the War Crimes Commission.

November: President Franklin D. Roosevelt (FDR) assigns the State Department authority over liberated territories.

1943

March 1: The U.S. Joint Chiefs of Staff (JCS) assume responsibility for training occupation officials.

November 2: The Moscow Declaration promises the trial of war criminals.

November 28–December 1: The Tehran Conference considers Germany's possible dismemberment.

1944

January: The European Advisory Commission (EAC)—set up by the United States, Great Britain, and the USSR—makes postwar plans.

April: An Anglo-American Combined Chiefs of Staff (CCS) plans military occupation strategy.

August: The U.S. State Department rejects the idea of partitioning Germany.

September: U.S. Secretary of the Treasury Henry Morgenthau, Jr., presents a plan to pastoralize Germany.

September: FDR approves Joint Chiefs of Staff Directive 1067 (JCS1067).

September 12: The EAC agrees to divide Germany into three zones of occupation.

November 11: The EAC adds France to the commission.

1945

February 4–11: At Yalta the United States, Great Britain, and the USSR agree to dismember Germany, if necessary for world peace.

May 8: Germany surrenders.

May 11: Truman approves a revised "Directive to Commander-in-Chief of U.S. Forces of Occupation

Field Marshall Wilhelm Keitel signs ratified surrender terms for the German Army at Soviet headquarters in Berlin, May 7, 1945. *(Library of Congress, Signal Corps Photo)*

Regarding the Military Government of Germany" (JCS 1067).

June 11–July 5: The western zones authorize German political parties.

July 3: Truman disavows the Morgenthau plan to pastoralize Germany.

July 7: The American Military Government in Germany (AMGOT) directs that all high-level civil servants who joined the Nazi party before May 1, 1937, be removed from office.

August 14: Japan surrenders.

August 15: Gen. Douglas MacArthur becomes supreme commander in Japan for the Allied Powers (SCAP).

October: An AMGOT public opinion survey unit begins operations in Germany.

October 1: The Allied Control Council (ACC) lifts the ban on fraternization in Germany.

October 4: A SCAP directive removes restrictions of political, civil, and religious liberties and discrimination on grounds of race, nationality, creed, or political opinion.

October 11: MacArthur orders Japan to institute woman suffrage, promote labor unions, and democratize the economy.

November 14–October 1, 1946: War crimes trials are held in Nuremberg, Germany.

December 12: AMGOT creates the German states of Bavaria, Greater Hesse, and Württemberg-Baden.

December 15: SCAP establishes the principle of the separation of religion and state.

1946

January 1: Japanese emperor Hirohito denies that he is a god in the Western sense but continues to claim descent from the sun goddess.

January 4: SCAP excludes from office seven categories of Japanese "militarists" or "ultranationalists," thus disqualifying about 90 percent of the existing members of the Diet; 200 members of the conservative Progressive party; almost 400 top officials in the Ministry of Home Affairs; and most ranking public servants in office between July 1937 and September 1945.

February: The United States starts a German-operated radio station in West Berlin.

February 9: Soviet premier Joseph Stalin declares that communism and capitalism are incompatible and that another war is inevitable.

March 5: In the "iron-curtain" speech in Fulton, Missouri, Churchill warns against communist expansionism.

March 5: The German states of Bavaria, Württemberg-Baden, and Hesse call for the trial of some 3.5 million Germans.

March 26: The ACC limits Germany's industrial production.

March 30: A *Report of the United States Education Mission to Japan* recommends a new philosophy, procedures, and structure for Japanese schools.

April 10: Women win 39 seats in the Japanese Diet.

May 3: The Tokyo trials of 28 accused war criminals begin.

June 29: The United States admits alien fiancées or fiancés of members of the U.S. armed forces.

September 6: Secretary of State James Byrnes calls for a self-sustaining German economy as necessary to European well-being and promises that "as long as any other foreign country's troops are in Germany we're going to be there."

1947

The U.S. House Un-American Activities Committee (HUAC) conducts hearings on alleged communist activity.

January: AMGOT creates the state of Bremen.

January: SCAP purges some wartime executives and removes thousands of public officials and candidates from politics.

January 31: MacArthur forbids a general strike in Japan.

March 12: Truman promulgates the Truman Doctrine, designed to contain communism.

May 3: The new Japanese Constitution goes into effect, replacing the Meiji Constitution of 1889.

July: The Paris Economic Conference institutes the European Recovery Program (Marshall Plan) of 1948–51.

July 11: JCS 1779, emphasizing Europe's need for stability and productivity in Germany, replaces JCS 1067.

November: AMGOT restores to the original owners property confiscated by the Nazis.

1948

March 19: The ACC ceases to function.

April 16: Seventeen European countries establish the Organization of European Economic Cooperation to assist developing countries.

June: The German currency is reformed, a necessary step toward economic revival.

June 24: The USSR cuts surface traffic to and from West Berlin. Until September 1949 the United States operates an airlift to sustain the city.

July 31: Japan forbids public servants, including teachers, to strike.

December: The United Nations (UN) General Assembly passes the Convention on the Prevention and Punishment of the Crime of Genocide.

December 20: The U.S. Supreme Court refuses to hear an appeal in the Tokyo war crimes trial, saying that it has no jurisdiction.

1949

January 1: The United States recognizes the new Republic of Korea.

February 1: The Dodge Plan for anti-inflationary economic recovery is instituted in Japan.

April 4: The United States, Canada, Belgium, Denmark, France, Great Britain, Iceland, Italy, Luxembourg, the Netherlands, Norway, and Portugal establish the North Atlantic Treaty Organization (NATO).

May 12: Stalin calls off the blockade of Berlin.

May 12: The Allied powers approve the establishment of a new German Federal Republic.

May 30: In the Soviet zone a People's Congress adopts a constitution for the German Democratic Republic.

June–September: SCAP orders wholesale purges of communists from Japanese educational institutions, government, labor, politics, and industry.

September 23: Truman announces that the USSR has exploded an atomic bomb.

1950

January 31: Truman announces the decision to build the hydrogen bomb.

February 9: Senator Joseph R. McCarthy claims that communists in the U.S. State Department control U.S. foreign policy, beginning a career of baseless accusations that destroy reputations and livelihoods.

April: John Foster Dulles of the U.S. State Department advocates a separate bilateral security treaty between the United States and Japan.

June 24: Communist North Korea invades South Korea, initiating a war that does not end until the armistice of July 27, 1953.

June 25: The UN Security Council calls for the immediate cessation of hostilities and withdrawal of North Korean forces to the 38th parallel.

June 26: The United States supports the UN resolution of June 25.

June 27: Truman orders U.S. forces to support the South Korean government.

July: SCAP authorizes and trains a Japanese "National Police Reserve"—in effect a little army.

November 1: Chinese Communist troops have entered the Korean War.

1951

April 11: Truman relieves MacArthur of all his commands for failing to support U.S. and UN policies.

April 19: MacArthur addresses a joint session of Congress and is mentioned as a potential presidential nominee.

June 25: Truman announces his willingness to negotiate a settlement of the Korean War, as the USSR has recently proposed.

September: The United States and 47 other Allies (but not the communist countries) sign a peace treaty with Japan.

1952

April 28: The occupation of Japan ends.

EYEWITNESS TESTIMONY

The Occupation of Germany

Everywhere [American soldiers] went the impression was exactly the same. The men were easygoing, generous, very much given to liquor and to women. They were very good to children and as a rule in most places were considered extremely gullible. They were taken in conspicuously in Germany where the ordinary people were pretty hard up. American soldiers were abused, swindled, . . . and lied to throughout Germany and to a certain extent in Italy. In England they succeeded the Canadians as favored lovers and seemed to have reached a not totally unjustified conclusion that any woman in England was available.

> *Herbert Pell, former congressman, U.S. minister to Portugal and Hungary, and U.S. representative on the United Nations War Crimes Commission from August 1943 to January 1945, speaking about the war years in England and the occupation years in Italy and Germany, interview, CUOHROC, 554–555.*

[While planning for postwar Germany] we were also very much influenced by the fact that we felt we would still be fighting a war against Japan. . . . We didn't realize that the bombing was going to make the Japanese quit. . . . For this reason, we didn't want to get too involved in Europe. I think we were willing to settle for such less than we would have if it hadn't been for this particular factor.

> *Gen. Lucius D. Clay, U.S. military governor for the American zone of Germany, remembering the late war years, 1974 interview, 4, available online. URL: www.trumanlibrary.org/oralhist/clay1.htm.*

In heart, body, and spirit . . . every German is Hitler! Hitler is the single man who stands for the beliefs of Germans. Don't makes friends with Hitler. Don't fraternize. If in a German town you bow to a pretty girl or pat a blond child . . . you bow to Hitler and his reign of blood.

> *Warning printed in the* Stars and Stripes, *probably in 1945, in line with a soon-to-be-abandoned policy, quoted in Davidson,* Death and Life, *54.*

[The situation in Germany as the war ended] could scarcely be believed by those who saw it—it cannot be appreciated by those who did not. It was [the] Wild West, [the] hordes of Genghis Khan, the Klondike Gold Rush and Napoleon's retreat from Moscow all rolled up into one.

> *Medical officer Lt. Col. Sanford V. Larkey, speaking about spring 1945, quoted in Cowdrey,* Fighting for Life, *280.*

They [Germans accused of war crimes] all had either of two explanations: a) they would have had to fear for their own life if they had refused to carry on, or b) they stayed because if they left a real nazi would take their job. And we had one standard question at the end of each interrogation: "what do you think will happen to you?" And some of the worst mass murderers, like Prince Subheit Veitheim who was the higher SS and Gestapo chief of the city of Kassell later executed in one of the follow-up trials, he had the nerve to say, "I'm completely innocent and I'm trusting in Anglo Saxon jurisprudence, so I'll be vindicated." . . . So at the end of these interrogations like many of my colleagues, I concluded that there had only been one nazi in all of Germany and he was conveniently dead. All the others had been against it.

> *Robert Lochner, who surveyed bomb damage in Germany immediately after the surrender in 1945 and interrogated accused Germans, interview, available online. URL: www.gwu.edu/~nsarchiv/coldwar/ interviews/episode-4/lochner1.html.*

Payment of reparations should leave enough resources to enable the German people to subsist without external assistance.

> *Protocol of Potsdam conference, July–August 1945, quoted in Grosser,* Germany in Our Time, *33.*

It is Saturday afternoon and the soldiers are still there with their frauleins [young German women]. In every park they are thick in couples and in groups on the grass. The first sugar ration for adults since V-E Day has only just been distributed, and the soldiers have plenty of PX supplies. More important, there are few young [male] Germans left. No sugar, no men. Thirty-two percent of the babies born in Bavaria last month were illegitimate.

> New York Times *correspondent Dana Adams Schmidt, May 1946, quoted in Shukert and Scibetta,* War Brides, *132.*

The question is not whether we want the Germans to suffer for their sins. Many of us would like to see them suffer the tortures they have inflicted on others. The only question is whether over the years a group of seventy million educated, efficient, and imaginative people can be kept within bounds on such a low level of subsistence as the [Morgenthau] proposals contemplate. . . . It would be just such a crime as the Germans themselves hoped to perpetrate upon their victims—it would be a crime against civilization itself.

Secretary of War Henry Stimson, 1947, in Stimson
On Active Service, 578.

Everywhere the pressures to give up the fight for freedom are almost irresistible. The fight for survival is so primitive, the submergence of the middle class so general, the individual so helpless, the sense of human dignity so blunted by inhuman transfers of people, the desire for change, and the feeling that any change must be for the better so overwhelming, that it is harder to stand fast than to follow the easier path—toward a Communist dictatorship or reaction. It cannot be said too often that the greatest danger to democracy . . . is the weariness and faltering spirit of democrats. . . .

The extent to which democratic government survives on that continent depends on how far this country is willing to help it survive.

Anne O'Hare McCormick, dispatch to the New York
Times, *February 1947, in Phillips,*
The 1940s, *304–305.*

The Cold War, The Truman Doctrine, the Marshall Plan, and NATO

[T]here can never be on Moscow's side any sincere assumption of a community of aims between the Soviet Union and powers which are regarded as capitalist. It must be invariably assumed in Moscow that the aims of the capitalist world are antagonistic to the Soviet regime. . . . Soviet pressure against the free institutions of the western world is something that can be contained by the adroit and vigilant application of counterforce at a series of constantly shifting geographical and political points corresponding to the shifts and maneuvers of Soviet strategy. . . .

U.S. ambassador to the USSR George B. Kennan,
telegram to the State Department, February 22, 1946,
available online. URL: balrog.sdsu.edu/
~putman/410b/kennan.htm.

In the spring of 1946 I met and became friendly with French socialist Irène Laure; on her first visit to the United States [in 1947] I accompanied her as her interpreter and guide. When I told her that the next day we were to go to the Senate hearings where Gen. George Marshall would testify on his plans for the rebuilding of Europe, she reacted negatively: "He's out to enslave Europe." But . . . hearing Marshall for herself changed her concept of America. . . . Later she expressed her gratitude for this nation, saying, "Twice your young men came to shed their blood on our shores because we Europeans had failed to resolve our differences."

Moral Rearmament international staff member Denise
Wood speaking of spring 1946, unpublished memoir.

One of the primary objectives of the foreign policy of the United States is the creation of conditions in which we and other nations will be able to work out a way of life free from coercion. . . . We shall not realize our objectives, however, unless we are willing to help free peoples to maintain their free institutions and their national integrity against aggressive movements that seek to impose upon them totalitarian regimes. This is no more than a frank recognition that totalitarian regimes imposed on free peoples, by direct or indirect aggression, undermine the foundations of international peace and hence the security of the United States.

President Harry S. Truman, Truman Doctrine address
before a joint session of Congress, March 12, 1947,
available online. URL: trumanlibrary.org.

The remedy lies in breaking the vicious circle and restoring the confidence of the European people in the economic future of their own countries and of Europe as a whole. . . . [It is logical] that the United States should do whatever it is able to do to assist in the return of normal economic health in the world, without which there can be no political stability.

Secretary of State General George Marshall speaking at
the Harvard commencement, June 5, 1947, available
online. URL: usaid.gov/multimedia/video/
marshall/marshallspeech.html.

While I cannot take the time to name all the men in the State Department who have been named as members of the Communist Party and members of a spy ring I have here in my hand a list of 205 that were known to the Secretary of State as being members of the Communist Party and who nevertheless are still working and shaping the policy of the State Department.

Senator Joseph R. McCarthy, speech in Wheeling, West Virginia, February 9, 1950, quoted in Halberstam, The Fifties, 50.

If the Communists were permitted to force their way into the Republic of Korea without opposition from the free world, no small nation would have the courage to resist threats and aggression by stronger Communist neighbors. If this was allowed to go unchallenged, it would mean a third world war, just as similar incidents had brought on the second world war.

President Harry Truman reflecting on the events of June 1950, quoted in McCullough, Truman, 776–777.

[MacArthur's politics of an aggressive stance toward China] would involve us in the wrong war at the wrong place at the wrong time with the wrong enemy.

Gen. Omar Bradley, Chair of the Joint Chiefs, at Senate hearings, summer 1951, quoted in Halberstam, The Fifties, 204.

The Occupation of Japan

[I favored keeping Emperor Hirohito on the throne] because otherwise we would have had nothing but chaos. The religion was gone, the government was gone, and he was the only symbol of control. Now, I know he had his hand in the cookie jar, and he wasn't any innocent little child. But he was of great use to us, and that was the basis on which I recommended to [MacArthur] that we keep him.

Intelligence specialist Brig. Gen. Elliott Thorpe speaking of the occupation years, quoted in Dower, Embracing Defeat, 327.

My Papa almost died with shame when I announced that since I had learned English I would take a job working with the American Army. He started to shout that I could never do such a thing, but Mama was firm and said it was all right but I mustn't fall in love with any of them, for she still didn't trust them completely.

Ryuko Ozawa, sometime during the occupation years, quoted in Shukert and Scibetta, War Brides, 187–188.

Marine Chaplain Edward Brubaker in occupied Japan talks with a Japanese Episcopal priest who acts as his interpreter. *(Collection of Ed Brubaker)*

It didn't take us long to learn we were the new law in Japan. At first, average people were very much afraid of us. . . . They really expected that we would treat them as they had treated the hapless Chinese, Filipinos, Koreans, and other Asians. When we walked down the street, they would stop and kneel until we passed. . . .

We were quartered four men to a room in a former hospital, and when we arrived, a group of ex-Japanese soldiers saluted us, unloaded our trucks, and carried our belongings into our rooms. They continued saluting us for the balance of our stay. We also had cleaning women who bowed to us each time we passed or when they came into our rooms. . . . We soon began feeling like conquerors.

Combat infantryman H. Stanley Huff, who arrived in Japan in September 1945, in Huff, Unforgettable Journey, 190, 198.

I mixed quite thoroughly with German POW's, [*sic*] and now the Japs. I've been to their homes for dinner and crowded into streetcars with them—and I find them as human as any people I've seen.

I don't think I've been taken in too easily. I'm pretty skeptical by nature, but who am I supposed to hate? Can I hate the boy who ran alongside my train window for 50 yards to pay me for a pack of cigarettes that I had sold him just before the train left the station? Can I hate the old man who took us to his home for dinner and made us accept his family heirlooms for souvenirs? Can I hate the kids that run up and throw their arms around me in the street? Or a Jap truck driver who went miles out of his way to drive me home one night? Or the little girl (about 4) who ran up to me and gave me her one and only doll for a present?

Sgt. Richard Leonard, November 3, 1945, quoted in Carroll, War Letters, *318–319.*

My mind has become empty. There is only resentment toward our incompetent government. With five children, I worked hard and even managed to meet the responsibility of saving a little in these hard times, but the government's incompetence regarding food supplies kept getting worse and finally I became unable to work even half the month. . . .

I have resolved to commit suicide. . . . Indirectly, I've asked neighbors and the head of the neighborhood association to look after my wife and children.

Letter signed "A Laborer," November 7, 1945, Asahi *newspaper (Osaka ed.), quoted in Dower,* Embracing Defeat, *97.*

With regard to the Emperor system, it is the opinion of observers especially as far as the middle classes are concerned that the Allies are unduly apprehensive of the effect on the Japanese if the Emperor were removed. It is claimed that at the most there might be demonstrations, particularly in the rural districts, but they would soon pass. People are more concerned with food and housing problems than with the fate of the Emperor.

Report of a U.S. intelligence unit in Tokyo, mid-December 1945, quoted in Dower, Embracing Defeat, *305.*

I ended up in the occupation. We went up and down the coast of southern Kyushu to make the

A Red Cross office on Okinawa *(Collection of Mildred Corey)*

Japanese think there were a lot of ships around. We'd go to Nagasaki, be there for a while, go to Yokohama. I got myself assigned to shore patrol—not regular shore patrol, they're cops, they lock you up. But every ship has its own shore patrol that it puts over when its sailors have liberty. Their job is to see to it that the real shore patrol doesn't do any paper work, because once they start the paper work, they've got your sailor, and there's no replacement for him. Whenever we were in port, I would have liberty one day, and the alternate day I would be on shore patrol. In Nagasaki, where we were more often and for longer than any place else, I talked to the real shore patrol and told them if they ever got a sailor off our ship to come and see me and I would take him away and guarantee he would never be a problem to them again.

Sailor Larry Reeves speaking of late 1945 and 1946, author interview.

I'd say that out of the rest of the list [of some 70 projects] the most important are . . . the study of all Jap companies working in the [Yokosuka] naval yard, control of VD, sisters of the Sacred Heart, the elections coming up, the reparations program, the police department, democratic education, roads, inspections of jails, hospitals, a dial telephone system, a look at the Social Democratic Party . . . and there's more.

Military government official Lt. Comdr. Wallace Higgins to his assistant, June 1946, in Higgins, From Hiroshima with Love, *121.*

Red Cross workers gather outside their donut shop on Okinawa.
(Collection of Mildred Corey)

I returned to Japan from the southern regions on May 20. My house was burned, my wife and children missing. What little money I had quickly was consumed by the high prices, and I was a pitiful figure. Not a single person gave me a kind word. . . . Tormented and without work, I became possessed by a devil.
Letter from an anonymous returning veteran, Asahi *newspaper, June 9, 1946, quoted in Dower,* Embracing Defeat, *60.*

If the conception that government is something imposed upon the people by an outstanding god, great man, or leader is not rectified, democratic government is likely to be wrecked. We fear, the day after MacArthur's withdrawal, that some living god might be searched out to bring the sort of dictatorship that made the Pacific War.
Newspaper editorial, Fiji Shimpo, *October 1946, quoted in Dower,* Embracing Defeat, *406.*

At Autumn Shinto festival, some people were forced to make big contribution by leader of our town. Boss of every street made his followers go house to house to collect ten *yen* in the least and 100 *yen* on basis of people's tax, all of which was spent for sake, food, and dramatic party of which people are now complaining.

I beg of you to investigate the matter and give a most severe punishment for social restraint against these supporters of feudalism who forced people to make a religious contribution.
Japanese citizen's letter to a military government team, October 29, 1946, quoted in Van Staaveren, American in Japan, *133.*

We've got to revise our reparations program to get Japan's economy back on its feet. It is a matter of Japan's survival. . . . [American experts] just completed a[n] exhaustive study of Japanese industry which shows that we just can't take reparations if Japan is ever going to become self-supporting again.
Military government officials, probably in 1947, quoted in Higgins, From Hiroshima with Love, *143, 144.*

Under the authority vested in me as Supreme Commander for the Allied Powers, I have informed the labor leaders, whose unions had federated for the purpose of conducting a general strike, that I will not permit the use of so deadly a social weapon in the present impoverished and emaciated condition of Japan, and have accordingly directed them to desist from the furtherance of such action. . . . While I have taken this measure as one of dire emergency, I do not intend otherwise to restrict the freedom of action heretofore given labor in the achievement of legitimate objectives.
Gen. Douglas MacArthur, January 31, 1947, quoted in Van Staaveren, American in Japan, *110–111.*

This Red Cross clubmobile served U.S. forces on Okinawa.
(Collection of Mildred Corey)

. . . [W]orkers go in a big way for marches, flag-waving, slogans, and listening to orators. When they have to engage in collective bargaining with employers, however, they are lost. So SCAP is distributing much literature on trade unionism so workers will be more knowledgeable about how to settle disputes with employers. This labor education effort is also for the purpose of combating Communism.

Although Socialists and Communists dominate the leadership of the major national trade unions in Tokyo, in this [Yamanashi] prefecture, it is not always clear who is a "Communist." Many citizens . . . are inclined to label as a "Communist" anyone who displays unusual initiative or appears aggressive.

Educator Jacob Van Staaveren, letter, February 10,
1947, in Van Staaveren, American in Japan,
113–114.

The postwar surrender document prepared in Washington by men experienced in Far Eastern Affairs was a very commendable and workable document but its implementation was placed in the hands of young and inexperienced persons who proceeded to carry out the letter and spirit of the directive with great zeal and with many embellishments. This was their great opportunity to prove their theories. The young man who was in complete charge, a virtual dictator, over the vast chemical industry of Japan had never had a days [sic] business experience. He went into the Army directly from college and after being tsar of the chem-

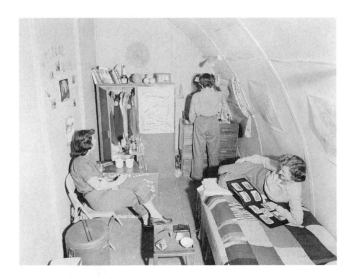

Red Cross workers shelter in this Quonset hut on Okinawa.
(Collection of Mildred Corey)

ical industry three or four years went back to finish college. . . .

One of the greatest mistakes of the occupation was the wholesale "purge" of all capable men in high positions in Banking, Business, Manufacturing, Education, and Government. Under the postwar surrender document it was intended to purge the leading militarists, government officials and those "directly responsible" for leading Japan into war. As implemented by SCAP the purge was extended to include hundred[s] of friends of America who happened to occupy positions of responsibility.

Comdr. Wallace L. Higgins, military governor of
Hiroshima, Japan, writing in 1960 about
the occupation years, quoted in Higgins,
From Hiroshima with Love, *302.*

German War Crimes Trials

Gentlemen, I must ask you to arm yourselves against all feeling of pity. We must annihilate the Jews.

Nazi governor general of Poland Hans Frank, wartime
speech introduced in evidence at the Nuremberg trials,
quoted in Davidson, Death and Life, *111.*

What happens to the Russians, the Czechs, does not interest me in the slightest. What the nations can offer in the way of good blood of our type we will take, if necessary, by kidnapping their children and raising them here with us. Whether the other nations live in prosperity or starve to death interests me only so far as we need them as slaves of our culture; otherwise, it is of no interest to me. Whether 10,000 Russian females fall down from exhaustion while digging an anti-tank ditch or not interests one only insofar as the anti-tank ditch for Germany is finished.

Nazi SS head Heinrich Himmler, speech of October 4,
1943, introduced in evidence at the Nuremberg trials,
quoted in Davidson, Death and Life, *110.*

Those German officers and men and members of the Nazi party. . . . who have been responsible for . . . atrocities, massacres and executions will be sent back to the countries in which their abominable deeds were done in order that they may be judged and punished according to the laws of these liberated countries. The above declaration is without prejudice to the case of the major war criminals whose offenses have no particular geographical localization and who will be punished by the joint decision of the governments of the allies.

Moscow Declaration signed by representatives of the USSR, United States, and Great Britain, November 1, 1943, quoted in Davidson, Trial, 5–6.

It has at all times been the position of the United States that the great industrialists of Germany were guilty of crimes charged in this indictment quite as much as its politicians, diplomats and soldiers.

Robert Jackson, lead prosecutor at the Nuremberg trials 1945–49, quoted in Davidson, Trial, 7.

[The German military leaders'] philosophy is so perverse that they regard a lost war, and a defeated and prostrate Germany, as a glorious opportunity to start again on the same terrible cycle. . . . We are at grips here with something big and evil and durable; something that was not born in 1933, or even 1921. . . . The tree which bore this fruit [human skins being used as lampshades in concentration camps] is German militarism.

American assistant prosecutor Brig. Gen. Telford Taylor, Nuremberg trials 1945–49, quoted in Davidson, Trial, 554.

There shall be established after consultation with the Control Council for Germany an International Military

At the Nuremberg trials, the defendants sit in their dock, ca. 1945–46. *(National Archives, 238-NT-592)*

Tribunal for the trial of war criminals whose offenses have no particular geographical location whether they be accused individually or in their capacity as members of the organizations or groups or in both capacities.

London Agreement signed by representatives of the United States, France, Great Britain, and the USSR, August 8, 1945, available online. URL: yale.edu.lawweb/avalon/imt/proc/imtchart.htm.

A thousand years will pass, and still this guilt of Germany will not be erased.

Former Governor General of Poland and defendant Hans Frank testifying at the Nuremberg trials, April 18, 1946, quoted in Davidson, Trial. *7.*

[The German General Staff and High Command] have been a disgrace to the honorable profession of arms. Without their military guidance the aggressive ambitions of Hitler and his fellow-Nazis would have been academic and sterile. Although they were not a group . . . they were certainly a ruthless military caste. The contemporary German militarism flourished briefly with its recent ally, National Socialism, as well as or better than it had in the generations of the past. Many of these men have made a mockery of the soldier's oath of obedience to military orders. When it suits their defense they say they had to obey; when confronted with Hitler's brutal crimes, which are shown to be within their general knowledge, they say they disobeyed. The truth is that they actively partici-

pated in all these crimes, or sat silent and acquiescent, witnessing the commission of crimes on a scale larger and more shocking than the world has ever had the misfortune to know.

Nuremberg tribunal, finding the German General Staff and High Command not guilty by virtue of not being an organization, 1949, quoted in Davidson, Trial, *563.*

Japanese War Crimes Trials

[The Japanese] had a belief that any enemy of the emperor could not be right, so the more brutally they treated their prisoners, the more loyal to the emperor they were being.

Chaplain Francis P. Scott testifying before the Tokyo War Crimes Tribunal sometime between 1946 and 1948, quoted in Brackman, The Other Nuremberg, *251.*

I am duty bound to see that every Japanese accused of atrocities is given a fair trial. . . . No right-thinking citizen would like to see the Philippines commit a historical blunder through its courts by allowing conviction of innocent people just because they were former enemies.

Filipino chief defense counsel, army captain, in trial of Gen. Shigenori Kuroda, 1947, quoted in Robert Barr Smith, "Justice Under the Sun," 9, available online. URL: www.thehistorynet.com/worldwarII/ articles/0996_text.htm.

10 Victory: At Home
June 1944–November 1952

The end of the war brought a new era all over the world. By best estimate, more than 50 million people had been killed and millions more displaced.[1] Even in the United States, untouched by enemy action, the end of the war found American society changed almost beyond recognition. Its people had gained self-confidence, as a nation they had triumphed, and as individuals they had found themselves capable of doing what they had to do.

Minorities in the United States had also changed. Japanese Americans who had fought for the country and those who had left the camps to take jobs in middle America had grown used to living and working outside the Japanese-American communities in which almost all of them had lived before the war. They now placed less emphasis on their own group, more on the individual. Black servicemen who had experienced life abroad free from prejudice returned with heightened expectations and a deepened sense of their own worth, and with a new determination that would lead to the Civil Rights movement of the 1960s and 1970s. Black workers who had tasted equality of opportunity in the workplace did not willingly subside into ill-paid, dead-end jobs. Thousands of black people had moved north and west.

The black sociologist Charles S. Johnson has written of the "profound and sustained social shock" and the "social upheaval of war"—in race relations and in the lives and thinking of all Americans.[2] War had upset social and economic hierarchies, introduced Americans to their fellows in record numbers, moved them around their country and the world, and changed their concepts of themselves and their abilities. It had submerged their private lives in their public duties. War's end left most of them eager to get on with their private lives.

The Veterans and Their Families

Americans wanted their servicemen back home. Clearly some were still needed in the armies of occupation in the defeated countries. The rest had to await transport. For fairness's sake, the military established a point system that would send home first those who had been prisoners of war, decorated service members, combat troops, those who had served longest, and those whose families most needed them. Service members received one point for each month in the military, one for each month overseas, 12 for each child, five for each battle star earned by their units, and five for a Purple Heart (awarded for a wound in combat). Eighty-five points bought a ticket home. Thanks to the planning of the Armed Forces Committee on Post-War Education for Service Personnel, formed in mid-1943, demobilization proceeded rapidly, so that by September 1945, 25,000 men were discharged daily. Each of them received mustering out pay; additionally, the Armed Forces Leave Act of 1946 provided for terminal leave pay.[3]

The families of the approximately 400,000 Americans who had died had to rebuild their lives without the husbands, fathers, sons, and brothers who would never return.[4] Luckier families had to readjust to the veterans, who had been away from home for years. Their wives and families had had to learn to function without them; now they had to relearn how to function with them—and vice versa. Many a returning veteran did not find the girl he had left behind, but in her stead a strong, independent woman accustomed to making her own decisions and perhaps earning her own living.

Not surprisingly, the postwar divorce rate mounted, climbing from the 1939 rate of 1.9 per 1,000 population to 4.3 in 1946.[5] Some had married hastily and repented in separation. Some were shocked by discoveries of infidelities and of children fathered overseas. The necessity of living with in-laws because of the housing shortage strained relationships. Moreover, divorce was becoming less disgraceful, more socially acceptable.

The British liner *Queen Mary* arrives in New York Harbor, June 20, 1945, with thousands of U.S. troops from European battles. *(National Archives, 80-GK-5645)*

For the families of most servicemen, reunion was a happy ending to the gray years of working and waiting, and a happy beginning for the rest of their lives. For combat veterans and for prisoners of war, reentry was harder. The postwar condition of POWs varied with their wartime treatment. As a group, the prisoners of the Japanese fared much worse than those of the Germans. Their prolonged suffering as POWs from beatings, torture, slave labor, starvation—many lost 40–60 percent of their body weight—and diseases caused by nutritional deficiencies and extreme anxiety inflicted permanent damage on their bodies and minds.[6] For some combat veterans physical and mental disabilities precluded a normal life. Many felt isolated, alienated from everyone but the old comrades who knew what the worst of war was like. Often they did not want their families and friends at home to know such horror, and they themselves wanted to forget, yet at the same time they were angry at their families' lack of understanding. Most tried to take the army's advice to repress the memories and get on with their lives—advice that tallied with their upbringing, which had taught them to keep their troubles to themselves and maintain a stiff upper lip. Still, some of them could not escape the nightmares that haunted their sleep. A 1955 study by the National Academy of Sciences revealed that a third of World War II veterans suffered emotional disorders.[7]

Meanwhile, in the military and Veterans Administration hospitals, the grievously wounded struggled—the paraplegics, the 14,648 amputees,[8] the blind, the men with head wounds that made their brain waves abnormal, and the psychiatric cases. The hospitals offered reconstructive surgery, physical and occupational therapy, education, and training for work, but the men had to rebuild their lives themselves. They did, to a surprising extent—even the victims of severe combat exhaustion. By 1951, according to a study conducted by the National Research Council and the Veterans Administration, of almost a million men diagnosed as psychoneurotics, only 8 percent were severely disabled, and some 85 percent were working.[9]

The American Legion and Veterans of Foreign Wars vigorously recruited the veterans, but many preferred the new Am Vets. Originally titled American Veterans of World War II but later opened to all who served honorably in the U.S. military, this group held its first convention in Chicago in October 1945. Smaller groups of veterans also banded together for mutual support in organizations such as the American Veterans Committee ("Citizens first, veterans second") and the Paralyzed Veterans of America. Others built organizations around their units or ships. Other veterans could not wait to be rid of everything military. A Bill Mauldin cartoon showed a war-worn soldier behind a desk at a discharge depot ironically asking, "Do you want to re-enlist? It says here I gotta ask." Most veterans soon discarded the lapel pins shaped like eagles, evidence of their military service, that they called "ruptured ducks." More mature, more responsible than when they went off to war, now they were ready to set their sights higher, go in new directions, and explore new fields, and their government was ready to help them.

The GI Bill (Servicemen's Readjustment Act of 1944)

Throughout the war, servicemen's advocates worked on the GI Bill. Former Governor John Stelle of Illinois and the American Legion proposed it, and others lobbied it through Congress, among them newspaper owner William Randolph Hearst and activist Cecile Kibre Bosworth.[10] President Roosevelt signed it into law on June 22, 1944. For the first time, the nation treated justly and generously the servicemen and servicewomen who had saved it.

For all veterans, the GI Bill eased the transition into civilian life by providing up to 52 weeks of unemployment compensation at $20 a week. Almost 9 million veterans used this "52-20 club" for shorter or longer periods.[11]

Far more important, the bill educated a generation, including many children of the Great Depression of 1929–41 who had never thought college possible. It subsidized tuition, fees, books, and educational materials and contributed to living expenses. Veterans could attend whatever educational institution would admit them. They leapt at the chance. In 1947 veterans constituted 49 percent of the college population. In the seven years following the war, millions of veterans, including a third of all servicewomen, took advantage of educational opportunities. Two million three hundred thousand veterans went to colleges and universities; another 3,500,000 received school training; and 3,400,000 of them learned on the job.[12] Among them were future presidents and Supreme Court justices of the United States, as well as people who distinguished themselves in every profession: 450,000 engineers; 238,000 teachers; 91,000 scientists; 67,000 doctors; and 22,000 dentists.[13]

The $14 billion spent on veterans' education bore rich returns. Senator Dale Bumpers of Arkansas termed it the best single investment the federal government ever made. The men and women so prepared built a flourishing postwar economy. Their education enabled them to earn more money, and they paid more taxes into the federal treasury. Challenging the old idea that higher education was only for a well-off elite, they also transformed the educational institutions they attended. In the late 1930s about 160,000 U.S. citizens graduated from college each year; by 1950 that number had increased to 500,000.[14] Matured by the war and eager to learn, the veterans inspired their professors and instructors with a new vision of what students could achieve. The nation's schools, colleges, and universities expanded their campuses, student bodies, and course offerings (particularly in business and engineering).

The GI Bill also offered veterans government-guaranteed mortgages. Millions took out such loans, forming a solid new middle class. Twenty percent of all single-family homes built in the 20 years after World War II were so financed.[15] Additionally, the bill helped veterans get started in business or on farm by guaranteeing loans for both. It also helped them protect the financial security of their families by offering them $10,000 worth of life insurance at minimal cost.

For millions the GI Bill underwrote a fresh start but not a free ride. They scraped and scrounged to get through college or job training on a monthly allowance of $65 for a single man and $90 for a married couple.[16] To make up for the lost years, they wanted to do everything at once—finish their education, establish new businesses, get new jobs, get married, and start their families.

War Brides

The American soldiers had made friends and conquests all over the world, as they continued to do throughout the occupation in the immediate postwar years. Many women of other nations found them attractive; as Monette

Goetinck wrote, "They were good guys, easy to like, easy to fall in love with."[17] They wooed, won, and sometimes married many a foreign young woman, though the military did its level best to put obstacles to marriage in their way—obstacles that prevented some GIs from deceiving women whom they merely wanted to seduce, that forced some young couples to think twice, and that sometimes were unreasonably applied. Defying them could cost the GI a court-martial or transfer to combat.

The regulations required servicemen to notify their commanding officers of their intention to marry at least two months in advance, though this requirement was sometimes waived if the bride-to-be was pregnant. Some commanding officers set up complicated procedures and deliberately delayed permissions. Additionally, some brides' families refused consent until they had investigated their prospective son-in-law. Australia enacted a bill requiring a waiting period of six months, character references, a doctor's certificate, and written permission from the bride's family. Strong social pressures sometimes made the brides feel like traitors. As late as 1948 German women who married foreigners lost their rights as German citizens.[18]

Interracial couples had a hard time getting both permission to marry and visas. Commanding officers withheld their approval, sometimes because of prejudice, and sometimes because most U.S. states did not recognize interracial marriages and might imprison women for marrying or cohabiting with men of other races. These difficulties affected not only black servicemen but also those who wanted to marry Asians. The Oriental Exclusion Act of 1924 prohibited most immigration from Asia, even for foreign-born wives and children of U.S. citizens of Asian ancestry. The War Brides Act of 1945 temporarily allowed Chinese and Filipina—but not Japanese—war brides to enter the United States, and subsequent legislation further opened the way for Asian brides of U.S. servicemen.[19] In 1952 the McCarran-Walter Act (Immigration and Nationality Act), by eliminating race as a basis for denying naturalization, cracked the doors wider for Japanese war brides: Only about 900 of them had been admitted up until that time, but that year alone 4,220 entered.[20]

All told, experts estimate that about a million American servicemen married women they met overseas in 50 different countries. About 75 percent of these war brides eventually arrived in the United States.[21] Some of the others were deserted; some were widowed; and some chose to remain in their own countries. Several thousand GIs settled down in their wives' homelands.

Only at war's end did the United States face the problem of reuniting these new families, transporting wives of servicemen from all over the world. In December 1945 Congress passed the War Brides Act. It waived for GI brides and their children, whether natural-born or adopted, both visa requirements and most provisions of immigration law, including restrictions based on race and the quotas for immigrants assigned to various nations. Each bride had to show her husband's sworn affidavit of support, demonstrating ability to care for her and her children, as well as her passport, two copies of her birth certificate, two copies of any police record, her marriage certificate, her discharge papers if she had served in the military, and evidence that once arrived in the United States she would have means to buy a railroad ticket. She had to undergo a humiliating semipublic physical examination, for which she had to undress completely, even if she was menstruating. She also had to meet security requirements. Quite naturally, these mostly young and inexperienced women felt put upon by restrictions designed to protect the American public good, like the refusal to admit women with a history of tuberculosis.

Some 30,000 British and Australian women managed to sail on troop and hospital ships before war's end,[22] but most had to wait for months or even years for transport, sometimes housed in army camps, sometimes fending for themselves and their babies, some of them in financial trouble. Long separations strained marriages: Even while they were waiting at the port of embarkation, some women received word that they were being divorced.

When they finally arrived in the United States these foreign-born women faced the problem of meeting their husbands' families and settling in communities the likes of which they had never imagined, whether in Blooming Prairie, Minnesota; in the lonely sand hills of Nebraska; or as Caucasian or Asian wives of black soldiers in the Deep South. Some could not handle the adjustment, but an astounding majority of them did.

Parents of many GIs swallowed hard and welcomed the daughters-in-law they had never seen and who perhaps could not speak their language. Some immigrant families were delighted with a daughter-in-law from their "old country." Others found it difficult to accept the new family member, particularly when she came from an enemy nation. Similarly, the general public varied from resentment of the war brides to warm hospitality and generosity.

The largest group of these women came from Great Britain—some 70,000 or more.[23] They were young, averaging 23 years of age. Most of them came from working- or lower-middle-class families. They, the Australians, and the New Zealanders had the advantage over other war brides of speaking English, but they still had to get used to new customs and new points of view.

Of all the brides, the Japanese may have faced the greatest difficulties. Typically their own parents disapproved of their marrying foreigners, sometimes even expunging them from family records. In the United States they faced more prejudice, a language barrier, and a culture and ethic markedly different from their own. Japanese Americans after years of struggle to prove their loyalty to the United States did not welcome them.[24] Nonetheless between 1947 and 1964 about 72,700 Asian women immigrated, of whom 45,853 were Japanese, 14,435 Filipina, about 6,000 Chinese, and 6,423 Korean.[25]

No reliable statistics exist on the success of all these international marriages, but most scholars agree that despite the extraordinary strains on them, the divorce rate among these couples was lower than among the U.S. population in general.[26] Of course every war bride had a lot invested in keeping the marriage going. If her husband died or they divorced, she had to raise and support her children alone in an alien land, or shamefacedly go back where she had come from. If she stayed, she usually had to work at a low-paid job such as a waitress, maid, or seamstress.

The arrival of the war brides continued the widening of experience and the increasing sophistication of Americans that had begun during the war. Changes of attitude were reflected in such modifications as California's 1948 repeal of its law banning interracial marriage. For years Filipino-American men, who outnumbered eligible Filipina-American women in the United States 40 to one, had been deterred by such laws from marrying at all. In liberating the Philippines, hundreds of Filipino-American soldiers met the young Filipinas they would marry.[27]

The Peacetime Economy

The whole nation faced the problem of changing from a wartime to a peacetime economy. It was complicated by the abrupt end to the war effected by the atom bomb: Government economists had based their plans for reconversion on the military estimate that the war would last minimally well into 1946. Within hours after Japan surrendered in August 1945 the government began canceling war contracts—$15 billion worth in less than a month.[28] Both planners and the population as a whole feared that unemployment would lead to a major depression as war plants laid off thousands of workers and millions of servicemen and servicewomen hit the civilian market, reclaiming their old jobs or looking for others. That did not happen, thanks in large part to the GI Bill and to the Veterans Preference Act of 1944, which granted preference in governmental employment to veterans and the wives and widows of disabled and deceased veterans.

What was more, Americans were ready to spend some of the $136.4 billion in savings that they had accumulated during the war,[29] when they had done without the housing and consumer goods they wanted. The returning GIs added to the demand: They needed everything, from civilian underwear on out. Young couples had put off marrying and buying furniture and appliances and houses. No one had been able to buy a new car since 1941, and almost every car on the road needed new tires. The pent-up demand spurred factory reconversion to the manufacture of consumer goods, and popular sentiment forced the abandonment of most controls in the spring of 1946.

The real danger turned out to be not depression and unemployment, but inflation, which threatened the country for several postwar years. When price controls were lifted inflation jumped by 5 percent in one month and by 15 percent by the end of the year.[30] Still, despite severe shortages of cars, housing, consumer goods, and even meat—and despite the over-hasty lifting of price controls—the nation escaped runaway inflation.

Government planning helped avert both inflation and a depression—at a heavy cost to working women. The GI Bill of Rights delayed veterans' entry (or reentry) to the job market by financing their education and training and jumpstarted the peacetime construction industry by guaranteeing their home loans. Far less satisfactory and beneficial was the joint effort of government, industry, and the media to get women out of the workplace, which in fact sent them back to low-paying jobs. In 1945 Kotex switched its ads from praising a teenager sticking to a factory job to depicting her being counseled on housework.[31] Government told women that now it was their duty to stay at home, making way for the returning veterans. Industry simply got rid of them, harassing them, putting them on the graveyard shift, transferring them to new locations, closing down the daycare on which they depended, demoting them to "women's jobs," or just firing them. As early as December 1944 women were rapidly being laid off. Though with the closing of the shipyards and other defense plants men were also affected, the layoff rate for women was 75 percent higher than that for men.[32]

That was all right with women who wanted to stay at home, but not with others. According to a *Wall Street Journal* report near the end of the war, 75 percent of working women wanted to continue to work.[33] Fifty percent of the women in war production areas who described themselves as former home-makers wanted to keep their jobs after the war.[34] Many a Rosie the Riveter had to work or just wanted to work. She was proud of her skills, disliked the only jobs now available to her, and resented the sharp reduction in her wages. Although between September 1945 and November 1946 2.25 million women voluntarily left their jobs and another million were laid off, in the same period 2.75 million women were hired. By 1947 female employment had regained its wartime levels quantitatively, but not qualitatively.[35] Women's participation in the workplace continued to grow in the years that followed, particularly among older women and married women. Although historians differ about the relationship of World War II and the women's liberation movement of the 1960s and 1970s, there is something to be said for columnist Max Lerner's observation: "When the classic work on the history of women comes to be written, the biggest force for change in their lives will turn out to have been war. Curiously, war produces more dislocations in the lives of women who stay at home than of men who go off to fight."[36]

In the postwar years the economy was beset with strikes, as labor tried to hold on to its wartime gains and expand its power. After major strikes in rail-roads, steel, and mines, in 1947 the Congress passed over President Harry Truman's veto the Taft-Hartley Act drastically limiting union power and banning strikes that endangered the national health and safety.

Postwar Politics

When on Roosevelt's death on April 12, 1945, Harry S. Truman entered the presidency, many Americans felt that he was not up to the task. When he ran for election in 1948, political experts almost with one voice predicted that he would lose to Republican candidate Thomas E. Dewey. Even though Truman ran ahead of Dewey all the while the election returns came in, the *Chicago Tribune* the next morning ran the headline "Dewey Defeats Truman"—an error that much amused Truman. Truman proved himself a competent, honest, outspoken, tough leader—one whom historians have since reevaluated admiringly. He dealt firmly with domestic crises and with the escalating cold war.

In the United States the cold war brought an atmosphere of distrust and suspicion. Opportunists such as Senator Joseph McCarthy[37] irresponsibly flung accusations of communist sympathies at anyone they did not like, destroying careers and reputations. Anyone who criticized hard-line U.S. policies against the USSR risked social and economic reprisals. Teachers, including those who had recently risked their lives for the country, were required to sign loyalty oaths. Federal employees were subject to dismissal if "reasonable grounds" could be found for the belief that they were disloyal; they had no recourse, no opportunity to confront their accusers, not even knowledge of the charges against them. From the spring of 1947 into 1951, the Civil Service Commission investigated and cleared 3 million employees and the FBI another 14,000. Several thousand resigned, but only 212 were fired for doubts about their loyalty.[38]

CHRONICLE OF EVENTS

1944

June: The Veterans Preference Act grants preference in governmental employment to veterans, wives of disabled veterans, and the widows of disabled veterans.

June 22: President Franklin D. Roosevelt (FDR) signs the GI Bill of Rights.

November: The Office of Civilian Defense is placed on standby status.

December 20: The Women's Airforce Service Pilots (WASP) is disbanded, the pilots' duties being assumed by male combat pilots who have completed their missions and male pilots formerly in the War Training Service.

1945

May: The War Department lifts blackout regulations.

June 30: The Office of Civilian Defense is closed.

Pfc. Lee Harper, who was wounded in Normandy, France, is greeted by his two-and-a-half-year-old sister, Janet, whom he had never seen before, on his arrival in New York City as his wife and mother observe, August 1, 1945. (*National Archives, 208-AA-2H-1*)

July: The government authorizes automobile plants to resume building cars.

August 14: The military services rapidly cancel war production contracts.

August 18: President Harry S. Truman authorizes government agencies to "continue stabilization of the economy" as provided by law, and simultaneously "to move as rapidly as possible without endangering the economy toward the removal of price, wage, production and other controls."

August 20: The War Production Board cancels controls on the production of 210 items, including radios, refrigerators, stoves, and washing machines.

October: The Brooklyn Dodgers sign Jackie Robinson to the first contract for a black player in major-league baseball.

October 26: The secretaries of war and navy warn that rapid demobilization threatens the country's strategic position; President Truman agrees.

November: The War Production Board ceases operations.

November 19: President Truman recommends to Congress a comprehensive, prepaid medical insurance program tied to Social Security.

November 21: The United Auto Workers strike against General Motors.

December: The U.S. Treasury Department conducts the last of eight War Loan drives.

December: Tire rationing ends.

December: President Truman restores controls on building materials, which were lifted in October.

December 12: Phil Murray, president of the Congress of Industrial Organizations, orders a steel strike.

December 28: Congress passes the War Brides Act, exempting from national quotas alien spouses and children of U.S. citizens serving in or honorably discharged from the armed forces.

1946

New housing starts reach 937,000.

Developer Bill Levitt founds Levittown near New York City, with simple houses of four and a half rooms on lots 60 feet x 100 feet designed for young families and priced from $7,990 to $9,500.

January 1: The Coast Guard is transferred from the navy back to the Treasury Department.

January 26: The first special shipment of British war brides leaves Southampton with 452 brides, 173 children, and one bridegroom (husband of a WAC). The brides are aged 16–44 and have husbands in 45 different states.

April 1: President John L. Lewis of the United Mine Workers calls a nationwide coal strike.

May 22: Truman orders seizure of the coal mines.

May 23: The Brotherhood of Railroad Trainmen and the Brotherhood of Locomotive Engineers strike, halting rail traffic across the nation.

May 24: Truman warns that if the railroad strike is not halted, he will call out the army and do whatever else is necessary to break it.

May 25: Truman asks Congress for authority to draft into the army all workers on strike against the government. As he speaks, word comes that the rail strike has been settled on terms he proposed.

May 29: The coal strike ends.

June: The Coast Guard's SPARs are disbanded.

August 13: The Armed Forces Leave Act provides terminal leave pay for veterans.

October 27: Truman signs into law the bill establishing the Atomic Energy Commission.

November 20: The United Mine Workers strike in defiance of an injunction.

December 4: A federal judge fines the United Mine Workers $3 million and their president John L. Lewis $10,000 for contempt of court.

December 7: John L. Lewis orders the United Mine Workers back to work.

1947

March 21: Truman issues an executive order establishing a Federal Employees Loyalty and Security Program, making all federal employees subject to loyalty investigations. The order also authorizes the attorney general to draw up a list of subversive organizations.

June: Over Truman's veto Congress passes the Taft-Hartley act, outlawing the closed shop, making unions liable for breach of contract, prohibiting political contributions from unions, requiring unions to make financial reports, and requiring union leaders to take a noncommunist oath.

June: Sugar rationing ends.

June 29: Truman becomes the first president to address the National Association for the Advancement of Colored People, calling for state and federal action against lynching and the poll tax, and equal opportunity in education and employment.

July 25: Congress passes Truman's National Security Act, unifying the armed services under a single department and a single Secretary of Defense, establishing the air force as a separate service, setting up a new National Security Council, and authorizing the Central Intelligence Agency.

December: Truman issues pardons to more than 1,500 people, including 282 Japanese Americans, convicted of Selective Service violations and restores their civil rights.

1948

New housing starts reach 1,118,000.

With the creation of the U.S. Air Force as a separate arm, the Women in the Air Force (WAF) is established.

May: Congress passes the Women's Armed Services Integration Act, giving women permanent status in the military, except in the Coast Guard.

June 30: The Cadet Nurse Corps graduates its last student.

July 27: Truman ends racial discrimination in the armed forces and guarantees fair employment in the civil service.

fall: Dick and Mac MacDonald redesign their business to achieve greater speed, lower prices, and higher volume by firing their carhops, cutting their menu from 25 items to 9, and mechanizing their kitchens.

1949

Radio is being overtaken by television, and 1,082,100 TV sets are operating in U.S. homes, mostly in urban centers.

December: Some congressional Republicans, charging communist infiltration into government, call for the resignation of Secretary of State Dean Acheson.

1950

New housing starts reach 1.7 million.

1951

Recognizing the growing numbers of highways and the increase in automobile travel, home builder Kemmons Wilson starts the first motel chain, Holiday Inn.

1952

The number of TV sets in U.S. homes reaches 19 million.

April 8: Truman seizes the steel mills to prevent a strike that might interrupt the flow of war materiel to Korea and to the North American Treaty Organization.

June 2: The U.S. Supreme Court declares Truman's action in seizing the steel mills unconstitutional. Steel workers strike.

June 27: The McCarran-Walter Act eliminates race as a barrier to naturalization and clears the way for legal recognition of Asian-GI marriages by the states.

July 24: Truman negotiates a settlement of the steel strike.

November: Gen. Dwight D. Eisenhower is elected president.

EYEWITNESS TESTIMONY

The Veterans and Their Families

The last two or three years of [the war] I was just sleepwalking. There are only two of us left from the outfit, and we're both half dead.

> *Congressional Medal of Honor winner Audie Murphy,*
> *who said that after the war he could not sleep without a*
> *weapon beside his bed, here speaking about the war*
> *years, quoted in Gosorski, "World War II's 'Silent*
> *Army,'" Veterans of Foreign Wars Magazine*
> *(October 1997), 5, available online. URL:*
> *www.vfw.org/magazine/oct97/32.shtml.*

[Back home] things seemed pretty tame to me, with all the excitement I went through. It was almost like I missed it.

> *Former army medic John Gill, who was wounded in the*
> *Normandy campaign of 1944, interview in the*
> *Wisconsin Veterans Museum Oral History Project*
> *(begun in 1994), quoted in Van Ells,*
> *To Hear Only Thunder Again, 60.*

There were a lot of cases [in which visitors would] come down to see their husbands or their boyfriends, [but then] were never heard from again, because they just couldn't . . . tolerate what war had done to them. . . . We dared these fellas to go out with us, take us out to dinner, take us out dancing, to get them used to going out into the public.

> *Mary Ann Renard, recalling her years during and after*
> *the war as a WAC medical technician in a Missouri*
> *army hospital, interview in the Wisconsin Veterans*
> *Museum Oral History Project (begun in 1994), quoted*
> *in Van Ells, To Hear Only Thunder Again, 99.*

[In the spring of 1951 at Harvard's Graduate School of Education] I learned . . . that the new student was from Nagoya. I decided to tell him of my visits to his city in March of 1945, as the copilot of a B-29 bomber crew. . . . In our two missions to Nagoya we quickly became acquainted with a diabolically placed searchlight battery in the mountains behind the city. As we flew in one at a time . . . this searchlight battery would nail us right now and right on, blinding the pilot, copilot, and bombardier in the nose of the B-29. Worse yet, our plane was lighted like a moth in a lamp. As a final insult, the distance from us to the searchlight battery was deceptively far away, so we used up thousands of .50 caliber rounds without even coming close. . . . It turned out [that the new student] had been one of the principal planners and designers of that fiend-begotten battery. . . . We shook hands on it . . . and became quite good friends.

> *Norman Thoburn, "Nagoya," reminiscing about 1945*
> *and 1951, in Thoburn and Knapp, "Perspectives," 5.*

Renate sailed from Portsmouth, Va., 31 March 1945 for Pearl Harbor where she took on passengers and cargo destined for Eniwetok, Ulithi, and Okinawa. Departing 14 May, she returned to Hawaii the day before the Japanese capitulation and was assigned to operation "Campus," the occupation of the defeated enemy's home islands. She got underway for Kyushu 1 September, mooring 16 days later at Sasebo where she disembarked units of the 5th Marines. Completing another occupation troop lift, from the Philippines to Sasebo, in early October, she joined in operation "Magic Carpet," the transportation of Pacific campaign veterans back to the United States. With San Francisco as her terminus she completed two "Magic Carpet" runs by mid-January 1946.

> *Description of the career of the USS Renate 1945–46,*
> *in Office of the Chief of Naval Operations, Dictionary*
> *of American Naval Fighting Ships, 1, available*
> *online. URL:www.ibiblio.org/hyperwar/usn/*
> *ships/dats/aka/aka36.html.*

When the war was over my husband was one of the first men discharged from the Navy, but all the plans we had made for the future, all of them were dashed. We didn't go back to West Virginia, we didn't build the brick house we had dreamed of, and we never had children.

When my husband returned from the Navy, he was unable to adjust to civilian life. He couldn't cope. When he joined the service, he was like most young men, a happy-go-lucky person. He came out very disillusioned, very bitter. The doctors said he had gone through too much trauma. . . .

We stayed together for seven years after the war, but things got worse and worse, so finally we divorced.

> *Service wife Marjorie Cartwright, speaking of a period*
> *from 1945 to 1952, quoted in Harris et al.,*
> *Homefront, 226, 227.*

We believed everything good about ourselves. Life was going to be glorious from now on, because we deserved it. Good times were going to go on and on; everything was going to get better. It was just a wonderful happy ending.

Service wife Laura Briggs speaking of the immediate postwar period, quoted in Harris et al., Homefront, 255.

My husband had been in the South Pacific. You could never get the father of my four children to talk about the war. It was like we put blinders on the past. . . . That's the way we lived in suburbia, raising our children, not telling them about war. I don't think it was just [us]. It was everybody. You wouldn't fill your children full of these horror stories, would you?

Army nurse Betty Hutchinson speaking of the postwar period, in Terkel, Good War, 133.

My husband did not care for my independence. He had left a shrinking violet and come home to a very strong oak tree. . . . I think the seeds of my liberation and many other women's started with the war. . . . [At a friend's house I heard the mother and grandmother talk about which drill would bite into a piece of metal at the factory.] My God, this was Sunday dinner in Middle America and to hear, instead of a discussion of the church service, a conversation about how to sharpen tools—it was a marvelous thing. I remember thinking that these women would never again be the same.

Dellie Hahne, probably in 1946, in Harris et al., The Home Front, 230.

But my very stomach turned over when I learned that Negro soldiers, just back from overseas, were being dumped out of army trucks in Mississippi and beaten.

President Harry S. Truman, letter to several southern congressmen, February 1948, quoted in McCullough, Truman, 588.

[The] final disposition [of my ship, on which I accompanied Marines during their assaults on the beaches of Guadalcanal, Tarawa, Peleliu, Palau, and other islands] . . . was to be sold for scrap to the Honda Motor Car Company. She lives, however, in my memory as a gallant little vessel, which took me

and a wonderful group of very young men as my shipmates in harm's way and brought us home.

Naval officer William B. Bell, "Short Record of One Ship," which he does not name, and the date of the final disposition of which he does not record, in Thoburn and Knapp, "Perspectives," 56–57.

The GI Bill (Servicemen's Readjustment Act of 1944)

[The GI Bill] meant that the children of bricklayers and laborers and machinists could enter those centers of higher education from which they had been barred by economics and class. And if very few of us were elected president and only a fortunate few played left field for the Dodgers, most of us realized lives that were beyond the imaginations of our parents.

Journalist Pete Hamill speaking of the immediate postwar years, quoted in Borreca, "GI Bill Propelled 1954's Democratic Revolution," available online. URL: starbulletin.com/1999/10/18/special/story1.html.

I was able to enroll at USC [University of Southern California] on the G.I. Bill of Rights. . . . We had a tremendous faculty, including Slavko Vorkapich, a former art director who pioneered the use of montages in such films as *David Copperfield*, *The Good Earth* and the earthquake sequence in *San Francisco*. It was a very exciting time. The cinema department was located in the old horse stables, because there was no room for us at the school. The last year and a half, I went to school five nights a week, because the best teachers were people from the industry who only taught at night.

Cinematographer William Fraker speaking of the immediate postwar years, in Fisher and Crudo, "A Conversation with William A. Fraker," available online.

We were young. The war was over. We all survived it. And I think there was a great sigh of relief that we survived it. America wanted to reward us. They gave us the G.I. Bill. So we had our choice of what we could do with our lives. They even said, "If you want to go to Paris, go to Paris." It was something that was all part of youth. Those of us that weren't married and

This Quonset hut, a building constructed for a variety of wartime uses, has been converted in peacetime for storage on the Santos Farm, Fremont, California. Tens of thousands of these huts served peacetime functions in locales from farms to college campuses. *(Library of Congress, HABS CA-2289-C)*

raising a family were pretty much free to do what we wanted.

> *Art Buchwald speaking of the immediate postwar years, quoted in Morris, "An American in Paris: Art Buchwald on the Good Life in Postwar France," available online. URL: www.bookpage.com/9609bp/nonfiction/ illalwayshaveparis.html.*

When I got out, I had the understanding that the GI Bill was only for those who did not have college degrees. . . . I went to college for teaching credits, which I paid for myself, because I did not know that I could go under the GI Bill.

> *New Hampshire woman veteran speaking of the immediate postwar years, quoted in Willenz, Women Veterans, 199–200.*

Listen, these GIs—and that includes the marines and the navy and the air force of course—these GIs made modern America, and they did it because the government had enough sense to say we're going to educate these guys. We're not going to be stingy as we were after World War I; we're going to give these guys an opportunity, and they could go to Harvard. They could go to Stanford. They could go to the University of Chicago. They could go, as Art Buchwald did, to the Sorbonne in Paris and get 50 bucks a month if

they weren't married, 75 if they were. Later on, that figure was moved up, and they could and did study and work and improve themselves, and the institutions that served them, that grew out of this—like the state teacher's colleges in Wisconsin—or like Harvard and all the others in between—they all benefited from it.

> *Historian Stephen Ambrose speaking of the early postwar years, Public Broadcasting System, "The G.I. Bill," December 2000, available online. URL: www.pbs.org/newshour/bb/mil/ july-dec00/gibill_7-4.html.*

Syracuse turned me down in the fall of 1945, [but] I jumped on a train from my home in Long Island and pounded my fist on the Dean's desk until he accepted me. . . . The returning GIs were older and more serious about academics and learning than ordinary freshmen.

> *Joseph Geary of the 291st Engineer Combat Battalion remembering 1945, quoted in Syracuse University, "Remembering the GI Bulge," available online. URL: sumweb.syr.edu/archives/exhibits/gi/serve.htm.*

The government paid me $20 a month [(sic; actually $20 per week) veterans' unemployment compensation] for 52 weeks. They called it 52/20. I wasn't sure I could collect that because you had to be available for a job, but I went back to school. . . . The man looked at me and said, "You go back to school and maybe you won't be called." . . . I never got called for a job. That's life. Sometimes you get lucky.

> *Dan Dander speaking probably of 1946, home page, available online. URL: www.groton.k12.ct.us/ www/wsms/dander.htm.*

War Brides

My parents offered John [a GI] £3,000—now about $12,000—to go away.

> *Australian Peggy Klaren speaking probably of the wartime years, quoted in Shukert and Scibetta, War Brides, 19.*

I had been cooped up for five years under the German Occupation, with no opportunity to move around, and I like to travel. When I met this lady [a U.S. servicewoman], I said to myself, rather than staying in Denmark, we'll go see some of the United States.

Danish war groom Jorgen Nielsen speaking of the period from 1943 to 1946, quoted in Shukert and Scibetta, War Brides, 163.

The lack of everything [in wartime Italy] led many naïve young girls into the arms of allied soldiers.

Italian war bride, who herself married for "love at first sight," speaking of the years from 1943 to 1946, quoted in Shukert and Scibetta, War Brides, 101.

[On shipboard a] squabble broke out between two girls who became quite raucous. A lieutenant yelled at the sergeant, whose chest was ablaze with medals. "For heaven's sake, Sarge, keep those women quiet!" To which the sergeant replied, "Not me, sir, I ain't going in there *noways.*"

Welch war bride Gwen Chushcoff speaking probably of 1945 or 1946, quoted in Shukert and Scibetta, War Brides, 65.

My first impression of America was of a husband (not mine) walking up the gang plank in a zoot suit. I remember thinking, "Oh God, I hope mine doesn't look like that."

British war bride Sheila Ochocki speaking probably of 1945 or 1946, quoted in Shukert and Scibetta, War Brides, 75.

Trudy was shocked to see how [her husband's] appearance had changed. He was wearing clothes that were more suited for a person in poverty, not the neat soldier she had remembered four months before. . . . They departed for Sweetwater [Tennessee] in Jim's cousin's old cramped pick-up truck. It was hot, and the Tennessee heat bothered her. She asked Jim if they could stop at a Hostel to get a cold beer. To her surprise he jabbed at her in the ribs and stated that women do not drink beer in Tennessee. . . . Her worst fears were realized when they pulled up to the home Jim had prepared for them. Trudy said . . . "I stood there appalled at what I was seeing. It was an unpainted wooden shack that sat on stones which supported the structure's four corners. There was not any running water or a bathroom. The water had to be drawn from an open well, and the bathroom was an outhouse. Our kitchen was a lean-to built onto the side of the house. The floors were rough wood slabs with

cracks large enough to see the ground underneath the house. Cardboard lined the walls to keep out the wind. I thought in all of war-torn Germany we may have lived in bombed out buildings out of necessity, but never would we have chosen to live in such a pig sty."

War bride "Trudy" speaking probably of 1945 or 1946, in an interview by Tennessee Technological University student Tim Daughtery, "Gender Roles," available online. URL: www2.h-net.msu.edu/~women/bibs/ bibl-germanwarbride.html.

My work in Tokyo took me repeatedly to the Provost Marshall's office, and I was never there without seeing at least four GIs with their Japanese girls applying for marriage licenses. I asked several of them what they were going to do when their wives had to go back to America to live and they said, "We aren't planning to go back. We intend to live here."

Author James A. Michener speaking probably of a period from 1945 to 1947, "Japan," in Michener, Voice of Asia, 17–18.

My parents said, "You made your own decision. If your husband leaves you, don't come back. Just slit your throat."

Japanese war bride Midori Langer speaking probably of a period from 1945 to 1947, in Glenn, Issei, Nisei, War Bride, 58.

I tell my husband I'm pregnant, but I don't want to marry. I'm afraid to go to the United States. My husband said, "If you don't want to marry me, I'd like to have the baby anyway." . . . My girlfriend said, "You're 28. It's hard for you to stay single. It's time you married. You're pregnant and he wants the child." So then I said, "Okay."

Japanese war bride Shizuko Howell speaking probably of a period from 1945 to 1947, in Glenn, Issei, Nisei, War Bride, 61.

[When I told my family about the American I was seeing, one relative] beat me about the hips with a bamboo cane. I still feel pain from the blows—even now, decades later—when the seasons change.

But my determination could not be broken. Two months after our initial meeting, the young man asked me to marry him. But our storms were not over. His mother in the United States worried about him because of his youth and took steps to have him recalled immediately. On the evening of our parting, he visited my room and assured me that he would come back. But, as he left, a sudden fit of despair seized me. The razor blade cut my wrist and the red blood spurted. When I awoke, I was in a hospital room.

Japanese war bride Julie Grant speaking probably of a period from 1945 to 1947, quoted in Shukert and Scibetta, War Brides, 193.

[In Bad Wildungen, Germany, after the war] the Third Division formed its own stage and floor shows to entertain the soldiers and officers. . . . In the summer of 1945, I applied for a position as actress and dancer, and was hired. There, in February of 1946, I met my future husband.

Congress passed a law in 1948 that American Army personnel can send for and marry German citizens. After two years of separation, while my husband earned a master's degree in psychology at the University of Michigan, I arrived—ten minutes after midnight New Year's Eve, 1949, at Willow Run airport.

We married March 29, 1949. . . . [I]n 1952, I became a U.S. citizen.

Helga Hover speaking of the years 1945 to 1949, "I Was a German War Bride," in Thoburn and Knapp, eds., "Perspectives," 28.

[When 236 Brisbane war brides were offloaded from the *Lurline* to make room for GIs going home] 150 of [them] had stormed the Matson office and were creating a riot. . . . Lt. Col. Jacobs . . . explained the facts to them. Although they were very bitter, no further commotion resulted.

To further complicate matters, that day a message was received from General Headquarters in Manila by the U.S. Army in Brisbane stating that all Military personnel had first priority and to please amend. This message was also somehow received by [the] Chargé d'Affaires of the American Legation at Canberra. He phoned the State Dept. in Washington. Evidently the Legation at Canberra took the stand that the war brides were all aboard and to remove them now and place Military personnel aboard would be close to complete chaos. He further stated that if the war brides were off-loaded by the U.S. Army he would not permit the vessel to sail until ordered to do so by the State Dept. in Washington. The situation was evi-

dently clarified with the War Dept., as the brides remained aboard and the vessel was set to sail at 11:00 A.M. the next morning.

Lurline purser's record, September 1945, quoted in Shukert and Scibetta, War Brides, 43–44.

Scattered throughout Britain . . . are somewhere between 700 and 1,000 children who are the helpless victims of racial intolerance and governmental red tape. They are the illegitimate half-caste babies born of the U.S. Negro servicemen and British girls. . . .

Scores of young couples to whom these children were born were genuinely and legitimately in love. Some had acquired parental permission to wed—*but could not get the permission of the U.S. Army authorities!*

"U.S. Race Prejudice Dooms 1,000 British Babies," Reynold's News (February 1947), quoted in Shukert and Scibetta, War Brides, 30.

When Ceth [my black husband] was promoted to Warrant Officer 3, the major made a toast, "To Mr. Hunter and his lovely [German-born] wife Ursula." I turned to the woman next to me, an officer's wife, and said, "Come on, you're supposed to drink," and she said, "I'm not thirsty." And she was black!

War bride Ursula Hunter speaking of the later postwar years, quoted in Shukert and Scibetta, War Brides, 151.

The Peacetime Economy

Industry must not be allowed to settle the employment problem by chaining women to kitchen sinks. . . . We must start planning immediately [for peacetime employment]. [S]ixty million jobs will not create themselves.

Labor leader Walter Reuther, quoted in the New York Times, December 10, 1944, 42.

America will never again permit the callous indifference, the economic and political ineptitude of the late twenties and early thirties to return to political power. No depression will be allowed to grow, like a Frankenstein monster, ultimately threatening our entire social structure.

Vice-President Harry S. Truman, April 8, 1945, quoted in Gosorski, "World War II's 'Silent Army,'" 4, available online. URL: www.vfw.org/magazine/oct97/32.shtml.

My whole life and that of my two children depends on my working eight hours each day. My little girl is 4 and the boy is 2 and one-half. The care and training they have received in this childcare center is the best possible thing that could have happened to them.

Former war worker Dorothy Thibault, quoted in Detroit Free Press, *June 14, 1945, 7.*

After the war fashions changed drastically, you were supposed to become a feminine person. . . . All this was part of the propaganda in magazines to put a woman back in her "rightful place" in the home. . . . I went home. And I did all the things that I had been feeling guilty about not doing during the war. . . . I tried it for three years, but it just didn't work out. All at once I took a good look at myself, and I said no.

Frankie Cooper speaking of the years from 1945 to 1948, in Harris, The Homefront, *249.*

[Television is] a device that permits people who haven't anything to do to watch people who can't do anything.

Comedian Fred Allen, 1949, quoted in Halberstam, The Fifties, *180.*

Postwar Politics

These various [congressional] committees, particularly the investigating committees, were the center of most of the criticism of the War Department, the Army and the Air Force. Even though the war in Japan was still going on, Congress started immediately criticizing how the war had been conducted in Europe. . . .

Another thing—the Committees would often pick out trifles for their criticism. I remember in one case later . . . after the war in the Pacific was over—one Committee presented . . . a photograph of troops pushing a jeep in Okinawa over the cliff into the ocean. The Committee made a great play about it—as showing reckless waste of property—at least of a particular jeep.

. . . . We finally got the facts - as to the age of the jeep and the weather conditions during this period. The vehicle was old and necessarily had to be depreciated. There was no market for such a jeep in Okinawa. We then got how much it would have cost to ship the jeep back to America. The fact was that all in all we would have lost about $100.00 more than by pushing it over a cliff.

Gen. Kenneth C. Royall speaking of a period that began in 1945, Columbia University Oral History Research Office Collection.

The proposed legislation to include women both in the Regular Navy and the Naval Reserve during peacetime was discussed [in the spring of 1945] with commanding officers and department heads at each activity. Each officer interviewed on this subject favored such legislation not only because the WAVES have proved their usefulness in the Naval establishment, but also because it is important to maintain a nucleus of trained personnel for planning purposes in case of any future national emergency.

Naval captain Joy Bright Hancock speaking of the spring of 1945, in Hancock, Lady in the Navy, *223–224.*

If the Congress does not get busy and expedite the release of these men from the armed forces—men who are needed at home, who have jobs to go back to, who have wives and children to look after or who have crops to gather, or young men who should finish their education—you will soon be in the hottest water you have ever been in since you have been in Congress—and ought to be.

Representative John E. Rankin, September 14, 1945, quoted in Donovan, Conflict and Crisis, *127.*

My convictions are not so much concerned with what I am against as what I am for—and that excludes a lot of things automatically.

Traditionally, democracy has been an affirmative doctrine rather than merely a negative one.

I believe in—and I conceive the Constitution of the United States to rest, as does religion, upon—the fundamental proposition of the integrity of the individual; and that all government and all private institutions must be designed to promote and protect and defend the integrity and dignity of the individual; that that is the essential meaning of the Constitution and the Bill of Rights, as it is essentially the meaning of religion.

Any form of government [including communism], therefore, and any other institutions, which make men means rather than ends in themselves, which exalt the state or any other institution above the importance of men, which place arbitrary power over men as a fundamental tenet of government, are contrary to this conception; and therefore I am deeply opposed to them. . . .

I deeply believe in the capacity of democracy to surmount any trials that may lie ahead provided only we practice it in our daily lives. . . .

And whether by administrative agencies acting arbitrarily against business organizations, or whether by investigative activities of the legislative branches, whenever those principles fail, those principles of the protection of an individual and his good name against besmirchment by gossip, hearsay, and the statement of witnesses who are not subject to cross-examination; then, too, we have failed in carrying forward our ideals in respect to democracy.

David Lilienthal answering a question on his views on communist doctrine at the January–April 1947 Senate confirmation hearings of his appointment to the Atomic Energy Commission, in Phillips, The 1940s, *298–299.*

11

The United Nations
January 6, 1941–July 27, 1953

HISTORICAL CONTEXT

Even before the United States entered World War II, President Franklin D. Roosevelt had begun to plan the peace, setting up a State Department team for that purpose and talking of a postwar international organization. In planning the postwar world, he compared the major Allied powers—Great Britain, the Union of Soviet Socialist Republics (USSR), China, and the United States—to four policemen, working within a station house. They would, he said, stop any aggressor nations who "started to run amok . . . before they got started."[1]

He laid the foundations for the United Nations (UN) in speeches and international agreements setting forth the aims of the Allies, such as his speech on the four freedoms, delivered before Congress on January 6, 1941, and the Atlantic Charter, issued jointly with British prime minister Winston Churchill in August of that year. Under Roosevelt's leadership and that of his successor, Harry S. Truman, at the end of World War II a majority of the people of the United States were persuaded of the necessity of an international organization to preserve the peace of the world. After World War I the United States had refused to join the League of Nations, thereby dooming it to failure. By the end of World War II even former American isolationists recognized that the country could not stand apart from the world.

The rudiments of the new institution existed in the association of the united nations who as Allies in World War II helped each other to win an unconditional surrender of their enemies. Roosevelt himself devised the name, first used in the "Declaration by United Nations" of January 1, 1942, in which 26 Allied nations pledged to continue fighting together against the Axis powers. At the Moscow conference in October 1943 Great Britain, the USSR, China, and the United States formally declared:

[1] That their united action, pledged for the prosecution of the war against their respective enemies, will be continued for the organization and maintenance of peace and security, . . .

[2] That they recognize the necessity of establishing at the earliest practicable date a general international organization, based on the principle of the sovereign equality of all peace-loving states, and open to membership by all such states, large and small, for the maintenance of international peace and security, . . . [and]

[3] That for the purpose of maintaining international peace and security pending the re-establishment of law and order and the inauguration of a system of general security they will consult with one another and as occasion requires with other members of the United Nations, with a view to joint action on behalf of the community of nations.[2]

From August to October of 1944 representatives of Great Britain, the USSR, China, and the United States conferred at Dumbarton Oaks in Washington, D.C., to draw up a blueprint for the organization.[3] Their proposals were somewhat modified at Yalta in February 1945, when Roosevelt, Stalin, and Churchill agreed to summon a conference of the united nations on the world organization to meet on April 25, inviting both current members of the united nations and others who had declared war on the Axis by March 1. They worked on details of voting within the proposed security council and on territorial trusteeships. Roosevelt and Churchill yielded to Stalin in agreeing to support for membership in the general assembly of two Soviet Socialist Republics. The United States was also to consult China and France about the Yalta decisions.

In response to the invitation, on April 25 representatives of 50 countries met at the United Nations Conference on International Organization in San

Prime Minister Winston S. Churchill, President Franklin D. Roosevelt (center), and Premier Joseph Stalin (right) meet at the Yalta Conference, February 1945. *(National Archives, 111-SC-260486)*

Francisco, California. They deliberated on the basis of the Dumbarton Oaks proposals as modified at Yalta. Individual countries hesitated to yield national autonomy and give up national power. Great Britain had no intention of losing the British Empire, and the USSR was set on expanding its influence through the creation of satellite states in eastern Europe and beyond. U.S. planners feared that if they gave the UN too much power the Senate would reject it. The British and Americans suspected the motives of the USSR, and the Soviets were afraid that the British and their dominions might combine with the United States and its Latin American allies to outvote them. A UN charter was achieved only through compromises that have weakened the organization and complicated its efforts.

Conferees agreed on a security council that could employ "any means necessary," including military force, to maintain the peace. It would be constituted of representatives of Great Britain, the USSR, the United States, China, and France—the Big Five—and a few rotating delegates from other countries. They also agreed that the five permanent members should have the power of veto, but they disagreed about whether the veto should be absolute—whether it could be invoked on trivial issues, whether it could be used by a nation involved in the matter in question, and whether or not it could be used to suppress discussion about a dispute. In the end they settled for the power of veto on everything except procedures, but with the proviso that a member of the council would abstain in peaceful disputes to which it was party.

Thus the UN would be an organization in which the Big Five were more powerful than the smaller nations, who could vote only in the general assembly. The smaller nations accepted that inequality mainly because they had no choice. As U.S. Senator Tom Connally told the San Francisco conference, "You may go home from San Francisco, if you wish, and report that you have defeated the veto. . . . But you can also say, "We tore up the charter."[4] So urgent and obvious was the need for an international peacekeeping institution that on June 25, 1945, when the San Francisco conference unanimously approved the UN Charter, "the delegates and the entire audience rose and cheered."[5]

The same argument won almost unanimous approval of the charter by the U.S. Senate when President Truman told them, "The choice before the Senate . . . is not between this Charter and something else. It is between this Charter and no charter at all."[6] The United States became the first nation to ratify. Ratification by all member nations was completed on October 24, 1945, and the charter then came into force:

We the peoples of the United Nations [its preamble began] determined to save succeeding generations from the scourge of war, which twice in our lifetime has brought untold sorrow to mankind, and to reaffirm faith in fundamental human rights, in the dignity and worth of the human person, in the equal rights of men and women and of nations large and small, and to establish conditions under which justice and respect for the obligations arising from treaties and other sources of international law can be maintained, and to promote social progress and better standards of life in larger freedom, and for these ends to practice tolerance and live together in peace with one another as good neighbours, and to unite our strength to maintain international peace and security, and to ensure, by the acceptance of principles and the institution of methods, that armed force shall not be used, save in the common interest, and to employ international machinery for the promotion of the economic and social advancement of all peoples, have resolved to combine our efforts to accomplish these aims.

When it was signed, the charter embodied the dream of the world for international peace and security. Less than a year later, on February 9, 1946, Premier Joseph Stalin of the USSR announced that "no peaceful international order is possible" between the communist and the capitalist worlds. The USSR exercised its veto frequently—in the view of the United States, frivolously. When the actions of the Security Council did not please him, the Soviet representative walked out. The Big Five, unlike the policemen of Roosevelt's plans, could not work together harmoniously. In the years that followed, the

The UN headquarters rises next to the East River in New York City. *(United Nations photograph, Library of Congress, LC-USZ62-118384)*

cold war between the USSR and the United States over the expansion of communism threatened the very existence of civilization with nuclear war, and the UN lacked power to stop it. Each side developed a multination military force outside UN control: the American-led North Atlantic Treaty Organization (NATO) and the Soviet-led Warsaw Pact.

Nonetheless, the UN went about its business. It acquired a permanent home complex on the East River in New York City. It intervened in international disputes, sometimes effectively, sometimes not. In 1948 it oversaw the creation of the state of Israel, although it could not persuade the Arab states to approve. With the prodding of the United States, from 1950 to 1953 it used military force to back up the international treaty that guaranteed the border between North and South Korea.

The workings of its various agencies encouraged international cooperation to better the lives of people everywhere and thus to eliminate the causes of war. These agencies—such as the International Labor Organization (ILO); the World Health Organization (WHO); the World Bank and International Monetary Fund; the UN Children's Fund (UNICEF); and the UN Educational, Scientific, and Cultural Organization (UNESCO)—worked around the globe for economic and social development, the improvement of health and education, and the preservation of cultures. Agency experts provided Third World countries with technical assistance, funded under the UN Development Program with moneys donated by richer nations.

Among the UN's most remarkable accomplishments was the adoption on December 10, 1948, of the Universal Declaration of Human Rights—achieved under the leadership of former U.S. first lady Eleanor Roosevelt, who used her prestige, her tact and sympathy, and her political skills to enable its passage. Its preamble, noting that "recognition of the inherent dignity and of the equal and inalienable rights of all members of the human family is the foundation of freedom, justice and peace in the world," proclaims "This Universal Declaration of Human Rights as a common standard of achievement for all peoples and all nations, to the end that every individual and every organ of society, keeping this Declaration constantly in mind, shall strive by teaching and education to promote respect for these rights and freedoms and by progressive measures, national and international, to secure their universal and effective recognition and observance, both among the peoples of Member States themselves and among the peoples of territories under their jurisdiction."

In the 30 articles that follow, the Declaration incorporates the principles of the U.S. Bill of Rights and rejects "distinction of any kind, such as race, color, sex, language, religion, political or other opinion, national or social origin, property, birth, or other status." It prohibits slavery and defends the right to privacy, the right to work, the right to join trade unions, the right to equal pay for equal work, the right to education—even the rights to leisure, a decent standard of living, and "a social and international order in which the rights and freedoms set forth in this Declaration can be fully recognized."

If the principles of the Universal Declaration of Human Rights cannot be actualized in any foreseeable future, it nonetheless provides a strong base from which to work toward peace, equality, freedom, dignity, and respect for all people.

CHRONICLE OF EVENTS

1941

January 6: President Franklin D. Roosevelt lays the foundation for the United Nations in a speech on the Four Freedoms delivered to Congress.

August 12: The Atlantic Charter calls for the postwar "establishment of a wider and permanent system of general security."

1942

January 1: The United States, the United Kingdom, the Union of Soviet Socialist Republics (USSR), the Republic of China, and 22 other nations at war with the Axis powers pledge their commitment to the war in a "Declaration by the United Nations."

1943

spring: The U.S. Senate passes a resolution to establish a postwar international organization.

summer: Senator Harry S. Truman goes on a speaking tour to propagandize for the United Nations Association.

October: In the name of the nations united against the Axis powers, the Big Four (the United States, Great Britain, USSR, and China) issue the Moscow Declaration, promising to prosecute the war to a victorious conclusion, to collaborate in the drawing and enforcement of peace terms, and to work toward "establishing at the earliest practicable date a general international organization . . . for the purpose of international peace and security."

November 28–December 1: At Tehran President Franklin D. Roosevelt of the United States, Prime Minister Winston Churchill of Great Britain, and Premier Joseph Stalin of the USSR further discuss plans for an international organization.

1944

September 21–October 7: Representatives of the United States, Great Britain, the USSR, and China meet at Dumbarton Oaks in Washington, D.C., to discuss the structure of a postwar security organization; the U.S. representatives propose a large assembly and a small security council.

1945

February: At Yalta Stalin accepts Roosevelt's voting proposals for the security council of the new international organization and cuts to two his demands for seats in the general assembly for Soviet republics. Negotiators agree that France should become a permanent member of the security council.

April 23: President Harry S. Truman warns USSR foreign minister Vyacheslav Molotov that failure to honor the agreement reached at Yalta for a Polish government based on free elections may endanger U.S. Senate approval of the new organization.

April 25–June 25: Representatives from 50 nations convene at San Francisco to set up the United Nations (UN).

June 26: Representatives of 50 nations sign the UN charter.

July 28: The U.S. Senate approves the UN charter by a vote of 89-2.

August 8: The United States deposits its notice of ratification of the UN Charter, the first nation to do so.

October 24: The Soviet bloc deposits its ratifications of the UN Charter, bringing the number of ratifications to the requisite 29, and the UN is created.

November: An organizing conference in London creates the UN Educational, Scientific, and Cultural Organization (UNESCO).

1946

January 10: The first UN General Assembly opens in Central Hall, Westminster, London, England.

January 17: The UN Security Council meets for the first time, in London.

January 19: The Iranian ambassador accuses the USSR of interfering in his country's internal affairs by encouraging the Azerbaijanis to secede and calls for a UN investigation. The USSR is also showing no signs of removing its troops, which along with other Allied troops (since removed) have occupied Iran during World War II.

January 29: The Security Council selects Trygve Lie of Norway as the first UN secretary-general.

February 9: Stalin alleges that "no peaceful international order is possible" between the communist and the capitalist worlds.

February 16: The USSR vetoes a U.S. resolution in the UN authorizing negotiations for the immediate withdrawal of British and French troops from Syria, alleging that the resolution is too weak. This is the first of 50 Soviet vetoes in the next seven years.

March 25: The U.S. opposes a USSR request for postponement of consideration of the Iranian complaint of January 19, 1946, even though the USSR promises that all its troops will leave Iran in six weeks.

March 27: When the Security Council refuses to postpone discussion of the Iranian affair, USSR representative, Andrey Gromyko, walks out.

April 16: After the Iranian-Soviet dispute is settled between the two countries, Secretary-General Lie supports Gromyko's request that it be expunged from the agenda, but it remains.

July 22: An international health conference in New York approves the constitution of the World Health Organization (WHO).

November: The UNESCO Constitution comes into force.

December 11: American John D. Rockefeller, Jr., offers the United States $8.5 million to buy lands in New York City as a site for the UN's permanent home.

1947

A World Health Organization Interim Commission organizes assistance to Egypt to combat a cholera epidemic.

The United States and the USSR, unable to agree on the division of power between North and South Korea, appeal to the UN. The General Assembly passes a resolution providing separate UN-supervised elections in the two zones for a united national assembly. The South elects a conservative government. The North refuses to hold elections, and the USSR installs a communist government there. Each government claims to represent the whole country. A UN commission stations observers along the 38th parallel dividing North Korea from South Korea.

May: The General Assembly names 11 representatives to a Special Committee on Palestine to study the issue of a Jewish homeland there, with African-American political scientist Ralph Bunche as a special assistant to the secretary-general's representative on the committee.

August: The majority report of the Special Committee on Palestine recommends that "Palestine within its present borders, following a transitional period of two years from 1 September 1947, shall be constituted into an independent Arab state, an independent Jewish state, and the [international] City of Jerusalem," the three entities to be economically unified.

These Jewish settlers are on their way to Palestine after having been released from the concentration camp at Buchenwald. The young woman on the left is from Poland; the young man in the center is from Latvia; and the young woman on the right is from Hungary, June 5, 1945. *(National Archives, 111-SC-207907)*

November 29: The UN votes for partition of Palestine into two states, one Arab, one Jewish.

1948

March 19: The U.S. ambassador to the UN, without President Truman's knowledge, calls for a temporary UN trusteeship over Palestine.

May 14: The new Jewish state of Israel is declared, and the United States recognizes it de facto (as an accomplished fact, rather than de jure, by law), to the embarrassment of U.S. delegates to the UN. Arab nations invade Palestine, beginning the first Arab-Israeli war.

June: The UN Truce Supervision Organization (Middle East) is formed.

Mid-June: The UN mediator for Palestine, Count Folke Bernadotte, negotiates a month-long truce.

July: Count Bernadotte and his chief aide, Ralph Bunche, persuade the Security Council to impose an extension of the Arab-Israeli truce.

September 16: The Israeli Stern Gang assassinates Count Bernadotte. Full-scale fighting erupts again in Palestine. Bunche succeeds Bernadotte.

December 10: The UN General Assembly adopts and proclaims the Universal Declaration of Human Rights.

1949

January: The UN Military Observer Group in India and Pakistan is formed.

February 24: Israel and Egypt sign an armistice negotiated by Bunche. At this point Israel is a fifth larger than the Jewish state envisioned in the original UN Palestine resolution. These borders hold until the Six-Day War of 1967. In the next few months Bunche mediates an armistice between Israel and the bordering nations of Jordan, Lebanon, and Syria.

April 4: Twelve nations sign the treaty creating the North Atlantic Treaty Organization (NATO).

October 24: The cornerstone is laid for the permanent UN headquarters in New York City.

1950

The fifth General Conference of UNESCO in Florence unanimously adopts a resolution authorizing UNESCO "to assist and encourage the formation and organization of regional centres and laboratories in order to increase and make more fruitful the international collaboration of scientists."

June 24: North Korea invades South Korea.

June 27: The UN Security Council calls for cessation of hostilities in Korea and the withdrawal of the North Korean forces to the 38th parallel and calls on UN member states to defend South Korea.

June 27: Truman orders U.S. air and sea forces to the aid of South Korea.

June 30: On the advice of Gen. Douglas MacArthur, Truman commits U.S. ground troops to Korea.

August 1: USSR representative Jacob Malik returns to the Security Council and rotates into its presidency for the month, thereby blocking more Security Council resolutions condemning North Korea.

September 22: Ralph Bunche wins the Nobel Peace Prize, the first African American so honored.

October 9: Under the authority of a UN General Assembly resolution, MacArthur's troops cross the 38th parallel into North Korea.

President Truman awards the Congressional Medal of Honor to a World War II veteran at the White House, November 1, 1950. At such award ceremonies Truman always said, "I'd rather have this medal than be president of the United States." *(Truman Library, 73-3412)*

October 31: Trick-or-Treat-for-UNICEF begins in Philadelphia, Pennsylvania.

November 24: MacArthur begins an unauthorized drive north toward the Chinese border with North Korea.

November 28: Chinese and North Korean troops drive UN troops back toward the 38th parallel.

1951

April 10: Truman relieves MacArthur of all his commands, and Gen. Matthew B. Ridgway assumes command of U.S. forces in Korea.

July: Negotiations to end the Korean War begin.

1952

The UN moves into its own complex on the East River in New York City.

February: Agreement is reached in the Korean War for a cease-fire, a two-mile demilitarized zone along the 38th parallel, an exchange of prisoners, and future talks about withdrawal of foreign troops and a permanent peace settlement, but the unwillingness of large numbers of Chinese and North Koreans to return to their countries forces the continuation of the war.

1953

July 27: The UN Command and the Chinese–North Korean Command sign the Korean armistice agreement.

Eyewitness Testimony

[The quarrel within the UN over voting stems from the] false major premise that the Dumbarton Oaks organization can and should be a universal society to pacify the world. The truth is that only in a reasonably pacified world can there be a universal society.

Columnist Walter Lippman, September 19, 1944, quoted in Steel, Walter Lippman, 411.

The structure of world peace cannot be the work of one man, or one party, or one nation. It cannot be an American peace, or a British, a Russian, a French, or a Chinese peace. It cannot be a peace of large nations—or of small nations. It must be a peace which rests on the cooperative effort of the whole world. . . . There can be no middle ground here. We shall have to take the responsibility for world collaboration, or we shall have to bear the responsibility for another world conflict.

Secretary of State Edward Stettinius, April 1945, quoting President Franklin D. Roosevelt's remarks of February 1945 speech at the opening of the United Nations Conference, available online. URL: www.whistlestop.org/ study-collections/un/large/st-conference/ um_sf6-1.htm.

I saw [American representatives to the UN] Stettinius and Nelson Rockefeller marshal the twenty Latin American republics in one solid bloc and steamroll [the membership of Argentina] through the United Nations. I remember . . . feeling this was an ominous thing for the future; if we were going to use that kind of a majority to dominate things, we were going to run into iron resistance to anything else from the Russians. . . . [Such tactics would make the great powers] more than ever determined to keep the things that really matter most to them away from the organization.

Columnist Walter Lippman, May 5, 1945, quoted in Steel, Walter Lippman, 420–421.

This is the great day. This is the day we have been looking for since December 7, 1941. This is the day when fascism and police government ceases [sic] in the world. This is the day for the democracies. This is the day when we can start on our real task of implementation of free government in the world.

President Harry S. Truman, impromptu speech on August 14, 1945, quoted in Brinkley, Washington, 277.

After the war while I was waiting in England for transport home, I wanted to attend a lecture by political scientist Harold Laski, but it conflicted with a required army indoctrination session on the UN. As I had been following the creation of the UN fairly closely, I tried to get excused—but no way. The army was hell-bent on seeing that all of us soldiers were properly informed.

Charles Taylor, speaking of fall 1945, author interview.

However, it was clear even before the San Francisco conference adopted the Charter that an evil fairy attended this beginning as well. The Soviet Union intended to use the UN as its instrument. Openly violating Stalin's promise at Yalta to permit democratic governments in Eastern Europe through free elections, the Soviet Union imposed communist regimes. . . . At one point, the Soviets insisted that the veto power cover also what the Security Council could discuss. The United States replied flatly that it would not join such an organization.

I was present when this was put to the test at the Council's first sessions in March, 1946 at New York's Hunter College. Moscow refused to withdraw its troops from Iran as agreed and set up a puppet republic in the Kurdish provinces. When the Council took this up over his objections, Foreign Minister Andrei Gromyko gathered his officials and marched out. Several days later he quietly returned.

Journalist Richard Hottelet speaking of March 1946, "Ups and Downs in UN History," 18, available online. URL: law.wustl.edu/igls/unconfpapers/p.

If you reach agreement, each of you will get one [of these plates inscribed "Rhodes Armistice Talks 1949"] to take home. If you don't, I'll break them over your heads!

Diplomat Ralph Bunche to warring Israelis and Palestinians, January 1949, quoted in Meisler, United Nations, 52.

You can't imagine what it takes to hold these monkeys together long enough to squeeze agreement out of them. . . . I swear by all that's holy, I will never come anywhere near the Palestine problem once I liberate myself from this trap.

> *Diplomat Ralph Bunche, letter to his wife about negotiating treaties between Palestinians and Israelis, spring 1949, quoted in Meisler,* United Nations, *53.*

[The North Korean invasion of South Korea in 1950 had] all the elements of surprise which reminded me of the Nazi invasion of Norway. . . . I consider my stand on Korea [determination to beat back North Korean aggression] the best justified act of seven years in the service of peace.

> *UN Secretary-General Trygve Lie writing about the beginning of the Korean War in 1950, memoirs, quoted in Meisler,* United Nations, *57.*

[The North Korean aggression constitutes a] clear-cut Soviet challenge which in our considered opinion US should answer firmly and swiftly as [a] . . . direct threat [to] our leadership of [the] free world against Soviet Communist imperialism.

> *Cable from the U.S. Moscow embassy to the State Department, June 25, 1950, quoted in Meisler,* United Nations, *60.*

Jack, in the final analysis I did this [sent troops to Korea] for the United Nations. I believed in the League of Nations. It failed. Lots of people thought it failed because we weren't in it to back it up. Okay, now we started the United Nations. It was our idea, and in this first big test we just couldn't let them down. If a collective system under the U.N. can work,

United Nations forces, having withdrawn from Pyongyang, the North Korean capital, recross the 38th parallel, 1950. *(National Archives, 306-FS-259-21)*

it must be made to work, and now is the time to call [the Soviet] bluff.

President Harry S. Truman speaking of his 1950 decision, as reported by Assistant Secretary of State John Hickerson, quoted in Meisler, United Nations, 60–61.

Forcing the withdrawal of the North Korean aggressors to the 38th parallel is not an end in itself. It is the means to what must be the true end for the UN and ourselves. . . . That is to abolish the partition which has ended in war and to achieve a united and independent Korea.

Columnist Walter Lippman, July 20, 1950, quoted in Steel, Walter Lippman, 626, n. 19.

Massacre Valley, Scene of Harry S. Truman's Police Action. Nice Going, Harry!

Sign erected by U.S. servicemen north of the village of Hoengsong, Korea, February 13, 1951, in Turbak, "Massacre at Hoengsong," available online. URL: www.landscaper.net/kortime.htm.

The enemy . . . must by now be painfully aware that a decision of the United Nations to depart from its tolerant effort to contain the war to the area of Korea through expansion of our military operations to his coastal areas and interior bases would doom Red China to the risk of imminent military collapse. . . . [I am ready to meet with the commander in chief of the enemy forces] to find any military means whereby the realization of the political objectives of the United Nations in Korea . . . might be accomplished without further bloodshed.

Gen. Douglas MacArthur, spring 1951, quoted in Meisler, United Nations, 68.

In early '52 our squadron was returning from a mission over North Korea. They were at high altitude, probably about 40,000 feet, when one of the F84's went into a dive. The other pilots tried to raise this particular aircraft on the radio, to no avail. Luckily, a characteristic of the F84 was that when it exceeded sound speed it would pitch up, which this aircraft did. When it stalled and again dove the other pilots knew that this pilot was in some kind of trouble, probably a faulty oxygen system. Two of them dove down to see what they could do. After another pitch-up and dive the two decided at the next pitch-up they, one on each side of the stricken aircraft, would attempt to catch and steady the plane on their wing tips. I don't know if they were successful on their first try but they did succeed and managed to get this plane to a lower altitude where the pilot came to and was able to fly back and land on his own.

Pilot Don Paul describing an experience in early 1952, in "Recollections," available online. URL: www.koreanwar.org.

APPENDIX A
Documents

1. Excerpts from the Neutrality Act of 1937, May 1, 1937
2. Excerpt from physicist Albert Einstein's letter warning President Franklin Roosevelt of the possibility of an atomic bomb, August 2, 1939
3. Excerpts from the statement of the Historic Peace Churches on conscientious objectors (COs), signed by representatives of the Friends, Mennonites, and Church of the Brethren, January 10, 1940.
4. Excerpt from Section 6 of the National Defense Act of May 1940
5. Conscientious objector clause in the Selective Training and Service Act, signed into law September 16, 1940
6. Notice to register for the draft, October 16, 1940
7. Excerpts from the Lend-Lease Act (An Act to Promote the Defense of the United States), March 11, 1941
8. Excerpt from Executive Order No. 8802, June 25, 1941
9. The Atlantic Charter, August 14, 1941
10. Excerpts from isolationist Charles A. Lindbergh's speech in Des Moines, Iowa, at an America First rally, September 11, 1941
11. President Franklin D. Roosevelt's address to Congress, December 8, 1941
12. Excerpt from the Japanese emperor's Declaration of War, December 8, 1941
13. Declaration by the United Nations (Allies), January 1, 1942
14. Excerpts from Executive Order No. 9066, February 14, 1942
15. Excerpts from A. Philip Randolph, "Keynote Address to the March on Washington Movement" for equal treatment in the military, September 26, 1942
16. Excerpt from Marine Corps Classification of Military Occupational Specialties, 1943
17. Excerpts from memorandum from General Benjamin O. Davis, Sr., to the inspector general, November 9, 1943
18. Excerpt from President Roosevelt's Fireside Chat of December 1943
19. Excerpt from Executive Order No. 9417 establishing a War Refugee Board, January 22, 1944
20. *In Re Summers* (325 U.S. 561 1944)
21. Excerpt from President Roosevelt's radio-broadcast prayer on D day, June 6, 1944
22. Dissent in the Case of *Korematsu v. United States* by Justice Robert H. Jackson, 1944
23. Opening paragraphs of Proposals for the Establishment of a General International Organization, Issued in the names of the United States, the United Kingdom of Great Britain and Ireland, the Union of Soviet Socialist Republics, and the Republic of China, October 7, 1944

1. Excerpts from the Neutrality Act of 1937, May 1, 1937

Export of Arms, Ammunition, and Implements of War

Section 1. (a) Whenever the President shall find that there exists a state of war between, or among, two or more foreign states, the President shall proclaim such fact, and it shall thereafter be unlawful to export, or attempt to export, or cause to be exported, arms, ammunition, or implements of war from any place in the United States to any belligerent state named in such proclamation, or to any neutral state for transshipment to, or for the use of, any such belligerent state.

(b) The President shall, from time to time, by proclamation, extend such embargo upon the export of arms, ammunition, or implements of war to other states as and when they may become involved in such war.

(c) Whenever the President shall find that such a state of civil strife exists in a foreign state and that such civil strife is of a magnitude or is being conducted under such conditions that the export of arms, ammunition, or implements of war from the United States to such foreign state would threaten or endanger the peace of the United States, the President shall proclaim such fact, and it shall thereafter be unlawful to export, or attempt to export, or cause to be exported, arms, ammunition, or implements of war from any place in the United States to such foreign state, or to any neutral state for transshipment to, or for use of, such foreign state. . . .

(g) Whenever, in the judgment of the President, the conditions which have caused him to issue any proclamation under the authority of this section have ceased to exist, he shall revoke the same, and the provisions of this section shall thereupon cease to apply with respect to the state or states named in such proclamation, except with respect to offenses committed, or forfeiture incurred, prior to such revocation. . . .

Export of Other Articles and Materials

Section 2. (a) Whenever the President shall have issued a proclamation under the authority of section 1 of this Act and he shall thereafter find that the placing of restrictions on the shipment of certain articles or materials in addition to arms, ammunition, and imple-

ments of war from the United States to belligerent states, or to a state wherein civil strife exists, is necessary to promote the security or preserve the peace of the United States or to protect the lives of citizens of the United States, he shall so proclaim, and it shall thereafter be unlawful, for any American vessel to carry such articles or materials to any belligerent state, or to any state wherein civil strife exists, named in such proclamation issued under the authority of section 1 of this Act, or to any neutral state for transshipment to, or for the use of, any such belligerent states or any such state wherein civil strife exists. . . .

Section 4. This Act shall not apply to an American republic or republics engaged in war against a non-American state or states, provide[d] the American republic is not cooperating with a non-American state or states in such a war. . . .

National Munitions Control Board

Section 5. (a) There is hereby established a National Munitions Control Board (herein after referred to as the "Board") to carry out the provisions of this Act. . . .

(b) Every person who engages in the business of manufacturing, exporting, or importing any of the arms, ammunition, or implements of war referred to in this Act, whether as an exporter, importer, manufacturer, or dealer, shall register with the Secretary of States his name, place of business, and places of business in the United States, and a list of the arms, ammunition, and implements of war which he manufactures, imports, or exports. . . .

American Vessels Prohibited from Carrying Arms to Belligerent States

Section 6. (a) Whenever the President shall have issued a proclamation under the authority of section 1 of this Act, it shall thereafter be unlawful, until such proclamation is revoked, for any American vessel to carry any arms, ammunition, or implements of war to any belligerent state, or to any state wherein civil strife exists, named in such proclamation, or to any neutral state for transshipment to, or for the use of, any such belligerent state or any such state wherein civil strife exists. . . .

Use of American Ports as Base of Supply

Section 7. (a) Whenever, during any war in which the United States is neutral, the President, or any person thereunto authorized by him, shall have cause to believe that any vessel, domestic or foreign, whether requiring clearance or not, is about to carry out of a port of the United States, fuel, men, arms, ammunition, implements of war, or other supplies to any warship, tender, or supply ship of a belligerent state, but the evidence is not deemed sufficient to justify forbidding the departure of the vessel as provided for by section 1, title V, chapter 30, of the Act approved June 15, 1917, and if, in the President's judgment, such action will serve to maintain peace between the United States and foreign states, or to protect the commercial interests of the United States and its citizens, or to promote the security or neutrality of the United States, he shall have the power and it shall be his duty to require the owner, master, or person in command thereof, before departing from a port of the United States, to give a bond to the United States, with sufficient sureties, in such amount as he shall deem proper, conditioned that the vessel will not deliver the men, or any part of the cargo, to any warship, tender, or supply ship of the belligerent state. . . .

Submarines and Armed Merchant Vessels

Section 8. Whenever, during any war in which the United States is neutral, the President shall find that special restrictions placed on the use of the ports and territorial waters of the United States by the submarines or armed merchant vessels of a foreign state, will serve to maintain peace between the United States and foreign states, or to protect the commercial interests of the United States and its citizens, or to promote the security of the United States, and shall make proclamation therefore, it shall thereafter be unlawful for any such submarine or armed merchant vessel to enter a port or the territorial waters of the United States or to depart therefrom, except under such conditions and subject to such limitations as the President may prescribe. Whenever, in his judgment, the conditions which have caused him to issue his proclamation have ceased to exist, he shall revoke his proclamation and the provisions of this section shall thereupon cease to apply.

Travel on Vessels of Belligerent States

Section 9. Whenever the President shall have issued a proclamation under the authority of section 1 of this Act it shall thereafter be unlawful for any citizen of the United States to travel on any vessel of the state or states named in such proclamation, except in accordance with such rules and regulations as the President shall prescribe: . . .

Arming of American Merchant Vessels Prohibited

Section 10. Whenever the President shall have issued a proclamation under the authority of section 1, it shall thereafter be unlawful, until such proclamation is revoked, for any American vessel engaged in commerce with any belligerent state, or any state wherein civil strife exists, named in such proclamation, to be armed or to carry any armament, arms, ammunition, or implements of war, except small arms and ammunition therefor which the President may deem necessary and shall publicly designate for the preservation of discipline aboard such vessels. . . .

2. EXCERPT FROM PHYSICIST ALBERT EINSTEIN'S LETTER WARNING PRESIDENT FRANKLIN ROOSEVELT OF THE POSSIBILITY OF AN ATOMIC BOMB, AUGUST 2, 1939

In the course of the last four months it has been made probable—through the work of [Frédéric] Joliot in France as well as [Enrico] Fermi and [Leo] Szilard in America—that it may become possible to set up a nuclear chain reaction in a large mass of uranium, by which vast amounts of power and large quantities of new radium-like elements would be generated. Now it appears almost certain that this could be achieved in the immediate future.

This new phenomenon would also lead to the construction of bombs, and it is conceivable—though much less certain—that extremely powerful bombs of a new type may thus be constructed. A single bomb of this type, carried by boat and exploded in a port, might very well destroy the whole port together with some of the surrounding territory. However, such bombs might very well prove to be too heavy for transportation by air.

The United States has only very poor ores of uranium in moderate quantities. There is good ore in Canada and the former Czechoslovakia, while the most important source of uranium is the Belgian Congo.

In view of this situation you may think it desirable to have some permanent contact maintained between the Administration and the group of physicists working on chain reactions in America. One possible way of achieving this might be for you to entrust with this task a person who has your confidence who could perhaps serve in an unofficial capacity. His task might comprise the following:

a) to approach Government Departments, keep them informed of the further development, and put forward recommendations for Government action, giving particular attention to the problems of securing a supply of uranium ore for the United States.

b) to speed up the experimental work, which is at present being carried on within the limits of the budgets of University laboratories, by providing funds, if such funds be required, through his contacts with private persons who are willing to make contributions for this cause, and perhaps also by obtaining the co-operation of industrial laboratories which have the necessary equipment.

I understand that Germany has actually stopped the sale of uranium from the Czechoslovakian mines which she has taken over. . . .

3. EXCERPTS FROM THE STATEMENT OF THE HISTORIC PEACE CHURCHES ON CONSCIENTIOUS OBJECTORS (COs), SIGNED BY REPRESENTATIVES OF THE FRIENDS, MENNONITES, AND CHURCH OF THE BRETHREN, JANUARY 10, 1940.

Memorandum to the Government Regarding Alternative Service in Time of War

1. That a civilian board be appointed . . . to judge the sincerity of COs, to assign them definite status . . . and authorize non-military service projects to which they might be assigned.
2. That draft boards be directed to route COs directly to this civilian board, leaving them at all times under civilian direction and control.
3. That appropriate organizations of the historic peace churches be permitted to set up and administer . . . service projects to which COs might be assigned. . . .

4. EXCERPT FROM SECTION 6 OF THE NATIONAL DEFENSE ACT OF MAY 1940

Whenever the President determines that it is necessary in the interest of national defense to prohibit or curtail the exportation of any military equipment or munitions, or component parts thereof, or machinery, tools, or materials or supplies necessary for the manufacture, servicing or operation thereof, he may by proclamation prohibit or curtail such exportation, except under such rules or regulations as he shall prescribe. . . .

5. CONSCIENTIOUS OBJECTOR CLAUSE IN THE SELECTIVE TRAINING AND SERVICE ACT, SIGNED INTO LAW SEPTEMBER 16, 1940

Section 5(g): Nothing contained in this Act shall be construed to require any person to be subject to combatant training and service in the land and naval forces of the United States who, by reason of religious training and belief, is conscientiously opposed to participation in war in any form.

Any such person claiming such exemption from combatant training and service because of such conscientious objections whose claim is sustained by the local draft board shall, if he is inducted into the land or naval forces under this Act, be assigned to noncombatant service as defined by the President, or shall, if he is found to be conscientiously opposed to participation in such noncombatant service, in lieu of such induction, be assigned to work of national importance under civilian direction.

6. NOTICE TO REGISTER FOR THE DRAFT, OCTOBER 16, 1940

Registration

If you are a man who has reached his 21st birthday but has not reached his 36th birthday, you must register today for selective service. If you have no valid reason for failing to do so you are liable to arrest, and if convicted you may be sentenced to as much as five years in prison and fined $10,000.

You are to register between 7 A.M. and 9 P.M. at the nearest school in the election district in which you live, or where you are staying if you are from out of town. If you have used your best efforts to locate your registration place and cannot find it, inquire at the police station nearest where you are staying.

7. Excerpts from the Lend-Lease Act (An Act to Promote the Defense of the United States), March 11, 1941

SEC. 3. (a) Notwithstanding the provisions of any other law, the President may, from time to time, when he deems it in the interest of national defense, authorize the Secretary of War, the Secretary of the Navy, or the head of any other department or agency of the Government—

(1) To manufacture in arsenals, factories, and shipyards under their jurisdiction, or otherwise procure, to the extent to which funds are made available therefor, or contracts are authorized from time to time by the Congress, or both, any defense article for the government of any country whose defense the President deems vital to the defense of the United States.

(2) To sell, transfer title to, exchange, lease, lend, or otherwise dispose of, to any such government any defense article. . . . The value of defense articles disposed of in any way under authority of this paragraph, and procured from funds heretofore appropriated, shall not exceed $1,300,000,000. . . .

(3) To test, inspect, prove, repair, outfit, recondition, or otherwise to place in good working order, to the extent to which funds are made available therefor, or contracts are authorized from time to time by the Congress, or both, any defense article for any such government, or to procure any or all such services by private contract.

(4) To communicate to any such government any defense information pertaining to any defense article furnished to such government. . . .

(5) To release for export any defense article disposed of in any way under this subsection to any such government. . . .

(b) The terms and conditions upon which any such foreign government receives any aid authorized under subsection (a) shall be those which the President deems satisfactory, and the benefit to the United States may be payment or repayment in kind or property, or any other direct or indirect benefit which the President deems satisfactory. . . .

(d) Nothing in this Act shall be construed to authorize or to permit the authorization of convoying vessels by naval vessels of the United States.

(e) Nothing in this Act shall be construed to authorize or to permit the authorization of the entry of any American vessel into a combat area in violation of section 3 of the Neutrality Act of 1939. . . .

The President from time to time, but not less frequently than once every ninety days, shall transmit to the Congress a report of operations under this Act except such information as he deems incompatible with the public interest to disclose. . . .

8. Excerpt from Executive Order No. 8802, June 25, 1941

It is the duty of employers and labor organizations to provide for the full and equitable participation of all workers in the defense industries without discrimination. . . . All departments and agencies of the Government of the United States concerned with vocational and training programs for defense production shall take special measures appropriate to assure that such programs are administered without discrimination. All contracting agencies of the Government of the United States shall include in all defense contracts hereafter negotiated by them a provision obligating the contractor not to discriminate against any worker. There is established in the office of Production Management a committee on fair employment practices, which shall consist of a chairman and four other members to be appointed by the President.

9. The Atlantic Charter, August 14, 1941

The President of the United States of America and the Prime Minister, Mr. Churchill, representing His Majesty's Government in the United Kingdom, being met together, deem it right to make known certain common principles in the national policies of their respective countries on which they base their hopes for a better future for the world.

First, their countries seek no aggrandizement, territorial or other.

Second, they desire to see no territorial changes that do not accord with the freely expressed wishes of the people concerned.

Third, they respect the rights of all peoples to choose the form of government under which they will live; and they wish to see sovereign rights and self-government restored to those who have been forcibly deprived of them.

Fourth, they will endeavor, with due respect for their existing obligations, to further the enjoyment by all states, great or small, victor or vanquished, of access, on equal terms, to the trade and to the raw materials of the world which are needed for their economic prosperity.

Fifth, they desire to bring about the fullest collaboration between all nations in the economic field, with the object of securing for all improved labor standards, economic advancement, and social security.

Sixth, after the final destruction of the Nazi tyranny they hope to see established a peace which will afford to all nations the means of dwelling in safety within their own boundaries, and which will afford assurance that all the men in all the lands may live out their lives in freedom from fear and want.

Seventh, such a peace should enable all men to traverse the high seas and oceans without hindrance.

Eighth, they believe that all the nations of the world, for realistic as well as spiritual reasons, must come to the abandonment of the use of force. Since no future peace can be maintained if land, sea, or air armaments continue to be employed by nations which threaten, or may threaten, aggression outside of their frontiers, they believe, pending the establishment of a wider and permanent system of general security, that the disarmament of such nations is essential. They will likewise aid and encourage all other practicable measures which will lighten for peace-loving peoples the crushing burden of armaments.

FRANKLIN D. ROOSEVELT
WINSTON S. CHURCHILL

10. Excerpts from Isolationist Charles A. Lindbergh's Speech in Des Moines, Iowa, at an America First Rally, September 11, 1941

It is now two years since this latest European war began. From that day in September, 1939, until the present moment, there has been an ever-increasing effort to force the United States into the conflict.

That effort has been carried on by foreign interests, and by a small minority of our own people; but it has been so successful that, today, our country stands on the verge of war. . . .

If you will look back over the record, you will find that those of us who oppose intervention have constantly tried to clarify facts and issues; while the interventionists have tried to hide facts and confuse issues. . . .

National polls showed that when England and France declared war on Germany, in 1939, less than 10 percent of our population favored a similar course for America. But there were various groups of people, here and abroad, whose interests and beliefs necessitated the involvement of the United States in the war. . . .

The three most important groups who have been pressing this country toward war are the British, the Jewish [sic] and the Roosevelt administration.

Behind these groups, but of lesser importance, are a number of capitalists, Anglophiles, and intellectuals who believe that the future of mankind depends upon the domination of the British empire. Add to these the Communistic groups who were opposed to intervention until a few weeks ago, and I believe I have named the major war agitators in this country. . . .

If it were not for her hope that she can make us responsible for the war financially, as well as militarily, I believe England would have negotiated a peace in Europe many months ago, and be better off for doing so. . . .

It is not difficult to understand why Jewish people desire the overthrow of Nazi Germany. The persecution they suffered in Germany would be sufficient to make bitter enemies of any race.

No person with a sense of the dignity of mankind can condone the persecution of the Jewish race in Germany. But no person of honesty and vision can look on their pro-war policy here today without seeing the dangers involved in such a policy both for us and for them. Instead of agitating for war, the Jewish groups in this country should be opposing it in every possible way for they will be among the first to feel its consequences. . . .

The danger of the Roosevelt administration lies in its subterfuge. While its members have promised us peace, they have led us to war heedless of the platform upon which they were elected. . . .

[These groups] planned: first, to prepare the United States for foreign war under the guise of American defense; second, to involve us in the war, step by step, without our realization; third, to create a series of incidents which would force us into the actual conflict. . . .

Our theaters soon became filled with plays portraying the glory of war. Newsreels lost all semblance of objectivity. Newspapers and magazines began to lose advertising if they carried anti-war articles. A smear campaign was instituted against individuals who opposed intervention. The terms "fifth columnist," "traitor," "Nazi," "anti-Semitic" were thrown ceaselessly at any one who dared to suggest that it was not to the best interests of the United States to enter the war. Men lost their jobs if they were frankly anti-war. Many others dared no longer speak.

Before long, lecture halls that were open to the advocates of war were closed to speakers who opposed it. A fear campaign was inaugurated. We were told that aviation, which has held the British fleet off the continent of Europe, made America more vulnerable than ever before to invasion.

The war groups have succeeded in the first two of their three major steps into war. The greatest armament program in our history is under way.

We have become involved in the war from practically every standpoint except actual shooting. Only the creation of sufficient "incidents" yet remains; and you see the first of these already taking place, according to plan. . . .

We are on the verge of a war for which we are still unprepared, and for which no one has offered a feasible plan for victory—a war which cannot be won without sending our soldiers across the ocean to force a landing on a hostile coast against armies stronger than our own. . . .

11. PRESIDENT FRANKLIN D. ROOSEVELT'S ADDRESS TO CONGRESS, DECEMBER 8, 1941

Yesterday, December 7, 1941—a date which will live in infamy—the United States of America was suddenly and deliberately attacked by naval and air forces of the Empire of Japan.

The United States was at peace with that nation, and, at the solicitation of Japan, was still in conversation with its government and its Emperor looking toward the maintenance of peace in the Pacific. Indeed, one hour after Japanese air squadrons had commenced bombing in Oahu, the Japanese Ambassador to the United States and his colleague delivered to the Secretary of State a formal reply to a recent American message. While this reply stated that it seemed useless to continue the existing diplomatic negotiations, it contained no threat or hint of war or armed attack.

It will be recorded that the distance of Hawaii from Japan makes it obvious that the attack was deliberately planned many days or even weeks ago. During the intervening time the Japanese Government has deliberately sought to deceive the United States by false statements and expressions of hope for continued peace.

The attack yesterday on the Hawaiian Islands has caused severe damage to American naval and military forces. Very many American lives have been lost. In addition, American ships have been reported torpedoed on the high seas between San Francisco and Honolulu.

Yesterday the Japanese government also launched an attack against Malaya.

Last night Japanese forces attacked Hong Kong.

Last night Japanese forces attacked Guam.

Last night Japanese forces attacked the Philippine Islands.

Last night the Japanese attacked Wake Island.

This morning the Japanese attacked Midway Island.

Japan has, therefore, undertaken a surprise offensive extending throughout the Pacific area. The facts of yesterday speak for themselves. The people of the United States have already formed their opinions and well understand the implications to the very safety and life of our nation.

As Commander-in-Chief of the Army and Navy, I have directed that all measures be taken for our defense.

Always will we remember the character of the onslaught against us.

No matter how long it may take us to overcome this premeditated invasion, the American people in their righteous might will win through to absolute victory. . . .

I ask that the Congress declare that since the unprovoked and dastardly attack by Japan on Sunday, December 7, a state of war has existed between the United States and the Japanese Empire.

12. EXCERPT FROM THE JAPANESE EMPEROR'S DECLARATION OF WAR, DECEMBER 8, 1941

Patiently have We waited and long have We endured, in the hope that Our government might retrieve the situation in peace. But Our adversaries, showing not the least spirit of conciliation, have unduly delayed a settlement; and in the meantime they have intensified the economic and political pressure to compel thereby Our Empire to submission. . . .

This trend of affairs would, if left unchecked, not only nullify Our Empire's efforts of many years for the sake of the stabilization of East Asia, but also endanger the very existence of Our nation. Our Empire, for its existence and self-defense, has no other recourse but to appeal to arms and to crush every obstacle in its path.

13. DECLARATION BY THE UNITED NATIONS (ALLIES), JANUARY 1, 1942

The Governments signatory hereto,

Having subscribed to a common program of purposes and principles embodied in the Joint Declaration of the President of the United States of America and the Prime Minister of the United Kingdom of Great Britain and Northern Ireland dated August 14, 1941, known as the Atlantic Charter;

Being convinced that complete victory over their enemies is essential to defend life, liberty, independence and religious freedom, and to preserve human rights and justice in their own lands as well as other lands, and that they are now engaged in a common struggle against savage and brutal forces seeking to subjugate the world, DECLARE:

(1) Each Government pledges itself to employ its full resources, military or economic, against those members of the Tripartite Pact and its adherents with which such government is at war.

(2) Each Government pledges itself to cooperate with the governments signatory hereto and not to make a separate armistice or peace with the enemies.

The foregoing declaration may be adhered to by other nations which are, or which may be, rendering material assistance and contributions in the struggle for victory over Hitlerism.

Signed by representatives of the United States, the United Kingdom of Great Britain and Northern Ireland, the Union of Soviet Socialist Republics, the Republic of China, and 22 other governments at war with the Tripartite Powers (Axis).

14. EXCERPTS FROM EXECUTIVE ORDER NO. 9066, FEBRUARY 14, 1942

Authorizing the Secretary of War to Prescribe Military Areas

Whereas the successful prosecution of the war requires every possible protection against espionage and against sabotage to national-defense material, national-defense premises, and national-defense utilities. . . .

Now, therefore, by virtue of the authority vested in me as President of the United States, and Commander in Chief of the Army and Navy, I hereby authorize and direct the secretary of war, and the military commanders whom he may from time to time designate, whenever he or any designated commander deems such actions necessary or desirable, to prescribe military areas in such places and of such extent as he or the appropriate military commanders may determine, from which any or all persons may be excluded, and with such respect to which, the right of any person to enter, remain in, or leave shall be subject to whatever restrictions the secretary of war or the appropriate military commander may impose in his discretion. The secretary of war is hereby authorized to provide for residents of any such area who are excluded therefrom, such transportation, food, shelter, and other accommodations as may be necessary, in the judgment of the secretary of war or the said military commander, and until other arrangements are made, to accomplish the purpose of this order. . . .

—Franklin D. Roosevelt

15. EXCERPTS FROM A. PHILIP RANDOLPH, "KEYNOTE ADDRESS TO THE MARCH ON WASHINGTON MOVEMENT" FOR EQUAL TREATMENT IN THE MILITARY, SEPTEMBER 26, 1942

. . . As one of the sections of the oppressed darker races, and representing a part of the exploited millions of the workers of the world, we are deeply concerned that the totalitarian legions of Hitler, Hirohito, and Mussolini do not batter the last bastions of democracy. We know that our fate is tied with the fate of the democratic way of life. And so, out of the depth of our hearts, a cry goes up for the triumph of the United Nations. But we would not be honest with ourselves were we to stop with a call for a victory of arms alone. We know this is not enough. We fight that the democratic faiths, values, heritages, and ideals may prevail.

Unless this war sounds the death knell to the old Anglo-American empire systems, the hapless story of which is one of exploitation for the profit and power of monopoly capitalist economy, it will have been fought in vain. Our aim then must not only be to defeat nazism, fascism, and militarism on the battle-field but to win the peace, for democracy, for freedom and the Brotherhood of Man without regard to his pigmentation, land of his birth or the God of his fathers. . . .

Thus our feet are set in the path toward equali-ty—economic, political and social and racial. . . .

Our nearer goals include the abolition of discrim-ination, segregation, and jim-crow in the Govern-ment, the Army, Navy, Air Corps, U. S. Marine . . . and defense industries; the elimination of discrimination in hotels, restaurants, on public transportation con-veyances, in educational, recreational, cultural, and amusement and entertainment places such as theaters, beaches and so forth.

We want the full works of citizenship with no reservations. We will accept nothing less. . . .

These rights will not be given. They must be taken. . . .

16. Excerpt from Marine Corps Classification of Military Occupational Specialties, 1943

Class I: Jobs in which women are better, more efficient than men. Examples: all clerical jobs, especially those involving typing or requiring fairly routine tasks but coupled with a high degree of accuracy in the work; administrative jobs connected with organization and administration of the Women's Reserve; and instruc-tional jobs of all types.

Class II: Jobs in which women are as good as men, and replaced men on a one-to-one basis. Examples: some cler-ical jobs in which men are especially good, such as accounting; some relatively unskilled service or cleri-cal jobs, such as messengers or Post Exchange clerks; some of the mechanical and skilled jobs, such as watch repairman, fire control instrument repairman, tailor, sewing machine operator—especially those jobs requiring a high degree of finger dexterity.

Class III: Jobs in which women are not as good as men, but can be used effectively when need is great, such as wartime. Examples: most of the jobs in motor trans-port—men are better as motor mechanics and even as drivers when the equipment is heavy and the job demands loading and unloading as well as driving, as it often does; most of the "mechanical" and "skilled" jobs; supervisory and administrative jobs, such as first-

sergeant (except in WR [Women's Reserve] units) where maximum proficiency depends on years of experience in the Marine Corps, and also some super-visory jobs where part of the personnel being super-vised is male; strenuous and physically tiring jobs, such as mess duty where experience showed that more women had to be assigned to cover the same amount of work because they could not endure the long hours and physical strain without relief as well as men.

Class IV: Jobs in which women cannot or should not be used at all. Examples: jobs demanding excessive physi-cal strength, such as driving extremely heavy equip-ment, stock handling in warehouses, heavy lifting in mess halls; jobs totally inappropriate, such as battle duty or jobs requiring that personnel be engaged at particularly unfavorable hours; jobs protected by spe-cial civil service regulations for civilians, such as librarians.

17. Excerpts from memorandum from General Benjamin O. Davis, Sr., to the Inspector General, November 9, 1943

During the last two months I have . . . visited the col-ored troops at the following stations: Fort Devens, Massachusetts; the New York Port of Embarkation . . . , Selfridge Field and Oscoda, Michi-gan. During 1941, 1942, and the early part of this year, my visits were made to the stations located in the Southeastern states, Indiana, Kentucky, Missouri, Oklahoma, Texas, Arkansas, Arizona, and Illinois.

I have reviewed inspection reports and investiga-tions made by other inspectors general from this office and the field. I was deeply impressed with the high morale and attitudes of the colored officers and soldiers stationed in the states visited in the past two months. They were so different from those of the colored offi-cers and soldiers at the stations located in the Southern states. While there has been an improvement in general conditions, there is still great dissatisfaction and dis-couragement on the part of the colored people and the soldiers. . . . The[y] . . . feel that they are denied the pro-tection and rewards that ordinarily result from good behavior and proper performance of duty.

Colored combat units, upon completion of train-ing, have not been sent to theaters of operations. The enlisted personnel of two battalions of Field Artillery has been recently transferred to service units. . . .

In the activation of new colored units, few commanding officers, if any, have been selected from among the colored field officers. Some of these colored field officers have successfully completed the courses at the service schools and have been serving in their present grades for long periods.

The Press news items and reports of Investigations show that there has been little change in the attitudes of civilian communities in Southern states. . . . The colored man in uniform is expected by the War Department to develop a high morale in a community that offers him nothing but humiliation and mistreatment. . . . The War Department has failed to secure to the colored soldier protection against violence on the part of civilian police and to secure justice in the courts in communities near-by to Southern stations. . . .

In fact, the Army, by its directives and by actions of commanding officers, has introduced the attitudes of the "Governors of the six Southern states" in many of the other 42 states of [the] continental United States.

I believe the time has come for the War Department to give some consideration to relieving the colored troops now located in [the South]. Some consideration should be given to the replacement of white commanding officers by colored officers of proven ability—those who have met War Department requirements for promotion and assignments. . . .

I have always tried to be wholly impersonal in connection with the performance of my duties. I have at all times received the kindest consideration and cooperation from those with whom I have been associated. I have striven at all times to successfully accomplish the missions assigned to me. I am grateful for the privilege of contributing to the war effort. . . . I believe a promotion is coming to me at this time, and a gradual relief of colored troops from Southern stations, and the assignment of colored officers of field grade in the command of colored units would go a long way toward inspiring confidence of colored people in the War Department.

18. Excerpt from President Roosevelt's Fireside Chat of December 1943

Britain, Russia, China, and the United States and their allies represent more than three-quarters of the total population of the earth. As long as these four nations with great military power stick together in determination to keep the peace, there will be no possibility of an aggressor nation arising to start another world war. . . . But at the same time we are agreed that if force is necessary to keep international peace, international force will be applied—for as long as it may be necessary.

19. Excerpt from Executive Order No. 9417 establishing a War Refugee Board, January 22, 1944

WHEREAS it is the policy of this Government to take all measures within its power to rescue the victims of enemy oppression who are in Imminent danger of death and otherwise to afford such victims all possible relief and assistance consistent with the successful prosecution of the war;

NOW, THEREFORE, by virtue of the authority vested in me by the Constitution and the statutes of the United States, as President of the United States and as Commander in Chief of the Army and Navy, and in order to effectuate with all possible speed the rescue and relief of such victims of enemy oppression, it is hereby ordered as follows:

1. There is established in the Executive Office of the President a War Refugee Board (hereinafter referred to as the Board). . . .

2. . . . The functions of the Board shall include without limitation the development of plans and programs and the inauguration of effective measures for (a) the rescue, transportation, maintenance and relief of the victims of enemy oppression, and (b) the establishment of havens of temporary refuge for such victims. To this end the Board, through appropriate channels, shall take the necessary steps to enlist the cooperation of foreign governments and obtain their participation in the execution of such plans and programs. . . .

3. It shall be the duty of the State, Treasury and War Departments, within their respective spheres, to execute at the request of the Board the plans and programs so developed and the measures so inaugurated. . . . The State Department shall appoint special attachés, with diplomatic status, on the recommendation of the Board, to be stationed abroad in places where it is likely that assistance can be rendered to war refugees[,] the duties and responsibilities of such

attachés to be defined by the Board in consultation with the State Department.

20. *In Re Summers* (325 U.S. 561 1944)

[In this case Clyde Wilson Summers allegedly was denied a certificate of good character because he was a conscientious objector; without such a certificate he could not be admitted to the Illinois bar.]

Mr. Justice Reed for the Court.

Disqualification under Illinois Constitution. The Justices justify their refusal to admit petitioner to practice before the courts of Illinois on the ground of petitioner's inability to take in good faith the required oath to support the Constitution of Illinois. His inability to take such an oath, the Justices submit, shows that the Committee on Character and Fitness properly refused to certify to his moral character and moral fitness to be an officer of the Court, charged with the administration of justice under the Illinois law. His good citizenship, they think, judged by the standards required for practicing law in Illinois, is not satisfactorily shown. A conscientious belief in nonviolence to the extent that the believer will not use force to prevent wrong, no matter how aggravated, and so cannot swear in good faith to support the Illinois Constitution, the Justices contend, must disqualify such a believer for admission.

Petitioner appraises the denial of admission from the viewpoint of a religionist. He said in his petition:

"The so-called 'misconduct' for which petitioner could be reproached . . . is his taking the New Testament too seriously. Instead of merely reading or preaching the Sermon on the Mount, he tries to practice it. The only fault of the petitioner consists in his attempt to act as a good Christian in accordance with his interpretation of the Bible, and according to the dictates of his conscience. We respectfully submit that the profession of law does not shut its gates to persons who have qualified in all other respects even when they follow in the footsteps of that Great Teacher of mankind who delivered the Sermon on the Mount. We respectfully submit that under our Constitutional guarantees even good Christians who have met all the requirements for the admission to the bar may be admitted to practice law."

Thus a court created to administer the laws of Illinois as it understands them, and charged particularly with the protection of justice in the courts of Illi-

nois through supervision of admissions to the bar, found itself faced with the dilemma of excluding an applicant whom it deemed disqualified for the responsibilities of the profession of law or of admitting the applicant because of its deeply rooted tradition in freedom of belief. The responsibility for choice as to the personnel of its bar rests with Illinois. Only a decision which violated a federal right secured by the Fourteenth Amendment would authorize our intervention. It is said that the action of the Supreme Court of Illinois is contrary to the principles of that portion of the First Amendment which guarantees the free exercise of religion. Of course, under our Constitutional system, men could not be excluded from the practice of law, or indeed from following any other calling, simply because they belong to any of our religious groups, whether Protestant, Catholic, Quaker or Jewish, assuming it conceivable that any state of the Union would draw such a religious line. We cannot say that any such purpose to discriminate motivated the action of the Illinois Supreme Court.

The sincerity of petitioner's beliefs are [sic] not questioned. . . .

The United States does not admit to citizenship the alien who refuses to pledge military service. . . . Even the powerful dissents which emphasized the deep cleavage in this Court on the admission to citizenship did not challenge the right of Congress to require military service from every able-bodied man. It is impossible for us to conclude that the insistence of Illinois that an officer who is charged with the administration of justice must take an oath to support the Constitution of Illinois and Illinois' interpretation of that oath to require a willingness to perform military service violates the principles of religious freedom which the Fourteenth Amendment secures against state action, when a like interpretation of a similar oath as to the Federal Constitution bars an alien from national citizenship.

Mr. Justice Black, dissenting:

The State of Illinois has denied the petitioner the right to practice his profession and to earn his living as a lawyer. It has denied him a license on the ground that his present religious beliefs disqualify him for membership in the legal profession. The question is, therefore, whether a state which requires a license as a prerequisite to practicing law can deny an applicant a license solely because of his deeply-rooted religious convictions. The fact that petitioner measures up to every other requirement for admission to the Bar set by the State demonstrates beyond doubt that the only reason for his rejection was his religious beliefs. . . .

The petitioner's disqualifying religious beliefs stem chiefly from a study of the New Testament and a literal acceptance of the teachings of Christ as he understands them. . . .

I cannot believe that a state statute would be consistent with our constitutional guarantee of freedom of religion if it specifically denied the right to practice law to all members of one of our great religious groups, Protestant, Catholic or Jewish. Yet the Quakers have had a long and honorable part in the growth of our nation, and an amicus curiae brief filed in their behalf informs us that under the test applied to this petitioner, not one of them if true to the tenets of their faith could qualify for the bar in Illinois. And it is obvious that the same disqualification would exist as to every conscientious objector to the use of force, even though the Congress of the United States should continue its practice of absolving them from military service. The conclusion seems to me inescapable that if Illinois can bar this petitioner from the practice of law it can bar every person from every public occupation solely because he believes in nonresistance rather than in force. . . .

The state's denial of petitioner's application to practice law resolves itself into a holding that it is lawfully required that all lawyers take an oath to support the state constitution and that petitioner's religious convictions against the use of force make it impossible for him to observe that oath. The petitioner denies this and is willing to take the oath. . . . In the *Schwimmer* and *Macintosh* cases aliens were barred from naturalization because their then religious beliefs would bar them from bearing arms to defend the country. Dissents in both cases rested in part on the premise that religious tests are incompatible with our constitutional guarantee of freedom of thought and religion. In the *Schwimmer* case dissent, Mr. Justice Holmes said that "if there is any principle of the Constitution that more imperatively calls for attachment than any other it is the principle of free thought—not free thought for those who agree with us but freedom for the thought that we hate. I think that we should adhere to that principle with regard to admission into, as well as to life within this country." In the *Macintosh* case dissent, Mr. Chief Justice Hughes said, "To conclude that the general oath of office is to be interpreted as disregarding the religious scruples of these citizens and as disqualifying them for office because they could not take the oath with such an interpretation would, I believe, be generally regarded as contrary not only to the specific intent of the Congress but as repugnant to the fundamental principle of representative government." I agree with the constitutional philosophy underlying the dissents of Mr. Justice Holmes and Mr. Chief Justice Hughes.

The Illinois Constitution itself prohibits the draft of conscientious objectors except in time of war and also excepts from militia duty persons who are "exempted by the laws of the United States." It has not drafted men into the militia since 1864, and if it ever should again, no one can say that it will not, as has the Congress of the United States, exempt men who honestly entertain the views that this petitioner does. Thus the probability that Illinois would ever call the petitioner to serve in a war has little more reality than an imaginary quantity in mathematics.

I cannot agree that a state can lawfully bar from a semi-public position a well-qualified man of good character solely because he entertains a religious belief which might prompt him at some time in the future to violate a law which has not been and may never be enacted. Under our Constitution men are punished for what they do or fail to do and not for what they think and believe. Freedom to think, to believe and to worship, has too exalted a position in our country to be penalized on such an illusory basis. Mr. Justice Douglas, Mr. Justice Murphy, and Mr. Justice Rutledge concur.

21. Excerpt from President Roosevelt's Radio-Broadcast Prayer on D Day, June 6, 1944

In this poignant moment I ask you to join with me in prayer; Almighty God: our sons, pride of our nation, this day have set on a mighty endeavor, a struggle to preserve our Republic, our religion, and our civilization, and to set free a suffering humanity. . . . They will need Thy blessings. Their road will be long and hard. For the enemy is strong. He may hurl back our forces. Success may not come with rushing speed, but we shall return again and again; and we know that by Thy grace, and by the righteousness of our cause, our sons will triumph. They will be sore tried, by night and by day, without rest—until the victory is won.

22. Dissent in the Case of *Korematsu v. United States* by Justice Robert H. Jackson, 1944

[Fred Korematsu was convicted of violating an order excluding persons of Japanese descent from a military area, and the U.S. Supreme Court upheld that conviction.]

Mr. Justice Jackson, dissenting:

Korematsu was born on our soil, of parents born in Japan. The Constitution makes him a citizen of the United States by nativity and a citizen of California by residence. No claim is made that he is not loyal to this country. There is no suggestion that apart from the matter involved here he is not law-abiding and well disposed. Korematsu, however, has been convicted of an act not commonly a crime. It consists merely of being present in the state whereof he is a citizen, near the place where he was born, and where all his life he has lived.

Even more unusual is the series of military orders which made this conduct a crime. They forbid such a one to remain, and they also forbid him to leave. They were so drawn that the only way Korematsu could avoid violation was to give himself up to the military authority. This meant submission to custody, examination, and transportation out of the territory, to be followed by indeterminate confinement in detention camps.

A citizen's presence in the locality, however, was made a crime only if his parents were of Japanese birth. Had Korematsu been one of four—the others being, say, a German alien enemy, an Italian alien enemy, and a citizen of American-born ancestors convicted of treason but out on parole—only Korematsu's presence would have violated the order. The difference between their innocence and his crime would result, not from anything he did, said, or thought different than they but only in that he was born of different racial stock.

Now, if any fundamental assumption underlies our system, it is that guilt is personal and not inheritable. Even if all of one's antecedents had been convicted of treason, the Constitution forbids its penalties to be visited upon him, for it provides that "no attainder of treason shall work corruption of blood or forfeiture except during the life of the person attainted." But here is an attempt to make an otherwise innocent act a crime merely because this prisoner is the son of parents as to whom he had no choice and belongs to a race from which there is no way to resign. If Congress in peacetime legislation should enact such a criminal law, I should suppose this Court would refuse to enforce it.

But the "law" which this prisoner is convicted of disregarding is not found in an act of Congress but in a military order. Neither the act of Congress nor the executive order of the President, nor both together, would afford a basis for this conviction. It rests on the orders of General DeWitt. And it is said that if the military commander had reasonable military grounds for promulgating the orders, they are constitutional and become law, and the Court is required to enforce them. There are several reasons why I cannot subscribe to this doctrine.

It would be impracticable and dangerous idealism to expect or insist that each specific military command in an area of probable operations will conform to conventional tests of constitutionality. When an area is so beset that it must be put under military control at all, the paramount consideration is that its measures be successful rather than legal. The armed services must protect a society, not merely its Constitution. The very essence of the military job is to marshal physical force, to remove every obstacle to its effectiveness, to give it every strategic advantage. Defense measures will not, and often should not, be held within the limits that bind civil authority in peace. No court can require such a commander in such circumstances to act as a reasonable man; he may be unreasonably cautious and exacting. Perhaps he should be. But a commander in temporarily focusing the life of a community on defense is carrying out a military program; he is not making law in the sense the courts know the term. He issues orders, and they may have a certain authority as military commands, although they may be very bad as constitutional law.

But if we cannot confine military expedients by the Constitution, neither would I distort the Constitution to approve all that the military may deem expedient. That is what the Court appears to be doing, whether consciously or not. I cannot say, from any evidence before me, that the orders of General DeWitt were not reasonably expedient military precautions, nor could I say that they were. But even if they were permissible military procedures, I deny that it follows that they are constitutional. If, as the Court holds, it does follow, then we may as well say that any military order will be constitutional and have done with it. . . .

A military order, however unconstitutional, is not apt to last longer than the military emergency. Even during that period a succeeding commander may revoke it all. But once a judicial opinion rationalizes such an order to show that it conforms to the Constitution, or rather rationalizes the Constitution to show that the Constitution sanctions such an order, the Court for all time has validated the principle of racial discrimination in criminal procedure and of transplanting American citizens. The principle then lies about like a loaded weapon ready for the hand of any authority that can bring forward a plausible claim of an urgent need. Every repetition imbeds that principle more deeply in our law and thinking and expands it to new purposes. All who observe the work of courts are familiar with what Judge Cardozo described as "the tendency of a principle to expand itself to the limit of its logic." A military commander may overstep the bounds of constitutionality and it is an incident. But if we review and approve, that passing incident becomes the doctrine of the Constitution. There it has a generative power of its own, and all that it creates will be in its own image. Nothing better illustrates this danger than does the Court's opinion in this case. . . .

I should hold that a civil court cannot be made to enforce an order which violates constitutional limitations even if it is a reasonable exercise of military authority. The courts can exercise only the judicial power, can apply only law, and must abide by the Constitution, or they cease to be civil courts and become instruments of military policy.

23. Opening Paragraphs of Proposals for the Establishment of a General International Organization, Issued in the names of the United States, the United Kingdom of Great Britain and Ireland, the Union of Soviet Socialist Republics, and the Republic of China, October 7, 1944

There should be established an international organization under the title of The United Nations, the Charter of which should contain provisions necessary to give effect to the proposals which follow.

The purpose of the organization should be:

1. To maintain international peace and security; and to that end to take effective collective measures for the prevention and removal of threats to the peace and the suppression of acts of aggression or other breaches of the peace, and to bring about by peaceful means adjustment or settlement of international disputes which may lead to a breach of the peace;
2. To develop friendly relations among nations and to take other appropriate measures to strengthen universal peace;
3. To achieve international cooperation in the solution of international economic, social and other humanitarian problems; and
4. To afford a center for harmonizing the actions of nations in the achievement of these common ends.

24. Opening Paragraphs of German Act of Military Surrender, May 8, 1945

1. We the undersigned, acting by authority of the German High Command, hereby surrender unconditionally to the Supreme Commander, Allied Expeditionary Force and simultaneously to the Supreme High Command of the Red Army all forces on land, at sea, and in the air who are at this date under German control.

2. The German High Command will at once issue order to all German military, naval and air authorities and to all forces under German control to cease active operations at 2301 hours Central European time on 8th May 1945, to remain in all positions occupied at that time and to disarm completely, handing over their weapons and equipment to the local allied commanders or officers designated by Representatives of the Allied Supreme Commands. No ship, vessel, or aircraft is to be scuttled, or any damage done to their hull, machinery or equipment, and also to machines of all kinds, armament, apparatus, and all the technical means of prosecution of war in general.

3. The German High Command will at once issue to the appropriate commanders, and ensure the carrying out of any further orders issued by the Supreme Commander, Allied Expeditionary Force and by the Supreme Command of the Red Army.

4. This act of military surrender is without prejudice to, and will be superseded by any general instrument of surrender imposed by, or on behalf of the United Nations and applicable to GERMANY and the German armed forces as a whole.

25. OPENING PARAGRAPHS OF RECOMMENDATIONS ON THE IMMEDIATE USE OF NUCLEAR WEAPONS BY THE SCIENTIFIC PANEL OF THE INTERIM COMMITTEE, JUNE 16, 1945

You have asked us to comment on the initial use of the new weapon. This use, in our opinion, should be such as to promote a satisfactory adjustment of our international relations. At the same time, we recognize our obligation to our nation to use the weapons to help save American lives in the Japanese war.

(1) To accomplish these ends we recommend that before the weapons are used not only Britain, but also Russia, France, and China be advised that we have made' considerable progress in our work on atomic weapons, and that we would welcome suggestions as to how we can cooperate in making this development contribute to improved international relations.

(2) The opinions of our scientific colleagues on the initial use of these weapons are not unanimous: they range from the proposal of a purely technical demonstration to that of the military application best designed to induce surrender. Those who advocate a purely technical demonstration would wish to outlaw the use of atomic weapons, and have feared that if we use the weapons now our position in future negotiations will be prejudiced. Others emphasize the opportunity of saving American lives by immediate military use, and believe that such use will improve the international prospects, in that they are more concerned with the prevention of war than with the elimination of this specific weapon. We find ourselves closer to these latter views; we can propose no technical demonstration likely to bring an end to the war; we see no acceptable alternative to direct military use.

26. PREAMBLE TO THE CHARTER OF THE UNITED NATIONS, JUNE 26, 1945

We the peoples of the United Nations determined to save succeeding generations from the scourge of war, which twice in our lifetime has brought untold sorrow to mankind, and to reaffirm faith in fundamental human rights, in the dignity and worth of the human person, in the equal rights of men and women and of nations large and small, and to establish conditions under which justice and respect for the obligations arising from treaties and other sources of international law can be maintained, and to promote social progress and better standards of life in larger freedom, and for these ends to practice tolerance and live together in peace with one another as good neighbours, and to unite our strength to maintain international peace and security, and to ensure, by the acceptance of principles and the institution of methods, that armed force shall not be used, save in the common interest, and to employ international machinery for the promotion of the economic and social advancement of all peoples, have resolved to combine our efforts to accomplish these aims.

Accordingly, our respective Governments, through representatives assembled in the city of San Francisco, who have exhibited their full powers found to be in good and due form, have agreed to the present Charter of the United Nations and do hereby establish an international organization to be known as the United Nations.

27. EXCERPT FROM THE POTSDAM DECLARATION, JULY 17, 1945

A. Political Principles

1. In accordance with the agreement on control machinery in Germany, supreme authority in Germany is exercised on instructions from their respective governments, by the Commander in Chief of the armed forces of the United States of America, the United Kingdom, the Union of Soviet Socialist Republics, and the French Republic, each in his own zone of occupation, and also jointly, in matters affecting Germany as a whole, in their capacity as members of the Control Council.

2. So far as is practicable, there shall be uniformity of treatment of the German population throughout Germany.

3. The purposes of the occupation of Germany by which the Control Council shall be guided are:

(i) The complete disarmament and demilitarization of Germany and the elimination or control of all German industry that could be used for military production....

(ii) To convince the German people that they have suffered a total military defeat and that they cannot escape responsibility for what they have brought upon themselves, since their own ruthless warfare and the fanatical Nazi resistance have destroyed German economy and made chaos and suffering inevitable.

(iii) To destroy the National Socialist Party and its affiliated and supervised organizations, to dissolve all Nazi institutions, to insure that they are not revived in any form, and to prevent all Nazi and militarist activity or propaganda.

(iv) To prepare for the eventual reconstruction of German political life on a democratic basis and for eventual peaceful cooperation in international life by Germany.

28. Excerpts from Instrument of Japanese Surrender, September 2, 1945

We, acting by command of and in behalf of the Emperor of Japan . . . hereby proclaim the unconditional surrender to the Allied Powers of the Japanese Imperial General Headquarters and of all Japanese armed forces and all armed forces under Japanese control wherever situated.

29. Excerpts from Secretary of State George Marshall's Harvard University Commencement Speech Outlining the Marshall Plan for Europe, June 5, 1947

In considering the requirements for the rehabilitation of Europe, the physical loss of life, the visible destruction of cities, factories, mines, and railroads was correctly estimated; but it has become obvious during recent months that this visible destruction was probably less serious than the dislocation of the entire fabric of European economy....

In many countries confidence in the local currency has been severely shaken.... The farmer has always produced the foodstuffs to exchange with the city dweller for the other necessities of life. This division of labor is the basis of modern civilization. At the pre-

sent time it is threatened with breakdown. The town and city industries are not producing adequate goods to exchange with the food-producing farmer. Raw material and fuel are in short supply. Machinery is lacking or worn out.

The farmer or the peasant cannot find the goods for sale which he desires to purchase. So the sale of his farm produce for money which he cannot use seems to him an unprofitable transaction. He, therefore, has withdrawn many fields from crop cultivation and is using them for grazing. He feeds more grain to stock and finds for himself and his family an ample supply of food, however short he may be on clothing and the other ordinary gadgets of civilization. Meanwhile, people in the cities are short of food and fuel. So the governments are forced to use their foreign money and credits to procure these necessities abroad. This process exhausts funds which are urgently needed for reconstruction....

The truth of the matter is that Europe's requirements for the next three or four years of foreign food and other essential products—principally from America—are so much greater than her present ability to pay that she must have substantial additional help, or face economic, social, and political deterioration of a very grave character....

Aside from the demoralizing effect on the world at large and the possibilities of disturbances arising as a result of the desperation of the people concerned, the consequences to the economy of the United States should be apparent to all. It is logical that the United States should do whatever it is able to do to assist in the return of normal economic health in the world, without which there can be no political stability and no assured peace.

Our policy is directed not against any country or doctrine but against hunger, poverty, desperation, and chaos. Its purpose should be the revival of a working economy in the world so as to permit the emergence of political and social conditions in which free institutions can exist. Such assistance, I am convinced, must not be on a piecemeal basis as various crises develop. Any assistance that this government may render in the future should provide a cure rather than a mere palliative.

Any government that is willing to assist in the task of recovery will find full cooperation, I am sure, on the part of the United States Government. Any government which maneuvers to block the recovery of other countries cannot expect help from us. Furthermore, governments, political parties, or groups which seek to perpetuate human misery in order to profit therefrom politically or otherwise will encounter the opposition of the United States. . . .

It would be neither fitting nor efficacious for this government to undertake to draw up unilaterally a program designed to place Europe on its feet economically. This is the business of the Europeans. . . . The program should be a joint one, agreed to by a number, if not all, European nations.

30. Excerpt from Nuremberg Trials Final Report (JCS 1023/10), August 15, 1949

The scope of individual responsibility for these crimes was to include not only "accessories" and those who had taken "a consenting part" in crime, but also "members of groups or organizations connected with the commission of such crimes" and (as to the crime of aggressive war only) "persons who have held high political, civil, or military positions in Germany or in one of its allies or in the financial, industrial or economic life of any of these countries."

To prepare for the carrying out of the directive by the initiation of criminal proceedings, the theater commander was directed "to identify, investigate, apprehend, and detain all persons whom you suspect to be criminals" under the foregoing definitions of the crimes and scope of responsibility, and "all persons whom the Control Council, any one of the United Nations, or Italy notifies to you as being charged as criminals." The theater commander was ordered to report the names of suspected criminals to the Control Council, and there were additional detailed provisions governing the delivery or "extradition" of suspects from one country to another. The directive provided in very general terms "that appropriate military courts may conduct trials of suspected criminals in your custody" but specified that these courts should be "separate from the courts trying current offenses against your occupation," and that their procedures should be "fair, simple, and expeditious . . . designed to accomplish substantial justice without technicality." As theretofore, the theater commander was to postpone trials of high political, civil, or military officials until it was ascertained whether such persons would be tried before an international military tribunal, as well as trials of persons wanted elsewhere.

31. Excerpts from "An American Promise," February 19, 1976

By the President of the United States of America, Gerald R. Ford
A PROCLAMATION

February 19th is the anniversary of a sad day in American history. It was on that date in 1942, in the midst of the response to the hostilities that began on December 7, 1941, that Executive Order No. 9066 was issued, subsequently enforced by the criminal penalties of a statute enacted March 21, 1942, resulting in the uprooting of loyal Americans. Over 100,000 persons of Japanese ancestry were removed from their homes, detained in special camps, and eventually relocated.

The tremendous effort by the War Relocation Authority and concerned Americans for the welfare of these Japanese Americans may add perspective to that story, but it does not erase the setback to fundamental American principles. Fortunately, the Japanese American community in Hawaii was spared the indignities suffered by those on our mainland.

We now know what we should have known then—not only was that evacuation wrong, but Japanese Americans were and are loyal Americans. On the battlefield and at home, Japanese Americans—names like Hamada, Mitsumori, Marimoto, Noguchi, Yamasaki, Kido, Munemori and Miyamura—have been and continue to be written in our history for the sacrifices and the contributions they have made to the well-being and security of this, our common Nation.

The Executive Order that was issued on February 19, 1942, was for the sole purpose of prosecuting the war with the Axis Powers, and ceased to be effective with the end of those hostilities. Because there was no formal statement of its termination, however, there is concern among many Japanese Americans that there may yet be some life in that obsolete document. I think it appropriate, in this our Bicentennial Year, to remove all doubt on that matter, and to make clear our commitment in the future.

Now, THEREFORE, I, GERALD R. FORD, President of the United States of America, do hereby proclaim that all the authority conferred by Executive Order No. 9066 terminated upon the issuance of

Proclamation No. 2714, which formally proclaimed the cessation of the hostilities of World War II on December 31, 1946.

I call upon the American people to affirm with me this American Promise—that we have learned from the tragedy of that long-ago experience forever to treasure liberty and justice for each individual American, and resolve that this kind of action shall never again be repeated.

IN WITNESS WHEREOF, I have hereunto set my hand this 19th day of February in the year of our Lord 1976, and of the Independence of the United States of America the 200th.

32. EXCERPT FROM CIVIL LIBERTIES ACT OF 1988

The Congress recognizes that as described by the Commission on Wartime Relocation and Internment of Civilians a grave injustice was done to both citizens and permanent resident aliens of Japanese ancestry during World War II. The excluded individuals of Japanese ancestry suffered enormous damages both material and intangible which resulted in significant human suffering for which appropriate compensation has not been made. For these fundamental violations of the civil liberties and constitutional rights of those individuals of Japanese ancestry, the Congress apologizes on behalf of the nation.

33. EXCERPT FROM THE WARTIME VIOLATION OF ITALIAN AMERICAN CIVIL LIBERTIES ACT, SIGNED INTO LAW NOVEMBER 7, 2000

The Congress makes the following findings:

1. The freedom of more than 600,000 Italian-born immigrants in the United States and their families was restricted during World War II by Government measures that branded them "enemy aliens" and included carrying identification cards, travel restrictions, and seizure of personal property.

2. During World War II more than 10,000 Italian Americans living on the West Coast were forced to leave their homes and prohibited from entering coastal zones. More than 50,000 were subjected to curfews.

3. During World War II thousands of Italian American immigrants were arrested, and hundreds were interned in military camps.

4. Hundreds of thousands of Italian Americans performed exemplary service and thousands sacrificed their lives in defense of the United States.

5. At the time, Italians were the largest foreign-born group in the United States, and today are the fifth largest immigrant group in the United States, numbering approximately 15,000,000.

6. The impact of the wartime experience was devastating to Italian American communities in the United States, and its effects are still being felt.

7. A deliberate policy kept these measures from the public during the war. Even 50 years later much information is still classified, the full story remains unknown to the public, and it has never been acknowledged in any official capacity by the United States Government. . . .

[After ordering a report on and the dissemination of information about the treatment of Italian Americans during World War II, this public law ends by recommending that] the President should, on behalf of the United States Government, formally acknowledge that these events during World War II represented a fundamental injustice against Italian Americans.

APPENDIX B
Biographies of Major Personalities

Acheson, Dean (April 11, 1893–October 12, 1971) *statesman, attorney, author*

Dean Acheson was born in Middletown, Connecticut, the son of the British-born Episcopal bishop of Connecticut and his well-off Canadian-born wife. Acheson was educated at Groton, Yale, and the Harvard Law School, where he became a protégé of Felix Frankfurter. On May 5, 1917, he married Wellesley graduate Alice Stanley, with whom he had three children.

After World War I, in which he served briefly in the U.S. Navy, he clerked for Supreme Court Justice Louis D. Brandeis. In 1921 he entered the firm of Covington and Burling in Washington, D.C., an association that became lifelong, with intervals of public service as assistant secretary of state for economic affairs (1941–45) in Franklin Roosevelt's presidency, and as undersecretary of state (1945–47) and secretary of state (1949–53) for President Harry S. Truman. Acheson worked closely and loyally with Truman throughout much of the cold war, during which the capitalist United States and the communist Union of Soviet Socialist Republics (USSR) confronted one another. During this period the United States with other Western nations formed the North Atlantic Treaty Organization (NATO) and forced the USSR to lift the blockade of Berlin. In cooperation with the United Nations the United States blocked Communist expansion in Korea. Truman and Acheson also supported the French in Indochina, an action that ultimately led to the Vietnam War.

When Dwight D. Eisenhower became president in January 1953, Acheson returned to practice law at Covington and Burling and to write six books and many articles on diplomatic affairs, consistently advocating a firm policy against the USSR. Subsequently he counseled several presidents on international affairs. He died suddenly, while working at his desk, on October 12, 1971.

Arnold, Henry Harley (Hap Arnold) (June 25, 1886–January 15, 1950) *general*

Born in Gladwyn, Pennsylvania, Arnold graduated from the U.S. Military Academy in 1907 and began his military service as a second lieutenant of infantry. He was taught to fly by Orville Wright in 1911. In World War I he won promotions from captain to executive officer to the air services chief, and in the years that followed he argued that air power would outmode traditional armies and navies. In 1941 he was promoted to brigadier general and named chief of the U.S. Army Air Corps, and the next year he became commanding general of that organization. In 1944 he was promoted to the five-star rank of general of the army. He retired to his California farm in 1946. Three years later he was named general of the U.S. Air Force.

Axis Sally (Mildred Elizabeth Gillars) (November 29, 1900–June 25, 1988) *American-born radio propagandist for the Nazis*

An aspiring actress, Gillars attended Ohio Wesleyan University, studied in Europe, and then worked in the theater. In 1933 she moved to Europe, living first in France and then in Germany, where she taught English and then worked for Radio Berlin. During the war she broadcast propaganda to American troops in a program called "Home Sweet Home." In a sultry voice, she taunted GIs about the alleged infidelities of their wives and sweethearts, delivered discouraging news about specific soldiers, and forecast the failure of their missions.

In August 1948 she was captured, and the next year she was tried for treason. At her trial witnesses testified that she had posed as a member of the International Red Cross, luring GI POWs into recording messages for their families that she then aired with such insertions as, "It's a disgrace to the American public that they don't wake to the fact of what Franklin D. Roosevelt is doing to the Gentiles of your country and my country." She was found guilty on one of the eight counts of treason with which she was charged and sentenced to 10–30 years in prison. On June 10, 1961, she was paroled. She taught for a while and finished her bachelor's degree before her death in 1988.

Baruch, Bernard Mannes (August 19, 1870–June 20, 1965) *financier, public adviser*
Baruch was born in Camden, South Carolina, his father a Jewish immigrant from East Prussia and his mother, Belle Wolfe, the daughter of a well-established southern Jewish family. In 1881 the Baruch family moved to New York City, where Bernard attended public school and graduated from the College of the City of New York in 1889. He joined the brokerage firm of A. A. Housman, where his speculations made him a millionaire at age 30. In 1897 he married Annie Griffen, by whom he had three children. In 1903 he established his own brokerage firm specializing in raw-material industries.

Influenced by his father's public spirit, Baruch used his wealth for civic causes and philanthropy. During World War I President Woodrow Wilson appointed him to a number of posts concerned with mobilization, including commissioner for raw materials in the War Industries Board. His successful service gained him a reputation for wisdom and common sense that followed him until his death.

He preferred to act behind the scenes and is typically pictured sitting on a bench in a Washington park dispensing advice to the politically powerful. As one of President Franklin D. Roosevelt's economic advisers he helped to shape plans to adapt industry to wartime requirements. In 1941 he was appointed adviser to the Office of War Mobilization chaired by James Byrnes; in 1942 he headed the Rubber Survey Committee to produce a plan to deal with the rubber shortage and develop a synthetic rubber industry; and in February 1944 he headed a committee to plan the transition to a peacetime economy.

After World War II president Harry S. Truman appointed Baruch ambassador to the United Nations Atomic Energy Commission, the last post in which he directly influenced governmental policy. His influence waned during the Truman administration, though he participated vigorously in many of the

public debates over current policy issues. He died in New York City.

Bourke-White, Margaret (June 14, 1904 [or 1906]–August 21, 1971) *photographer, journalist, war correspondent*
Margaret Bourke-White was born in New York City, the daughter of naturalist and engineer-designer Joseph White and Minnie Bourke, who worked in publishing. In 1922 she entered Columbia University, where she studied first herpetology and then photography; after several transfers she graduated from Cornell in 1927. Meanwhile, in 1925, she had married graduate student engineer Everett Chapman, but they divorced the next year.

Drawn to images of machinery and derricks, she gained early recognition as an industrial photographer in Cleveland, Ohio. Her pictures caught the attention of Henry Luce, who hired her to work on his magazines *Fortune* and *Life*. In 1931 after an assignment in the Soviet Union as the first Western photographer allowed in, she published *Eyes on Russia*. For the rest of the decade she roamed the United States covering everything from dam construction to floods. Most famously she traveled the American South with the writer Erskine Caldwell, with whom in 1937 she published a book on the living conditions of poor tenant farmers, *You Have Seen Their Faces.* After their marriage in 1939, they published *North of the Danube* (1939) on Czechoslovakian life, and *Say, This Is the U.S.A.* (1941). The Caldwells divorced in 1942.

The only foreign correspondent in the USSR when war broke out, Bourke-White spent the war as an accredited war correspondent, photographing action in North Africa and Italy, crossing the German border with Gen. Patton's troops, and documenting the death camps in pictures later collected as *The Living Dead of Buchenwald.* After the war she was assigned to India and South Africa, then to the Korean War. Her life was studded with danger: She was torpedoed in the Mediterranean, strafed by the Luftwaffe, stranded on an Arctic island, bombarded in Moscow, and doused in the Chesapeake River when her helicopter crashed. Her interest in the people and things she photographed led her to say, "The camera is a remarkable instrument. Saturate yourself with your subject and the camera will all but take you by the hand."

In the mid-1950s Parkinson's disease gradually disabled her and ended her career; she fought it bravely, saying, "If you banish fear, nothing terribly bad can happen to you." Her autobiography, *Portrait of Myself,* appeared in 1963. She died in Connecticut.

Bowles, Chester (April 5, 1901–May 25, 1986)
businessman, diplomat, governor of Connecticut
Chester Bowles was born in Springfield, Massachusetts, and educated at Choate and Yale, receiving a B.S. in 1924. He earned his fortune in advertising in New York. During World War II President Franklin D. Roosevelt appointed him chief of the Office Of Price Administration in 1943. From 1946 to 1948 he served as director of the Office of Economic Stability, and from 1949 to 1951 as governor of Connecticut. His work with the United Nations led to his appointment as U.S. ambassador to India in 1951, a post to which he was reappointed in 1963. He wrote three books, including *The Makings of a Just Society.*

Brown, Willa B. (January 21, 1906–July 18, 1992)
African-American aviator, black aviation advocate, educator
Willa Brown was born in Glasgow, Kentucky. Having received a bachelor's degree in 1927 at Indiana State Teacher's College, she began teaching business in Gary, Indiana. Thereafter she moved to Chicago, where she learned to fly. In 1937 she earned both her pilot's license and a master's degree from Northwestern University.

The same year she and her flight instructor, Cornelius R. Coffey, founded the National Airmen's Association of America to promote African-American aviation and to lobby Congress for the racial integration of the Army Air Corps. The next year they started the Coffey School of Aeronautics, which was later selected by the Civil Aeronautics Administration to offer the Civilian Pilot Training Program. Some of the 200 pilots they trained at the Coffey School in the next seven years became Tuskegee Airmen, a unit that Brown had lobbied to create. In 1941 she began work as a training coordinator for the Civil Aeronautics Administration and as a teacher in the Civil Air Patrol, in which she was a commissioned officer. After the war she continued her interest in aviation, in 1972 joining the Women's Advisory Committee on Aviation in the Federal Aviation Agency. She died in 1992.

Byrnes, James Francis (May 2, 1879 [or 1882]–April 9, 1972) *governor of South Carolina, U.S. representative and senator, U.S. Supreme Court justice, director of Economic Stabilization, director of the Office of War Mobilization, secretary of state*
Born in Charleston, North Carolina, Byrnes was educated in that city's public schools. From 1900 to 1908, he worked as a court reporter, adding to that task in 1903 the editorship of the *Aiken Journal and Review.* In 1903 he also was admitted to the bar, having read law privately. In 1906 he married Maude Busch.

Byrnes devoted his life to public service, adopting Tolstoy's philosophy: "The sole meaning of life is to serve humanity." He rose rapidly, becoming solicitor for the Second Circuit for two years. In the federal government he also served in the U.S. House of Representatives from 1911 to 1925 and in the Senate from 1931 to 1941, after which he was appointed to the U.S. Supreme Court. The next year he resigned to become director of the Office of Economic Stabilization under President Franklin D. Roosevelt—an office in which he was popularly called the "assistant president." From there he moved to the directorships successively of the Office of War Mobilization and the Office of War Mobilization and Reconversion. Under President Harry Truman he served as secretary of state from 1945 to 1947, exercising his skills in peaceful negotiation.

After this remarkable career in the legislative, judicial, and executive branches of the national government, Byrnes returned to his home state, which he governed from 1951 to 1955, significantly improving the state's mental-health-care system. He rounded off his public service as U.S. delegate to the United Nations in 1953. He died in 1972 in South Carolina.

Cochran, Jacqueline (ca. May 11, 1908–August 7, 1980) *pilot*
Orphaned at an early age, Cochran grew up in poverty in a lumber mill town in northern Florida, perhaps as a child laborer in a cotton mill. At 13 she began cutting hair; at the urging of one of her customers, she trained as a nurse, but dislike of medical practice made her return to the beauty industry. She landed a job as beautician at Saks Fifth Avenue in New York City. Soon thereafter, on the advice of her future husband, millionaire Floyd Oldham, she began to take flying lessons, obtaining her pilot's license in 1932 with only three weeks of instruction. On May 11,

1935, she married Oldham. That year she set up the Jacqueline Cochran Cosmetic Company, the profits of which she used to finance her flying. In 1938 she won the transcontinental Bendix race, the first to finish the course nonstop. She went on to win the Harmon trophy and to break speed records and the women's altitude record.

After the outbreak of World War II, she ferried U.S.-built Hudson bombers to England. In 1941, she studied the British system of ferrying planes around the country by using women pilots, and the next year she led 25 American women to join that service (the British Air Transport Auxiliary). Meanwhile she developed plans for using women pilots in the U.S. Army Air Corps. In August 1943 she joined with Nancy Harkness Love to form the Women's Airforce Service Pilots (WASPs), in which women ferried planes across the continent, trained male pilots and B-17 turret gunners, towed targets for antiaircraft gunnery practice, and tested planes at repair depots. Her work with this group earned Cochran the U.S. Distinguished Service Medal.

After the war Cochran continued her career in aviation, in 1953 becoming the first woman to break the sound barrier. In 1964 she set a record of 1,429 miles per hour in the F-104 Starfighter. After heart trouble grounded her in the early 1970s, she spent the rest of her life driving a recreational vehicle around the country, gardening, and cycling around her ranch. She died in 1980, having, as she wished, traveled "with the wind and the stars."

Davis, General Benjamin O., Sr. (July 1, 1877–November 26, 1970) *U.S. Army's first black general*

Born in Washington, D.C., Davis as a young man spent a year at Howard University, leaving in 1898 to serve as a first lieutenant of volunteers in the Spanish-American War. Mustered out in 1899, he enlisted as a private in the regular army. During service in the Philippines, he was promoted to second lieutenant in 1901. From 1905 to 1909 he taught military tactics at Wilberforce University, from 1909 to 1912 he served as military attaché in Liberia, and from 1912 to 1915 he was on garrison duty and border patrol in the American Southwest. Thereafter he spent much of his time teaching at Tuskegee and Wilberforce, reaching the rank of colonel in 1930. In 1938 he received his first independent command, and two years later he became the first black general. He retired in 1941 but was immediately summoned to active duty in the office of the inspector general.

In World War II Gen. Davis served as adviser on race relations. On assignment with the army's inspector general, he conducted inspections involving black troops stationed at northern and southern posts. In a memorandum of November 9, 1943, he pointed to the difficulty for the black soldier to maintain "a high morale in a community that offers him nothing but humiliation and mistreatment." He accused the army of introducing southern attitudes into other states. After investigating racial clashes between white soldiers or civilians and black soldiers, he recommended that black soldiers gradually be removed from southern posts and that black officers be assigned to command black troops.

After the war Davis briefly returned to the inspector general's office and then again retired in 1948, after 50 years of service. He died in Chicago on November 26, 1970. He held the Bronze Star Medal, the Distinguished Service Medal, the croix de guerre with palm from France, and the Grade of Commander of the Order of the Star of Africa from Liberia. Atlanta University awarded him an honorary LL.D.

Donovan, William Joseph (Wild Bill Donovan) (January 1, 1883–February 8, 1959) *lawyer, major general, diplomat, the only American to hold his nation's four highest awards: the Medal of Honor, the Distinguished Service Cross, the Distinguished Service Medal, and the National Security Medal*

Born in Buffalo, New York, the son of a railroad yard superintendent, Donovan studied for the priesthood but in 1904 transferred to Columbia University to study law. He set up as a lawyer in Buffalo in 1907. In 1914 he married Ruth Rumsey, who bore him two children.

With other young Buffalo men, in 1912 he organized a military unit that was called into service during the 1916 Mexican border crisis but saw no combat. The unit did serve in World War I, however, where Donovan distinguished himself as an officer in the 69th New York Infantry. In 1922 he embarked on a public career as U.S. attorney for western New York and entered Republican politics. For a time he alternated between public service and private law, strongly supporting military preparedness. He collected intelligence for the United States on several trips abroad.

After war broke out in Europe in 1939, Donovan advocated the creation of a central intelligence bureau. President Franklin D. Roosevelt listened and appointed him first coordinator of information in 1941 and, the next year, head of the new Office of Strategic Services (OSS). This office was staffed both by specialists who collected and evaluated data on which national policy and tactical decisions were based, and by agents engaged in covert activities abroad—espionage, guerrilla warfare, aid to local resistance groups, and rescuing Allied soldiers. At war's end Donovan resigned, strongly urging the creation of a peacetime agency to replace the OSS. He returned to his law practice and also assisted in the prosecution of the Nuremberg war crimes trials.

But when the Central Intelligence Agency was formed, President Dwight Eisenhower passed him over as its possible director, instead offering him the ambassadorship to Thailand, where he served in 1953 and 1954. He died in Washington, D.C., in 1959.

Drew, Charles Richard (June 3, 1904–April 1, 1950) *black physician and researcher, founder of the American Red Cross blood bank, organizer of the first blood bank drive*
Charles Richard Drew was born in Washington, D.C., and educated in the public schools of Washington, at Amherst College, and at the medical school of McGill University in Montreal, Canada, at all of which he was a star athlete. At Montreal General Hospital and at Columbia University Medical School he conducted experiments demonstrating that in many cases blood plasma could be used instead of whole blood, had a longer shelf life, and was less likely to become contaminated. Having earned his doctorate of medical science from Columbia, Drew became the medical supervisor in England of the "Blood for Britain" project. He returned to the United States to take the post of director of the Red Cross Blood Bank and assistant director of the National Research Council, in charge of blood collection for the U.S. military. In this work he spoke out against the separation of blood from blacks and whites. When on April 1, 1950, he was seriously injured in a one-car accident in Alabama, doctors at a white hospital struggled to save him, but he died from having lost too much blood.

Ebel, Miriam Davenport Burke (June 6, 1915–September 13, 1999) *artist, sculptor*
Miriam Davenport was born in Boston, Massachusetts. After taking an undergraduate degree in art

and architecture history at Smith College and spending a year in New York University's Graduate Institute of Fine Arts, she studied in Paris. After the German invasion of France in May 1940, she spent several months in Marseilles working with Varian Fry at the Centre Américain de Secours, founded to rescue prominent people wanted by the Gestapo. In October she went to Yugoslavia to rescue her desperately ill fiancé; they married secretly in April 1941 and managed to return to the United States in December of that year.

Over the next decade she worked for the International Rescue and Relief Committee and other worthy causes, and later for the American Council of Learned Societies' Committee for the Protection of Cultural Treasures in War Areas. For a while she managed the Princeton office of the Emergency Committee of Atomic Scientists. In 1951 her husband took a job at the University of Iowa, where she began graduate work in art and exhibited both as a sculptor and as a painter. After her husband's death in 1961 she taught art and French to children in Riverside, Iowa, where she met and married archaeologist Charles Ebel. She then earned a Ph.D. in French literature at the University of Iowa.

Eisenhower, Dwight David (October 14, 1890–March 28, 1969) *supreme commander in the European Theater of Operations in World War II, supreme commander of the North Atlantic Treaty Organization, 34th president of the United States*
Born in Denison, Texas, and raised in Abilene, Kansas, Eisenhower graduated from West Point in 1915. The next year he married Mamie Geneva Doud. During World War I he served within the United States, earning two promotions, and thereafter he continued to rise rapidly, at posts both in the United States and overseas. He gained recognition through writing a guidebook to World War I battlefields (1927–29) and through his service under Gen. Douglas MacArthur (1933–36).

During the early part of World War II he was assigned to Washington, D.C. More promotions followed, and in December 1943 he was designated the commanding general of the European Theater of Operations; the success of the invasion on June 6, 1944, brought promotion to General of the Army in December of that year, a rank made permanent in April 1946. After a stint as military governor of the

American-occupied zone in Germany, Eisenhower was named army chief of staff in November 1945.

In June 1948 he assumed the presidency of Columbia University in New York City, but in December 1950 he was called back to the army to become the supreme allied commander of the North Atlantic Treaty Organization and of American forces in Europe. He retired from active service and resigned his commission to announce his candidacy for the U.S. presidency in June 1952; he was elected that November. During his two terms the Korean War ended, and Alaska and Hawaii joined the union. After they left the White House on March 4, 1961, the Eisenhowers lived on their farm near Gettysburg, Pennsylvania, where he died in 1969.

Gildersleeve, Virginia Crocheron
(October 3, 1877–July 7, 1965) *college administrator, leader in international affairs*
Virginia Gildersleeve was born in New York City and educated at the Brearly School; at Barnard College, where she graduated with an A.B. in 1899; and at Columbia University, where she earned an A.M. in medieval history in 1900, and a Ph.D. in English and comparative literature in 1908. After a term as lecturer at Barnard, she accepted the deanship in 1911 and held the post for the next 36 years. She maintained close friendships with the British Shakespearean scholar Caroline Spurgeon and with Elizabeth Reynard, Barnard professor of English who became second in command of the WAVES.

Gildersleeve is known not only for her brilliant administration but also for her work as an advocate for the expansion of women's education, with particular emphasis on entry into the professions. She fought the isolationism rampant in the United States between the two world wars, achieving stature in both national and international affairs. From 1942 to 1945 she chaired the advisory council of the WAVES, and during World War II she also set up an important code-breaking program at Barnard, established a program in international relations to prepare women for the foreign service, and found jobs for anthropologists with the army and navy.

In February 1945 she was the lone woman in the U.S. delegation to the founding conference of the United Nations and helped to draft the charter of that organization: She and Reynard drafted the opening paragraph of the preamble, and Gildersleeve insisted that the charter require a Commission on Human Rights. She went on to serve on the U.S. Educational Mission in Japan that restructured the Japanese educational system. She retired in 1947 and died in 1965, in Centerville, Massachusetts.

Hallaren, Mary A. (1907–) *Women's Army Corps (WAC) director, director of Women in Community Service*
Massachusetts born, as a young woman, Mary Hallaren taught junior high school, in the summers hitchhiking across Canada, Mexico, Europe, and China. As soon as the Women's Auxiliary Army Corps (later the Women's Army Corps) was organized in 1942, she went to enlist. "You don't have to be six feet tall to have a brain that works," she told the recruiter who questioned what a woman of five feet could do in the army. A year later as a captain she commanded the first battalion of WAACs to serve in Europe, the largest contingent of U.S. women serving overseas. She directed the WAC from 1947 to 1953, working with Gen. Dwight D. Eisenhower to assure a permanent place for women in the military, an achievement embodied in the Women's Armed Services Integration Act of 1948. That year "the Little Colonel" became the first woman commissioned in the regular army, where she served until 1960.

In 1965 she became the executive director of Women in Community Service (WICS), an organization sponsored by church women to assist young women in poverty, which Hallaren had helped to establish. There she worked for the next 34 years, developing the organization from the recruitment wing for the U.S. Job Corps to a variety of services, like helping women about to be released from prison and moving women from welfare to self-support. In retirement from this third career she continued her civic work and her lecturing on the history of military women.

Halsey, William F. (Bull Halsey)
(October 30, 1882–August 16, 1959) *admiral*
Born in Elizabeth, New Jersey, and educated at various schools in California, Pennsylvania, Maryland, and Virginia, Halsey graduated from the naval academy in 1904. In 1909 he married Frances Cooke Grandy, who bore him two children.

Through 23 rather undistinguished years of service, he specialized in torpedo warfare. In World War I he commanded two destroyers on antisubmarine escort duty. In the 1930s he earned the designation of naval aviator. In 1921 he was promoted to commander, in 1927 to captain, and in 1938 to rear admiral. World War II brought him fame, with his promotion to vice admiral and appointment as commander of Aircraft Battle Force, which made him senior carrier admiral in the Pacific. His aggressiveness and quotability increased his renown, though as a commanding officer he suffered several disastrous defeats as well as winning several notable victories. Although some naval professionals questioned the thoroughness of his planning and his efficiency, he was promoted to Fleet Admiral in December 1945. He retired in 1947 and in 1959 died at Fishers Island, New York.

Harriman, W. Averell (William Harriman)
(November 15, 1891–July 26, 1986) *businessman, public official*

Born in New York City, Harriman as a child traveled around the world and participated in scientific exploration with his family. He was formally educated at Groton and Yale, where he studied history and economics. After graduation and the death of his father, he went to work in 1913 for the Union Pacific railroad, where he won rapid promotions. With the money his mother settled on him, he invested in shipping and organized an international investment house and an international banking firm. These experiences increased his interest in European affairs. He stopped doing business with Germany even before Hitler came to power, and in 1926 decided that the Bolshevik revolution was "a reactionary development."

In 1928 he departed from his Republican upbringing by voting for the Democratic candidate for president, Al Smith. Harriman's eldest sister, founder of the Junior League, encouraged his interest in politics, especially after the election in 1932 of Franklin Delano Roosevelt (FDR), and in 1933 he entered national public service by serving on the Business Advisory Council to mobilize support for FDR's economic recovery program. From then on he devoted much of his time and energy to public affairs, serving in such positions as FDR's personal representative to Great Britain (1941–43), ambassador to the USSR (1943–46), secretary of commerce (1946–48), governor of New York (1955–59), undersecretary of state (1963–65), ambassador-at-large (1965–68), and chief U.S. negotiator at the Paris peace talks on Vietnam (1968).

Henderson, Leon (May 26, 1895–October 19, 1986) *economist, government administrator*

Born poor in Millville, New Jersey, Henderson worked his way through Swarthmore College and two years of graduate study at the University of Pennsylvania. After several years of teaching economics and acting as a consultant to the governor of Pennsylvania, he joined the Russell Sage Foundation, where he worked from 1925 to 1934. He advised President Franklin D. Roosevelt in such posts as director of research and planning for the National Recovery Administration and director of the Office of Price Administration (OPA) (1941–42), where he fought Congress for a workable price-control law, arguing against the "business as usual" mentality, and outraged auto manufacturers by ordering a 50 percent decrease in auto production.

After the many enemies he had made by his work in the OPA forced his resignation, he made his career in business. However, he continued his interest in public affairs, notably as chair of Americans for Democratic Action.

Hillman, Sidney (March 23, 1887–July 10, 1946) *labor leader*

Hillman was born in Lithuania and educated as a rabbi. As a member of the trade union movement and an advocate of labor reforms, he was imprisoned by the czarist government. Released in 1905, he emigrated first to England and then two years later to the United States.

Carrying his prolabor sentiments into his employment in the Chicago clothing industry, he led a successful strike in 1910. In 1914 he was elected president of the Amalgamated Clothing Workers, a position he held for the rest of his life. He led the growing union into political action: securing unemployment insurance, creating a model arbitration system, building cooperative housing developments, and organizing two banks. From 1935 to 1940 he served as a vice-president of the Congress of Industrial Organizations (CIO), a group of unions that broke off from the American Federation of Labor in 1936.

During World War II he acted as associate director of the Office of Production Management and later served on the War Production Board. In 1943 he took the chair of the CIO Political Action Committee. He died in 1946.

Hobby, Oveta Culp (January 19, 1905–August 16, 1995) *first commanding officer of the Women's Army Corps, first secretary of the Department of Health, Education, and Welfare*

Oveta Culp was born in Killeen, Texas, and educated in the public schools there and at Mary Hardin Baylor College in Belton, Texas. She then taught elocution, became a cub reporter on the Austin *Statesman,* and from 1925 to 1931, while continuing her studies, served as legislative parliamentarian of the Texas House of Representatives. Deeply involved in politics, she became a clerk of the state banking commission, codified the state banking laws, clerked for the legislature's judiciary committee, and acted as assistant to the city attorney. At 25 she was defeated in her only campaign for elective office, as a state legislator.

On February 23, 1931, she married 53-year-old William Pettus Hobby, president of the Houston *Post-Dispatch* and former governor of Texas, with whom she had two children. Meanwhile she worked on the *Post-Dispatch,* which the Hobbys bought, becoming executive vice president in 1938. She also published a handbook of parliamentary law.

In 1941, she reluctantly agreed to draw up an organizational chart recommending ways for women to serve in the army and to head the Women's Interest Section in the War Department Bureau of Public Relations; after Pearl Harbor, yielding to her husband's belief that citizens must do whatever their country asks of them, she consented to put the plan into operation. As the first commander of the Women's Auxiliary Army Corps, established in 1942, Hobby gradually persuaded the army to increase the number of job classifications open to women from 54 to 239, and oversaw the incorporation of the corps into the regular army, as the Women's Army Corps. She resigned, exhausted, in July 1945.

Soon however she took up a career as director of the Hobby-owned radio station KPRC, KPRC-TV, and executive vice president of the Houston *Post,* as well as heavy responsibilities as a volunteer. In 1948 she served as a delegate to the United Nations and in 1949 as president of the Southern Newspaper Publishers Association.

In 1953 President Dwight Eisenhower appointed her chair of the Federal Security Agency and invited her to sit in on cabinet meetings. On April 11, 1953, she became the first secretary of the newly created Department of Health, Education, and Welfare, over-seeing medical research, planning for the education of the baby boomers, administering the teacher-student exchange program with foreign countries, and assuming responsibility for the public health. In 1955 her husband's illness necessitated her resignation, after which she resumed her work with the *Post* and her volunteer work. Her husband died on June 7, 1964, but thereafter she continued to participate in public affairs on the local, state, national, and international levels. She died in 1995.

Hopkins, Harry Lloyd (August 17, 1890–January 29, 1946) *social worker, federal administrator, diplomat*

An Iowan by birth and upbringing, Hopkins began his career as a social worker in New York City, with an intense interest in politics. In October 1913, he married Ethel Gross, his colleague, with whom he had four children. In 1929 he divorced his first wife to marry secretary Barbara Duncan, who in 1932 bore him a daughter, Diana.

In 1931 he began to run an agency set up by New York governor Franklin D. Roosevelt, which provided jobs for more than a million New Yorkers during the Great Depression. When Roosevelt moved to the White House in 1933, he appointed Hopkins director of the Federal Emergency Relief Administration, modeled on the New York program. That fall Hopkins persuaded Roosevelt to create the Civil Works Authority to provide work relief for people with limited skills, putting 4 million people to work within 30 days. In 1934 he undertook responsibility for the new Works Progress (Projects) Administration. He also helped develop the Social Security system.

Despite bad health, the death of his second wife in 1937, and the defeat of his presidential ambitions, Hopkins continued to serve as secretary of commerce, in the development of special projects, and as a speech writer. In March 1941 he assumed responsibility for the Lend-Lease program, and that fall Roosevelt appointed him his assistant—according to Robert Sherwood, "Roosevelt's own personal foreign office." In that role, Hopkins directly negotiated with Churchill, de Gaulle, Stalin, and Molotov; provided liaison with American generals; and acted as the president's aide at every major conference. Off and on he and his daughter Diana lived in the White House, until he married Louise Macy on July 30, 1942. In 1945, summoning almost his last ounce of strength, he eased the transition into Truman's presidency after

Roosevelt's death, supporting the new president's resolve to build the United Nations. In July of that year, Hopkins accepted the chair of the Women's Cloak and Suit Industry in New York City.

Horton, Mildred McAfee See MCAFEE, MILDRED.

Hull, Cordell (October 2, 1871–July 23, 1955)
U.S. secretary of state, 1933–1944
Born in a log cabin in Pickett County, Tennessee, Hull was educated in a one-room school, a private academy, a Kentucky normal school (for the training of teachers), the National Normal University in Ohio, and Tennessee's Cumberland University, where he earned a law degree in 1891.

At 19 he began practicing law in Celina, Tennessee, and at 21 ran for the state legislature, serving as a member of its House of Representatives from 1893 to 1897. After service in the Spanish-American War, he resumed practicing law in Tennessee, and from 1903 to 1907 served on the Fifth Judicial District bench. From 1907 to 1931 he represented the state in the U.S. House of Representatives. He moved on to the Senate in 1931, resigning to become President Franklin D. Roosevelt's secretary of state in 1933. In the almost 12 years of his tenure in that office he laid the foundation for the Good Neighbor Program with Latin and South America; battled the Great Depression through a series of treaties that lowered tariffs and stimulated trade; carried the heavy burdens that World War II imposed on his office; and drew a blueprint for the United Nations. In 1944 he retired because of ill health, but in 1945 he served on the American delegation to the first United Nations conference. He died in 1955.

Jones, Jesse Holman (April 5, 1874–June 1, 1956)
businessman, head of the Reconstruction Finance Corporation, secretary of commerce
Jesse Jones was born in Robertson County, Tennessee. When he finished the ninth grade he took charge of one of his father's tobacco factories. After a period at Hill's Business College in Dallas, Texas, he entered the lumber business, eventually setting up for himself in Houston and expanding into real estate, banking, and development. In World War I he took charge of military relief for the American Red Cross, thereafter returning to Houston.

President Herbert Hoover appointed Jones to the board of the Reconstruction Finance Corporation (RFC), an agency established to combat the Great Depression that began in 1929, and President Franklin D. Roosevelt (FDR) made him its chair. In this position he pumped money into the economy to stave off the breakdown of the system. In 1939 he became head of the Federal Loan Agency (FLA), continuing to control the RFC. Beginning in 1940, Jones served in the dual capacity of secretary of commerce and head of the FLA.

His conservatism and political differences with FDR prompted a request for his resignation in 1945. Jones then broke with the Democratic Party. Refusing other appointments, he returned to life as a Houston businessman and philanthropist. He died in 1956.

Kaiser, Henry John (May 9, 1882–August 24, 1967) *industrialist, entrepreneur*
The son of poor German immigrants, Henry J. Kaiser was born in Canajoharie, New York. At 13, he began working in a dry-goods store and as a photographer's apprentice. At 19, he bought the photography business and thereafter traveled to summer and winter resorts photographing tourists. Eager to marry Bessie Hannah Fosburgh, daughter of a wealthy lumberman, he turned to the hardware business, establishing himself in Spokane, Washington. They were married in 1907, and during their 44-year marriage they had two children. After Bessie's death in 1951, he married Alyce Chester.

Taking as his motto, "Find a need and fill it," Kaiser established business after business, building highways, aqueducts, pipelines, levees, bridges, and dams (including the Grand Coulee and the Hoover) in the United States, Cuba, and Mexico, and constructing naval defense installations on Wake, Guam, and the Hawaiian Islands. Willing to delegate authority, he himself concentrated on visualizing a whole problem in its complexity and adapting or creating new means to solve it.

His talents served the nation well when in 1939 he turned from the international construction business to shipbuilding. In his seven yards in the Pacific Northwest, he produced more than a thousand Liberty ships desperately needed to transport goods to the Allies. For speed of production, when he discovered that his largest cranes could not carry the superstructure of a ship off the assembly line, he cut the finished structure into four pieces, moved them, and welded them back together. To insure a steady supply of steel to his shipyards, he built a steel plant in California. He also supplied lightweight metals for aircraft by entering the magnesium industry.

Kaiser failed in his postwar dream of creating a low-cost, lightweight automobile made of aluminum, but Kaiser Aluminum became the second-largest corporation in the industry. He valued his reputation as a humanitarian businessman, maintaining excellent relations with unions. The health-maintenance organization that he founded for his workers, Kaiser Permanente, expanded to serve millions of Americans. Kaiser died in Hawaii, having started more than 100 companies, many of which still exist.

Kappius, Jupp (unknown–unknown) *the first Office of Strategic Services agent parachuted into Germany*
Kappius was a German trade unionist driven from Germany by the Nazis. He was trained by the British, who also arranged the logistics for his jump into Germany. Posing as Wilhelm Leineweber, an architect of German military construction searching for his mother on the way to a new assignment, he landed near Bochum in the late summer of 1944 and by prearrangement found shelter with fellow trade unionists. At the end of September, his wife, Anne Kappius, began acting as courier between him and his U.S. Office of Strategic Services (OSS) superiors in Switzerland, as well as for other OSS agents within the Reich. By then he had organized a resistance cadre, mostly among factory workers and miners, in several Ruhr cities, with links to other major German cities. While he waited for an arms drop, he collected information on conditions in the Ruhr until, on November 4, Allied planes began bombing. He also encouraged industrial sabotage. He remained in Germany until April 9, 1945, when he made contact with invading American troops, providing U.S. intelligence with a list of trustworthy anti-Nazis in Ruhr cities. Soon thereafter, he was flown to England, where he told authorities that in his opinion few Germans had known of the existence of the death camps. After the war Jupp and Anne Kappius returned to Germany, where he was eventually elected to the state legislature of North Rhine–Westphalia.

Kelly, Colin (ca. 1915–December 10, 1941) *U.S. Army pilot*
In the early days of World War II Kelly became a legendary hero erroneously credited with sinking a Japanese battleship by crashing his bomber into it, an exploit for which he reputedly received the Congressional Medal of Honor; after his death his infant son was given a scholarship to West Point. In fact Captain Kelly attacked a Japanese force landing in the Philippines; when his plane was irreparably hit he ordered the crew to bail out; the plane exploded near Clark Field in the Philippines, killing Kelly. He was posthumously awarded the Distinguished Service Cross.

Kennedy, Joseph P., Sr. (September 6, 1888–November 19, 1969) *businessman, U.S. ambassador to Great Britain, founder of a political dynasty*
Born in Boston, Massachusetts, the son of a saloon keeper, Kennedy was educated at Roman Catholic schools, the Boston Latin School, and Harvard University. Ambitious and eager for acceptance in the Protestant social world, he worked hard and successfully to make his fortune. In 1914, at age 25, he married Rose Fitzgerald, the daughter of Boston's mayor; they had nine children.

That year he became at 25 the youngest bank president in the country. As an entrepreneur he profitably explored business after business—investment banking, movie theaters, film production, real estate, stocks, and a franchise on Scotch whiskey and British gin. He accumulated an immense fortune. He was devoted to his growing family, whom he and his wife raised for competition and success. At the same time he adventured with other women, most notoriously the movie star Gloria Swanson.

In 1932 Kennedy supported Franklin D. Roosevelt for the presidency, for which he was rewarded successively with the chair of the Securities and Exchange Commission, the directorship of the Maritime Commission, and in 1938 the ambassadorship to Great Britain. The last appointment proved disastrous, for his isolationism alienated him both from the British government and from Roosevelt, forcing Kennedy's resignation in 1940.

Thereafter he concentrated on enabling the political careers of his sons until, in 1961, he suffered a series of strokes. He died in 1969 at Hyannis Port, Massachusetts.

King, Ernest Joseph (November 23, 1878–June 25, 1956) *Fleet Admiral, ninth chief of naval operations*
King was born in Lorain, Ohio, and graduated from the naval academy in 1901. After serving there he

served in the Spanish-American War. His career in the navy flourished. During World War I he worked on the staff of the commander of the Battleship Force of the Atlantic Fleet. During the 1920s he went to submarine school and qualified as a naval aviator as well as serving on an aircraft tender, winning two Distinguished Service Medals for submarine salvage work and commanding an air base. The 1930s held equally varied and ever more important posts for him, but he believed that he could never rise to the top because the statutory retirement age would overtake him first.

The outbreak of World War II in Europe changed his prospects. He returned to sea as commander of the Patrol Force in December 1940; on January 22, 1941, he became commander in chief of the Atlantic fleet, and after Pearl Harbor he assumed command of the entire U.S. fleet. King, Chief of Naval Operations Adm. Harold R. Stark, Gen. George Marshall, and Gen. Hap Arnold coordinated the actions of the army and navy and advised the president on strategy. In March 1942 King took on Stark's duties as chief naval officer in addition to his own. As one of the joint chiefs of staff he attended the conferences of Allied leaders in Washington, Casablanca, Quebec, Cairo, Tehran, Malta, Yalta, and Potsdam from 1942 to 1945.

Acting on the slogan "Do all that we can with what we have," he urged more aggressive pursuit of the war in Europe to enable the assignment of more men and supplies in the Pacific. "No fighter ever won his fight by covering up—merely fending off the other fellow's blows," he wrote. "The winner hits and keeps on hitting even though he has to be able to take some stiff blows in order to keep on hitting." At FDR's behest King served throughout the war, although he passed the statutory retirement age of 64 in 1942. After the war, on December 15, 1945, he resigned, receiving from Congress a gold medal honoring his career as submariner, destroyerman, and aviator. In August 1947, he suffered a stroke. Thereafter he lived at the Bethesda Naval Medical Center and the U.S. naval hospital at Portsmouth, New Hampshire, where he died.

LeMay, Curtis E. (ca. 1906–October 3, 1990) *U.S. Army Air Corps general*
Born in Columbus, Ohio, LeMay graduated from Ohio State University with a degree in civil engineering. In 1928 he joined the army as a flying cadet

and was commissioned in 1929. In the 1930s he flew bombers and pioneered air routes. In World War II he developed new formations and tactics that dramatically increased the potency of strategic bombing in Europe. Transferred to the Pacific in July 1944, he directed heavy bombardment activities in the China-Burma-India theater. As chief of staff of the Strategic Air Forces in the Pacific, recognizing that high-altitude bombing of Japan was not working, he stripped down B-29s and sent them in low, dumping so many incendiary bombs that they destroyed most major Japanese cities and their communications systems.

After the war he served as the first deputy chief of air staff for research and development, facilitating the transition to jet bombers and in-flight refueling. In 1947 he took command of the U.S. Air Forces in Europe, in which capacity he developed and implemented the Berlin airlift. The next year he returned to Washington to reorganize the Strategic Air Command, creating an enormous organization capable of reaching every industrial center in the Soviet Union. From 1957 to 1965 he served as vice-chief and then chief of staff of the air force. LeMay's retirement in 1965 relieved those who thought that his belligerence endangered the nation.

Lewis, John Llewellyn (February 12, 1880–June 11, 1969) *labor leader*
John L. Lewis was born in Lucas County, Iowa, the son of a farm laborer and coal miner. In 1897 he left high school to begin work as a coal miner and activist in the United Mine Workers of America (UMW), becoming secretary of a local union by 1901. After several years of wandering the West and a business venture that failed, he made his career in trade unionism. In 1920 his leadership of a nationwide coal strike won him election as president of the UMW, a position that he held until he retired in 1960.

In 1935 he created a new union alliance that became the Congress of Industrial Organizations (CIO), organizing thousands of blue-collar workers, negotiating contracts with General Motors and U.S. Steel, acquiring heft in the Democratic Party, and leaving the American Federation of Labor in the dust. By 1940, however, Lewis was losing power, opposing U.S. entry into World War II, splitting with President Franklin D. Roosevelt, and taking the UMW out of the CIO. The national coal miners' strike that he led in 1943, in the midst of the war, made enemies for him and the UMW among the American populace; the numbers of these enemies grew with the successive, almost annual strikes from 1945 to 1950. While the membership of the UMW declined thereafter, union members enjoyed better wages and conditions, and mine owners supported Lewis as a labor statesman and friendly collaborator. He retired in 1960.

Lindbergh, Charles Augustus (February 4, 1902–August 26, 1974) *pilot who made the first solo nonstop flight across the Atlantic, isolationist, U.S. Army colonel*

Lindbergh was born in Detroit. He studied engineering at the University of Wisconsin, leaving after two years to barnstorm as a stunt pilot at country fairs. Trained as an army reserve pilot, in 1925 he took a job flying mail between St. Louis and Chicago. Two years later he persuaded St. Louis businessmen to help him buy a plane, which he helped design, so that he could compete for the Orteig prize of $25,000 offered to the first aviator to fly nonstop from New York to Paris. His 1927 flight in the *Spirit of St. Louis* in 33 1/2 hours brought him fortune and international acclaim as "the Lone Eagle."

For almost a dozen years he was an idolized hero. He was employed by several airlines as a technical adviser. He and his wife, Anne Morrow, whom he married in 1929, promoted aviation and charted new routes for airlines. The sympathy of the world was stirred when their infant son was kidnapped and murdered. In search of privacy for themselves and their second son, the family moved to Europe in 1935. There Lindbergh came to admire the aircraft industry of Nazi Germany, accepting a medal from Hitler's government. After the family's return to the United States in 1939, he joined the isolationist America First committee, arguing against American involvement in World War II and alleging that British, Jewish, and pro-Roosevelt groups were inveigling the United States into the war. He resigned his army commission.

After the Japanese attack on the United States on December 7, 1941, Lindbergh tried to reenlist but was rejected. He then worked as a test pilot and technical adviser until in 1944 he was invited to advise the military in the Pacific. There he flew 50 combat missions and helped to improve fighter planes. In the years after the war he acted as consultant to the chief of staff of the air force and to Pan American World Airways. He and his wife wrote extensively and successfully. In the late 1960s he publicly advocated conservation.

MacArthur, Douglas (January 26, 1880–April 5, 1964) *U.S. general, supreme commander in the occupation of Japan*

Douglas MacArthur was born in Little Rock, Arkansas, the son of infantry officer Arthur MacArthur, Jr., and his ambitious wife, Mary Pinkney, Hardy MacArthur, but he spent his early years in remote forts of New Mexico and Kansas. He was educated at the West Texas Military Academy and West Point, where he made history academically and as the first captain of the cadet corps; he graduated in 1903. As a young soldier he served in the Philippines and elsewhere in Asia, where he grew to believe his country's future and his own lay. In 1915 as a major he became the army's first public relations officer, persuading Americans to accept selective service for World War I. In that war as leader of the Rainbow Division, he became the most decorated American soldier, known for his boldness in battle and for his battle dress—riding crop but no helmet, gas mask, or weapon—and winning from his commanding officer the description "the bloodiest fighting man in this army" and promotion to brigadier general.

He was further rewarded by a postwar appointment as the youngest superintendent ever of West Point, where he modernized the academy. After another tour of duty in the Philippines, in 1930 he was appointed chief of staff of the army. During the Great Depression he scarred his reputation by personally leading troops to evict from makeshift shanties in the nation's capital a pathetic group of World War I veterans seeking a bonus; MacArthur alleged that there was "incipient revolution in the air."

Again assigned to the Philippines in 1935, MacArthur failed to build a force able to oppose the Japanese. After defeat there he retreated to Bataan and then to Corregidor, leaving that island on President Roosevelt's orders just before the U.S. surrender but promising, "I shall return." MacArthur disagreed with the basic Allied policy of defeating Germany first, intimating that the Americans who agreed to that priority were dominated by "Communists and British Imperialists." He talked of "the navy cabal that hates me, and the New Deal cabal," and complained that Roosevelt "acted as if he were the directing head of the army and navy."[1] Nonetheless from Australia

MacArthur fought his way back through New Guinea, and in October 1944 he waded ashore at Leyte to liberate the rest of the Philippines. On September 2, 1945, he received the Japanese surrender that ended World War II.

For the next five and a half years MacArthur as the supreme commander of the Allied powers in Japan oversaw its rebuilding as a nonmilitaristic nation with a relatively democratic constitution. He sapped the powers of the 10 Japanese families who had controlled 90 percent of industry there, and he redistributed the land by having the government buy it up and resell it to farmers.

In 1950 during the Korean War MacArthur commanded United Nations forces. Initially he experienced success with his brilliant amphibious assault at Inchon, behind North Korean lines. Thereafter, however, the entry into the war of the Communist Chinese forced his retreat, and in a disagreement over strategy he so defied the authority of President Harry Truman that Truman removed him on April 11, 1951. Many U.S. citizens and officials sided with MacArthur and gave him a hero's welcome home, but as he had predicted in an address to a joint session of the U.S. Congress, despite efforts in some Republican quarters to make him a presidential candidate, he "faded away" into retirement in New York.

Marshall, George Catlett (December 31, 1880–October 16, 1959) *chief of staff of the U.S. Army during World War II, secretary of state, Nobel Peace Prize recipient for the Marshall Plan*
Marshall was born and grew up in Uniontown, Pennsylvania. Rejected by the U.S. military academy, he earned a degree at Virginia Military Institute and in 1902 entered the army, where his talents were quickly recognized. He solidified his reputation as a brilliant staff officer in World War I.

In the period between the wars he gained experience in working both with civilians and with his military colleagues, keeping evaluations of them in the little black book that later helped him decide promotions and appointments. In the fall of 1938 he was named deputy chief of staff and, only months thereafter, chief of staff of the army. In this position he showed his virtuosity as administrator and global strategist. His achievements defeated his own ambition—to lead Operation Overlord in the invasion of France—for President Franklin D. Roosevelt felt that he could not do without him in Washington. He retired from the army on November 20, 1945.

In 1947 President Harry S. Truman appointed him secretary of state. During his tenure he developed the European Recovery Program, better known as the Marshall Plan, and persuaded the American people to put aside thoughts of revenge against Germany and Italy in favor of generosity, to the benefit of the world. He served as Truman's strong right arm in opposing the Soviet Union, but he held to his own position when he thought Truman wrong, insisting that political considerations must not weigh in foreign policy. Bad health caused Marshall to resign in 1949.

The next year, however, Truman called him back to serve as secretary of defense during the Korean War. He supported Truman in the firing of General Douglas MacArthur, upholding civilian over military authority. After all his years of service to the United States, Marshall had to endure the unfounded attack made on him by Senator Joseph McCarthy on June 14, 1951. Marshall retired again in 1951, but he was called on for military advice until near the end of his life.

Mayer, Frederick (unknown–unknown) *Jewish agent of the Office of Strategic Services*
The Mayer family fled Germany in 1938 and settled in Brooklyn, where Frederick Mayer took a job in a Ford plant. A volunteer in the U.S. Army, he was on maneuvers with the Rangers when the Office of Strategic Services (OSS) recruited him for his German background and his mastery of French, Spanish, German, and English. Imaginative and courageous, he was sent to a reconnaissance battalion to work behind the lines and stationed in Bari, Italy. There he was teamed with Hans Wynber, a Dutch Jewish professor of chemistry, and Franz Weber, an Austrian deserter volunteer, for a mission called GREENUP. In the spring of 1945 they parachuted onto a glacial ridge and after a hair-raising trip down the mountains took refuge in a village near Innsbruck, where they began to gather intelligence and to contact anti-Nazis. Mayer procured and wore the uniform of a lieutenant in the German Alpine troops and acquainted himself with German officers. He also recruited a thousand partisans and proposed a takeover of Innsbruck ahead of airborne landings, but his controllers told him to stick to intelligence gathering.

On April 21 he missed an appointment to meet an OSS courier carrying papers for him. He had adopted a new pose as a foreign laborer fleeing before the Russian advance, registered as a French electrician, and found a job working in a radio shop owned by an anti-Nazi, Robert Moser. He set about collecting information on important Nazis rallying to a final stand in Innsbruck, but about April 10 he was captured by the Gestapo. Under torture, and having discovered that the Gestapo had already extracted much information about him and his operation from another OSS agent, he reportedly talked, although evidence is conflicting and he himself denied the accusation. In any case the other members of his team were not caught. Sent to the concentration camp of Reichenau, he escaped, arranged the surrender of a local Nazi leader, rode out to meet the American troops preparing to take Innsbruck, and negotiated the surrender of the city.

McAfee, Mildred Helen (Mildred Horton)
(May 12, 1900–September 2, 1994) *educator, first commander of the WAVES*
Mildred McAfee was born in Parkville, Missouri, and educated at Vassar and the University of Chicago. She made a career in higher education, in 1936 accepting the presidency of Vassar, where she was affectionately known as "Miss Mac."

On August 3, 1942, on leave from Vassar, she was commissioned a lieutenant commander in the naval reserve—the first woman naval line officer—to command the newly established Women's Reserve, later called Women Accepted for Volunteer Emergency Service (WAVES). She was promoted to captain in November 1943. Under her direction the WAVES grew to more than 40,000 women, serving in various occupational specialties and freeing men for sea duty. She returned to civilian life in February 1946, resuming her duties as president of Vassar. In August 1945 she married the Rev. Dr. Douglas Horton.

Miller, Dorie (October 12, 1919–presumed dead November 25, 1944) *black naval hero*
Born in Waco, Texas, after high school Dorie Miller worked on his father's farm and then on September 16, 1939, enlisted as a mess attendant in the navy. Restricted by his race to menial assignments, he eventually won advancement to ship's cook. He served on the ammunition ship USS *Pyro* and on January 2, 1940, was transferred to the USS *West Virginia,* where

he became the ship's heavyweight boxing champion. The *West Virginia* was in Pearl Harbor on December 7, 1941, when the Japanese attacked. At the alarm for general quarters, Miller headed for his battle station, only to find it wrecked; he went on deck, where he was assigned to carry wounded sailors to places of greater safety, and then ordered to the bridge to aid the mortally wounded captain of the ship.

Although he had not been trained to operate the weapon, he manned a 50-caliber Browning antiaircraft machine gun until he ran out of ammunition and was ordered to abandon ship as the *West Virginia* sank. "It wasn't hard," he said. "I just pulled the trigger and she worked fine. I had watched the others with these guns. I guess I fired her for about fifteen minutes. I think I got one of those Jap planes. They were diving pretty close to us." For his heroism Miller was commended by the secretary of the navy and received the Navy Cross.

After a national personal appearance tour to encourage enlistments, he began service on the escort carrier USS *Liscome Bay,* on which he participated in the seizure of Makin and Tarawa atolls in the Gilbert Islands. On November 24, 1944, that ship was torpedoed and sunk, and the next day Miller was presumed dead. Besides his Navy Cross, Miller also earned the Purple Heart; the American Defense Service Medal, Fleet Clasp; the Asiatic-Pacific Campaign Medal; and the World War II Victory Medal.

Morgenthau, Henry, Jr. (May 11, 1891–February 6, 1967) *secretary of the treasury from 1934 to 1945*
Morgenthau was born in New York City. He attended private schools and for two years studied architecture and agriculture at Cornell. A gentleman farmer, in World War I he worked on a plan to send tractors to France. After that war he published *The American Agriculturalist.* In 1929 his former neighbor, Governor of New York Franklin D. Roosevelt (FDR), appointed him to state posts on agriculture and conservation.

During the Great Depression that began in 1929, Morgenthau defended the dollar against the devaluation plotted by Nazi Germany, making it the world's strongest currency. As president, FDR appointed Morgenthau secretary of the treasury, a position in which he served from 1934 until 1945. In that post he successfully financed the war effort, particularly through the sale of defense bonds, which both supported the war needs and averted runaway inflation.

His proposal to reduce postwar Germany to an agricultural nation was rejected in favor of the Marshall Plan, but he succeeded in establishing postwar economic policies and currency stabilization.

Morgenthau resigned soon after FDR died. Thereafter he devoted himself to Jewish philanthropies, particularly in support of the new nation of Israel.

Nelson, Donald Marr (November 17, 1888–September 29, 1959) *corporation executive, government official, diplomat*

Born in Hannibal, Missouri, Nelson graduated from the public schools and entered the University of Missouri, earning a chemical engineering degree in 1911. The next year he went to work as a chemist for Sears, Roebuck, where he rose rapidly, becoming executive vice-president in 1939. In May 1940, President Franklin D. Roosevelt appointed him acting director for procurement for the U.S. government. In early 1942 he moved to the chair of the new War Production Board, his first task being to convert the economy from civilian to war production. He had to redirect the output of the manufacturing companies while also coping with relationships between management and labor. Additionally, he had to decide whether limited supplies should be allocated to the needs of another country or to those of the United States, and to arbitrate between a disputatious army and navy none too happy to accept the rulings of a civilian.

In August 1944, feuding with the army over such matters as the preparation for reconverting to a civilian economy, he accepted the president's assignment to confer with Soviet and Chinese leaders on economic matters, and in May 1945 he returned to private life. He wrote a book, *Arsenal of Democracy,* presided over the Society of Independent Motion Picture Producers, chaired the board of a chemical corporation, and in 1950 became president of a silver mining company.

Nimitz, Chester W. (February 24, 1885–February 20, 1966) *commander of the Pacific Fleet in World War II*

Born in Fredericksburg, Texas, Chester Nimitz worked from the age of eight but earned high grades in school. Denied an appointment to West Point, he went instead to the naval academy, graduating in 1905. In the navy he saw sea duty in the Far East and became an expert on submarines.

In World War I he served on the staff of the chief of the submarine force in the Atlantic. During the interval between the wars he earned regular promotions as a line officer, making rear admiral in 1938. From 1939 to 1941 he headed the Bureau of Navigation, so impressing Secretary of the Navy Frank Knox that after the Japanese attack on the United States on December 7, 1941, he was given command of the Pacific Fleet and in 1942 of the Pacific Ocean Area, so that he also commanded designated army ground and air units.

In these capacities, he used his leadership skills to rebuild morale, pick able subordinates, and delegate responsibility to them. Under his command the Pacific Fleet stopped the advance of the Japanese at the battle of Midway in 1942. The next year Nimitz masterminded the Allied central Pacific offensive. Using carrier attacks, amphibious assaults, and the imaginative strategy of leapfrogging some enemy strongholds, the Pacific Fleet advanced in nine months to the Marianas, from which U.S. B-29s bombed Japan.

On December 16, 1945, Nimitz succeeded Admiral Ernest J. King as chief of naval operations. In his two years in that position, he oversaw demobilization and peacetime retrenchment, planned a strategy to deal with the Soviet threat, and advocated the development of nuclear-powered submarines—though the potential of such weapons for mass destruction later worried him. He retired from the navy in 1947, refusing all offers to enter private industry. Instead, as a regent for the University of California, he struggled vainly to prevent the imposition of a loyalty oath on the faculty. From 1949 to 1952 he also traveled widely as a goodwill ambassador for the United Nations.

Pack, Amy Thorpe (November 2, 1910–December 1, 1963) *Allied spy*

The beautiful daughter of a Marine Corps colonel and his socially ambitious wife, Amy Thorpe made her debut in Washington, D.C., in 1929. She attracted many suitors among embassy attachés, among them the Englishman Arthur J. Pack, by whom she became pregnant. They married in 1936. When he was posted to Poland, he became involved with another woman, and she attracted much notice from men in the Polish foreign service. In 1937 the British took advantage of her popularity to recruit her to spy for them, assigning her the critical task of gathering information about the German Enigma coding machine, which

Polish mathematicians and engineers had helped develop. Her success enabled the British to acquire an Enigma machine, which allowed them to read Hitler's secret messages throughout the war.

The British Foreign Office then got Arthur Pack out of the way by sending him to South America, gave Amy Pack the code name *Cynthia,* and established her in a Washington, D.C., house. She renewed acquaintance with the Italian naval attaché who had courted her before her marriage and who now confided his arrangements to blow up 27 Italian merchant ships held in American ports, and she passed along that secret to the Office of Naval Intelligence in time for the Americans to save and seize a few of these ships. She also extracted from the infatuated man the Italian navy's code books. With the help of the French embassy's press attaché, Captain Charles Brousse, she arranged for the French navy's code books to be handed to FBI agents, who copied and returned them within an hour. Some time after Pack's suicide in 1945, she married Brousse, and after the peace they lived in the south of France.[2]

Patton, George Smith (November 11, 1885–December 21, 1945) *U.S. Army general*
George Patton was born in Pasadena, California, in a wealthy family with a military tradition. He grew up on a ranch, reading widely but not attending school until he was 12. He was then formally educated at Dr. Stephen Cutter Clark's Classical School for Boys in Pasadena, at Virginia Military Institute, and finally at West Point, where he graduated and was commissioned in 1909. By then he had shown himself a moody romantic—intuitive, intermittently energetic, and superstitious. He believed that he had fought with great warriors of the past, like Napoleon.

In Gen. John Pershing's chase after Pancho Villa in 1916, Patton led a motorized patrol in what may have been the first combat use of the automobile by the U.S. Army. The next year he was detailed to the Tank Corps, studying the training methods of the British and French, and in World War I as a lieutenant colonel, he briefly commanded a tank brigade. After the war he switched to cavalry because at that point the U.S. Army paid little attention to tanks. The German use of tanks in 1939 changed that attitude, and in July 1940 Patton took command of an armored brigade.

On November 8, 1942, Patton directed amphibious operations near Casablanca, Morocco, in the invasion of North Africa. In March 1943 he led successful operations in Tunisia, and on July 11, 1943, he commanded the U.S. Seventh Army in the invasion of Sicily. Exasperated when the campaign stalled, he committed the court-martial crimes of slapping two hospitalized victims of battle fatigue, whom he called cowards, cursing them and threatening one of them with his pearl-handled revolver. He aggravated the resulting scandal by publicly announcing that "it is the evident destiny of the British and Americans to rule the world." Nonetheless the higher command let him off lightly, thinking him too valuable to lose. Gen. Dwight Eisenhower told Patton, "You owe us some victories. Pay off and the world will deem me a wise man."[3] Beginning in late July 1944, Patton paid off with brilliant leadership of the Third Army in France during the Battle of the Bulge and the crossing of the Rhine into Germany.

After the war, Patton's tendency to chum with former Nazis—and his conviction that the United States and the Soviet Union would soon be at war—embarrassed the government, as when he told a reporter that most ordinary Nazis joined the party in the same manner that Americans became Republicans or Democrats. Eisenhower removed him from command of the Third Army. Shortly thereafter Patton broke his neck in an auto accident on December 9, 1945, and died 12 days later.

Pyle, Ernest Taylor (Ernie Pyle) (August 3, 1900–April 18, 1945) *journalist*
Born and raised on a farm near Dana, Indiana, Pyle studied journalism at Indiana University. In 1927 he began the country's first daily aviation column for the *Washington Daily News*. Thereafter for several years he roamed the United States, reporting what he saw in columns later collected in *Home Country*. In 1940 he began reporting the bombing of England; some of his columns from that period went into *Ernie Pyle in England*.

He gained fame during the war as a syndicated columnist who traveled with U.S. troops, often at or near the front lines, carefully identifying by rank and hometown the fighting men featured in his stories. His columns both in the newspapers and in his books *Here Is Your War* and *Brave Men* gave Americans intimate experience of the war in North Africa and Europe as the GIs knew it. As the war in Europe wound down, he went to the Pacific. When he was killed by a Japanese sniper on an island off Okinawa, GIs marked his grave: "At This Spot the 77th Infantry Division Lost a Buddy, Ernie Pyle, 18 April, 1945." He left behind notes for a projected column on the end of the war in Europe. He would not soon forget, he said, "the unnatural sight of cold dead men scattered over the hillsides and in the ditches along the high rows of hedge throughout the world. . . . Dead men by mass production—in one country after another—month after month and year after year. Dead men in winter and dead men in summer. . . . Dead men in such familiar promiscuity that they become monotonous. . . . Dead men in such monstrous infinity that you come almost to hate them."[4]

Randolph, A. Philip (Asa Philip Randolph) (April 15, 1889–May 16, 1979) *black leader, president of the Brotherhood of Sleeping Car Porters*

Born in Crescent City, Florida, the son of an itinerant Methodist minister, Randolph was schooled at the Cookman Institute. Moving to New York as a young man, he took classes at City College and affiliated with the Socialist Party. With his fellow radical Chandler Owen, he edited and published *The Messenger,* which advocated "scientific socialism." During World War I he served time in prison for pacifism.

Regarding the struggle for the rights of workers as a holy crusade, in 1925 he organized the Brotherhood of Sleeping Car Porters, beginning a long bitter struggle with the Pullman Company. In 1935 the Brotherhood affiliated with the American Federation of Labor, and two years later won a contract with Pullman, the first contract between a company and a black union.

During World War II Randolph labored to open defense jobs to blacks. The threat of a black march on Washington finally persuaded President Franklin D. Roosevelt to issue an executive order banning discrimination based on race within the government and among industries with government contracts. After the war Randolph successfully pressured President Harry S. Truman to end racial discrimination in the military. In the 1950s he fought inside the AFL-CIO (American Federation of Labor-Congress of Industrial Organizations) for equal opportunities for blacks in the workplace, and at the end of the decade he called for a black march on Washington—a call that was answered on August 28, 1963, when a quarter of a million Americans peacefully demonstrated for civil rights.

Rankin, Jeanette Pickering (June 11, 1880–May 18, 1973) *suffragist, the first woman elected to the House of Representatives, the only member of Congress to oppose U.S. participation in both world wars*

Jeanette Pickering was born in the Montana Territory and grew up on the frontier, attending public schools and graduating from the University of Montana in 1902. Later she went to the New York School of Philanthropy and the University of Washington. There she joined the successful state campaign for woman suffrage, coming to believe that the suffrage movement should work not only for votes for women but also for peace. Her work for the movement across the country enabled her in 1916—three years before the woman suffrage amendment—to win a Republican congressional seat.

In April 1917, she was one of the 57 members of Congress to vote against American entry into World War I, a position that she sustained throughout her life. She failed in her bid for the Republican nomination to the Senate in 1918. The next year she served as a delegate to the Second International Congress of Women (later the Women's International League for Peace and Freedom). For many years, from 1919 on, Rankin worked for better working conditions for women, improved health services for women and children, and world peace. In 1940 Montana Republicans again elected her to Congress, where she argued against aid to Britain and preparedness measures. On December 8, 1941, she cast the sole vote against the declaration of war. She was not reelected.

For the rest of her life she continued to work for peace, again rising to public notice with the organization of the Jeannette Rankin Brigade in 1967 to oppose the Vietnam War. At 88 she made up her mind to run again for Congress, but bad health prevented her.

Roosevelt, Anna Eleanor (October 11, 1884–November 7, 1962) *social activist, first lady, teacher, columnist*

Eleanor Roosevelt was born in New York City in a wealthy and socially prominent family and privately educated. From 1899 to 1902 she studied at a London boarding school. There Mlle Marie Souvestre recognized and cultivated her talents and interested her in politics. In 1905 she married her distant cousin Franklin Delano Roosevelt, with whom she had six children.

The couple had marital difficulties but matured into a unique, mutually respectful political team, in which she nurtured his social conscience and he her political expertise. Besides her duties as first lady successively of New York State and the United States, she worked independently as a teacher, columnist of "My Day," and writer. She also became a powerful friend to whom American organizations and individuals appealed for help. During World War II she traveled widely, visiting military bases and hospitals and carrying messages back to the families of GIs.

After her husband died in April 1945, Eleanor Roosevelt became a senior adviser for the Democratic Party and U.S. ambassador to the world. As a delegate to the United Nations in the late 1940s she shaped the Universal Declaration of Human Rights and secured its adoption. She fought for civil rights and for women's rights. Throughout her life she never deserted her principles or the causes to which she had devoted herself.

Roosevelt, Franklin Delano (January 30, 1882–April 12, 1945) *32nd president of the United States*

Franklin D. Roosevelt (FDR) was born on his father's estate in Hyde Park, New York, and educated privately at Groton, Harvard, and Columbia Law School, passing the bar in 1906. He married his distant cousin, Eleanor Roosevelt, who became his lifelong political partner and adviser. After a few years with a New York law firm, in 1910 he was elected to the New York State Senate, where he made a reputation by opposing the political bosses of New York City and championing upstate farmers and conservationists. In the 1912 presidential election he campaigned for Woodrow Wilson, who rewarded him with an appointment as assistant secretary of the navy. In 1920 he ran unsuccessfully as the Democratic vice-presidential candidate.

Out of office, he again practiced law in New York City but continued his political activities, even after he was stricken with polio in 1921. By 1928 he had recovered sufficiently to run for the governorship of New York. In his two terms in this office, he extended his reputation as a moderate progressive. In 1932, in the depths of the Great Depression, he was elected president of the United States, a position he held for the rest of his life. His strong leadership and optimistic outlook strengthened the nation and began economic recovery.

As the 1930s ended, FDR, recognizing the threat to world peace presented by Nazi Germany, fascist Italy, and militaristic Japan, gradually prepared for war, which he regarded as inevitable. To the extent politically possible, he supported the Allied cause. After the Japanese attack on the United States on December 7, 1941, he led the nation in a rapid conversion to a wartime economy, simultaneously building the strength of both industry and the military. With Prime Minister Winston Churchill of Great Britain he created the doctrine of the Four Freedoms to which all humans are entitled: freedom from want, freedom from fear, freedom of religion, and freedom of speech. With Churchill and Premier Joseph Stalin of the Union of Soviet Socialist Republics, he coordinated the Allied war efforts and strategy. Victory was in sight when, a few months after his election to an unprecedented fourth term, FDR was stricken with a fatal cerebral hemorrhage in the spring of 1945.

Sebold, William (unknown–unknown) *double agent for Germany and the United States*

A German native, Sebold served in the German army in World War I, then wandered the world for 12 years as a seaman, machinist, and engineer, finally settling in New York. He became a naturalized American citizen in 1936. On a trip back to Germany in 1939, he was, he claimed, told that he must spy for the Nazis on pain of harm to his family, sent to a training facility, and thereafter given a new identity as native-born American Harry Sawyer. He warned the American consulate about his situation, and on arrival in the United States in February 1940 he contacted the FBI, who signed him on as a double agent. He was stationed on Long Island, where for 16 months, while he became acquainted with several Nazi spies in the New York area, he radioed messages intercepted and screened by the FBI to Germany. In June 1941, the FBI arrested 33 Nazi spies whom Sebold had come to know: The FBI had filmed his conversations with them. All were found guilty and sentenced to prison for varying terms.

Stettinius, Edward Reilly, Jr. (October 22, 1900–October 31, 1949) *businessman, secretary of state under Franklin D. Roosevelt and Harry S. Truman*

Stettinius was born in Chicago, educated at the University of Virginia, and swiftly rose in the management of General Motors and thereafter at U.S. Steel. He held key positions in the national defense program: chair of the War Resources Board in 1939, Lend-Lease administrator from 1941 to 1943, undersecretary of state from 1943 to 1944, and secretary of state from 1944 to 1945. As secretary of state he attended the Yalta conference of Allied leaders and led the U.S. delegation at the 1945 San Francisco conference that organized the United Nations.

Stimson, Henry Lewis (September 21, 1867–October 20, 1950) *secretary of war under President Taft, secretary of state under President Hoover, secretary of war under President Franklin Roosevelt*

Stimson was born in New York City and educated at Phillips Andover Academy, Yale University, and Harvard Law School. He was appointed a U.S. district attorney in New York by President Theodore Roosevelt, and secretary of war by President William Taft. In the First World War he commanded an artillery unit in France. After a stint as governor of the Philippines from 1927 to 1929, he served as secretary of state to President Herbert Hoover.

Stimson, a Republican, left office when Democratic President Franklin D. Roosevelt (FDR) was elected in 1932, but his advocacy for support of the Allies and a need for political unity prompted FDR to call him back to public service as secretary of war, a position in which he served until September 21, 1945, although he objected on moral grounds to the conventional and atomic bombing of cities. He was the author of several books on foreign affairs.

Stratton, Dorothy C. (March 24, 1899–) *first director of the Coast Guard women's reserve (SPARS)*

Stratton was born in Brookfield, Missouri, and educated in the public schools, Ottawa University in Kansas, the University of Chicago, and Columbia University, from which she earned a doctorate in student personnel administration. While she did her graduate work she taught in several public schools, and in 1933 she was appointed dean of women at Purdue. There she devised a curriculum in the sciences for women and created an employment placement office for women.

In June 1942 she took a leave of absence to join the WAVES and received a commission as a lieutenant. On November 23, 1942, she was appointed director of the newly established Coast Guard women's reserve with the rank of lieutenant com-

mander. She suggested calling these women SPARs, explaining, "As I understand it, a spar is often a supporting beam, and that is what we hope each member of the Women's Reserve will be." She was promoted to commander on January 1, 1944, and to captain the next month.

After the war she was director of personnel for the International Monetary Fund in Washington, D.C., from 1947 to 1950, and she spent the next decade as national executive director of the Girl Scouts of America. From 1962 until she retired, she served on the President's Commission on the Employment of the Handicapped and as a consultant on vocational rehabilitation for the Department of Health, Education, and Welfare.

Streeter, Ruth Cheney (October 2, 1895–September 30, 1990) *first director of the U.S. Marine Corps Women's Reserve*

Born in Brookline, Massachusetts, Streeter was educated abroad and at Bryn Mawr, from which she graduated in 1918. On June 23, 1917, she married businessman Thomas Cheney, with whom she had four children. During the Great Depression years after 1930 she worked in public health and welfare in New Jersey. In 1940 she learned to fly and received her commercial pilot's license in 1942. She served as director of the Women's Reserve of the Marine Corps from its activation on February 13, 1943, until she resigned on December 7, 1945, rising from major to colonel.

After her return to civilian life she participated in public affairs in Morristown, New Jersey. In 1947 she was a delegate to the state constitutional convention.

Taylor, John Hedrick (1908–unknown) *orthodontist, Office of Strategic Services agent*

Jack Taylor was practicing dentistry in Los Angeles when the United States entered the war. An adventurer at heart, he was a yachtsman and a licensed pilot who had gone on an expedition to the Yukon. When war broke out, he rejected a commission in the medical corps and became a naval office on a sub-chaser. The Office of Strategic Services brought him to Washington, D.C., to instruct agents in boat-handling, navigation, seamanship, and underwater demolition. He later completed 15 missions into Corfu, Yugoslavia, and Albania, in the course of which he survived alone for 45 days on an enemy-held island, but these missions produced little useful intelligence. Although he spoke almost no German, on October 13, 1944, Taylor and three Austrian "deserter volunteers" (enemy aliens who agreed to work for the Allies) parachuted into Austria. From the beginning, the mission went badly; they gathered much intelligence, but with their radios lost in the drop and a contact killed in an air raid, they had no means of transmitting it. In time the whole team was captured by the Gestapo and found guilty of espionage.

On April 1, 1945, Taylor arrived at Mauthausen concentration camp, where he was beaten, assigned to a work gang constructing a new crematorium, and subjected to an experiment to see how much sawdust could be substituted for flour in bread. On the chance that he might survive and, as an American, be a credible witness to their suffering, inmates confided to him the tortures they had undergone; he insisted upon two eyewitnesses to each story. When he was liberated and had recovered somewhat, he went back to the camp to collect documents and gather information about camp officials from former prisoners. There he learned that only the intervention of a Czech trusty had forestalled his own execution in April 1945. He was discharged from the navy in October of that year and returned to dentistry in California.[5] In 1946 the navy recalled him and promoted him to lieutenant commander, and he testified in the war crimes trial.

Tokyo Rose (Iva Ikuko Toguri D'Aquino) (July 4, 1916–unknown) *radio propagandist for the Japanese*
This name was applied to several female radio announcers who with their broadcasts tried to rob American servicemen of the will to fight by making them homesick. Iva Ikuko Toguri D'Aquino was one of them. She was a second-generation Japanese American who had learned her English growing up in the United States. Convicted of treason in 1949, she spent six years in prison and was pardoned by President Gerald Ford in 1977.

Truman, Harry S. (May 8, 1884–December 26, 1972) *senator, 33rd president of the United States*
Born in the Missouri countryside, Harry Truman grew up on his grandmother's farm in Jackson County and in Independence and Kansas City, Missouri. He graduated from the Independence high school in 1901. When his father died in 1917, he took over the management of the 600-acre farm, doing much of the

work himself. In World War I he helped organize a regiment from a National Guard company, trained and went overseas with it, and served as captain of an artillery battery.

After his demobilization, Truman set up in the haberdashery business, the venture ending in bankruptcy in the recession of 1922. He then entered politics and, with the endorsement of the Kansas City Pendergast machine, won the office of Jackson County commissioner. Except for a brief period of selling memberships in the Kansas City Automobile Club from 1924 to 1926, he thereafter made his career in politics. In 1934, after 10 years in county government, he won a seat in the U.S. Senate, where he remained, gaining a solid reputation for probity. In his first term he focused on learning about national transportation problems and enacting important legislation to correct them. In his second term he chaired a special committee to root out fraud in the massive military procurement going on in preparation for and during World War II, saving American taxpayers millions of dollars and gaining national prominence.

In 1944 Democratic leaders chose him over his vigorous protests as their vice-presidential candidate. Upon President Roosevelt's death on April 12, 1945, Truman, telling reporters, "If you fellows know how to pray, pray for me now," shouldered the responsibility of bringing the war to a victorious conclusion and actualizing the position of the United States as a major world power in peacetime. His was the ultimate burden of deciding whether to drop atomic bombs, a decision he made in the belief that he was saving unknown numbers of American and Japanese lives by bringing the war to a speedy end. With little previous experience in foreign affairs and diplomacy, he negotiated the peace and carried out the establishment of the United Nations.

During the early years of the cold war with the Soviet Union, Truman sturdily defended the interests of the United States. On March 12, 1947, he announced the Truman Doctrine, stating that the United States would support any nation threatened by Soviet communism. That year he also announced the Marshall Plan, which enabled the economic recovery of Western Europe. Under his leadership the North Atlantic Treaty, a military pact of 12 nations (later 16), was signed in April 1949. On June 25, 1950, perceiving in North Korea's invasion of South Korea a communist threat and a challenge to the authority of the United Nations, he sent American troops to the aid of the invaded country.

After refusing to run for a third term, Truman spent his retirement in Independence, Missouri, where he wrote his memoirs and oversaw the construction of the Truman Library.

Willkie, Wendell Lewis (February 18, 1892–October 8, 1944) *politician, statesman, diplomat*
Wendell Willkie was born in Elwood, Indiana, and educated at the University of Indiana, graduating from law school there in 1915 at the head of his class. After World War I, in which he spent two years in the army, he practiced law in Akron, Ohio, and entered local Democratic politics, though he refused to run for political office. In 1929 he moved to New York as the general counsel for the Commonwealth and Southern Corporation, and in 1932 he assumed the presidency of that utility. His sustained opposition to the Tennessee Valley Authority made him the hero of those who opposed President Franklin D. Roosevelt's New Deal. In 1936 he turned Republican. His 1939 victory in selling Commonwealth and Southern to the government inspired talk of him as a presidential candidate, and in 1940 the Republicans nominated him. After defeating Willkie, Roosevelt sent him to England as his emissary and in 1942 frequently consulted him on foreign and domestic issues. In 1943 Willkie wrote the best-selling *One World*, a plea for an international organization. These actions precluded his obtaining the Republican nomination for president in 1944, as he had hoped. That fall he suffered a series of heart attacks, and died.

Winant, John Gilbert (February 23, 1889–November 3, 1947) *governor of New Hampshire, first chair of the Social Security board, director of the International Labor Office, U.S. ambassador to Great Britain during World War II*
Born in New York City, John Winant was educated at St. Paul's School in Concord, New Hampshire, Princeton, and Dartmouth, earning two master's degrees. As a history teacher at St. Paul's, in 1917 he was elected to the state legislature but volunteered to go to France in World War I. After the war he again taught and reentered state politics, serving in the legislature from 1922 and as governor from 1930 to 1934.

As a Republican governor during the Great Depression, he cooperated closely with the Franklin D. Roosevelt administration to sustain the economy. In the mid-1930s he directed the International Labor Organization in Switzerland and the Social Security Administration in Washington, D.C. In 1940 he was appointed U.S. ambassador to Great Britain, where he served throughout World War II, until 1946. After that he functioned briefly as U.S. representative to the United Nations Economic and Social Council. In 1947 he killed himself at his Concord home.

APPENDIX C
Maps

1. Growth of the Japanese Empire, 1931–1941
2. Jewish Refugees from Nazi Europe, 1933–1944
3. World War II in Europe and the Middle East, 1939–1945
4. War Deaths in Europe, 1939–1945
5. The Holocaust, 1939–1945
6. The Battle of the Atlantic, 1940–1943
7. Japanese Attack Pearl Harbor, December 7, 1941
8. War in the Pacific, December 7, 1941–April 1, 1942
9. Japanese Attacks, 1941–1942
10. Japanese-American Concentration Camps, 1942–1945
11. War in the Pacific, Allied Offensives, 1942–1945
12. Defeat of Japan, 1942–1945
13. Allied Advances in North Africa and Italy, 1942–1945
14. D Day, June 6–July 5, 1944
15. Post–World War II Occupation Zones of Germany, 1945–1948
16. Division of Berlin after World War II, 1945–1990
17. Population Displacement after World War II, 1945–1948
18. Nations in the Marshall Plan, 1948

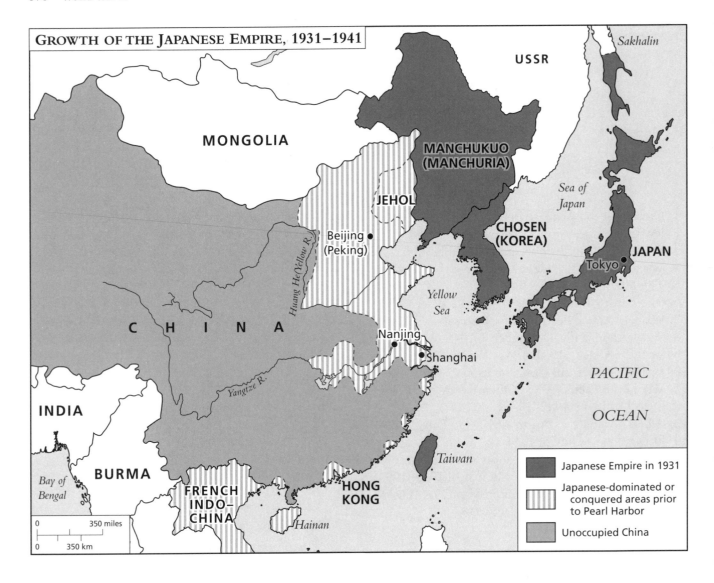

GROWTH OF THE JAPANESE EMPIRE, 1931–1941

USSR

Sakhalin

MONGOLIA

MANCHUKUO
(MANCHURIA)

JEHOL

Beijing
(Peking)

CHOSEN
(KOREA)

Sea of
Japan

Tokyo

JAPAN

C H I N A

Huang He/Yellow R.

Yellow
Sea

Nanjing

Shanghai

Yangtze R.

PACIFIC

INDIA

OCEAN

BURMA

Bay of
Bengal

Taiwan

FRENCH
INDO–
CHINA

HONG
KONG

Hainan

	Japanese Empire in 1931
	Japanese-dominated or conquered areas prior to Pearl Harbor
	Unoccupied China

0   350 miles

0   350 km

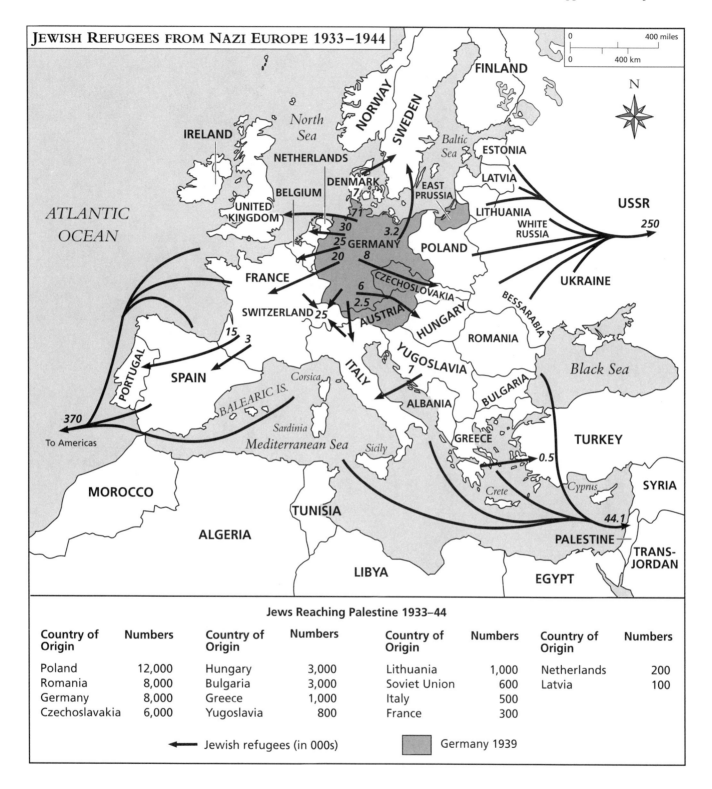

JEWISH REFUGEES FROM NAZI EUROPE 1933–1944

Jews Reaching Palestine 1933–44

Country of Origin	Numbers	Country of Origin	Numbers	Country of Origin	Numbers	Country of Origin	Numbers
Poland	12,000	Hungary	3,000	Lithuania	1,000	Netherlands	200
Romania	8,000	Bulgaria	3,000	Soviet Union	600	Latvia	100
Germany	8,000	Greece	1,000	Italy	500		
Czechoslavakia	6,000	Yugoslavia	800	France	300		

← Jewish refugees (in 000s)   Germany 1939

WORLD WAR II IN EUROPE AND THE MIDDLE EAST, 1939–1945

FINLAND

NORWAY

SWEDEN

USSR

North Sea

Helsinki

ESTONIA

Leningrad besieged
(Sept. 1941–
Jan. 1944)

June 1944

Nov. 1942

Dec. 1944

Riga

LATVIA

Baltic Sea

Moscow
Germans repulsed
(Dec. 1941)

GREAT
BRITAIN

IRELAND

LITHUANIA

Minsk

Stalingrad
(Aug. 21, 1942–
Jan. 31, 1943)

June 1944

Dec. 1943

Peenemünde

Danzig

EAST
PRUSSIA

Coventry

Dresden

Warsaw

Nov. 1942

London

Amsterdam

May 1945

Berlin surrendered
(May 2, 1945)

POLAND

Dec. 1944

Kiev

Plymouth

Brussels

Dec. 1944

GERMANY

Prague

late June 1944

Normandy
D day
(June 1944)

Paris liberated
(Aug. 25, 1944)

Battle of
the Bulge
(Dec. 16, 1944–
Jan. 31, 1945)

Nuremberg

CZECHOSLOVAKIA

Vienna

Budapest

ATLANTIC
OCEAN

*Bay of
Biscay*

Vichy

AUSTRIA

HUNGARY

ROMANIA

Yalta

SWITZERLAND

Bordeaux

FRANCE

ITALY

Dec. 1944

YUGOSLAVIA

Belgrade

Bucharest

Black Sea

Marseilles

*late June
1944*

Adriatic Sea

Dec. 1944

BULGARIA

PORTUGAL

SPAIN

Rome liberated
(June 4, 1944)

Anzio

Dec. 1943

ALBANIA

Ankara

Naples

TURKEY

Gibraltar

Reggio

GREECE

Syria
(Fr.)

IRAQ
(Br.)

Tangiers

SP. MOROCCO

Algiers

Tunis

Mediterranean Sea

Oran

Kasserine Pass
(Feb. 14–22, 1943)

TUNISIA

El Alamein
(Oct. 23–Nov. 5, 1942)

Jerusalem

Palestine
(Br. Mandate)

TRANS-
JORDAN
(Br.)

Morocco
(Fr.)

N

Algeria
(Fr.)

Dec. 1942

Tobruk

EGYPT (Br.)

Nov. 1942

SAUDI
ARABIA

0   300 miles

0   300 km

LIBYA
(It. until 1943/
then Br.-Fr.)

Maximum extent of territory under Axis control	Area under Allied control by December 1942	Soviet advance
Territory that remained under Soviet control	Neutral	Western Allied advance
		Major battle

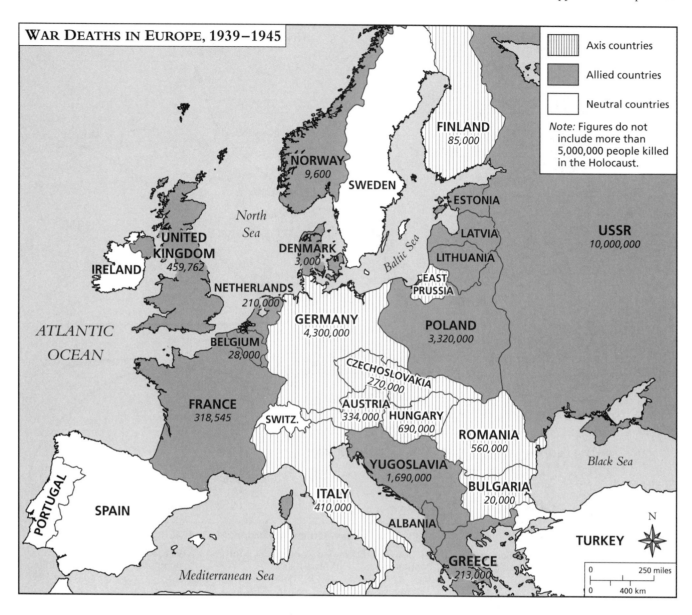

WAR DEATHS IN EUROPE, 1939–1945

Axis countries

Allied countries

Neutral countries

Note: Figures do not include more than 5,000,000 people killed in the Holocaust.

FINLAND
85,000

NORWAY
9,600

SWEDEN

ESTONIA

LATVIA

LITHUANIA

USSR
10,000,000

North Sea

UNITED KINGDOM
459,762

DENMARK
3,000

EAST PRUSSIA

IRELAND

Baltic Sea

NETHERLANDS
210,000

GERMANY
4,300,000

POLAND
3,320,000

ATLANTIC OCEAN

BELGIUM
28,000

CZECHOSLOVAKIA
270,000

FRANCE
318,545

SWITZ.

AUSTRIA
334,000

HUNGARY
690,000

ROMANIA
560,000

YUGOSLAVIA
1,690,000

Black Sea

PORTUGAL

SPAIN

ITALY
410,000

BULGARIA
20,000

ALBANIA

N

TURKEY

GREECE
213,000

Mediterranean Sea

0   250 miles

0   400 km

THE HOLOCAUST, 1939–1945

Jews Killed in Europe, 1941–1945

Country	1941 Jewish Population	Estimated Number of Jews Killed by 1945	Country	1941 Jewish Population	Estimated Number of Jews Killed by 1945
Austria	70,000	60,000	Hungary	710,000	200,000
Belgium	85,000	28,000	Italy	120,000	9,000
Bulgaria	48,000	40,000	Netherlands	140,000	104,000
Czechoslovakia	81,000	60,000	Poland	3,000,000	2,600,000
Denmark	6,000	100	Romania	1,000,000	750,000
France	300,000	65,000	Soviet Union	2,740,000	924,000
Germany	250,000	180,000	Yugoslavia	70,000	58,000
Greece	67,000	60,000			

Legend:

— German border, 1939

← Movement of Einsatzgruppen (Special-Action Groups)

■ Extermination camp

▼ Concentration camp

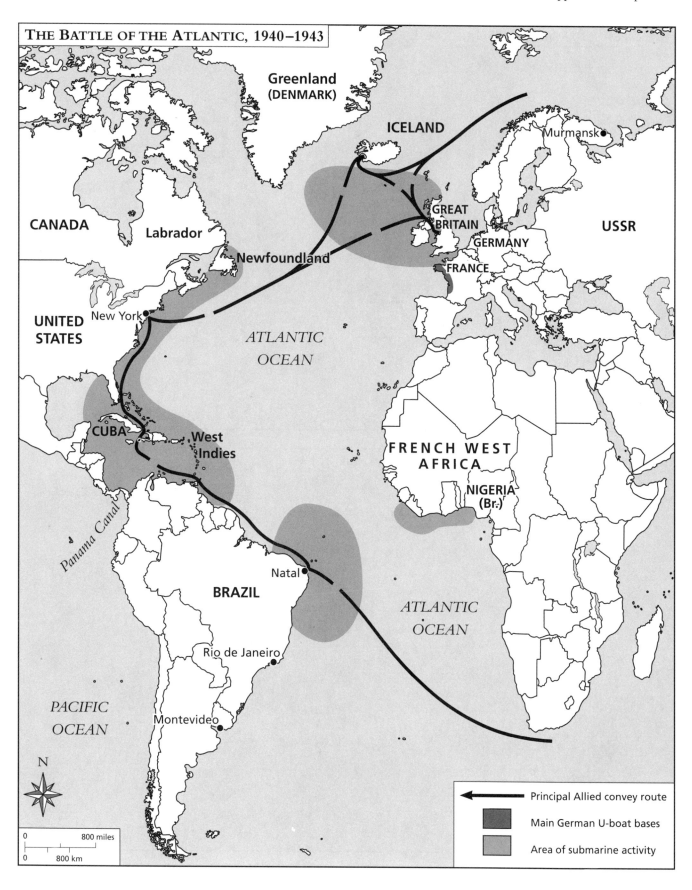

THE BATTLE OF THE ATLANTIC, 1940–1943

Greenland
(DENMARK)

ICELAND

Murmansk

CANADA

Labrador

Newfoundland

GREAT
BRITAIN

GERMANY

FRANCE

USSR

UNITED
STATES

New York

ATLANTIC
OCEAN

Panama Canal

CUBA

West
Indies

FRENCH WEST
AFRICA

NIGERIA
(Br.)

BRAZIL

Natal

ATLANTIC
OCEAN

Rio de Janeiro

PACIFIC
OCEAN

Montevideo

N

→ Principal Allied convey route

Main German U-boat bases

Area of submarine activity

0   800 miles
0   800 km

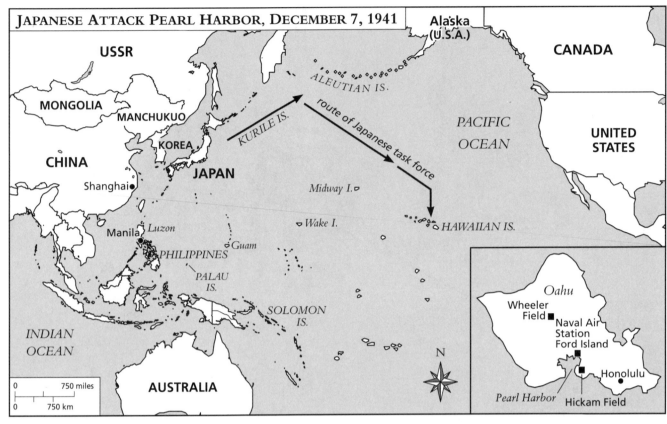

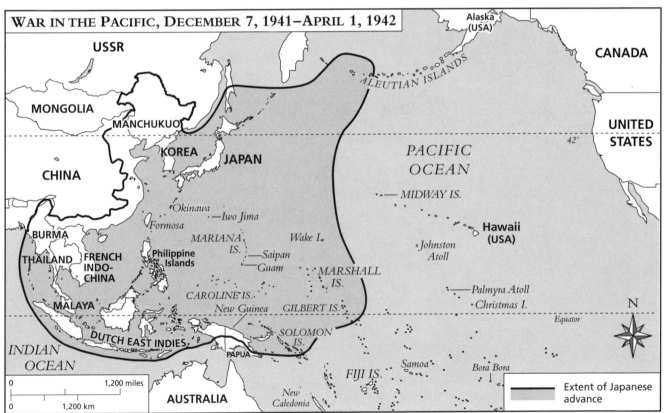

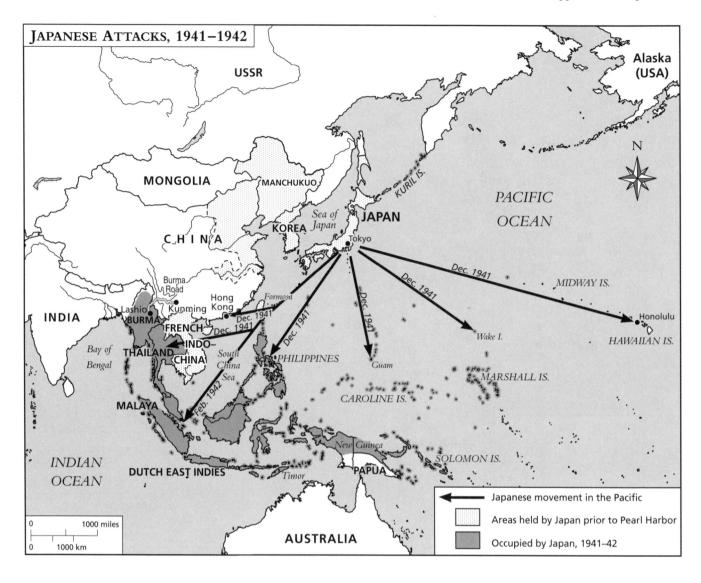

JAPANESE ATTACKS, 1941–1942

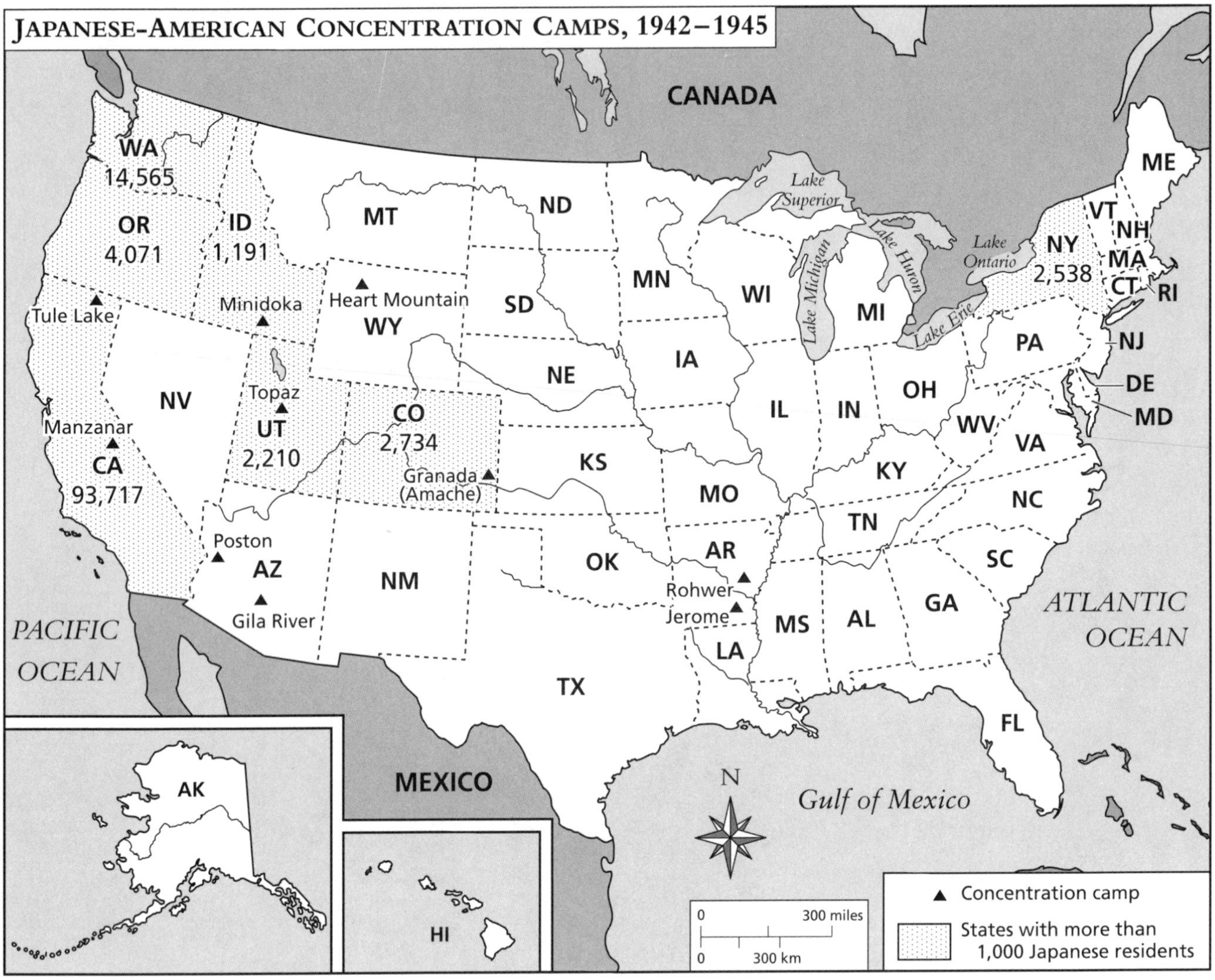

JAPANESE-AMERICAN CONCENTRATION CAMPS, 1942–1945

CANADA

Lake Superior

Lake Huron

Lake Michigan

Lake Ontario

Lake Erie

WA
14,565

OR
4,071

ID
1,191

MT

ND

MN

WI

MI

ME

VT

NH

NY
2,538

MA

CT   RI

NJ

DE

MD

▲ Minidoka

▲ Heart Mountain
WY

SD

NE

IA

PA

▲ Tule Lake

NV

▲ Topaz
UT
2,210

CO
2,734

IL

IN

OH

WV

VA

▲ Manzanar

CA
93,717

▲ Poston

▲ Granada
(Amache)

KS

MO

KY

TN

NC

SC

▲ AZ

NM

OK

AR ▲

Rohwer
Jerome ▲

MS

AL

GA

▲ Gila River

TX

LA

FL

PACIFIC
OCEAN

MEXICO

Gulf of Mexico

*ATLANTIC
OCEAN*

AK

HI

N

0 ——— 300 miles

0 ——— 300 km

▲ Concentration camp

States with more than
1,000 Japanese residents

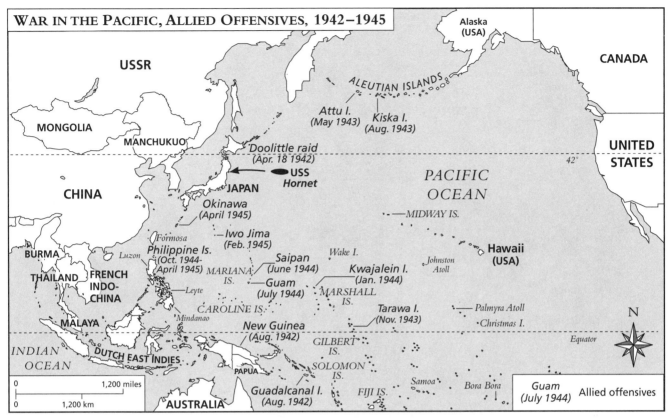

WAR IN THE PACIFIC, ALLIED OFFENSIVES, 1942–1945

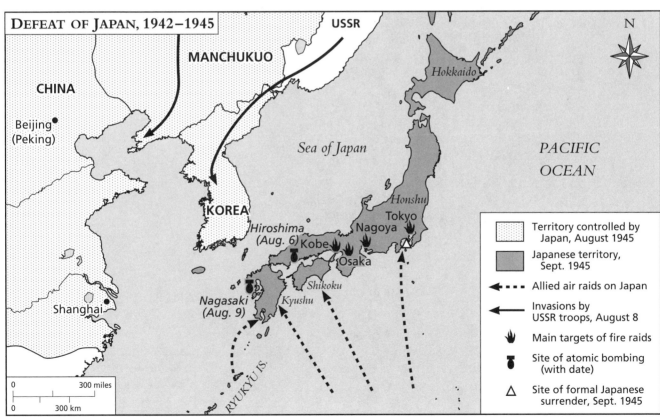

DEFEAT OF JAPAN, 1942–1945

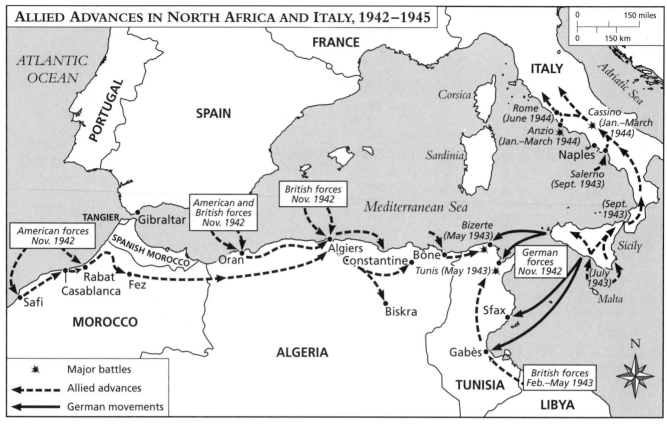

ALLIED ADVANCES IN NORTH AFRICA AND ITALY, 1942–1945

0   150 miles
0   150 km

ATLANTIC OCEAN

FRANCE

ITALY

Adriatic Sea

Corsica

PORTUGAL

SPAIN

Rome (June 1944)

Cassino (Jan.–March 1944)

Anzio (Jan.–March 1944)

Sardinia

Naples

American and British forces Nov. 1942

British forces Nov. 1942

Salerno (Sept. 1943)

Mediterranean Sea

(Sept. 1943)

TANGIER

Gibraltar

American forces Nov. 1942

SPANISH MOROCCO

Oran

Algiers
Constantine

Bône

Bizerte (May 1943)

German forces Nov. 1942

Sicily

Rabat
Casablanca

Fez

Tunis (May 1943)

(July 1943)

Safi

Biskra

Sfax

Malta

MOROCCO

ALGERIA

Gabès

British forces Feb.–May 1943

N

✶   Major battles

◄----   Allied advances

◄—   German movements

TUNISIA

LIBYA

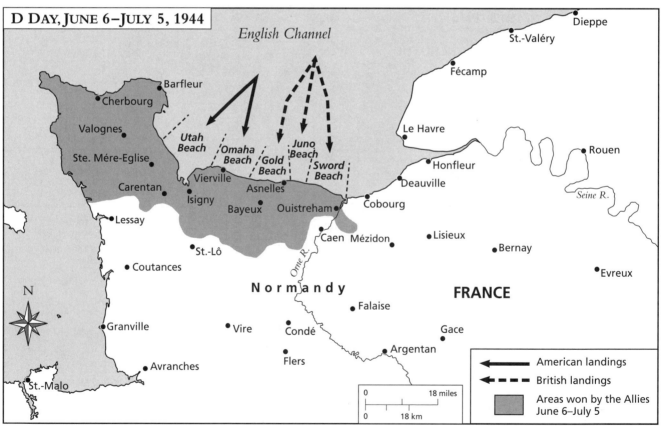

D DAY, JUNE 6–JULY 5, 1944

English Channel

Dieppe

St.-Valéry

Fécamp

Barfleur

Cherbourg

Valognes

Ste. Mére-Eglise

Utah Beach

Omaha Beach

Gold Beach

Juno Beach

Sword Beach

Le Havre

Rouen

Vierville

Carentan

Isigny

Asnelles

Bayeux

Ouistreham

Honfleur

Deauville

Cobourg

Seine R.

Lessay

St.-Lô

Caen   Mézidon

Lisieux

Bernay

Coutances

Orne R.

N o r m a n d y

FRANCE

Evreux

N

Granville

Vire

Condé

Falaise

Gace

Avranches

Flers

Argentan

St.-Malo

0   18 miles
0   18 km

◄—   American landings

◄----   British landings

     Areas won by the Allies June 6–July 5

POST–WORLD WAR II OCCUPATION ZONES OF GERMANY, 1945–1948

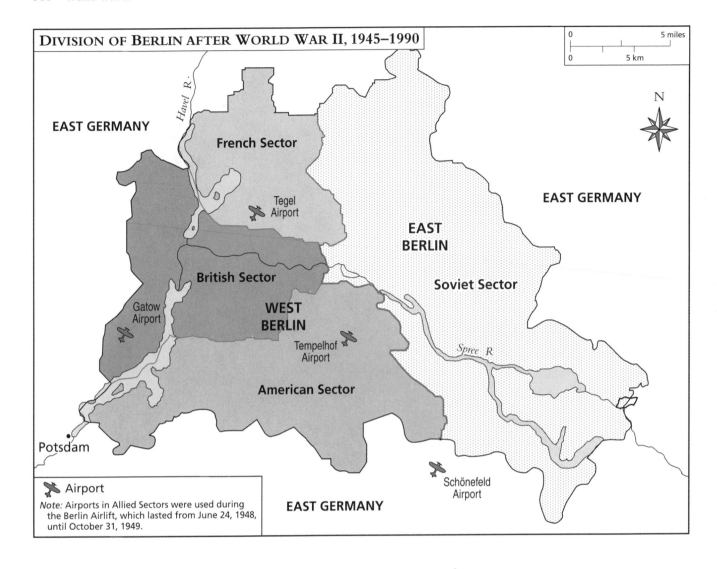

DIVISION OF BERLIN AFTER WORLD WAR II, 1945–1990

0 ___ 5 miles
0 ___ 5 km

N

EAST GERMANY

Havel R.

French Sector

Tegel Airport

EAST GERMANY

EAST BERLIN

British Sector

Soviet Sector

Gatow Airport

WEST BERLIN

Tempelhof Airport

Spree R.

American Sector

Potsdam

Schönefeld Airport

✈ Airport

Note: Airports in Allied Sectors were used during the Berlin Airlift, which lasted from June 24, 1948, until October 31, 1949.

EAST GERMANY

POPULATION DISPLACEMENT AFTER WORLD WAR II, 1945–1948

| 0 | | 300 miles |
| 0 | | 300 km |

60 Number of people (000s)

◀—·— Germans and
         German speakers

◀— — Baltic peoples

◀—— Russians

◀—··— Poles

◀— — Czechs

◀········ Prisoners of war
            and slave laborers

▨ Territory added to
     Soviet Union by 1945

Destruction caused by World War II (1939–45) and boundary changes agreed by the victorious Allies at the Yalta (Feb. 1945) and Potsdam (July 1945) Conferences resulted in the mass movement of peoples all over Europe.

MAJOR MOVEMENTS OF PEOPLES

Germans in conquered lands to the east fled the approaching Soviet (USSR) armies in 1945.

Russians moved into territories added to the USSR in the Baltic region and Eastern Europe.

Native German-speaking people in the Eastern European nations were expelled.

Prisoners of war and slave laborers held by Germans were released by the Allied advance and sent home or temporarily resettled.

NATIONS IN THE MARSHALL PLAN, 1948

Nations in the Marshall Plan, 1948

N

ICELAND

FAEROE IS.

SHETLAND IS.

NORWAY

SWEDEN

FINLAND

USSR

UNITED
KINGDOM

IRELAND

DENMARK

NETHER-
LANDS

EAST

POLAND

BELGIUM   WEST

GERMANY

LUXEMBOURG

CZECHOSLOVAKIA

GERMANY

FRANCE

SWITZ.

AUSTRIA

HUNGARY

ROMANIA

LIECHTENSTEIN

MONACO

ITALY

YUGOSLAVIA

BULGARIA

PORTUGAL

SPAIN

Corsica

Sardinia

ALBANIA

TURKEY

BALEARIC IS.

Gibraltar

GREECE

Sicily

Cyprus
(UK)

Malta

Crete

| 0 | 300 miles |
| 0 | 300 km |

APPENDIX D
Glossary

absolutist conscientious objector Conscientious objectors to war whose beliefs do not allow them to do any work that directly or indirectly contributes to the war effort.

Allies The side on which the United States fought. From 1939 to 1940: Great Britain (and its empire), France, and Poland; 1941: Britain and the Soviet Union; from 1942: Britain, the Soviet Union, the United States, and many smaller nations. After the fall of France, the Free French fought for the Allies. Early in the war the Allies began to refer to themselves as the United Nations.

assembly center A temporary place at which the U.S. military held Japanese-American evacuees.

Axis The powers arrayed against the Allies, chiefly Germany, Italy, and Japan. Italy broke away in 1943, and thereafter Italians fought on both sides.

banzai charge A suicidal mass attack by Japanese servicemen, common in the Pacific theater when their command considered the military situation hopeless. The charge was often accompanied by yelling and screaming. Banzai literally means "10,000 years."

blitzkrieg Meaning "lightning war," chosen for the speed with which Hitler's armies moved through Europe in the early days of the war. The shortened term *blitz* was often used for air raids.

booby trap A disguised bomb or mine set to be exploded by some action of the intended victim, as when some seemingly harmless object is lifted.

Civil Air Patrol (CAP) A volunteer organization, serving without pay, that trained hundreds of pilots, sailors, and coastguardsmen; spotted enemy submarines and survivors of sinkings; and performed other auxiliary services for the armed forces.

Civilian Pilot Training Program A program begun in 1939 in which the Civil Aeronautics Board contracted with more than 1,000 educational institutions to provide ground training and with private flight schools to provide flight training for pilots. In December 1942 the military took over the program and renamed it the War Training Service.

Civilian Public Service (CPS) The organization in which conscientious objectors worked in lieu of military service.

Coast Guard Auxiliary A civilian organization of small boat owners willing to serve in patrol work at their own expense.

coast watchers Men, mostly Australian, who at great risk hid in the jungles of Pacific islands, to observe Japanese activities, and reported to the Allies by radio.

C-rations A portable meal consisting of canned meat and vegetables with hard biscuits, providing 3,800 calories a day in battle conditions.

D day The day designated for the commencement of a specific military operation, most often used to refer to June 6, 1944, when Operation Overlord—the Allied invasion of France—began.

"Dear John" A letter to a soldier from his wife or sweetheart explaining that she had found someone else.

deserter volunteer An enemy alien who agreed to serve the Allies as a spy or informer.

dog tag   A metal identification disk engraved with the name, serial number, and blood type and worn around the neck by all military personnel.

dollar-a-year men   Business executives who worked for the U.S. government for $1 a year, usually retaining their company salaries.

European theater of operations (ETO)   The geographical area of Europe in which World War II was fought.

fifth column   Group of people who aid the enemy from within their own country.

fireside chat   A radio address by President Franklin D. Roosevelt, in which he talked directly to the American people as if he were sitting with them in their living rooms. So many people listened to these addresses that during the broadcasts the sale of movie tickets sagged and the home use of electricity soared, as millions turned on their radios.

flak   Antiaircraft fire; by extension, harassing verbal protests.

Free French   French people who refused to accept the surrender of their government to the Germans in June 1940. Under the leadership of General Charles de Gaulle the war against the Nazis was continued by clandestine resistance groups in France and by French armed forces organized in Britain.

GI   Government issue. This term was widely used as a noun to refer to American military personnel, particularly male enlisted soldiers, and as an adjective to refer to the strict following of regulations: "He's very GI."

GGs   Government girls, mostly in Washington, D.C., working for the expanding federal bureaucracy.

H-hour   The exact hour of the beginning of a specific military operation.

Historic Peace Churches   Friends (Quakers), Mennonites, and Church of the Brethren.

issei   Japanese immigrants.

Kamikaze corps   A special Japanese air corps, organized in 1944, in which pilots were trained to crash their planes into enemy ships, an action that set the ships on fire by the spread of gasoline and exploded them with bombs. The name, which means "divine wind," derives from a 16th-century event in which, according to legend, the gods sent a typhoon to scatter and destroy a Mongol fleet attacking Japan. According to Doug Stanton in *In Harm's Way*, kamikaze pilots sometimes wore ceremonial robes and clutched dolls given them by their daughters. See also *kikusui*.

kibei   Japanese Americans born in the United States but sent back to Japan for work or education.

kikusui   Massed kamikaze attacks. The name means "floating chrysanthemum."

"Kilroy was here"   Graffiti words and images inscribed in unlikely places marking the previous passage of an imaginary character. Sgt. Francis J. Kilroy of the Air Force among several others claimed to be the originator, but such claims were widely contested.

kitchen police (KP)   The military assignment of helping cooks by preparing vegetables, washing pots and pans, etc.

K-ration   A day's combat ration of dried and concentrated foods, cigarettes, gum, water purification and salt tablets, and matches.

Liberty ship   An ungainly freighter turned out in large numbers during World War II to transport goods to Allies.

Luftwaffe   The German air force.

merchant marine   Mostly civilian ships, subject after February 7, 1942, and throughout the war to the authority of the War Shipping Administration.

milk run   An easy air combat mission.

military occupational specialty (MOS)   The particular tasks for which a service member is specially trained.

military police (MP)   Those army personnel assigned to perform police functions within the military, keep order, and ensure the good conduct of servicemembers on and off duty.

North Atlantic Treaty Organization (NATO)   An association formed on April 4, 1949, by Belgium, Canada, Denmark, France, Iceland, Italy, Luxembourg, the Netherlands, Norway, Portugal, the United Kingdom, and the United States to prevent aggression, or, if necessary, to resist attack against any alliance member. In 1952, Greece and Turkey joined NATO, followed by the Federal Republic of Germany in 1955 and by Spain in 1982; Spain in 1982; Hungary, Poland, and the Czech Republic in 1999; and Bulgaria, Estonia, Latvia, Lithuania, Romania, Slovakia, and Slovenia in 2002.

nisei   American-born children of Japanese immigrants.

Pacific theater of operations (PTO)   The geographical area on and around the Pacific Ocean in which World War II was fought.

Quonset huts   Prefabricated, lightweight, multipurpose, half-tubular buildings measuring 36 ft x 16 ft, with a skin of ribbed galvanized steel sheathing over a frame of steel arch ribs, insulated, and set on a floor of wood or concrete.

relocation center   A camp to which Japanese-American evacuees were assigned.

ruptured duck   Originally a cloth insignia depicting an eagle inside a wreath, worn on uniforms above the right breast pocket by World War II servicemen and women; on discharge they were given a lapel pin of the same design.

Seabees (C-Bs)   Naval construction battalions.

serial number   Each member of the U.S. armed services was assigned an identification number. The number was engraved on a "dog tag" that was worn around the neck. He or she had to give this number to be paid, to receive mail, etc. Mail addresses had to include such a number. Anyone captured was under orders to give the enemy only his or her name, rank, and serial number.

skip bombing   A method of aerial bombing in which a bomb is released from such a low altitude that it slides or glances along the surface of the water or ground and strikes the target at or above water level or ground level.

SNAFU   An acronym for "situation normal, all f---ed up." Used both as a noun and as a verb.

shore patrol (SP)   Those naval, marine and Coast Guard personnel assigned to perform police functions within the military, keep order, and ensure the good conduct of service members on and off duty.

SS (Schutzstaffeln)   Fanatic Nazi elite troops.

Tokyo Rose   Radio name used by some 20 women broadcasting from Japan. Tokyo Rose broadcasts were intended to undermine the morale of American servicemen, and often included supposedly secret information about ship sailings and unit names.

U-boat (*Unterseeboot*)   German submarine.

V-1 and **V-2**   Pilotless rocket-powered missiles launched from bunkers in German-occupied northern France against England. The V-1 carried more than 12,000 pounds of high explosives; the V-2 was even more deadly because of its supersonic speed and heavier warhead.

V-E Day   Victory in Europe day, May 7, 1945.

Vichy France.   The term applied to that part of France not directly occupied by the Germans and its government seated in the city of Vichy. Headed by the World War I hero marshall Henri Philippe Pétain, the Vichy regime collaborated with the Nazis. In November 1942 the Germans occupied the Vichy-ruled part of France and Pétain's government became irrelevant.

victory girls   Also known as "khaki-whackies" and "cuddle-bunnies," young females who had sex with servicemen not for money but allegedly out of patriotism.

V-J Day   Victory in Japan day, August 14, 1945.

Willie and Joe   The long-suffering, hardened combat infantrymen of Bill Mauldin's cartoons.

Zero   Japanese fighter plane.

zoot-suit riots   Riots that broke out in Los Angeles in June 1943 between white servicemen on leave and Mexican-American youths wearing zoot suits. The servicemen typically stripped the youths and destroyed their suits. The riots escalated in violence as they spread to other cities; black zoot-suiters were also involved.

zoot suits   Outfits worn by young men in rebellion. The suits flouted the rationing regulations by their excessive use of material in long coats and draped pants with peg-legged bottoms. The suits were often worn with pork-pie hats and by youths with ducktail haircuts. In the public mind they became associated with juvenile delinquents, particularly Mexican-American and black gang members who were also draft dodgers.

APPENDIX E
Refugees

HISTORICAL CONTEXT

"The [U.S. State] department does not refuse visas. It merely sets up a line of obstacles stretching from Washington to Lisbon and on around to Shanghai.... It is as if we were to examine laboriously the curricula vitae of flood victims clinging to a piece of floating wreckage and finally to decide that, no matter what their virtues, all but a few had better be allowed to drown."

—Freda Kirchwey[1]

All through World War II, Europeans who had been made refugees by reason of their ethnicity or their opposition to the Nazi dictator Adolf Hitler tried desperately to get to the United States. However, the Great Depression of the 1930s had caused the nation to all but close its gates. In 1938 it opened them slightly but began shutting them again in the fall of 1939, by July 1941 leaving only a crack. The immigration quotas for Europeans totaled 154,000 a year, of which about 84,000 were for the British and Irish, but in fact immigration was held to about 10 percent of the quota limits.[2] Fears of renewed unemployment after the war, nativism, and anti-Semitism kept the numbers to these lows throughout the war. A few refugees with money or influence got in; the rest did not.

During his first term as president, Franklin D. Roosevelt worked quietly to admit more. Between 1933 and 1940, nearly 105,000 refugees from Nazism reached the United States.[3] However, anti-Semitism hindered the president's efforts: In 1939 a Roper poll reported that 53 percent of the respondents believed Jews differed from everyone else and should be restricted in business and social life, and other surveys from 1940 to 1945 showed that 15 to 24 percent of respondents looked on Jews as a menace to the United States.[4] Moreover, Americans—even the president—feared infiltration by foreign agents. So strong was the opposition to the reception of refugees that the Alaskan Development Bill introduced in late 1940 died in committee: It had proposed only to bring 10,000 settlers to Alaska, half of whom would be European refugees who promised to stay in Alaska for five years, after which they would be allowed to enter the United States under the existing quotas.[5]

First Lady Eleanor Roosevelt accepted the president's argument that the best way to help refugees was to win the war as fast as possible, but she could not ignore their plight. She tried in vain to help the 930 Jews aboard the *St. Louis,* which sailed from Germany to Cuba in May 1939, each refugee armed with a valid Cuban visa. Nonetheless the Cuban government denied them entry, and so did the U.S. government, to whom they next appealed. They were forced to return to Europe, where many of them died in concentration camps.

Again in June 1940, with representatives of such groups as the American Friends Service Committee, the German-Jewish Children's Aid, and the Committee for Catholic Refugees, Eleanor Roosevelt organized the U.S. Committee for the Care of European Children. The committee easily found families to care for the children, but they had trouble persuading the State Department to let them in, even as visitors, and finding transport for them. A direct order from the president resulted in temporary visas for British children, and Congress acted to permit unarmed, unescorted American ships to transport them. In late August of that year Eleanor Roosevelt also successfully appealed to her husband to admit 83 Jewish refugees who had escaped from occupied France and sailed on the Portuguese freighter *Quanza*. But all her many subsequent efforts to save refugees failed.

After the Germans conquered France in 1940, many Europeans endangered by Hitler fled to the relative safety of Vichy France, where the Germans allowed a puppet French government to operate. The refugees remained in peril, however, for the Germans could force the Vichy French to surrender on demand any non-French person. Several American organizations set out to do what they could to help, most of them by relief efforts that by the end of July 1942 did somewhat ameliorate conditions in the Vichy detention camps.

A group of prominent Americans (including journalists Elmer Davis, Raymond Gram Swing, and Dorothy Thompson and the presidents of several colleges and universities) formed the Emergency Rescue Committee to save European artists, intellectuals, trade unionists, and anti-Nazi political figures. In July 1940 the first lady helped the committee persuade the State Department to issue visitors' visas for such endangered people. The President's Advisory Committee on Political Refugees was to certify the good faith of these refugees, who would then be issued visas by U.S. consuls abroad. With this encouragement the Emergency Rescue Committee in August 1940 sent Varian Fry to Marseilles (in Vichy France), ostensibly as a representative of the World Committee of the YMCA. The 32-year-old Fry, an editor from Foreign Policy Association Books, had no previous experience in relief work or clandestine operations, but he spoke French and German and knew the work of many of the refugees on the rescue list.

However, a middle-management group within the State Department, led by Breckenridge Long, battled all efforts to admit refugees to the United States. According to Fred L. Israel, his biographer in the *Dictionary of American Biography,* Long "linked communism and international Jewry, and he had a strong dislike for both" and believed that he was "protecting the nation against an invasion by those whom he considered radicals and foreign agents."[6] Long instructed consuls to put every obstacle in the refugees' way, indefinitely postponing the issuance of visas.

Nonetheless, in cooperation with workers from the American Friends of Czechoslovakia, the American Federation of Labor, and the Unitarian Service Committee, Fry and his motley international staff of the Centre Américain de Secours managed to help thousands of refugees[7] and transport to the United States several hundreds of them, including artist Marc Chagall; sculptor Jacques Lipchitz; weaver Alma Mahler; pianist Wanda Lendowska; painter-poet Max

Ernst; authors Lion Feuchtwanger and Franz Werfel; scientists Fritz Kah, Jacques Hadamard, and Otto Meyerhof; and political philosopher Hannah Arendt. Fry also helped stranded soldiers from the British Expeditionary Force get back to England.

Imperturbable, sensitive, and witty, Fry himself dealt with the American consulate, the police, friendly priests, and workers from other agencies, while his staff handled the streams of refugees seeking aid. Together they invented their methods as they went, getting Czech, Lithuanian, and Polish passports; securing Siamese, Chinese, or Belgian Congo overseas visas and false French demobilization papers or identity cards; working out escape routes by train or on foot into Spain or by sea or plane to North Africa. About a month after he arrived, Fry was reprimanded by the U.S. State Department for evading French laws; later he was arrested and detained by the Vichy French. Nonetheless he persisted in his efforts until September 1941, when he was expelled from France and forced to return to the United States. He died in obscurity, his work unrecognized.

American Jewish organizations disagreed about goals and methods. Some insisted on the formation of a Jewish state and some did not. Some wanted to ransom Jews from the Nazis and some did not. Nonetheless they were working to discover what was happening to European Jews and to spread the word of their plight. The State Department impeded that task by questioning the validity of information passed from European to American Jews and delaying its transmission. Many Americans, disillusioned by the discovery of British use of false propaganda in World War I, could not believe the atrocities the reports relayed and dismissed the rumors of a Nazi plan to eradicate Jews. Still, reports seeped through: As early as October 1941 the *New York Times* reported the machine-gunning of thousands of Jews in Poland and the Ukraine, and accounts of torture and murder multiplied thereafter. Newspaper stories and editorials, advertisements, and statements from prominent people gradually made it impossible to doubt that European Jews were facing unimaginable horrors.

Roosevelt and other Allied leaders denounced the persecutions and issued warning after warning to the Axis powers that punishment for war crimes would follow. By late 1942 American agencies were permitted to send food parcels to specific addresses in Axis Europe. A day of mourning and prayer for European Jews was observed in 30 countries, including the United States. But, at a time when even the State Department was confirming news of the Nazi plans of genocide, Congress refused to give the president power to suspend laws hampering the unimpeded movement of persons, property, and information into and out of the United States. Private agencies went on trying to rescue refugees; the U.S. government did not. Any talk of rescuing sizable numbers was always silenced by the question, "Where would we put them?"

By 1944, however, concern for the European Jews was mounting. On January 26, at the urging of Treasury Secretary Henry Morgenthau and Interior Secretary Harold Ickes, Roosevelt created a War Refugee Board (WRB). The president mandated the board to take "all measures within [U.S.] power to rescue the victims of enemy oppression who are in imminent danger of death" and to provide "relief and assistance consistent with the successful prosecution of the war."[8] He instructed the Departments of State, Treasury, and War to execute the programs the WRB formulated and supply it with information and assistance. Instead, after a short period of cooperation, the State Department reverted to its old habits and hindered the WRB's work. The board acted mainly as facilitator and coordinator of projects carried out by private organizations, and Jewish private agencies financed and implemented most of its projects.

The WRB did relieve the plight of some Jews by such relief measures as sending food parcels to concentration camp inmates and investigating ways and means of rescuing the victims of persecution and finding places they could go. Thousands of Hungarian Jews were saved by the protective papers issued them by neutral nations at the suggestion of the WRB. The board cooperated in schemes to ransom Jews held by the Germans by payments of money and materiel, though it was careful not to offer large enough sums to help the German war effort. It used psychological measures aimed at preventing deportations and atrocities, particularly by reminders of Allied determination to try war criminals. It tried to persuade the War Department to bomb the railroad tracks to concentration camps and commanders in theaters of war to assist rescue efforts. It pleaded with neutral countries to announce that they would permit all refugees who reached their borders to enter and promised these countries that the board would arrange to evacuate the refugees so admitted. To prevent murders of Jews with Latin American passports, it encouraged the Nazis to hope for exchanges of these Jews for German nationals held abroad. The diplomatic pressures that the board exerted as the war wound down helped to move 48,000 Jews to safe areas of Romania and end Hungarian deportation of Jews to the death camps. All in all, the board helped to save about 200,000 Jews.[9]

The WRB had high hopes for the "free ports" proposal put forth in April 1944 by *New York Post* writer Samuel Grafton. Grafton suggested allowing refugees to live in the United States for the duration of the war, not as immigrants but as internees behind fences—a proposal that immediately won the support of churches, the President's Advisory Committee on Political Refugees, labor unions, and the National Farmers Union. The board hoped that by this means the United States would offer temporary havens for all who could escape from Hitler.

But the United States offered such a refuge to only 982 people, most of them Jews. On June 2, 1944, Roosevelt announced plans to bring a thousand refugees to the United States for the duration of the war, to live in a camp "under appropriate security restrictions." Secretary of the Interior Harold Ickes sent his personal assistant, Ruth Gruber, to escort these men, women, and children, who had escaped from 18 countries, to the haven of Ft. Ontario in Oswego, New York. Restrictions were severe: The refugees lived behind a fence, could not travel, and could not receive overnight visitors—not even a husband or wife—and they faced the prospect of a return to Europe after the war. But they were safe, they were physically comfortable, and the children were allowed to go to school in Oswego. In December 1945 a vigorous campaign to permit them to stay in the United States resulted in President Harry Truman's admitting, under unused immigration quotas, those of them who so wished.

During World War II the United States broke the promise symbolized in the Statue of Liberty. In the decade from 1933 to 1943 the country had accepted fewer than 250,000 refugees from the Nazis, while in Europe millions died. Between December 7, 1941, and September 2, 1945, only about 21,000 refugees, mostly Jewish, were permitted to enter the United States—about 10 percent of the quota places legally available to people from Axis-controlled European countries in those years.[10]

CHRONICLE OF EVENTS

1938

In the United States, four separate polls indicate that from 71 to 85 percent of the American public oppose increasing immigration quotas to help refugees, and 67 percent want refugees completely barred.[11]

Concerned about German persecution of the Jews, President Franklin D. Roosevelt (FDR) opens the U.S. quotas for Europeans for full use.

August: The International Intergovernmental Committee on Refugees is created but remains moribund.

1939

In the United States, a survey shows that 66 percent of Americans object to a one-time exception to allow 10,000 refugee children to enter in excess of the quota limits.[12]

spring: The 930 Jewish refugees aboard the *St. Louis* are refused entry to the United States and the ship is forced to return to Europe.

November: The Vaad ha-Hatzala is founded by the Union of Orthodox Rabbis of the United States and Canada, mainly to rescue European rabbinic leaders.

1940

The U.S. State Department tightens requirements for immigration, cutting admissions by half.

summer: Through the efforts of the U.S. Committee for the Care of European Children and Eleanor Roosevelt, British children are brought to the United States on visitors' visas.

August: Eleanor Roosevelt gains admission to the United States for 83 Jewish refugees who escaped from occupied France and sailed on the Portuguese freighter *Quanza.*

August: The Emergency Rescue Committee sends Varian Fry to Marseilles, France, where in the next year he succors thousands of refugees.

1941

The Committee for a Jewish Army of Stateless and Palestinian Jews is formed to exert pressure on the U.S. and British governments to permit the establishment of a separate Jewish army, based in Palestine, to fight with the Allies.

July: New York Yiddish daily newspapers report the Nazi murders of hundreds of Jewish civilians.

July: U.S. refugee immigration is again cut, to about 25 percent of the relevant quotas, on the grounds that Axis spies are entering as refugees. The State Department institutes strict interdepartmental committee security reviews.

July 31: German Reichsmarshal Hermann Goering instructs the Reich Security Office to organize "a complete solution of the Jewish question in the German sphere of influence in Europe."

October: Jews are denied exit from German-held territory.

October: The *New York Times* carries a small inside article reporting the machine-gunning of thousands of Jews in Poland and the Ukraine.

December: The U.S. State Department tightens visa procedures for enemy aliens.

1942

March: A representative of the American Jewish Joint Distribution Committee holds a press conference to publicize a report based on eyewitness testimony, estimating that the Nazis have already massacred 240,000 Jews in the Ukraine.

May: The *New York Times* publishes the report of a United Press correspondent caught in Germany when the United States entered the war, revealing that Germans had killed more than 100,000 Jews in the Baltic states, nearly that many in Poland, and more than twice as many in western Russia.

May: A Zionist conference in New York agrees on the Biltmore Program, which calls for unlimited Jewish immigration into Palestine and the establishment of Palestine as a Jewish commonwealth.

June 29: In a London press conference the World Jewish Congress estimates that the Nazis have already killed more than a million Jews, mostly in Poland, Lithuania, Russia, and Romania, and alleges the existence of Nazi policy to exterminate the Jews. The press conference is reported by both the Associated Press and the United Press.

July: U.S. State Department inquiries uncover numerous reports of the murders of Jews.

July 21: At Madison Square Garden in New York City more than 20,000 people protest Nazi atrocities and hear a message from President Roosevelt declaring that the American people "will hold the perpetrators of these crimes to strict accountability in a day of reckoning which will surely come."

August: News of the existence of the Nazi plan for the systematic extermination of Europe's Jews reaches American Jewish leaders.

August 21: Roosevelt again warns the Axis that perpetrators of war crimes will be tried after Germany's defeat.

August 27: American Jewish organizations in a letter to the State Department call on the United States to protest to the French Vichy government its deportations of Jews.

September: At the suggestion of American relief workers in France, their headquarters appeal to the State Department for a thousand immigration visas for Jewish children stranded in France; their plea is supported by Eleanor Roosevelt and the President's Advisory Committee on Political Refugees.

September: A group of Jewish leaders organizes a council of representatives of the major American Jewish organizations to plan a response to Nazi persecution of the Jews.

September 18: The State Department authorizes a thousand visas for Jewish children stranded in France—a number raised to 5,000 by the end of the month. But the Vichy government never releases the children.

October: Efforts by the United States and other governments to persuade the Vatican to condemn Nazi atrocities fail.

November 24: The U.S. State Department confirms news of the Nazi plan to exterminate European Jews.

November 25: American Jewish leaders resolve to announce to the press Nazi genocide of the Jews, to ask 500 newspapers to publish editorials on the issue, to ask a few prominent non-Jews to make statements on the European Jewish situation, to hold a day of mourning and prayer, and to meet with President Roosevelt.

late 1942: The U.S. State Department permits American relief agencies to send $12,000 worth of food parcels per month to specific addressees in Axis Europe, the food to be produced in neutral European countries.

December: Journalist Dorothy Thompson proposes several measures to stir resistance to mass murders of Jews within Germany; as a result 50 prominent Americans of German descent, including theologian Reinhold Niebuhr, news correspondent William L. Shirer, baseball player Babe Ruth, and orchestra conductor Walter

Damrosch, sign a "Christmas Declaration" published in the *New York Times* denouncing the "cold-blooded extermination of the Jews" and other atrocities. The declaration is broadcast over all major American radio networks, and the Office of War Information beams it to the U.S. armed forces and to Axis Europe.

December: At the instigation of the President's Advisory Committee on Political Refugees, an appeals process is instituted for would-be immigrants rejected by the State Department.

December: The U.S. State Department at the instigation of private agencies and the President's Advisory Committee on Refugees agrees to admit some 200 Jewish children who have escaped to Spain and Portugal and their mothers, but during 1943 only about 125 children reach the United States under this program, to be followed by another dozen before war's end.

December: Jewish groups urge that German citizens living in the United States and Latin America be exchanged for Jews in Axis Europe.

December 2: A day of mourning and prayer for European Jews is observed in 30 countries, including the United States.

December 8: American Jewish leaders confer with FDR, asking him to issue warnings about war crimes and to form a commission to collect evidence of Nazi barbarism.

December 17: The Allies and the governments of eight occupied countries issue the "U.N. Declaration" condemning Nazi plans to exterminate the Jews.

1943

January: A poll indicates that 78 percent of Americans believe that "it would be a bad idea to let more immigrants come into the country after the war."[13]

January: Quaker David Blickenstaff establishes in Madrid the Representation in Spain of American Relief Organizations, which frees hundreds of Jewish refugees by supplying money for their maintenance, sends aid to those still incarcerated, and seeks out emigration possibilities.

January 7: In a Gallup poll, 47 percent of the respondents believe it true that 2 million Jews have been killed in Europe since the war began, 29 percent think it rumor, and 24 percent have no opinion.[14]

March: The council of representatives of the major American Jewish organizations becomes the Joint Emergency Committee on European Jewish Affairs, usually called the Temporary Committee.

March 1: The American Jewish Congress holds a "Stop Hitler Now" demonstration in Madison Square Garden in New York City, cosponsored by other Jewish organizations, the American Federation of Labor, the Congress of Industrial Organizations, the Church Peace Union, and the Free World Association. The meeting calls for action to rescue European Jews and provide havens for them.

March 3: The U.S. State Department reveals plans for a diplomatic conference to deal with the refugee problem.

March 9: The Committee for a Jewish Army presents a pageant in Madison Square Garden in New York City as a memorial to the murdered Jews of Europe.

March 15: The Joint Emergency Committee (JEC) on European Jewish Affairs replaces the Temporary Committee. It includes representatives from the American Jewish Committee, the American Jewish Congress, B'nai B'rith, the Jewish Labor Committee, the Synagogue Council of America, Agudath Israel of America, the Union of Orthodox Rabbis, and the American Emergency Committee for Zionist Affairs. In the following weeks the JEC sponsors 40 rallies in 20 states to mobilize public opinion for rescue of European Jews.

April: Seven Jewish congressmen ask FDR to simplify State Department procedures, which are holding immigration to less than 10 percent of the quotas.

April 19: A joint British-American meeting is held in Bermuda for a "preliminary . . . discussion on the refugee problem" and the revival of the Intergovernmental Committee on Refugees.

May: Senator William Langer of North Dakota calls on the Senate to act to save Jews from extermination.

May 2: The Federal Council of the Churches of Christ in America sponsors a "Day of Compassion" focusing on the Nazi persecution of European Jews.

July: The U.S. State Department requires that a visa application form more than four feet long must be filled out on both sides by a sponsor for each refugee and submitted in six copies.

July 20–25: The Emergency Conference to Save the Jewish People of Europe is held in New York City, sponsored by the Committee for a Jewish Army, but most Jewish organizations refuse to support it. At its end the conference forms the Emergency Committee to Save the Jewish People of Europe.

mid-August: Eleanor Roosevelt records a message of encouragement to the Jews of Europe for broadcast overseas by the Office of War Information.

August 29–September 2: An American Jewish Conference in New York City, in which 65 national Jewish organizations participate, calls for unlimited Jewish immigration into Palestine and the reconstitution of Palestine as the Jewish commonwealth.

fall: U.S. State Department policy says that refugees "not in acute danger" (e.g., those who have escaped to Spain, Portugal, and North Africa) may be denied visas. The Department also stipulates that visas may be granted only to refugees not accepted for a refugee depot in North Africa.

fall: Refugee-aid and social-service organizations launch a campaign to head off further curtailment of immigration.

September: American Federation of Labor (AFL) and Congress of Industrial Organizations (CIO) leaders ask that the United Nations (Allies) take in all Jews who can get out of Europe and declare the rest legally prisoners of war. Soon thereafter, the AFL convention resolves that the United Nations, and specifically the United States, should temporarily suspend immigration restrictions to provide havens for Jews. The National Republican Club and the National Democratic Club issue a joint statement calling on Congress to admit 100,000 refugees on condition that they return to Europe soon after war's end. Bills are introduced in Congress to allow refugees who would not endanger the public safety to come to the United States temporarily.

October 6: Four hundred Orthodox rabbis under the sponsorship of the Emergency Committee to Save the Jewish People of Europe, the Union of Orthodox Rabbis, and the Union of Grand Rabbis make a pilgrimage to Washington to petition for rescue of European Jews.

November: Identical resolutions are introduced in the House of Representatives and the Senate to create a commission to save the remaining Jews of Europe (the Rescue Resolution).

November: Roosevelt suggests to the State Department the creation of additional refugee camps and small offices staffed by Americans in Spain, Portugal, North Africa, Italy, and Turkey.

November: With Allied advances in southern Italy, thousands of refugees stream across the Adriatic to Italy, their movement facilitated by the Yugoslav resistance and the Allied military. The British army then transports many of them to camps in Egypt.

December: The Senate Foreign Relations Committee calls for sending food to populations in occupied Europe, but British opposition defeats the implementation of the plan.

1944

January 22: Roosevelt issues Executive Order 9417 establishing the War Refugee Board.

February: The War Refugee Board sends department-store executive Ira Hirschmann to Turkey to help Jews in the Balkans pass through Turkey to Palestine. With the help of the Jewish Agency, the executive arm of the World Zionist organization, nearly 8,000 refugees pass through Turkey from the Balkans and Greece. Hirschmann also later arranges the protection of 48,000 Jews still living in Romania and persuades Bulgaria to abolish anti-Jewish laws and reinstate Jewish property rights for the 45,000 Jews there.[15]

March: A camp for 2,000 refugees opens at Fedala, near Casablanca, North Africa.

March: After long delays, the International Red Cross obtains informal guarantees from individual Nazi concentration camp commanders that they will relay food parcels to internees.

spring: The flow of Yugoslav refugees to Italy is reduced by Allied military orders.

spring: The War Refugee Board appoints Roswell McClelland, director of the American Friends Service Committee's refugee-relief program in Switzerland, to head War Refugee Board operations there. These operations enjoy considerable success, extending into France, Germany, Italy, Czechoslovakia, and Hungary, and enable thousands of endangered people to survive and other thousands to escape.

April: The War Refugee Board begins a series of protests to Hungary against deportation of its Jews and appeals to neutral nations to grant protective citizenship documents to Hungarian Jews with ties to their countries.

April: In a "free ports" proposal *New York Post* writer Samuel Grafton advocates setting aside fenced-off land in the United States where refugees may stay for the duration of the war.

May: On President Roosevelt's order the flow of refugees from Yugoslavia to Italy and Egypt is resumed.

June 2: President Roosevelt announces plans to bring 1,000 refugees from southern Italy to the United States for the duration of the war; they are to be kept in camp "under appropriate security restrictions."

mid-1944: A camp for 7,000 refugees opens at Philippeville, Algeria.

Summer: A War Refugee Board operation in Sweden sends rescue teams into Estonia, Latvia, and Lithuania and rescues 1,200 non-Jews.

July: Hungary offers to permit emigration of all Jewish children under 10 who have visas to other countries and all Jews of any age who have permission to immigrate to Palestine. Germany prevents the emigration.

July 31: The American Jewish Conference holds a mass demonstration in New York City to generate pressure for efforts to save the Hungarian Jews.

August: The War Refugee Board begins a limited program of sending food parcels into concentration camps.

August: The United States allows 982 refugees, the majority Jews, to enter Fort Ontario in Oswego, New York, where they live fenced in with the understanding that they will return to Europe after the war.

November 7: Gen. Dwight D. Eisenhower warns the Germans not to "molest, harm or persecute" concentration-camp inmates, "no matter what their religion or nationality may be."

1945

January: Eight hundred Germans interned in the United States and Latin America are exchanged for 800 American and Latin American citizens in Europe, including 149 Jews from Bergen-Belsen concentration camp with Latin American passports.[16]

February: With the USSR in control of Bulgaria and Romania, the War Refugee Board office in Turkey closes.

July 1: The U.S. visa system reverts to prewar practice.

fall: President Harry Truman calls on Britain to permit 100,000 Jews to enter Palestine.

late 1945: A poll indicates that 32 percent of Americans believe the same number of Europeans as before the war should be allowed to immigrate each year; 37 percent think fewer should enter; 14 percent want no immigrants; and 5 percent want more than before the war.[17]

December: The U.S. Congress resolves in favor of a Jewish state.

December 22: President Truman rules that the refugees at Fort Ontario, Oswego, New York, may enter the United States under unused immigration quotas.

EYEWITNESS ACCOUNT

With the advent of Hitler, things changed rapidly. I was termed Jewish. As it turned out, being of mixed background, at that time I could still finish my high-school education *Abitur* (which in the USA includes two years of college). It also helped that my father was a decorated soldier during the First World War. However, I knew I could never finish any prolonged academic studies. What now?

My family had hoped to emigrate to the USA and I certainly needed to learn something quickly to support myself in another country. I still could attend a dressmaker trade school, a two-year program strictly supervised by the Dressmaker Guild. May I assure you, I was not their best student. I liked to design and it was recognized by my teachers, but the precision needlework was not for me. Still, I learned, passed the rigorous bi-monthly exam and got through until *Kristallnacht* (when all Jewish stores were smashed and plundered) and rules and regulations were changed. I had to leave school six weeks before graduation, but what I had learned helped me later.

Then came a number of tough happenings, like forced labor and so on, too unpleasant to report. Rather I will talk about the joyous time when finally the immigration papers for the USA arrived, and in May 1941 we arrived in New York City. My mother soon became a companion to a rich American lady. My father could not do much with a German law degree, but finally he started as a cutter for a comforter quilting company—a most unsuitable job for him with his analytical mind, but he forced himself to do this work. I got a job in the garment industry, at first running a sewing machine, and later designing. After three months we were able to rent an apartment, furnishing it with two sleeping couches, paid on installment, a kitchen table, three chairs from the Salvation Army, and, after another month, a used Baldwin piano, also bought on installments.

Well, this was the beginning. Father got a better job and after the war represented some German cutlery firms in the United States. Mother, who by profession was a fashion artist, developed a washable paint, suitable for clothing, on which she was granted a patent. In the evenings I was a bit of a technical advisor, and we both worked out a method to produce a painted, decorated nylon stocking. Mother created some beautiful designs and successfully marketed them to fancy department stores. When mother presented her merchandise at Bonwit Teller, the stocking buyer was enchanted. She suggested that Mother should also paint a clock on the stockings. Well, mother came home saying that the people in the fashion industry are crazy, and we all laughed at the suggestion, but Mother finally painted a small watch fob from which a tiny watch was hanging, placed it at the ankle, and set the hands at five minutes to five o'clock; we figured that it should be cocktail time and a little diamond-encrusted painted watch would be appropriate. When Mother showed her work to the Bonwit buyer, she burst out laughing and explained to my poor embarrassed mother that the word *clock* has another meaning—a decoration going up the side of a stocking from the ankle. But the tiny painted watch was so well liked that it was produced over quite some time. My mother became a well-known fashion artist.

Eve T. Karr, unpublished memoir.

People [refugees] came with their personal problems, housing problems, psychological problems of husbands who had had big positions and finally got a position here but their ego was so damaged that living with them was practically impossible. That could happen at midnight. You could get a phone call, and you would walk over to Oxford Street and sit and talk with them, and there are millions of stories like that.

Austrian-Jewish Mary Mohrer, first refugee employee of the Window Shop, a food and crafts shop established by Harvard faculty wives in Cambridge, Massachusetts, about 1940 to help recently arrived European Jews, quoted in Haber, From Hardtack to Homefries, *163.*

They all came together [fleeing from Austria]—[Alice Perutz] and her husband, and her husband's lady [mistress], and the Perutz' two boys, but they weren't divorced then, and very sensibly. I wouldn't be surprised if it was Alice Perutz who saw to it that they didn't get to this country unless they were all one family. And then they could get a divorce. I don't know this for a fact, but that's what I suspected. Then when they were divorced, very quietly she and this lovely Mr. Broch got married. . . .

Alice De Normandie Cope, a director of the Cambridge, Massachusetts, Window Shop from 1942 to 1954, quoted in Haber, From Hardtack to Homefries, *167. This food and crafts shop was established by Harvard faculty wives about 1940 to help recently arrived European Jews.*

NOTES

1. THE DEBATE: ISOLATIONISM V. INTERVENTIONISM, JANUARY 30, 1933–DECEMBER 11, 1941

1. Cole, *Charles A. Lindbergh*, 4.
2. Doenecke, *Storm on the Horizon*, 324.
3. Anne Lindbergh, *War Within and Without*, 57.
4. *Dictionary of American Biography*, Supp. 9: 591.
5. Quoted in Doenecke, *Storm on the Horizon*, 325.
6. *New York Times*, September 17, 1939, 5.
7. Paul Johnson, *Modern Times*, 309. Johnson gives the figure of 132,069, citing Manchester, *The Glory and the Dream*, 7.
8. Smith, *The Army and Economic Mobilization*, 122, Table 16.
9. Quoted in Craig, "The X-Files," review of Bendersky, *"The Jewish Threat," New York Review of Books*, April 12, 2001, 4.
10. Quoted in *New York Times*, September 17, 1939, 5.
11. Quoted in Burns, *Roosevelt*, 46.
12. Lardner, *The Lardners*, 268.
13. Goossen, *Women against the Good War*, 16–17.
14. *Dictionary of American Biography*, Supp. 9: 640.
15. Cole, *Charles A. Lindbergh*, 208.
16. Doenecke, *Storm on the Horizon*, 60.
17. Quoted in Schlesinger, *A Life*, 231.
18. Steel, *Walter Lippman*, 386.
19. Anne Lindbergh, *War Within and Without*, page xx; see also O'Neill, *Democracy at War*, 45.
20. Charles Lindbergh, "Who Are the War Agitators," available online.
21. U.S. Department of the Interior, map of the presidential election of 1940, available online.
22. Boston speech quoted in Goodwin, *No Ordinary Time*, 256.
23. Quoted in Cole, *Charles A. Lindbergh*, 128.
24. Poll of August 31, 1939, reported in Cardozier, *Mobilization*, 11–12.
25. Quoted in Colville, *The Fringes of Power*, 347.
26. Ever since the end of World War II, however, right-wing Japanese historians and a minority of American historians have argued that President Roosevelt deliberately provoked the attack at Pearl Harbor. The earliest of these was Charles A. Beard, in *President Roosevelt and the Coming of War, 1941: A Study in Appearances and Reality* (New Haven, Conn.: Yale University Press, 1948), and among the most recent is Robert A. Stinnett, *Day of Deceit: The Truth about FDR and Pearl Harbor* (New York: Touchstone, 2001). In the 21st century, evangelist Pat Buchanan repeats the argument that if the United States had not entered World War II, nothing much would have happened to the country. In his 1995 book *America First!* Bill Kauffman extends the argument, asserting that the United States and the United Nations are acting in a "destructive and unconstitutional" manner, asking, "Do we want to live in an America in which the flickering image of a starving Rwandan on CNN is more immediate to us than the plaintive cries of the hungry girl down the road; a world in which young Americans don blue helmets and travel halfway around the globe to enforce the resolutions of the United Nations, while in small towns across America volunteer fire departments are undermanned?"
27. Doenecke, *Storm on the Horizon*, 166.
28. Challener, "Veterans of Future Wars," available online.

2. GEARING UP: NATIONAL DEFENSE, MILITARY, AND ECONOMIC MOBILIZATION, 1939–DECEMBER 7, 1941

1. Gailey, *War in the Pacific*, 25.
2. Schubert, *Mobilization in World War II*, 8.
3. Quoted in Loewenheim et al., eds. *Roosevelt and Churchill*, 109, n. 2.

4. Lukacs, *Five Days in London,* passim.

5. Lukacs, *Five Days in London,* passim.

6. Quoted in Loewenheim et al., eds. *Roosevelt and Churchill,* 108.

7. Kimball, *Most Unsordid Act,* 70.

8. Franklin Roosevelt, fireside chat, December 29, 1940, available online; see also McCullough, *Truman,* 254.

9. Walker et al., *Our Glorious Century,* 194.

10. Steel, *Lippmann,* 389.

11. Perret, *Days of Sadness,* 37.

12. Calvocoressi et al., *Penguin History,* 214.

13. Rossiter, *Constitutional Dictatorship,* 267.

14. Sherwood, *Roosevelt and Hopkins,* 271.

15. Ibid.

16. Ibid.

17. Sherwood, *Roosevelt and Hopkins,* 274.

18. Astor, *Mighty Eighth,* 1–2.

19. Kennedy, *Freedom from Fear,* 661.

20. These restrictions had been imposed by the Neutrality Act of 1935, as later revised. Merchant Mariners greeted the arming of their ships as long overdue.

21. CIA home page, "COI Came First" and "What Was OSS?," available online.

22. Sherwood, *Roosevelt and Hopkins,* 270.

23. Letter from Gen. Arthur R. Wilson to Harry Hopkins, quoted in Sherwood, *Roosevelt and Hopkins,* 101.

24. Sherwood, *Roosevelt and Hopkins,* 76.

25. Sherwood, *Roosevelt and Hopkins,* 100.

26. Fleming, *Operation Sea Lion,* 308, n. 1.

27. Perrett, *There's a War to be Won,* 63.

28. Schubert, *Mobilization in World War II,* 8.

29. Perret, *Days of Sadness,* 87–88.

30. Fesler, *Industrial Mobilization,* 147.

31. Sherwood, *Roosevelt and Hopkins,* 160.

32. Riddle, *Truman Committee,* 53.

33. Schubert, *Mobilization in World War II,* 6.

34. Riddle, *Truman Committee,* 54.

35. Sherwood, *Roosevelt and Hopkins,* 157.

36. Sherwood, *Roosevelt and Hopkins,* 161.

37. Kennedy, *Freedom from Fear,* 473, 651.

38. Cardozier, *Mobilization,* 135.

39. Sherwood, *Roosevelt and Hopkins,* 289.

40. Carruth, *Encyclopedia,* 522.

41. Milward, *War, Economy and Society,* 63–72.

42. Quoted in Lash, *Roosevelt and Churchill,* 223.

43. Lash, *Roosevelt and Churchill,* 226.

3. Crisis Government, December 7, 1941–September 2, 1945

1. Nelson, *Arsenal of Democracy,* 208–209.

2. Smith, *The Army and Economic Mobilization,* 8.

3. Cardozier, *Mobilization,* 105.

4. R. Elberton Smith, *The Army and Economic Mobilization,* 143.

5. R. Elberton Smith, *The Army and Economic Mobilization,* 352–353.

6. Baruch, *Baruch,* 274.

7. Cardozier, *Mobilization,* 110.

8. Catton, *War Lords of Washington,* 115.

9. Nelson, *Arsenal of Democracy,* 389–390.

10. Cardozier, *Mobilization,* 109; and Gropman, *Mobilizing U.S. Industry,* chap. 6, available online.

11. Nelson, *Arsenal of Democracy,* 359.

12. Nelson, *Arsenal of Democracy,* 360.

13. Ibid.

14. Cardozier, *Mobilization,* 110.

15. Ibid.

16. Polenberg, *War and Society,* 13.

17. Baruch, *Baruch,* 286.

18. Polenberg, *War and Society,* 16.

19. Polenberg, *War and Society,* 18.

20. Ibid.

21. Baruch, *Baruch,* 287.

22. Gropman, *Mobilizing U.S. Industry,* chap. 6, available online.

23. *Singer in World War II, 1939–1945,* 1946, available online.

24. Nelson, *Arsenal of Democracy,* 288–289.

25. Nelson, *Arsenal of Democracy,* 218.

26. Senator Maury Maverick, chair of the Smaller War Plants Corporation, quoted in Catton, *War Lords of Washington,* 138.

27. Polenberg, *War and Society,* 13.

28. Polenberg, *War and Society,* 12.

29. Polenberg, *War and Society,* 18. This discussion of transportation relies heavily on Polenberg, 18ff.

30. Polenberg, *War and Society,* 19.

31. Palmer and Johnson, "Big Inch and Little Big Inch," in *The Handbook of Texas Online,* available online.

32. McCullough, *Truman,* 287–288.

33. McCullough, *Truman,* 287–288.

34. Riddle, *Truman Committee,* 13, quoting the Congressional Record, February 10, 1941, 830, 838.

35. R. Elberton Smith, *The Army and Economic Mobilization,* 351 and 457.

36. Quoted in Polenberg, *War and Society,* 174.

37. Polenberg, *War and Society,* 30–33.

38. Gropman, *Mobilizing U.S. Industry,* chap. 7.

39. Gropman, *Mobilizing U.S. Industry,* chap. 10.

40. R. Elberton Smith, *The Army and Economic Mobilization,* 707.

41. Polenberg, *War and Society,* 165.

42. Polenberg, *War and Society,* 167.

43. Polenberg, *War and Society,* 20–21.

44. Polenberg, *War and Society,* 22.

45. *Columbia Encyclopedia,* 6th ed., s.v. "War Production Board," and Robert Cuff's commentary in Titus, *The Home Front,* 113.

46. Morison, *Invasion of France and Germany,* 633.

47. Gropman, *Mobilizing U.S. Industry,* chap. 1. See also Koistinen, "Warfare and Power Relations in America," in Titus, *The Home Front,* 101.

4. Civilian Daily Life, 1940–June 1945

1. Cardozier, *Mobilization,* 185.

2. Cardozier, *Mobilization,* 189.

3. Cardozier, *Mobilization,* 188. At war's end the CAP became a civilian auxiliary of the U.S. Air Force.

4. "V-Mail," available online.

5. O'Neill, *Democracy at War,* 253.

6. Bellow, *It All Adds Up,* 28–29.

7. O'Neill, *Democracy at War,* 252.

8. Quoted in Kennett, *For the Duration,* 141.

9. Phillips, *The 1940s,* 173.

10. O'Neill, *Democracy at War,* 254.

11. Wattenberg, *The First Measured Century,* 8:2, available online.

12. Reynolds, *Rich Relations,* 47.

13. Gluck, *Rosie,* 4.

14. Quoted in Hoopes, *Americans Remember,* v.

15. Quoted in Litoff and Smith, *Since You Went Away,* 170.

16. Campbell, *Women at War,* 173.

17. "The only truly substantial and persistant black market was in meat." Brinkley, *Washington,* 136.

18. Cardozier, *Mobilization,* 241.

19. Phillips, *The 1940s,* 173.

20. O'Neill, *Democracy at War,* 263.

21. Ambrose, *Americans at War,* 142.

22. Phillips, *The 1940s,* 173.

23. Brokaw, *Greatest Generation,* 231.

24. Butt, "Wartime Housing at Atchison Village," 2, available online.

25. Cardozier, *Mobilization,* 226.

26. Goodwin, *No Ordinary Time,* 356.

27. Cardozier, *Mobilization,* 228–229.

28. "With the elimination of many New Deal programs, poverty increased, even with rising wages for many Americans. One committee reported that 20 million Americans were on the border of subsistence and starvation. 25% of all employed Americans earned less than 64 cents an hour, while skilled workers often earned $7 or $8 an hour." Schultz, "World War II, The Home Front," available online.

29. American Citizens Abroad, "A Brief History of U.S. Law on the Taxation," available online.

30. Winke Tax Services, "Maximum Individual Rates," available online.

31. Cardozier, *Mobilization,* 128.

32. Twight, "Evolution in Federal Income Tax Withholding," *Cato Journal* 14:3, 1, available online.

33. O'Brien and Grice, *Women in the Weather Bureau,* 6, available online.

34. Campbell, *Women at War,* 68.

35. O'Brien and Grice, *Women in the Weather Bureau,* 9, available online.

36. Colman, "Rosie the Riveter," 2, available online.

37. The Museum of the City of New York has at least one of these in its collection.

38. Schultz, "World War II: The Home Front," available online.

39. Cantril and Strunk, *Public Opinion, 1935–1946,* 1178.

40. About 8 percent of the more than 65 million American women were married to servicemen. Gluck, *Rosie the Riveter Revisited,* 13.

41. Ambrose, *Americans at War,* 143.

42. See the oral history of Barbara De Nike in Harris et al., *Homefront,* 194.

43. Brokaw, *Greatest Generation,* 231.

44. Campbell, *Women at War,* 90–92.

45. O'Neill, *Democracy at War,* 250.

46. Costello, *Virtue under Fire,* 87.

47. Campbell, *Women at War,* 208.

48. O'Neill, *The First Measured Century,* 2:2, available online.

49. Keegan, *The Second World War,* 537.

5. CIVILIANS AT WORK, SEPTEMBER 1941–SEPTEMBER 2, 1945

1. Nolan, "Willow Run," 6, available online.
2. Inscription on the plaza, Riverfront, Wilmington, Delaware.
3. Phillips, *The 1940s,* 105.
4. Nolan, "Willow Run," 4, available online.
5. Schwarz, "Henry J. Kaiser," Supp. 8, 308.
6. "Century's Top East Bay Movers and Shapers," 2, available online.
7. Goodwin, *No Ordinary Time,* 318–319.
8. Goodwin, *No Ordinary Time,* 399.
9. *Dictionary of American Biography,* Supp. 4:499.
10. Phillips, *The 1940s,* 140.
11. Goodwin, *No Ordinary Time,* 477.
12. Schultz, "World War II: The Home Front," 4, point 8, available online.
13. Goodwin, *No Ordinary Time,* 333.
14. Nolan, "Willow Run," 4, available online.
15. Cardozier, *Mobilization,* 131.
16. Morgan, "Native Americans in World War Two," *Army History,* 23.
17. "Overall Unemployment Rate in the Civilian Labor Force, 1920–2000," available online.
18. Cardozier, *Mobilization,* 149.
19. In March 2001, some of these Mexicans and their heirs filed a class-action lawsuit against the governments of the United States and Mexico for the 10 percent of their wages deducted and held in savings accounts in accordance with an agreement between the two governments. "Some advocates and academics estimated the amount of money owed now, including interest, could be $500 million or more." Bulluck, "Mexican Laborers in the U.S.," *New York Times,* April 21, 2001, 1. On August 23, 2002, U.S. district judge Charles R. Breyer, on motions of the Mexican defendants and Wells Fargo (a bank in which some of the money was deposited) and of the United States, dismissed the claims against them in the case of *Senorino R. Cruz et al. v. U.S.A. et al.,* saying that the palintiffs were not entitled to any relief from the Mexican defendants or Wells Fargo in a U.S. court of law, and that the plaintiffs were not entitled to relief from the United States "because their claims are time-barred." Judge Breyer conceded, "The Court does not doubt that many braceros never received Savings Fund withholdings to which they were entitled. The Court is sympathetic to the braceros [sic] situation." His decision is available online at URL:www. cand.uscourts.gov. After the ruling Governor Gray Davis of California, on September 29, 2002, signed legislation giving the Mexican workers more time to recover the funds withheld. "Companies and Human Rights Abuses during World War II," available online. URL:www.businesshumanrights.org/Companies. WW2.htm.
20. Cardozier, *Mobilization,* 154.
21. Gruber, *Haven,* 194.
22. Cardozier, *Mobilization,* 264.
23. Goodwin, *No Ordinary Time,* 432.
24. Wattenberg, *The First Measured Century,* 8:2, available online.
25. O'Neill, *Democracy at War,* 249.
26. Cardozier, *Mobilization,* 150.
27. Honey, *Creating Rosie the Riveter,* 22.
28. Phillips, *The 1940s,* 93.
29. Cardozier, *Mobilization,* 151.
30. Cardozier, *Mobilization,* 151. By 1944 women constituted more than 20 percent of union members. Cardozier, *Mobilization,* 163.
31. Cardozier, *Mobilization,* 150.
32. Phillips, *The 1940s,* 169.
33. Quoted in Wattenberg, *The First Measured Century,* 8:2, available online.
34. Wattenberg, *The First Measured Century,* 8:3, available online.
35. Brown, "Rosie the Riveters," *New York Times,* October 22, 2000, 16.
36. Wattenberg, *The First Measured Century,* 8:4, available online.
37. Wattenberg, *The First Measured Century,* 8:3, available online.
38. Campbell, *Women at War,* 77.
39. Wynn, *The Afro-American and the Second World War,* 56.
40. Wattenberg, *The First Measured Century,* 2:3, available online.
41. Quoted in O'Brien and Grice, *Women in the Weather Bureau,* 8, available online.
42. Cardozier, *Mobilization,* 161.
43. Honey, *Creating Rosie the Riveter,* 35.
44. Honey, *Creating Rosie the Riveter,* 45.
45. Honey, *Creating Rosie the Riveter,* 48.
46. Quoted in Honey, *Creating Rosie the Riveter,* 127–128. The condescending tone of this passage is typical of the period.

47. Wynn, *The Afro-American and the Second World War,* 57.

48. Honey, *Creating Rosie the Riveter,* 19.

49. Gluck, *Rosie the Riveter Revisited,* 153.

50. Campbell, *Women at War,* 96.

51. Wattenberg, *The First Measured Century,* 8:4, available online.

52. Wattenberg, *The First Measured Century,* 8:4, available online.

53. O'Brien and Grice, *Women in the Weather Bureau,* 6, available online.

54. Goodwin, *No Ordinary Time,* 555.

55. Goodwin, *No Ordinary Time,* 416.

56. Honey, *Creating Rosie the Riveter,* 19; and Campbell, *Women at War,* 77. Nancy Gabin, however, says that "49 percent of the women employed in war industries in March 1944 had not worked before the war"—a figure that apparently includes young women newly old enough to enter the workforce. Gabin, "The Hand that Rocks the Cradle," 19.

57. Wattenberg, *The First Measured Century,* 8:5, available online.

58. Campbell, *Women at War,* 97.

59. Honey, *Creating Rosie the Riveter,* 22.

60. Campbell, *Women at War,* 136.

61. Campbell, *Women at War,* 108.

62. Campbell, *Women at War,* 109.

63. Campbell, *Women at War,* 125.

64. Campbell, *Women at War,* 82.

65. Goodwin, *No Ordinary Time,* 416. Campbell says that although at any one time during the war 9 out of 10 mothers with children under six were not in the labor force, 20 percent of working women had children to care for. Campbell, *Women at War,* 82.

66. Goodwin, *No Ordinary Time,* 416.

67. Goodwin, *No Ordinary Time,* 418.

68. Campbell, *Women at War,* 97. Campbell adds that of 740,000 women employed in 10 major war centers in March 1944, only 1 percent used public or private day care. Ibid., 97.

69. For an extended description of these musicians, see Tucker, *Swing Shift,* passim.

70. Cardozier, *Mobilization,* 260, 161.

71. Victory ships were designed as an improvement on the slow Liberty ships. Designs for the 15-knot Victory ships were begun in 1942. The first of the 534 Victory ships was launched on February 28, 1944. "American Merchant Marine Heroes and their Gallant Ships in World War II," available online.

72. "U.S. Merchant Marine in World War II," 1, 2, 6, available online.

73. "U.S. Merchant Marine in World War II," 10, available online.

74. Harmon Collection, available online.

75. "U.S. Merchant Marine in World War II," 1–2, and "African Americans in the Merchant Marine," 1, available online.

76. Bowerman, "U.S. Naval Armed Guard and World War II Merchant Marine," 1, available online. Friction sometimes developed between the naval personnel and the unionized merchantmen interested in pay, bonuses, and overtime.

77. "U.S. Merchant Marine in World War II," 3–4, available online.

78. "U.S. Merchant Marine in World War II," 7, available online.

79. "U.S. Merchant Marine in World War II," 9, available online.

80. Horodysky, "Recognition Sought," 1, available online.

6. Military Life: The U.S. Army and the European Theater of Operations, September 3, 1939–May 8, 1945

1. Quoted in the Indiana Historical Society, Ernie Pyle website, 1, available online.

2. Morgan, "Native Americans in World War II," 23.

3. Linderman, *World within War,* 1. See also the PBS program, Wattenberg, *The First Measured Century,* Program Segment 8. For Mexican Americans, see Carey McWilliams, *North From Mexico,* (New York: Praeger, 1990), particularly his chapter on Mexican Americans: McWilliams estimates the number of Mexican Americans who served in the armed forces at 375,000–500,000.

4. U.S. Department of Defense, Table T-23, "Principal Wars in Which the United States Has Participated: U.S. Military Personnel Serving and Casualties," available online.

5. Cardozier, *Mobilization,* 92.

6. Walker, *Our Glorious Century,* 195; and Rich Anderson, "The United States Army in World War II," available online.

7. Fussell, *Wartime,* 16.

8. Goodwin, *No Ordinary Time,* 372, 425.

9. Cardozier, *Mobilization,* 195–196.

10. Astor, *Mighty Eighth,* 322.

11. Fussell, *Wartime,* 276; and Linderman, *World within War,* 1.

12. Gosorski, "World War II's 'Silent Revolution,'" 2, available online.

13. Quoted in Tapert, *Lines of Battle,* 160–161.

14. Cardozier, *Mobilization,* 144.

15. In November 1942 in a Gallup poll, only 6 percent of respondents considered "Germans" the enemy, but 74 percent named the German government as the enemy. As the war went on more Americans—but still a minority—came to think of the German people as weak and too easily led by ruthless leaders. Merritt, *Democracy Imposed,* 38.

16. Linderman, *World within War,* 138.

17. "Rules violations remained exceptional—and generally unacceptable—because powerful amelioristic forces rooted in battlefield terrain and cultural propinquity continued to ensure that assumptions of the enemy's treachery never became entrenched." Linderman, *World within War,* 97–98. German conduct in the war against the USSR differed dramatically, for even "before the start of the Russian campaign Fuehrer [Hitler's] directives demanded that the Army fight without paying any attention to the rules of war." Davidson, *Trial,* 574.

18. Keegan, *Second World War,* 327.

19. Doubler, *Closing with the Enemy,* 9.

20. Keegan, *Second World War,* 343.

21. Calvocoressi et al., *Second World War,* 397.

22. Keegan, *Second World War,* 356.

23. Keegan, *Second World War,* 369.

24. Szasz, "Peppermint and Alsos," 406–407.

25. Linderman, *World within War,* 243.

26. Keegan, *Second World War,* 378.

27. Keegan, *Second World War,* 383.

28. Keegan, *Second World War,* 387.

29. Doubler, *Closing with the Enemy,* 31.

30. Anecdote related by Sgt. Buddy Gianelloni, quoted in Ambrose, *Victors,* 229.

31. Quoted in Keegan, *Second World War,* 406.

32. Keegan, *Second World War,* 410.

33. Ambrose, *Citizen Soldiers,* 106.

34. Keegan, *Second World War,* 533.

35. Kennett, *G.I.,* 72.

36. Secretary of War Henry Stimson called Americans "the most homesick troops in the world." Laffin, *Americans in Battle,* 134.

37. Astor, *Mighty Eighth,* 395.

38. Astor, *Mighty Eighth,* 385.

39. Astor, *Operation Iceberg,* 422–423.

40. Astor, *Operation Iceberg,* 370.

41. Ambrose, "The Last Barrier," 531.

42. Astor, *Mighty Eighth,* 176.

43. Ambrose, "The Last Barrier," 537.

44. Astor, *Mighty Eighth,* 59.

45. Astor, *Operation Iceberg,* 414–415.

46. Fussell, *Wartime,* 145.

47. Fussell, *Wartime,* 102–103.

48. Linderman, *World within War,* 65.

49. Quoted in Fussell, *Wartime,* 275.

50. Congressional Medal of Honor Citations, available online.

51. Keegan, *Second World War,* 430.

52. Linderman, *World within War,* 39.

53. Bellafaire, *Army Nurse Corps,* 3, available online.

54. Cowdrey, *Fighting for Life,* 101.

55. On April 16, 1943, President Roosevelt signed a bill allowing women to practice as physicians in the military because of the shortage of male doctors. Hill, "Women Physicians 1945–1960," 1, available online.

56. Cowdrey, *Fighting for Life,* 125, 123.

57. Cowdrey, *Fighting for Life,* 96–97.

58. Bellafaire, *Army Nurse Corps,* 3, available online.

59. Bellafaire, *Army Nurse Corps,* 8, available online.

60. Goossen, *Women against the Good War,* 74.

61. Bellafaire, *Army Nurse Corps,* 8–9, available online.

62. Bellafaire, *Army Nurse Corps,* 11, available online.

63. Nonetheless Allied hospital ships were bombed on at least three occasions: en route to Salerno in September 1943, at Anzio in January 1944, and off Leyte Island in April 1945. Bellafaire, *Army Nurse Corps,* 14, 16.

64. Bellafaire, *Army Nurse Corps,* 15, available online.

65. Bellafaire, *Army Nurse Corps,* 20, available online.

66. Bellafaire, *Army Nurse Corps,* 23, available online.

67. Ibid.

68. Bellafaire, *Army Nurse Corps,* 31, available online.

69. Cowdrey, *Fighting for Life,* 105.

70. Persico, *Piercing the Reich,* 334–335.

71. Holm, *Women in the Military,* 56.

72. Campbell, *Women at War,* 20.

73. Campbell, *Women at War,* 21.

74. Quoted in Campbell, *Women at War,* 22.

75. Bellafaire, *Women's Army Corps,* n.p., available online.

76. Bellafaire, *Women's Army Corps,* n.p.; and Japanese American National Museum, "Frequently Asked Questions"; both available online.

77. Cardozier, *Mobilization,* 171.

78. Bellafaire, *Women's Army Corps,* n.p., available online.

79. Ibid.

80. Ibid.

81. Campbell, *Women at War,* 25.

82. Campbell, *Women at War,* 23.

83. Campbell, *Women at War,* 24–25.

84. Campbell, *Women at War,* 37.

85. Campbell, *Women at War,* 44.

86. Bellafaire, *Women's Army Corps,* n.p., available online.

87. Ibid.

88. Ibid.

89. Holm, *Women in the Military,* 64; and Jacqueline Cochrane's final report for the WASP, available online.

90. Granger, *On Final Approach,* 160.

91. Holm, *Women in the Military,* 314.

92. David Reynolds, *Rich Relations,* 242.

93. David Reynolds, *Rich Relations,* 406.

94. David Reynolds, *Rich Relations,* 260.

95. David Reynolds, *Rich Relations,* 414.

96. Quoted in Dyer, *War,* 101.

97. Fussell, *Wartime,* 132.

98. Doubler, *Closing with the Enemy,* 243.

99. Bellafaire, *Army Nurse Corps,* 7, available online. David M. Gosorski, writing in the *Veterans of Foreign Wars Magazine* for October 1997 says that battle fatigue afflicted 1,393,000 Americans. He cites Richard Gabriel's statement in his book *No More Heroes: Madness and Psychiatry in War* that 37.5 percent of World War II ground troops were discharged for psychiatric reasons. Gosorski, "World War II's 'Silent Army' Produced 'Silent Revolution,'" n.p., available online.

100. Statistics furnished by the American Ex-Prisoners of War, available online.

101. Ambrose, *Citizen Soldiers,* 362.

102. Charles Taylor interview by the authors.

103. Astor, *Mighty Eighth,* 417.

104. Astor, *Mighty Eighth,* 241.

105. Astor, *Mighty Eighth,* 393–394.

106. Astor, *Mighty Eighth,* 416.

7. MILITARY LIFE: THE NAVY, THE MARINE CORPS, THE COAST GUARD, AND THE WAR IN THE PACIFIC, SEPTEMBER 3, 1939–SEPTEMBER 9, 1945

1. Aspects of the navy and the Pacific experience are also treated in Chapter 6.

2. On May 1, 1944, the navy, Marine Corps, and Coast Guard together numbered 3,400,646 officers and enlisted men and women. Walsh, "The Decline and Renaissance of the Navy, 1922–1944," n.p., available online.

3. Naval Historical Center, "Frequently Asked Questions," personnel strength, available online.

4. U.S. Marine Corps Headquarters Information, available online.

5. Per U.S. Coast Guard Historian's office (G-IPA-4), Washington, DC 20593.

6. Morison, "Thoughts on Military Strategy," n.p., available online. As late as the fall of 1944, only 30 percent of the U.S. arsenal was allocated to the fight against Japan. Dunne, "Hardest War," 50.

7. Holt, "The Deceivers," 385–386.

8. Alexander, "The Turning Points of Tarawa," 303.

9. Sgt. Henry Manion, quoted in Astor, *Operation Iceberg,* 85.

10. Gailey, *War in the Pacific,* 296. Gailey also says (on p. 332) that on Tinian, Japanese soldiers used hand grenades to blow up civilians and pushed some over cliffs and that defeated Japanese on Guam murdered hundreds of civilians.

11. Dower, *Embracing Defeat,* 33–34.

12. Gudmundsson, "Okinawa," 638.

13. Whyte, "Patrolling Guadalcanal," 193.

14. Quoted in Astor, *Operation Iceberg,* 98.

15. Astor, *Operation Iceberg,* 148.

16. Cook, "The Myth of the Saipan Suicides," 597.

17. Quoted in Linderman, *World within War,* 177. Linderman also cites (on p. 176) Keene discovered that every month the Japanese executed 5 to 20 Koreans to furnish a supply of liver as medicine for high-ranking Japanese officers—a practice that he called "sordid brutality—worse, utter degeneracy."

18. Manchester, "The Bloodiest Battle," 42.

19. "The Pearl Harbor Attack," U.S. Naval History Center, available online. The first sign of the attack came when at 4:40 A.M. on December 7, the USS *Ward* sighted and sank a small submarine, presumably Japanese. The commander of U.S. Destroyer Division 80 reported on December 12: "U.S.S. *Ward* on Pearl Entrance Patrol at 1640 on the morning of December 7 sighted a small submarine on the surface but trimmed down, following the U.S.S. *Antares* towards Pearl Entrance. *Ward* promptly attacked with 4" 50 gunfire 0645. At a range of fifty yards a shell from Gun #3 was seen to strike the base of the conning

tower. The submarine submerged or sank almost directly over the blast from a depth charge which had been dropped as the submarine passed close aboard. The depth of water was about 1200 feet. [I]t is considered that the submarine was destroyed." On December 13 the commander of the *Ward* filed a more detailed report. Both reports are available online at URL:http://www.history.navy.mil/docs/wwii/pearl/ph9.htm.

20. U.S. Department of the Navy, Naval History Center, available online.

21. Stanton, *In Harm's Way,* 77–78. The top-secret code-breaking program ULTRA was based at Pearl Harbor and Washington, D.C., where intelligence workers transcribed and transmitted to a decrypting machine Japanese radio signals sent in "PURPLE" code. Use of information obtained in this way at the Battle of Midway tipped off the Japanese that their code had been broken, and they changed it. ULTRA broke the new code and reprogrammed the decrypting machine; thereafter information derived from the machine was aboslutely protected, even to refraining from sinking Japanese ships whose whereabouts were known.

22. Keegan, *The Second World War,* 293.

23. Led by U.S. brigadier general Frank Merrill.

24. Keegan, *The Second World War,* 546–547.

25. Keegan, *The Second World War,* 560.

26. U.S. Marine Corps History, available online.

27. Keegan, *The Second World War,* 572–573. Gudmundsson notes that 10,000 Koreans enslaved by the Japanese also died in the battle, "Okinawa," 638.

28. Gailey, *War in the Pacific,* 448.

29. Keegan, *The Second World War,* 576–577.

30. Keegan, *The Second World War,* 578.

31. Keegan, *The Second World War,* 575.

32. Quoted in Ferrell, *Off the Record,* 55–56.

33. Quoted in Tibbetts, "The Event," available online.

34. Keegan, *The Second World War,* 584; and the Avalon Project, available online.

35. Allen, "The Voice of the Crane," 677–687.

36. Astor, *Operation Iceberg,* 440.

37. Gudmundsson, "Okinawa," 638. Efforts to estimate the total numbers killed during the 1945 battle for Okinawa are ongoing, though some historians claim exact numbers can never be known, as many Okinawans killed themselves by jumping off cliffs or in mass suicides in caves, and skeletons and bone fragments are still being discovered on the island. To date

the most likely figures range from 219,000 to 239,000: 12,000 American troops, 107,000 Japanese and Okinawan troops, and 100,000–120,000 Okinawan civilians. The Itoman memorial in southern Okinawa shows a total of 237,318. See http://danshistory.com/ww2/atombomb.shtml.www.spartacus.schoolnet.co.uk/2WWokinawa. htm, and www.globalsecurity.org/military/facility/okinawa-battle. htm. Http://danshistory.com/ww2/atombomb.shtml, using data from the U.S. Strategic Bombing Survey, Japanese official counts, and U.S. government/military documents, estimates 70,000–80,000 Japanese dead and missing at Hiroshima and 35,000–40,000 at Nagasaki, for a maximum total of 120,000. The Avalon Project (http://www.yale.edu/lawweb/avalon/abomb/mp10.htm), which bases its estimates on "the Manhattan Engineer District's best available figures," shows similar numbers: 66,000 killed instantly at Hiroshima and 39,000 at Nagasaki. If one assumes that as many as half those injured but not immediately killed—69,000 at Hiroshima and 25,000 at Nagasaki, according to the Avalon Project—died later from the effects of the blasts, that speculatively adds 47,000, for an estimate of 167,000 killed by the two atomic bombs.

The U.S. Strategic Bombing Survey (http://www.anesi.com/ussbs01.htm#taaatjhi) says: "Total civilian casualties in Japan, as a result of 9 months of air attack, including those from the atomic bombs, were approximately 806,000. Of these, approximately 330,000 were fatalities. These [civilian] casualties probably exceeded Japan's combat casualties which the Japanese estimate as having totaled approximately 780,000 during the entire war."

38. Cowdrey, *Fighting for Life,* 64.

39. Kerr, *Surrender and Survival,* 43.

40. Hanson, "The Right Man," 647; and Kerr, *Surrender and Survival,* 266.

41. Kerr, *Surrender and Survival,* 89.

42. Waterford, *Prisoners of the Japanese,* 178.

43. Stenger, "American Prisoners of WWI, WWII, etc.," 2. The introductory video shown by the National Park Service at Andersonville National Historic Site in Georgia shows slightly different figures: 95,532 American POWs held in German camps, of whom 1,124 died there, for a 1 percent death rate; 43,648 American POWs held in Japanese camps, of whom 12, 935 died there, for a 37 percent death rate. Letter from Don Pettijohn, park ranger

44. Waterford, *Prisoners of the Japanese*, 180–181.

45. Kaminski, *Prisoner in Paradise*, 2.

46. McKinley, interview by Dorothy Schneider.

47. Kaminski, *Prisoners in Paradise*, 182–185.

48. Quoted in Astor, *Operation Iceberg*, 120, 211, 253, and 451.

49. Stafford, *Camp X*, 78.

50. Lord, *Coastwatchers*, 62–64.

51. Mohr, "Navajo Code Talkers," 1, available online.

52. Mohr, "Navajo Code Talkers," 1, available online.

53. Holm, *Women in the Military*, 32.

54. Campbell, *Women at War*, 14.

55. Ebbert and Hall, *Crossed Currents*, 99–100.

56. Campbell, *Women at War*, 32.

57. Ebbert and Hall, *Crossed Currents*, 97.

58. Ebbert and Hall, *Crossed Currents*, 98–99.

8. CIVIL LIBERTIES AND "MILITARY NECESSITY," JUNE 8, 1938–DECEMBER 23, 2000

1. Abraham Lincoln's record on civil liberties has been criticized because of his declaration of martial law during the Civil War. Rehnquist, "Civil Liberties in Wartime," available online.

2. Cardozier, *Mobilization*, 47.

3. Hoover, "Martial Law," n.p.

4. For the opinion of the court, see "U.S. Supreme Court, Duncan v. Kahanamoku," available online.

5. Some American citizens related to Italian and German enemy aliens were involved.

6. Allen, *Fight for Peace*, 597.

7. Frazer and O'Sullivan, *We Have Just Begun*, xiv.

8. Except for Seventh-Day Adventists, no one knows the religious affiliations of all the COs. For instance, 60 CPS members described themselves as Jewish, but other Jews identified themselves as without religious affiliation. Eller, *Conscientious Objectors*, 118, no. 60. Richard Anderson gives figures for the CPS showing 10,838 as identified with denominations, 449 as nonaffiliated, and 709 with unidentified denominations. Anderson, *Peace Was in Their Hearts*, 286.

9. Sibley and Jacob, *Conscription of Conscience*, 84; Eller, *Conscientious Objectors*, 28; and Zinn, *People's History*, 409.

10. Frazer and O'Sullivan, *We Have Just Begun*, xiii.

11. For the text of this clause, see Appendix A, document 5.

12. Flynn, "Lewis Hershey and the Conscientious Objector" in *Lewis B. Hershey: Mr. Selective Service*, available online.

13. Frazer and O'Sullivan, *We Have Just Begun*, xxi.

14. Wynn, *The Afro-American in the Second World War*, 103.

15. These hopes were ended in 1943 by the passage of a rider to the Military Establishment Appropriations Act authored by Joseph Starnes of Alabama, banning COs from engaging in foreign relief and prohibiting colleges from hosting relief training units. Goossen, *Women against the Good War*, 100.

16. Goossen, *Women against the Good War*, 105.

17. Keim, *CPS Story*, 33, 40, 106–110.

18. Frazer and O'Sullivan, *We Have Just Begun*, xix.

19. Keim, *CPS Story*, 100.

20. Daniels, *Concentration Camps*, 104.

21. Inada, *Only What We Could Carry*, 113.

22. Goodwin, *No Ordinary Time*, 428.

23. Brokaw, *Greatest Generation*, 221.

24. Daniels, *Concentration Camps*, 114.

25. Daniels, *Concentration Camps*, 116.

26. Nevertheless in *Korematsu v. United States* Justice Murphy in his dissent commented that the internment "bore a melancholy resemblance" to the Nazi treatment of the Jews. Morison et al., *A Concise History*, 637.

27. Inada, *Only What We Could Carry*, 333.

28. Phillips, *The 1940s*, 114.

29. Inada, *Only What We Could Carry*, 204.

30. Daniels, *Concentration Camps*, 34.

31. Ponting, *Armageddon*, 216.

32. Hacker, "Aliens in Montana," *American History* (June 2001): 33–36.

33. Harris, *Homefront*, 92.

34. Wynn, *The Afro-American and the Second World War*, 49.

35. From April 1940 to April 1944 the total number of Afro-Americans in work rose by a million. Wynn, *The Afro-American and the Second World War*, 55.

36. Morison et al., *A Concise History*, 636.

37. McGuire, *Taps for a Jim Crow Army*, xxx. An estimated 909,000 African-American men and women served in the army during World War II; in 1944 they constituted a peak of 700,000, or 8.7 percent of total army strength. African-American women in the WAAC/WAC numbered 150,000 and made up

about 4 percent of that force. Moore, *To Serve My Country,* 26.

38. Polenberg, *War and Society,* 123.

39. Kennett, *G.I.,* 83 and Williams, "The Invisible Cryptologists," chap. 1.

40. Morison et al., *A Concise History,* 636.

41. Goodwin, *No Ordinary Time,* 330.

42. Morison et al., *A Concise History,* 636. The Tuskegee Airmen were commanded by Colonel Benjamin O. Davis, Jr.

43. Wynn, *The Afro-American and the Second World War,* 37.

44. Goodwin, *No Ordinary Time,* 567.

45. McGuire, *Taps for a Jim Crow Army,* 251.

46. McGuire, *Taps for a Jim Crow Army,* 251.

47. Rehnquist, "Civil Liberties," available online.

48. Shipler, review of Diane McWhorter's *Carry Me Home, New York Times Magazine,* March 18, 2001, 9.

9: VICTORY: THE ENEMY, JANUARY 13, 1942–APRIL 28, 1952

1. "The treasury secretary's [Henry Morgenthau's] proposal proved popular with the Soviets and the French, both of whom had suffered appalling casualties and had vowed to prevent any revival of German power. It initially appealed to U.S. military authorities as well, because it seemed relatively simple to implement. Inspired in part by the Morgenthau Plan, Franklin D. Roosevelt approved in September 1944 a Joint Chiefs of Staff directive (JSC 1067), the final version of which came in April 1945. JCS 1067 ordered the dismantling of iron, steel, and chemical industries; the decentralization of large business cartels; the abolition of the German military; and a vigorous program of denazification designed to bar all Nazis and Nazi sympathizers from employment in government and business. At Yalta in February 1945 Roosevelt, Churchill, and Stalin endorsed the idea of a punitive peace by dividing Germany into four occupation zones: French, British, and American zones in western Germany and a Soviet zone in the east." *The Documentary History of the Truman Presidency,* III, available online. URL: http://www.lexisnexis.com/academic/2upa/Aph/truman_docs/guide_intros/tu3.htm. Downloaded December 17, 2002.

2. Clay, interview, 4.

3. Clay, interview, 5.

4. Merritt, *Democracy Imposed,* 68.

5. Clay, interview, 14–15.

6. Byrnes, Stuttgart speech, available online.

7. Churchill, "Iron Curtain Speech," *Modern History Sourcebook,* available online.

8. "The Marshall Plan," available online. This was in addition to the $6 billion of aid that the United States had poured into European relief projects in the two years after the German surrender. Phillips, *The 1940s,* 310.

9. Davidson, *Death and Life,* 212, 220.

10. Dower, *Embracing Defeat,* 47.

11. Dower, *Embracing Defeat,* 45.

12. Dower, *Embracing Defeat,* 103.

13. Van Staaveren, *American in Japan,* 84; and Dower, *Embracing Defeat,* 51–52.

14. Dower, *Embracing Defeat,* 532.

15. State Shintoism was abolished.

16. Schonberger, *Aftermath of War,* 9.

17. Quoted in Davidson, *Trial,* 12.

18. Robert Barr Smith, "Justice under the Sun: Japanese War Crime Trials," 3, available online.

10. VICTORY: AT HOME, JUNE 1944–NOVEMBER 1952

1. Young, *World Almanac of World War II,* 614. On the Public Broadcasting System program, *The First Measured Century,* Segment 8, available online. Ben Wattenberg said that 80,000,000 people were killed worldwide in World War II. "All told, American forces suffered 293,131 killed in action, 115,185 non-combat deaths and 670,846 wounded." Gosorski, "World War II's 'Silent Army,'" 2, available online.

2. Quoted in Wynn, *Afro-American and the Second World War,* 60.

3. Gosorski, "World War II's 'Silent Army,'" 3, available online.

4. Public Broadcasting System program, *The First Measured Century,* Segment 8, available online.

5. Condon-Rall, *Historical Statistics,* 1; Tables B216–220.

6. Waterford, *Prisoners of the Japanese,* 94.

7. Gosorski, "World War II's 'Silent Army,'" 5, available online.

8. Gosorski, "World War II's 'Silent Army,'" 4, available online.

9. Gosorski, "World War II's 'Silent Army,'" 4, available online.

10. "G.I. Bill," *West's Encyclopedia of American Law*, 1, available online; and Oliver, "Creator of the G.I. Bill," *Los Angeles Times*, April 24, 1997, available online.

11. Gosorski, "World War II's 'Silent Army,'" 6, available online.

12. "G.I. Bill Facts," available online; and Jenny J. Lee, "G.I. Bill of Rights," available online.

13. Haydock, "G.I. Bill," *American History*, available online.

14. "G.I. Bill Facts," available online.

15. "G.I. Bill," *West's Encyclopedia of American Law*, 2, available online.

16. Shukert and Scibetta, *War Brides*, 227.

17. Publisher's advertisement for Monette Goetinck's *Bottled Dreams*, available online.

18. Shukert and Scibetta, *War Brides*, 153. This loss of citizenship resulted from a law from the Hitler regime, still on the books. These women became stateless people.

19. For instance, the Soldier Brides Act of 1947 provided that "The alien spouse of an American citizen by marriage occurring before 30 days after the enactment of this Act shall not be considered as inadmissible because of race, if otherwise admissible under this Act." Quoted in Shukert and Scibetta, *War Brides*, 209.

20. Shukert and Scibetta, *War Brides*, 216.

21. Shukert and Scibetta, *War Brides*, 1–2.

22. Shukert and Scibetta, *War Brides*, 39.

23. More than 100,000 GIs married British women during and just after World War II; 16,000 married Australian and New Zealand women. Shukert and Scibetta, *War Brides*, 2, 7.

24. Unsigned review of a book in Japanese, available online.

25. Simpson, "Out of an obscure place," in *Differences: A Journal of Feminist Cultural Studies* 10.3 (1998), 51, available online.

26. For instance, Elfrieda Berthiaume Shukert and Barbara Smith Scibetta think that "by far the majority of these couples had no regrets." *War Brides*, 3. These authors obtained information from more than 2,000 war brides.

27. Jung, "War Brides," *Mercury News*, available online.

28. McCullough, *Truman*, 469.

29. Phillips, *The 1940s*, 275.

30. Cardozier, *Mobilization*, 229.

31. Honey, *Creating Rosie the Riveter*, 180.

32. Goodwin, *No Ordinary Time*, 557.

33. Gluck, *Rosie the Riveter Revisited*, 16.

34. Honey, *Creating Rosie the Riveter*, 123.

35. Schneider and Schneider, *Women in the Workplace*, 297. See also Gluck, *Rosie the Riveter Revisited*, 16–17.

36. Quoted in Ambrose, *Americans at War*, 145.

37. Senator Joseph McCarthy was later censured by his Senate colleagues.

38. McCullough, *Truman*, 552.

11. THE UNITED NATIONS, JANUARY 6, 1941–JULY 27, 1953

1. President Franklin D. Roosevelt to reporters when he announced the Dumbarton Oaks conference, quoted in Meisler, *United Nations*, 3.

2. Moscow Conference Declaration, October 1943, available online.

3. For specifics of these proposals, see Dumbarton Oaks proposals, available online.

4. Quoted in Meisler, *United Nations*, 19.

5. Official minutes, quoted in Meisler, *United Nations*, 19.

6. Quoted in Meisler, *United Nations*, 19.

APPENDIX B: BIOGRAPHIES OF MAJOR PERSONALITIES

1. Ambrose, *Americans at War*, 116.

2. Brinkley, *Washington Goes to War*, 42–45; and Deac, "Amy Elizabeth Thorpe," available online.

3. Ambrose, *Americans at War*, 135, 136.

4. Quoted by Indiana Historical Society, Ernie Pyle website, 3.

5. Persico, *Piercing the Reich*, passim.

APPENDIX E: REFUGEES

1. Quoted in Goodwin, *No Ordinary Time*, 175.

2. Wyman, *Abandonment*, 6, text and note.

3. Goodwin, *No Ordinary Time*, 101.

4. Goodwin, *No Ordinary Time*, 102; and Wyman, *Abandonment*, 15.

5. Gruber, *Haven*, 5.

6. *Dictionary of American Biography*, Supp. 6: 389–390.

7. Fry's coworker Mary Jayne Gold in "Crossroads Marseilles 1940" (available online) synopsis esti-

mates the number at 2,000, and coworker Miriam Davenport Ebel in "Memoir" (available online) says 4,000.

8. "Establishment of the War Refugee Board." Unsigned article, available online.

9. Wyman, *Abandonment of the Jews,* 285, and Jewish Virtual Library, "The War Refugee Board," available online.

10. Wyman, *Abandonment of the Jews,* 106, 136.

11. Wyman, *Abandonment of the Jews,* 8.

12. Ibid.

13. Ibid.

14. Wyman, *Abandonment of the Jews,* 79.

15. Wyman, *Abandonment of the Jews,* 219–220.

16. Wyman, *Abandonment of the Jews,* 277.

17. Wyman, *Abandonment of the Jews,* 8–9.

BIBLIOGRAPHY

"African Americans in the Merchant Marine." Available online. URL: http://www.usmm.org/African-americans.html. Downloaded October 13, 2000.

Akune, Harry. Citation for induction into the Military Intelligence Hall of Fame. Available online. URL: http://www.thedropzone.org/pacific/akune.html. Downloaded September 14, 2001.

Alexander, Joseph H. "The Turning Points of Tarawa." In *No End Save Victory: Perspectives on World War II,* edited by Robert Cowley, 292–305. New York: G. P. Putnam's Sons, 2001.

Aline, Countess of Romanones. *The Spy Wore Red: My Adventures as an Undercover Agent in World War II.* New York: Random House, 1987.

Allen, Devere. *The Fight for Peace.* New York: Macmillan, 1930.

Allen, Thomas B. "The Voice of the Crane." In *No End Save Victory: Perspectives on World War II,* edited by Robert Cowley, 677–688. New York: G. P. Putnam's Sons, 2001.

Ambler, Barbara. "Pre-Kendal Memory." Undated unpublished manuscript, Kendal Library, Kennett Square, Pa.

Ambrose, Stephen. *Americans at War.* Jackson: University of Mississippi Press, 1997.

———. *Citizen Soldiers: The U.S. Army from the Normandy Beaches to the Bulge to the Surrender of Germany.* New York: Simon & Schuster, 1997.

———. "The Last Barrier." In *No End Save Victory: Perspectives on World War II,* edited by Robert Cowley, 527–551. New York: G. P. Putnam's Sons, 2001.

———. *The Victors: Eisenhower and His Boys: The Men of World War II.* New York: Simon & Schuster, 1998.

American Citizens Abroad. "A Brief History of U.S. Law on the Taxation." Available online. URL: http://www.aca.ch/hisustax.htm. Downloaded May 10, 2001.

American Civil Liberties Union, Northern California Branch. "Annual Report, June 1, 1944–June 1, 1945." San Francisco, Calif.: American Civil Liberties Union, 1945.

American Ex-Prisoners of War. Available online. URL: www.axpow.org/nso_msg.htm. Downloaded September 3, 2001.

American Heritage. *A Sense of History: The Best Writing from the Pages of American Heritage.* New York: American Heritage, 1985.

"American Merchant Marine Heroes and their Gallant Ships in World War II." Available online. URL: http://www.usmm.org/men_ships.html#anchor514404. Downloaded October 25, 2001.

"American POWs Held in World War II." Available online. URL: http://www.lewiston.k12.id.us/ldahl/Title%20Pages%20Links/pows_of_the_japanese.htm. Downloaded December 17, 2002.

Amonette, Ruth Leach. *Among Equals: The Rise of IBM's First Woman Corporate Vice President.* Berkeley, Calif.: Creative Arts Book Company, 1999.

Anderson, Rich. "The United States Army in World War II." Available online. URL: http://www.militaryhistoryonline.com/wwii/usarmy/introduction.asp. Downloaded August 13, 2001.

Anderson, Richard C. *Peace Was in Their Hearts: Conscientious Objectors in World War II.* Watsonville, Calif.: Correlan, 1994.

Angle, Paul M. *The American Reader.* New York: Rand McNally, 1958.

———. *By These Words: Great Documents of American Liberty.* New York: Rand McNally, 1954.

Anthony, Carl Sferrazza. *First Ladies: The Saga of the Presidents' Wives and Their Power, 1789–1961.* New York: William Morrow, 1990.

Antrim, Richard Nott. Congressional Medal of Honor Citation. Available online. URL: http://www.army.mil/cmh-pg/mohiial.htm. Downloaded August 4, 2001.

Astor, Gerald. *The Mighty Eighth: The Air War in Europe as Told by the Men Who Fought It.* New York: D. I. Fine, 1997.

———. *Operation Iceberg: The Invasion and Conquest of Okinawa in World War II.* New York: D. I. Fine, 1995.

Avalon Project at Yale Law School: Documents in Law, History, and Diplomacy. Available online. URL: http://www.yale.edu/lawweb/avalon/avalon.htm. Downloaded on various dates.

Bailey, R. H. *The Home Front: USA.* Alexandria, Va.: Time-Life Books, 1977.

Baker, Russell. *Growing Up.* New York: Congdon & Weed, 1982.

Balkoski, Joseph. *Beyond the Beachhead: The 29th Infantry Division in Normandy.* Harrisburg, Pa.: Stackpole, 1989.

Baluch, Vivian M., and Patricia Zacharias. "The 1943 Detroit Race Riots." In "Rearview Mirror" of the *Detroit News.* Available online. URL: http://www.detnews.com/history/riot. Downloaded July 27, 2001.

Bartlett, Charlotte. "Pre-Kendal Memory." Undated unpublished manuscript. Kendal Library, Kennett Square, Pa.

Baruch, Bernard M. *Baruch. The Public Years.* New York: Pocket Books, 1982.

Baruma, Ian. Letter in reply to Gore Vidal. *The New York Review of Books* (May 17, 2001), 67–68.

Bassett, John. *War Journal of an Innocent Soldier.* Hamden, Conn.: Shoe String Press, 1989.

"Battle of Okinawa." Available online. URL: http://www.globalsecurity.org/military/facility/okinawa-battle.htm. Downloaded December 30, 2002.

Beard, Charles A. *President Roosevelt and the Coming of War, 1941: A Study in Appearances and Realities.* New Haven, Conn.: Yale University Press, 1948.

Becker, Carl M., and Robert G. Thobaben. *Common Warfare: Parallel Memoirs by Two World War GIs in the Pacific.* Jefferson, N.C.: McFarland, 1992.

Belden, Jack. *Still Time to Die.* New York: Harper, 1943.

Bellafaire, Judith. *The Army Nurse Corps.* Washington, D.C.: U.S. Army Center for Military History. Available online. URL: http://www.army.mil/cmh-pg/books/wwii/72-14/72-14.htm. Downloaded August 21, 2001.

———. *The Women's Army Corps. A Commemoration of World War II Service.* Washington, D.C.: U.S. Army Center for Military History. Available online. URL: http://www.army.mil/cmh-pg/brochures/wac/wac.htm. Downloaded August 22, 2001.

Bellow, Saul. *It All Adds Up. From the Dim Past to the Uncertain Future.* New York: Viking, 1994.

Belluck, Pam. "Mexican Laborers in U.S. During War Sue for Back Pay," *New York Times,* April 29, 2001.

Bendersky, Joseph W. *The "Jewish Threat": Anti-Semitic Politics of the U.S. Army.* New York: Basic Books, 2000.

Bergerud, Eric M. *Fire in the Sky: The Air War in the South Pacific.* Boulder, Colo.: Westview, 2000.

Bernstein, Bernice Lotwin. Interview, 1965. Columbia University Oral History Research Office Collection.

Bernstein, Burton. *Family Matters: Sam, Jennie, and the Kids.* New York: Summit, 1982.

Bisson, T. A. "Japan as a Political Organism." *Pacific Affairs,* December 1944, 417–420.

Bix, Herbert. *Hirohito and the Making of Modern Japan.* New York: HarperCollins, 2000.

Blair, Joan, and Clay Blair. *Return from the River Kwai.* New York: Simon & Schuster, 1979.

Block, Herbert. *Herblock: A Cartoonist's Life.* New York: Macmillan, 1993.

Boesch, Paul. *Road to Huertgen—Forest in Hell.* Houston, Tex.: Gulf, 1962.

Boroughs, Ralph Zeigler. *A Private's View of World War II.* Greenwood, S.C.: Clew, 1987.

Borreca, Richard. "GI Bill Propelled 1954's Democratic Revolution," *Honolulu Star-Bulletin,* October 18, 1999. Available online. URL: http://www.starbulletin.com/1999/10/18/special/story1.html. Downloaded November 13, 2001.

Bourke-White, Margaret. *Purple Heart Valley.* New York: Simon & Schuster, 1944.

Bowerman, Tom. "U.S. Naval Armed Guard and World War II Merchant Marine." Available online. URL: http://www.armed-guard.com. Downloaded June 4, 2001.

Bowles, Chester. *Promises to Keep: My Years in Public Life, 1949–1969.* New York: Harper and Row, 1971.

Bowman, Constance. *Slacks and Calluses.* New York: Longmans, Green, 1944.

Boyle, Peter G. "The Roots of Isolationism: A Case Study." *Journal of American Studies* 6 (April 1972): 42.

Bracchini, Miguel A. "The History and the Ethics Behind the Manhattan Project." *Undergraduate Engineering Review* (fall 1997). Available online. URL: http://www.me.utexas.edu/~uer/manhattan/project.html. Downloaded October 8, 2001.

Brackman, Arnold C. *The Other Nuremberg: The Untold Story of the Tokyo War Crimes Tribunals.* New York: Morrow, 1987.

Bradlee, Ben. *A Good Life: Newspapering and Other Adventures.* New York: Simon & Schuster, 1995.

Brinkley, David. *David Brinkley.* New York: Knopf, 1995.

————. *Washington Goes to War.* New York: Knopf, 1988.

Broadfoot, Barry, ed. *Six War Years, 1939–1945: Memories of Canadians at Home and Abroad.* Toronto: Doubleday, 1974.

Brokaw, Tom. *The Greatest Generation.* New York: Random House, 1998.

Brown, Harry. *A Walk in the Sun.* New York: Knopf, 1944.

Brown, Patricia Leigh. "'Rosie the Riveters' Honored in California Memorial." *New York Times,* October 22, 2000, 16.

Brubaker, Ed. "Pre-Kendal Memories." Undated unpublished manuscript, Kendal Library, Kennett Square, Pa.

Buchwald, Art. *Leaving Home: A Memoir.* New York: G. P. Putnam's Sons, 1993.

Buhmann, Shirley E. Kodalen. "Personal View." In *Women in the Weather Bureau During World War II,* edited by Kaye O'Brien and Gary K. Grice, 14–16. Available online. URL: http://www.lib.noaa.gov/edocs/women.html. Downloaded June 13, 2001.

Burdick, Charles B. *An American Island in Hitler's Reich: The Bad Nauheim Internment.* Menlo Park, Calif.: Markgraf, 1987.

Burns, James MacGregor. *Roosevelt: Soldier of Freedom.* New York: Harcourt Brace Jovanovich, 1970.

Butt, Thomas K. "Wartime Housing at Atchison Village." Available online. URL: http://www.rosietheriveter.org/parkav.htm. Downloaded June 19, 2001.

Buxco, Ralph A., and Douglas D. Adler. "German and Italian Prisoners of War in Utah and Idaho." *Utah Historical Quarterly* 39 (1971): 64.

Byers, Jean. "A Study of the Negro in Military Service." Washington, D.C.: U.S. War Department, June 1947.

Byrnes, James F. Stuttgart speech, September 6, 1946. Available online. URL: http://www.usembassy.de/usa/etexts/ga4-460906.htm. Downloaded January 1, 2002.

Caldwell, Oliver J. *A Secret War: Americans in China, 1944–1945.* Carbondale: Southern Illinois University Press, 1972.

Calvocoressi, Peter, Guy Wint, and John Pritchard. *The Penguin History of the Second World War.* New York: Viking, 1989.

Campbell, D'Ann. *Women at War with America: Private Lives in a Patriotic Era.* Cambridge, Mass.: Harvard University Press, 1984.

Canedy, Susan. *American Nazis: A Democratic Dilemma: A History of the German-American Bund.* New York: Markgraf, 1990.

Cantril, Hadley (ed.) and Mildred Strunk, *Public Opinion, 1935–1945.* Princeton, N.J.: Princeton University Press, 1951.

Caraccilo, Dominic J. "Americans." *American History* 36, no. 2 (June 2001): 20.

Cardozier, V. R. *The Mobilization of the United States in World War II. How the Government, Military and Industry Prepared for War.* Jefferson, N.C.: McFarland, 1995.

Carney, Frank. Quoted in an Associated Press dispatch, August 2, 1944.

Carroll, Andrew. *War Letters.* New York: Scribner's, 2001.

Carroll, Gordon. *History in the Writing.* New York: Duell, Sloan & Pearce, 1945.

Carroll, Peter. Letter to the editor. *New York Times Book Review,* December 17, 2000, 3.

Carruth, Gorton. *The Encyclopedia of American Facts and Dates,* 8th ed. New York: HarperCollins, 1987.

Carter, Ross. *Those Devils in Baggy Pants.* New York: Appleton-Century-Crofts, 1951.

Catton, Bruce. *The War Lords of Washington.* New York: Harcourt, Brace, 1948.

Cawthon, Charles R. "St. Lo." In *A Sense of History: The Best Writing from the Pages of American Heritage,* 705–727. New York: American Heritage, 1985.

"Century's Top East Bay Movers and Shapers," staff report for the *Contra Costa Times,* December 12, 1999. Available online. URL: http://www.contracostatimes. com/biztech/movers/stories/jan00737.htm. Downloaded May 29, 2001.

Chadakoff, Rochelle, ed. *Eleanor Roosevelt's My Day: Her Acclaimed Columns 1936–1945.* New York: Pharos, 1989.

Chafe, William H. *The Paradox of Change: American Women in the 20th Century.* New York: Oxford University Press, 1991.

Challener, Richard D. "Veterans of Future Wars." Available online. URL: mondrian.princeton.edu/CampusWWW/Companion/veterans_future_wars. html. Downloaded March 1, 2002.

Chamberlain, John. *A Life with the Printed Word.* Chicago: Regnery Gateway, 1982.

Chambers, Dorothy Hurd. "Personal View." In *Women in the Weather Bureau during World War II,* edited by Kaye O'Brien and Gary K. Grice. Available online. URL: http://www.lib.noaa.gov/edocs/women.html. Downloaded June 13, 2001.

Chapin, Emily. Interview, December 1977, Columbia University Oral History Research Office Collection.

Chernitsky, Dorothy. *Voices from the Foxholes, by the Men of the 110th Infantry.* Uniontown, Pa.: Dorothy Chernitsky, 1991.

"Chest Surgery in Wartime." Editorial in *Military Surgeon* 97 (October 1945): 331.

Chicago Tribune. News item, September 22, 1942, 1.

Children's Bureau. Department of Labor Records, Record Group 1027, National Archives, Washington, D.C., 1942.

Churchill, Winston. "Iron Curtain Speech," March 5, 1946. In *Modern History Sourcebook.* Available online. URL: http://www.fordham.edu/halsall/mod/churchill-iron.html. Downloaded October 5, 2001.

CIA home page, "Coordinator of Information." Available online. URL: http://www.cia.gov/cia/publications/oss/. Downloaded November 21, 2001.

Ciardi, John. *Saipan.* Fayetteville: University of Arkansas Press, 1988.

Clarke, Thurston. "Sons of Pearl." *Modern Maturity,* July/August 2001, 5–7. Available online. URL: http://www.modern.maturity.org. Downloaded October 24, 2001.

Clay, Lucius D. Interview conducted by Richard D. McKinzie in New York City, 16 July 1974. Available online. URL: http://www.trumanlibrary.org/oralhist/clayl.htm. Downloaded December 31, 2001.

Cochrane, Jacqueline. Final report on the WASP. Available online. URL: http://www.wasp-wwii.org. Downloaded August 23, 2001.

Cohen, Marshall, Thomas Nagel, and Thomas Scanlon, eds. *War and Moral Responsibility.* Princeton, N.J.: Princeton University Press, 1974.

Cole, Wayne S. *Charles A. Lindbergh and the Battle against American Intervention in World War II.* New York: Harcourt Brace Jovanovich, 1979.

Colley, David P. *Blood for Dignity: The Story of the First Integrated Combat Unit in the U.S. Army.* New York: St. Martin's, 2002.

Colman, Penny. "Rosie the Riveter: Author Questionnaire." Available online. URL: http://ourworld.compuserve.com/homepages/pennycolman/rosiefaq.htm. Downloaded May 15, 2001.

Colville, John Rupert. *The Fringes of Power: 10 Downing Street Diaries, 1939–1955.* New York: Norton, 1985.

Commager, Henry S. *The Story of the Second World War.* Boston: Little, Brown, 1945.

Commander Destroyer Division Eighty, U.S. Navy. Report of the sinking in the early morning of December 7, 1941, of an unidentified submarine that was following a U.S. naval ship into Pearl Harbor, filed December 12, 1941. Available online. URL: http//www.history.navy.mil/docs/wwii/pearl/ph9.htm. Downloaded January 8, 2002.

Commander USS *Ward*. Detailed report of the sinking in the early morning of December 7, 1941, of an unidentified submarine that was following a U.S. naval ship into Pearl Harbor, filed December 13, 1941. Available online. URL: http://www.history.navy.mil/docs/wwii/pearl/ph9.htm. Downloaded January 8, 2002.

"Companies and Human Rights Abuses during World War II." Business and Human Rights Resource Center. Available online. URL: http:www.business-humanrights.org/Companies-ww2.htm. Downloaded January 10, 2002

Compton, A. H., E. O. Lawrence, J. R. Oppenheimer, and E. Fermi. "Recommendations on the Immediate Use of Nuclear Weapons, June 16, 1945." Available online. URL: http://www.dannen.com/decision/scipanel.html. Downloaded July 12, 2002.

Condon-Rall, Mary Ellen. *Historical Statistics of the United States: Colonial Times to 1970*. Washington, D.C.: Government Printing Office, 1989.

Congressional Medal of Honor Citations. U.S. Army Center for Military History. Available online. URL: http://www.army.mil/cmh-pg/mohl.htm. Downloaded August 28, 2001.

Cook, Haruko Taya. "The Myth of the Saipan Suicides." In *No End Save Victory: Perspectives on World War II,* edited by Robert Cowley, 583–597. New York: G. P. Putnam's Sons, 2001.

Cook, Theodore F., Jr. "Tokyo, December 8, 1941." In *No End Save Victory: Perspectives on World War II,* edited by Robert Cowley, 131–143. New York: G. P. Putnam's Sons, 2001.

Cooke, Elliot D. *All but Thee and Me: Psychiatry at the Foxhole Level*. Washington, D.C.: Infantry Press Journal, 1946.

Costello, John. *Virtue under Fire: How World War II Changed Our Social and Sexual Attitudes.* New York: Fromm International, 1985.

Cowdrey, Albert E. *Fighting for Life: American Military Medicine in World War II.* New York: Free Press, 1994.

Cowley, Robert, ed. *No End Save Victory: Perspectives on World War II.* New York: G. P. Putnam's Sons, 2001.

Coy, Wayne. *New Republic,* April 15, 1946, p. 547.

Craig, Gordon A. "The X-Files." Review of Bendersky, *"The Jewish Threat,"* *New York Review of Books,* April 12, 2001, 4.

Crandell, Bradshaw, artist. "Are You a Girl with a Star-Spangled Heart?" Women's Army Corps recruiting poster. Library of Congress Collection POS-World War II-US .J22 1943; color transparency LC-USZC4-1653. Available online. URL: http://catalog.loc.gov. Downloaded November 27, 2001.

Crowder, Ray. *Iwo Jima Corpsman.* Gadsden, Ala.: R. Crowder, 1988.

Curtis Mina, ed. *Letters Home.* Boston: Little Brown, 1944.

Dander, Dan. Home page. Available online. URL: http://www.groton.k12.ct.us/WWW/wsms/DANDER.htm. Downloaded November 13, 2001.

Daniels, Roger. *Concentration Camps USA: Japanese Americans and World War II.* New York: Holt, Rinehart and Winston, 1972.

Daniels, Roger, Sandra C. Taylor, and Harry H. L. Kitano, eds. *Japanese Americans from Relocation to Redress.* Salt Lake City: University of Utah Press, 1986.

Danner, Dorothy Still. *What a Way to Spend a War: Navy Nurse POWs in the Philippines.* Annapolis, Md.: Naval Institute Press, 1995.

Daughtery, Tim. "Gender Roles—They Are Always Shifting." Student paper at Tennessee Technological University, April 15, 1997. Available online. URL: http://www2.h-net.msu.edu/~women/bibs/bibl-germanwarbride.html. Downloaded October 8, 2001.

Davidson, Eugene. *The Death and Life of Germany: An Account of the American Occupation.* New York: Knopf, 1959.

———. *The Trial of the Germans.* New York: Macmillan, 1966.

Davis, Barbara. "POW Nurses: So Proudly We Hail." *The Retired Officer,* March 1974.

Davis, Kenneth S. *Experience of War.* Garden City, N.Y.: Doubleday, 1965.

Deac, Wilfred P. "Amy Elizabeth Thorpe: World War II's Mata Hari," *World War II Magazine* (February 1996). Available online. URL: http://womenshistory.about.com/library/prm/blamythorpe1.htm. Downloaded December 23, 2002.

Delaney, Edmund. *Me Voilà: Recollections of Three Quarters of a Century.* Chester, Conn.: Connecticut River Publications, 1994.

D'Este, Carlo. "Falaise: The Trap Not Sprung." In *No End Save Victory: Perspectives on World War II,* edited by Robert Cowley, 460–473. New York: G. P. Putnam's Sons, 2001.

Detroit Free Press, June 14, 1945.

Devereux, James P. S. *The Story of Wake Island.* New York: J. B. Lippincott, 1947.

DeWan, George. "The Hunger for Learning." Available online. URL: http://www.lihistory.com/8/hs805a.htm. Downloaded September 22, 2001.

Diamond, Sander A. *The Nazi Movement in the United States, 1924–1941.* Ithaca, N.Y.: Cornell University Press, 1974.

"The Diary of a World War II Veteran." Available online. URL: http://users.vnet.net/jterrell/wwdiary/everettlt.htm. Downloaded February 13, 2001.

Dictionary of American Biography. 10 vols., 10 supp. New York: Scribner's, 1988.

Directive to the Commander-in-Chief of U.S. Forces of Occupation Regarding the Military Government of Germany, April 1945. U.S. State Department Bulletin, October 17, 1945. Washington, D.C.: Government Printing Office, 1945.

Doenecke, Justus D. *Storm on the Horizon: The Challenge to American Intervention, 1939–1941.* Lanham, Md.: Rowman & Littlefield, 2000.

Donovan, Robert J. *Conflict and Crisis: The Presidency of Harry S. Truman, 1945–1948.* New York: Norton, 1977.

Doss, Desmond. Citation for Congressional Medal of Honor. Available online. URL: http://www.armymedicine.army.mil/history/MOH/dossd.htm. Downloaded July 12, 2002.

Doubler, Michael D. *Closing with the Enemy: How GIs Fought the War in Europe, 1944–1945.* Lawrence: University of Kansas Press, 1994.

Dower, John W. *Embracing Defeat: Japan in the Wake of World War II.* New York: Norton, 1999.

Dreux, William B. *No Bridges Blown.* Notre Dame, Ind.: University of Notre Dame Press, 1971.

Drez, Ronald J., ed. *Voices of D-Day: The Story of the Allied Invasion Told by Those Who Were There.* Baton Rouge: Louisiana State University Press, 1994.

Dryden, Charles W. *A-Train: Memoirs of a Tuskegee Airman.* Tuscaloosa: University of Alabama Press, 1997.

Duer, Caroline King. Interview, 1950. Columbia University Oral History Research Office Collection.

Dumbarton Oaks Washington Conversations on International Peace and Security Organization, October 7, 1944. Proposals. Available online. URL: http://www.ibiblio.org/pha/policy/1944/. Downloaded March 19, 2002.

Dunne, John Gregory. "The Hardest War." *New York Review of Books,* December 20, 2001, 50–56.

Durr, Virginia Foster. *Outside the Magic Circle: The Autobiography of Virginia Foster Durr,* edited by Hollinger F. Barnard. University: University of Alabama Press, 1985.

Dyer, Gwynne. *War.* New York: Crown, 1985.

Eaker, Ira C. *Air Force Times,* December 6, 1976, 4.

Earley, Charity Adams. *One Woman's Army: A Black Officer Remembers the WAC.* College Station: Texas A&M University Press, 1989.

Ebbert, Jean, and Marie-Beth Hall. *Crossed Currents: Navy Women in a Century of Change.* 3d ed. Washington, D.C.: Brassey's, 1999.

Ebel, Miriam Davenport. "Memoir." Available online. URL: http://www.chambon.org/ebel%20memoir.htm. Downloaded June 25, 2001.

"Eight-Hour Orphans." Unsigned article, based on research by Grace Thorne Allen, Maxine Davis, and Warren Oliver. *Saturday Evening Post,* October 10, 1942, 10.

Einstein, Albert. Letter to President Franklin D. Roosevelt, August 2, 1939. Available online. URL: www.wsmr.army.mil/paopage/Pages/Einstn.htm. Downloaded September 12, 2001.

Eisenhower, Dwight D. Cable to War Shipping Administration, June 28, 1944. Available online. URL: http://www.usmm.org/quotes.html#anchor2778810. Downloaded November 19, 2002.

———. *Crusade in Europe.* New York: Doubleday, 1948.

Elkins, Paul. "The Bomb Hastened the End of World War II," guest column, *Los Alamos Monitor,* August 3, 1995. Available online. URL: http://www.childrenofthemanhattanproject.org/LC/I-006.htm. Downloaded December 17, 2002.

Eller, Cynthia. *Conscientious Objectors and the Second World War: Moral and Religious Arguments in Support of Pacifism.* New York: Praeger, 1991.

Ellis, John. *On the Front Lines: The Experience of War Through the Eyes of the Allied Soldiers in World War II.* New York: John Wiley, 1980.

"Establishment of the War Refugee Board." Unsigned article. Available online. URL: http://www.pbs.org/wgbh/amex/holocaust/peopleevents/pandeAMEX102.html. Downloaded December 27, 2002.

Eustis, Edith Morton. *War Letters of Morton Eustis to his Mother.* New York: Spiral, 1945.

Facts On File. "Nuremberg Trials." Available online. URL: http://www.facts.com/icof/nurem.htm. Downloaded December 4, 2001.

Fager, Chuck, ed. *Friends in Civilian Public Service: Quaker Conscientious Objectors in World War II Look Back and Look Ahead.* Wallingford, Pa.: Pendle Hill, 1966.

Faubus, Orval. *In This Faraway Land.* Conway, Ark.: River Road Press, 1971.

Feis, Herbert. *Japan Subdued.* Princeton, N.J.: Princeton University Press, 1961.

Fermi, Enrico. "Eyewitness Report of the Trinity Test," July 16, 1945. U.S. National Archives, Record Group 227, OSRD-S1 Committee, Box 82 folder 6, "Trinity." Available online. URL: http://www.nuclearfiles.org/docs/manhattan.html. Downloaded October 8, 2001.

Ferrell, Robert H. *Off the Record: The Private Papers of Harry S. Truman.* New York: Harper & Row, 1980.

Fesler, James W., et al. *Industrial Mobilization for War—History of the War Production Board and Predecessor Agencies, 1940–45: Program and Administration.* Washington, D.C.: Government Printing Office, 1947.

"The First Measured Century." Segment 8. PBS program, available online. URL: http://www.pbs.org/fmc/segment/progseg8.htm. Downloaded December 17, 2002.

Fisher, Bob, and Richard Crudo. "A Conversation with William A. Fraker, ASC, BSC." Available online. URL: www.cameraguild.com/interviews/chat_fraker/Fraker_conversation.htm. Downloaded November 13, 2001.

Fleming, Peter. *Operation Sea Lion: The Projected Invasion of England in 1940, An Account of the German Preparations and the British Countermeasures.* New York: Simon & Schuster, 1957.

"Fly Girls." PBS program. Available online. URL: www.pbs.org/wgbh/amex/flygirls/peopleevents/pandeAMEX-07.html. Downloaded October 25, 2001.

Flynn, George B. *Lewis B. Hershey: Mr. Selective Service.* Chapel Hill: University of North Carolina Press, 1985. Available online. URL: members.macconnect.com/users/k/knelson/co/ch2/ch202.html.Downloaded December 14, 2002.

Fort, Cornelia. "At the Twilight's Last Gleaming." *Ladies Home Companion,* July 1, 1943. Available online. URL: http://www.wpafb.af.mil/museum/history/wasp/wasp17.htm. Downloaded June 20, 2002.

Francis, Charles E. *The Tuskegee Airmen: The Men Who Changed a Nation.* Boston, Mass.: Branden, 1988.

Frankel, Nat, and Larry Smith. *Patton's Best: An Informal History of the 4th Armored Division.* New York: Hawthorn Books, 1978.

Frazer, Heather T., and John O'Sullivan. *We Have Just Begun to Not Fight: An Oral History of Conscientious Objectors in Civilian Public Service during World War II.* New York: Twayne, 1996.

Friederich, David R. "World War II Memoirs." Available online. URL: http://www.geocities.com/TheTropics/7621/navyindex.html. Downloaded July 3, 2001.

Friends of George C. Marshall. "The Plan." Available online. URL: http://www.lcsys.net/fayette/history/plan.htm. Downloaded November 13, 2001.

Fussell, Paul. *Wartime: Understanding and Behavior in the Second World War.* New York: Oxford, 1989.

Gabay, John. "Diary of a Tail Gunner." In *No End Save Victory: Perspectives on World War II,* edited by Robert Cowley, 259–277. New York: G. P. Putnam's Sons, 2001.

Gabin, Nancy. "The Hand That Rocks the Cradle Can Build Tractors, Too." *Michigan History Magazine* (March–April 1992): 12–21.

Gabriel, Richard A. *No More Heroes: Madness and Psychiatry in War.* New York: Hill and Wang, 1988.

Gailey, Harry A. *War in the Pacific: From Pearl Harbor to Tokyo Bay.* Novato, Calif.: Presidio, 1995.

George, John B. *Shots Fired in Anger.* Plantersville, S.C.: Small Arms Technical Publishing Co., 1947.

Gesensway, Deborah, and Mindy Roseman. *Beyond Words: Images from America's Concentration Camps.* Ithaca, N.Y.: Cornell University Press, 1987.

"G.I. Bill." *West's Encyclopedia of American Law.* Available online. URL: http://www.wld.com/conbus/weal/wgibill.htm. Downloaded September 21, 2001.

"G.I. Bill Facts." Available online. URL: http://www.syr.edu/archives/exhibits/ti/serve.htm. Downloaded September 22, 2001.

Gildersleeve, Virginia. *Many a Good Crusade.* New York: Macmillan, 1954.

Giles, Janice Holt. *The G.I. Journal of Sergeant Giles.* Boston: Houghton Mifflin, 1965.

Glendon, Mary Ann. "What Would My Mother Have Thought of Women's Freedom Network?" *Women's Freedom Network Newsletter* 7, no. 3 (May–June 2000): 1.

Glenn, Evelyn Nakano. *Issei, Nisei, War Bride: Three Generations of Japanese American Women in Domestic Service.* Philadelphia: Temple University Press, 1986.

"Glider Pilot Humor." In "Tribute to the Glider Pilots of World War II." Available online. URL: http://www.pointvista.com/WW2GliderPilots/gliderpilothumor.htm. Downloaded November 17, 2001.

Gluck, Sherna. *Rosie the Riveter Revisited: Women, the War and Social Change.* Boston: Twayne, 1987.

Goetinck, Monette. *Bottled Dreams.* Publisher's advertisement. Available online. URL: http://www.abbott-adele.com. Downloaded October 5, 2001.

Gold, Mary Jayne, comp. "Crossroads Marseilles 1940." Synopsis of the novel so entitled. Available online. URL: http://www.chambon.org/gold_cm_summary.htm. Downloaded June 22, 2001.

———. "The Original Officers of the Emergency Rescue Committee." Available online. URL: http://www.chambon.org/emergency_rescue_list.htm. Downloaded June 25, 2001.

Goodwin, Doris Kearns. Landon Lecture, Kansas State University, April 22, 1997. Available online. http://gos.sbc.edu/g/goodwin.html. Downloaded December 27, 2002.

———. *No Ordinary Time: Franklin and Eleanor Roosevelt: The Home Front in World War II.* New York: Simon and Schuster, 1994.

Goossen, Rachel Waltner. *Women against the Good War: Conscientious Objection and Gender on the American Home Front, 1941–1947.* Chapel Hill: University of North Carolina Press, 1997.

Gosorski, David M. "World War II's 'Silent Army' Produced 'Silent Revolution,'" *Veterans of Foreign Wars Magazine,* October 1997. Available online. URL: http://www.vfw.org/magazine/oct97/32.shtml. Downloaded August 14, 2001.

Granger, Byrd Howell. *On Final Approach: The Women Airforce Service Pilots of W.W.II.* Scottsdale, Ariz.: Falconer, 1991.

Grant, David N.W. "Work of the Flight Surgeon." *Military Surgeon* 94 (March 1944): 131–35.

Grant, Katie. "Wartime Memories." Available online. URL: http://www.rosietheriveter.org/memory.htm. Downloaded June 19, 2001.

Graydon, Bob. Letter to the editor. *New York Times,* October 29, 2000, "The News in Review," sec. A, 8.

Gropman, Alan L. *Mobilizing U.S. Industry in World War II.* MacNair Paper No. 50. Washington, D.C.: Institute for National Strategies Studies, August 1996. Available online. URL: http://www.ndu.edu/inss/macnair/macnair.html. Downloaded March 12, 2002.

Grosser, Alfred. *Germany in Our Time: A Political History of the Postwar Years.* New York: Praeger, 1971.

Gruber, Ruth. *Haven: The Dramatic Story of 1,000 World War II Refugees and How They Came to America.* New York: Three Rivers, 2000.

Gudmundsson, Bruce I. "Okinawa." In *No End Save Victory: Perspectives on World War II,* edited by Robert Cowley, 625–638. New York: G. P. Putnam's Sons, 2001.

Haas, Mary E. Coleman. "Personal View." In *Women in the Weather Bureau During World War II,* edited by Kaye O'Brien and Gary K. Grice, 35–38. Available online. URL: http://www.lib.noaa.gov/edocs/women.html. Downloaded June 13, 2001.

Habe, Hans. *Our Love Affair with Germany.* New York: G. P. Putnam's Sons, 1953.

Haber, Barbara. *From Hardtack to Home Fries: An Uncommon History of American Cooks and Meals.* New York: Free Press, 2002.

Hacker, Doug. "Aliens in Montana." *American History* 36:2 (June 2001), 33–36.

Hadley, Arthur T. *The Straw Giant: Triumph and Failure, America's Armed Forces.* New York: Random House, 1986.

Halberstam, David. *The Fifties.* New York: Villard, 1993.

Hancock, Joy Bright. *Lady in the Navy: A Personal Reminiscence.* Annapolis, Md.: Naval Institute Press, 1972.

Hanson, Victor Davis. "The Right Man." In *No End Save Victory: Perspectives on World War II,* edited by Robert Cowley, 639–657. New York: G. P. Putnam's Sons, 2001.

Hardwick, James C. "Pearl Harbor." *Modern Maturity,* July/August 2001. Available online. URL: http://www.modernmaturity.org. Downloaded September 7, 2001.

Hareven, Tamara. *Eleanor Roosevelt: An American Conscience.* Chicago: Quadrangle, 1968.

Harmon Collection. Available online. URL: http://www.npg.si.edu/exh/harmon/mulzharm.htm. Downloaded October 15, 2000.

Harper, Dale P. "American-born Axis Sally Made Propaganda Broadcasts for Radio Berlin in Hitler's Germany." *World War II Magazine,* November 1995. Available online. URL: http://www.thehistorynet.com/WorldWarII/articles/1195_text.htm. Downloaded September 21, 2001.

Harriman, W. Averell, and Elie Abel. *Special Envoy to Churchill and Stalin, 1941–1946.* New York: Random House, 1975.

Harris, Mark Jonathan, Franklin Mitchell, and Steven J. Schechter. *The Homefront: America during World War II.* New York: Putnam, 1984.

Hastings, Max. *Overlord: D-Day and the Battle for Normandy.* New York: Simon & Schuster, 1984.

Haydock, Michael D. "The G.I. Bill." *American History.* Available online. URL: www.thehistorynet.com/AmHistory/articles/1999/10992_cover.htm. Downloaded September 23, 2001.

Hayes, Winifred. "Woman's Place in the Future World Order." *Catholic World,* August 1943, 482–486.

Heide, Robert, and John Gilman. *Home Front America: Popular Culture of the World War II Era.* San Francisco: Chronicle Books, 1995.

Hersey, John. *Into the Valley: A Skirmish of the Marines.* New York: A. A. Knopf, 1943.

Higgins, Raymond A. *From Hiroshima with Love: The Allied Military Governor's Remarkable Story of the Rebuilding of Japan's Business and Industry after World War II.* Central Point, Oreg.: Hellgate, 1997.

Hill, K. "Women Physicians 1945–1960: Background Information." Interview by Dena Miller, November 5, 1982. In Norfolk Women's History, Special Collections, Perry Library, Old Dominion University, Hampton Boulevard, Norfolk, Va. 23529. Available online. URL: www.lib.odu.edu/aboutlib/spccol/oralhistory/womenhistory/khillpaper.html. Downloaded October 22, 2001.

"An Historical Look at The Honorable Elijah Muhammad." Unsigned article on the Nation of Islam website. Available online. URL: http://www.noi.org/history-elijah.html. Downloaded December 27, 2002.

Hobbie, Katherine. "Reminiscences of Fourth-grade Teaching at Tule Lake Internment center." Manuscript for Japanese-American publication *Grains of Rice.* Private collection.

Holm, Jeanne. *Women in the Military: An Unfinished Revolution.* Novato, Calif.: Presidio, 1982.

Holt, Thaddeus. "The Deceivers." In *No End Save Victory: Perspectives on World War II,* edited by Robert Cowley, 385–404. New York: G. P. Putnam's Sons, 2001.

———. "King of Bataan." In *No End Save Victory: Perspectives on World War II,* edited by Robert Cowley, 155–172. New York: G. P. Putnam's Sons, 2001.

Honey, Maureen. *Creating Rosie the Riveter: Class, Gender, and Propaganda During World War II.* Amherst: University of Massachusetts Press, 1984.

Hoopes, Roy. *Americans Remember the Home Front.* New York: Hawthorn, 1973.

Hoover, Will. "Martial Law Darkened War Years for Hawai'i." *Honolulu Advertiser,* December 7, 2000.

Horodysky, Daniel. "Recognition Sought by Heroic Wartime Merchant Marine Veterans." *San Francisco Examiner,* April 21, 1997. Available online. URL: www.usmm.org/recognitionsought.html. Downloaded June 4, 2001.

Hottelet, Richard. "Ups and Downs in UN History." *Journal of Law and Policy* 5, no. 17: 17–25. Available online. URL: http://law.wustl.edu/igls/ Unconfpapers/p. Downloaded January 9, 2002.

Houck, Herbert. Obituary. *Los Angeles Times,* March 7, 2002. Available online. URL: www.latimes.com/news/obituaries. Downloaded March 7, 2002.

Hough, Frank O. *The Island War; the United States Marine Corps in the Pacific.* Philadelphia: J. B. Lippincott, 1947.

Houston, Jeanne Wakatsuki, and James D. Houston. *Farewell to Manzanar.* New York: Bantam, 1974.

Hovsepian, Aramais Akob. *Your Son and Mine.* Culver City, Calif.: Murray & Gee, 1950.

Huebner, Klaus. *Long Walk through War: A Combat Doctor's Diary.* College Station: Texas A&M University Press, 1987.

Huff, H. Stanley. *Unforgettable Journey: A World War II Memoir.* Fort Wayne, Ind.: Bridgeford, 2001.

Hummel, Jeffrey Rogers. "Not Just Japanese Americans: The Untold Story of U.S. Repression During 'The Good War.'" *Journal of Historical Review* 7: 285ff. Available online. URL: http://ihr.org/jhr/v07/v07p285_Hummel.html. Downloaded December 17, 1999.

Hunt, George P. *Coral Comes High.* New York: Harper, 1946.

Hynes, Jean Elizabeth Williams. "Pearl Harbor," in *Modern Maturity,* July/August 2001. Available online. URL: http://www.modernmaturity.org. Downloaded September 7, 2001.

Hynes, Samuel. *The Soldiers' Tale: Bearing Witness to Modern War.* New York: Penguin, 2001.

Inada, Lawson Fusao, ed. *Only What We Could Carry: The Japanese Internment Experience.* Berkeley and San Francisco, Calif.: Heyday and the California Historical Society, 2000.

Indiana Historical Society. Ernie Pyle website. Available online. URL: http:// www.indianahistory.org/heritage/pyle.html. Downloaded October 31, 2001.

Intelligence Officer, An. "The Japanese in America." *Harper's Magazine,* October 1942. (The author has since been identified as Lt. Comdr. Kenneth D. Ringle of the Office of Naval Intelligence, on loan to the War Relocation Authority.)

Irons, Peter. *Justice at War: The Story of the Japanese American Internment Cases.* New York: Oxford, 1983.

Isenberg, Sheila. *A Hero of Our Own: The Story of Varian Fry.* New York: Random House, 2001.

Jansen, Marius. *The Making of Modern Japan.* Cambridge, Mass.: Harvard University Press, 2000.

Japanese American National Museum. "Frequently Asked Questions." Available online. URL: http://www.janm.org/nrc/q&a.html. Downloaded August 23, 2001.

Jarrell, Mary, ed. *Randall Jarrell's Letters.* New York: Houghton Mifflin, 1985.

Jewish Virtual Library. "The War Rescue Board." Available online. URL: http://www.us-israel.org/jsource/Holocaust/wrb.html. Downloaded June 29, 2001.

"Johnnie." "My Thoughts on the Home Front during World War II." Available online. URL: http://www.eagnet.com/edipage/user/joanie/news.htm. Downloaded June 13, 2001.

Johnson, Amirah. *Modern Maturity,* July/August 2001, 50.

Johnson, Paul. *Modern Times. The World from the Twenties to the Eighties.* New York: Harper & Row, 1983.

Jones, James. Quotation in "Glider Pilot Humor." Available online. URL: http://www.pointvista.com/WW2GliderPilots/GliderPilotHumor.htm. Downloaded June 19, 2002.

Jones, Stacy. "The Rural World War II Homefront in Homer, Illinois." Available online. URL: http://wwdangpow.com/tildafelixia/thesis.html. Downloaded March 5, 2001.

Judd, Junior. Letter home, printed in a newspaper in Colfax, Indiana. Available online. URL: http://members.tripod.com/~GenFamily/ww2.html. Downloaded June 21, 2001.

Juergensen, Hans. *Beachheads and Mountains: Campaigning from Sicily to Anzio.* Tampa, Fla.: American Studies Press, 1984.

Jung, Caroline. "War Brides." *San Jose Mercury News,* October 20, 1995. Available online. URL: http://www.ignacio.org/warbride.html. Downloaded October 17, 2000.

Kahn, Sy M. *Between Tedium and Terror.* Urbana: University of Illinois Press, 1993.

Kaminski, Theresa. *Prisoners in Paradise: American Women in the Wartime South Pacific.* Lawrence: University Press of Kansas, 2000.

Karig, Walter, et al. *Battle Report, Prepared from Official Sources.* New York: Published for the Council on Books in Wartime by Farrar & Rinehart, ca. 1944.

Karoly, Steve. "Seabee Food Service in WW II: The Story of the Can Do! Cooks and Bakers." Available online. URL: http://www.seabeecook.com/cooks/navy/cbinww2.htm. Downloaded May 17, 2001.

Karr, Eve T. "Pre-Kendal Memories." Unpublished undated manuscript, Kendal Library, Kennett Square, Pa.

Kauffman, Bill. *America First: Its History, Culture, and Politics.* Amherst, N.Y.: Prometheus, 1995.

Kauffmann, Stanley. *Albums of Early Life.* New York: Ticknor & Fields, 1980.

Keats, John. *They Fought Alone.* Philadelphia: J. B. Lippincott, 1963.

Keegan, John. "Berlin." In *No End Save Victory: Perspectives on World War II,* edited by Robert Cowley, 565–580. New York: G. P. Putnam's Sons, 2001.

———. *The Second World War.* New York: Viking, 1989.

———. *Six Armies in Normandy: From D-Day to the Liberation of Paris, June 6th–August 25th, 1944.* London: Cape, 1982.

Keim, Albert N. *The CPS Story: An Illustrated History of Civilian Public Service.* Intercourse, Pa.: Good Books, 1990.

Keith, Agnes Newton. *Three Came Home.* Boston, Mass.: Little, Brown, 1947.

Kennan, George. Telegram to the State Department, February 22, 1946, later published as "The Sources of Soviet Conduct," *Foreign Affairs* (July 1947). Available online. URL: balrog.sdsu.edu/~putman/410b/kennan.htm. Downloaded January 10, 2002.

Kennedy, David M. *Freedom from Fear: The American People in Depression and War, 1929–1945.* New York: Oxford, 1999.

Kennett, Lee. *For the Duration . . . The United States Goes to War: Pearl Harbor—1942.* New York: Scribner, 1985.

———. *G.I.: The American Soldier in World War II.* New York: Scribner, 1989.

Kernan, Alvin. "The Day the Hornet Sank." In *No End Save Victory: Perspectives on World War II,* edited by Robert Cowley, 202–209. New York: G. P. Putnam's Sons, 2001.

Kerr, E. Bartlett. *Surrender and Survival: The Experience of American POWs in the Pacific, 1941–1945.* New York: William Morrow, 1985.

Ketchum, Carlton G. *The Recollections of Colonel Retread, USAAF 1942–1945.* Pittsburgh, Pa.: Hart, 1976.

Kiester, Edwin, Jr. "G.I. Bill of Rights." Available online. URL: http://www.mcn.org/c/irapilgrim/edu24.html. Downloaded September 22, 2001.

Kilroy Legends and Logo. Available online. URL: http://www.kilroywashere.org/001-Pages/01-0KilroyLegends-2.html. Downloaded March 6, 2002.

Kimball, Warren S. *The Most Unsordid Act: Lend-Lease, 1939–1941*. Baltimore, Md.: Johns Hopkins University Press, 1969.

———, ed. *Churchill & Roosevelt: The Complete Correspondence*. 3 vols. Princeton, N.J.: Princeton University Press, 1984.

King, Mollie Parry. Letter to the editor. *Athens Daily News,* May 22, 1998. Available online. URL: http://www.geocities.com/Heartland/Meadows/9710/WW2warbrides/WBLINKS.html. Downloaded October 1, 2001.

Koistinen, Paul A. C. "Warfare and Power Relations in America: Mobilizing the World War II Economy." In *The Home Front and War in the Twentieth Century,* edited by James Titus, 91–110. Washington, D.C.: U.S. Air Force Academy and Office of Air Force History, 1984.

Krock, Arthur. "In the Nation." *New York Times,* December 14, 1937, sec. 4.

Kuralt, Charles. *A Life on the Road*. New York: Ivy, 1990.

"Labor, Women—Now!" Unsigned article, *Business Week,* January 9, 1943, 72.

Laffin, John. *Americans in Battle*. New York: Crown, 1973.

Landstrom, Elsie H., ed. *Hyla Doc: Surgeon in China through War and Revolution, 1924–1949*. Fort Bragg, Calif.: Q.E.D. Press, 1991.

Langer, William L., and Everett S. Gleason. *Undeclared War: 1939–1940*. New York: Harper & Row, 1952–53.

Lardner, Ring, Jr. *The Lardners: My Family Remembered*. New York: Harper & Row, 1976.

Lash, Joseph. *Roosevelt and Churchill, 1939–1941: The Partnership That Saved the West*. New York: Norton, 1976.

Laurence, William L. *Men and Atoms*. New York: Simon & Schuster, 1959.

Lawrence, W. H. "Dr. Facts Digs In." *New York Times,* August 16, 1942, sec. 7, 5.

Lawton, Manny. *Some Survived*. Chapel Hill, N.C.: Algonquin, 1985.

Lea, Tom. *Peleliu Landing*. El Paso, Tex.: Carl Hertzog, 1945.

Lee, Bruce. *Marching Orders: The Untold Story of World War II*. New York: Crown, 1995.

Lee, Jenny J. "GI Bill of Rights." Available online. URL: http://www.gseis.ucla.edu/courses/ed191/assignment1/gibill.html. Downloaded September 21, 2001.

Lee, Robert E. *To the War.* New York: Alfred A. Knopf, 1968.

Lee, Ulysses G. *The Employment of Negro Troops: U.S. Army and World War II.* Washington, D.C.: Office of the Chief of Military History, 1966.

Leighton, Alexander H. *The Governing of Men: General Principles and Recommendations Based on Experience at a Japanese Relocation Camp.* Princeton, N.J.: Princeton University Press, 1945.

Leinbaugh, Harold P., and John D. Campbell. *The Men of Company K.* New York: Bantam, 1987.

Levine, Ellen. *A Fence Away from Freedom: Japanese Americans and World War II.* New York: G. P. Putnam's Sons, 1995.

Levitt, Saul. "Down and Go: Two Stories by and of Our Airborne Troops in France." *Yank,* July 2, 1944, 5.

Levy, Peter B., ed. *100 Key Documents in American Democracy.* Westport, Conn.: Greenwood, 1994.

Life, September 17, 1945, 115.

Lindbergh, Anne Morrow. *War Within and Without: Diaries and Letters, 1939–1944.* New York: Harcourt Brace Jovanovich, 1980.

Lindbergh, Charles A. *New York Times,* May 20, 1940, 8.

———. "Who Are the War Agitators?" Speech delivered at an America First rally in Des Moines, Iowa, September 11, 1941. Available online. URL: http://www.charleslindbergh.com/americanfirst/speech.asp. Downloaded June 5, 2001.

Lindbergh, Reeve. *Under a Wing: A Memoir.* New York: Simon & Schuster, 1998.

Linderman, Gerald F. *The World within War: America's Combat Experience in World War II.* Cambridge, Mass.: Harvard University Press, 1997.

Litoff, Judy Barrett, and David C. Smith, eds. *Since You Went Away: World War II Letters from American Women on the Home Front.* New York: Oxford University Press, 1991.

Lochner, Robert. Interview, undated. Available online. URL: http://www.gwu.edu/~nsarchiv/coldwar/interviews/episode-4/lochner1.html. Downloaded October 22, 2001.

Loewenheim, Francis L., Harold D. Langley, and Manfred Jonas, eds. *Roosevelt and Churchill: Their Secret Wartime Correspondence.* New York: Saturday Review Press/E. P. Dutton, 1975.

London Agreement, August 8, 1945. Available online. URL: http://www.
yale.edu/lawweb/avalon/imt/proc/imtchart.htm. Downloaded August 27, 2001.

Long, Breckenridge. *The War Diaries of Breckinridge Long,* edited by Fred L.
Israel. Lincoln: University of Nebraska Press, 1966.

Longo, Bill. "Operation 'Magic Carpet.'" Available online. URL: http://
members.aol.com/_ht_a/troopship/index.htm. Downloaded June 21, 2001.

Lord, Walter. *Incredible Victory.* New York: Harper & Row, 1967.

———. *Lonely Vigil: Coastwatchers of the Solomons.* New York: Viking, 1977.

Love, Spencie. *One Blood: The Death and Resurrection of Charles R. Drew.* Chapel
Hill: University of North Carolina Press, 1996.

Lucas, Jim. *Combat Correspondent.* New York: Reynal and Hitchcock, 1944.

Lukacs, John. *Five Days in London, May 1940.* New Haven: Yale University
Press, 1999.

Lyons, Jane. "Pre-Kendal Memory." Undated unpublished manuscript, Kendal
Library, Kennett Square, Pa.

Malone, Ruth. "Pre-Kendal Memories." Undated unpublished manuscript,
Kendal Library, Kennett Square, Pa.

Manchester, William. "The Bloodiest Battle of All." *New York Times Magazine,*
June 14, 1987, 15.

———. *The Glory and the Dream: A Narrative History of America.* Boston: Little,
Brown, 1974.

———. *Goodbye, Darkness: A Memoir of the Pacific War.* Boston: Little, Brown,
1979.

Marks, Leo. *Between Silk and Cyanide: A Codemaker's War.* New York: Free Press,
1998.

Marlowe, David H. *Psychological and Psychosocial Consequences of Combat and
Deployment with Special Emphasis on the Gulf War.* Santa Monica, Calif.: Rand,
2001. Available online. URL: http://www.gulflink.osd.mil/randrep/
marlowe_paper/mr1018_11_ch7.html. Downloaded September 10, 2001.

Marshall, George C. "The Marshall Plan." Available online. URL: http://usinfo
.state.gov/usa/infousa/facts/democrac/57.htm. Downloaded January 1, 2002.

———. The Marshall Plan speech, Harvard University commencement, June
5, 1947. Available online. URL: http://www.usaid.gov/multimedia/video/
marshall/marshallspeech.html. Downloaded March 15, 2002.

———. Memorandum of December 1, 1941. Archives, George C. Marshall Foundation, P. O. Drawer 1600, Lexington, Virginia, 24450.

Mater, Gene. "The Freedom Forum." Available online. URL: http://www. newseum.org/berlinwall/essay.htm. Downloaded December 5, 2001.

Mathias, Frank F. *G.I. Jive: An Army Bandsman in World War II.* Lexington: University Press of Kentucky, 1982.

McCarthy, Abigail. *Private Faces/Public Places.* Garden City, N.Y.: Doubleday, 1972.

McCormick, John. *The Right Kind of War.* Annapolis, Md.: Naval Institute Press, 1992.

McCullough, David. *Truman.* New York: Simon & Schuster, 1992.

McDermott, Andrew. "The War Bride Inverted." Available online. URL: http://eserver.org/zine375/issue1/portrt4.html. Downloaded April 2, 2001.

McGuire, Philip. *Taps for a Jim Crow Army: Letters from Black Soldiers in WWII.* Santa Barbara, Calif.: ABC-Clio, 1983.

McKeown, Harry. "B-29 Letter." Available online. URL: http://www. wasp-wwii.org/. Downloaded August 23, 2001.

McKinley, James. Interview by Dorothy Schneider, ca. 1945, Gloucester, Mass. Collection of the authors.

McWilliams, Carey. *North From Mexico.* 1949. Reprint, New York: Praeger, 1990.

———. *Prejudice: Japanese Americans, Symbol of Racial Intolerance.* Boston: Little, Brown, 1944.

Meisler, Stanley. *United Nations: The First Fifty Years.* New York: Atlantic Monthly Press, 1995.

Menuhin, Yehudi. *Unfinished Journey.* New York: Alfred A. Knopf, 1977.

Merillat, Herbert L. *The Island: A History of the First Marine Division on Guadalcanal.* Washington, D.C.: Zenger, 1944.

Merrill, Dennis K., ed. *The Documentary History of the Truman Presidency.* 34 volumes to date. Bethesda, Md.: University Publications of America, 1995–.

Merritt, Richard L. *Democracy Imposed: U.S. Occupation Policy and the German Public, 1945–1949.* New Haven, Conn.: Yale University Press, 1995.

Meyer, Robert, Jr., ed. *The* Stars and Stripes *Story of World War II.* New York: David McKay, 1960.

Michel, Ernest W. *Promises to Keep: One Man's Journey against Incredible Odds.* New York: Barricade Books, 1993.

Michener, James A. *The Voice of Asia.* New York: Random House, 1951.

Miller, Arthur. "The Face in the Mirror: Anti-Semitism Then and Now." *New York Times Book Review,* October 14, 1984, 3.

———. *Situation Normal.* New York: Reynal and Hitchcock, 1944.

Milward, Alan S. *War, Economy and Society, 1939–1945.* Berkeley: University of California Press, 1977.

Minear, Richard H. *Dr. Seuss Goes to War: The World War II Editorial Cartoons of Theodor Seuss Geisel.* New York: New Press, 1999.

Mohr, Alexander. "Navajo Code Talkers: World War II Fact Sheet." Available online. URL: http://www.history.navy.mil/faqs/faq61-2.htm. Downloaded October 2, 2002.

Moore, Brenda L. *To Serve My Country, To Serve My Race: The Story of the Only African American WACs Stationed Overseas during World War II.* New York: NYU Press, 1996.

Morgan, Thomas D. "Native Americans in World War II." *Army History* 35 (fall 1995): 22–27.

Morison, Samuel Eliot. *The Invasion of France and Germany: 1944–1945.* Vol. 11 in the series *History of United States Naval Operations in World War II.* Boston: Little, Brown, 1957.

———. "Thoughts on Military Strategy, World War II." Available online. URL: http://www.nwc.navy.mil/press/Review/1998/winter/art6-w98.htm. Downloaded September 5, 2001.

———. *The Two-Ocean War: A Short History of the United States Navy in the Second World War.* Boston: Little, Brown, 1963.

Morison, Samuel Eliot, Henry Steele Commager, and William E. Leuchtenberg. *A Concise History of the American Republic.* New York: Oxford University Press, 1977.

Moritz, Garrett. "Coupons and Counterfeits: World War II and the U.S. Black Market." Available online. URL: http://www.gtexts.com/college/papers/j2.html. Downloaded June 19, 2001.

Morris, Edward. "An American in Paris: Art Buchwald on the Good Life in Postwar France." Available online. URL: http://www.bookpage.com/9609bp/nonfiction/illalwayshaveparis.html. Downloaded November 13, 2001.

Moscow Conference Declaration. Moscow Conference. October 1943. Available online. URL: http://www.yale.edu/lawweb/avalon/imt/moscow. Downloaded March 19, 2002.

Moser, John E. *Presidents from Hoover through Truman, 1929–1953: Debating the Issues in Pro and Con Primary Documents.* Westport, Conn.: Greenwood, 2001.

Muirhead, John. *Those Who Fall.* New York: Random House, 1986.

Murray, Williamson. "Did Strategic Bombing Work?" In *No End Save Victory: Perspectives on World War II,* edited by Robert Cowley, 494–512. New York: G. P. Putnam's Sons, 2001.

"My History Is America's History." Millennium project of the National Endowment for the Humanities. Available online. URL: http://www.myhistory.org/history_files/articles/conscientious_objection.html-18k. Downloaded October 15, 2000.

Mydans, Seth. "Japanese Veteran Writes of Brutal Philippine War," *International New York Times,* September 2, 2001. Available online. URL: http://www.nytimes.com/2001/09/02/international/asia/02FILI.html. Downloaded December 26, 2002.

National Atomic Museum. "The Manhattan Project." Available online. URL: http://www.atomicmuseum.com/tour/manhattanproject.cfm. Downloaded September 12, 2001.

National Park Service. "Aleut Internment." Available online. URL:http//www.nps.gov/AleutInternmentAndRestitution.htm. Downloaded February 24, 2003.

Nelson, Donald M. *Arsenal of Democracy: The Story of American War Production.* New York: Harcourt, Brace, 1946.

Nichols, David, ed. *Ernie's War: The Best of Ernie Pyle's World War II Dispatches.* New York: Random House, 1986.

Nimitz, Chester. Quotation on Iwo Jima. Available online. URL: http://www.usmc.mil/History.nsf/Table+of+Contents. Downloaded March 7, 2002.

Nishimoto, Warren. *An Era of Change: Oral Histories of Civilians in World War II Hawai'i,* 3 vols. Honolulu: Ethnic Studies Oral History Project, University of Hawaii at Manoa, ca. 1980.

Nolan, Jenny. "Willow Run and the Arsenal of Democracy." *Detroit News,* n.d. Available online. URL: http://detnews.com/history/arsenal/arsenal.htm. Downloaded May 29, 2001.

Norris, Robert W. "Civilian Public Service Conscientious Objectors in World War II." Available online. URL: http://www2.gol.com/users/norris/copaper. html. Downloaded September 25, 1999.

Noyes, John. "Pre-Kendal Memory." Undated unpublished manuscript, Kendal Library, Kennett Square, Pa. 19348.

O'Brien, Kaye, and Gary K. Grice, eds. *Women in the Weather Bureau During World War II.* Available online. URL: http://www.lib.noaa.gov/edocs/women.html. Downloaded June 13, 2001.

O'Donnell, Patrick. Interview with Earl Walker. Available online. URL: http://www.thedropzone.org/pacific/walters.htm. Downloaded August 22, 2001.

Office of the Chief of Naval Operations, Naval History Division. *Dictionary of American Naval Fighting Ships.* Washington, D.C.: Naval History Division. Available online. URL: http://www.ibiblio.org/hyperwar/USN/ships/dafs/AKA/aka36.html. Downloaded November 13, 2001.

"Okinawa." Available online. URL: http://www.spartacus.schoolnet.co.uk/2WWokinawa.htm. Downloaded December 30, 2002.

Oliver, Myrna. "Creator of the G.I. Bill of Rights Dies at 100." *Los Angeles Times,* April 24, 1997. Available online. URL: http://www.voice.bloomu.edu/4-24-97/news/news9.html. Downloaded September 21, 2001.

Olsson, Johan. "The North Atlantic Treaty Organization. An Alliance without an Enemy?" International Institutions (POLSCI 440), Hawaii Pacific University, December 8, 1994. Available online. URL: http://www.geocities.com/TimesSquare/1848/nato.html. Downloaded January 2, 2002.

O'Neill, William L. *A Democracy at War: America's Fight at Home and Abroad in World War II.* New York: Free Press, 1993.

———. Interview. PBS program *The First Measured Century,* Segment 8. Available online. URL: http://www.pbs.org/fmc/interviews/oneill.htm. Downloaded June 1, 2001.

O'Reilly, Bill. *World Net Daily.* Available online. URL: http://www.wnd.com/news/article.asp?ARTICLE_ID=23430. Downloaded December 17, 2002.

Ottley, Roy. *New World A-Coming.* New York: Ayer, 1968.

"Overall Unemployment Rate in the Civilian Labor Force, 1920–2000." Available online. URL: http://www.infoplease.com/ipa/A0104719.html. Downloaded May 28, 2001.

Overy, Richard. *Why the Allies Won.* New York: W. W. Norton, 1995.

Palmer, Jerrell Dean, and John G. Johnson, "Big Inch and Little Big Inch," in "The Handbook of Texas Online." URL: http://www.tsha.utexas.edu/handbook/online/articles/view/BB/dob8.html. Downloaded March 11, 2002.

Parkinson, Roger. *The Origins of World War Two.* New York: G. P. Putnam's Sons, 1970.

Paul, Don. "Recollections." Available online. URL: http://www.koreanwar.org. Downloaded March 18, 2002.

Paul, Doris A. *The Navajo Code Talkers.* Pittsburgh, Pa.: Dorrance, 1973.

Paull, William Trewhella. "From Butte to Iwo Jima." Available online. URL: http://www.sihope.com/~tipi/marine.html. Downloaded July 3, 2001.

"The Pearl Harbor Attack." U.S. Naval Historical Center. Available online. URL: http://www.history.navy.mil/faqs/faq66-1.htm. Downloaded September 5, 2001.

Pell, Herbert. Interview, 1951. United States representative on the United Nations War Crimes Commission from August 1943 to January 1945. Columbia University Oral History Research Office Collection.

Penniman, Anne. Interview by the authors, tape recording, Essex, Conn., April 2000.

Penniman, Caleb. Interview by the authors, tape recording, Essex, Conn., April 2000.

———. Unpublished memoir on his experiences as an aircraft navigator in the Pacific during World War II, 2000. Collection of the authors.

Perret, Geoffrey. *Days of Sadness, Years of Triumph; the American People, 1939–1945.* New York: Coward, McCann & Geoghegan, 1973.

———. *There's a War to Be Won: The United States Army in World War II.* New York: Ballantyne, 1991.

Persico, Joseph E. *Piercing the Reich: The Penetration of Nazi Germany by American Secret Agents during World War II.* New York: Barnes and Noble, 1979.

Phibbs, Brendan. *The Other Side of Time: A Combat Surgeon in World War II.* Boston: Little, Brown, 1987.

Phillips, Cabell B. H. *The 1940s: Decade of Triumph and Trouble.* New York: Crown, 1975.

———. *The Truman Presidency.* New York: Macmillan, 1966.

Pitt, Thomas F., Jr. "The Waal River Crossing." Interview conducted by Thomas F. Pitt, Jr. Available online. URL: http://www.thedropzone.org/europe/Holland/pitt.html. Downloaded July 4, 2001.

Pittsburgh Courier. Letter to the editor from 15 sailors aboard the USS *Philadelphia,* mid-September 1940.

PM. Washington, D.C., newspaper, December 8, 1941.

Polenberg, Richard. *War and Society: The United States, 1941–1945.* Philadelphia: Lippincott, 1972.

Ponting, Clive. *Armageddon: The Reality behind the Distortions, Myths, Lies, and Illusions of World War II.* New York: Random House, 1995.

Potsdam Conference Protocol. Available online. Avalon project. URL: http://www.yale.edu/lawweb/avalon/decade/decade17.htm. Downloaded July 10, 2001.

Potter, Lou, William Miles, and Nina Rosenblum. *Liberators: Fighting on Two Fronts in World War II.* New York: Harcourt Brace Jovanovich, 1992.

Public Broadcasting System. *The First Measured Century,* Segment 8. Available online. URL: http://www.pbs.org/fmc/interviews/2seg3.htm. Downloaded October 25, 2001.

———. "The G.I. Bill." December 2000. Available online. URL: http://www.pbs.org/newshour/bb/mil/july-dec00/gibill_7-4.html. Downloaded September 21, 2001.

Putney, Martha Settle. *When the Nation Was in Need: Blacks in the Women's Army Corps During World War II.* Metuchen, N.J.: Scarecrow, 1992.

Pyle, Ernie. *Brave Men.* New York: Henry Holt, 1944.

Ramsey, Norman. Interview, 1960. Columbia University Oral History Research Office Collection.

"Rationing Situation in the New York Area," *New York Times,* June 6, 1943, 38.

Recommendations on the Immediate Use of Nuclear Weapons (by the Scientific Panel of the Interim Committee, June 16, 1945). Available online. URL: http://www.nuclearfiles.org/docs/1945/450616-ic-sc-panel.html. Downloaded December 26, 2002.

Reeves, Larry. Interview by the authors, Ajijic, Mexico, July 2001.

Rehnquist, William H. "Civil Liberties in Wartime." Speech of November 17, 1999. Available online. URL: http://wwics.si.edu/NEWS/speeches/rehnquist.htm. Downloaded January 15, 2002.

Reischauer, Edwin O. *The United States and Japan.* Cambridge, Mass.: Harvard University Press, 1965.

"Remembering the GI Bulge." Syracuse University Archives. Available online. URL: http://sumweb.syr.edu/archives/exhibits/gi/serve.htm. Downloaded September 22, 2001.

Reporting Civil Rights. 2 vols. New York: Library of America, 2003.

"Reporting World War II: American Journalism 1938–1946." In *Reporting World War II: American Journalism 1938–1946.* 2 vols. New York: Library of America, 1995.

Reuther, Walter. Speech at national women's conference. *New York Times,* December 10, 1944, 42.

Reynolds, David. *Rich Relations: The American Occupation of Britain, 1942–1945.* New York: Random House, 1995.

Reynolds, Quentin. *Officially Dead: The Story of Cmdr. C. D. Smith.* New York: Random House, 1945.

Riddle, Donald H. *The Truman Committee.* New Brunswick, N.J.: Rutgers University Press, 1964.

Ridgway, Matthew B. "D-Day Minus One: U. S. Paratroopers Leave for France." Available online. URL: http://www.rjgeib.com/heroes/draper/ridgway.html. Downloaded June 13, 2001.

Roberts, Ray. *Survivors of the Leopoldville Disaster.* Available online. URL: http://members.aol.com/rayandlu/book.html. Downloaded June 21, 2001.

Roosevelt, Eleanor. Collection of "My Day" columns. Archives, Marist College, 3399 North Road, Poughkeepsie, N.Y. 12601.

———. Radio broadcast. *New York Times,* December 8, 1941, 4.

Roosevelt, Elliott, and James Brough. *A Rendezvous with Destiny: The Roosevelts of the White House.* New York: Dell, 1975.

Roosevelt, Franklin D. Arsenal of democracy speech, December 29, 1940. Available online. URL: http://www.mtholyoke.edu/acad/intrel/WorldWar2/arsenal.htm. Downloaded December 26, 2002.

———. Chautauqua speech, August 14, 1936. Available online. URL: http://web.mala.bc.ca/davies/H324War/FDR.Chautauqua.Speech.Aug14.1936.htm. Downloaded May 25, 2002.

———. Fireside chat, May 26, 1940. Available online. URL: http://www.politicalsource.net. and http://www.mhric.org/fdr/chat15.html. Downloaded May 24, 2002.

———. Fireside chat, April 28, 1942. Available online. URL: http://www.mhric.org/fdr/chat21.html. Downloaded May 27, 2002.

———. Fireside chat, Columbus Day 1942. Available online. URL: http://www.mhric.org/fdr/fdr.html. Downloaded June 17, 2002.

———. Pearl Harbor speech, December 8, 1941. Available online. URL: http://bcn.boulder.co.us/government/national/speeches/spch2.html. Downloaded May 25, 2002.

———. Press conference proposing Lend-Lease. *New York Times,* December 18, 1940, 1.

———. Press conference. *New York Times,* July 28, 1943, 9.

———. *The Public Papers and Addresses of Franklin D. Roosevelt.* New York: Random House, 1938–1950.

———. Quarantine speech, October 5, 1937. Available online. URL: http://www.ku.edu/carrie/docs/texts/fdrquarn.html. Downloaded May 25, 2002.

———. Quoted in *New York Times,* September 11, 1941, 4.

———. Speech delivered at commencement exercises at the University of Virginia, Charlottesville, June 10, 1940. Available online. URL: http://usinfo.state.gov/usa/infousa/facts/democrac/52.htm. Downloaded May 24, 2002.

———. Speech to Congress, December 8, 1941. Available online. URL: bcn.boulder.co.us/gov/national/speeches/spch2.html. Downloaded December 4, 2002.

———. State of the Union address. *New York Times,* January 7, 1941, 5.

———. State of the Union address. *New York Times,* January 12, 1944, 3.

Ross, Ishbel. *Grace Coolidge and Her Era.* New York: Dodd, Mead, 1962.

Rossiter, Clinton L. *Constitutional Dictatorship: Crisis Government in the Modern Democracies.* Westport, Conn.: Greenwood, 1979.

Royall, Kenneth C. Interview, 1963. Columbia University Oral History Research Office Collection.

Rudd, Hughes. "When I Landed, the War Was Over." In *A Sense of History: The Best Writing from the Pages of American Heritage,* 744–59. New York: American Heritage Press, 1985.

Rupp, Leila J. *Mobilizing Women for War: German and American Propaganda 1939–1945.* Princeton, N.J.: Princeton University Press, 1978.

Rustin, Bayard. Letter to his draft board, November 16, 1943. Collection of Walter Naegle.

Ryan, Cornelius. *A Bridge Too Far.* London: Hamilton, 1974.

Sanborn, Frederic R. *Design for War: A Study of Secret Power Politics, 1937–1941.* New York: Devin-Adair, 1951.

Sareyan, Alex. *The Turning Point: How Men of Conscience Brought about Major Change in the Care of America's Mentally Ill.* Washington, D.C.: American Psychiatric Press, 1993. Reviewed in *New England Journal of Medicine* 330, no. 21 (May 26, 1994).

Sayama, Etsuo. Interview by Warren Nishimoto, March 16, 1992. *An Era of Change: Oral Histories of Civilians in World War II Hawai'i,* Vol. 3, University of Hawai'i Center for Oral History, p. 976. Available online. URL:http:www2.soc.hawaii.edu/css/oral_hist/war.html. Downloaded March 8, 2003

Scheina, Robert. "The Coast Guard at War." Available online. URL: http://www.uscg.mil/hq/g-cp/history/h_CGatwar.html. Downloaded September 5, 2001.

Schlesinger, Arthur M., Jr. *A Life in the Twentieth Century: Innocent Beginnings, 1917–1950.* Boston, New York: Houghton Mifflin, 2000.

Schlissel, Lillian, ed. *Conscience in America; A Documentary History of Conscientious Objection in America, 1757–1967.* New York: Dutton, 1968.

Schmidt, William E. "Jewish Vet May Finally Get Medal." *Ann Arbor News,* November 5, 1989, 139.

Schneider, Dorothy, and Carl J. Schneider. *The ABC-Clio Companion to Women in the Workplace.* Santa Barbara, Calif.: ABC-Clio, 1993.

Schonberger, Howard B. *Aftermath of War: Americans and the Remaking of Japan, 1945–52.* Kent, Ohio: Kent State University Press, 1989.

Schubert, Frank N. *Mobilization: The U.S. Army in World War II.* Pub. 72–32. Washington, D.C.: U.S. Army Center of Military History, ca. 1994.

Schultz, Stanley K. "World War II, The Home Front," University of Wisconsin American History course 102. Available online. URL: http://us.history.wisc.edu/hist102/lectures/lecture21.html. Downloaded May 14, 2001.

Schwarz, Jordan A. "Henry John Kaiser." In *Dictionary of American Biography,* supp. 8, 308. New York: Scribner's, 1988.

Senorino R. Cruz et al. v. U.S.A. et al. Decision available online. URL:http://www.cand.uscourts.gov. Downloaded January 10, 2002.

Sevareid, Eric. *Not So Wild a Dream.* 1946. Reprint, New York: Atheneum, 1976.

Sherwood, Robert E. *Roosevelt and Hopkins.* New York: Harper, 1948.

Shipler, David K. Review of Diane McWhorter's *Carry Me Home. New York Times Magazine,* March 18, 2001, 9.

Shirer, William L. *Berlin Diary: The Journal of a Foreign Correspondent, 1934–1941.* New York: Knopf, 1941.

Shomon, Joseph J. *Crosses in the Wind*. New York: Stratford, 1947.

Shukert, Elfrieda Berthiaume, and Barbara Smith Scibetta. *War Brides of World War II*. Novato, Calif.: Presidio, 1988.

Sibley, Mulford Q., and Philip E. Jacob. *Conscription of Conscience: The American State and the Conscientious Objector, 1940–1947*. Ithaca, N.Y.: Cornell University Press, 1952.

Simpson, Caroline Chung. "'Out of an obscure place': Japanese War Brides and Cultural Pluralism in the 1950s," in *differences: A Journal of Feminist Cultural Studies* 10.3 (1998): 47–81. Available online. URL: muse.jhu.edu/demo/dif/10.3simpson.html. Downloaded October 4, 2001.

"Singer in World War II, 1939–1945." (1946). Available online. URL: http://www.home.cfl.rr.com/featherweight/crinklg.htm. Downloaded March 12, 2002.

Slater, Robert. *Portraits in Silicon*. Cambridge, Mass.: MIT Press, 1987.

Sledge, Eugene B. *With the Old Breed at Peleliu and Okinawa*. New York: Oxford University Press, 1981.

Smith, R. Elberton. *The Army and Economic Mobilization*. Washington, D.C.: Center of Military History, 1991.

Smith, Robert Barr. "Justice under the Sun: Japanese War Crime Trials." Available online. URL: http://www.thehistorynet.com/World War II/articles/0996_text.htm. Downloaded December 4, 2001.

Smith, Robert Ross. *The Approach to the Philippines*. Washington, D.C.: Office of the Chief of Military History, Department of the Army, 1953.

Soper, Robert T. "Pearl Harbor," in *Modern Maturity*, July/August 2001. Available online. URL: http://www.modernmaturity.org. Downloaded September 7, 2001.

Soucy, Lee. "Report from the Battleship *Utah*." Oral history. U.S. Naval History Center. Available online. URL: http://www.history.navy.mil/nhc3.htm. Downloaded September 6, 2001.

Stafford, David. *Camp X*. New York: Dodd, Mead, 1986.

Stanton, Doug. *In Harm's Way: The Sinking of the USS* Indianapolis *and the Extraordinary Story of Its Survivors*. New York: Henry Holt, 2001.

Stars and Stripes. Letter to the editor, signed by hundreds of GIs, October 21, 1944, European edition, 3.

Steel, Ronald. *Walter Lippmann and the American Century*. Boston: Little, Brown, 1980.

Steinbeck, John. *Once There Was a War.* New York: Viking, 1958.

Stenger, Charles A. "American Prisoners of War in WWI, WWII, Korea, Vietnam, Persian Gulf, Somalia, Bosnia, Kosovo and Afghanistan: Statistical Data Concerning Numbers Captured, Repatriated and Still Alive as of January 1, 2002. Prepared for the DVA [Department of Veterans' Affairs] Advisory Committee on Former Prisoners of War, Mental Health Strategic Health Care Group, VHA [Veterans' Health Administration], DVA, American Ex-Prisoners of War Association." Available from American Ex-Prisoners of War National Headquarters, 3201 East Pioneer Parkway, #40, Arlington, Texas 76010-5396.

Stettinius, Edward R., Jr. Address at the Opening of the United Nations Conference on International Organization, April 25, 1945. Available online. URL: http://www.whistlestop.org/study_collections/un/large/sf_conference/un_sf61.htm. Downloaded January 10, 2002.

Stewart, Sidney. *Give Us This Day.* New York: Norton, 1956.

Stimson, Henry L., and McGeorge Bundy. *On Active Service in Peace and War.* New York: Harper, 1947.

Stinnett, Robert B. *Day of Deceit: The Truth about FDR and Pearl Harbor.* New York: Touchstone, 2001.

Stoff, Michael B., et al., eds. *The Manhattan Project: A Documentary Introduction to the Atomic Age.* Philadelphia: Temple University Press, 1991.

Stokes, Isaac N.P., interview by Richard D. McKinzie, July 3, 1973, in the Truman Library, Independence, Missouri. Available online. URL: http://www.trumanlibrary.org. Downloaded February 14, 2002.

Stone, I. F. *The Nation,* May 3, 1941, 519.

———. *The War Years, 1939–1945.* Boston: Little, Brown, 1988.

Stonecypher, LaMar. "Kilroy Was Here," *Kudzu Monthly.* Available online. URL: http://www.kudzumonthly.com/kudzu/ju101/Kilroy.html. Downloaded February 25, 2003.

Stout, D. B. "Race, Cultural Groups, Social Differentiation," *Social Forces,* (October 1942): 81.

Stremlow, Mary V. *A History of Women Marines: 1946–77.* Working draft. Washington, D.C.: HQ USMC, March 1979.

Suzuki, Kanji. "A Kamikaze's Story," as told to Tadao Morimoto, translated by Kan Sugahara. In *No End Save Victory: Perspectives on World War II,* edited by Robert Cowley, 616–624. New York: G. P. Putnam's Sons, 2001.

Syracuse University. "Remembering the GI Bulge." Available online. URL: sumweb.syr.edu/archives/exhibits/gi/serve.htm. Downloaded November 13, 2001.

Szasz, Ferenc M. "Peppermint and Alsos." In *No End Save Victory: Perspectives on World War II,* edited by Robert Cowley, 406–418. New York: G. P. Putnam's Sons, 2000.

Tapert, Annette, ed. *Lines of Battle: Letters from American Servicemen, 1941–1945.* New York: Pocket Books, 1987.

Taylor, Charles. Interview by the authors, Kennett Square, Pa., May 21, 2001. Collection of the authors.

Taylor, Dorothy. Interview by the authors, Kennett Square, Pa., May 21, 2001. Collection of the authors.

Terkel, Studs. *"The Good War": An Oral History of World War II.* New York: Pantheon, 1984.

Terrell, J. "The Diary of a W W II Veteran." Available online. URL: http://users. vnet.net/jterrell/wwdiary/everettlt.htm. Downloaded June 21, 2001.

Thibault, Dorothy. *Detroit Free Press,* June 14, 1945, 7.

Thoburn, Catherine, and Janet Knapp, eds. "Perspectives on World War II: Personal Narratives." Ann Arbor, Mich.: Learning in Retirement, Turner Geriatric Services, University of Michigan Medical Center, May 8, 1995.

Thompson, Paul W., et al. *How the Jap Army Fights.* New York: Penguin, 1942.

Tibbetts, Paul W. Available online. URL: http://www.theenolagay.com. Downloaded September 12, 2001.

Titus, James, ed. *The Home Front and War in the Twentieth Century: Proceedings of the Tenth Military History Symposium, USAF Academy, 1982.* Washington, D.C.: U.S. Air Force Academy and the Office of Air Force History, Headquarters USAF, 1984.

Toczko, Wilfred J. "Pearl Harbor," *Modern Maturity,* July/August 2001. Available online. URL: http://www.modernmaturity.org. Downloaded September 7, 2001.

Toland, John. *The Last 100 Days.* New York: Random House, 1966.

Toole, John H. *Battle Diary.* Missoula, Mont.: Vigilante, 1978.

"Town's Fond Memories of the Enemy: German P.O.W.'s Gathered Potatoes and Friends in 1940's Maine," *New York Times,* March 17, 2002, 37.

Treadwell, Mattie. *U. S. Army in World War II: Special Studies—the Women's Army Corps.* Washington, D.C.: Department of the Army, 1954.

Tregaskis, Richard. *Invasion Diary.* New York: Random House, 1944.

Treml, William. "Mine Patrol," *Ann Arbor News,* June 3, 1984.

Truman, Harry S. *Diary. Memoirs of Harry S. Truman: Year of Decisions.* New York: Doubleday, 1955.

———. Papers of Harry S. Truman, President's Secretary's Files, Truman Library, Independence, Mo. Available online. URL: http://www.trumanlibrary.org.

———. Truman Doctrine address to Congress. March 12, 1947. Available online. URL: http://www.trumanlibrary.org. Downloaded July 10, 2001.

Trumble, Thomas G. Reminiscences, 1962. Columbia University Oral History Research Office Collection.

Tsuchida, William S. *Wear It Proudly.* Berkeley: University of California Press, 1947.

Tucker, Sherrie. *Swing Shift: "All-girl" Bands of the 1940s.* Durham, N.C.: Duke University Press, 2000.

Turbak, Gary. "Massacre at Hoengsong." *VFW Magazine,* February 2001. Available online. URL: http://www.landscaper.net/kortime.htm. Downloaded March 18, 2002.

Twight, Charlotte. "Evolution in Federal Income Tax Withholding." *Cato Journal* 14: no. 3: 1. Available online. URL: http://www.cato.org/pubs/journal/cj14n3-1.html. Downloaded April 3, 2000.

Unsigned review of Japanese book. Available online. URL: http://photojpn.org/book/theme/enari.html. Downloaded October 13, 2001.

U.S. Air Force Museum. Woman Pilots History Gallery. URL: http://www.wpafb.af.mil/museum/history/wasp/wasp17.htm.

U.S. Department of Defense. "Principal Wars in Which the United States Has Participated: U.S. Military Personnel Serving and Casualties," Table T-23. Available online. URL: http://www.members.aol.com/TeacherNet/WWII.html. Downloaded August 14, 2001.

U.S. Department of the Interior. Map of the U.S. presidential election of 1940. Available online. URL: http://teachpol.tcnj.edu/amer_pol_hist/thumbnail358.html. Downloaded June 11, 2001.

U.S. Department of Labor and Women's Bureau. Leaflet, April 1943. Division of Research, Record Group 86, Women's Bureau, National Archives, Washington, D.C.

U.S. Department of the Navy, Naval Historical Center. Available online. URL: http://www.history.navy.mil/nhc3.htm. Downloaded September 5, 2001.

U.S. Marine Corps Headquarters Information. Available online. URL: http://www.hqmc.usmc.mil. Downloaded September 5, 2001.

U.S. Marine Corps History. Available online. URL: http://www.usmc.mil/History.nsf/Table+of+Contents. Downloaded March 28, 2002.

U.S. Merchant Marine. "Quotes About American Merchant Marine by Military Leaders during World War II." Available online URL: http://www.usmm.org/quotes.html#anchor2778810. Downloaded June 17, 2002.

"U.S. Merchant Marine in World War II." Available online. URL: http://www.usmm.org/ww2.html. Downloaded November 19, 2002.

U.S. National Park Service. Letter from Don Pettijohn, park ranger at Andersonville National Historic Site, December 26, 2002, collection of the authors.

U.S. Naval Historical Center. "Frequently Asked Questions." Available online. URL: http://www.history.navy.mil/. Downloaded July 23, 2001.

U.S. Navy Department, Bureau of Naval Personnel. *U. S. Naval Administration in World War II: Women's Reserve.* 2 vols. Washington, D.C.: Government Printing Office, 1947.

U.S. Strategic Bombing Survey. "Summary Report (Pacific War), 1 July 1946." Available online. URL: http://www.anesi.com/ussbs01.htm#taaatjhi. Downloaded December 30, 2002.

"U.S. Supreme Court, Duncan v. Kahanamoku." Available online. URL: http://caselaw.lp.findlaw.com/scripts/getcase.pl?court=US&vol=327&i nvol=304. Downloaded December 30, 2002.

"U.S. Women in the British Air Transport Auxiliary." Available online. URL: http://www.wpafb.af.mil/museum/history/wasp/wasp13.htm. Downloaded October 24, 2001.

Van Ells, Mark D. *To Hear Only Thunder Again: America's World War II Veterans Come Home.* Lanham, Md.: Lexington, 2001.

Van Staaveren, Jacob. *An American in Japan 1945–1948: A Civilian View of the Occupation.* Seattle: University of Washington Press, 1994.

"Varian Fry." Varian Fry Foundation Project of the International Rescue Committee. Available online. URL: http://www.almondseed.com/vfry/fryfoun.htm. Downloaded June 25, 2001.

Vatter, Harold G. *The U.S. Economy in World War II.* New York: Columbia University Press, 1985.

Vidal, Gore. Letter to the editor. *New York Review of Books,* May 17, 2001, p. 67.

Vietor, John A. *Time Out: Our American Airmen at Stalag Luft I.* New York: Richard R. Smith, 1951.

Villard, Oswald Garrison. "Issues and Men." *The Nation,* June 29, 1940, 13.

"V-Mail." Available online. URL: http://www.si.edu/postal/learnmore/vmail.html. Downloaded March 23, 2002.

Wagner, Jacob. "World War II Naval Strength, 1939." Available online. URL: http://www.warcity.net/navy1939.html. Downloaded September 4, 2001.

Walker, Bryce, et al. *Our Glorious Century.* Pleasantville, N.Y.: Reader's Digest Association, 1994.

Walsh, David I. "The Decline and Renaissance of the U.S. Navy, 1922–1944." Washington, D.C.: Senate Committee on Naval Affairs, 1944. Available online. URL: http://www.ibiblio.org/pha/navywwii.html. Downloaded September 5, 2001.

Walzer, Michael. "World War II: Why Was This War Different?" In *War and Moral Responsibility,* edited by Marshall Cohen, Thomas Nagel, and Thomas Scanlon. Princeton, N.J.: Princeton University Press, 1974.

War Manpower Commission. "Policy on Women." *Manual of Operations: War Manpower Commission.* October 17, 1942, Record Group 86, Woman's Bureau, National Archives, Washington, D.C.

Waterford, Van. *Prisoners of the Japanese in World War II: Statistical History, Personal Narratives, and Memorials Concerning POWs in Camps and on Hellships, Civilian Internees, Asian Slave Laborers, and Others Captured in the Pacific Theater.* Jefferson, N.C.: McFarland, 1994.

Wattenberg, Ben. Interview with David Kennedy, Alice Kessler-Harris, William O'Neill, and William Julius Wilson. PBS program *The First Measured Century,* Segment 8: "World War II: The Homefront." Available online. URL: http://www.pbs.org/fmc/segments/progseg8.htm. Downloaded June 1, 2001.

Weglyn, Michi. *Years of Infamy: The Untold Story of America's Concentration Camps.* New York: William Morrow, 1976.

Welker, Robert H. *A Different Drummer.* Boston: Beacon, 1958.

Welles, Sumner. *The Time for Decision.* New York: Harper & Row, 1944.

Wells, Bob. "Pre-Kendal Memory." Undated unpublished manuscript. Kendal Library, Kennett Square, Pa.

Whelan, Frank. "Rosie the Riveter." In *The Morning Call.* Available online. URL: http://www.mcall.com/html/decades/43355.htm. Downloaded on May 31, 2001.

White, Robert W. Letter to *Aerial Gunners Association Magazine.* Available online. URL:http://www.kensmen.com/tokyoroseb.html. Downloaded July 4, 2001.

White, Walter. Letter to the editor. *New York Post,* March 6, 1941, 14.

Whyte, William H. "Patrolling Guadalcanal." In *No End Save Victory: Perspectives on World War II,* edited by Robert Cowley, 191–201. New York: G. P. Putnam's Sons, 2001.

Wickard, Claude. Interview, 1953. Columbia University Oral History Research Office Collection.

Wilde, Louise. Memo to Capt. Mildred McAfee, February 23, 1945. Fourteenth Naval District (1943–53), folder 50, box 7, series I, ACNP(W), Navy Operational Archives, Naval Historical Center, Washington, D.C.

Wiley, Alexander. Interview, 1964. Columbia University Oral History Research Office Collection.

Willenz, June. *Women Veterans: America's Forgotten Heroines.* New York: Continuum, 1983.

Williams, Jeannette, with Yolande Dickerson, Researcher. *The Invisible Cryptologists: African-Americans, WWII to 1956.* Fort George G. Meade, Md.: National Security Agency, Revised 2001. Available online. URL: http://www.nsa.gov/wwii/papers/invisible_cryptologists.htm. Downloaded December 16, 2002.

Wills, Mary. "Daylight Come." *Modern Maturity,* May–June 1948, pp. 55–59, 87.

Wilson, George. *If You Survive.* New York: Ivy Books, 1987.

Wingfield, R. M. *The Only Way Out.* London: Hutchinson, 1955.

Winke Tax Services. "Maximum Individual Rates." Available online. URL: http://www.winke.com/wts/wts/wtsthis.htm.

Wise, Nancy Baker, and Christy Wise. *A Mouthful of Rivets: Women at Work in World War II.* San Francisco: Jossey-Bass, 1994.

Wolfe, Don M., ed. *The Purple Testament.* Garden City, N.Y.: Doubleday, 1947.

Wolfe, Wade H. "Why I Volunteered to Help Refurbish 'Fi Fi.'" In *Westwind Online.* Available online. URL: http://www.wwc.edu/about-us/publications/westwind. Downloaded October 8, 2001.

Wollenberg, Charles, comp. and introd. *Photographing the Second Gold Rush: Dorothea Lange and the Bay Area at War, 1941–45.* Berkeley, Calif.: Heyday, 1995.

"Women Mariners in World War II." Available online. URL: http://www.usm.org/ww2.html. Downloaded February 1, 2001.

Women's Army Corps. Recruiting poster. See Crandell, Bradshaw.

Wood, Denise. "Pre-Kendal Memory." Undated unpublished memoir. Kendal Library, Kennett Square Pa. 19348.

Wood, Robert E. Interview, 1961. Columbia University Oral History Research Office Collection.

"World War II Air Power: The Atom Bomb." Available online. URL: http://danshistory.com/ww2/atombomb.shtml. Downloaded December 30, 2002.

World War II Survey, Historical Services Division, U.S. Army Historical Institute, Carlisle Barracks, Pennsylvania.

Wyman, David S. *The Abandonment of the Jews: America and the Holocaust, 1941–1945.* New York: Pantheon, 1984.

Wynn, Neil A. *The Afro-American and the Second World War.* New York: Holmes and Meier, 1975.

Young, Peter, ed. *The World Almanac Book of World War II.* Rev. ed. New York: Bison Books, 1981.

Zinn, Howard. *A People's History of the United States, 1942–Present.* Rev. ed. New York: HarperPerennial, 1995.

INDEX

Page numbers in **boldface** indicate biographical entries. Page numbers in *italics* indicate an illustration.
Page numbers followed by *g* indicate glossary entries. Page numbers followed by *m* indicate maps.